The Illustrated History Of
LEEDS

by
Steven Burt and Kevin Grady

Breedon Books
Publishing Company
Derby

Published in Great Britain by
The Breedon Books Publishing Company Limited
Breedon House, 44 Friar Gate, Derby, DE1 1DA.
1994

ISBN 1 873626 35 5

Printed and bound by Hillman Printers, Frome, Somerset.
Jackets printed by BDC Printing Services of Derby

Contents

Sources of Illustrations

Thanks are due to the following bodies, societies and individuals who have kindly granted us permission to reproduce their material. Illustrations not listed below are from the authors' own collections.

Peter Brears: 19, 60 (top), 61 (bottom), 78 (bottom).

City Varieties: 244 (top).
Corn Exchange: 251.
Robert Finnigan: 216, 218 (bottom).
Derek Green: 37 (bottom), 39 (middle), 42 (left), 43, 59 (top).
W.R.Lee: 113.
Leeds City Council (Dept of Housing): 183 (bottom).
Leeds City Council (Lord Mayor's Office): 88 (top).
Leeds City Libraries (Dept of Leisure Services): 33, 37, 38-9, 40, 41, 42 (top), 48, 50, 62, 69 (left), 72 (bottom), 73, 76 (top), 78 (top), 79, 83, 88 (bottom), 91, 93, 94, 95, 96-7, 98, 101, 102, 107, 108, 109 (top), 110, 114, 117 (top), 119, 123, 129, 133, 134, 135, 136 (bottom right), 137, 138 (top and bottom), 139, 141, 142, 143, 144, 147 (bottom), 149, 150, 154, 155, 156, 164, 165, 166, 167, 168, 171, 172, 174, 175 (top), 177 (right and bottom), 178, 179, 181, 182 (right), 183 (top), 186, 188, 193, 194 (bottom), 196, 201 (top), 202 (bottom), 206, 210, 226 (bottom), 227.

Photographs were taken for the authors by Mel Hulme: 81, 146 (bottom), 236 (bottom), 248 (bottom), 250, 252.
Leeds City Council (Depts of Planning, Highways and Engineering) 205, 232.

Leeds City Museums: 10 (right), 32, 109 (bottom), 117 (bottom), 159, 197 (top), 201 (bottom), 208 (right).

Leeds Civic Trust: 100, 146 (top), 191, 192 (bottom), 198 (top), 202 (top), 211, 218, 220 (bottom), 223, 229, 235, 236 (top), 237, 238-9, 240, 248 (top).

Leeds Parish Church: 28 (top), 35 (bottom), 38 (bottom), 47 (top).
E.Lunn: 225.
Opera North: 244 (middle).
Public Record Office: 14 (bottom), E31/2 fos 315 & 379a.
Robert Preedy: 224.
St James's University Hospital, Medical Illustrations Department: 173.
Thoresby Society: 15, 18, 26, 60 (right), 75, 122.

Tim Green Photography: 194 (top).
West Yorkshire Archive Service, Leeds District Office: 23 DB 204/2p79.
147 (top).

University of Leeds, Art Collections: 90.
University of Leeds: Dept of Geography: 27, 67.
Yorkshire Evening Post: 92, 138 (right), 175 (bottom), 195, 213, 226 (top), 243, 244 (bottom), 245.

YTV: 231.

The Authors

STEVEN BURT is President of the Thoresby Society and a historical advisor to Leeds Civic Trust. He is particularly well known for his extensive adult education teaching and public lectures on the history of Leeds. He was born and bred in the city and, since graduating, has complemented his teaching at Alwoodley Primary School with running courses for teachers on historical sources. His publications include *Roundhay Park — an Illustrated History* (1984); *Criminal Leeds — from earliest records to 1879 (1985);* The Lord Mayor's Centenary Trails (1993), and with Kevin Grady, *War, Plague and Trade — Leeds in the Seventeenth Century* (1985), *The Merchant's Golden Age, Leeds 1700-1790* (1987); and *A History of Kirkgate Market* (1992).

KEVIN GRADY is Director of Leeds Civic Trust. He has lived in Leeds (with a three-year break) since 1969, graduating from Leeds University in Economic History. His Ph.D thesis was published as a Thoresby Society Monograph in 1989 entitled *The Georgian Public Buildings of Leeds and the West Riding of Yorkshire.* His other publications, in addition to those with Steven Burt, include articles on English charities and the history of Leeds in the *Urban History Yearbook* and *Thoresby Society Publications*. He lectured at Leeds Polytechnic, Exeter University and Leeds University before taking up his present post.

Steven Burt (left) and Kevin Grady toast the completion of their book, which has been sponsored by Joshua Tetley & Son, outside the city's latest family visitor attraction, Tetley's Brewery Wharf.

Acknowledgements

The authors' are indebted to the following people for their help without which this book would not have been possible:
Leeds City Libraries (Department of Leisure Services): Joyce Hainsworth, Peter Kelly, Sandra Smith, Ann Heap, Jennifer Horne, Colin Price, Moya Barker and David Sheard.
West Yorkshire Archive Service, Leeds District Office: Bill Connor and Brett Harrison.
Leeds City Museums: Peter Brears, Peter Kelley, Alan Garlick and Liz Pirie.
Leeds Development Agency: Tony Shelton.
Thoresby Society: Mary Forster
A special mention must be made of the staff of the Local and Family History Library who have cheerfully brought us literally thousands of photographs, pamphlets, booklets, books, maps, microfilms and newspapers over the past ten years.

Our thanks are also due to Karen Guest, Yvonne Ambrosen and Barbara Nixon, who did a marvellous job in deciphering our manuscripts in the word processing of the first drafts of the book. Our very special thanks go to Don Cole and Linda Biran who painstakingly and perceptively commented on each chapter of the book, and made many helpful suggestions which have made the book much more readable than it might otherwise have been. Very special thanks too are due to Maurice Beresford who has been an inspiration and a friend over many years, and advised on the medieval chapter. Peter Brears, too, has helped in many ways, providing illustrations and advice, and not least of all by introducing us to the publishers. We have also benefited considerably from the comments of Stan Kenyon and Bob Wolfe on city planning in the twentieth century. Thank you also to the many friends who have shared their knowledge with us.

Dedicated to
Lynda Burt and Sally Grady
whose love, patience and support
allowed us to fulfil our
ambition to write this book.

The authors warmly thank Joshua Tetley & Son for its generous sponsorship of this book.

Conversion Table – Money and Measurement

1 guinea	=	21 shillings (s.)	1 yard	=	3 feet
1 pound	=	20 shillings	1 foot	=	12 inches
1 shilling	=	12 pence (d.)	1 metre	=	39.37 inches

Preface

THIS book is the culmination of just over twenty years of research by both authors into the history of Leeds. The book itself has been in active preparation for ten years. We have written it simply because we feel that Leeds has a rich and fascinating history and we want to share our knowledge and enthusiasm with our fellow citizens.

Through our evening class teaching over many years, we recognised that there was a major need for a comprehensive history of Leeds, that would be both lively to read and serve as a useful work of reference. No author since Edward Parsons in 1834 has attempted to write such a work. The excellent series of essays in Derek Fraser's, *History of Modern Leeds*, published in 1980, covered a good deal of ground, but inevitably major aspects of the history of the city were omitted, and important themes were pursued for only limited spans of years. We hope that this publication will be a major contribution to the understanding of how the city has developed over the centuries and how people lived their lives.

In writing this book, between us we have attempted to draw on all the major secondary works on the history of Leeds. Thanks in particular to the splendid work of the Thoresby Society's editors, the research literature on the history is vast. We have also drawn extensively on the results of our archival research over many years. Working in partnership has been immensely enjoyable. To sustain a major project of this kind, we have relied greatly on the shared excitement of new research discoveries and mutual encouragement when the exhaustion of countless evenings and weekends' work periodically took its toll.

Inevitably, in a co-operative venture people will be looking for the joins in the work! Steven Burt wrote Chapter One on medieval Leeds and researched and drew the maps. Kevin Grady wrote Chapters Seven and Eight on twentieth century Leeds. For the intervening chapters, we each wrote various sections. While Kevin Grady was editing these together, Steven Burt was undertaking the picture research.

It was our good fortune to be approached by Anton Rippon of Breedon Books soon after we had decided to move on from writing a series of booklets to writing a full-blown history of the city. Breedon Books' excellent track record in publishing books of the sort that we wanted to write, produced an instant yes to their offer of a contract. We owe them a great debt for their patience in allowing us an additional 18 months to complete the book. The book is almost twice as long as we originally intended!

Perhaps our boldest decision was to bring the story of Leeds right up to the present day. We concluded that this is important so that readers can see the direct link between themselves and the inhabitants of the medieval manor of Leeds, and so that we provide future Leeds historians with a useful supply of contemporary comment.

CHAPTER ONE

Medieval Leeds

The Origins of Leeds

Of Leeds of yesterday and the day before, there is little of importance to chronicle, at any rate from the picturesque historian's point of view. The sumptuary, tilt and tournamental element is well-nigh wanting in her annals; her streets are not known to have been hallowed by the footsteps of the noble or illustrious. Persons who would find within her boundaries some obvious traces 'of an age that is long since past' are wont to avail themselves of the steam cars and proceed to Kirkstall.

Leeds – Illustrated, 1892[1]

These rather dismissive remarks made just over a century ago convey a somewhat misleading and yet still commonly held view of the origins and history of Leeds. Certainly, the medieval village or town of Leeds was not an important administrative centre, nor was it a stage for the playing out of major national events. But the absence of substantial physical remains of earlier ages does not deny it the possibility of an illustrious past.

The centre of Leeds has been continuously occupied at least since the Middle Ages and virtually all evidence of earlier settlement has been destroyed by the extensive digging of cellars in the city centre. Most were dug before local people became interested in antiquarian remains, and so for archaeological evidence of early Leeds we must rely primarily on brief descriptions of random archaeological finds made from the eighteenth century onwards. By ingeniously combining this information with the somewhat oblique evidence in pre-Norman literature and a limited range of surviving artefacts, historians and archaeologists have arrived at some fascinating insights into the early history of the settlement we now know as Leeds.

In the prehistoric period around 4000BC the landscape of the region in which Leeds is sited today, and through which the River Aire runs, was dominated by considerable tracts of carr (boggy ground) and marsh, and vast areas of oak and birch woodland. By the end of the Bronze Age (*c*.500BC) settlers had probably extensively cleared the woodland to create farmland. The cultivated areas no doubt were surrounded by a predominantly open landscape which had either been cleared for rough grazing or to obtain supplies of timber for buildings and fuel, or simply had been abandoned when earlier cultivation had exhausted its fertility. This process of woodland clearance continued throughout the Iron Age.[2]

The existence of settlements in the region of Leeds in the Bronze and Iron Ages is confirmed by a variety of small archaeological finds including an urn containing burnt bones and a flint axe head, discovered near

Ancient pre-Roman urn, containing ashes, bones, and a stone axe, found in 1745 by a carpenter sinking a tenter post in a field near the top of Briggate.

Neolithic axe found in Neville Street, near City Station.

Briggate in 1745, and two important hoards found at Carr Moorside (near Hunslet Moor) and at Roundhay.[3] Surviving present-day physical evidence and observations made in earlier centuries point to the existence of prehistoric defensive sites (*c.*1500BC to 150BC) with mounds and ditches at Gipton, Hawcaster Rigg (Chapel Allerton), Woodhouse Moor (on the line of Rampart Road), Temple Newsam, Seacroft and Quarry Hill.[4]

The question which has tantalised historians for centuries is whether the Romans had a settlement in or near the present-day Leeds city centre. The surrounding towns of Ilkley, Castleford and Tadcaster were all Roman settlements of some size. Closer to home, the large quantities of Roman materials uncovered at Adel (five miles to the north of Leeds) establish the site as a Roman settlement of some importance, in all probability including a fort.[5] But what of Leeds itself? Ralph Thoresby, the Leeds antiquary, noted some intriguing features on Quarry Hill in 1715:

> Upon the ascent of the Hill are the Vestigia [surviving traces] of a very large Camp; the Trenches considering its Nearness to the Town, and the Interposition of so many Ages, are very deep: But whether it was a Roman, or a Saxon Camp, I dare not positively assert; tho', from the single Vallum [earth rampart] and Conveniency of the Water (which the Romans always made sure of) at the Foot of the Hill, I suppose it to be the former ...Somewhat of the Vallum is yet retained in the Name Wall-flat.[6]

Minor Romanised civilian settlements occur throughout Yorkshire, almost always located on Roman roads and spaced at intervals between important settlements and forts. Adel, for example, lies on the route from York to Ilkley. The stretch of road between York and Manchester is known to have been divided off by the settlements of Tadcaster and Cambodunum, but the location and present-day identity of Cambodunum is lost in the mists of time. Probably it originated either in a fort or a convenient stopping place for travellers and officials moving between the major centres of Roman Britain. The most likely meaning of its name is 'the fort by the river-bend'. By combining knowledge of the topography of Quarry Hill with other archaeological evidence, and information given in early literature, including Bede's *Ecclesiastical History* written *c.*AD730, archaeologists have recently concluded that Leeds and more specifically Quarry Hill is the most likely site of Cambodunum.[7]

Even if this speculation turns out to be wrong, archaeologists are almost certain that Leeds was a Roman site of some note. In 1819 workmen clearing land to the south of Leeds Bridge discovered a 'compact and hard

The pieces of this eighth- or ninth-century cross were found in 1838 during the demolition of the parish church tower. Today it stands in the parish church.

trajectus', which was believed to have been a Roman ford. Moreover, a 'strongly cemented' pavement discovered while digging a cellar in Briggate in the eighteenth century sounds very much like the remains of a Roman road. Pottery, coins and other Roman artefacts found in Leeds over the past two centuries, give further support to this theory.[8]

When the Romans left Britain *c.*AD400 the country broke up into a number of small independent British kingdoms. The area which Leeds now occupies was situated in the British kingdom of Elmet. In AD617 Edwin, the Anglo-Saxon king of Northumbria conquered the area and expelled its king, Ceretic. Bede in his *Ecclesiatical History*, when recounting the activities of the monk Paulinus, tells us that:

> In Campodunum, where there was a villa regia [royal palace], he built a church which was afterwards burnt down, together with the whole of the buildings, by the heathens who slew King Edwin. In its stead, later kings built a dwelling for themselves in the region known as Loidis.[9]

If Cambodunum, or Campodunum as Bede referred to it, was on the site of the present-day Leeds, then it would appear that in the seventh century Leeds was the site of a church, and the administrative centre of an Anglo-Saxon royal estate which was sacked by Penda of Mercia in AD633. It is possible that the earthworks on Quarry Hill were the remains of this ancient settlement and that it was the major early Anglo-Saxon site in West Yorkshire.

Perhaps the most clear cut evidence of the great antiquity of Leeds as a human settlement is its name. Historians and experts in the derivation of place names generally agree that the region which Bede called 'Loidis' in his *Ecclesiastical History* was the region in which Leeds is situated. 'Leeds' was originally a two-syllable word, which must have been pronounced as 'Leedis' throughout the Middle Ages, and is certainly a corruption or merely a change in the spelling of 'Loidis'. Bede's 'Loidis', which has also survived in the names of two neighbouring villages, Ledsham and Ledston, was a region, possibly a subdivision of the British kingdom of Elmet. 'Loidis' perhaps perpetuated the Anglian pronunciation of the British name of the River Aire and was at first the name of the people living by the river. It is thought that, having started as the name of the region, the name was later restricted to the chief place in it, namely Leeds. Thus, perhaps over time, 'Cambodunum' became 'Campodunum' and then 'Loidis', and then 'Leedis'; though it may be that simultaneously the different races referred to it under different names.[10]

Inevitably, given the tenuous nature of the information available, all theories must be treated with great care. The first compelling evidence that Leeds was an important early settlement lies in the substantial remains of at least five stone crosses, dating from the ninth and tenth centuries, which were discovered at Leeds parish church in 1838 during the demolition of the church tower. There can be little doubt that these impressive artefacts belonged to an earlier church on the site. When Christianity was being re-established in the seventh century, crosses were sometimes used as preaching centres before a church could be built. But by the time of the Leeds crosses, preaching crosses were unnecessary, since churches were well established. This group of crosses confirms Leeds as an important eighth and ninth century settlement because they must have been memorials to prominent individuals who thought the settlement of sufficient distinction to choose it as their place of burial.[11]

The eleventh century *Life of St Cadroe* also suggests that tenth-century Leeds (the saint died *c.*976) was an important settlement on the borders of the British kingdom of Strathclyde, the Norse-Danish kingdom of York and the Anglo-Saxon kingdom of Alfred the Great's successors to the south.[12] In the story, the saint, having visited Domnall, the king of Strathclyde, was conducted by him to the city of Loidis:

> King Domnall was chief of that people, and as he was a relative of the man [St Cadroe], he went to meet him with all joy, and keeping him with him for some little time, he conducted him to the city of Loidis, which is the border between the Norsemen and the Cumbrians; and there he was taken up by a certain nobleman, Gunderic, by whom he was led to King Eric in the city of York, which king indeed had a wife who was a relative of the divine Cadroe himself.[13]

If Leeds at this time had a church where people of importance chose to be buried, and it was a border-town, where the king might hand over an honoured guest for safe conduct through a neighbouring kingdom, then clearly it was a place of consequence.

We can only guess at the precise pattern of landholding in the vicinity of Leeds during the four or five hundred years before the Norman Conquest. Possibly the land contained within the medieval parish of Leeds had once been one large British estate. Perhaps, as first Anglo-Saxon and then Scandinavian settlers occupied the area, this estate was subdivided into lesser estates served by the mother church in the village of Leeds. In the Domesday survey we find the manor of Leeds recorded and these lesser estates as individual manors bearing names now familiar to us as the out-townships and suburbs of the city of Leeds.[14]

Quite how everyday life on the manor of Leeds was organised on the eve of the Norman Conquest we cannot be sure. Undoubtedly, there would have been a system of communal farming under which the people of the village were required to meet various dues and obligations to an overlord. In classifying Leeds as a 'manor', the Norman surveyors thought not so much in terms of a unit of land, as in a unit of feudal obligations, rights, and sources of income associated with land accruing to an individual overlord. The land of the manor of Leeds, they noted, had been divided into the holdings of seven lesser landlords – 'seven thegns for seven manors'. The seven thegns with their families and dependents probably made up a sizeable village for the time. Undoubtedly, a well-structured system of farming had evolved, based on the central village whose cottages lined the street known today as Kirkgate.[15]

The Manor of Leeds

Medieval records of the manor of Leeds enable us to piece together a picture of Leeds in the eleventh century and beyond. When the Norman Domesday officials and clerks arrived in the village in 1086 to begin their task of valuing the manor, they saw a group of large open fields, undivided by hedges, stretching away into the distance towards the settlements of Knostrop, Hillhouse (Richmond Hill), Woodhouse and Buslingthorpe. Meadowland hugged the sides of the River Aire and its tributaries, the Hol and Sheepscar becks. Wood, so vital to the medieval economy for building, fuel, furniture, fencing and the production of domestic implements, was a diminishing resource; only two major areas of woodland remained in the manor – the manorial park to the west of the village, and Woodhouse Ridge to the north. The only large area of common land – uncultivated pasture land upon which all tenants, except cottagers, could graze their animals – was Woodhouse Moor. Throughout the manor there were large areas of 'waste', probably uncultivated rough moor and scrubland, used for grazing as well as for the collection of berries, nuts and fungi which supplemented the diet of the inhabitants. The roads were poor trodden trackways despite being on the routes to York and London.[16]

The village itself must have consisted of crude timber-framed houses stretching along the street, later called Kirkgate, down to the parish church. Apart from this small grouping of buildings, there was a separate cluster of buildings to the west, centred on the manorial mill and the manor house. The church, with its group of ancient crosses was the ecclesiastical centre for a much larger area than the manor. The Domesday clerks noted the presence of a priest, who ministered to his parish which comprised not only the inhabitants of the manor of Leeds but also those of the manors of Allerton, Gipton, Osmondthorpe, Beeston, Hunslet, Holbeck, Wortley, Farnley, Bramley, Armley and Headingley; in all some 32 square miles. The mill was an important source of income for the lord of the manor, since his tenants were bound to grind their corn there. The millstones were driven by the waters of the Aire, carefully diverted through a clever system of channels, dams and sluices, to ensure that supplies were not wasted.

Domesday states that there were 27 villeins (unfree tenants), 4 sokemen (free tenants) and 4 bordars

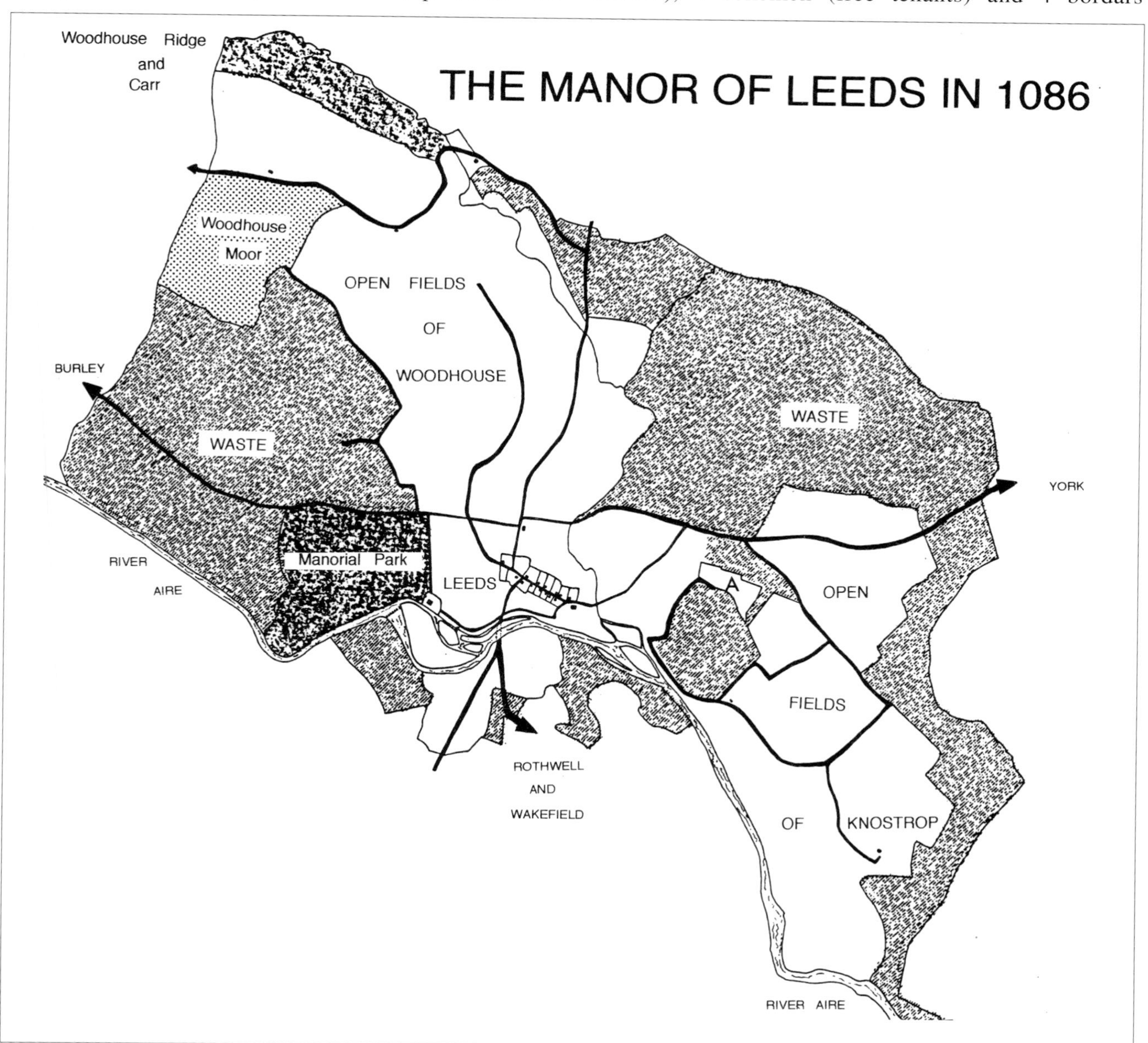

A reconstruction of the features of the manor in 1086, based on the evidence of manorial documents and later maps. The main village stands near a key crossing point on the River Aire. Timber-framed cottages with gardens line the street of Kirkgate. To the west lie the fortified manor house and the wooded manorial park. A series of cultivated open fields stretch towards Woodhouse where the moor provides the only substantial tract of common land. Woodhouse Ridge is one of the few remaining wooded areas in the manor. To the east are the open fields of Knostrop, with the lord's rabbit warren (A) on their western boundary. There are still large areas of scrubby waste land providing rough grazing for sheep, pigs and cattle.

(cottagers) working on the land. These men and their families and dependents constituted a population of probably around two hundred. The surrounding manors had been badly affected by the harrying of the North, the ruthless military campaign aimed at eradicating opposition to William the Conqueror. Seventeen years earlier Norman soldiers had rampaged through the district burning farmhouses, destroying crops, killing people and driving away cattle. The Domesday survey reveals that the surrounding manors of Headingley, Halton, Seacroft and Garforth had been greatly reduced in value, whilst places such as Eccup, Bramley and Beeston were simply recorded as being 'waste'. In contrast, Leeds, one of the larger and more valuable manors in the district, appears to have come through largely unscathed. It had risen in value from £6 to £7 since the Conquest and more men and ploughing teams seem to have been brought in. Because of the strategic importance of the settlement, a fortified structure with a moat had been built to the west of the village, on what today is Mill Hill. This was the Normans' local administrative base.[17]

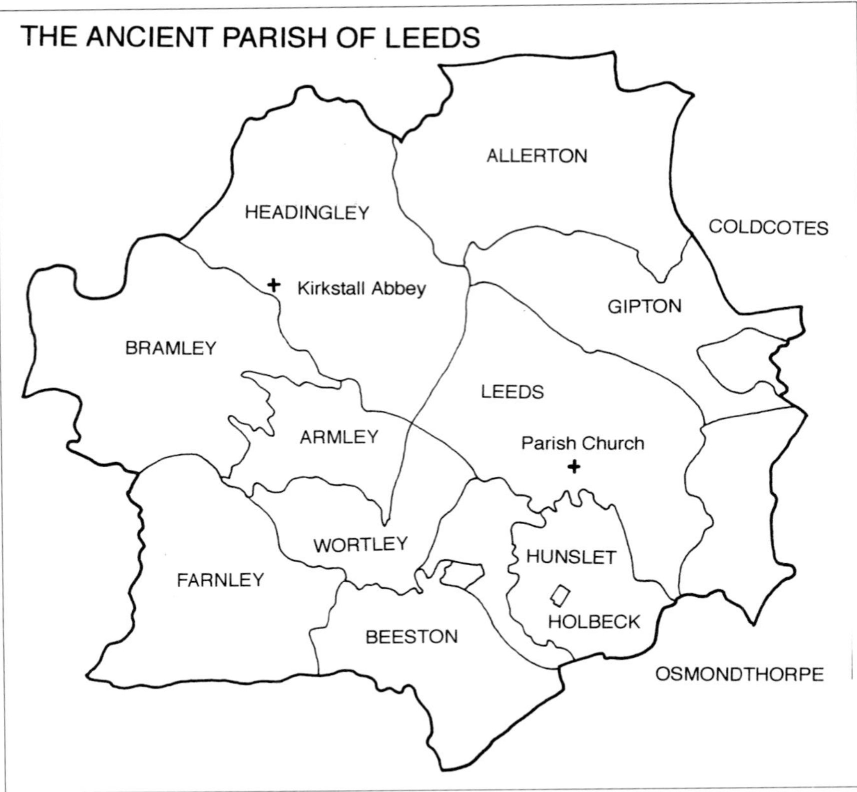

This plan of the vast parish of Leeds shows the boundaries of the main medieval townships and hamlets.

Domesday Book tells us that after the invasion William the Conqueror vested the manor of Leeds in Ilbert de Lacy, an important Norman baron who held large estates in France, Lincolnshire and the Midlands, as well as being lord of the honour of Pontefract, of which Leeds was only a minor part. Shortly after 1086, Ilbert granted lands in Leeds, constituting pretty well the whole of the manor, to another wealthy Norman baron, Ralph Paynel. This grant was followed by a process of asset stripping which left the manor without its main village, the income from the mills, and certain small parcels of land. In 1089, soon after acquiring the manor, Paynel, as an act of piety, made a highly significant gift of Leeds property to Holy Trinity Priory at York. This included not only Leeds parish church with its income, but also the village immediately around it, the 'tithe of the hall', and certain lands including some in Holbeck. Henceforth, these properties and lands were known as the rectory manor of Leeds Kirkgate-cum-Holbeck. Though mainly within the boundaries of the manor of Leeds, they were no longer part of it, and were administered from a separate manor house near the parish church. This building and the courts held there are recalled even today in the name of High Court Lane in the Calls. Ralph's son, William, further reduced the value of the manor by granting the income from the tithes of 'all the mills in Leeds' to Drax Priory which he founded in Yorkshire.

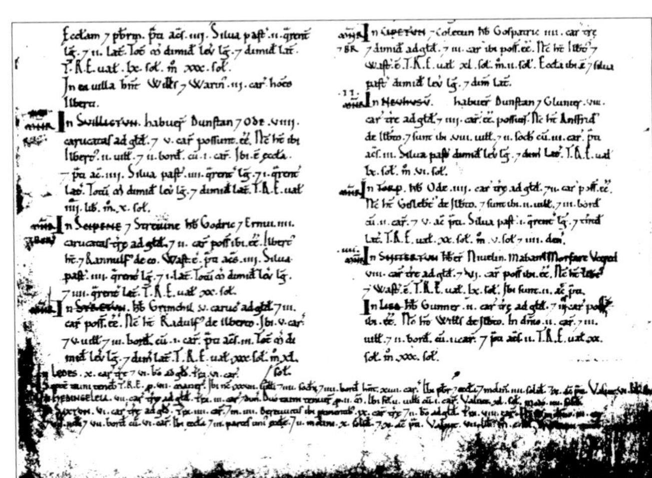

One of the two Leeds entries in Domesday Book: 'In Leeds, 10 carucates of land and 6 bovates to be taxed and land for 6 ploughs. Seven thanes held it in the time of King Edward as 7 manors. Now there, 27 villeins [unfree tenants], 4 sokemen [free tenants], and 4 bordars [cottagers] who have 14 ploughs. There, a priest and church, and a mill of 4s. and 10 acres of meadow. The value was £6; now £7.'

This process was compounded by gifts to the two great medieval military orders involved in the Crusades, the Knights Hospitallers and Templars. Amongst the gifts the Templars received was what eventually became the manor of Whitkirk. Its assets primarily comprised the church and lands at Whitkirk (four miles to the east of Leeds) but also included some small parcels of land within the village of Leeds. As a result, in the following centuries, some of the landholders in central Leeds were exempt from the obligation to have their corn ground at the manorial corn mill, and marked their houses with Templar crosses to confirm that they were part of the manor of Whitkirk.[19] Further land was taken from the manor with the creation of the manor of North Hall around 1180. Its main hall was located near the junction of Vicar Lane and Lady Lane, its lands stretching down to Sheepscar Beck and beyond, with further holdings upstream.[20]

This process had two results which were highly significant for the future development of Leeds. Firstly,

Templar cross on the late sixteenth-century Pack Horse Inn in the Pack Horse Yard, off Briggate.

in economic terms the manor was left a much less valuable asset – something which a future lord of the manor might attempt to remedy. Secondly, the village and its inhabitants, who had hitherto farmed the manorial open fields, became detached from the manor. This led to the increased importance of the settlements of Woodhouse and Knostrop as the centres of the manor's agricultural activity.

By the late-twelfth century the manor was in the possession of Robert de Gant, the husband of Ralph Paynel's great granddaughter, Avice. When he died in 1191 he owed Aaron the Jew of Lincoln £26, money which he had obtained by mortagaging the manors of Leeds and Irnham in Lincolnshire. When Robert and Avice's son Maurice came of age (*c.*1200-1205) he gained possession of the manor of Leeds. Sometimes styling himself 'de Gant' and sometimes 'Paynel', after his mother, Maurice found himself with pressing debts and a manor which was both impoverished and mortgaged. He realised immediately that some radical action was required if the manor was ever to provide him with a substantial income.[21] It was fashionable at the time to create boroughs within manors which gave their inhabitants freedoms from manorial restrictions. It was hoped that the privilege of being left free to follow their trade would encourage skilled craftsmen to settle in the borough and in return they would pay relatively high rents.

In 1207, in a bid to make the manor more profitable, Maurice granted a charter creating the borough of Leeds, a 'new town' grafted on to the top of Kirkgate, extending up to the southern boundary of the Woodhouse open fields and down to the important crossing point on the river where Leeds Bridge now stands. Thirty plots were marked out on either side of the new street, which later became known as Briggate. The inhabitants living on these burgage plots were known as burgesses, and in addition to the parcel of land on Briggate, they were given an allotment of half an acre at Burmantofts (burgage-men's tofts). In return they paid a fixed rent of 16d. per annum. These were 'townsmen'; they were to earn their living from a craft or trade and not from agriculture. The street was unusually wide so that a regular market could be held, close to the place of manufacture. The charter permitted the burgesses to build upon the plots and to sub-divide and sell their holdings. Though they had to attend the new borough court, its procedures were more flexible than the ordinary manorial court, acknowledging the difficulties encountered by people whose business would regularly take them outside the manor. Significantly, the charter did not give any rights of self-government and Maurice was unable to grant extensive trading privileges. The burgesses were to be classed as freemen, but the freedoms granted were minimal and they pursued their activities under the watchful eyes of the bailiff, the lord's representative on the manor.[22]

The 'new town' was not an immediate success and initially it contributed little to manorial income. Nevertheless, it was of major significance for the physical pattern of Leeds. Briggate soon become the most important street in the village, and even today the layout of the medieval burgage plots is clearly discernable in the Briggate arcades and yards. As we shall see, the main sources of manorial revenue were to remain income from the agricultural land and the manorial amenities.

Life in the Manorial Fields

In the thirteenth and fourteenth centuries Leeds was essentially an agricultural manor.[23] The well being of its inhabitants was heavily dependent on the success of the harvest. A poor harvest brought with it the real threat of hardship and starvation in the winter months. The peasants lived by cultivating their ridge and furrow strips of land in the open fields and by grazing sheep and cattle. Their diet was supplemented by small amounts of vegetables and dairy products produced on the plots of land attached to their cottages.[24] The principal agricultural feature of the manor was two systems of open fields. The first, cultivated by the inhabitants of the hamlet of Knostrop, was probably a group of three fields farmed using a simple system of crop rotation where each field changed its function each year. The second system, which may well have consisted of four open fields, stretched out to Woodhouse.

In the first half of the thirteenth century the main tenants of the field systems were the bondmen. They were the 'villeins', so familiar to us from school textbooks, the peasants who, if they wished to retain possession of their land, were obliged to provide a range of services and meet a range of financial obligations to the lord of the manor. In this sense they were not 'free' men. Originally, the bondmen held standard customary holdings of perhaps two bovates (approximately 40 acres), but certainly from the 1320s onwards, perhaps because of population pressure, such customary holdings had been reduced to one bovate. We cannot be sure in what proportion a bondman's 20 acres was divided between arable land in the open fields, and areas of the meadows and rights of pasture on the common land. But on the reasonable assumption that at least half of it was arable land, he would have had more than forty 'selions' or strips dotted about the open fields; the manorial records indicate that four selions occupied one acre of land. The open fields would have been minutely subdivided between the tenants to ensure a fair division of good and poor land.[25]

This intermingling of tenants' land, combined with the absence of hedges and the usual inability of any one bondman to provide the eight oxen usually needed to pull a plough, meant that cultivating the open fields required considerable co-operation between the peasants. Neighbours shared oxen, ploughs and other farming implements. They grew wheat and rye for bread, oats for porridge and oatcakes, and barley for brewing beer. Peas and beans were a popular crop by the fourteenth century, with additional vegetables being grown in the gardens abutting their homes. Each year one of the fields in each field system was left fallow, and the animals left to graze on it, thus manuring the land. Hens, pigs, sheep, goats and cows were also kept because meat, milk, butter, cheese and eggs were important additions to the peasants' diet. The pasture and meadowland, which complemented the open fields, were carefully tended. The hay from the meadows was especially valuable for feeding the animals and other purposes.[26]

The lord of the manor reserved land on the manor for himself – his demesne. This comprised some of the strips in the open fields, referred to in the manorial records as 'old demesne', and the home farm in the central area, known as the 'new demesne'. The home farm comprised four elements: Hall Flatt, a fifteen-acre field bounded by the Headrow to the north, the gardens of the Briggate burgages to the east, Boar Lane to the south, and the manorial park to the west; Margaret Holmes, south of the manorial park; Gallowhill Flatt; and the Holmes – a twenty-acre field just south of the river.[27] In a traditional manorial system, lords of the manor, in addition to receiving rents from their bondmen, profited by imposing an onerous range of obligatory duties on them including farming the demesne. This was the case in Leeds, as is shown by an inventory and valuation of the manor land and tenancies, known as an 'extent', produced in 1341 just a few years before the outbreak of the Black Death. The extent records the services and dues of Robert Knostrop, bondman. For his cottage and small adjoining plot of land or garden (together known as a messuage) and one bovate of land in the open fields of Knostrop he paid a rent of 4s. 9d. a year. In addition, he was required at Christmas to give the lord of the manor 4 hens worth 6d. plus 40 hens' eggs or 2d. at Easter. The extent, written in Latin, then enumerated a long list of services he had to perform for the lord:

> He owes ploughing-service for 2 days at the winter sowing and 3 days at the Lent sowing, receiving each day [in return from the lord of the manor] 2 loaves of rye bread and 4 herring [as well as 5d.]; Also he owes harrowing-service with one man and one horse for 2 days at the winter sowing and 3 days at the Lent sowing, receiving each day one loaf of the same size and 2 herring [plus the payment of 5d.]. Also he must mow the lord's meadow which is called Hall Ing and with the other bondmen, spread, lift and carry the hay until the work is fully done, receiving each day one rye loaf and 2 herring, pottage [soup] and his share of 15d. for the meadow services aforesaid, in common with his neighbours [plus an additional payment of 3d.]; And he must reap the lord's corn in the autumn for 6 days with 2 men, receiving one rye loaf and 2 herring for each man on each day [plus 12d.]. And he must carry the lord's corn for three days in the autumn [receiving in return one loaf, 2 herring and 9d.]; And he must repair the dam of the water-mill when necessary, receiving one loaf of rye bread and 2 herring from the lord; and this service is not valued because it occurs irregularly, though he must always be ready to do it. Also he must fence the park with the lord's timber when necessary in company with his neighbours from Hall Flatt to Margaret Holmes. Also he must serve as reeve when chosen, receiving from the lord, in time of wainage [during the time of agricultural activity] 4 bushels of wheat in Lent and 4 bushels of wheat in autumn and the right to pasture 4 beasts in the meadow.[28]

In addition his son could not become a monk or priest nor his daughter be married without the permission of the lord. If his daughter was deflowered payment had to be made. He was also bound to attend the lord's court when summoned, and on his death the land reverted to the lord until a relative had paid an entry fine (the sum of money required to permit him to take over the dead man's tenancy). On the benefit side, bondmen were allowed into the communal woods of Tameclyff, Lolloweker and Ryngbank where, for a small fee, they could gather timber blown down by the wind. They also had the jealously guarded privilege of grazing a carefully controlled number of cattle on the common. Extra payment, however, had to be made for pannage, the privilege of your pigs being permitted to forage in the woods.

The manorial records show that in addition to the bondmen there were two other categories of inhabitant on the manor living by agriculture. Alongside the bondmen, and farming in a very similar manner, were the free men or freeholders. They also farmed strips in the open fields but they had the advantage of merely paying rent for their land and were 'free' from the obligations which the lord imposed on the bondmen. In the first half of the fourteenth century the free men represented about one-sixth of the thirty or so tenants of the open fields.[29] Despite the aura of feudal servitude which the obligations, such as those on a bondman like Robert Knostrop, implied, in relative terms a bondman was a person of some substance and standing in the community. He employed not only his family but wage labourers on his land. Indeed, the 1341 extent shows that Robert Knostrop farmed over 55 acres of land.

Below the freeholders and bondmen in the manorial hierarchy was the humble cottar. He merely rented a cottage with an adjoining plot of land, rarely more than an acre, and eked out a living as an agricultural labourer for the free men, bondmen, or the lord of the manor. Surname evidence suggests that the cottars were supplementing their income by spinning, weaving and dyeing cloth. The 1258 extent of the manor lists 20 cottars. In 1341 there were about a dozen.[30]

For the lord, the manor was primarily a source of revenue. He, or his agents, would aim to manage it in a way which would generate the greatest income possible within the constraints of manorial custom and practice and the economic conditions of the day. During the fourteenth century in England as a whole, there was a sharp decline in population and a corresponding rise in wage levels. We cannot be precise about the impact of the Black Death of 1348-9 and other devastating occurrences of plague in fourteenth-century Leeds, but it is likely that plague killed up to half the adult population of the manor.[31] Recovery in numbers, if it came, was probably slow. Given the sharp fall in population it became difficult for manorial lords to hold on to tenants and to enforce the existing terms of tenancies. The manorial accounts show a fall in income due to lapsed holdings and reduced values in the last decades of the fourteenth century. Successive reeves found it difficult to ensure that all the bondmen performed their duties to the full, and it seems unlikely that any agricultural services were demanded of the bondmen from the Black Death onwards and they were commuted for monetary payments. Though the 1399 manorial accounts stressed that the commutation was viewed as a temporary measure, perhaps the lord of the manor knew that the writing was on the wall.

Falling agricultural prices combined with rising wage levels, due to labour shortages, made farming the manorial demesne a much less profitable proposition for the lord. As the years went by, the lord's paid officials hired labour to farm the land and only at busy times of the farming year called upon the bondmen to perform

This reconstruction of the manor as it was by 1350 shows the village of Leeds still growing, but the planned town of 1207 (Briggate), with its neatly divided plots stretching down to the bridge, beginning to prosper. The 'allotments' or 'tofts' which belonged to the holders of the Briggate burgages had been created from an area of scrubland to the north-east (B), later known as Burmantofts. The park and Woodhouse Ridge remained partly wooded, but the community's supply of timber had to be supplemented from the woods at Rothwell and Roundhay. The settlements of Woodhouse and Knostrop had grown and land had been taken from the waste and brought into agricultural use.(C). The rabbit warren (A) had been abandoned and was now farmed.

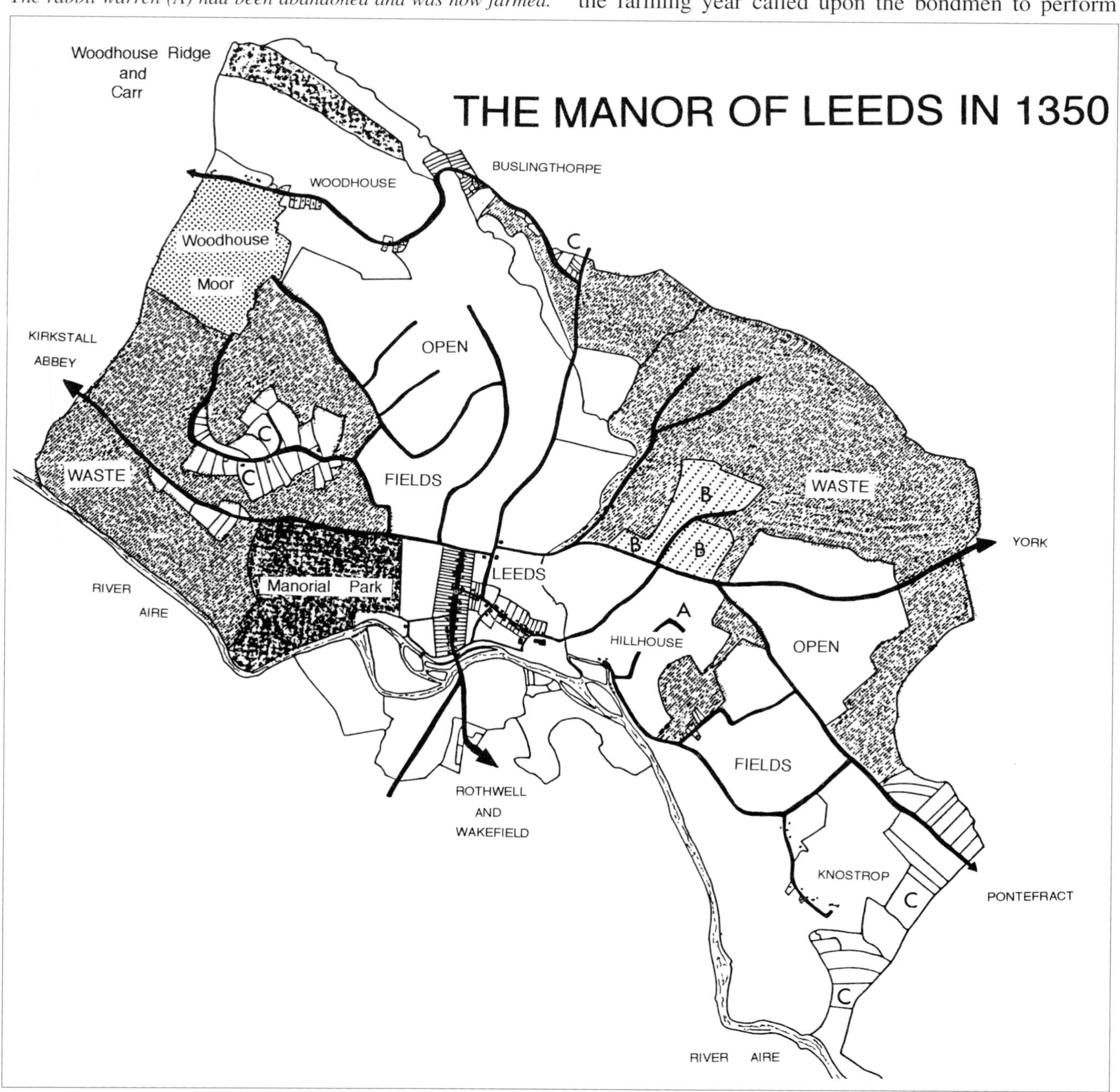

A medieval bell pit revealed during the digging of the foundations of a hotel just off Briggate c. 1900. Recent building work has revealed that the land between the Calls, Kirkgate and Briggate is peppered with similar pits from which miners extracted ironstone and occasionally coal as well.

their obligatory services. The 'new demesne', or home farm, was finally rented out in parcels to 22 tenants in 1343, and in 1399, though it was still farmed largely by the bondmen of Knostrop and Woodhouse, they worked it as leasehold tenants rather than by villein service.[33] By the end of the fourteenth century, therefore, the manor had ceased to be farmed or managed in the classic medieval manorial style. By virtue of the commutation of labour services and the disappearance of the demesne, the status and the style of life of a free man and a bondman were very much the same – perhaps the main distinction being the difference in the level of rents they paid for their holdings.

The movement away from the traditional system of farming was compounded by the process of assarting. Not all the land cultivated on the manor was arranged in the open field strip system. All the manorial accounts record rents paid for assarts. These were parcels of land cleared from the lord's waste by people who wished to increase the size of their holding. As the population of the manor increased in the century before the Black Death, more land had to be brought into cultivation to feed the inhabitants. Accordingly, one of the most important changes to the landscape was the reduction of the manor's wasteland and the emergence of these small enclosed areas, often on the periphery of the open field system.[34]

The Early Town

During the thirteenth and fourteenth centuries the life of the majority of the inhabitants of the manor was dominated by the demands of the farming year, ploughing, sowing, weeding, watering, harvesting, threshing and tending their animals. But even at the beginning of the period, not all the inhabitants were directly involved in farming. As far as possible agricultural communities were self-supporting, and skilled craftsmen such as carpenters and blacksmiths were needed. These craftsmen lived and worked in the village around the church and, increasingly after 1207, in the new borough on Briggate. Indeed, as we have seen, the borough had been established specifically to encourage non-agricultural activities. The occupants of the Briggate burgage plots paid a money rent for their dwellings and workshops and were free to carry out their trade without having to labour in the lord's fields.The surnames of some of the tenants of the manor in 1258, Shoemaker, Carpenter, Taylor, Smithson, and Baker, perhaps give a clue to some of the trade which were plied. Certainly, by then, Maurice Paynel's attempt to found a centre of commercial and industrial activity was beginning to bear fruit. The manorial extent of 1258 refers to a market in the borough, and the accounts of 1322/23 refer to both a market *and* fairs being held. By 1341 the market in Briggate took place on Mondays and there were two fairs, the lord levying tolls at 'the fairs held for one day on the feast of the apostles Peter and Paul [29 June] and for one other day on the feasts of the apostles Simon and Jude [28 October]'. The fairs, in particular, brought a range of goods to the manor which were not normally available in the district and, no doubt, entertainment as well. Probably there were originally twelve stalls in the market, but more were added during the fourteenth century. At the same time a number of shops were built at the northern end of the market-place.[35] The Poll Tax returns give us an idea of the range of occupations in the village by 1379. The highest taxed inhabitants included three smiths, two hostlers, two tailors, a cobbler, a baker, a dyer, a butcher, a mason and a merchant.[36] In addition to these village-based activities, coal mining was another notable non-agricultural activity on the manor; manorial documents make frequent reference to the valuable mines at Carlton Cross and Knostrop.[37]

Also within the manor in the thirteenth century were the beginnings of the industry which was to become central to the history of Leeds – the making of woollen cloth. The soils of the manor could only comfortably support a limited number of people, and as its population increased in the thirteenth century there was a major incentive, if not a necessity, for some of its inhabitants to look to a craft or trade as a major source of income. One of the key advantages of the manor was the soft water of the River Aire, ideal for use in the cloth finishing processes. Surnames derived from occupations are a clue to early textile activity in Leeds. The names listed in the 1258 extent include: Webster (weaver), Lister (dyer), and Taylor (tailor). Moreover, a Robertus Tynctor (dyer) de Ledes was a witness to a thirteenth-century Kirkstall Abbey charter.[38] The making of woollen cloth required skill rather than a great deal of capital, for only relatively small amounts of money were required to purchase a spinning wheel and loom. The initial development of woollen cloth making in Leeds was fairly slow because this manufacture was dominated by towns such as York and Beverley, where careful supervision by guilds ensured that the cloth produced was of high quality. Equally, though there were good wool supplies in the area from the sheep introduced by the Cistercian monks of Kirkstall, a large proportion of this was sold to merchants from the Low Countries and Italy.[39]

Perhaps the most laborious and arduous stage of woollen cloth making was fulling – the finishing process whereby the cloth, after weaving, was soaked in a mixture of water, urine and fuller's earth and pounded. As the cloth shrank it became thicker and the pounding knitted its fibres together. This gave the cloth a smoother and softer surface and made it much more hard-wearing. Teams of twelve or fourteen people had to 'walk' or trample the cloth in large troughs to achieve this task. During the Middle Ages, however, water-powered fulling mills were invented which pounded the cloth with wooden hammers while it lay in troughs. This was a major technological breakthrough which was of immense benefit to clothiers. Significantly, the first reference to a fulling mill being used in England is to one powered by a stream on the Templar's manor of Temple Newsam in 1185, only four miles from Leeds.[40] The adoption of these water-powered fulling mills in the thirteenth century in the rural areas of Yorkshire, where fast flowing rivers and streams were available, adversely affected the prosperity of towns such as York and Beverley. Fulling mills were expensive to build, and therefore were a scarce facility, but they were very profitable because clothiers very readily paid to use them. By 1322 the lord of the manor had erected a fulling mill in Leeds on the east side of Leeds Bridge and this must have greatly encouraged the growth of cloth production in the district.[41] Specialist workers, such as dyers, found employment, and Leeds gained a reputation as a finishing centre for the surrounding villages. By 1356 there was enough business to warrant the lord constructing a second fulling mill, this time on the western side of the bridge.[42] Another indicator of the growth of the woollen industry in Leeds was the erection of tenter frames. After cloth had been fulled it was taken into fields where it was dried and stretched to the required size on rows of wooden posts with hooks in them known as tenter frames. From at least the thirteenth century, frames occupied the fields skirting the north bank of the river.[43]

The Manorial Administration

From the Norman Conquest the manor was held by absentee landlords and, probably for this reason, by the fourteenth century the fortified manor house or 'castle' on the site today partly occupied by the Scarbrough public house in Bishopgate Street, had been demolished. The extent of 1341 noted under the heading 'Capital Messuage' that 'there is there the site of the manor [house] without any building, enclosed by a moat, together with an enclosure for a courtyard and another enclosure for a grange [a granary or group of farm buildings] now built'.[44] The existence of the building and earthworks was recalled by a reference in the manorial records of 1499 to 'Castelhyll'. Thoresby suggested that the stone from the manor house were used to build the medieval bridge.[45]

In the lord's absence the manor was administered by his representatives. The affairs of the manor and borough were regulated by manorial courts which had jurisdiction over much of the property on the manor. The court baron enforced the customs of the manor and dealt with matters such as surrenders of land and the use of the open fields and wastes, and protected the ancient rights of both lord and tenant. Those who held land in the manor had the terms of their leases recorded at the court and could then purchase a copy of the entry in the court rolls. In theory

Leeds manor house with its moat in the early eighteenth century, shown on a woodcut included in Thomas Gent's, History of Ripon published in 1733. Today the site is occupied by the Scarbrough public house in Bishopgate Street.

the court was supposed to meet every three weeks with all leaseholders in attendance, but in practice there was insufficient business to warrant such regular meetings. In the financial year 1383/4, for example, only three courts were held. In addition to the court baron, there was the twice yearly court leet, where every adult resident had to be present. Here minor criminal matters and personal actions under £2 were dealt with. For the townsmen of Briggate there was a separate borough court. The courts baron and leet were presided over by the lord's steward, whereas the borough court was presided over by the manorial bailiff. The day-to-day affairs of the manor were supervised by the reeve, a local man, who was appointed by the lord of the manor. He was responsible for collecting all monies due to the lord, and each year he presented his accounts to the lord's steward and receiver. These accounts give a vital insight into life within the manor, particularly because none of the court rolls have survived. The reeve also supervised the repair and maintenance of all manorial buildings, often disbursing large sums of money. Meanwhile the day-to-day affairs of the borough were supervised by the bailiff.[46]

In 1258 the manor was reckoned to produce an annual profit for the lord of over £38. For most of the fourteenth century the profit was in the region of £70-£80, although it did decline a little at the end of the century. Taking as a rule of thumb that a craftsman, for example a carpenter, earned around 4d. per day in the first half of the fourteenth century and a labourer 2d., a profit of around £75 per annum in the early fourteenth century was equivalent to at least seventeen times a skilled worker's annual wages and thirty-four times that of a labourer.[47] Surprisingly, perhaps, only about half of the manorial income came from the rents from the land and payments in lieu of labour services. The second largest source of income was from the manorial amenities. When the tenant had gathered in his corn, threshed it and stored it, he was not free to grind it into flour or bake it into bread on his own premises. He was bound to use the lord's corn mill, situated on Swinegate, and the manorial oven, located at the top of Kirkgate. These were valuable monopolies, as were the first fulling mills the lord built in the manor, and he thought it well worth while to invest considerable sums in them. Such facilities were a major benefit for the manor's inhabitants and, in view of the very high construction and maintenance costs, initially the lord's monopoly was justified. In later years, however, the inhabitants came to see it as an unjust imposition. In 1258, out of the manorial revenue of £38 4s. 7d., the lease of the mill contributed £12 and the fees from the market and oven £10.[48]

Without doubt, the most valuable asset on the manor was the corn mill which generated around £14 per annum throughout the Middle Ages. The River Aire provided the necessary substantial head of water but from time-to-time its powerful flood waters damaged the mill and dams. The maintenance of High Dam (now under City Station) and Bondman Dam (which diverted water to the corn mill) was a constant drain on manorial income, as well as the natural resources of the manor. They were complex structures. The dams were faced at front and back by parallel rows of wooden piles driven into the bed of the river or goit. A timberwork frame, constructed by local carpenters, was placed between the piles, and the core of the dam was filled with stones, sand, clay, turves and faggots. The sheer scale of constructing and maintaining the mill is demonstrated by the manorial accounts for 1383/84 which record the massive outlay of £15 required to repair the High Dam when the river burst its banks:

The remains of a medieval tomb in Leeds Parish Church. The beautiful effigy carved in limestone depicts a knight in chain mail. On his left he has a shield, the armorial bearings suggesting that he was from the Manston family.

> And 68s. 7½d. for the wages of 40 carpenters for four days (60s.) and 23 carpenters as for one day (8s. 7½d.) felling timber in Rothwell Park and Seacroft Wood, cutting into posts, preparing it for transport ...constructing "scultrees", piles and beams from it and with these repairing a breach by the High Dam there caused by the exceptional floods during the winter of this year coming suddenly from the broken

banks, and on account of this breach the water flowed out, leaving the water-course leading to the mill completely dry, each carpenter receiving 4½d. a day; and 24s. 6d. for the wages of sundry carters transporting the said timber from the aforesaid places to the breach, that is making 21 journeys from Rothwell Park ...and 28 journeys from Seacroft Wood; ...and 20s. for part of a quarry bought from Roger Leeds at Leeds Townend to obtain stone for completing these works; and 104s. wages of 60 workmen as for 4 days (60s.), 52 workmen as 1 day (13s.) ...each drawing 3d a day ...all removing a bank of sand and gravel which had been piled up in the bed of the stream near the breach, ...breaking stones, ...loading the stones, ...carrying and laying them there and so completely filling the said breach with the stones and also with turves, sand and faggots, ...driving piles and helping the aforesaid carpenters to lift the timber and set in position.[49]

Stone came from Headingley Moor, and Armley as well as the quarry at Town End specially purchased for the purpose.

The fulling mills, too, produced the much smaller but valuable income of around £2-£3 per annum in the fourteenth century.[50] A similar income was obtained from the manorial oven or 'bakehouse'. The oven was in constant need of repair, and was regularly rebuilt. In the 1323/4 accounts 13s. 10d. was paid for 'repairing the ruined building of the common oven, together with the carriage of the said timber to the said building, purchase of pegs and straw for the same, cutting posts for the roof and repairing the walls in places.'[51] The lord also made money out of the fish in the river. The fishing rights were let to the highest bidder. In 1356 the lord received 2s. 6d., though the reeve noted that it used to yield 6s. 8d.[52] The Normans introduced rabbits into the district, keeping them in special enclosures called conygers or conygarths. Rabbit meat was highly prized and their fur was in much demand. The field name 'Conyshaw' suggests that the Leeds warren was on the western edge of the Knostrop field system. This, however, was not one of the lord's more successful ventures for the land was quickly let to tenants.[53]

To simplify the task of administering the manor it became the habit of the lord to 'farm out', that is to lease out, the manor's amenities. A local man of substance would pay a fixed annual sum for the lease of the corn mill or manorial oven, for example, and would collect and keep all the profits they made. It also became the habit to farm out the bailiwick of the manor, the office of bailiff with the accompanying revenues. Sir Roger Leeds of North Hall, for example, at the end of the fourteenth century held a twelve year lease of the town. As bailiff he was entitled to the profits of the borough court over which he or his deputy presided and to the tolls levied on goods sold in the Monday market and at the two annual fairs. As lessee of the manorial oven and the corn mill he also exercised the seigneurial monopolies of baking and milling. His levies in respect of each would have been a notable charge on the inhabitants.[54]

Though the manorial courts could deal with some criminal matters and disputes between tenants, they could not deal with serious crime. In such instances the inhabitants had to look outside the manor for justice, perhaps to the county sheriff, the Justices of the Peace (whose role began to develop in significance from the later years of the fourteenth century), or to the higher courts of the land. The most infamous instance, and one which brings medieval Leeds to life, concerned the death of William de Wayte. In August 1318 Robert of North Hall, the son of one of the wealthiest men in Leeds, and William de Wayte had a furious row over a gambling game they were playing before church. Neighbours intervened and the matter seemed to have been settled peacefully. After church, however, William, his page and John de Manston loitered in the churchyard. As Robert left the church John de Manston taunted him and William and his page rounded the corner with their swords drawn. Robert ran back to the church but finding the door barred he had to defend himself against William with his buckler (a small shield). In the ensuing fight he fatally wounded William with his sword. In revenge John de Manston, Thomas Nesant and the chaplain dragged Robert to the area between the cemetery and the ditch of the churchyard and brutally attacked him, leaving him for dead. His brothers found him and took him to a nearby house where he subsequently recovered. Despite his innocence, Robert was accused of murder and, since this was far too serious a matter to be dealt with by the manorial courts, he was arrested and detained in Marshalsea prison in London to await trial. Fortunately, witnesses supported his claim of self-defence and he was released without conviction. Such an incident reminds us that though Leeds was predominantly an agricultural community peopled by peasants, it was part of a wider world in which knights and gentlemen frequently fought with each other and violence and lawlessness were problems of the age.[55]

St Peter's, the religious centre of the vast parish of Leeds, was one of the largest medieval churches in the West Riding.

Church and Abbey

So far little has been said of

The ruins of Kirkstall Abbey as they appeared in Ralph Thoresby's, Ducatus Leodiensis published in 1715.

the Church, and yet it underpinned society in medieval Leeds. At some time during the reign of Edward III (1327-1377) a disastrous fire destroyed the old parish church, and as a result a fine new building, shaped like a cross, with choir, transepts, nave and aisles was built on the same site. Its crowning glory was the tower, 96 feet high, whose rubble infill incorporated the stone from the ancient crosses, which by then were regarded as pagan artefacts. The new church dwarfed all other buildings in the district and dominated the sky-line. It must have been one of the largest in the West Riding, and a source of great pride for the parishioners, reflecting the increasing importance of the settlement.[56] The Church had a great influence upon the everyday lives of the people, but this came at a price. All men had to pay the tithes. One tenth of their produce had to be taken to the huge tithe barn sited on the west side of the parish church. This additional burden was resented by many, particularly because much of the income accrued from the sale of tithe produce went to institutions and individuals outside the parish.[57]

Only three miles north-west of the parish church, on a remote wooded site beside the River Aire, stood an even more important religious institution – the mighty Cistercian abbey of Kirkstall.[58] In 1152, at the behest of Henry de Lacy, the site was given for the foundation of an abbey to Abbot Alexander and twelve monks and ten lay brothers, who moved there after an unhappy attempt to establish an abbey at Barnoldswick in Lancashire. Henry continued to support the small community and, before the death of the first abbot in 1182, the impressive range of stone buildings including the church, chapterhouse, dormitories and dining halls, whose ruins are familiar to us today, had been erected.

The community was able to finance the construction of such impressive buildings because it was extremely successful at acquiring gifts of land, particularly on the barren sandstone lands on the western and northern borders of Leeds, where the devastating effects of the 'harrying of the North' were still in evidence. Within a relatively short period the order had become owners of very large tracts of land within the parish of Leeds including Allerton, Moor Allerton, Allerton Gledhow, Potternewton, Meanwood, Weetwood, Beeston, Bramley, Armley, East Headingley and West Headingley. Moreover, its estates came to include land outside the parish, not only in Cookridge, Eccup, Adel, Seacroft and Roundhay, but also further afield in Bessacar near Doncaster and at Barnoldswick. Significantly, no grants were received of land on the highly fertile edge of the Aire Valley at Leeds and Knostrop. The abbot of Kirkstall therefore became the most influential landowner in the Leeds district. The estates generated considerable income. In 1288, for example, when the manor of Leeds was bringing in around £70-80 per annum, the abbey's estates yielded £207. By 1459 while the manor was still producing around £70-80, the abbey's rents had increased to £354.[59]

Initially it was the Cistercians' skill as agricultural pioneers which accounted for the growth in their wealth. They cleared woodlands, encouraged cattle breeding, and created granges (farms) such as those at Allerton Grange, Moor Grange, and Bar Grange, which became bases for their extensive sheep grazing activities. Wool became a vital source of income for the community. By 1301 the abbey owned around 4,500 sheep.[60] Much of the produce from the abbey's estates including grain, wool, and dairy products were brought to Kirkstall by road and river. By the mid-fourteenth century the abbey was much less involved in the direct cultivation of its lands than hitherto. The practice of including lay brothers in the community, who were responsible for working on and supervising work on the farm lands, was in decline, and by 1381 only six remained. Gradually more and more of the estates were leased out for a money rental.

It is difficult to assess the impact of the existence of the abbey on the village and manor of Leeds. Certainly, the abbey had a significant involvement in the manor in the later years of its existence. By the late fifteenth century the abbot was the most substantial copyhold tenant in Woodhouse and in consequence was reeve of the manor in 1499-1500 and 1536-37.[61] Equally, local families were tenants on the abbey's lands, and, indeed, local men such as William de Leeds and Roger de Leeds held the position of abbot in 1269-75 and 1349-1351 respectively.[62] The degree of contact between the inhabitants and the monks is a matter for speculation. In theory it should have been very restricted, for parishioners would not normally have worshipped in the abbey and the church authorities would have taken a very dim view if they had. In 1314, for example, Archbishop Greenfield of York called the abbot to account before the archdeacon for admitting parishioners of Leeds to the small chapel on the first floor of the abbey gatehouse and for allowing others to be buried in the abbey.[63] Perhaps we will never know whether the solemnity of religious life gave way to periods of ribald and high living. In other parts of the country by the late-fourteenth and fifteenth centuries, some monks were to be found going hunting and hawking, and frequenting both taverns and women. Some abbots were living more like country gentlemen than men devoted to a secluded life of worship.[64] All we can say for certain is that Kirkstall Abbey offered hospitality to passing lords, gentlemen and wayfarers. It stood on the route between the major administrative centres of Pontefract and Clitheroe, and possessed an extensive range of costly stone buildings to the west of its church, including a main hall, chamber block, kitchen, bakehouse, and stables, which must have provided luxurious self-contained accommodation for visitors and longer-stay guests. Furthermore, though the abbot, under the rules of the order, was supposed to sleep in the same unheated dormitory as his monks, in practice he had his own very pleasant set of rooms with fireplaces and a gallery.

To some degree the abbey must have constrained the early economic development of Leeds. Though it was a centre of great economic activity, the wool produced on its estates immediately to the west and north of the manor was sold in the thirteenth and early fourteenth centuries directly to Italian merchants, who probably stayed in its Guest House on their visits. This denied Leeds the opportunity to be the market place for this important commodity, though it is likely that some of the abbey's other produce was sold in the market.[65] Restrictions on the export of wool in the fourteenth century, however, encouraged the Cistercians to sell their high quality wool locally, and this no doubt gave a major stimulus to the growth of cloth-making in the parish. Equally as the abbey leased out more and more of its lands, its control on the distribution and sale of local produce must have diminished. Certainly, the abbey had some commercial involvement in Leeds, for the abbot held the tenancy of two 'shops' at the top of the butchers' shambles in the early-sixteenth century.[66]

By the end of the fourteenth century the lord of the manor of Leeds had good reason to be pleased. Despite war and pestilence all the customary holdings on the manor were taken and the woollen industry was beginning to bring real prosperity to the market town. Leeds, nevertheless, still had a long way to go before it could be viewed as a town of the first or second rank in Yorkshire. The Poll Tax returns for 1379 show that York, Beverley, Kingston upon Hull and Scarborough were the wealthiest towns in county, followed by Doncaster and Pontefract. Leeds rated only fourteenth in the list of West Riding places which contributed to the tax. Significantly, however, it was already the second most highly assessed town in the Aire and Calder valleys. Of the listed 157 inhabitants (almost exactly two-thirds of whom were married) only 14 individuals paid above the minimum rate of 4d. The returns are a highly imperfect guide to the size of the town, but they suggest that the population of the parish might have been around 1000, of which roughly half lived in the timber-framed houses that abutted the central streets of the town.[67]

At the very tail end of the fourteenth century Leeds became a royal manor. By a long and circuitous route, the manor had passed from the hands of Maurice Paynel into the great inheritance of Henry of Lancaster. Leeds thereby became the property of the Crown when Henry became king, as Henry IV, in 1399. Thereafter, as a royal manor, it was part of the honour of Pontefract and its courts were presided over by the steward of the honour, who in turn was answerable to the council of the Duchy of Lancaster.[68]

The Rise of the Leeds Gentry

For much of the fifteenth century the manor was less profitable than it had been, its profits having declined to around £62-£66 per annum in the period 1383-1471 compared to £70-£80 in the earlier part of the fourteenth century. The impact of this fall in income was compounded by the lord's rising costs. Daily wage rates rose to around 5d. for a skilled worker and 4d. for a labourer in the fifteenth century as a result of labour shortages, Nevertheless, the manor remained a valuable asset producing a profit of at least twelve times the annual wages of a skilled worker and fifteen times those of a labourer.[69] The decline in profitability was due in part to higher maintenance costs. Major expense was incurred, for example, in 1438 with the complete rebuilding, on its moated site, of the manorial oven with the manorial court house, known as the Hall of Pleas, above it.[70] But lower revenues also resulted from the fall in population. In 1425 the manor had only 62 tenants compared with 100 in 1343.[71]

There seems to have been a considerable turnover in the population between the mid-fourteenth century and the first quarter of the fifteenth century. By 1425 there remained only 11 families whose surnames indicated that they had occupied lands in Leeds before the Black Death.[72] The breaking down of the traditional pattern and tenure of landholding, and the increased availability of land to rent due to the clearing of the manorial waste, coupled with the renting out of the demesne and some subdivision and sale of customary holdings, created a land market in Leeds. The local gentry were quick to perceive the advantages of investing in the manor.

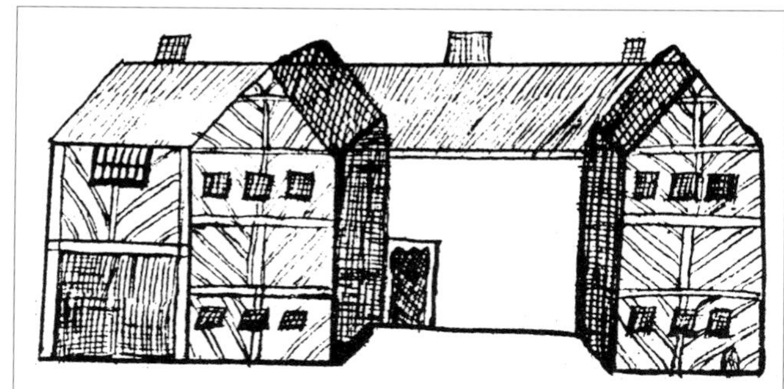

Rockley Hall, sited near the junction of the Headrow and Vicar Lane, was the impressive home of Henry Rockley, the town bailiff and farmer of the manorial oven, who died in 1502.

During the fifteenth century the Romes of Cat-Beeston, the Nevilles of Cundall, the Scargills of Thorpe Stapleton and the de Ledes family of North Hall invested heavily, acquiring most of the freehold land in the manor, which they then sub-let at a profit. They had great influence in the town, where they held many of the burgage plots. As bailiffs of the town during most of the first half of the fifteenth century, the Scargills were entitled to the rents of the sixty burgages, the tolls levied on the goods sold in the Monday market and at the two annual fairs, and the perquisites of the Court of Burgesses. The de Ledes family chose to live near the town, at North Hall, but few of the gentry resided in the central township. One of the few exceptions was Henry Rockley, who built a most impressive house for himself on the Headrow. For a period he was bailiff of the town, farmed the manorial oven, and leased land in the manorial park. Probably he was also involved in collecting the tax paid on cloth. His great influence in the town is reflected in the fact that he had his own chapel in Leeds Parish church, where he was eventually buried in September 1502.[73]

The dissolution of Kirkstall Abbey on 22 November 1539 also had a dramatic impact on the local land market. In the post-dissolution period former monastic lands around Leeds were eagerly purchased or leased, not only by old established families like the Killingbecks of Chapel Allerton or the Arthington family of Arthington, but new businessmen like the Wades and the Foxcrofts who saw an opportunity to increase their income.[74] The arrival of these new, dynamic families acted as a spur to economic development. While the gentry took advantage of the supply of land, it was clear that the inhabitants involved in the textile industry also continued to successfully exploit opportunities for growth. More mills were built as the woollen manufacture continued to expand. Growth of the industry was considerable in the fifteenth century: Gilbert Legh of Middleton was willing to speculate a very large sum in 1455 when he was granted land on which to build a fulling mill at a place called Steander, close to where the river and Sheepscar Beck met.[75] Two more mills were erected in the next fifty years. Equally, there were regular additions to other cloth making facilities. Nine new tenters, for example, were being erected on the river banks on both sides of Leeds Bridge in the decade after 1455.[76]

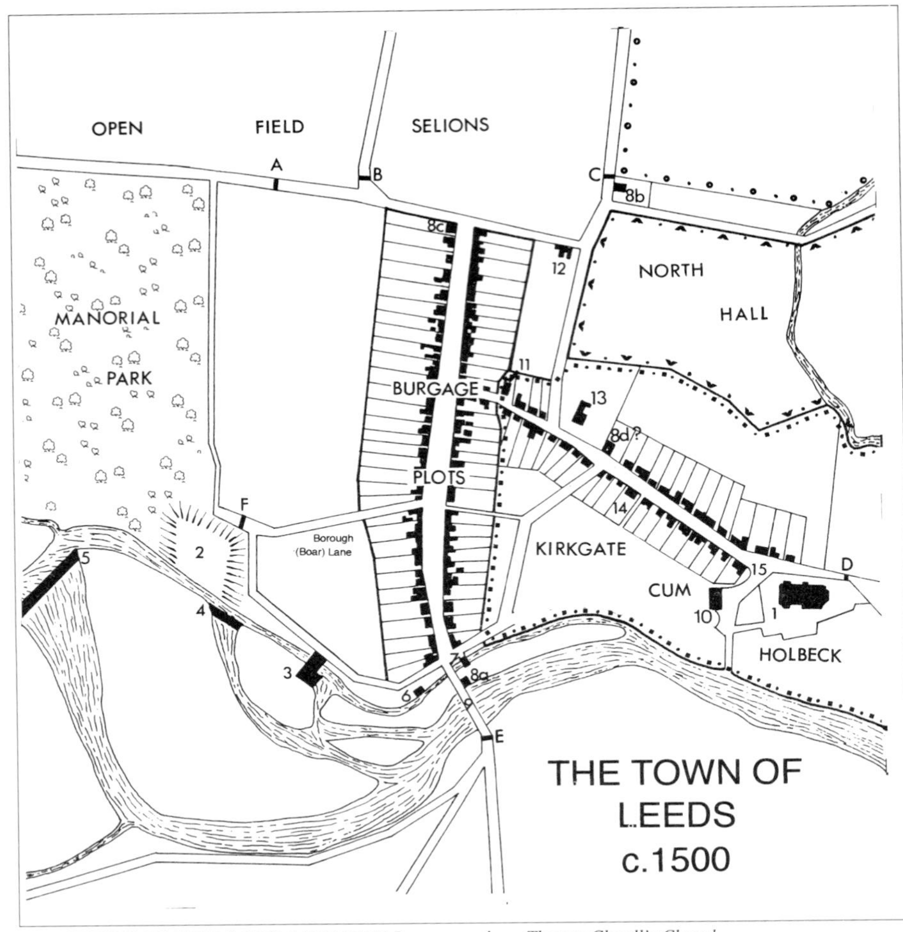

LEEDS IN THE LATE MEDIEVAL PERIOD.

KEY:

1. *St. Peter's — the parish church*
2. *Castelhyll — site of the former fortified manor house*
3. *Manorial Corn Mill*
4. *Bondman Dam*
5. *High Dam*
6. *Fulling mill*
7. *Fulling mill*
8. *Chantry Chapels:*
   - a. *St. Mary's on the Bridge*
   - b. *Lady Chapel*
   - c. *Sir William Eures' Chapel*
   - d. *Thomas Clarell's Chapel*
9. *Leeds Bridge*
10. *Tithe Barn*
11. *Manorial Oven with Hall of Pleas above*
12. *Rockley Hall*
13. *The Vicarage*
14. *The Hospitium.*
15. *Manor house of Kirkgate-cum-Holbeck.*

The Bars — the boundaries of the medieval town

- A. *Burley Bar.*
- B. *Woodhouse Bar.*
- C. *North Bar.*
- D. *East or York Bar.*
- E. *South Bar.*
- F. *West Bar.*

The parish church of St Peter's continued to dominate the religious life of the huge parish, for though masses were celebrated and baptisms performed in the out-lying chapelries when they were erected, all parishioners had to be buried at the mother church. It was the final resting place for the élite, whose brasses, funeral monuments and effigies cluttered the interior of the building. Recent additions, repairs and alterations had improved the fine old structure. Grateful clergy and parishioners generously provided funds for the creation of chapels, including the chapel of Jesu Guild, the chantry of St Katherine and Rockley Quire.[77]

There were also chantry chapels scattered around the town. On the north side of the bridge there was St Mary's chantry chapel for the use of travellers. Another was built in Vicar Lane. The fashion continued into the sixteenth century. By his will dated 1524 William Eure, Vicar of Leeds, left money for the construction of a chantry and further funds to support a priest who, besides ministering at the altar, was 'to pray and keep a yearly obit of 7s. to be distributed for the weal [benefit] of the soul of the founder' and had to serve in the choir at divine service on festivals and Holy Days. The chapel was built on the west side of Briggate, at the junction with the Headrow. Leeds was thus well served by priests and religious buildings. Further chapels were built outside the central area at Chapel Allerton, Farnley, Holbeck and Beeston.[78]

Sixteenth-Century Expansion

The sixteenth century saw major growth and change in Leeds. In 1500 agriculture still dominated the life of the manor, but the development of the town in the previous two centuries ensured that it would benefit from the phenomenal growth of the woollen cloth industry in the West Riding during the sixteenth century and the drift of production away from the ancient chartered boroughs. John Leland (1506-1553), noted the importance of the cloth industry to Leeds when he made his famous tour through England begun in 1534: 'Ledis, 2 miles lower than Christal Abbay, on Aire Ryver, is a praty Market,

These sixteenth-century timber-framed houses of one and two storeys, on the west side of Briggate just below Boar Lane, were to survive into the 1860s.

having one Paroche Chirche reasonably welle buildid, and as large as Bradeford but not so quik as it. The Toun standith most by Clothing.'[79]

The West Riding clothiers, producing cloth in their cottages in rural hamlets and small towns such as Leeds, were free from the onerous guild restrictions and high rents of chartered boroughs. They constantly exploited new markets and made in-roads into the traditional markets in which the cloth produced in the centres of York and Beverley had once predominated. The situation was summarised by a York writer commenting on the state of trade in the city in 1561:

> The cause of the decay of the ...weavers and loomes for woollen cloth within the sayd cite as I doe understand and learn is the lak of cloth makyng in the said cite as was in old tyme accustomed, which is nowe encreased and used in the townes of Halyfax, Leedes and Wakefield, for that not only the comodytie of the watermylnes is ther nigh at hande, but also the poor folk as speynners, carders, and other necessary work-folkes for the said webbyng, may ther besyde ther hand labor, have rye, fyre, and other releif good cheape, which is in the cite very deare and wantyng.[80]

The successful expansion of woollen cloth production was responsible for a remarkable growth of population in Leeds in the later years of the sixteenth century and the early seventeenth century. Estimates for this period are fraught with difficulties, but the evidence of very extensive population growth in the parish, particularly towards the end of the century, is unmistakable. Between 1576-80 and 1621-5 the rate of baptisms, marriages, and burials more than doubled, suggesting a doubling in the population of the parish, and almost certainly a doubling in the population of the town. By 1600 the population of Leeds stood perhaps at around 4,000, while by the 1620s it had reached about 5,000 to 6,000.[81]

People anxious to enjoy a more prosperous life in the bustling market town were drawn to Leeds in large numbers. Not only were there low rents, cheap fuel and easy access to fulling and dyeing facilities, but small plots of land were available for craftsmen who wished to keep livestock, grow their own vegetables or erect a tenter frame. Moreover, seasonal work was available on the surrounding farmland. Manorial restrictions were no longer sufficiently burdensome to be a deterrent.

The expansion of cloth production in Leeds in the Elizabethan period was considerable. A survey of the Yorkshire industry dated 1595 noted: 'At Wackefeilde, Leedes, and some other smale villages, nere there aboutes, there is made about 30 packes of brode cloths every weecke, and ev'y packe is four whole clothes; the sort made in Wackefeilde are pukes, tawneys, browns, blues, and some reddes; in Leeds of all colours.'[82] Leeds possessed clothiers with considerable initiative who were prepared to seek out new opportunities. An outstanding example was Randall Tenche, who placed several tenter frames on a large tract of land which he leased near the bridge. In 1589 he successfully negotiated a contract to make fancy cloth for Sir Francis Willoughby of Wollaton Hall, near Nottingham. The work he undertook to perform included 'the dyeing of Sir Francis Willoughby's wool, and the spinning, dyeing, and working of Arres work (tapestry work) of all sorts, which he is emboldened to do, more especially as he has found out a workman or two who will join with him or be under him, who will work any work that shall be set unto them by a painter in colours, and to work the same in woollen yarn, …or in silk or silver or gold or altogether'. For this he received the handsome sum of £50 per annum plus the wages of his workmen at 6s. 8d. Tenche was renowned as an honest workman, and became one of the searchers of the town charged with seizing all pieces that did not conform to legal standards.[83]

The demolition of this house in North Street in 1896 revealed a timber-framed structure with pargetting (decorative plasterwork) placed on the frontage to make the building more impressive.

As the clothiers of Leeds became increasingly successful, part of their wealth was used to construct more elaborate timber-framed houses, which were no longer just single storey dwellings. The contents of their houses remained relatively simple, yet they owned far more than their forebears. A very detailed inventory dated 1576 has survived listing the contents of the house of John Pawson, a clothier living in Kirkgate. On his death he left £69 18s. 5d. to his wife and son, and a further £23 4s. 8d. was shared between other relatives, the poor and gifts for the repair of highways. In his kitchen, the only room with a fireplace, there was an iron range for cooking, along with various pots and pans, two salts and three candlesticks. Its furniture consisted of a cupboard, a long table, two chairs and two stools. His purse, with 16d. in coin, a girdle, a dagger and his clothes were also found in the kitchen. In the unheated bedroom there were five valuable silver spoons and 30s. in money. In a cupboard there were blankets, covers, towels, pillows and sheets. There was also 'one counter[pane] and two pairs of bedstocke'. Also stored there were twelve flitches of salted beef for the winter. The chamber was the main store room where the white and coloured wool was kept, along with butter for use in weaving, and alum, a fixative for dye. There were sacks of barley, rye and wheat, as well as kneading tubs for making bread. Two huge arks contained the flour for the household and meal for the pigs. In his shop and loomhouse were rolls of finished cloth and the tools of his trade, namely, spinning wheels, a loom, a shearboard and various specialist implements. As the officials making the inventory moved into the back yard they noted a leadhouse for the dyeing of wool and cloth, together with assorted tubs and baskets. To the rear they found a barn full of hay and grass, and a quantity of wool, coals and sawn boards. There were hens, cows and pigs and John's horse with a pair of saddles. Surprisingly, perhaps, John Pawson did not own the freehold of his Kirkgate home, though he did own three tenements in Marsh Lane and some land in Woodhouse.[84]

While the cloth industry was expanding rapidly there was very considerable change in the agricultural framework of Leeds. Many people from the West Riding and elsewhere were attracted to Leeds, particularly after the dissolution of Kirkstall Abbey in 1539, when land flooded on to the market. Much of this was purchased by the sons of yeomen farmers and clothiers, who farmed the land more intensively, as well as producing cloth. It is perhaps significant that 24 of the 29 families which were represented on Leeds corporation created in 1626 were either first or second generation newcomers to the district, several of whom were descended from yeoman families who had settled on former abbey lands.[85] This in-migration, coupled with a rise in the birth rate amongst the existing population led to the marked increase in population already noted.

Such large numbers of people placed new demands upon the land, one of the most notable changes being the eventual abandonment of communal farming. In 1538 the ancient manorial park, by then almost totally denuded of trees, was divided up into enclosed arable fields by Sir Arthur Darcy, an act which caused some consternation in the manor.[86] By 1548 the majority of tenants holding land in the remaining open fields were successful townsmen, who either sub-let these large units or sought to break them down into small enclosed areas, which could be used for a variety of agricultural or industrial purposes.

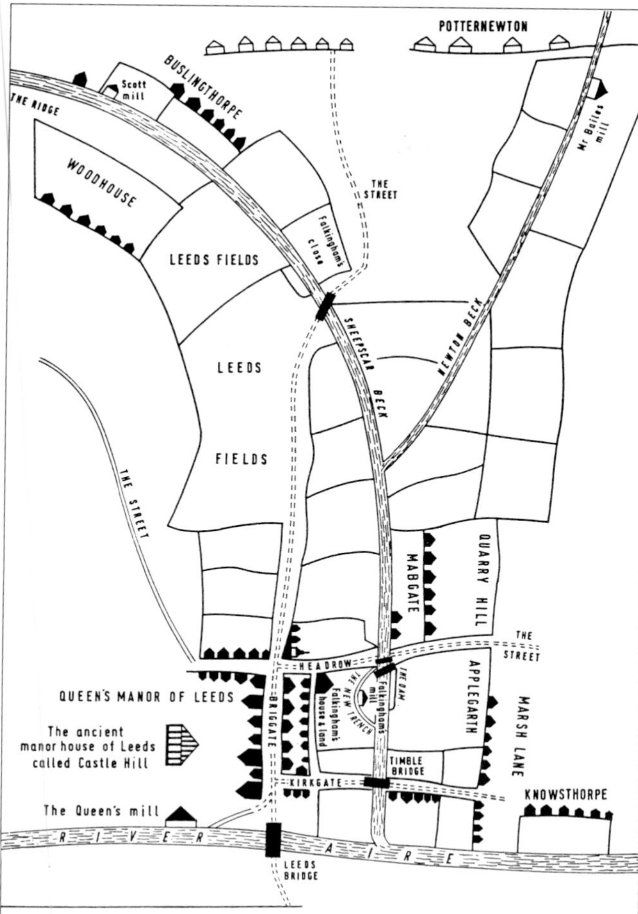

The first surviving plan of Leeds, 1560. This plan, which has been redrawn, was produced as evidence in a law-suit over mill rights. It indicates the main locations of the houses, and the positions of the ancient manor house, the Queen's Mill and Falkingham's Mill. The central streets, as well as the outlying hamlets, are clearly shown.

Over the next fifty years this process accelerated, and by the end of the century most of the traditional open field strips of land had, by exchange and agreement, been made into long, narrow fields surrounded by either walls, fences or hedges. Almost all the remaining lands of the home farm had been enclosed by 1548. There appears to have been little opposition to the total abandonment of communal farming, and the lord no doubt welcomed the money raised by granting licences allowing enclosure.[87]

While landholders still paid him rents, their value or burden was much eroded. Generally they had been fossilised at rates set centuries before, and the Tudor inflation, amounting to around 450 per cent over the sixteenth century, caused their real value to plummet. Thus in 1548 tenants who still held a customary bovate of land – a holding for which they had been obliged to perform extremely onerous labour services in the thirteenth century – paid a yearly rent of a mere 6s. 8d. to the lord, at a time when the wages of a skilled craftsman were around 4s. a week. By 1612, when a craftsman's weekly wages were around 6s., the rent due to the lord for 12 acres of land in Woodhouse, for example, was 2s., while the tenants of a complete burgage plots on Briggate paid 1s. 4d.[88]

The town had outgrown the manorial framework created for raising revenue for the lord and for controlling a much smaller population, whose livelihood was based mainly on the land. In the fourteenth and fifteenth centuries it had been the local gentry, the non-aristocratic small landed families, who dominated the life of Leeds and held the important manorial offices. In the sixteenth century, however, it was the wealthier clothiers and tradesmen, and resident landlords who sought to gain control of the town and its industry.[89] Growth and prosperity could only be sustained if the woollen industry continued to thrive. Many of the wealthier clothiers and merchants-clothiers became concerned that the good name of Leeds cloth would be damaged unless steps were taken to ensure its quality. To this end attempts were made in the 1570s to secure a charter creating a corporation in Leeds whose members would have powers to inspect cloth produced in the district, remove substandard material and prosecute offenders. For the moment this attempt failed.[90]

Denied such powers, the close-knit upper ranks of Leeds inhabitants sought to occupy existing positions of importance in the town. By 1553 the chief officers in Leeds were residents. John Casson, for example, a clothier of some repute, became steward, presiding over the court leet. The town bailiff, Henry Ambler, had jurisdiction over the Monday market and annual fairs. As well as sharing in the perquisites of the courts, he exercised the monopoly over baking. Even minor posts, such as ale conners, inspectors and appraisers of goods were much prized, because to occupy these positions improved a person's standing in the community.[91]

The more dynamic and independent-minded townsmen were increasingly frustrated by influences and controls on their lives from outside the town. Major irritants were the archaic manorial monopolies. As the population expanded, the work at the manorial corn mill in Swinegate (now known as either the King's or the Queen's Mills depending whether the monarch was male or female) increased to such an extent that it found it difficult to cope. Thomas Falkingham of the manor of North Hall decided to construct a new mill on his land at Mill Garth. The Queen's miller, having paid a considerable sum for the monopoly of grinding the corn of the inhabitants of Leeds, immediately challenged the legality of Falkingham's actions. The ensuing law suit dragged on for over twenty years. Fortunately for us, it had the incidental benefit in around 1560 of producing the first map of Leeds.[92] Further quarrels between the Queen's miller and the miller of Hunslet regarding the rights of the inhabitants of Kirkgate to grind their corn where they wished, also led to protracted legal action.[93]

Turning to religious life in Leeds, the dissolution of the chantries in 1547 drastically reduced the number of priests at work in the district. Edward VI's commissioners noted that besides the Vicar and his curates, there were eight priests attached to the chantry chapels in the parish. They were not replaced, as the property that provided them with an income was confiscated by the king and sold. After their deaths the number of clergy fell dramatically, so that by the accession of Elizabeth I there were only three or four members of the clergy ministering to the needs of the parishioners. As well as taking services in church, they were responsible for all marriages, baptisms and funerals. With the population increasing so rapidly this became a heavy workload, leaving them little time to help comfort the sick and needy. With so few left ministering to the needs of so many, the traditional bond between priest and parishioner diminished. This, combined with the recent confiscation of both abbey and chantry lands and property, made benefactors, once generous in their wills to both the church and the poor, cautious, and the amount given to charity dried to a trickle, despite greater prosperity.[94]

One benefit of the dissolution of the chantries was the formal establishment of a grammar school in the town. William Sheffield, by his will of 6 March 1547, vested his lands and tenements in the hands of trustees, who were to pay him a regular income until his death, but thereafter use the money to provide part of the stipend of a schoolmaster in Leeds. As a chantry priest he may have fulfilled both the role of priest and teacher. His benefaction gave the trustees some income, but they were left with the responsibility of establishing the school, and ensuring that the schoolmaster had an adequate salary and lodgings. Many of the old chantry buildings had fallen into disrepair, and it seems likely that the trustees purchased the chapel at Bridge End for use as a 'reading' school, and the 'New Chapel' on Vicar Lane for the grammar school.[95]

The state of the church in Leeds was another matter to

The funeral monument of Thomas Hardwick at Leeds Parish Church. Hardwick, a successful lawyer who lived at Potternewton Hall, died in 1577. The monument depicts Thomas, with his two sons behind him, opposite his wife Anne, with two of her children by a previous marriage.

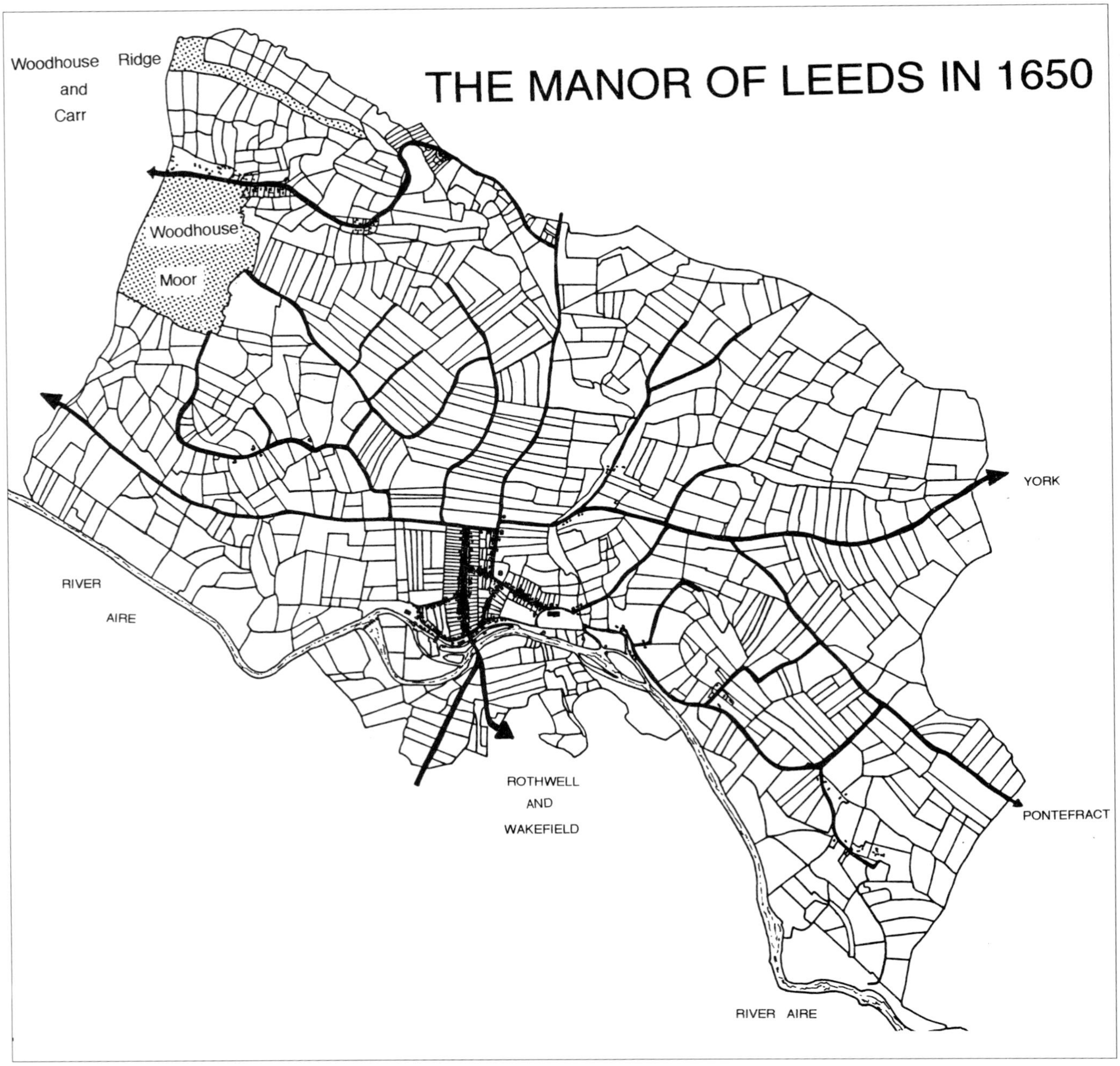

THE MANOR OF LEEDS IN 1650

Woodhouse Ridge and Carr

Woodhouse Moor

YORK

RIVER AIRE

ROTHWELL AND WAKEFIELD

PONTEFRACT

RIVER AIRE

which senior townsmen also turned their attention towards the end of the sixteenth century. After the dissolution of the monasteries, Henry VIII gave the manor of Leeds Kirkgate-cum-Holbeck with the associated tithes of the parish church to the newly founded, Christ Church, Oxford. In addition the advowson, the right to appoint the vicar, was sold to Thomas Culpepper, gentleman of London. As the vicar was one of the most influential people in the parish, the fact that his successor would be chosen by a stranger in the capital was a cause for much consternation. As a result the parishioners had foisted upon them a series of vicars whom they regarded as unlearned and incompetent. In 1588 some of the townsmen decided to rectify this highly unsatisfactory arrangement and bought the advowson on behalf of the parishioners for the princely sum of £130. Their purpose was clear: that 'they might be furnished with honest, learned and able ministers to succeed in the said vicarage.' Accordingly, on the death of Revd. Alexander Fawcett (an aged and blind man) in 1590, a 'famous and learned man', Robert Cooke was chosen by the purchasers to succeed him. Cooke laid the foundations of the Puritan tradition which was to be so marked a feature of the life of the parish in the seventeenth century. Indeed, by 1600 there is little evidence of recusancy, the clinging to Roman Catholic traditions and practices, in the town. This episode demonstrated how the new breed of leading townsmen were willing to spend large sums in order to gain greater control of their own affairs and to reduce interference from outside the parish.[96]

While concentrating on the growth of Leeds and its domestic affairs it is too easy to think of it as an island little affected by events in the outside world. In practice, the well-being of its cloth industry was considerably affected by the vicissitudes of international trade. Likewise, the decisions by Henry VIII and Edward VI to close down first the monasteries and then the chantries had had a profound impact on the town. Its inhabitants, too, had responsibilities connected with the defence of the realm. The passageway, known as Butt's Court, in the centre of Leeds today, is a reminder of the place where the people of Leeds practiced their archery. The Muster records of the Skyrack Wapentake for 1539 list the 162 Leeds people who were liable to be called upon to serve at times of war. There were 78 archers of whom 22 were fully armed, 11 partly armed and 45 not armed, and 84 'Bills' of whom 21 were fully armed, 26 partly armed and 37 not armed. The 'Bills' were men who would fight with axes with long wooden handles, and hatchets and swords. Those described as 'fully armed' would have had full body armour and helmets.[97]

Fortunately for Leeds, the Tudor period was one in which its inhabitants were not called upon to fight on domestic soil, and the town prospered. By 1600 the economic growth of the previous centuries had transformed the settlement. The vill of Kirkgate and the 'new town' of Briggate had joined together to form the basic structure of the in-township. Around 3000 people now lived in the timber-framed houses that abutted Briggate and Kirkgate, and occupied the new plots that fronted the Headrow, Boar Lane, Vicar Lane, Mill Hill and Marsh Lane. The tenter fields, orchards and gardens ensured that even the central, built up area retained a semi-rural atmosphere, yet the northern bank of the River Aire was lined with fulling mills and tenter frames, the physical evidence that here was a cloth finishing centre of importance. The landscape of small enclosures peppered with houses and cottages was in stark contrast to the sparcely populated manor dominated by wasteland and open fields that had been viewed by the Domesday clerks over five hundred years earlier. The manor had long since failed to produce enough food to feed its people, and Leeds was now a bustling market town, where farm produce was purchased by the townsfolk, the majority of whom earned their living in the textile industry. As the Aire valley developed as a cloth-producing district, so the number of workers employed in Leeds in the finishing processes increased. The cheap kerseys and northern dozens were popular, and an increasing proportion of the cloth was exported to the Low Countries through the port of Hull. The wealth created by this trade enabled the townsmen to dominate the parish and seek to gain control of their own affairs. The gentry still owned a significant number of the burgage plots, and retained the fishing and fowling rights, but their position of dominance had gone forever.

Left: [The Manor of Leeds in 1650].
By 1650 the landscape of the manor had been completely transformed. The manorial park was denuded of trees and had been divided into fields. Kirkgate and Briggate had coalesced to form the town of Leeds. The two open field systems, based on Knostrop and Woodhouse, had been abandoned and groups of the former strips of land had been enclosed as long, narrow fields. All the former 'waste' was now farmed. One of the few visible reminders of the old manorial system was Woodhouse Moor, upon which tenants with the jealously guarded common right of pasturage still grazed animals. Visitors to the manor now viewed a landscape dominated by small fields, bounded by walls, fences and hedges. The land was intensively farmed, though fields near to the centre often were used for tenter frames. The lords of the manor now had minimal control over land use. Land ownership was fragmented into the hands of hundreds of freeholders, the majority of whom lived in the parish.

References

1. Robinson, Son & Pike, publishers, *Leeds - Illustrated, 1892* (Brighton, 1892), p.4.
2. R.Yarwood, 'The Historical Landscape of Colton and Newsam', *Leeds Arts Calendar*, No. 92 (1983).
3. West Yorkshire Metropolitan County Council, *West Yorkshire: an Archaeological Survey to A.D. 1500* (Wakefield, 1981), (hereafter, *Archaeological Survey*) I, pp. 99, 107.
4. *Ibid.*, pp. 123, 128-30.
5. *Ibid.*, pp. 141-6.
6. Ralph Thoresby, *Ducatus Leodiensis* (second edition, ed. Rev. T.D.Whitaker, Leeds, 1816), (hereafter, *Ducatus Leodiensis*), p. 104.
7. *Archaeological Survey*, I, pp. 146, 157-63.
8. *Ibid.*
9. Venerable Bede, *Historia Ecclesiastica*, ed. Plummer (1896), p. 115.
10. J.Le Patourel, ed., 'Documents Relating to the Manor and Borough of Leeds, 1066-1400', *Thoresby Soc.*, XLV (1956), (hereafter, *Manor Documents, 1066-1400*), p. xi.
11. A.McGuire and A.Clark, *The Leeds Crosses* (Leeds City Museums, 1987).
12. *Manor Documents, 1066-1400*, pp. xi-ii.
13. W.F.Skene, *Chronicles of the Picts: Chronicles of the Scots* (1867), p. 116.
14. G.R.Jones, 'To the Building of Kirkstall Abbey', in M.W.Beresford and G.R.Jones, eds., *Leeds and its Region* (1967), pp. 119-30.
15. *Ibid.*, pp. 121-4.
16. The account in this chapter of the development of the manor of Leeds is based primarily on two printed selections of manorial records. That of Le Patourel, *Manor Documents, 1066-1400*, already cited, and J.W.Kirby, 'The Manor and Borough of Leeds, 1425-1662: An Edition of Documents, *Thoresby Soc.*, LVII (1983), (hereafter, *Manor Documents, 1425-1662*).
17. J.Le Patourel, 'The Norman Conquest of Yorkshire', *Northern History*, VI (1971), pp. 1-21; G.D.Lumb, 'Leeds Manor House and Park', *Thoresby Soc.*, XXIV (1917), pp. 399-400. Using conversion figures for Domesday Book entries suggested in M.M.Postan, *The Medieval Economy* (1975) the population could have been in the range 120 to 262 people.
18. *Manor Documents, 1066-1400*, pp. xii-xxiii describes the descent of the ownership of the manor.
19. G.E.Kirk, *History of the Parish Church of St Mary, Whitkirk, Leeds* (Leeds, 1935), pp. 1-20.
20. *Archaeological Survey*, II, pp. 427-8.
21. *Manor Documents, 1066-1400*, pp. xiv-v.
22. G.Woledge, 'The Medieval Borough of Leeds', *Thoresby Soc.*, XXXVII (1945), pp. 288-309.
23. Few manorial documents survive prior to the fourteenth century, we must use later evidence therefore to deduce how the manor was run in the thirteenth century.
24. H.S.Bennett, *Life on the English Manor* (Cambridge, 1937), pp. 231-7.
25. *Manor Documents, 1425-1662*, pp. xli-xliv; J.B.Place, 'Woodhouse in the Manor of Leeds', *Thoresby Soc.*, XXXVII (1945), pp. 345-65.
26. Bennett, *op. cit.*, p. 43; Postan, *op. cit.*, pp. 49-58.
27. *Manor Documents, 1425-1662*, p. xlv.
28. *Manor Documents, 1066-1400*, pp. 35-38.
29. Approximation based on the table in *Manor Documents, 1425-1662*, p. xlviii.
30. *Manor Documents, 1066-1400*, pp. 10-11, 29-42.
31. Postan, *op. cit.*, chapter 3 on the impact of plague countrywide.
32. *Manor Documents, 1425-1662*, pp. xlvii-xlix.
33. *Ibid.*, pp. xxiv, xlii, xlv.
34. *Manor Documents, 1066-1400*, pp. 13, 38-40, 46; *Manor Documents, 1425-1662*, pp. xliii, 259, 263.
35. *Manor Documents, 1066-1400*, pp. xxix, 10-11, 16, 31, 35.
36. 'West Riding Poll Tax Returns, 1379', *Yorkshire Archaeological Journal*, VII (1882).
37. *Manor Documents, 1066-1400*, pp. 13, 23; *Manor Documents, 1425-1662*, p.56.
38. *Manor Documents, 1066-1400*, pp. 10-11.
39. H.Heaton, *The Yorkshire Woollen and Worsted Industries* (2nd edn, Oxford, 1965), (hereafter, *Woollen Industries*), pp. 1-2; and chapter 1, passim.
40. E.M.Carus-Wilson, 'An Industrial Revolution of the Thirteenth Century', *Economic History Review*, XI (1941).
41. *Manor Documents, 1066-1400*, pp. 13, 70-1.
42. *Ibid.*, pp. 47, 59, 70-1.
43. *Ibid.*, pp. 35, 51.
44. *Ibid.*, p. 29.
45. *Manor Documents, 1425-1662*, p.28; *Ducatus*, p. 77.
46. *Manor Documents, 1425-1662*, pp. xxvi, lxi-ii.
47. *Manor Documents, 1066-1400*, pp. 10-11, 18-22, 43-8, 50-5, 61-4, 67-77; *Manor Documents, 1425-1662*, pp. 8-13, 252-4. These wages, given in the manorial accounts for 1324/25 and the higher levels in those for 1383/84 given later, are consistent with the trends identified in J.L.Bolton, *The Medieval Economy, 1150-1500*, (1980), p.71; and E.H.Phelps Brown and S.V.Hopkins, 'Seven Centuries of Building Wages', *Economica*, (1955).
48. *Manor Documents, 1066-1400*, pp. 10-11.
49. *Ibid.*, p. 61.
50. *Ibid.*, pp. 47, 52, 70.
51. *Ibid.*, p. 19.
52. *Ibid.*, p. 47.
53. *Ibid.*, p. 30.
54. *Manor Documents, 1425-1662*, p. xxv.
55. E.K.Clark, 'A Brawl in Kirkgate', *Thoresby Soc.*, IV (1895), pp. 125-38.
56. J.Rusby, *St Peter's at Leeds* (Leeds, 1896), pp. 17-26.
57. *Ibid.*
58. An excellent recent account of the history of Kirkstall Abbey from which this section draws extensively is: G.D.Barnes, 'Kirkstall Abbey, 1147-1539: An Historical Study', *Thoresby Soc.*, LVIII (1984).
59. *Ibid.*, pp. 41-2; *Manor Documents, 1425-1662*, p. 250; *Manor Documents, 1066-1400*, p.17.
60. Barnes, *op. cit.*, p. 40.
61. *Manor Documents, 1425-1662*, pp. xlvi, 23, 33.
62. C.T.Clay, 'The Early Abbots of Yorkshire Cistercian Houses', *Yorkshire Archaeological Journal*, XXXVIII (1952).
63. Barnes, *op. cit.* p. 71.
64. M.Keen, *English Society in the Later Middle Ages, 1348-1500* (1990), pp. 260-265.
65. Barnes, *op. cit.*, pp. 38-40; W.G.Rimmer, 'The Evolution of Leeds to 1700', *Thoresby Soc.*, L (1967), p. 101.
66. W.T.Lancaster, 'The Possessions of Kirkstall Abbey in Leeds', *Thoresby Soc.*, IV (1895), p. 39.
67. R.B.Dobson, 'Yorkshire Towns in the Late Fourteenth Century', *Thoresby Soc.*, LIX (1985), pp. 1-21.
68. *Manor Documents, 1066-1400*, pp. xii-xxiii. The administration of the manor was subsequently streamlined. It seems likely that by the 1450s the court baron and court leet had effectively merged. Likewise after the 1470s the borough court seems to have merged with the other courts. See *Manor Documents, 1425-1662*, pp. xxvi, lxi-ii.
69. *Manor Documents, 1066-1400*, pp. 10-11, 18-22, 43-48, 50-56, 67-77; *Manor Documents, 1425-1662*, pp. 8-13, 252-4. Wage rates taken from the 1438/39 manorial accounts.
70. *Manor Documents, 1425-1662*, pp. 6-7.
71. *Ibid.*, pp. xlvii-xlix.
72. *Ibid.*
73. J.W.Kirby, 'The Rulers of Leeds: Gentry, Clothiers and Merchants, *c.*1425-1626', *Thoresby Soc.*, LIX (1983), pp. 22-26.
74. A.Lonsdale, 'The Last Monks of Kirkstall Abbey, *Thoresby Soc.*, LIII (1973); J.M.Collinson, 'Weetwood and the Foxcroft Family', *University of Leeds Review*, Vol 30 (Leeds, 1987/88), pp. 27-35.
75. *Manor Documents, 1425-1662*, pp. lx, 10-11.
76. *Ibid.*, p. lx.
77. Rusby, *op. cit.*
78. T.Marshall, 'Leeds Chantries of the Blessed Virgin Mary', *Thoresby Soc.*, IV (1895), pp. 73-8; R.V.Taylor, *Leeds Worthies* (Leeds, 1865), p. 73.
79. *Leland's Itinerary* (first published in 1710), vii, 41-2.
80. York Corporation Minute Books, XXIII, f. 20a, 8 June 1561, cited in Heaton, *Woollen Industries*, pp. 54-55.
81. Heaton, *Woollen Industries* , p.220; M.Yasumoto, 'Urbanisation and Population in an English Town', *Keio Economic Studies*, X (1973), pp. 62-64; R.G.Wilson, *Gentlemen Merchants: The Merchant Community in Leeds, 1700-1830* (Manchester, 1971), p. 197.
82. Heaton, *Woollen Industries*, p. 79.
83. *Ibid.*, pp. 99-100.
84. C.B.Norcliffe, 'Inventory of the Goods of John Pawson', *Thoresby Soc.*, IV (1895), pp. 163-6.
85. W.G.Rimmer, 'The Evolution of Leeds to 1700', *Thoresby Soc.*, L (1967), p. 119.
86. *Manor Documents, 1425-1662*, pp. xlv-vi.
87. J.Kirby, 'A Leeds Élite: The Principal Burgesses of the First Leeds Corporation', *Northern History*, XX (1984), pp. 88-9.
88. R.B.Outhwaite, *Inflation in Tudor and Early Stuart England* (1969), passim; *Manor Documents, 1425-1662*, pp. 38, 85, 100, 141.
89. J.Kirby, 'The Rulers of Leeds: Gentry, Clothiers and Merchants, *c.*1425-1626', *Thoresby Soc.*, LIX (1985), pp. 30-4.
90. Kirby, 'A Leeds Élite', p. 90.
91. Kirby, 'The Rulers of Leeds', pp. 26-7.
92. E.Wilson, 'A Leeds Law Suit in the Sixteenth Century', *Thoresby Soc.*, IX (1899).
93. *Manor Documents, 1425-1662*, lxiii.
94. C.Cross, 'The Development of Protestantism in Leeds and Hull, 1520-1640: the Evidence of Wills', *Northern History*, XVIII (Leeds, 1982), and 'Urban Magistrates and Ministers: Religion in Hull and Leeds from the Reformation to the Civil War', *Borthwick Papers*, No. 67 (York, 1985).
95. A.C.Price, *A History of Leeds Grammar School from its Foundation to the end of 1918* (Leeds, 1919), pp. 56-69; Rushby, *St Peter's at Leeds*, pp. 27-31.
96. R.Thoresby, *Vicaria Leodiensis* (1720), pp. 48-60.
97. Cited in Price, *op. cit.*, pp. 46-7. Regarding Park Butts see, *Ducatus*, p. 94.

CHAPTER TWO

War, Plague and Trade

Seventeenth-Century Expansion

LEEDES is an Ancient Markett Towne some 10 or 12 miles Northwest beyond Pontfract, and 6 miles Northward beyond Wakefeilde (another great Markett Towne). It standeth pleasantlie in a fruitefull and enclosed vale; upon the North side of the same River of Eyre, over or beyond a stone bridge, from whence it hath a large and broad street (paved with stone) leadinge directlie North and continuallie ascendinge. The houses on both sides thereof are verie thicke, and close compacted together, beinge ancient meane and lowe built; and generallie all of Tymber; though they have stone quarries frequent in the Towne, and about it, only some fewe of the richer sort of the Inhabitants have theire houses more large and capacious: yett all lowe and straightened on theire backsides. In the middle of the streete (towards the upper end wheare the Markett place standeth) is built the Court or Moot House (as they terme it) and from thence upward are the shambles, with a narrow streete on both sides, much annoyinge the whole Towne; yett for theire Conveniencie, and want of roome, not to be avoided, or placed elsewhere.

Corporation of London survey of the manor of Leeds (1628)[1]

The Corporation of London surveyors visiting in 1628 clearly were not impressed by the town of Leeds, and yet it was certainly now a town of substance. By 1698, however, the traveller Celia Fiennes, though perhaps not using London as a yardstick to the same degree, gave a description suggesting remarkable progress:

> Leeds is a large town, severall large streetes cleane and well pitch'd and good houses, all built of stone, some have good gardens and steps up to their houses and walls before them; this is esteemed the wealthyest town of its bigness in the Country, its manufacture is the woollen cloth the Yorkshire Cloth in which they are all employ'd and are esteemed very rich and very proud; they have provision soe plentifull that they may live with very little expense and get much variety.[2]

Her description of the town is well supported by William Lodge's beautiful prospect of Leeds drawn in the 1680s.[3] He shows Briggate extending from the old bridge, and Boar Lane leading across to the Nonconformist chapel at Mill Hill. The old parish church and St John's stand out as buildings of importance, and it is possible to see Red Hall and the top of the market cross. Rich and poor lived next to one another, although poorer dwellings tended to be found on the lower land. The humble cottages clustered near the bridge were close to the more impressive homes of some of the wealthy members of the community. Tenter frames dominate the riverside scene, which shows men fishing in the still relatively pure waters of the Aire.

The hearth tax returns for the town in 1664 give us an idea of the relative wealth and poverty of its inhabitants in the middle of the century by counting the number of fireplaces in their homes.[4] Over two-fifths of the recorded households were taxed on only one hearth. These people must have lived near the poverty line, being employed as servants, labourers, or journeymen. Their poor housing and low income must have put them heavily at risk at times of plague and bad harvests. A further two-fifths of the households had two or three hearths. These would have been the homes of craftsmen, shopkeepers, and clothiers. Their higher incomes allowed them to live in a greater degree of comfort, but by modern standards they too would appear poor. The remaining fifth of the households with four or more hearths, however, were people with significant wealth and possessions. These were the substantial clothiers, merchants, retailers, clergymen, lawyers, small landowners and gentry.

During the century significant improvements had been made in the ways in which houses were built. Initially, oak, wattle and daub buildings with thatched roofs predominated, but stone and brick buildings with either stone slabs or tiles on the roofs became fashionable. Several important houses were erected for leading townsmen – Red Hall (1628) for Thomas Metcalf, Wade Hall (1630-40) for Thomas Jackson, and an impressive brick house for John Harrison.[5] By the end of the century the wealthy merchants began to build expensive residences on the edge of the town, and in the newly fashionable areas of Boar Lane and Town End (north of the Headrow around North Street).

Lodge's Prospect of Leeds. This engraving was based on a sketch by William Lodge (1649-89) made c. 1680. It appeared in Ralph Thoresby's history of Leeds, Ducatus Leodiensis published in 1715.

This timber-framed house with jettied storeys c. 1600, survives today in Lambert's Yard on the east side of Lower Briggate.

For the wealthy at least, life had become distinctly more comfortable. In 1694 George Sorocold constructed a water-pumping engine near the bridge, which pumped water from the Aire and stored it in a reservoir near St John's Church. By a series of pipes it was taken to houses within the town. Ralph Thoresby wrote in his diary on 1 October 1694: 'Was several times with Mr. Sorocold's workmen who this day first began in Kirkgate to lay the lead pipes to convey water to each family.' On 7 December he obtained a full supply when a branch from the main pipe was fixed into his kitchen.[6]

In 1600 the population of Leeds was around 3,000, but by 1700, despite the ravages of the Civil War and the plague, it had possibly reached 6,000.[7] The town had attained Lodge's accolade of being one of the 'most remarkable towns in the North of England for the Clothing Trade'. The central township had become increasingly crowded, and new houses were regularly being constructed in the yards, orchards, gardens and other open spaces bordering the main streets.

Before looking at the great expansion in the industry and trade of the town, it is helpful to look at how the adventurous and dynamic leaders of the town step by step took control of almost every aspect of town life. We have already seen how in 1588 leading townsmen purchased the advowson of the parish and thereby gained the right to appoint the vicars of Leeds. This was of critical importance not merely for religious reasons but because, as manors became of less importance in administrative terms, the ecclesiastical parish had become the basic unit of local government in England. Parish officers, on whom the vicar would have had considerable influence, administered a whole range of local affairs. There were the church wardens who were mainly responsible for the fabric of the church, the collection of the church rates, and the morals of the parishioners. Then there were the overseers of the poor who collected the poor rate, relieved the poor and dealt with vagrants and beggars passing throught the parish.

Red Hall, built in 1628 for Alderman Thomas Metcalf. Probably the first brick house in Leeds. The site is today occupied by part of the Schofield's Centre.

The roads were repaired under the supervision of the surveyors of highways, while the parish constable was the chief parish official with responsibilities connected with law and order.[8]

The principal figures of authority in the neighbourhood, however, were the West Riding Justices of the Peace. While the church wardens were chosen by the parishioners, the other parish officers were appointed by the Justices. As well as administering the criminal law, the Justices had the tasks of overseeing poor relief, fixing wages, having vagabonds flogged, apprenticing children, deciding the paternity of illegitimate children, regulating the price of corn and other foods, and many other matters.[9] When the West Riding Justices visited Leeds to carry out their duties, life cannot have been all that comfortable for them. In 1598 it appears that their sessions were held in the old medieval court house in 'a roome beinge directly over the Comon Ovens and furnaces there, which by the smoke and heate of the same ovens and furnaces dayly ascendinge into the said Courthouse, is very inconvenient, noysom and greate hyndrance to such as were to exercise her Majestie's service there.'[10]

Smoke or no smoke, there can be no doubt that the leading merchants of Leeds coveted the power and influence which these 'outsiders' had over the affairs of their town. In 1615, a new Moot Hall was built for the magistrates on a piece of ground in the middle of Briggate just above Kirkgate, and it was not long before the magistrates who sat there were the merchants themselves.[11]

The merchants had grand aspirations: how might the wealth of the town grow if they could gain powers to carefully regulate cloth production and the cloth trade, to ensure high quality and favourable conditions, not merely within the town but the whole 32 square miles of the parish? What if at the same time they could become Justices of the Peace for the locality? In 1626, supported by Sir John Savile of Howley, a neighbouring landowner, courtier and supporter of the 'cloth interest' in the West Riding, they successfully petitioned the Crown for a charter. On 13 July 1626 Charles I incorporated Leeds as 'a free borough' and 'a body corporate and politic'. This was the most important landmark in the history of Leeds, for the charter gave the town important powers of self-government.[12]

The government of the town and borough was placed in the hands of one alderman, nine principal burgesses and twenty assistants. The first office-holders named in the charter were to hold office for life; vacancies were to be filled by co-option and fines were to be imposed on those refusing to serve, once chosen. The corporation was to choose two sergeants at mace; a coroner; a clerk of the market; and constables. The alderman (later known as the mayor), the nine principal burgesses and the recorder were to be Justices of the Peace for the borough and in future the important day-to-day local government duties of the magistrates were now to be in their hands. Not surprisingly, great opposition was aroused amongst the clothiers of the parish, for the parish and the newly created borough had the same boundaries.[13] At a stroke this small group of men, by virtue of the establishment of this self-electing corporation, had in perpetuity gained considerable powers over the everyday lives of the people. The protests of the clothiers were to no effect, though in the event the establishment of the corporation was of major benefit to the development of the town. Since the chief role of magistrates was to maintain law and order, the charter required the corporation to build a prison. Most probably they used the manorial gaol, but in 1655 the old prison near the market cross in Briggate was demolished and a new one erected at the top of Kirkgate.[14]

Almost the final link in the chain of control of Leeds was the manor. When Charles I came to the throne in 1625, part of his inheritance was the manor of Leeds. He was always short of money and in the early years of his reign borrowed heavily from the Corporation of London. In 1628 in order to settle his debts and raise more money, he gave many estates, including the manor of Leeds, to this corporation. 'Leeds' thus became owned by 'London'.[15] The London Corporation, however, had only one thing in mind – to sell as soon as possible at a large profit. In 1628 it sent representatives to make a survey and report on the likely resale value. Their survey, part of which has already been quoted, offers a fascinating description of Leeds. The manor was certainly a valuable asset as its main yearly revenues show: rent £54; coal mines at Knostrop and Woodhouse Moor £100; the office of bailiff (the bailiwick) £70; the weighing of wool and tallow £30; and entry fines £139. The surveyors had been instructed to seek out potential buyers for either the whole or part of the manor and to inform tenants wishing to buy their holdings that they were prepared to sell at a reasonable price. This presented the leading merchants with a great opportunity.

In 1629 the purchase of the whole manor was negotiated by Richard Sykes, a wealthy merchant and the mayor of Leeds, for £2,710 8s. 10d. – a profit of about 80 per cent for the Corporation of London.[16] Although Sykes was named as the sole purchaser in the corporation's records, in fact the manor was conveyed to a group of six, William Skelton, William Marshall, John Thwaites,

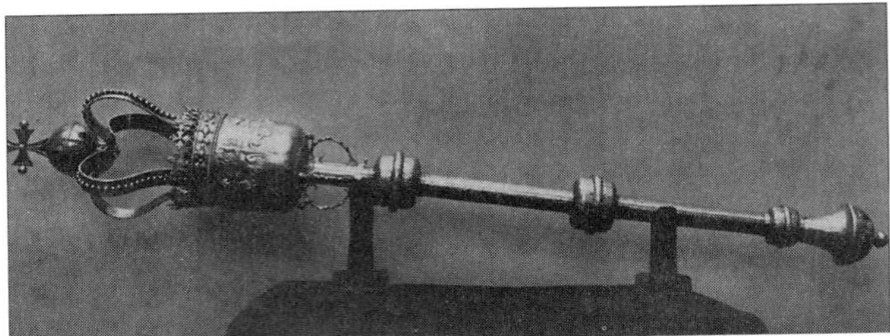

A silver mace was made for the corporation of 1626, but in 1694 was replaced by the current mace shown above.

The Corporation Seal of 1626. The seal was used to stamp or seal important legal documents. On it we see the borough coat of arms. This consisted of a fleece, to symbolize the importance of the woollen manufacture, and two owls ducally crowned. The owls were part of the arms of Sir John Savile, the first alderman.

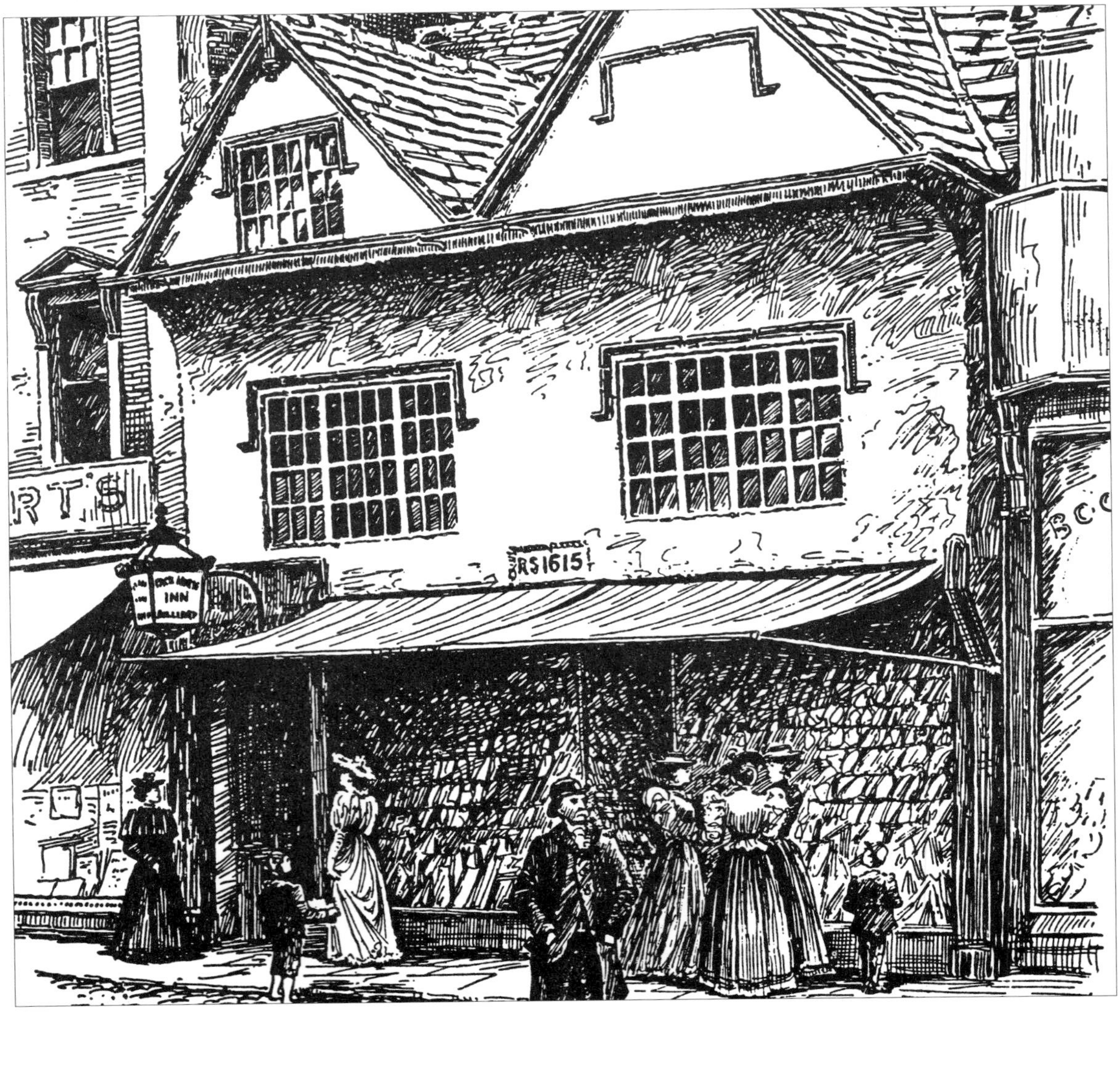

Richard Sykes, merchant, alderman and owner of a one-ninth share of the manor, had this fine house built on Briggate, opposite the Moot Hall.

The Corporation Seal 1662. The grant of a new charter in 1661 brought a change to the town seal and coat of arms. Three mullets argent (silver stars) were added to the arms, being part of the coat of arms of Thomas Danby, the first mayor under the new charter. Curiously, the owls were left off the seal.

The front of the mayor's pew, showing the 1661 borough coat of arms, now displayed at the parish church.

Henry Watkinson, John Wade, and Richard Symson. At the same time a lease of manorial rights was granted to nine people, including Richard Sykes, most of whom were leading members of the newly established Leeds corporation. In this way the manor effectively came under corporation control. There were great advantages for the corporation, since the manor courts had authority over the bulk of property in Leeds and consequently had a significant influence in the affairs of many townsmen. In 1655 the corporation's control of the manor was put on a more formal footing when it bought, from John Harrison and others, five one-ninth shares of both the lease and ownership of the manor. The shares were placed in the hands of trustees who were to use the manorial income, including that from the oven and bakehouse, as the corporation directed. Curiously, the rights over the manorial corn mills had not been sold in 1628 and remained in the Crown's hands, but the obligation to grind corn at the mill continued.

The outbreak of the Civil War turned Leeds society upside down: Royalist supporters were removed from the corporation and incomers introduced to civic office against the provisions of the charter.[17] In 1661 complaints from the members of the corporation ousted for Royalism led to the dismissal of the Parliamentarians and the issue of a new charter in November 1661. No essential change was made to the role of the corporation by this second charter although its members now consisted of a mayor, twelve aldermen and twenty-four assistants.[18] Additional powers were given to appoint a common clerk to levy rates, but the most important change was the acquisition of the right to hold borough quarter sessions. This was important because it increased the seriousness and range of matters which the Leeds magistrates could deal with, almost completely excluding magistrates from outside Leeds from having any say in local affairs. This charter remained the basis of Leeds town government until 1835, with a short hiccup in 1684-89 when Charles II temporarily revoked it and substituted one which gave him more control over the corporation.

During the course of the seventeenth century, because the corporation and its members became influential in so many aspects of local affairs, the distinction between the activities and jurisdictions of the parish, the manor and the corporation became increasingly blurred. In 1620 a body of trustees known as the Committee of Pious Uses was established to manage the charitable bequests given to relieve the poor, support the church, and repair the highways.[19] Though these functions overlapped with those of the other bodies in the town, confusion was avoided because once again the members of the committee usually were members of the corporation. The achievement of the leading merchants in gaining complete control of town and parish affairs in the comparatively short period of forty years from 1588 to 1628 was a remarkable one. Their only disappointment, and a highly significant one for the future of Leeds, was their failure to gain a seat in Parliament for the borough. The promoters of the charter in 1626 had clearly hoped that it would include this important privilege and that they would then have a voice at national level on matters affecting the cloth trade. In the event the wait was a very long one, for, except for brief representation in the Cromwellian parliaments of 1654 and 1656, Leeds did not secure its first Members of Parliament until 1832.[20]

Industry, Markets and Trade

The wealth of Leeds in the seventeenth century was founded on the woollen cloth industry, as the West Riding, with the West Country and East Anglia, came to make up the great cloth producing areas of England.[21] The rapid growth in the West Riding's textile industry experienced in the sixteenth century continued apace. The region around Leeds specialised in coarse cloth known as Yorkshire broadcloths or northern dozens and, as a result of its cheapness and excellent value, there was a vast boom in output between 1560 and 1640. The making of cloth went on both in Leeds and for many miles to the west of the town. Manufacture was on the 'Domestic System'. Most clothiers carried on the crafts of spinning and weaving in their cottages or workshops attached to them. The surveys of the Manor of Leeds in 1612 and 1628 show the centre of the town with many such cottage workshops and also tenter grounds, where cloth was stretched and dried on frames. Though most clothiers had just their families to help them, a petition of 1629 tells us that Leeds also had a number of large clothiers who were 'dayly setting on worke about forty poor people in theire trade'.[22] West Riding clothiers often combined cloth-making with part-time farming and the clothiers on the fringe of Leeds township were no exception. As we have seen, the manorial common fields had been enclosed, and those on the northern and southern outskirts had been broken into smallholdings where the cottagers engaged in farming as well as cloth making.

The small-scale methods of cloth manufacture and the scattering of clothiers over the rural West Riding were crucial to the growth and increasing prosperity of Leeds. These clothiers required markets at which they could both buy raw materials and sell their cloth. They needed the services of people who could finish and if required, dye their cloth. Moreover, there were a host of services and goods which could only be obtained in a town.

Clothiers carrying their cloth by pack horse to Leeds market.

Travellers through the Riding were constantly struck by the specialisation of the area in cloth-making and the inability of the clothiers to provide sufficient food for themselves, despite part-time farming. Here was one of the keys to the success of Leeds. It lay at the junction of a thriving agricultural district to the east – the Vale of York – and the large cloth-producing district to the west. It was an important crossing point on the Aire, and was on the main route from Chester to York. Other roads led to Knaresborough, Ripon, Wakefield and Pontefract, and to Ferrybridge, from which transport was available to London. It became not only the West Riding's principal cloth market and cloth finishing centre, but it also acted as a funnel through which food and other necessities of life could be passed to the cloth-making area. Though smaller and of less importance than Halifax and Wakefield as a textile centre in the sixteenth century, it now rapidly outgrew them both. Indeed, the taxes on hearths in 1664 and 1672 show that Leeds now had three times as many houses as Wakefield, even though Wakefield was the second largest town in the textile area.

Above all, it was the Leeds merchants who made the town nationally, indeed internationally, famous in this period. Early in the century the merchants of York and Hull complained bitterly of the appearance of a small but very successful group of cloth merchants in Leeds, 'young adventurers lately sprung up who at little or no charge buy and engross as they please'.[23] By the end of the century there were at least 30 well-established merchant families. Their great success early in the century was highlighted by their winning of the charter of incorporation in 1626. The charter permitted them to take measures to protect their dominance in the town and to ensure that the cloth they purchased was of good and consistent quality. They were able to regulate the cloth and wool markets and to exclude non-Leeds merchants from them. In addition they were empowered to enforce a system of apprenticeship within the borough and lay down standards of cloth manufacture.

An important aspect here was the establishment of trade guilds or fraternities to which Leeds cloth workers were obliged to belong. Fines and other penalties could be imposed on the workers for failure to produce cloth in the approved manner and of the proper quality. Not surprisingly, many clothiers opposed these guilds because of their restrictiveness, but the corporation had its way. Regrettably few records of the guilds survive, but by 1661 they were probably defunct and the corporation, restored to its former position by its second charter, immediately set up a new company of cloth workers. Though this survived to the end of the century, its activities probably were of little value and it was allowed to die a natural death.

Meanwhile, these ever ambitious merchants pondered the problem that whilst they could control the quality of cloth produced within the borough, much of the cloth they purchased came from areas outside their jurisdiction. In 1662 they achieved a major success by obtaining an Act of Parliament setting up a corporation to control cloth-making in the whole of the West Riding. Leeds people were to have the principal say in its running but, once again, we know little of its actual work. Perhaps, in the event, the task of controlling the whole of the Riding's cloth industry proved impossible, and in 1685 the body disappeared.[24]

One of the most impressive aspects of the Leeds merchant community was the extent of its foreign contacts. During the seventeenth century woollen cloth made up well over three-quarters of England's total exports and at least one-fifth of this cloth came from the West Riding. Probably over two-fifths of the cloth passing through Leeds was exported to Holland and Germany, and from there to the rest of Europe. Leeds merchants developed very strong foreign connections and it was common for them to spend part of their apprenticeship abroad. The town's merchants congregated in large numbers in Holland, in particular, and Ralph Thoresby's experience was probably quite typical when he was well entertained by them during his brief period of training in 1678. Many merchants stayed far longer, and in the 1690s, Leeds merchants such as William Milner and James Ibbetson spent five years training there.[25]

After the late 1630s the cloth trade was hit by many years of depression made particularly severe in Leeds by the major shocks of the Civil War, the Plague, and political disturbances abroad. The stagnation of trade was mirrored in the slow down in the growth of population and building in the town. The great showpiece of seventeenth century Leeds was its huge cloth market held on Tuesdays and Saturdays on and near Leeds bridge. Though the expansion of trade may have been slow during the mid-century, growth clearly occurred, for in 1684, pressure of business obliged the corporation to move the market into the lower part of Briggate. In the 1680s foreign markets began to grow rapidly again and a flood of prosperity returned to the town.

Above: The Butchers' Shambles in the centre of Briggate behind the Moot Hall.

Left: The Market Cross of 1619 in Briggate above the Moot Hall, where diary produce was sold on Tuesday and Saturday.

Though cloth dominated the economic life of Leeds, the town was also thronged with other trades and professions. These were sufficiently numerous for the corporation, when it set up the cloth workers guild in 1661, to also form five guilds for these other trades. The first largely consisted of building workers – millwrights, carpenters, joiners, plasterers, bricklayers and coopers (barrel makers); the second of shopkeepers – mercers, grocers, salters and drapers. The other three consisted of cordwainers (shoemakers); tailors; and workers in hardware – ironmongers, smiths, glaziers, cutlers and pewterers.[26] To this list of occupations the records of the corporation add doctors, lawyers, barbers, goldsmiths, stationers, booksellers, innkeepers, butchers, bakers and many more. Coal mining and quarrying continued to be highly important industries in the borough.

At the very end of the century, the wealth and prosperity of the merchant community and its confidence in the future were demonstrated by its investment of large sums of money in a major new venture. In 1699, in company with Wakefield merchants, the Leeds merchants embarked on a scheme to make the Aire and Calder rivers navigable to Hull. The result was the Aire and Calder Navigation which, in overcoming many of the problems of transporting cloth and other goods between Leeds and Hull, greatly enhanced the future importance of Leeds as a commercial centre for the West Riding.[27]

Charities and Poor Relief

It was essential to the well-being and dignity of Leeds in the seventeenth century that its poor should be looked after, its roads should be maintained, and its children should be educated or trained in a craft. The leading inhabitants had both a business and a humanitarian interest in ensuring that these matters were well conducted. One of the principal sources of funds for these activities was charitable bequests, and it was concern that these monies were being misappropriated which led senior townsmen in 1620 to petition King James to establish a commission to investigate. Sir John Savile, John Kaye, Esq., Alexander Cooke (the vicar) and William Lister (probably a curate at the parish church) were appointed commissioners, and their report and orders for the reform of the town charities, the 'First Decree for a Committee of Pious Uses in Leedes', gives a wonderfully detailed picture of Leeds charities in 1620.[28]

The commission at once revealed the corrupt activities of John Metcalfe, the manorial bailiff.[29] The building of the Moot Hall in Briggate in 1615 had been paid for out of funds given for poor relief on condition that the rents should go to the needy, but the commission found that only £15 out of the £20 rental had been so used. For the last two years the £5 from the upper rooms had gone straight into Metcalfe's pocket. This was not all. Metcalfe had also disregarded the custom that the money he derived from the corn he collected as a toll at the

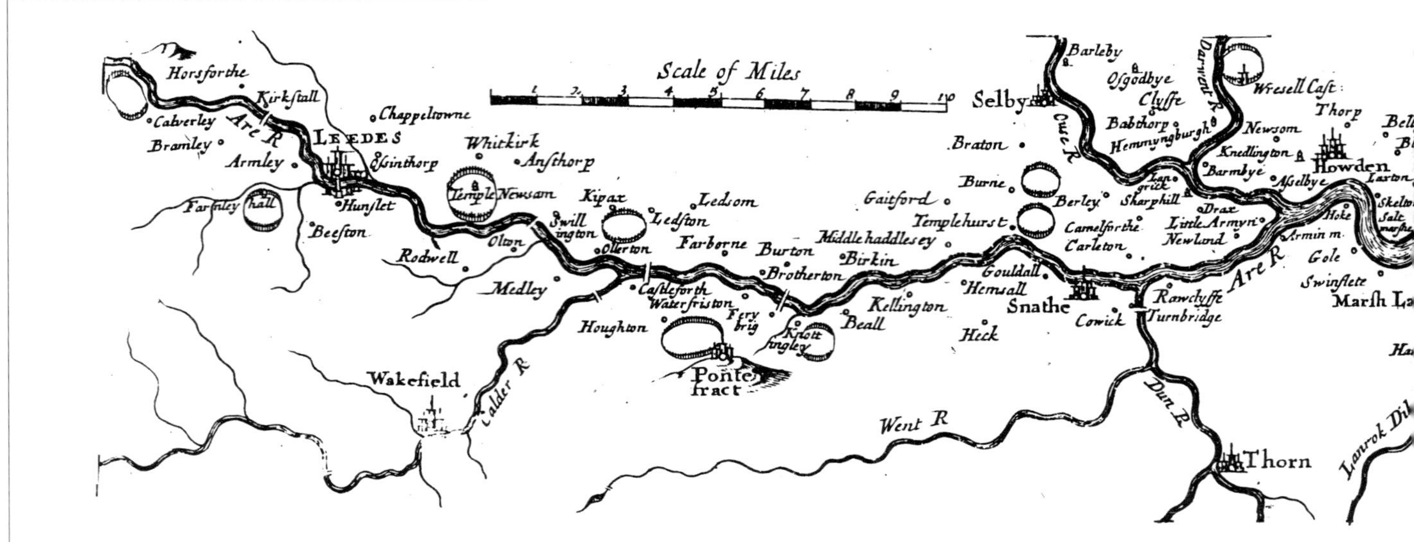

The Aire and Calder Navigation from Sutton Nicholl's map of 1712.

town's markets (the Toll Dish) should be divided three ways – between himself, the repair of the market place and highways, and the poor. Since 1617 the tolls of eight or nine shillings per week had all gone into his pocket. The commission ordered Metcalfe to repay the £10 arrears on the Moot Hall and insisted that in future the shops beneath the hall and the hall itself should be managed by a newly established body called the Committee of Pious Uses. Metcalfe was forced to pay the committee the arrears on the Toll Dish of £37 18s. 8d., and in future the toll of corn was to be collected by two people, one representing the bailiff and the other, the committee. It was the establishment of the Committee of Pious Uses which was the commission's principal act. As a body of trustees it was given the task of the future management of the town's charities. It consisted of the vicar and twelve of the town's leading inhabitants.

Space does not permit more to be said about the other bequests existing in 1620 for the poor, the highways and the church. One charity, however, deserves especial mention – the Grammar School. The commissioners reported that in 1552 the Rev. William Sheaffield had given nine cottages and eight acres of meadow and pasture land near Sheepscar Bridge, the income from which was to be used for paying:

> one honest and substantial learned man, to be a schoolmaster, to teach and instruct freely for ever all such young scholars, youths and children as should come and resort to him from time to time to be taught, instructed, and informed in such a schoolhouse as should be founded, erected, and builded by the parishioners of the said town and parish of Leeds.[30]

The school was still going strong and, as we will shortly see, it was soon to receive an impressive boost to its endowment.

When Charles II was restored to the throne in 1660 it was decided that Leeds charities needed to be investigated again to ensure that any abuses which had occurred during the Civil War and the Interregnum could be put right. Again, it is our great good fortune that another commission consisting of the mayor and principal members of the new corporation was set up in 1661 to investigate, and in 1663 it produced the 'Second Decree for a Committee of Pious Uses in Leedes'.[31] This decree reappointed the trustees of the Committee of Pious Uses and gave quite a detailed report on the history of Leeds charities between 1620 and 1661.

The Pious Uses Chest? All the documents concerning the town's charities were kept in 'a strong Chest in the vestry of the Parish Church locked with Three Strong Locks, one of the keys to remain with the vicar of Leeds and the other Two with [members] of the Committee'. This chest is in the vestry today.

The activities of these years turned out to be of great significance for the centuries to come. Perhaps the most important event recorded was the building of a workhouse. The decree reads as follows:

> About four and twenty years agoe there was a house built by Master Richard Sykes, Master Robert Benson, Master Ralph Croft, Master Josiah Jenkinson, Master Samuell Casson, Master Francis Jackson & diverse other Inhabitants of the Borough of Leeds which said house is built on the place where the old free Schoole formerely stood and in the yard belonging to the same schoole which said house soe there built was designed & since soe used & exercised as a Comon Workehouse soe commonly called a House of Correction for the reliefe & setting on Worke the poor of the said Parish of Leeds.[32]

From this and other evidence it appears that in 1636-7 Richard Sykes, the mayor who had recently negotiated the purchase of the manor, and other leading members of the corporation decided to build the town's first workhouse. Evidently workhouses were becoming popular in the West Riding at this time for one had just been set up in Halifax. The terms 'workhouse' and

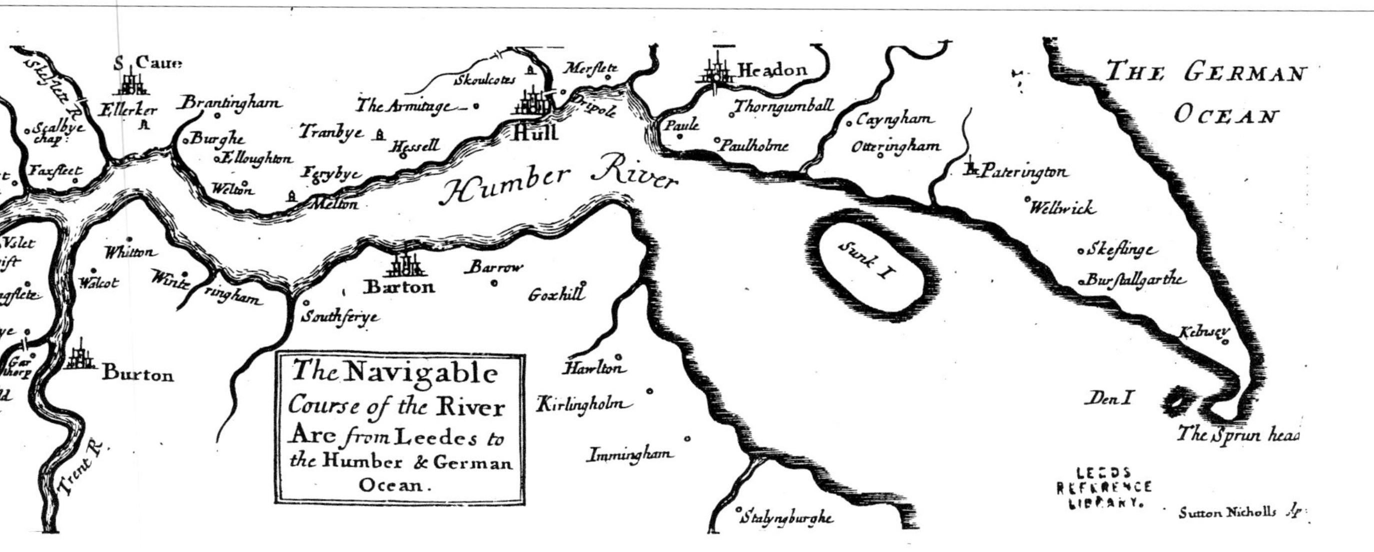

The workhouse (built 1636-7) stood on the north corner of the junction of what are now North Street and Lady Lane.

'house of correction' suggest that it was not intended to be a pleasant place to live. Laziness was thought to be the cause of poverty and unemployment; if people were put in workhouses and forced to earn their living, all would be well – or so it was thought. Predictably, the workhouse neither ended poverty nor raised enough money to support the poor of the parish. Many with no family to look after them were often too ill or too old to work, and young, healthy people were often unable to find work no matter how much they feared the workhouse.

Almost certainly, attempts to 'set the poor on work' had been abandoned by the 1660s, for in 1663 the commissioners ordered that the Committee of Pious Uses should appoint a person 'knowing in the art, Mystery or trade of a Clothier' to be the master of the workhouse and 'all the poor Persons there set on Work or hereafter to be set on Work'. By the time the decree was made the corporation had already acted. In 1662 they had appointed William Morris, a Leeds clothier, as 'master or keeper of the House of Correction'. His efforts, however, were probably fairly short-lived. Thoresby noted in his *Ducatus Leodiensis*, published in 1715, that for many years the workhouse had been used only as an almshouse for the aged poor and that in 1705 it had been closed and converted into the town's new charity school.[33]

In the years before the workhouse opened, and quite probably even while it remained open, the main source of support for the poor would have been money given out by the parish overseers of the poor. These funds, raised from the poor rate levied on inhabitants, would have provided only a miserable existence for the poor. Undoubtably, such assistance was administered in a haphazard way and in 1662 the corporation stepped in. It drew up an elaborate scheme to prevent begging and to

John Harrison (1579-1656). Despite all his charitable acts, he was fined £464 18s. by the Parliamentary Commissioners for supplying two horses to the Royalist Army.

ensure that the poor rate was assessed on a regular basis. The town was divided into six wards, in each of which aldermen and others were ordered to supervise the parish officers dealing with the poor.[34] In their role as borough magistrates, members of the corporation continued to apprentice pauper children.

The workhouse apart, the outstanding feature revealed in the Second Decree is the benevolence of John Harrison. The history of Leeds charities is dominated by this wealthy merchant. Harrison was a trustee of the Grammar School and in 1624, to quote Thoresby, at his

Leeds Free Grammar School erected in 1624 in a field between the present-day Grand Theatre and North Street.

own expense 'removed it from so inconvenient a Situation to a pleasant Field of his own, which he surrounded with a substantial Wall, and then in the midst of the Quadrangle built the present Fabrick of the School'.[35] The future of the school was guaranteed. Substantial as this benefaction was, it was merely one of a series. In 1631, as we shall see, Harrison began the erection of Leeds' oldest surviving place of worship, St John's Church. Having catered for the mind and soul, he then turned to the bodily comfort of the poor. In 1653 he conveyed to trustees a set of almshouses with a large yard which he had built on the west side of St John's. The 'hospital', as almshouses were often called in those days, consisted of two sets of almshouses each containing twenty separate apartments. This hospital was endowed with a yearly income of £80 so that the forty poor women who lived there would each have a small pension and the buildings could be kept in good repair. How must the poor in the workhouse or receiving parish relief have envied these almspeople.[36]

Harrison's almshouses were undoubtedly the finest in seventeenth century Leeds but they were not the only ones. The decree of 1620 makes it clear that there were already small almshouses dating from earlier centuries but they were in a decrepit state. Thoresby tells us that Lancelot Iveson, before his death in 1673, built three almshouses near the Grammar school to replace three decayed cottages at Kirk-gate-end which had been used as almshouses before they had fallen down. He also mentions two almshouses in Vicar Lane, which are referred to in the survey of the manor in 1612, and another old hospital in Kirkgate which merely provided lodgings for the poor.[37] Much more important, however, were Jenkinson's almshouses. The decree of 1663 tells us that in his will dated 1643, Josiah Jenkinson vested in trustees eight cottages erected by him for almshouses in Leeds to the intent that they should place therein such impotent and aged persons inhabiting Leeds. Thoresby tells us that the almshouses were just off Boar Lane close to Mill Hill Chapel and housed sixteen poor people.[38] The names of such benefactors live on in the homes for old people in Leeds today as a vivid reminder of past benevolence.

Troubles in the Church

Religion was a central feature of life in seventeenth-century Leeds. Any idea that it was a sphere of semi-rural harmony needs to be dispelled at once. On the contrary, it was the cause of fierce argument, violence and harsh persecution, and lay at the root of serious grievances felt by many inhabitants throughout the century. The first major controversy broke out in 1615 on the death of the vicar, Robert Cooke.[39] The advowson having been purchased in 1588, the parishioners expected to have the major say in the appointment of his successor. It tells something about the corruption and conflicts in the public life of those days that, though the parishioners had refunded the money to the individuals who had bought the advowson on their behalf, the surviving purchasers refused to place the advowson in the hands of trustees for the parish, and worse still attempted to sell it for £1500. Happily, after a legal battle the Court of Chancery ruled that the advowson should be vested in trustees led by Sir John Savile for the benefit of the parish. Alexander Cooke succeeded his brother and thereafter the vicars of Leeds were men who had strong family ties with the neighbourhood.

Though Alexander Cooke was the choice of the parish his fierce Puritanism made him unpopular with some of his parishioners; though exactly how widespread his unpopularity was, is impossible to say. Certainly he was a hell-fire preacher. On his own admission he would denounce members of the parish from the pulpit calling them 'unreligious atheists, whoremongers, drunkards, epicures, infidels and abbey-lubbers'. He believed in strict observance of the Sabbath and regularly sought to bring parishioners to book for moral offences, non-attendance at church and working or playing games on Sundays. In these activities he fell foul of John Metcalfe, the manorial bailiff whom we have already met. In 1619 he reported Metcalfe to the authorities for failing to

The medieval parish church of St Peter (demolished 1838).

attend church and later led the attack on him over the misuse of charitable funds. In 1622 Metcalfe hit back by filing a complaint in the Court of Star Chamber alleging amongst other things that the vicar was defaming his character by reciting a rhyme accusing him of immorality and corruption. Though the complaint was probably unsuccessful, the evidence presented shows that Metcalfe had attempted to stir up popular opinion against the vicar and had had some success. The highlight had been his encouragement of a rush-bearing ceremony in the church on St Bartholomew's Day, 1619. By tradition, rushes and garlands were carried into the church to decorate it – an event normally accompanied by much drinking and merry-making. It appears that knowing the vicar hated such ceremonies, he had hired a drummer to beat a drum in the parish a week before the ceremony to encourage a very large attendance. In the event many non-parishioners in addition to Leeds people came to enjoy the fun. In the drunken revels that followed, a door of the church had been broken open and a man wearing a visor and ram's horns had danced about during the service. Amidst the abandonment of the service the vicar was threatened by the crowd and in return assaulted at least one member of the congregation. Clearly, these were turbulent times and the vicar felt almost constantly under threat. He told the Star Chamber that it was his habit to wear loaded pistols and a dagger for his own protection.

Cooke died in 1632, but a new controversy was already under way. Though there were six chapels serving the out-townships of the parish, the parish church was too small for its congregation. A complaint to the Court of Chancery in 1615 by the town's leading inhabitants had already remarked that the town and parish consisted of over five thousand worshippers and, though many lived three or four miles from the church, three or four thousand usually attended services on Sundays.[40] 'Those most happy days', Thoresby exclaimed – a view no doubt shared by the Rector of Leeds today. But the fact remained that the church, though large, was inadequate for the demands placed upon it. The 1628 survey of the manor noted the overcrowding: 'The Church of Leeds (which is a verie faire church built after a cathedrall structure and having one side thereof double Iled) is soe besett with scaffold over scaffold [wooden galleries] soe as noe place is voide to heare ye Minister'.[41]

The solution came in 1631 when the great benefactor John Harrison began to build St John's – now the oldest and most beautiful church in Leeds. The problem was that the Archbishop of York initially refused to consecrate the church. The Archbishop was a leader of the movement to shift the Church of England back to the more elaborate ceremonies typical of Roman Catholicism. Undoubtedly, he suspected Harrison of attempting to set up St John's as a stronghold of Puritanism to rival the parish church. This view was supported by Harrison's choice of Robert Todd, a fervent Puritan, as the curate. Despite this, in 1634 after assurances that the vicar would have a say in the appointment of future curates, the Archbishop gave in and consecrated the church. But tradition has it that he soon regretted his decision. It is said that on hearing Todd's first sermon he immediately suspended him, and only with the help of Sir Arthur Ingram of Temple Newsam was Harrison able to persuade the Archbishop to restore Todd to the church.[42]

Though the ministers at both St Peter's and St John's

St John's Church was built 1631-34, entirely at the expense of John Harrison, on a plot he owned just north of Upper Head Row.

over the next quarter of a century were Puritans, this did not prevent further trouble during the Civil War. Todd was a staunch Parliamentarian and continued his ministry in Leeds during the war and the period of the Commonwealth. The vicar, Henry Robinson, John Harrison's nephew, on the other hand, was a Royalist and was forced to flee the town in 1643 when the Parliamentary forces took it. Not surprisingly, his successor in 1646, Peter Saxton, was almost certainly a Parliamentarian. It is likely that the wealthy Anglican merchants who dominated the corporation were unhappy about having a vicar with Parliamentarian sympathies and eventually got their own way. Saxton's successor in 1652, William Styles, had in 1649 refused to signify his loyalty to the Commonwealth without a king, and while vicar of Leeds publicly prayed for the king in exile.[43]

The Restoration of the monarchy in 1660 brought further trouble and great ill-feeling because Puritanism was now out of favour. The new Royalist parliament aimed to make all the people of England members of a single national church, the Church of England, with one set of beliefs and ceremonies.[44] To this end, the Act of Uniformity of 1662 required 'every parson, vicar or other minister whatsoever to declare his unfeigned assent and consent to all and everything contained and prescribed in and by the Book of Common Prayer'. The choice was to conform or be outlawed.

Approximately two thousand Puritan clergy refused to abide by the Prayer Book and were thrown out of their churches. Thereafter such people and their followers became known as Nonconformists or Dissenters. The vicar of Leeds faced no such problem. When Styles had died in 1661 change was already afoot and he had been succeeded by John Lake, an ardent Royalist, and 'model of uniformity'. Given the Puritan tradition in Leeds, local feelings ran high and a large group of the younger inhabitants opposed the choice of Lake. They barred the church doors to prevent his induction ceremony and the service was held only after a party of soldiers had been called.[45] Robert Todd, however, was ejected from St John's in 1662 because he refused to conform and afterwards was obliged to use his house for preaching.

The second half of the seventeeth century therefore saw the rise of the Nonconformists and Dissenters. As well as ejecting Nonconformist ministers, Parliament passed a series of laws to fine or imprison people attempting to worship separately from the Church of England and to prevent them from holding public offices. The persecution of the Dissenters thus became a common feature of life in Leeds and they were forced to worship in secret. The Nonconformists and Dissenters aspired to their own places of worship but it was not until the Declaration of Indulgence by Charles II in 1672 that they dared to come out into the open to take up royal licences to establish public places of worship. The Presbyterians (some of whom later became Unitarians) were quick off the mark and in the same year began building their first meeting house, Mill Hill Chapel, on the site of the present day building in Park Row.[46] The Independent Dissenters (or Congregationalists) were more guarded and waited until the position of Dissenters was more formally protected by the Toleration Act of 1689. Their meeting house 'a stately chapel' in Call Lane was opened in 1691.[47] The Friends of Truth, better known as the Quakers, were now also allowed to worship publicly. In 1689 they leased a house in Boar Lane for their meetings and in 1699, more confident of the future, erected their first purpose-built meeting house.[48] Judging from the size of these chapels, there were perhaps 1,000-1,500 adult Dissenters in Leeds by 1700. Indeed, the town merited its reputation as a hotbed of Nonconformity for this

Left: Mill Hill Presbyterian Chapel built 1672-74.

Below: Call Lane Chapel built in 1691 for the Independent Dissenters.

amounted to perhaps a quarter or one third of all worshippers in Leeds.[49]

Of the various sects, the Quakers were the worst affected by official persecution because they were hated almost as much as Catholics by conformists and other Dissenters alike.[50] A meeting of magistrates, ministers and inhabitants in Leeds in 1659 complained bitterly to the government about 'that unruly sect of people called Quakers whose principles are to overturn magistracy, ministry and ordinances [sacraments and ceremonies]. They meet by hundreds in or near public places of worship on purpose to disturb the preacher and the people assembled'. In 1658 a Quaker, George Watkinson, was jailed for trying to preach after the vicar at the parish church, and there were widespread arrests of Quakers in the West Riding in 1661. In 1671 Bartholomew Horner, a Leeds cloth merchant, was fined £55 for holding a Friends' meeting for worship at his house. Towards the end of Charles II's reign persecution became much more severe. One of the worst incidents occurred on 18 November 1683 when the Leeds magistrates ordered the arrest of 52 Friends who 'were hurried out of their peaceable Meetings', and put into the Moot Hall in extremely cold weather and kept there for four days and nights without a fire or bedding and then marched to the county gaol in York Castle. On 23 November Ralph Thoresby saw them go down Kirkgate where he lived and was greatly touched: 'I cannot wholly omit my concern', he wrote, 'for some deluded Quakers, who were hurried down this street to York Castle, in greater numbers than was ever known in these parts. The Lord open the eyes of the one party and tender the hearts of the other!'

The lot of other Dissenters was also difficult even after the Declaration of Indulgence in 1672.[51] One national scare or another could prompt the authorities to clamp down on them. Ralph Thoresby as a prominent member of Mill Hill Chapel recorded such misfortunes in his diary. In July 1682 we find him 'advising' with Mr Sharp, the minister of the chapel 'touching the order of court for suppressing conventicles'. The authorities had surprised Brook (perhaps the caretaker at Mill Hill) and got the keys of the chapel, so preventing the holding of services. The chapel was closed and the congregation was obliged to worship in secret for the next five years. Groups of the faithful met here and there but at times the inconvenience of crowded rooms and 'the unmannerliness of some of the ruder sort of folk' interrupted services. The feeling of being hounded is reflected in Thoresby's fear of informers and his description of a meeting which he attended at Hunslet. The officers came upon them before they could get away. Mr Sharp escaped but Thoresby was chased to a neighbour's house and narrowly avoided discovery. In 1687, however, matters eased and on 3 April Mr Sharp preached at Mill Hill Chapel for the first time in almost five years. In adversity there was co-operation and in 1691 the Call Lane congregation worshipped at Mill Hill while their meeting house was being built. Mr Sharp and Mr Whitaker (the Call Lane minister) shared the preaching.[52]

The Friends' Meeting House built in 1699 on Water Lane.

Even now life could still be difficult for ministers of the Church of England. John Milner, who succeeded Marmaduke Cooke as vicar in 1677, was an ardent Royalist and was ejected from the vicarage in 1689 because he refused to swear allegiance to King William and Queen Mary when James II was deposed. His successor, John Killingbeck, the son of a former mayor of Leeds, had a more peaceful existence, and it was his impressive preaching which won Ralph Thoresby over to the Church of England in 1698.[53]

We hear little of Roman Catholics in Leeds during the seventeenth century. If there were any, they would be few in number and have worshipped in the greatest secrecy. Not only was Catholicism regarded as a very superstitious religion, but Catholics were thought of as traitors and enemies of the nation. Undoubtedly some parishioners would have Catholic sympathies but on the whole they would have been as horrified as Ralph Thoresby whenever they saw anything in a religious service which smacked of 'popery'.

Clearly, religion had a much greater impact on the minds of the mass of Leeds people in the seventeenth century than it does today. Superstition was much greater and people were much more aware of a supreme being constantly watching over them, as Ralph Thoresby's diary brings home to us quite vividly. He noted in 1678: 'On Thursday night, about two or three o'clock, there was a most terrible storm of rain, hail, and violent winds, accompanied with such dreadful thunder and lightning, that some started up half-distracted, thinking it to be the Day of Judgement.'

The Civil War

By the late 1630s Leeds was developing extremely fast. As we have seen, the merchants had gained control of the charities in 1620; they had been granted the charter of incorporation in 1626; and they had bought the manor in 1628. The town's amenities had improved significantly: there was the new Moot Hall in 1615; the new grammar school in 1624; St John's Church in 1631-4; a new set of almshouses; and the workhouse in 1636-7. The last thing the merchants can have wanted at this point was a war which would disrupt trade, destroy property, and create great uncertainty, fear and instability. Yet on 22 August 1642 King Charles I raised his standard at Nottingham and his dispute with Parliament had become the English Civil War. Unlike the Wars of the Roses, this time Leeds, as a prosperous market town, was in the thick of things. It was fought over by the Royalists and Parliamentarians on several occasions, and as one set of troops left in retreat or to fight elsewhere, the other side seized the opportunity and moved in. There can be little doubt that the principal merchants were Royalist in sympathy – after all it was the king who had granted them their charter – but there were conflicting views in the town. Tensions existed between merchants and clothiers, Puritans and Anglicans, the corporation and clothiers.[54] Reviewing the events of the next few years, it is difficult to avoid the conclusion that in their heart of hearts most

Left: William Cavendish, Earl of Newcastle (1593-1676) the intelligent but over-cautious leader of the Royalist forces in Yorkshire.

Right: Sir Thomas Fairfax (1612-71), the valiant leader of the fighting arm of the Parliamentarian forces in Yorkshire. He strongly objected to the execution of Charles I and was partly responsible for the restoration of Charles II.

of the people of Leeds just wanted a quiet time to go about their business. Perhaps the majority of merchants sided with the king because they considered his party to be the one most likely to quickly restore peace.

Having said this, in the middle of September 1642, Lord Ferdinando Fairfax, the Parliamentarian leader in Yorkshire, went to Leeds where he found 'the commonalty of the town wholly at his command'. Indeed, the common people of the Leeds, Halifax and Bradford area did appear to have supported him, but Leeds soon became a Royalist stronghold. A Parliamentary broadsheet noted, 'In Leeds the malignant humour being predominant, [the Royalists] easily converted the town into their temper'.[55] At the start of the war the Yorkshire gentry tried to keep danger of battle from their county. The leading men on both sides in Yorkshire signed a neutrality treaty on 29 September 1642 agreeing to disband their troops, to gather no more, to keep out marauders of both sides and to keep the peace.[56] By mid-October 1642, however, the climate had changed and hostilities began. The Royalists, using York as their base, on 23 October sent an army to Leeds. The force of some 500 foot and 240 horse, with two cannon was under the command of Sir Thomas Glemham, Sir William Savile, Sir John Kay and Captain Sir John Goodricke. Their sole purpose was to take Bradford; but the attack on Bradford failed, and Parliamentarian reinforcements led a counter attack on Leeds. Glemham found himself so outnumbered that he took his forces back to York. In December the Earl of Newcastle arrived at York to mastermind the Royalists' strategy in Yorkshire. He sent Sir William Savile to re-establish a presence in Leeds and, in an attempt to make their grip on the town more secure, he improved its defences by constructing a long defensive trench in an arc around the western side of the town from St John's Church down to the river.[57]

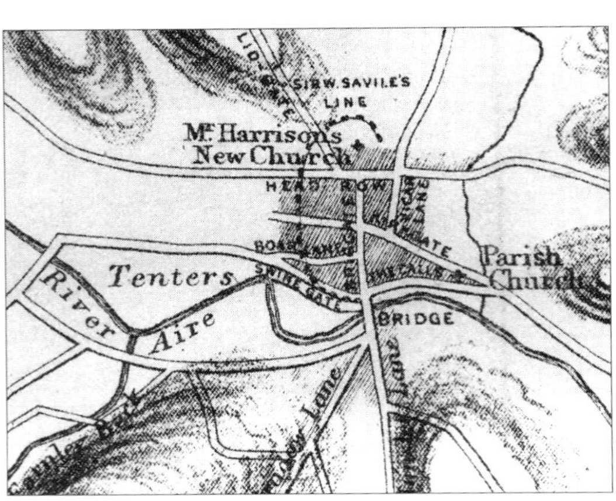

The Royalist fortifications of Leeds in 1643.

The Parliamentarian forces were meanwhile in some disarray. Lord Fairfax was short of funds to pay his troops, but resisted giving his soldiers free quarter upon the country in order to avoid losing local sympathies. In an effort to raise further money he wrote to his superiors in London:

> I have hitherto supported this army by the loans and contributions, for the most part, of the parishes of Leeds, Halifax, & Bradford, and some other small clothing towns adjacent, being the only well-affected people of the country, who, I much fear, may now suffer by this popish [Royalist] army of the North, merely for their good affection to religion and public liberty.[58]

The Royalists were still keen to capture Bradford, and on 18 December 1642 Sir William Savile launched a fierce attack on the town. The men of Bradford fought back well with scythes and clubs and Sir William's troops were obliged to return to Leeds unsuccessful.[59] Though the forces of Lord Fairfax's son, Sir Thomas Fairfax, were small, he was anxious to relieve Leeds. On 9 January 1643 he wrote to his father:

> These parts grow very

impatient of our delay in beating them [the Royalists] out of Leeds and Wakefield, for by them all trade & provisions are stopped, so that the people in these clothing towns are not able to subsist, and, indeed, so pressing are these wants, as some have told me, if I would not stir with them, they must rise of necessity of themselves in a thing of so great importance.[60]

The letter clearly prompted a positive response. On 23 January 1643 an enlarged Parliamentary army of well over two thousand men, many recently recruited in Halifax and Bradford, made its way towards Leeds. They found Kirkstall bridge destroyed and so crossed the Aire at Apperley Bridge. The army moved towards Woodhouse Moor, but torrential rain had made the moor difficult to cross, and this forced the troops southwards into the Aire Valley. A large number of men, commanded by Captain Mildmay, established themselves south of the river, on Hunslet Moor. Another sizeable group was based to the north-west of the town, near St John's Church. At this point Sir Thomas Fairfax requested the surrender of the town, to which Sir William Savile 'disdainfully answered' that he did not 'give answer to such frivolous tickets'.[61] The attack began.

In his memoirs Sir Thomas described the battle for Leeds in some detail:

Every commander in their several stations gave charges and commands, and riding from place to place encouraged their men to fall resolutely, who being mightily emboldened by their valiant leaders, performed the same with admirable courage; and although most of them were but inexperienced fresh water-men, taken up about Bradford and Halifax upon the Saturday before, yet they came on most resolutely and violently, especially the musketeers under Sir William Fairfax, commander of the foot, who most courageously at the head of his regiment and in the face of the enemy, stormed the town most furiously, whereupon began very hot servise: Capt. Forbes behaved himself most valiantly about the enemy's endeavour to oppose us, together with the assistance of their cannon, which were often discharged upon our men, yet they soon killed their cannoneers, and after a furious fight of two hours, our men most bravely beat them quite from works: When bullets flew about our men's ears as thick as hail, yet myself, Sir William Fairfax, and Sir Henry Fowles, on the one side, and the resolute Capt. Forbes with his brave company on the other side, made way into the town most furiously sword in hand, and violent force of arms, being closely followed by the dauntless clubmen, and so with much difficulty got possession thereof within the space of two hours, wherein were found two brass cannon, and good store of arms and ammunition, which we presently seized; we took also four colours, and five hundred prisoners, among whom were six commanders, most of the rest were common soldiers, who upon taking a common oath never in this cause against the King and Parliament, were set at liberty and suffered to depart, but unarmed. There were not above forty slain, whereof ten or twelve at the most on our side, the rest on theirs: Sergeant-Major Beaumont, in his flight endeavouring to cross the river to save his life, lost it by being drowned therein; and Sir William Savile, their General, in his flight also crossing the same river, hardly escaped the same fate.[62]

Despite the fortified state of the town, and the courage of Sir William Savile, the raw recruits on the Royalist side appear to have panicked when the town had been violently stormed.

It was only a matter of weeks before the Royalists sought to recapture Leeds. On 22 February 1643 Queen Henrietta Maria arrived at Bridlington with arms and ammunition which were immediately transported to York. This boosted the confidence of Newcastle and the Royalists, and prompted Lord Fairfax to gather the Parliamentarian forces in Leeds. To divert attention from the movement of his troops, Lord Fairfax ordered his son to make a show around Sherburn and Tadcaster. In doing this on 30 March, Sir Thomas lost his grip on the situation. On the return journey over Seacroft Moor many of his troops stopped for refreshment, and fell prey to the Royalists under General Goring. While Sir Thomas managed to fight his way back to Leeds, there were many casualties, and eight hundred Roundhead prisoners were carted away to York. Had Goring chosen to follow through the attack immediately and stormed Leeds with Lord Fairfax's forces unprepared, it could have brought the war in Yorkshire to a speedy conclusion.[63]

Leeds now came virtually under siege. On 23 April the queen informed King Charles:

Our troops followed them [the Parliamentarians], and it was resolved to besiege Leeds: on that the approaches were made with very little resistance, and very fair success, although they shot perpetually from the town, but when our cannon came to play, it produced no effect, on which a council of war was called, to know whether the town should be forced by an assault, or by a siege. General King, and all the old officers from Holland were of the opinion that an assault was too dangerous and might cause the ruin of all that army, by too severe a slaughter, and also that a siege was impossible, as we were not enough to make lines of circumvallation, the town being of very large circumference, and the weather also being bad: so that they resolved to raise the siege. General Goring and the fresh commanders were all for an assault, and I was with them.[64]

Newcastle decided to move with caution and, after an unsuccessful attempt at a treaty, ordered his Royalist army to retire to Wakefield. Fairfax was so fearful of a siege that he had written to London asking for money to strengthen himself. Parliament voted him the princely sum of £7000. Once again the Royalists had missed their opportuntiy of wiping out the fighting wing of the Parliamentarian army in Yorkshire. The presence of a large Royalist force nearby at Wakefield created difficulties for the town and surrounding area. In a letter to the House of Commons, Lord Fairfax complained about a worrying lack of provisions, the increasing number of poor people, the loss of faith in his army, and the mutinous state of his troops. He was desperate and reported that 'upon Saturday last 21 May 1643 in the night, I caused to be drawn out of the Garrisons in Leeds, Bradford, Halifax and Howley, some horse, foot, and Dragooners, in all about 1500, and sent them against Wakefield'. This attack on Wakefield was a complete success and drove the Royalists out.[65]

Nevertheless the Royalists regrouped and successfully stormed the Parliamentary stronghold of Howley Hall, near Morley. On 30 June they had another success on

Adwalton Moor and quickly took Bradford. Sir Thomas Fairfax escaped to Leeds, where his father was desperately trying to organise an orderly retreat to Hull.[66] This proved impossible, and the Royalist prisoners, held in the town, took full advantage of the chaotic situation as a contemporary account revealed:

> Came a captain of ours, who among divers other prisoners at Leeds, finding that my Lord Fairfax and his son were inclined to leave the town attended with three or four troops of horse, 200 dragoons and 300 foot, broke out of prison, possessed themselves of the magazine, took all the arms, which were 1500 at least, 8 barrels of powder, and 12 pieces of ordnance, with a very great proportion of match and ball.[67]

Lord Fairfax retreated to Hull and Newcastle's forces now dominated Yorkshire.

January 1644, however, brought the arrival of the Scottish army fighting for Parliament.[68] The Royalists were now weakened by having to fight on more than one front. Newcastle appointed John Belasyse as a governor of York while he went to deal with the Scots. Belasyse redeployed the royalist forces and chose Leeds as his headquarters. But this was the last time the Royalists occupied Leeds for, sensing weakness, on the night of 5-6 March, a small Parliamentarian raiding party under Major General Lambert attacked the Royalists at Hunslet and met with 'good success'. Perhaps Belasyse had only left a small force in Leeds by this time. On 7 April Sir Thomas Fairfax followed this up by retaking Leeds and from that date until the end of the war the town remained under the control of a Parliamentarian military governor.[69]

After the battle of Marston Moor later that year, the Parliamentarian armies dominated Yorkshire. The Scots began to move out of the county. As this army passed through the area it demanded money and destroyed property. John Hodgson of Beeston claimed that he had spent £73 6s. 8d. on the Scots and that they burnt down a mansion house and its outbuildings.[70] At the end of the Civil War, Charles I surrendered to the Scots. He was taken to Newcastle where the Parliamentary Commissioners received him. On 9 February 1647 he was brought to Leeds where he was held in Red Hall in a room which was later called the King's Chamber. Tradition has it that John Harrison came to him in the chamber with a tankard of ale which the king found to his delight when he opened the lid was full of gold sovereigns. This story is depicted today in the Harrison Window at St John's Church.[71]

It was widely believed that if the king touched the hand of someone with scrofula (King's Evil), an unpleasant skin complaint, the sufferer would be cured. When Charles arrived in Leeds hundreds of people came to see him. The Parliamentary Commissioners were so worried that they issued a declaration while they were in Leeds:

> Whereas divers people do daily resort unto the court, under pretence of having the Evil; and whereas many of them are in truth affected with other dangerous diseases, and are therefore altogether unfit to come into the presence of his majesty; these are therefore strictly to require and charge all persons whatsoever, which are diseased, not to presume hereafter to repair unto the court, wheresoever it be, upon pain of being punished severely for their intrusion; and we do further require all sheriffs, mayors, bailiffs, constables, and other officers to see this our order published.[72]

Both during and in the aftermath of the war, the pockets of Leeds merchants were hit very hard. One of the ways in which Parliament paid its own armies and that of the Scots was to make rich Royalists within its area pay heavy fines. Many of the papers relating to these fines still exist, and in describing the merchants' excuses for their inability to pay the fines, they give a fascinating insight into the scale of destruction in Leeds. Richard Sykes, for example, owned 'in the towneshippe and parish of Leedes two mansion houses, seven cottages and eighty five Acres of lande worth before the warres £180 ...but since these warres the houses have beene defaced and the lands soe spoyled, that they are not now worth £110'.[73] Robert Benson, attorney at Law, claimed that:

> His house hath been several times plundered and defaced, his debt books, writings, bonds, bills and the evidences of sundry gents, and the records of the Sessions in his custody burnt and embezzled, that he hath been forced to absent himself from his habitation most part of three years last, that he hath been deprived of his practise and Clerkship of the Peace and all profits thereof, and of a little land he hath not received one penny rent or any other debt since the beginnings of the troubles.[74]

The parliamentary commissioners sent to investigate confirmed that,'He is seized of an estate in Leeds intended for two habitations, all the glass broken and the floor and doors pulled up, no partition left but only the walls, and it rains into every room'. Nevertheless, Benson was fined £200 for being a 'commissioner to raise moneys' and 'very active for the king'. He died in Newgate prison.

Paul Freeman and some others residents of Leeds were so badly affected that on 19 July 1647 they petitioned the House of Commons claiming that:

> By direction of Lord Fairfax, their dwelling houses were, for the greater safety of the town, burnt to the ground, and all they possessed destroyed. They have attended nine months, but have had no relief, being obliged to seek their bread from strangers, whilst their poor children are left in the country harbourless. They implore the House to consider their wretched condition, and grant them some present supply to enable them to return to their callings.[75]

The financial demands of the occupying armies, the food shortages, the serious interruption of trade, the damage to property and the loss of life made these turbulent years in the history of the town. Leeds had suffered greatly during the Civil War.

The Plague

The Parliamentarians' dominance in Yorkshire after the Battle of Marston Moor in 1644, little though the Leeds merchants may have liked it, at least offered the prospect of the return of stability to life and better trading conditions. Fate, however, was soon to deliver another grievous body blow to the people of Leeds – the plague. Throughout the first half of the seventeenth century, England was rarely free of bubonic plague. Black rats, carrying the 'blocked' fleas whose bites transmitted the disease, were regular passengers on the trading ships.[76] Leeds had suffered visitations before 1645, but the outbreak of that fateful year was catastrophic. Alice Musgrave of Vicar Lane, who was buried on 11 March,

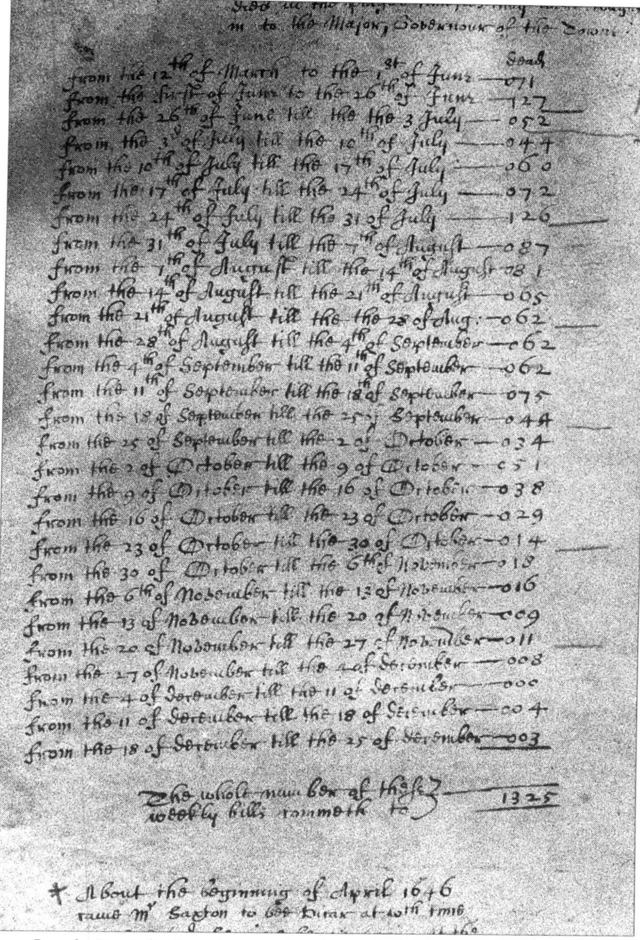

in to the Major, Governour of the Towne:

from the 12th of March to the 1st of June — 071
from the first of June to the 26th of June — 127
from the 26th of June till the 3 July — 052
from the 3rd of July till the 10th of July — 044
from the 10th of July till the 17th of July — 060
from the 17th of July till the 24th of July — 072
from the 24th of July till the 31 of July — 126
from the 31th of July till the 7th of August — 087
from the 7th of August till the 14th of August — 081
from the 14th of August till the 21th of August — 065
from the 21th of August till the 28 of Aug: — 062
from the 28th of August till the 4th of September — 062
from the 4th of September till the 11 of September — 062
from the 11 of September till the 18 of September — 075
from the 18 of September till the 25 of September — 044
from the 25 of September till the 2 of October — 034
from the 2 of October till the 9 of October — 051
from the 9 of October till the 16 of October — 038
from the 16 of October till the 23 of October — 029
from the 23 of October till the 30 of October — 014
from the 30 of October till the 6th of November — 018
from the 6th of November till the 13 of November — 016
from the 13 of November till the 20 of November — 009
from the 20 of November till the 27 of November — 011
from the 27 of November till the 4 of December — 008
from the 4 of December till the 11 of December — 000
from the 11 of December till the 18 of December — 004
from the 18 of December till the 25 of December — 003

The whole number of these weekly bills commeth to — 1325

About the beginning of April 1646

Leeds Parish Register at the time of the Plague. This page records 1,325 deaths: 'The several Numbers or bills that weekly died, in the plague time, as they were brought in to the Major, Governor of the Towne'.

The Plague Stone stood on Chapeltown Moor and probably marked the edge of the infected area at times of the plague. It is said that the hollowed out top was a money trough into which vinegar was poured as a disinfectant; contributions for the relief of plague victims were placed here. Despite the date on the stone it is probably much older, possibly 1604.

appears to have been the first victim. The numbers dying increased rapidly and it was not long before the weekly totals of deaths presented to Major Carter, the military governor of the town, were running into dozens. The outbreak was particularly bad in the area of Marsh Lane, the Calls, the lower part of Briggate and in Mill Hill, but it appears to have been worst in Vicar Lane.[77] As the fleas were carried by rats, the disease tended to affect the poor, who lived in the most squalid, crowded conditions where the rats could breed.

The worsening situation forced the Justices of the Peace into action. Under the authority of a statute of James I they were allowed to:

> Appoint within their limits' examiners, searchers, watchmen, keepers and 'buryers', [and to] tax and assess all and every ye inhabitants, and all houses of habitation, land, tenements and hereditaments within such borough or town corporate; and within five miles of such places infected, att such reasonable weekly taxes, rates and payments as they shall thinke fitt for the reasonable reliefe of such affected persons.

These measures were thought necessary to stop people from 'wandring abroade for their necessary reliefe' and sought to isolate the community and contain the disease. The initial sum thought necessary in May 1645 was ten pounds per week. This soon proved inadequate.[78]. Searchers kept a vigilant watch for possible victims. Once suspected of having the disease the sufferer, and members of the household, were transferred to cabins specially constructed on Quarry Hill, in an area near Mabgate that later became known as 'Cabin Closes'. Watchmen were appointed to feed these people and to ensure that they stayed in the cabins, and their homes remained locked and empty.[79] No one could leave or enter the town without a special certificate.

The large number of deaths proved a problem for the authorities. People were buried in Vicar's Croft and North Hall Orchard as well as in the churchyards of St Peter's and St John's. Such burials are evidenced by the discovery on 7 April 1779 of nine skeletons at Droney Laithe, said to be from Mill Hill and buried there 'in order not to traverse the stricken town'. In November 1790, 50 oak coffins were also discovered in George Street.[80] While later accounts conflict, it seems likely that the markets in the town were suspended and held on Woodhouse Moor, Hunslet Moor and Chapletown Green. Here corn, wool, cloth and other commodities were brought for sale by those who held a certificate declaring them free of the disease.[81]

The problem was, of course, that people were unsure what the cause of the plague was and they clutched at straws in attempting to deal with it. Was it, for example, transmitted through the atmosphere? A supposed contemporary account of the visitation claimed that in June 'the air was then very warm, and so infectious that dogs and cats, rats and mice died, also several birds in their flight over the town dropped dead'.[82] In reality, the warm, dry weather created ideal breeding conditions for the fleas. In desperation Colonel Charles Fairfax of Menston, a local Justice of the Peace, wrote to Lord Fairfax for advice on combatting the outbreak:

> The advice of the London Physicians, in a printed book, hath been of excellent use, but there not being any directions at all concerning cleansing, we are in a little time after in as ill a condition: for if we had any of skill to be got that will undertake it, as some there are, but their rates are so high and the country so poor, they [the people of West Riding] are not able to pay them …Be pleased my good lord, that divers of the physicians be consulted with for the best and cheapest means for cleansing the houses, furniture and stuff … Your lordship knows their trading consists much in wool, and therefore there would be particular directions how to use it in the fleece, yarn, cloth, etc.[83]

In an effort to keep the cloth trade going, Colonel Fairfax recommended that: 'Woolen cloth, Carsy

Wade Hall built by Thomas Jackson c.1630-40. Today its site is occupied by the St John's Centre. Fined £345 for supporting the king in the Civil War, Jackson claimed that he could not pay because of some of his lands had been devalued by plague victims being buried there.

(kersey) peeces etc. to be putt in a running stream 2 days att least, then dried on ye ground or on tenters. Woole is to be opened and wash't in a runninge water, dry itt on ye ground or on stakes, with sunne, winde or fyer.'[84]

Cleansing buildings and possessions, and isolating victims was the principal course of action taken to try to combat the disease. But the epidemic continued. Over three hundred people died in July, and the parish register noted that 'the infection was very hote, and baptizing children was given over because of the present danger'. On 2 July it recorded: 'Here the ould church doores was shut up and prayers and sermons onely at New church, and so no names of burials came to bee certified to us save the following, untill Mr. Saxton came to bee Vicar at Easter following'.[85] Public gatherings for church services became dangerous; only Robert Todd, curate of St John's, continued to work. The Leeds historian, Thomas Whitaker, noted: 'The minister, desiring to attune the minds of his hearers to the due state of humility befitting the great affliction, preached repeatedly on "Hezekiah's boil".'[86]

August proved a disastrous month and by September the weekly relief for plague sufferers had been increased to £50. Not surprisingly, the wealthier families abandoned the town. Charles Fairfax reported that about 270 householders of Leeds had left their homes and that many of them had 'removed their whole families into the countrey'. Whitaker remarked in his history of Leeds that he could not find evidence of 'any person of name', that is to say of importance, having died of the plague.[87] By November 1645 the plague was waning and a decree issued at the time creates the impression of the anti-plague operation being wound up:

> The houses infected are to be shutt upp for a monethe after ye sickness be ceased. The clothes well aired before they be used, but not to be medled with for six months tyme; if any remove them within twoe monethes, his house is to be shutt upp for twenty dayes. Beinge thinges of vallue they must be perfumed and washt & well aired, all houses throughly clensed; the meane stuff burnt & ye pore owners repaired out of ye collections of ye country. And for ye better performance of this necessary service th'examiners are to be continued for twoe moneths longer.[88]

The weekly returns indicated that the number of deaths was declining, and it was widely known that cold weather often extinquished the disease completely.[89] In the week before Christmas only three people died – the worst was over. In all between 12 March and 25 December 1645 over 1,325 people died from the plague in Leeds, probably one-fifth of the population. Leeds had seen nothing on this scale since the Black Death. An account amongst Thoresby's documents recorded that £339 18s. 9½d. had been distributed to the poor during the calamity.[90] Whereas the Civil War damaged the town physically and seriously depleted the wealth of its principal inhabitants, the plague gravely reduced its population and no doubt many skilled workers were lost. It was a testament to the great dynamism and resilience of the community that in the second half of the seventeenth century the town bounced back from these two great shocks and resumed its path to even greater prosperity.

Social Life

After the trials and tribulations of the Civil War and the plague, life in Leeds was brought back on to a more even keel. With the restoration of the monarchy in 1660 and the granting of a second charter to the town in 1661 the merchants were back in full control. Before this period few details survive of how people spent their leisure time in Leeds. Thanks, however, to the minutes of the corporation and, above all, the diaries, correspondence and publications of Ralph Thoresby, the great historian of Leeds, we are at last able to gain a much fuller picture of how the more affluent members of the community, at least, enjoyed themselves.

The ordinary workers and the poor who formed the majority of the town's population have left few records, and we must be content with scanty details. Undoubtedly they would have gathered in the numerous ale houses of Leeds where refreshment and entertainment were provided. A cheap meal called a Brig-End-Shot was available for the clothiers on their visits to Leeds at public houses near the bridge. As Thoresby put it, 'The Brig-End-Shots have made great noise among the vulgar, where the clothier may, together with his Pot of Ale, have a Noggin o'Pottage, and a Trencher of either Boil'd or Roast Beef for Two Pence.'[91] Despite the disapproval of the town and church authorities the common people were determined to enjoy the one free day in the week. The corporation records for 1662 noted:

> Many masters of familyes and parents of children, doe give liberty to their servants and others to

Ralph Thoresby (1658-1725), the great Leeds antiquarian, historian and numismatist.

profane the Sabbath by their open playing in the streets, sitting in publique places in great companyes, to the great dishonour of God in poynte of divine worship, in scandall of Christian profession, and to the bad example of the younger sort in poynte of education.[92]

The most was made of special events such as the Hunslet Feast which in 1679 'ended in great discontents, troubles and misunderstandings'.[93]

From 1677 the diaries and correspondence of Ralph Thoresby give not only a picture of middle-class life, but also interesting glimpses of the lower orders. Thoresby's father, John, had been a successful cloth merchant and in 1679 Ralph inherited from him his house in Kirkgate, and a collection of coins, medals and pictures which were to form the basis of his famous museum. Ralph was unsuccessful in business as a merchant and, after the failure of his rape seed mill at Sheepscar, devoted much of his time to antiquarian pursuits. As we have seen, for many years he was a leading Nonconformist, but in 1698 he became an Anglican and was instantly made a member of the corporation. In 1685 he married Anna Sykes and they had ten children only three of whom survived to adulthood. In one vicious attack of smallpox he lost two of his daughters. He regularly attended the spas on Quarry Hill, at Gledhow and at Woodhouse Carr in the hope of maintaining his own health.[94]

Weddings, funerals and christenings were times for social gatherings as his diary records:

12 February 1680
All day at Holbeck, assisting to my utmost at dear uncle's funeral; but such vast multitudes, what bidden and what unbidden, that abundance of confusion must unavoidably happen (of 130 dozen of cakes not one left).

28 March 1681
At the funeral of Lawyer Bathurst's brother, who was interred with the greatest state has been known in this town, near one hundred torches carried in state; the room hung with black, and escutcheons, and carried by the chief gentry, who had gloves and scarfs; all the company had gloves, with sack and biscuits.

1 June 1682
Spent the whole day at the wedding house and most of the night, it being too late ere I could get away.

He commented on his own wedding: 'Notwithstanding our designed privacy, we were met at our return to Leeds by about 300 horse'.[95]

Social events such as the Great Frost Fair of 1684 also attracted his attention. The winter was so cold that year that tents and booths were erected on the frozen River Aire and sports held. This lasted for about a month and 'ox-roasting on the ice formed no unimportant part in the carnival'. To begin with, he was grateful for the races on Chapeltown Moor (first noted 12 June 1682) because they were attended by all the local officials and this allowed the Dissenters time to meet without fear of interruption. The horses were weighed at the Talbot Inn, Briggate, and then taken to the Moor. A two mile course was marked out for the contest. Running races were also held. Edward Preston of Chapel Allerton, a butcher, was such a noted runner that he was given the title 'Harefoot'. Betting on 'Harefoot' was heavy and the diary records that 'several persons in Leeds advanced their fortunes mightily by laying wages upon his expeditious peregrinations'.

Not all recreation pleased Thoresby. He noted with feeling:

24 January 1681
Up early about five; Uncle Idle called to go to Ardington; was but indifferently furnished with company to follow the dogs; the first time I was a-hunting, and, I think, will be the last.

24 March 1682
Sent for by Mr. I. of Lynn, to the Talbot, stayed too late, and was much troubled to see the besottedness of some persons there.

2 February 1683
Spent not the evening so well at dancing school with Madam Dawkrey.

We read of Thoresby attending a firework display on 5 November 1681, and watching a rope dancer and tumbler in the town, but his diary is full of remorse for the time wasted in this manner. Above all he was a serious-minded man who spent much of his time reading, writing, visiting friends and attending chapel and church. His attitude to social events is best summarised by his diary entry for 21 July 1680: 'Afternoon, at Mr. Morris's banquet, had some learned company, the Vicar and two antiquaries, that made the entertainment abundantly more acceptable'.

Though the social life of Leeds primarily revolved around the clothiers and merchants, the town and neighbourhood had associations with many titled families. The proud, social group which possessed such surnames as Savile, Arthington, Calverley and Gascoigne, had influence far outside the locality of Leeds.[96] In the 1620s Sir John Savile had shown great interest in Leeds as a stepping-stone to power and influence but Sir Arthur Ingram soon became the local magnate. Sir Arthur (1567-1642) had made a fortune from the sale of Crown lands, and various other unscrupulous business ventures. He had connections

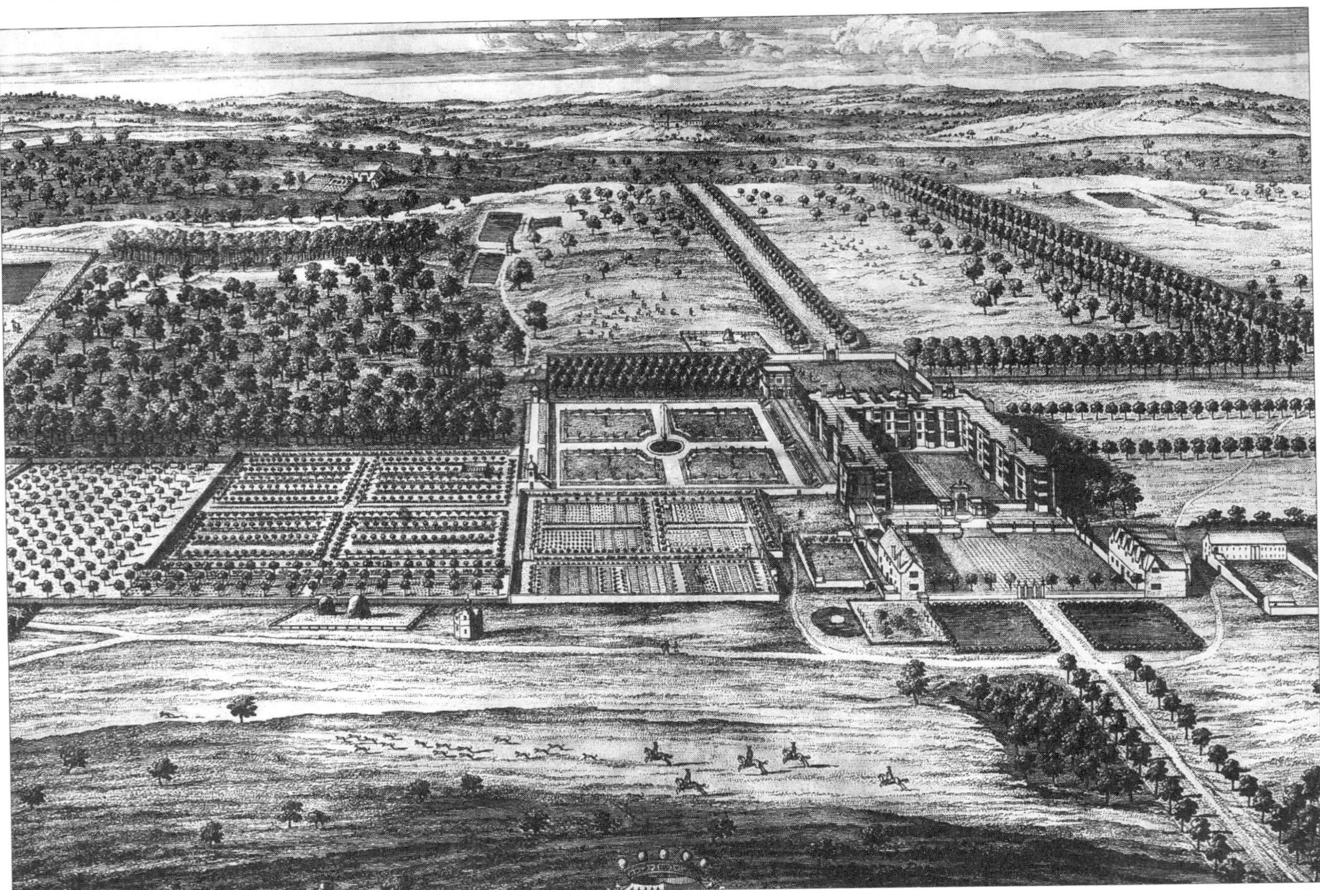

Temple Newsam in 1699 (engraving by Jan Kip after Leonard Knyff). The deer in the park, the hunting party and the stable block all reflect the way in which the estate was dominated by sport. Note the bowling green behind the house and the banqueting hall on a raised mound at one end of the south terrace.

with both James I and Charles I, and had given advice to leading members of the court. With the collapse of his hopes for high office in London he focused his attention on the North, intending to establish his family as one of importance. In 1622 he purchased the estate of Temple Newsam and remodelled the house for his son. He owned the manor of Leeds-Kirkgate-cum-Holbeck and, as we have seen, probably helped John Harrison in his difficulties concerning St John's Church.[98]

The fortune he amassed enabled his ancestors to enjoy the finest foods, wine and spirits; to purchase expensive furniture, paintings and clothes; and to follow a wide variety of hobbies. The vast quantity of bills, receipts and account books surviving give an insight into the family's taste. A note of household expenses for the period 7-13 August 1641 runs as follows:

> Imprimis for 12 ships [sheep] 3/8d for 36 pigeons 4/6d for 13 chickins 4/2d for 4 ducks 2/8d for 2 ducks more 16d for a plover 4d for 2 partrages 18d for a pigge 2/5d for 5 teales 16d for 2 baskets 12d for earthe vessell 2/4d for 4 couple rabits 3/10d for a cabage 6d for carrots 4d for turneps 6d for a bushell pease 20d for 4 harte chocks 12d for a watch light 10d for milk 3d for Kitchinge Chimnie sweepinge 6d for 2 litle salmon troutes 12d for egs 2/4d for 5 lemons and 6 origes 2/4d for quere paper 4d for 4 chickens more 14d for a pinte of creme 4d for 3 plovers 12d for 9 partrages 4/6d for 2 ducks 12d for a quart of red wine for my ladie 12d – £2 9s 6d. Item for fish 7s for three capon 2 pullets to meet master, 9/6d & 2 capons & 2 pullets more this night 7/2d for 2 quarts red wine at Mr. Bellwoods for Cooke 16d – £1-5-0d.[99]

The family regularly had visitors at Temple Newsam who they wined and dined, and to supplement the home-produced meat, fruit and vegetables they purchased luxury items like lobster, turkey and crab meat. Herbs and spices were increasingly used, as were tea, coffee, and sugar. They entertained on a lavish scale, and even had a banqueting hall built, overlooking the gardens, where the final course was served. After 1660 those fortunate enough to be of private means had time to relax and enjoy their wealth. The Ingram family had been granted the title of Viscount Irwin and the third Viscount Irwin, who died in 1702, appears to have indulged himself more than most. His bill for Port, Canary and French Claret from 4 December 1696 to 20 April 1700 comes to the astonishing total of £300 6s. 1d. (twice the cost of building the Friends' Meeting House in the 1690s). On top of this he purchased ale, spirits, and a wide variety of wines. He was a keen sportsman and made full use of the facilities available at Temple Newsam. Fox hunting, deer stalking, partridge and pheasant shooting all featured prominently in his life.[100] He regularly attended the races at York, Ripon and Northallerton, as well as those held on Chapeltown Moor. The family had their own racehorses.

The third Viscount enjoyed cock-fighting and appears to have gambled heavily at such events. Sir Walter Calverley recorded in his diary for 1700:

> At a cocking at Leeds, where Mr Nevile and Mr. Ameroyd went sides against Sir Thomas Gascoigne, who got far more battles, though I won something there. Sir Walter Hawksworth and I made a match for cocking with my Lord Irwin and Sir William Ramsden; were to shew one and thirty cocks a side,

Arthur Ingram, 3rd Viscount Irwin (died 1702). He succeeded to the family title and estate at the age of 23, and married Isabella Machell or Horsham, by whom he had nine sons!

> out of which we had eighteen matches, and fought at Mr. Nottingham's (the Old King's Arms) for one guineay a side, a cock, and ten guineays the main, out of which my Lord Irwin and partner got six battles and we got twelve. I won some money beside the wagers.[101]

The Ingram's journeys to the social centres of York, Bath and London allowed them to become familiar with the fashions of the day. Lavish spending was necessary to maintain their status in the community. With their property interests in Leeds and their local influence, they no doubt set the lifestyle and manners to which the Leeds merchant families aspired. In the eighteenth century, as the merchants grew even more wealthy, many of them began to live in considerable style, as we will see very shortly.

References

1. Transcript in: M.W.Beresford, 'Leeds in 1628: A "Ridinge Observation" from the City of London', *Northern History*, X (1975).
2. C.Morris, ed., *The Journeys of Celia Fiennes*, (1949), pp. 219-20.
3. T.F.Friedman, 'The Ingenious Mr Lodge's View of Leeds', *Leeds Arts Calendar*, No. 79 (1976).
4. G.C.F.Forster, 'The Foundations' in *Modern Leeds*, pp. 18-19. For a transcription of the Hearth Tax returns see: J.Wardell, *The Municipal History of the Borough of Leeds in the County of York* (Leeds, 1846), pp. lxxxii-cxiii.
5. Red Hall, see J.Sprittles, 'Links with Bygone Leeds', *Thoresby Soc.*, LII (1969), pp. 74-7; Wade Hall, see G.D.Lumb, 'The Old Hall, Wade Lane: Leeds and the Jackson Family', *Thoresby Soc.*, XXVI (1924); Harrison's house, see G.D.Lumb, 'The Family of Harrison the Leeds Benefactor', *Thoresby Soc.*, (1909), pp. 50-5.
6. J.Hunter, ed., *The Diary of Ralph Thoresby* (1830).
7. W.G.Rimmer, 'The Industrial Profile of Leeds 1740-1840', *Thoresby Soc.*, L (1967), p. 130; R.G.Wilson, *Gentlemen Merchants: The Merchant Community in Leeds, 1700-1830*, (Manchester, 1971), (hereafter *Gentlemen Merchants*), p. 197. An estimate supported by the Hearth Tax Returns of 1664.
8. See W.E.Tate, *The Parish Chest* (third edition, 1969), passim.
9. E.Moir, *The Justice of the Peace* (1969), chapters 2 and 3.
10. LDA, DB 213/47: Littlewood petition, 1598.
11. First Decree for a Committee of Pious Uses in Leeds, 1620 (hereafter, First Pious Uses Decree) transcribed in J.A.Symington, *Old Leeds Charities* (Leeds, 1926).
12. G.C.F.Forster, 'The Early Years of Leeds Corporation', *Thoresby Soc.*, LIV (1979), pp. 251-61. A transcript of the charter can be found in J.Wardell, *op. cit.*, pp. xxxi-xliii.
13. *Woollen Industries*, pp. 225-6, quotes clothiers' petition against creation of guilds, dated 1629.
14. *Ducatus* (1715), pp. 16, 37.
15. Beresford, *op. cit.* ('A Ridinge Observation').
16. For details of the purchase and subsequent history of the manor in the seventeenth century, see: W.G.Rimmer, 'The Evolution of Leeds to 1700', *Thoresby Soc.*, L (1967), pp. 123-4; J.W.Kirby, 'The Manor and Borough of Leeds, 1425-1662: An Edition of Documents, *Thoresby Soc.*, LVII (1983), pp. lxiv-lxvii; *Ducatus* , pp. 265-6.
17. Forster, *op. cit.* (Early Years), pp. 254-5.
18. *Ibid.*, pp. 256-60.
19. First Pious Uses Decree.
20. See corporation's petition to the king requesting parliamentary representation, dated 1639, quoted in *Woollen Industries*, pp. 226-7.
21. This account of the growth of the woollen textile industry in Leeds and the West Riding is based on: *Woollen Industries*, chs. 5-8; *Gentlemen Merchants*, pp. 1-17; W.G.Rimmer, 'The Evolution of Leeds to 1700', *Thoresby Soc.*, L (1967).
22. *Woollen Industries*, pp. 99, 226.
23. Gentlemen Merchants, pp. 12-4.
24. *Woollen Industries*, pp. 230-47.
25. *Gentlemen Merchants*, pp. 44-5.
26. 'The Court Books of the Leeds Corporation' (hereafter, Corporation Court Books), *Thoresby Soc.*, XXXIV (1933), p. 11.
27. R.W.Unwin, 'The Aire and Calder Navigation, Part I: The Beginnings of the Navigation', *Bradford Antiquary*, XLII (1964).
28. First Pious Uses Decree, pp. 1-5.
29. *Ibid.*, pp. 8, 11-12, 17.
30. *Ibid.*, pp. 7-8; A.C.Price, *A History of Leeds Grammar School from its Foundation to the end of 1918* (Leeds, 1919), chs. 3, 4, 5.
31. Second Decree for a Committee of Pious Uses (hereafter, Second Pious Uses Decree), transcribed in J.A.Symington, *Old Leeds Charities* (Leeds, 1926).
32. *Ibid.*, pp. 41-2.
33. *Ibid.*, p. 46; Corporation Court Books, p. 4; *Ducatus*, pp. 84, 107.
34. Corporation Court Books, p. 6.
35. *Ducatus*, p. 83.
36. *Report on the Endowed Charities of the City of Leeds*, PP 1898, LXVI, pp. 7-8; *Ducatus*, p. 13. Regarding the life and benefactions of John Harrison, see: M.A.Hornsey, 'John Harrison, The Leeds Benefactor and his Times', *Thoresby Soc.*, XXXIII (1935).
37. *Ducatus*, pp. 84 (Iveson's), 38 (Vicar Lane), 38-9 (Kirkgate).
38. *Ibid.*, p. 4; Second Pious Uses Decree, pp. 39-40.
39. The following account of the controversies surrounding the parish clergy between 1615 and 1632 is based on: R.Thoresby, *Vicaria Leodiensis: or The History of the Church of Leedes in Yorkshire* (1724) (hereafter *Vicaria*), pp. 60-3; G.C.F.Forster, 'Parson and People: Trouble at Leeds Parish Church', *University of Leeds Review*, VII (1961).
40. R.Thoresby, *Vicaria*, pp. 51-3.
41. Beresford, *op. cit.* (A "Ridinge Observation").
42. This paragraph is based on: Hornsey, *op. cit.*, pp.126-33. For further information about St John's, see: 'St John's Church, Leeds: The Trustees' (Feofees') Account Book, 1660-1766', *Thoresby Soc.*, XXIV (1919).
43. Thoresby, *Vicaria*, pp. 79-106.
44. This paragraph and those dealing with the impact of the Act of Uniformity are based on: C.Hargrove, *The Unitarian Chapels of Yorkshire*; W.L.Schroeder, *Mill Hill Chapel, 1674-1924 (Leeds, 1925)*.
45. *Thoresby*, Vicaria, p. 100.
46. Schroeder, *op. cit., pp. 25-6.*; Ducatus, p. 4; J.G.Miall, *Congregationalism in Yorkshire* (1868), p. 305.
47. *Ducatus*, pp. 76; Miall, *op. cit.*, p. 305.
48. For the history of the Quakers in Leeds see: W.Allott, 'Leeds Quaker Meeting', *Thoresby Soc.*, L (1965); J. and R.Mortimer, 'Leeds Friends Minute Book, 1692-1712', *Yorkshire Archaeological Society Record Series*, CXXXIX (1980), esp. pp. xv-xvi; J.E.Mortimer, 'Thoresby's "poor deluded Quakers": the Sufferings of Leeds Friends in the Seventeenth Century', *Thoresby Soc.* 2nd series, I (1991).
49. See K.Grady, 'The Georgian Public Buildings of Leeds and the West Riding', *Thoresby Soc.* (monograph), LXII (1989), p. 161.
50. This paragraph is based on Allott, *op. cit.*, pp. 8- 11.
51. Schroeder, *op. cit.*, passim.
52. *Ibid.*, p. 31.
53. Thoresby, *Vicaria*, pp. 115-33.
54. J.W.Kirby, 'The Rulers of Leeds: Gentry, Clothiers and Merchants, *c*.1425-1626', *Thoresby Soc.*, LIX (1985), pp. 45-7.
55. J.W.Clay, 'Events in Yorkshire during the Civil War', *Yorkshire Archaeological Journal*, XXIII (1914-5), p. 392; B.Manning, *The English People and the English Revolution* (1978), pp. 230-2.
56. G.Trease, *Portrait of a Cavalier: William Cavendish, First Duke of Newcastle* (1979), p. 95.
57. J.W.Clay, 'The Gentry of Yorkshire at the Time of the Civil War', *Yorkshire Archaeological Journal*, XXIII (1914-5), pp. 349-91; T.Fairfax, 'Short Memorials of the Civil War', *Yorkshire Archaeological Journal*, VIII (1884), p. 208.
58. R.Bell, ed., *Memorials of the Civil War* (1849).
59. T.Wright, *The Autobiography of Joseph Lister* (Leeds, 1842), pp. 14-6.
60. Bell, *op. cit.*.
61. T.Underhill (printer), *A True Relation of the Passages at Leeds on Munday the 23 of January* (1643).
62. Sir Thomas Fairfax, *The Memoirs of General Fairfax* (1776), pp. 32-7.
63. P.R.Newman, 'The Royalist Army in Northern England, 1642-5' (Unpublished Ph.D. thesis, 1978, University of York), pp. 165-7; P.R.Newman, 'The Defeat of John Belasyse: Civil War in Yorkshire, January to April 1644', *Yorkshire Archaeological Journal*, LII (1980), pp. 123-33; Thomas Fairfax, *op. cit.* ('Short Memorials'), p. 211.
64. M.A.E.Green, *Letters of Queen Henrietta Maria* (1857), p. 189.
65. G.Trease, *Portrait of a Cavalier: William Cavendish, First Duke of Newcastle* (1979), pp. 114-6.
66. E.Parsons, *The Civil, Ecclesiastical, Literary, Commercial and Miscellaneous History of Leeds* (Leeds, 1834), (hereafter *Parsons' History*), I, pp. 50-4.
67. D.H.Atkinson, *Old Leeds: Its Bygones and Celebrities by an Old Leeds Cropper* (Leeds, 1868), pp. 117-8.
68. P.Wenham, *The Great and Close Siege of York, 1644* (1970), p. 102.
69. P.R.Newman, 'The Defeat of John Belasye', *Yorkshire Archaeological Journal*, 52 (1980).
70. J.W.Clay, 'The Royalist Composition Papers', *Yorkshire Archaeological Society Record Series* (hereafter, *YASRS*), XX (1896), p.174.
71. *Ducatus*, pp. 25: Whitaker's notes describe the efforts of a servant girl to help the king escape from Red Hall.
72. Atkinson, *op. cit.*, pp. 127-8.
73. Clay, 'Composition Papers', *YASRS*, XV (1893): Richard Sykes, pp. 177-180, Thomas Jackson, pp. 47-50.
74. Clay, 'Composition Papers', *YASRS*, XVIII (1895), p. 89.
75. D.H.Atkinson, *op. cit.*, p. 162.
76. J.F.D.Shrewsbury, *A History of the Bubonic Plague in the British Isles* (1970).
77. T.D.Whitaker, *Loidis and Elmete* (Leeds, 1816), p. 76.
78. S.J.Chadwick, 'Some Papers Relating to the Plague in Yorkshire', *Yorkshire Archaeological Journal*, XV (1900), pp. 437-58.
79. *Ducatus*, p. 104.
80. *Parsons' History*, I, p. 100; R.Jackson, *Guide to Leeds* (Leeds, 1889), p. 39.
81. LCR: The Diary of John Lucas, 1712-50 – Master of Leeds Charity School (Microfilm 923.7 1962).
82. Whitaker, *op. cit.*, p. 76.
83. Bell, *op. cit.*, p. 303.
84. Chadwick, *op. cit.*, p. 499.
85. G.D.Lumb, ed., 'The Registers of the Parish Church of Leeds from 1639-67', *Thoresby Soc.*, VII (1897), p.52.
86. Whitaker, *op. cit.*, p. 94.
87. *Ibid.*, p. 76.
88. Chadwick, *op. cit.*, pp. 458-9.
89. Cambridge Group for the History of Population, *The Plague Reconsidered* (1977), p. 6.
90. *Ducatus*, The catalogue of antiquities, p. 79.
91. *Ibid.*, p. 17.
92. Corporation Court Books, pp. 7-8.
93. Hunter, *op. cit.*, I, p. 31.
94. For a general description of Thoresby's life see: D.H.Atkinson, *Ralph Thoresby the Topographer: His Town and Times (Leeds, 1887).*
95. *For diary entries see: Hunter,* op. cit..
96. *Ibid*; J.T.Cliffe, *The Yorkshire Gentry from the Reformation to the Civil War (1969).*
97. R.V.Taylor, Biographia Leodiensis: Worthies of Leeds (Leeds, 1865), pp. 78-9 (re. Savile).
98. A.F.Upton, *Sir Arthur Ingram, 1565-1642: a Study of the Origins of an English Landed Family* (1961).
99. This and subsequent references to the Ingrams are based on papers relating to Temple Newsam: LDA, TN: EA/12, 14; F/8 Temple Newsam papers.
100. P.C.D.Brears, *The Gentlewoman's Kitchen: Great Food in Yorkshire, 1650-1750* (Wakefield, 1984).
101. J.J.Cartwright, ed., *The Diary of John Reresby* (1875).

CHAPTER THREE

Georgian Leeds

A Town of Distinction

Leeds is a large, wealthy and populous Town, it stands on the North Bank of the River *Aire*, or rather on both Sides the River, for there is a large Suburb or Part of the Town on the South Side of the River, and the whole is joined by a stately and prodigiously strong Stone Bridge, so large and so wide, that formerly the Cloth Market was kept in neither Part of the Town, but on the very Bridge it self; and therefore the Refreshment given the Clothiers by the Inn-keepers is called the *Brigg-shot* to this Day.

The Encrease of the Manufacturers and of the Trade, soon made the Market too great to be confined to the Brigg or Bridge, and it is now kept in the High-street, beginning from the Bridge, and running up North almost to the Market-House, where the ordinary Market for Provisions begins, which also is the greatest of its kind in all the North of *England*, except *Hallifax*. It is the Cloth Market, which is indeed a Prodigy of its Kind, and is not to be equalled in the World.

The Street [Briggate] is a large, broad, fair and well-built Street, beginning, as I have said, at the Bridge, and ascending gently to the North.

The Town of *Leeds* is very large, and there are abundance of wealthy Merchants in it. Here are two Churches, and two large Meeting-Houses of Dissenters, and six or seven Chapels of Ease, besides Dissenters Chapels, in the adjacent, depending Villages; so that *Leeds* may not be much inferior to *Hallifax* in Numbers of People: It is really a surprising Thing to see what Numbers of People are thronged together in all the Villages about these Towns, and how busy they all are, being fully employed in this great Manufacture.

Daniel Defoe (1724)[1]

It is one of the great joys for those interested in the history of Leeds that the period around the beginning of the eighteenth century produced a relative profusion of visual images of the town. Previously having been limited to one crude plan produced in 1560, first we have William Lodge's prospect in the 1680s, then Francis Place's prospect of 1715 and then Samuel Buck's of 1720. The production of these views owes much to the enthusiasm and stimulus of Ralph Thoresby, who both encouraged the artists, Place and Buck, and accompanied them during their work.[2] Thoresby was also anxious that Leeds should join the largest English cities in having a plan drawn on a scale large enough to do justice to its topography. It was just after his death, however, that in 1726 John Cossins produced his splendid *New and Exact Plan of the Town of Leeds* which so wonderfully complements Daniel Defoe's description of the town.[3] Cossins' plan is a proclamation of civic pride if ever there was one (*see* p56/7). In its borders we see depicted the fine houses of the leading merchants – a testament to their good taste and the rising wealth of the town. It shows the street pattern with tenter frames in the more central open spaces and a patchwork of narrow fields at its edges. Mills, dye houses and warehouses line the north bank of the river. The churches of St Peter's, St John's and Holy Trinity are boldly portrayed, while the images of the Presbyterian, Quaker and Call Lane meeting houses acknowledged the increasing importance of Nonconformity. The Vicarage dominates the corner of Kirkgate and Vicar Lane, with the first White Cloth Hall of 1711 another significant landmark.

Certain notable merchants' houses are also depicted on the Plan itself. The mansion house of the Wilson family, later responsible for the development of Park Row, Park Place and Park Square, is to be found at Mill Hill. Alderman Atkinson's house of 1704, with its distinctive dome, is an impressive feature of the Calls. Alderman Cookson's house, near St Peter's, is set in its own formal gardens, with a fence near the river to prevent unwanted visitors landing. A small summer-house placed on the river bank added further character.[4]

Contemporary evidence reveals that Briggate was lined with a variety of dwellings; fine mansion houses often adjoining more humble timer-framed buildings. As Defoe's description indicates, the street was a focal point for commercial activity, many of its buildings were shops, offices and workshops. The plan shows the Moot Hall dominating the street, its central position making it a nuisance to traffic. The Shambles behind provided meat for the growing population. The most important charitable institutions, namely, the Free School, Harrison Hospital and the Workhouse are all clearly delineated, as is Sorocold's water engine, which pumped water from Leeds Bridge to a reservoir near St John's.

As Cossins shows, early in the eighteenth century Leeds retained much of its late medieval pattern based on the ancient streets of Briggate, Kirkgate, Boar Lane, Vicar Lane, and the Upper and Lower Headrow. Between 1700 and 1771 the town grew at a remarkable pace by the standards of the time, its population rising from about 6,000 to 16,380.[5] Remarkably, as the next map of Leeds to be drawn, Jefferys' Plan of 1770, shows, the physical boundaries of the built-up area hardly grew at all and most of the additional numbers were housed in buildings constructed in the yards, folds and gardens extending from the main thoroughfares.

Careful examination of Jefferys' plan offers fascinating indications of how the town had advanced since 1726 (*see* p58). The Methodist Meeting House at Quarry Hill, the Mixed Cloth Hall at the end of Boar Lane, and the Infirmary overlooking the open fields, were the amongst the most important new public buildings. The first White Cloth Hall, on Kirkgate, had become the Assembly Room, and cloth sales had been transferred to a new hall in Meadow Lane. Expansion had taken place south of the river, along Meadow Lane;

Francis Place's, Prospect of Leeds c. 1715, which appeared in Ducatus Leodiensis. Note the domed house of Alderman Atkinson near the river, Call Lane Chapel with its hipped roof and dormers just behind the imposing Parish Church of St Peter's, and St John's on the hillside.

by this time over 1,000 people lived in this district. New merchants' houses had been built along the lane leading to Woodhouse, and Little Woodhouse was witnessing a flurry of building activity.

John Tuke's map of the borough drawn in 1781 (the only other eighteenth-century plan of the town) showed Leeds during the most rapid phase of growth in its history. In 1772 there were 3,347 houses in Leeds township: a mere two decades later in 1793 there were 6,691. The number of houses was now growing at a phenomenal five per cent every year. As houses for the lower classes were crammed into every available yard, garden or patch of land with access from the central streets, the better off began to flee from the noise and overcrowding. Some merchants abandoned the town and moved to the villages and surrounding country areas. Others moved to fine new houses on the Park Estate, built in the fields north of the Mixed Cloth Hall and east of the fashionable and elegant Park Row. Their old houses were often subdivided and let for both commercial and residential use. By 1790 the population of Leeds had grown to approximately 25,000 (a four-fold increase since 1700) and it had become the sixth or seventh largest town in England.[6] Much will be said in succeeding pages about the manufacturing, marketing and merchanting of woollen cloth for, as Defoe said, it was the 'very life blood of these parts'. But the phenomenal expansion of the woollen industry in the eighteenth century pulled along with it many crafts and trades which became important in their own right. In 1700 probably four-fifths of Leeds workers were engaged in textile trades, but by 1790, though the woollen trade had grown enormously, it now employed only about half the town's workers. Sources for the early eighteenth century identify at least 50 different trades and crafts practised in Leeds, only about a quarter of which had direct associations with cloth. By the 1790s the number of such occupations had trebled. A host of crafts had taken root as Leeds became the commercial capital of the clothing district of the West Riding.[7]

In 1715 Thoresby marvelled at the wide range and quantity of goods to be had in the market:

> Once the Cloth and Benches are removed, the Street [Briggate] is at Liberty for the Market People of other Possessions, as the Country Linen-Drapers, Shoo-makers, Hard-ware-men, and the Sellers of Wood-Vessels, Wicker-Baskets, Wanded-Chairs [cane], Flakes [fencing], &c. Fruit of all Sorts are brought in so vast Quantities, that Hallifax, and other considerable Markets, are frequently supplied from hence.[8]

He remarked on the large markets higher up Briggate and in other streets for cattle, horses, pigs, fish, poultry, meat, wool, corn and 'whatever is necessary for the comfortable sustenance of mankind'.

Early in the century the town could boast salters, chandlers, braziers, coachmakers, white and blacksmiths, jewellers, clockmakers, tailors, shoemakers and a host of people connected with food, drink, lodgings and tobacco. Booksellers, wine merchants, printers, undertakers, building craftsmen, doctors, teachers and clergymen could also be found. Many of these trades and professions grew in step with the town's population, others raced ahead. By the 1790s amongst the trades

which might be added to the list were flax dressers, ropers, glovers, woodcarvers, gearmakers, flax and worsted spinners, timber merchants and insurance agents. Leeds increasingly became a centre for entertainment and wholesale distribution, for books and newspapers, wallpaper, chinaware, bricks, tailoring, and the best wigs, medical treatment and furniture.[9] The town's great advantage of being surrounded by coal was capitalised upon to the full. By 1779 the Brandling's well-known Middleton Colliery was supplying a minimum of 48,000 tons of coal to the town each year. The availability of cheap coal had stimulated the appearance of brick makers, potters, soap boilers and even chemical manufacturers and sugar refiners. The famous Leeds Pottery was built in 1770 on the north side of Jack Lane in Hunslet. By 1790 it produced creamware of such perfection that its goods found a ready market throughout England and abroad. The enormous upsurge in housebuilding particularly after 1770 gave a great stimulus to brick-making and the building industry.[10] Kirkstall Forge prospered too. For much of the century it had concentrated on producing iron rods, bars and plates, but after the Butler family took over in 1779 it was realised that more money could be made by making finished articles. Fourteen workshops were added for the manufacture of spades, shovels, screws and patten rings. By 1790 the forge employed about 70-80 workers.[11]

A significant landmark in the town's development was the arrival of banking. The first bank, Lodge and Arthington, was founded in 1758. In 1770 John Beckett became a partner and in the ensuing year took control. Beckett's Bank, as it became known, lives on today as the National Westminster Bank. A second establishment with the highly original name of Leeds New Bank was set up in 1777.[12]

A distinctive feature of the years from 1700 to 1790 was that the small workshop remained typical in Leeds. Few firms employed more than a handful of workers and the use of water power, let alone steam power, in production was a rarity.

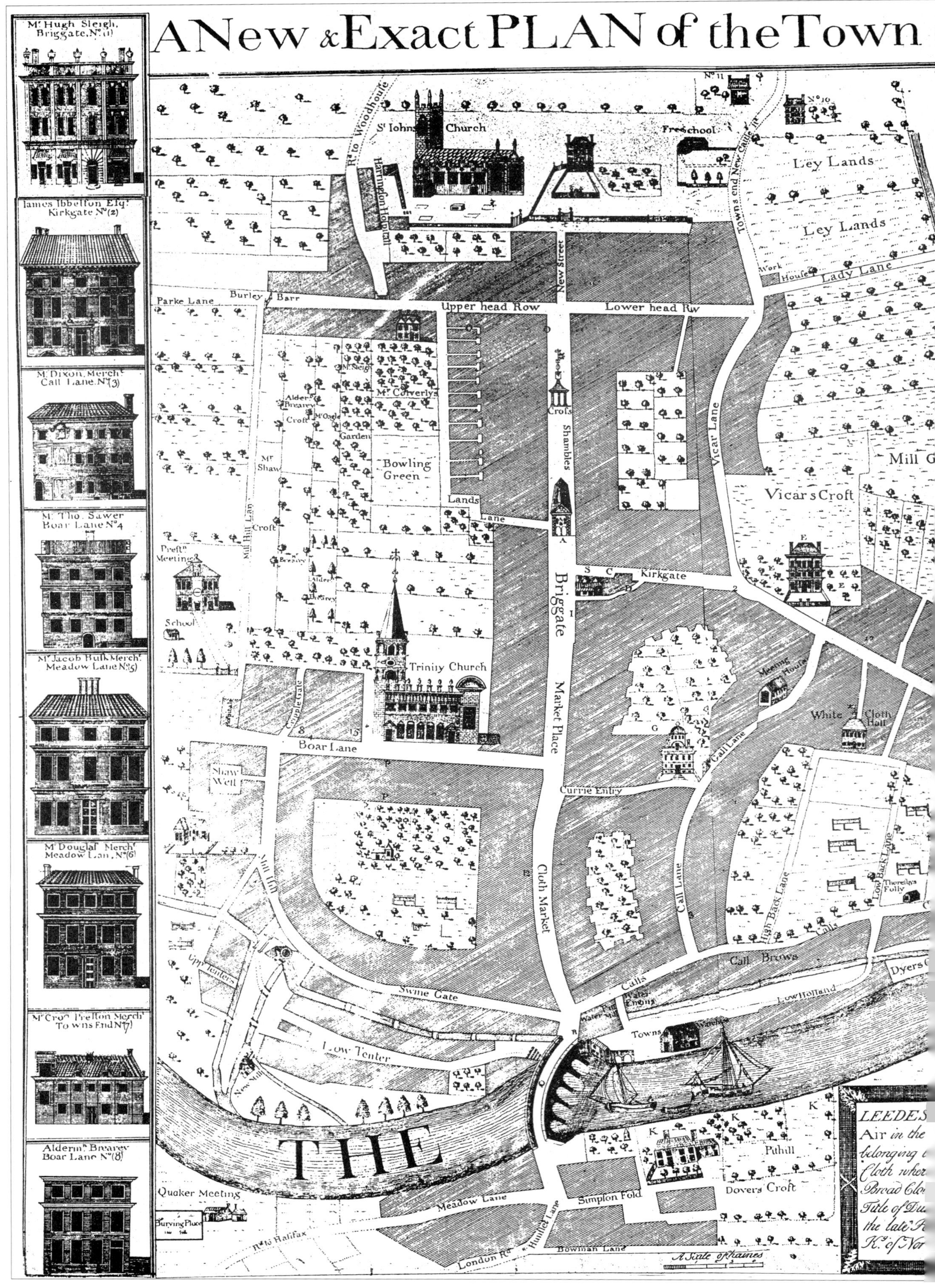

A New & Exact PLAN of the Town
Mr. Hugh Sleigh, Briggate, No. (1)
James Ibbetson Esq. Kirkgate No. (2)
Mr. Dixon, Merch. Call Lane. No. (3)
Mr. Tho. Sawer Boar Lane No. 4
Mr. Jacob Busk Merch. Meadow Lane No. (5)
Mr. Douglas Merch. Meadow Lan, No. (6)
Mr. Cro. Preston Merch. Towns End No. (7)
Aldermn. Brearey Boar Lane No. (8)
St. Johns Church
Free school
Ley Lands
Lady Lane
Parke Lane
Burley Barr
Upper head Row
Lower head Row
New Street
Vicar Lane
Cross
Shambles
Bowling Green
Mill Hill Lane
Vicars Croft
Kirkgate
Briggate
Trinity Church
Boar Lane
Market Place
Meeting House
White Cloth Hall
Call Lane
Currie Entry
Shaw Well
Cloth Market
High Back Lane
Low Back Lane
Call Brows
Calls
Swine Gate
Low Tenter
Low Holland
Dyers
THE
Pitfall
Dovers Croft
Quaker Meeting
Burying Place
Meadow Lane
Simpson Fold
Hunslet Lane
Bowman Lane
London Rd.
Rd. to Halifax
A Scale of Chaines
LEEDES

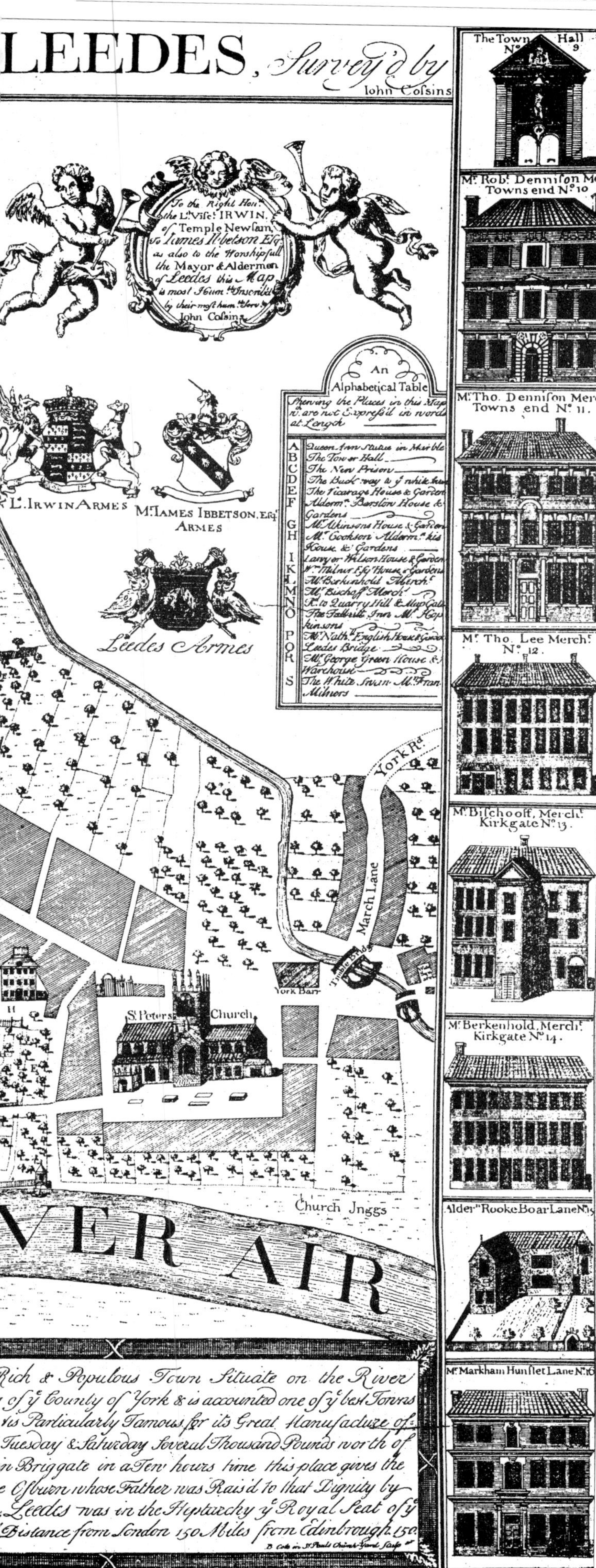

John Cossins' Plan of Leeds, 1726.

Merchants, Markets and Cloth

The great source of the remarkable growth and prosperity of Leeds in the eighteenth century remained the woollen cloth industry. As we have seen, most of Yorkshire's cloth-making was concentrated in the West Riding, particularly in the area between the market centres of Halifax, Bradford, Wakefield, Huddersfield and Leeds. As the adjoining plan shows, there were three largely distinct regions of production. The first region, that closest to Leeds, specialised in producing coloured or mixed broad cloth – cloth made from wool which had already been dyed. It included parts of the parish of Leeds but chiefly comprised the area to the west in the Aire Valley, as far distant as Guiseley and Baildon, and villages to the south such as Hunslet, Churwell, Morley, Batley, Dewsbury and Ossett. The second region specialised in making white or undyed broad cloth and lay roughly between Wakefield, Huddersfield and Bradford. It included villages such as Idle, Shipley, Birstall, Dewsbury, Gomersal, Cleckheaton and Kirkheaton. The fact of paramount importance is that throughout the eighteenth century, Leeds was the principal market for the vast quantity of broad cloths produced in these two regions. In these areas clothiers in their thousands lived in small cottages and made a living by combining cloth making with small-scale farming activities. A clothier, assisted by his family and perhaps a few journeymen, would produce one broad cloth each week ready to take to market.

Serving as the market-place for this cloth was a huge boon for the town but its advantage went still further. Many Leeds merchants dealt not only in woollen broad cloths marketed on their doorsteps, but also in the woollen narrow cloths and worsteds produced in the third main region of production in the West Riding. This region, which lay around Bradford, Halifax and Huddersfield, in 1700 specialised in narrow woollen cloths, especially kerseys, but as the century progressed, the district near Hudderfield turned to making fancy cloths, and Halifax, and later Bradford, switched to worsteds. By buying cloth at the markets in these towns as well as their home town, Leeds merchants came to handle almost two-thirds of all the West Riding's cloth exports by the 1770s. The importance of this cannot be overstated.[13]

During the century the West Riding's output of woollen cloth grew eight-fold, while its share of national output of woollen cloth rose from under 20 per cent to around 60 per cent.[14] Leeds was at the very heart of an industry experiencing a phenomenal growth. By the 1770s Leeds merchants handled approximately one-third of all woollen cloth exported from England. This was a vital service to the nation since woollen cloth accounted for over half England's home produced exports. In a good year in the 1770s, exports of cloth from Leeds amounted to £1,500,000; a very impressive sum when it is considered that the cost of a massive building like the Mixed Cloth Hall was a little over £5,000.

Without doubt, the aspect of Leeds which most fascinated visitors was the institution which brought

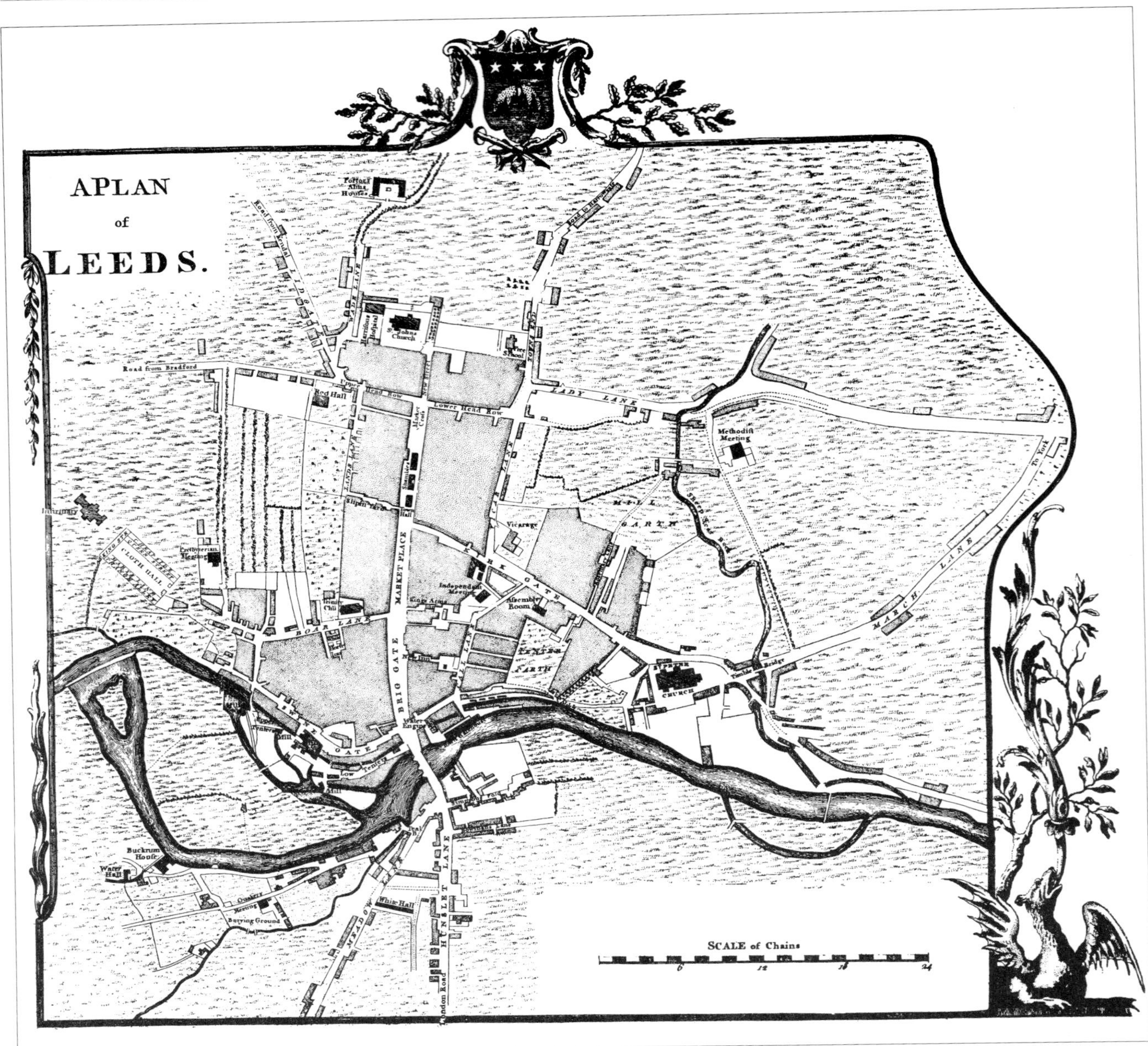

Jefferys' Plan of Leeds, 1770.

merchants and clothiers together, the cloth market. In the first half of the eighteenth century it was still held in Briggate on Tuesdays and Saturdays. Daniel Defoe's description brought fame to the market in the 1720s:

> Early in the morning, there are trestles placed in two rows in the street, some times two rows on a side, but always one row at least; then there are boards laid cross those trestles, so that the boards lie like long counters on either side, from one end of the street the other. The clothiers come early in the morning with their cloth; and as few clothiers bring more than one piece, the market being so frequent, they go into the inns and public-houses with it, and there set it down.
>
> At seven a clock in the morning, the clothiers being supposed to be all come by that time, even in the winter, the market bell rings; it would surprise a stranger to see in how few minutes, without hurry or noise, and not the least disorder, the whole market is filled; all the boards upon the trestles are covered with cloth, close to one another as the pieces can lie long ways by one another, and behind every piece of cloth, the clothier standing to sell it.
>
> This indeed is not so difficult, when we consider that the whole quantity is brought into the market as soon as one piece, because as the clothiers stand ready in the inns and shops just behind, and that there is a clothier to every piece, they have no more to do, but, like a regiment drawn up in line, every one takes up his piece, and has about five steps to march to lay it upon the first row of boards, and perhaps ten to the second row; so that upon the market bell ringing, in half a quarter of an hour the whole market is filled, the rows of boards covered, and the clothiers stand ready.
>
> As soon as the bell has done ringing, the merchants and factors, and buyers of all sorts, come down, and coming along the spaces between the rows of boards, they walk up the rows, and down as their occasions direct. Some of them have their foreign letters of orders, with patterns sealed on them, in rows, in their hands; and with those they match colours, holding them to the cloths as they think they agree to; when they see any cloths to their colours, or that suit their occasions, they reach over to the clothier and whisper, and in the fewest words

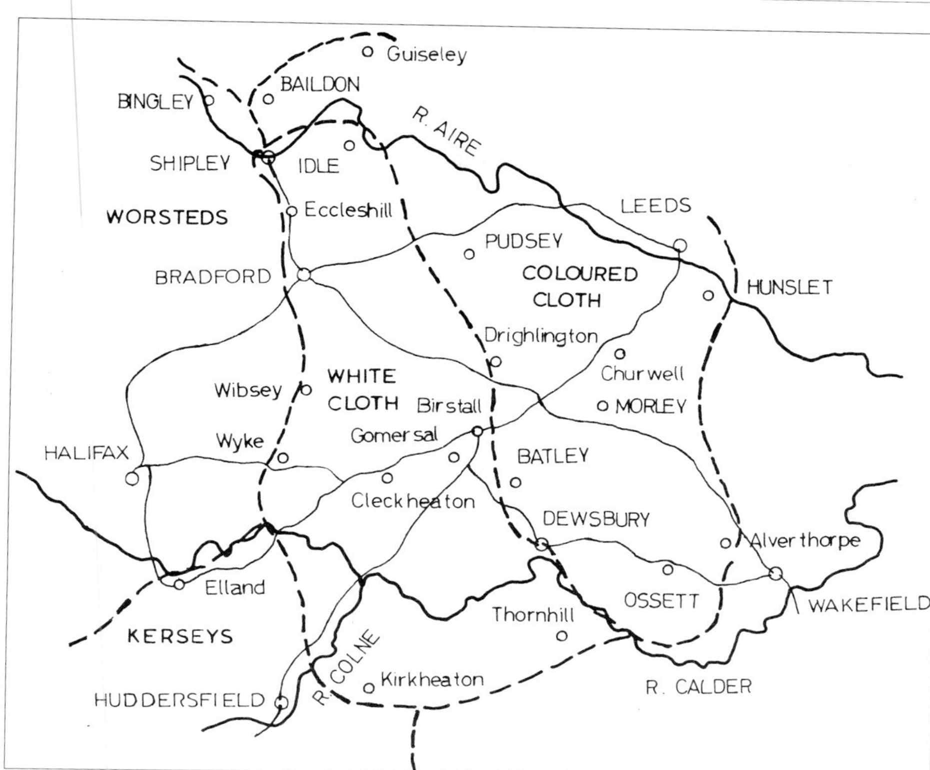

imaginable the price is stated; one asks, the other bids; and 'tis agree, or not agree, in a moment.

The merchants and buyers generally walk down and up twice on each side of the rows, and in little more than an hour all the business is done; in less than half an hour you will perceive the cloths begin to move off, the clothier taking it up upon his shoulder to carry it to the merchant's house; and by half an hour after eight a clock the market bell rings

The West Riding Cloth-making district in 1775. Leeds, the principal market for West Riding broad cloths, lay on the eastern edge of the district. The coloured or mixed broad cloth area began on the western outskirts of the town, the white broad cloth area six miles to the south-west.

Left: Spinning in a clothier's cottage. After purchasing his wool at market, the clothier's family washed it to remove the natural grease. Then the wool was dyed (if it were to be a mixed or coloured cloth) and blended, for example white and black wool making grey. In preparation for spinning, the wool was beaten and hand combed and then carded with wires set in leather (like a square hair brush). This created small pieces of sliver which could be spun into yarn.

Bottom left: A broad loom with fly-shuttle. The clothier now prepared the loom. Some of the yarn was used to make the warp (the threads running longways) and was coated in a type of glue to protect it from the shuttle. These threads were transferred to the back of the loom and the ends threaded through small hoops so that they could be alternately raised and lowered to let the shuttle pass through. The weft yarn was put on a bobbin using a winding wheel and then the bobbin placed in the shuttle. Weaving took place on either a broad or narrow loom. Once removed from the loom, the cloth was checked and any faults mended. Eighteenth-century statutes fixed the minimum width of a broad cloth as 5½ quarters (49½ inches/125 cms.) and its maximum length as 46 yards (42 metres). Narrow cloths were usually between 27 and 30 inches wide (68-76 cms.).

Bottom right: Water-powered fulling stocks. At the carding stage, wool was separated into long and short fibres (the long for the worsted cloth, the short for the woollens). Worsted cloth was stronger and lighter, and because it did not need fulling the pattern of the weave remained visible. Woollen cloth, on the other hand, after weaving, was taken to a fulling mill, placed in the stocks and washed in fuller's earth to remove the oil, glue and dirt. The pounding by the wooden hammers of the stocks thickened the cloth and strengthened it by 'felting' together the wool fibres. After fulling, the piece was washed and stretched to the correct proportions on a tenter frame, where it was allowed to dry.

The First White Cloth Hall opened in Kirkgate in 1711. Thoresby described it as 'a stately hall, built on pillars on arches in the form of an exchange, with a quadrangular court within'. The hall's facilities included a series of store rooms for the clothiers of individual townships and hamlets. Names such as Bradford, Heckmondwike, Batley, and Heaton were found on the doors. Peter Brears has drawn this beautiful reconstruction of the hall. The much altered building still survives today.

Right: The Second White Cloth Hall opened in 1756 just south of the river in Meadow Lane.

Below: The Mixed (or Coloured) Cloth Hall, built in 1756-7, stood on the site of City Square and Infirmary Street. The hall was the largest ever built in Leeds, being 127 yards by 66 yards. It was financed by the clothiers themselves, who contributed from £2 10s. to £7 10s. each. £2 10s. bought one of the 1,770 stalls. Its cost was £5,300. Its yard, which could hold 20,000 people, was often used for public meetings. It was demolished in 1890.

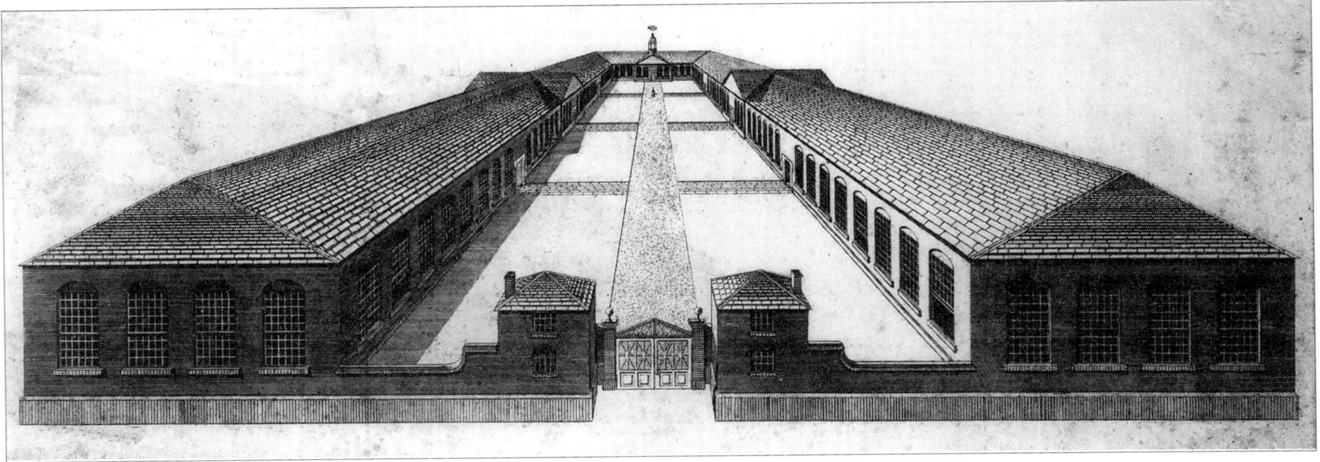

again; immediately the buyers disappear, the cloth is all sold, or if here and there a piece happens not to be bought, 'tis carried back into the inn, and, in a quarter of an hour, there is not a piece of cloth to be seen in the market. Thus, you see, ten or twenty thousand pounds value in cloth, and sometimes much more, bought and sold in litle more than an hour, and the laws of the market the most strictly observed as ever I saw done in any market in England.

By nine a clock the boards are taken down, the trestles are removed, and the street cleared, so that you see no market or goods any more than if there had been nothing to do; and this is done twice a week. By this quick return the clothiers are constantly supplied with money, their workmen are duly paid, and a prodigious sum circulates through the county every week.[15]

During the century it was the habit of merchants from towns such as Wakefield to visit Leeds to buy broad cloths, just as Leeds merchants attended markets elsewhere to buy narrow cloths and, later in the century, worsteds.[16] But considering that Leeds was on the very edge of the cloth producing district, how long could its merchants reasonably expect clothiers to make the tiring trek to the town to sell their cloth? Surely a more central site would be preferred? In 1710 the first real threat to prosperity came when the merchants of Wakefield made a bid to attract business away from Leeds by providing their own cloth market with a superior facility – a cloth hall. Leeds merchants reacted immediately. Thoresby wrote in his diary on 14 August 1710: 'Rode with the Mayor and others to my Lord Irwin's at Temple Newsam, about the erection of a hall for white cloths in Kirkgate, to prevent the damage to this town of one lately erected at Wakefield, with design to engross the woollen trade'. By April 1711 the proposed White Cloth Hall in Kirkgate was built and open for business.[17]

The Mixed (or coloured) Cloth Hall interior. Within the hall the stalls were arranged in rows or 'streets' so that trading operated as it had done in Briggate.

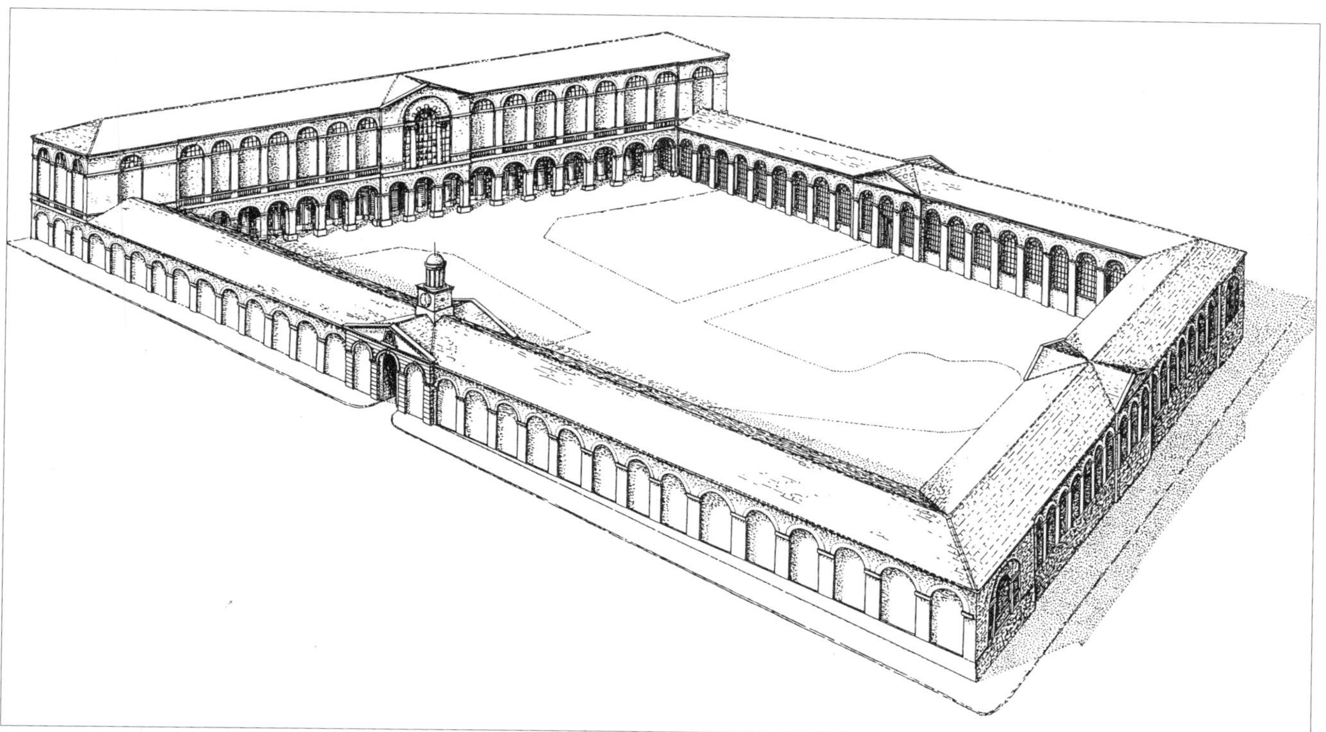

The Third White Cloth Hall, built between the Calls and Kirkgate, was opened in September 1776 at a cost of £4,300. At 99 yards by 70 yards with 1,213 stalls, it was somewhat smaller than the Coloured Cloth Hall, but imposing nevertheless. In 1765 between four and five thousand clothiers attended the Leeds cloth halls each week. This beautiful reconstruction has been drawn by Peter

The provision of high quality amenities such as cloth halls was clearly important to maintain the attraction of Leeds as a market centre. The expansion of trade was such that the first hall became too small, and in 1756 it was replaced by a new White Cloth Hall in Meadow Lane, just south of the river. This was financed by the clothiers and was much larger than its predecessor being seventy yards by ten and three storeys high. The Mixed Clothiers also wanted better facilities and shortly after left Briggate for a massive hall on the site of the present-day City Square.[18] In the 1770s the merchant community financed a new White Cloth Hall in the Calls. This had

The main gateway of the Third White Cloth Hall. This still survives today.

the additional advantage of a luxurious assembly rooms over its northern end. Early in the century a clothier needed to have served an apprenticeship of seven years before being allowed to display his wares in a cloth hall. By 1790 this term had been reduced to five years. In 1793 the sale of cloth made by unapprenticed clothiers came under cover too when a cloth hall known as the Irregulars' or Tom Paine Hall was opened on the ground floor of the newly built Music Hall in Albion Street.[19]

We have already encountered the names (and houses) of several Leeds cloth merchants, and we will meet more later, but how did they go about their business? In 1782 at least 46 of the 73 merchant firms in Leeds were partnerships. Even many of the firms which were nominally one-man businesses were in fact family enterprises. The Denisons, Blayds, Bischoffs and Oates are notable examples. Thirty-nine of the firms engaged solely in the export trade and, since three-quarters of the cloth passing through Leeds merchants' hands was exported, these included most of the largest and wealthiest firms. Eighteen firms were solely in the inland trade and 16 combined both.[20]

Almost all Yorkshire broad cloths were exported so they were the staple goods of the export houses. Meanwhile, the firms engaging in the inland trade dealt chiefly in kerseys (narrow cloths) and worsteds. The firm of Ibbetson and Koster, a medium-sized partnership engaging in both the export and inland trades in the 1750s dealt in kerseys, Leeds broad cloths (cloths, plains and coatings) and a whole range of worsteds including everlastings, amens, barragons, flannels, bays, tammies, serges and shalloons.[21]

At the start of the century a merchant having bought his cloth, arranged for it to be dyed, where necessary, and finished by a master dresser, usually based in Leeds, who employed a number of journeymen and apprentices. By the 1750s many merchants were taking over the finishing processes. Now almost all advertisements for merchants' premises made reference to dressing shops, dye-houses and tenters. By the 1790s the number of independent master dressers had fallen dramatically.[22]

Partnerships were often formed for convenience. The West Riding trade required the merchant to perform three distinct operations: he had to attend cloth markets throughout the county; supervise the cloth finishing in Leeds; and occasionally visit his correspondents to renew acquaintances, solicit new orders and collect bad debts. It was not easy for one man to combine all these functions especially if he had to go abroad or wished to enjoy any social life. Though the merchants' success generated much employment they themselves were not major employers. Even the largest of firms employed directly no more than half a dozen packers, pressers and clerks, besides at most thirty cloth dressers.[23]Probably the merchants bought the bulk of their broad cloths through the cloth halls, but the practice of buying cloth by direct order from clothiers was well established by the mid-eighteenth century. Direct orders probably occurred mainly in the case of worsteds and other cloths made at some distance from Leeds. Perhaps one-third of the cloth

Raising the Nap. Having purchased their cloth, Leeds merchants organised the finishing processes, including dyeing where necessary. Once dyed, the nap of the cloth was raised by drawing handles filled with teasels across the surface. The 'preemer boy' in the foreground of the picture is removing wool fibres from the teasels.

Cropping. Once the nap or pile had been raised, it was cropped to a uniform length, using large hand shears. This was a highly skilled job. The cloth was then pressed and bundled ready for sale.

exported by Leeds merchants by mid-century by-passed the halls.[24] The capital tied up in a merchant firm was substantial. In the 1750s Ibbetson and Koster were worth about £10,000. In 1737 the business of William Milner, the leading merchant of his day was worth about £25,000. Certainly, before 1780 an individual merchant had to be able to raise at least £1,500 capital to be able to trade and ensure a fair livelihood. Thereafter inflation and the increased importance of trade with America made £10,000 a more likely minimum.[25] Inevitably, with a trade so dominated by overseas sales, fluctuations in conditions abroad such as wars and trade embargoes produced periodic fluctuations in prosperity in Leeds. In the years from 1700-1730 Leeds merchants traded principally with Northern Europe, and Yorkshire cloth was distributed from Amsterdam, Rotterdam, Hamburg and Danzig. The decline of the Dutch and German markets between 1710 and 1730 brought relative depression to the town, but by the late 1720s its merchants were making major inroads into the markets of Southern Europe, notably Portugal, Spain and Italy. As a result the West Riding industry and Leeds in particular was able to enjoy a virtually unbroken generation of prosperity and progress between the late 1720s and 1750.

The 1750s were years of relative stagnation but at the same time Leeds merchants were in the forefront of the rapid expansion of trade with America. By the early

The Spinning Jenny. The initial technical changes and inventions in the woollen industry in the eighteenth century greatly increased clothiers' productivity. Until the 1790s, however, the devices required only human power and were cheap enough to be used by ordinary clothiers in their cottages. Kay's 'flying shuttle' speeded up weaving and enabled a broad loom to be manned by one instead of two weavers. Hargreaves' Spinning Jenny permitted one spinner to spin at least eight threads of yarn at one time. Both inventions were in common use around Leeds by the 1780s.

1770s the 13 American states, with the West Indies, took 30 per cent of English woollen exports. Gradual growth in the 1760s turned to a boom between 1769 and 1772. America was a major market for worsteds and by this time worsteds constituted about half the output of the West Riding cloth industry. The ensuing depression became chronic between 1778 and 1783 as a result of the war with America and France. The end of the war in 1783 brought great prosperity. The West Riding output of broad cloth trebled between 1781 and 1800, and the American market grew almost without check.[26] In part the great rise in the output of the West Riding cloth industry in the eighteenth century was at the expense of the industries of the West Country and East Anglia which it largely supplanted. There were two main reasons why this was so. In the first place the West Riding concentrated on cheap cloth which improved in quality as the century progressed. This represented excellent value against goods produced in the other regions which, though of higher quality, cost two to three times as much. In the second place the output of the West Riding was increasingly handled by a pushing group of merchants from Halifax, Wakefield and above all Leeds. The Leeds merchants were quite simply expert and highly trained specialists in the sale of cloth who keenly and adventurously exploited new market opportunities as older markets faded. The London merchants who organised the sale of cloth produced in the West Country and East Anglia could not hold a candle to them.[27]

Roads, Waterways and the Press

For the growing town, with its heavy reliance on trade and commerce, transport links were absolutely vital. The importance of roads to its success in the eighteenth century is often under-rated. Throughout the century they were major carriers of food, people, livestock and light compact goods, despite the heavy wear and tear imposed by the growing volume of traffic. Even in 1729 the *Leeds Mercury* advertised a weekly carrier service between

Leeds and many other towns, including London.[28] The degree to which roads improved during the century is debatable. Early in the century the state of local roads was appalling, in part because their maintenance remained the duty of the parish. As late as 1729 advertisements might be found in the local newspaper summoning the men of the parish to perform their obligatory six days labour repairing them.[29] Though changes occurred, as we shall see, Arthur Young in 1770 still considered the road between Leeds and Wakefield to be 'stony and very ill made'.[30]

In the 1740s Leeds merchants and tradesmen despaired of the existing system of road repairs, and spearheaded efforts to obtain Acts of Parliament to permit the most important routes to be turnpiked. Turnpike trusts were bodies of trustees empowered to raise capital to improve and manage stretches of road. Expenditure was to be recouped by levying tolls on road users at the turnpike gates. The paramount concerns of the promoters were to improve communications with the cloth producing areas to the west and the inland ports to the east, and to foster dealings between the West and North Ridings in wool and agricultural produce. The most important Leeds Acts were for routes which are very familiar to us today: Selby-Leeds-Halifax and Bradford (1741), Leeds-Tadcaster (1751), Leeds-Harrogate-Ripley-Boroughbridge-Ripon (1752), Leeds-Otley-Skipton (1755), and Leeds-Wakefield-Sheffield (1758). Initially, the trusts' finances were very poor, but they improved rapidly with the expansion of traffic and trade in the 1780s.[31] Charges for the use of the roads were not popular and in 1753 they caused several riots. At the worst, a troop of dragoons stationed in Leeds had to be called out to quell a mob attacking the King's Arms in Briggate where the borough magistrates were assembled. Thirty-seven people were killed or wounded, and a guard had to be kept on the houses of the mayor and recorder for several weeks after the event. Edward Parsons described the main events:

> The exaction of tolls excited an immense ferment among the people, and they determined to destroy the turnpike gates, and to demolish the houses of the collectors. In an attempt upon the gate and house at Harewood Bridge, they were defeated by Mr. Lascelles and some of his tenantry, and several were severely wounded. In other places they were more successful; they demolished the gate which had been erected between Bradford and Leeds; they destroyed the bar at Halton Dial, and repeated the same act of violence at Beeston. Three of the rioters were apprehended at the latter place, and were conveyed before the magistrates of the borough, then assembled at the King's Arms Inn in Briggate. The mob having on the morning of the same day liberated a carter who had been seized by the soldiery for refusing to pay toll at Beeston, assembled before the inn with the determination of rescuing the prisoners, and they soon broke the windows and shutters of the house with stones which they procured from the pavement of the street. The magistrates finding the civil power totally inadequate to preserve the peace of the town, ordered out a troop of dragoons then stationed in Leeds; the mob, however, so far from being intimidated, furiously assaulted the soldiers as well as the constables. Orders having been issued that each shop should be closed, and each family secured as far as possible from injury, the troops were commanded to fire first with powder, and this producing no effect, with ball. The people fled in all directions, but a considerable number were either killed or mortally wounded.[32]

In 1754 the first direct coach service to London began. In 1785 a mail coach started on the route, the fares being £3 3s. 0d. for each of the five passengers inside, and half-fare for the one passenger on top. Despite complaints about the state of the roads, the journey time had fallen from four days to twenty-six hours over the period. By 1790 daily coaches were also operating from Leeds to York, Hull, Sheffield, Birmingham, Manchester and Carlisle, and in 'the season' to Scarborough and Harrogate.[33]

The increased demand for road transport brought ancillary services. By mid-century it was possible to hire post-chaises 'to any part of England'.[34] In 1760 coach and coach-harness makers, like Scott and Ridyard, and Murdo Mackenzie trading from the old tythe barn off Kirkgate, advertised their wares and services to 'Gentlemen and others'.[35] Rather like the second-hand car dealers of today, there was a lively market in second-hand carriages – and the adverts were much the same:

> To be Sold. Two Four-wheel'd POST-CHAISES, the one London-made, which has not run one Year and little worse for wear; the other in good condition. Also one Single-horse CHAISE, little worse for wear . . .Gentlemen and Innkeepers may be accommodated with either coach or Post-chaise, 'til their own be repaired.[36]

Even the dead might be assured of transport in style:

> Atkinson, Smallpage, Randall, and Crosland beg leave to inform the Public that they have entered into Partnership in the UNDERTAKING LINE, having purchased New Coaches, Hearse, &c. with able Horses, and flatter themselves that they have it in their Power to Furnish Funerals completely, and in the most approved Manner. Coaches, Hearse, Pall, Cloaks, Hoods, Scarfs, Hatbands, Gloves &c. on the Shortest Notice.[37]

November 1700 saw the opening of an enterprise of almost incalculable importance to the commercial success of Leeds – the Aire and Calder Navigation. The scheme involved the canalisation, deepening or by-passing of unnavigable sections of the Rivers Aire and Calder to permit goods to be carried in large boats directly from Leeds and Wakefield to Hull.[38] For a merchant community so involved in the export trade, the link to the coast was vital. Though a joint venture between Leeds and Wakefield merchants, the lion's share of the finance came from the wealthiest woollen merchants in Leeds. The early outward trade was woollen goods, whilst wool and corn came inwards, much of it from Lincolnshire and East Anglia. Thereafter coal became an important cargo. In 1744 the eastern terminus was moved from Rawcliffe to Airmyn closer to where the Aire joined the Ouse.

By 1720, £26,700 had been invested in the navigation but profits were extremely low. In succeeding years, however, as the cloth industry expanded, the waterway became a gold mine for the small group of people who held shares in it. The volume of traffic increased seven-fold between 1712 and 1771, and by the 1790s annual dividends had reached an incredible 150 per cent. In 1778, in response to a proposal for a rival canal from Leeds to the Ouse at Selby, the proprietors opened their

Plan of the Leeds and Liverpool Canal. This plan was published in the Gentleman's Magazine in 1772. Contemporaries marvelled at the length of the canal, but much more awesome was the mountainous landscape which had to be negotiated between the two towns. The difference in the water levels at Leeds Bridge and the canal basin at North Lady's Wells in Liverpool was a mere 21 feet, but, in its eventual course of 127 miles, the canal climbed 411 feet over undulating terrain necessitating 844 feet of lockings, 8 aqueducts, a massive embankment two-thirds of a mile long and over one and a quarter miles of tunnel.

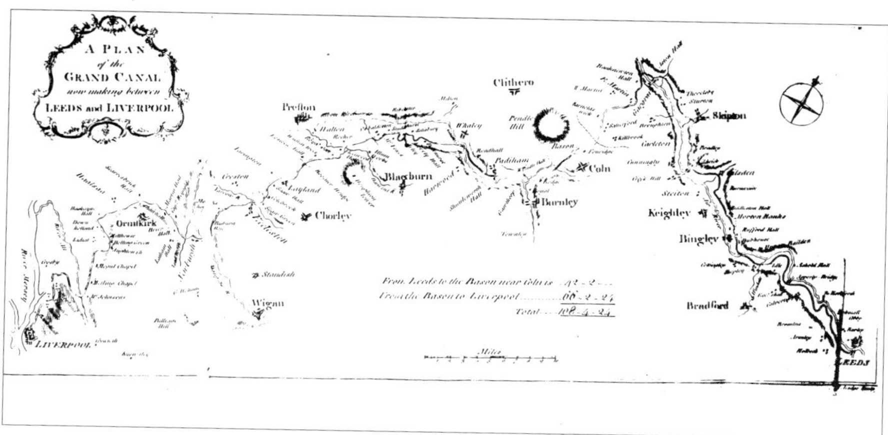

Leeds and Livepool Canal Warehouse built in 1777.

own canal to Selby from the Aire at Haddlesey. This was followed by £70,000 worth of improvements to the navigation itself, including five new cuts (short canals eliminating difficult streches of river) and a new set of locks completed by 1785. The end result was that Selby became the principal eastern terminus of the navigation.

With the clothing area to the west of Leeds and the growing trade with Lancashire and America, the potential benefits of a waterway running west of Leeds were enormous. But there was no convenient river. In 1766 the recent success of the Duke of Bridgewater's canal from Worsley to Manchester gave the Halifax engineer, John Longbotham an idea. The result, the Leeds and Liverpool Canal, was an extraordinary venture.[39] Half a century later, Joseph Priestley, the chief clerk of the Aire and Calder Navigation, believed it had been 'one of the boldest and most magnificent projects hitherto attempted in Great Britain'.[40] In May 1770 an Act of Parliament empowered the canal's promoters to raise £260,000 in £100 shares. By 1775 a 28-mile section from Liverpool to Newburgh costing £125,000 was open for trade. Meanwhile, a 33-mile stretch from Leeds to Holmbridge, near Gargrave, costing £175,000 was nearing completion. The grand opening ceremony for this section was held in Leeds on 4 July 1777 before a crowd of 20-30,000 people. On the arrival of the procession of boats, the canal's proprietors accompanied those of the Aire and Calder to a splendid dinner at the White Cloth Hall. Though only half the canal had been completed it was a great success. A much needed link between Leeds and the clothing districts had been created. Moreover, not only cloth and agricultural products passed up and down the canal, for in easy reach of its banks were immense quantities of stone for paving and building, limestone for the repair of roads and burning into lime for manure, and large beds of coal.

The Leeds Mercury, Issue no. 455, 5 March 1734. The woodcut on the left shows the cheerful scene of a postman in a low-crowned, broad-brimmed hat, blowing a horn, and galloping on a heavy bob-tailed horse; the one on the right shows the fleece, part of the borough coat of arms, wreathed around and suspended from the head of the Leeds mace.

THE Leeds Mercury.

From Tuesday February 26. to Tuesday March 5. 1733-4 (No. 455.)

Advertisements are desired to be sent in (also the Pay for publishing them) on every Monday *in the Forenoon.*

Thursday's Post.

From the Evening-Post, Feb. 26.

Since our last arrived one Mail from France, *one from* Holland, *and one from Flanders.*

Madrid, Feb. 17.

THE 9th Instant dy'd the Cardinal Archbishop of Toledo, aged 70. The 15th the Venetian Ambassador had Audience of their Majesties, as had the Pope's Nuncio the same Afternoon, and the former notified, that the Republick had accepted the Neutrality, and the latter had signified, that his Holiness could not grant Leave for the Spaniards to march thro' his Territories for Naples. 'Tis talked, that our Fleet next Spring will consist of 40 Ships of War, and great Preparations are making for a new Transport of Troops to attack both Naples and Sicily.

Paris, Feb. 22. The Merchants of St. Malo are said to have offered the King several Millions per Annum in Case of a War; for Leave to cruize on the Ships of Great-Britain, without a Tax upon their Booty.

Ratisbon, Feb. 25. Further Particulars of what passed in the Dyet of the Empire last Friday, upon the Imperial Decree for declaring War with France, are as follows: 'Tis observed in the first Place, that France having broken the Peace of Baden, attacked and carried by Force the Fortress of Kehl, exacted Contributions in the Empire by Force of Arms, and having in Conjunction with Spain and Sardinia taken the Dutchy of Milan, a Fief depending on the Empire, it was now become absolutely necessary to declare War against that Court, and the associated Enemies of the Empire, without giving into any Negotiation of what Kind soever for a Neutrality: In like Manner it was incumbent upon them to declare the King of Sardinia Enemy of the Empire, &c. Certain Ministers, amongst whom were those of Bavaria, reply'd; that the Affair of Poland having given the sole Occasion to the present War, the Empire had properly no Business with it, & ought rather to follow the Example of some other Powers and declare Neuter: That France had engaged to restore Fort Kehl, and reimburse what Contributions had been exacted. After which having expatiated a long while on the Ills which an offensive War would bring upon the Empire, they concluded that a Neutrality was far preferable to the present Conjuncture, &c. But after many Debates 'twas at length resolved by the Majority last mentioned, to take the most vigorous Measures possible against the hostile Attempts of France. This Resolution was concluded the 23d, and this Day put an End to the Business.

Dantzick, Feb. 20. The Saxon Minister having not comply'd with the Orders sent him to depart this City, an Officer and six Musqueteers were sent to him, and likewise to the Russian Minister, to put them both under Arrest; and on the 15th Inst. they were both conducted out of this City under a Guard of 36 Men, towards Demmers. On the 17th Inst. a Trumpeter arrived at the Barrier of this City from General Lascy, with a Letter for the Magistrates importing, that he had been informed, that the Russian and Saxon Ministers had been put under Arrest, as likewise two Couriers, and requiring their being set at Liberty. The Magistrates have returned for Answer, that all that had passed was without their Knowledge; that the two Couriers were not in their Hands, but in those of the Court. The Quarters of General Lascy are at Protest, about a Mile from this Place. By Disserters and Letters, we have the Confirmation of the weak State of the Russian Army, and that they are not as yet in Condition to undertake any Thing against this City.

(Price Two-Pence.)

COUNTRY-NEWS.

Bristol, Feb. 23. Thursday last his Highness the Prince of Orange honoured this City with his Presence, attended by Sir Clement Cottrell and some other Gentlemen from Bath.

He was met at a proper Distance by our Sheriffs, in a Chariot and six, accompanied by near a thousand Gentlemen on Horseback, and many others in Coaches, Chariots, &c. preceeded by about 200 Woolcombers in white Shirts, wearing on their Heads a sort of Wigs of Orange coloured Wool, diversify'd with a Mixture of Blue, and these were followed by a large Body of Weavers distinguished in a different Manner.

Our Churches and other Publick Buildings, Custom-house, Post-house, Ships, and many private Houses, were adorn'd with Flags, Streamers and other Decorations, indicating the Joy of the People, whilst ringing of Bells, firing of Guns, Orange Cockades, and all possible Demonstrations of Respect to the present Royal Family, as well as a grateful Remembrance of our once Glorious Deliverer, discovered a general and almost inexpressible Satisfaction.

To prevent Accidents, too common among Crowds of the giddy Populace, and to keep an open *Passage* in High-street, each Side thereof was lined with a Regiment of the Hon. Col. Montague, and the Consequence answered the Intention.

His Highness quitting his Coach at the Tolzey, was received by the Mayor and Corporation in their Formalities, when entering the Council-house, he was harrangued by our Town Clerk, in a short but pathetick Speech, which his Highness answered with a Sweetness of Temper peculiar to himself; and from thence proceeded to Mr. Alderman Day's, where taking a View of the Square, &c. for some Time, he removed next to the Merchants-Hall, at which Place he was treated with an elegant and magnificent Dinner. After which his Highness went to view the Hot-well, and tasted the Waters; from whence he returned to the Merchants-hall, where he gave the Gentlemen and Ladies the Honour of his Company at a Ball, in which his Highness distinguished himself in a most agreeable and polite Manner. He then proceeded once more to Mr. Alderman Day's, where he lodged, and yesterday Morning returned to Bath.

His Highness expressed great Satisfaction in the Honours paid him by Persons of all Degrees; and if the Face may be allowed to be an Index of the Mind, a more universal Pleasure could never possess a People, than what was visible in every Countenance on the foregoing Occasion.

The Affability, good Nature, and courteous Deportment of his Highness, and his great Prudence and Knowledge in Men and Things, struck every Spectator with Surprize When to finish the Characters of a Person every Way Princely, his Generosity to the Wool-combers, Weavers and many others, was much greater than could have been expected, or his Modesty (we apprehend) would willingly permit to be made Publick.

LONDON, Feb. 26.

On Thursday last his Majesty was pleased to appoint Augustus Schutz, Esq; Privy-Purse, and Master of the Robes to his Majesty, to be Avener, and Clerk Marshal of his Majesty's Stables, vacant since the Death of the late Col. Negus. On

More money was raised as a result of Acts of Parliament passed in 1790 and 1794 and the canal was finally completed in 1816 at a total cost of £1,200,000.

The railway age in the nineteenth century was to be the next major phase of development in British transport, but Leeds can claim a major first here of which it is justly proud. In 1758 Charles Brandling obtained an Act to build a waggon-way from his colliery at Middleton to Cassons Close near Leeds Bridge.[41] Though the wagons were drawn by horses along wooden rails, this piece of legislation was England's first railway Act.

For a trading community the communication of news and information was as important as physical communications. For most of the eighteenth century the town's post office was merely a branch of the main office at Ferrybridge, but in 1785 it gained full status.[42] In relative terms the local press was rather more advanced.[43] The town's first newspaper, *The Leeds Mercury*, began publication in 1718. In 1754 it was joined by *The Leeds Intelligencer*. Perhaps the town was too small to support two weekly papers at that time for in 1755 the *Mercury* closed down. In 1767, however, the paper was revived.

Before the 1790s the political preferences of the editors were well concealed. Thereafter, the Tory sympathies of the *Intelligencer* and the Whig views of the *Mercury* became plain for all to see. The papers drew the bulk of their information from the London press and chiefly contained Continental news and the 'latest' news from London. Remarkably little local news was reported, possibly because gossip made it common knowledge and readers such as the merchants were more interested in events in their export markets. Nevertheless, the notices and advertisements in the papers provide the historian with much fascinating and valuable local detail. By modern standards the papers were very expensive. The *Intelligencer* cost 3d. in the 1770s and 6d. by the 1790s. Both its price and its tone reflected that it was directed at the middle and upper classes. On 7 January 1755, for example, the editor of the *Intelligencer*, while condemning a customer of a public house in the Lowerhead Row for viciously killing a dog, remarked: 'I would advise that such men should herd only among the savages of HOLBECK'.

Justice and Improvement

In the eighteenth century, as in the century before, the pinnacle of government in Leeds was the corporation. Here the merchants' influence was total, for membership of this self-electing body was permitted only to those of the highest social status. Between 1700 and 1780 the twelve leading merchant families (Atkinson, Blayds, Cookson, Denison, Hall, Ibbetson, Kitchingman, Lodge, Milner, Preston, Rooke and Wilson) provided almost half of the aldermen, and three-fifths of corporation members were woollen merchants. To modern eyes, however, the corporation as a body seems remarkably inactive. Though established principally to regulate the cloth trade and manufacture, by 1700 it had largely abandoned this role. In truth, now that the bulk of cloth sold and finished in Leeds came from outside its boundaries the corporation could have little influence. Without Members of Parliament for the borough there was very limited scope for political intrigue, and with minimal corporation property or revenue from rates there was little money to spend. The corporation played a major part in the establishment of the Aire and Calder Navigation and the building of the cloth halls of 1711 and 1776, but these were isolated events.[44]

It was in their individual roles as Justices of the Peace for the borough and as members of the various committees and commissions, which were virtually sub-committees of the corporation, that the members of the corporation can be seen as active and even dynamic participants in local government. From the Moot Hall a rota of aldermen (automatically magistrates for the borough) dispensed justice on a day-to-day basis at petty sessions, and every three months, together with the mayor and recorder, at the much grander borough quarter

The Moot Hall. This view dated 1816 shows the hall as it was rebuilt on the site of its seventeenth-century predecessor in the centre of Briggate in 1710-11. It had butchers' shops on its ground floor and a court room above. It was here that the meetings of Leeds Corporation and Quarter Sessions were held. Note the way the hall divided Briggate in two. The town prison stood at Kirkgate-end (see 'C' on Cossins' Plan).

sessions. In this way they supervised the entire administration of the town.[45] They managed the collection of the poor and highway rates and kept a close watch on the activities of the poor law overseers and the constables. There were periodic attempts to clean up

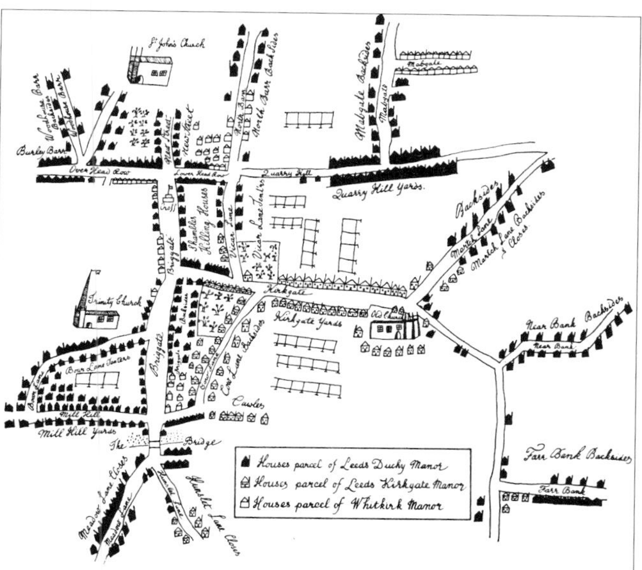

In the eighteenth century, Leeds people were still obliged to take their corn to the King's Mills to be ground. Many sought to escape this obligation by falsely fixing Templar Crosses on their houses. This map was drawn to clearly identify those who could lawfully grind their corn elsewhere. Houses in the manors of Leeds-Kirkgate and Whitkirk were exempt. The lines of squares with feet are tenter frames.

those vices which lured the working-class into sin: ale house, prostitutes, gaming dogs, and billiard tables. Even where offenders were not consigned to prison, the penalties could be vicious. In 1770 William Preston was ordered to be publicly whipped 'for stealing three pairs of spurrs from Mr Myers at the New Inn', and Ann Watson was ordered to be privately whipped 'for stealing a piece of Venetian stuff from Mr Frankland'.[46]

From the middle of the century the sheer growth in the size of Leeds and the diversification of its trades made it extremely difficult for the magistrates to manage the town. The parish administration, the vestry (in effect the assembled meeting of the vicar and ratepayers of Leeds) experienced difficulties too. As it had done in the seventeenth century, it elected the church wardens and the workhouse trustees, and under the close supervision of the magistrates was responsible for maintaining the highways, caring for the poor and infirm, and maintaining law and order.[47]

As the problems multiplied, attempts were made to transfer responsibilities to other hands or deal with them in a new manner. We have already seen how turnpike trusts were established to repair major roads, and later we will hear of the founding of the Infirmary to treat the sick. One of the most fascinating features of the period, however, was the establishment of the Leeds Improvement Commission. The Improvement Commission was set up by an Act of Parliament obtained on the initiative of the inhabitants of Leeds in 1755.[48] The clauses of the Act bring the place names and everyday lives of the people of mid-eighteenth century Leeds vividly out of the mists of time. Its preamble gives an impression of the vibrance of the town and the reasons for obtaining the Act:

Whereas the Town of Leeds, in the County of York, is a Place of great trade and large extent, consisting of many Streets, narrow Lanes, and Alleys, inhabited by great numbers of Tradesmen, Manufacturers, Artificers, and others, who in the prosecution and carrying on their respective Trades and Manufactures, are obliged to pass and repass through the same, as well in the night as in the day-time: And whereas several Burglaries, Robberies, and other Outrages and Disorders have lately been committed, and many more attempted within the said Town, and the Streets, Lanes, Alleys, and Passages thereof, and the enlightening the said Streets and Lanes, and regulating the Pavements thereof, would be of great advantage, and tend not only to the security and preservation of the Person and Properties of the Inhabitants of the said Town, but to the benefit and convenience of strangers and persons resorting to the several markets kept within the said Town ...May it please your Majesty that ...

As we have seen, by 1755 the centre of Leeds had become increasingly congested and much more densely populated. As a result the condition of the streets had deteriorated and the dark, narrow network of alleys and streets had been the scene of a wave of attacks and burglaries. The commissioners' task was to provide street lighting and to create well-made and easily negotiated pavements within the town bars. The five bars stood on the principal routes into Leeds and marked the medieval boundaries of the built-up area. The East or York Bar was at the bottom of Kirkgate by the parish church; the South Bar was just south of Leeds Bridge; the West Bar was at the west end of Boar Lane; Burley Bar, at the north western entrance to the town, stood at the junction of the present-day Headrow and Albion Street; and finally, the North Bar was sited beside the workhouse at the junction of Vicar Lane and Lady Lane.[49]

In no sense was the commission a rival to the corporation, for it was to consist of fourteen principal inhabitants living within the town bars, nominated by the ratepayers, plus the mayor, recorder and Justices of the Peace for the borough. After organising the purchase and setting up of street lamps, the commissioners were to employ lamp keepers and lamp lighters and to appoint assessors who would levy appropriate rates on the owners and occupants of property within the bars. The provision of street lighting financed out of rates is perhaps the first genuine example of modern style local government services in Leeds. The clauses dealing with the improvement of the streets paint a lurid picture of their current state. In an effort to deal with the dirt and filth the Act required that the occupants of houses fronting the street should sweep and clean the street in front of their property between one and three o'clock every Saturday afternoon and put the refuse in a heap ready to be carried away. People were to cease to throw 'ashes, rubbish, dust, timber, dirt, dung, filth, tubs or other annoyances' into the streets and allow them to remain there for more than twenty-four hours. Furthermore, in future, the slaughtering of cattle, calves, sheep, lambs and swine in the public streets, with the exception of the Shambles, was to cease.

To deal with congestion and inadequate pavements the Act insisted that no cart, waggon or carriage was to be permitted to remain in the public streets and passages any longer than was necessary for loading and unloading. Occupants were made responsible for the making and maintenance of the pavements in front of their property. The Act was to be enforced by the magistrates, who were to exact heavy penalties from people failing to comply with it.

Both the success and the inadequacy of the 1755 Act prompted the inhabitants of Leeds to obtain a second improvement Act in 1790.[50] Its purpose was two-fold: to improve the town's water supply and to extend the powers of the Improvement Commissioners. The water system created by Sorocold in 1694 for a population of 6,000 was grossly inadequate for a population of some 25,000. The Act established the Leeds Water Works Commission which was empowered to compulsorily purchase the old water works and modernise and extend the whole system to provide 'a sufficient and regular supply of good and wholesome water'. Water was to be taken from the River Aire between Armley Mill and the old water works at Pitfall Mill just beside Leeds Bridge. Consumers were required to pay a water rate and particularly heavy users such as brewers, distillers, merchants, cloth dressers, dyers, maltsters and innkeepers were to pay special levies in proportion to use. The interests of the poor were apparently assisted because the commissioners were specifically required to place cisterns and water-cocks at convenient distances in the public streets for the use of the poor without charge.

Applying for an Act of Parliament was an expensive business and so to get their money's worth the Leeds worthies had clauses tacked on to the Act to extend the powers of the Improvement Commissioners. Firstly, the clauses recognised the town's growth since 1755. Streets such as those on the Park estate were not within the town bars, so the powers under the original Act were now extended to the streets and passages within 1000 yard of the bars. Despite the execution of the earlier Act, Leeds was clearly an even more congested and chaotic place than it had been in 1755. The commissioners were further empowered to order the removal of all signs and boards projecting into the streets and passages; in future all signs were to be fixed flat against the walls of the premises concerned. Pedestrians were obviously in grave danger of being knocked down by vehicles or marauding cattle, for in future people were to be fined for placing or running wheelbarrows, trucks, drays or carriages on the footpaths, rolling barrels on them, riding or driving horses or cattle on them, or fastening animals on them or across them. Here we get the real flavour of Leeds as a horse and cattle market. People were expressly prohibited from letting loose, exercising and breaking horses, and exposing their stallions for the purpose of mating with mares in the public streets.

Today the principal decisions in local government are taken by unpaid, elected representatives of the people, but their decisions are implemented by a large army of administrators and workers. The Improvement Commissioners and Water Works Commissioners were both elected and unpaid, but their powers under the 1790 Act to employ workers represented a major step forward in the development of local government organisation. The optimism of the 1755 Act that the streets could be cleaned up largely by the voluntary efforts of the people of Leeds had proved unfounded. The 1790 Act empowered the commissioners to employ scavengers to clean the streets.

The Growth of Nonconformity

The quadrupling of the population of Leeds between 1700 and 1790 put great pressure on the accommodation provided by the town's places of worship. In response several new churches and chapels were built and the capacity of existing buildings was often increased.[51] Since Nonconformists were barred from holding public offices, the whole of the corporation were Anglicans during the eighteenth century, and it was Anglican church building which received their attention. Thoresby described the parish church as being 'very spacious ...of strong Fabrick ...black, but comely', but the ancient structure was always in need of repair.[52] Between 1712 and 1715 large sums were spent on improvements. The redecoration of the interior by fine craftsmen produced a particularly impressive east end. A new altarpiece, with the Decalogue, Creed and Lord's Prayer inscribed in gilt, was made by John Seymour, a local artisan. The French artist, Jacques Parmentier, surrounded it with an oil painting on plaster that portrayed Moses and Aaron 'Giving of the Law, (with) the Thunder & Lightning at the ending of the thick Clouds ...expressed ...upon the Roof in suitable Terror, but qualified by the lovely Aspects of a Choir of Angels & Cherubs'. Beneath, there was a painting of the Last Supper. An ornate brass candlestick with thirty branches was added and the screen choir seats, galleries and piers were painted. Over £250 was spent on a 'very fine large Organ ...adorned with very curious carved work'.[53]

Despite the beautification of the church, pressure on accommodation, and probably the desire for a socially more exclusive Anglican church nearer their homes, induced a group of merchants to set about providing another church. In 1714 the vicar, the mayor, three aldermen and Ralph Thoresby began to raise money. They quickly collected £1,000, but Mr Layton of Rawdon, who had promised to provide a similar sum, failed to fulfil his side of the bargain. Nearly six years elapsed before new impetus was given by the gift of £1,000 by Lady Elizabeth Hastings, a personal friend of Ralph Thoresby. Suitable land was purchased on Boar Lane and fund-raising activities resumed with vigour. On 27 August 1722 the Rev. Henry Robinson laid the foundation stone for Holy Trinity Church, and within five years it was open for worship. Most of the pews were sold or rented to private individuals, and this effectively excluded the lower orders.[54]

The principal churches for those outside the merchant élite remained the parish church, St John's and the Anglican chapels in the out-townships. Galleries were added at St Peter's and St John's to cater for the large number of worshippers. Numbers varied, however, and in 1743 only around four hundred attended monthly communion at the parish church. St Peter's remained the dominant force within the parish, and most weddings and funerals took place there. Weekly services were held at St John's and Holy Trinity, compared with three a day at the parish church.[55]

As we have seen, the appointment of the vicar of Leeds was of great concern to the leading Anglicans of the town. The merchant group dominated the process of selection of vicars and curates throughout the century. The vicar was usually a son or son-in-law of a local merchant. Arguments about the appointment were rare, but in 1746, when the Revd Joseph Cookson died, major problems arose. Twenty-five trustees should have gathered to elect his successor. Unfortunately, the untimely death of one of them meant that only twenty-

The Parish Church interior. Fine craftsmen were responsible for the redecoration of the interior in 1712-15 and the east end (shown here) was made particularly impressive.

Holy Trinity Church, Boar Lane, built 1721-7 (architect, William Etty).

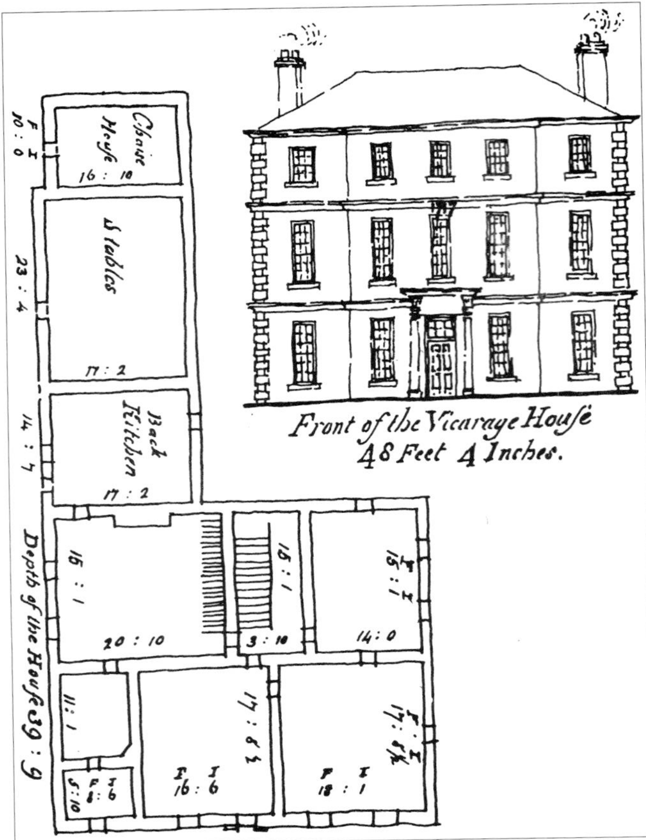

Leeds Vicarage in Vicar's Croft, Kirkgate, built in 1717. Redrawn from a terrier at the Borthwick Institute.

four were available. Samuel Kirshaw and James Scott (incumbent of Holy Trinity), both of whom were related to merchant families, were deemed suitable candidates for the post. Imagine the consternation when each received twelve votes! Nearly five months elapsed before the death of one of Kirshaw's supporters spurred Scott's friends into action. They hurriedly organised a meeting at which Scott was, not surprisingly, elected. The election was disputed and the Attorney General ruled that the parishioners and not the trustees should elect the vicar. Kirshaw and Edward Cookson, son of the deceased vicar, were the candidates; Scott felt that he had already won and was not prepared to entertain an election. Only males aged 16 and over could vote. There were confused reports as to who had won, but eventually it was accepted that Kirshaw was the victor.

Scott and his supporters appealed to the Court of Chancery, which ruled that the choice rightfully lay with the trustees, whose complement should be made up. An appeal to the House of Lords led to further delays, but eventually in March 1751, Kirshaw was appointed vicar.[56] The argument had raged for nearly five years, during which the Archbishop had licensed 'Mr. Fawcett, the Curate' to fulfil the duties of vicar. He was, throughout the dispute, a firm supporter of Kirshaw, and was soon to be rewarded for his loyalty. The opportunity presented itself when the curacy of Holbeck fell vacant in 1754. On the very day the old curate was buried, the vicar appointed his friend to the position. This incensed many of the people of Holbeck who had been led to believe that they would elect the next curate. When Fawcett first tried to take a service, the people would not let him near the church. He returned, a week later, with 18 constables but found himself opposed by 'a furious, frantic, lawless Rabble of Holbeckers, who assaulted him with Dirt, Stones, and Brickbats, and whatever Instrument of Violence that Fury could furnish'.

After the failure of a third attempt, the Constable of Holbeck was informed that 50 dragoons were being quartered in the village. On Wednesday 11 September, Fawcett at last succeeded in holding a service. Despite a party of Dragoons some 'evil disposed people' broke the windows of the chapel and threw a brickbat at Mr. Fawcett while he was at his reading-desk. After a few days of calm, some 'profane, Sacrilegious Villains broke into the Chapel, cut the Common Prayer Book in Pieces, and besmear'd the Seats with human Excrements'. Fawcett resigned and eventually returned to the parish church. The vicar of Leeds was to be plagued by several similar local controversies.[57]

Internal disputes, unsuitable clerics and a lack of leadership led to an apathetic approach by the Church to the new problems faced by the expanding town. Symptomatic, perhaps, was the fact that the vicar and curates held a monthly meeting at the Angel Inn. The Revd Henry Crooke, the conscientious curate of Hunslet, lamented 'all clergymen and yet not one word of spiritual things among us'.[58] It was not until the emergence of Evangelicalism, towards the latter part of the century, that the Anglican Church became more purposeful.

The initial fervour of the older kinds of Nonconformity appears to have dissipated as the century progressed. Many merchants who had initially subscribed to the chapels of Mill Hill and Call Lane, were lured back to Anglicanism. Ralph Thoresby, whose father had been a leading figure in the establishment of Mill Hill, was just such a convert. The Quaker Society remained insular.[59] It was not until the visits of John Nelson, George Whitfield and Charles and John Wesley that a new dynamism appeared within the religious life of the town. Initially viewed with curiosity, the Methodist preachers required both courage and stamina. John Nelson of Birstall (1707-1774) remembered that when he crossed Leeds Bridge two men had warned him that if he attempted to preach in the town he should not expect 'to come out again alive, for there is a company of men that swear they will kill you'.[60] Despite such threats, he did preach regularly in Leeds. In 1743 Charles Wesley noted that he 'met the infant society, about fifty in number'. One of its leading members was a barber called Shent and from his premises, near the corner of Briggate and what is today Duncan Street, Charles 'cried to thousands "Ho everyone that thirsteth, come ye, to the waters"!'[61]

Despite the fact that such impromptu gatherings were well attended, few joined the movement and by February 1746 John Wesley recorded in his journal:

> Sat 22 Feb 1746 to Leeds. I preached at five. As we went home a great mob followed, and threw whatever came to hand. I was struck several times, once or twice in the face, but not hurt at all. I walked on to the Recorder's, and told him the case. He promised to prevent the like for the time to come.[62]

Three years later, however, the situation had changed. He noted, with pride:

> At noon we spent an hour with several of our preachers, on exhortation and prayer. About one I preached to a crowded audience of high & low, rich & poor, but their number was abundantly enlarged at five; as was my strength both of soul & body. I cried aloud to them all, to look unto Jesus; and scarce knew when to leave off.[63]

Eventually, with the establishment of the 'Leeds

Mill Hill Chapel built 1672-4, but shown here refashioned in the modern eighteenth-century style.

Joseph Priestley (1733-1804). Minister of Mill Hill Chapel 1767-1773. He was a founder of the Leeds Library and published over 30 books and pamphlets while living in Leeds. He was an eminent scientist, most famous for the discovery of oxygen.

Circuit', the town regularly attracted talented authorised lay preachers such as John Easton, John Floyd, Christopher Hopper and Joseph Benson. A permanent meeting place at Ingram Hall was established.[64] In 1753 'travelling preacher Edwards' stood against Wesley's itinerary rules for preachers and his supporters formed an Independent congregation, eventually with premises in Casson Close, off Hunslet Lane. The 'White Chapel' opened in 1755 and Edwards remained here until his death in 1785.[65] Methodism drew its main support from tradesmen and the lower orders, though incurring opposition from all ranks of society. The Leeds Methodists were harrassed on their way to worship at Ingram Hall and a new venue was sought. Eventually the house of Matthew Chippendale, a basket maker, of Boggart Close was used. Persecution remained sporadic but this chapel continued to administer to the needs of the Leeds Methodists until 1801.[66]

Members of the Anglican Church became increasingly worried by the apparent popularity of the new movement. As early as 1743 the vicar had reported in the Visitation returns that 'we are disturbed with some Methodist preachers who appear almost every Sunday in the open streets'.[67] The Anglicans were not alone in expressing concern. Joseph Priestley, minister at Mill Hill from 1767 to 1773 felt it necessary to put pen to paper in order to persuade his congregation to remain faithful. He noted that:

> The Methodists being very numerous in Leeds and many of the lower sort of my own hearers listening to them, I wrote 'An Appeal to the Serious Professors of Christianity', 'An Illustration of Particular Texts'. and republished the 'Trial of Elwall', all in the cheapest manner possible. Those small tracts had a great effect in establishhing my hearers in liberal principles of religion, and in a short time had a far more extensive influence than I could have imagined.[68]

It was not until August 1778 that the Baptists had a permanent place of worship in Leeds.[69] Part of the first White Cloth Hall was utilised for the purpose, but

The Revd Mr Whitfield preaching in Leeds in 1749. George Whitfield (1714-70) was one of the most important figures in the evangelical revival. Whilst at Oxford he came under the influence of the Wesleys, but by 1741 he had parted company with them. He was a far better orator than John Wesley and is little remembered today simply because he did not found a denomination. He toured Britain and America, often preaching to huge crowds in the open air.

The Old Wesleyan Chapel, St. Peter's Street. According to the 1806 Guide to Leeds this 'exceedingly large and extensive building' was erected in 1771. The chapel was often referred to as `The Old Boggard House' because it was built on Boggart Close.

quickly proved inadequate and early in 1780 work began on the construction of the Stone Chapel.[70] The chosen pastor was Thomas Langdon, but he had not completed his studies in Bristol. This meant that a 'temporary' preacher was appointed; his name was the Revd William Price, and when Langdon returned to take up the appointment some of the congregation felt that William Price was the better candidate. As a result Price returned to the town and Ebenezer Chapel was built for him. This building was eventually purchased in the late 1790's by the newly formed Methodist New Connexion.[71] In 1786 Roman Catholics were allowed a place of worship in the town, and within seven years they had started building a chapel in Templar Street. Their influence remained small.[72]

The eighteenth century was a time of mixed fortune for the Anglicans; Methodism established itself in the town, and the variety of Dissent broadened.[73] Despite this, the increasing number of people who shunned religion of any sort must have been a worry to Christians of all denominations, and was to become the subject of major activity in the nineteenth century.

The Jacobite Rebellions

Unlike the seventeenth century, the period 1700-90 did not have a prolonged spell of civil turmoil like the Civil War to disturb peace and prosperity in Leeds. Nevertheless, the momentous challenges to the Crown

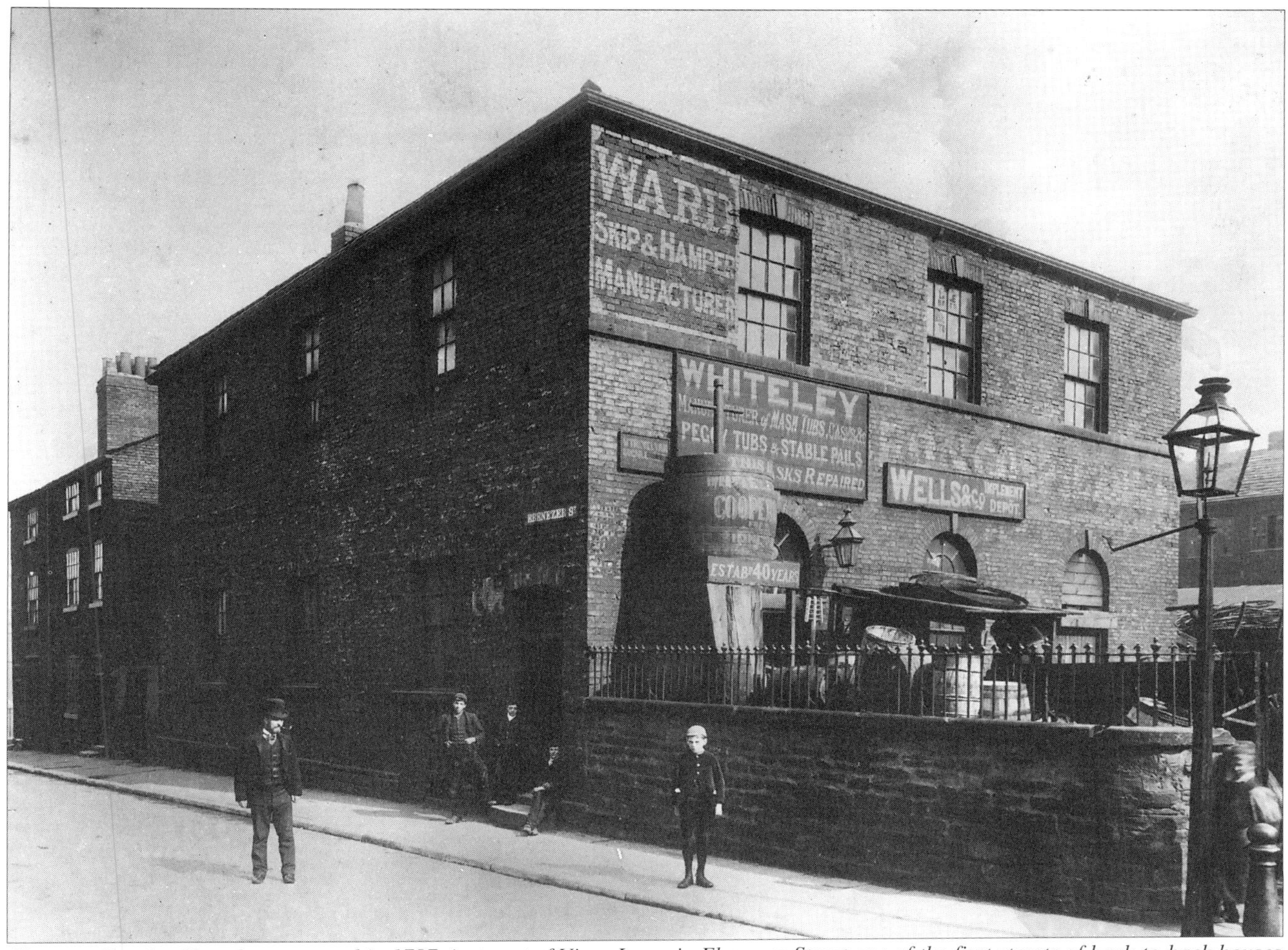

Ebenezer Baptist Chapel was opened in 1787, just east of Vicar Lane, in Ebenezer Street one of the first streets of back-to-back houses in Leeds.

posed by the Jacobite rebellions of 1715 and 1745, which attempted to regain the throne for the male line of the Stuarts, caused a great deal of anxiety in Leeds. The town was physically untouched by the rising of 1715, but the suspicions of central government fell on several of the town's most influential inhabitants as a result of the 'Leeds Riot'. It tells us much about the nervousness surrounding the accession of George I in 1714, and the acrimony between certain people in Leeds, that an almost laughable incident could end up with one of the town's most senior merchants, indeed only recently mayor, imprisoned in London.

In mid-1715 Whig government ministers were greatly worried about a potential rebellion by disaffected Tories supported by a French invasion. They were anxious to nip in the bud any signs of opposition in the provinces. The Tory corporation of Leeds was monitored with care, especially because the mayor, Solomon Pollard, was reported to have said that the taking of the oath of loyalty to George I at the Leeds sessions had been 'the bitterest pill' he had ever swallowed.[74] It was the events of one Friday night in June that caused the problem. In an account given to Lord Irwin it was said that the Leeds parish church bellringers, who normally practised on a Thursday night had – whether for devilment or from serious conviction we do not know – 'put off their ringing till the next day, which was the Pretender's birthday' and then had continued ringing for two or three hours longer than usual. Mr Ibbetson, Mr John Dodgson and Hugonot, lieutenant of the dragoons, seem to have chosen to interpret this as the start of a rising. The lieutenant put his men under arms and between 10 and 11 at night went through the streets beating a drum. Such was the commotion that a crowd of people gathered to see what all the fuss was about, though it quickly disbanded.[75] A report was sent to Secretary of State Stanhope in London that the people of Leeds had celebrated the Pretender's birthday with the 'Ringing of Bells, Bonfires, & all other marks of Publick Joy, that there was a great meeting of Magistrates clergy etc …who drank his Health, & that if the Soldiery had not awed the Mob the Issue wou'd have been of ye worst Consequence'.[76]

Solomon Pollard and Hugh Sleigh and a 'Mr Ormrod' were summoned to London to give an account of themselves. Alderman William Cookson wrote to Thoresby in alarm on 29 June asking him to take action on their behalf: 'Mr. Mayor, Mr. Sleigh & Mr. Ormrod have been sent for. I hope (as you have opportunity to see persons of distinction as much as any man) you'l take all occations to acquit your native & informed town from the villainous aspersions that are set up.'[77] Hugh Sleigh, a leading attorney in the town, whose house is shown on Cossins' Plan, under examination claimed that he had been out of town all day and returned around six o'clock. He admitted that he had heard the bells, but simply assumed that it was the ringers' weekly practice session. He denied knowing that it was the Pretender's birthday and claimed that it was not until the next morning that information regarding a bonfire had reached him. This transpired to be nothing more than some small pieces of wood and shavings set alight by mischievous children. Sleigh asserted that the allegations against him had been laid by Lieutenant Pausey, an officer in the town, who had an old score to settle with him. He was at pains to point out that he had only recently sworn allegiance to the House of Hanover at the town Sessions.[78]

It is not surprising that William Cookson was alarmed, for other leading figures were suspected of colluding with the Jacobites, and just over three months after his letter to Thoresby, he found himself in custody. William Milner thought it advisable to write to Lord Irwin to ask him to use his influence in London to help get the charges against his fellow corporation member quashed:

> My Lord
>
> Yor Lord-ship has without doubt heard that Aldr William Cookson of this Town had the misfortune about 10 days agoe to be sent for to London by a Messinger, and the only reason that I can learn is that he, being att the Bath upon account of his health, drew a bill from thence for £100 – upon his Bro John Cookson of London payble to some freind of his att sight, and in his letter of advice to his Bro. he desired him to pay itt immediately, for itt was upon a great Exigencie, and his letter being opend at the post office the word exigencie gave some occasion of suspition att this conjuncture, in so much that the letter or the coppy of itt was given to Lord Townsend, who sent his Warrant for Aldr Cookson to explaine the meaning of the word Exigencie, by which was only meant, that his freind had urgent occasion for the money, for his own private use and not otherwise, I have had a long and intimate acquaintance with Mr. Cookson and have known him to be very active upon all occasions in the Kings bussines and very serviceable to the publyck and doe beleive him in my consience to be a very honest worthy good man and well affected to King George, and as I have had ample experience of Your Lord-ships great goodness and readynes to serve your freinds, espesially those of this Corporation, I humblely request your Lordship to write a line to whom you shall thinke propper att London in Mr. Cookson's behalf, to procure him a speedy hearing and discharge, which will be ever ownd as an additional favour to our Corporation and recorded with the rest, and will particularly oblige.
>
> Yor Lordships most humble & Obedient Servt.
> William Milner.[79]

Cookson was soon released. By the middle of 1716 the Jacobite scare was over, but the episode should be a sharp reminder to us when we admire the bucolic charm of Francis Place's prospect of 1712, and the elegance depicted in Cossins' Plan of 1726, that in reality Leeds was a society possessing great tensions and uncertainties.

Any Jacobite sympathies which Leeds merchants possessed had probably disappeared by the middle of the century, but to their evident dismay the Jacobites had not. On 23 July 1745 the Old Pretender's son, Bonnie Prince Charlie, landed at Eriskay in Scotland. Most of the country's forces were stationed on the Continent and England was vulnerable to attack. Henry Ingram of Temple Newsam was horrified at the news. His new ceiling in the Long Gallery, by Thomas Perritt and William Rose of York, incorporated plasterwork heads of members of the king's family.[80] In September he received an assurance from the Duke of Newcastle that 'Marshal Wade will immediately march northward with an army of near 10,000 men'. Nevertheless he remained nervous, fearing that many would support the Scots. Addresses loyal to the king, however, began to flood in.[81]

The county worthies organised a fund and volunteers were quickly attracted to the defence of 'King George and the Illustrious House of Hanover'. In Leeds, Henry Ibbetson of Red Hall offered to raise a hundred men at his own expense to join the county companies. He was later to receive a baronetcy for his patriotism.[82] With Ibbetson, Richard Wilson, Thomas Pullyne and several other important figures, Ingram began to organise the defence of the district. Houses were searched, horses of Catholics seized and anonymous notes investigated.[83]

In October the English army, under General Wade, arrived in the area. Ingram was relieved to see the troops, despite the fact that some companies of the county troop were already quartered in the inns of the district. Wade's visit was brief, and he soon pressed on towards Newcastle. Within a few weeks his troops had been completely out-manoeuvred and the Scots, having rested around Edinburgh, crossed the Tweed. John Wesley brought this alarming news when he arrived in Leeds on 5 November, Bonfire Night. He wrote:

> In the evening I came to Leeds, and found the town full of bonfires, and people shouting, firing of guns, cursing & swearing, as the English manner of keeping holidays is. I immediately sent word to some of the magistrates, of what I had heard on the road. This ran through the town, as it were, in an instant, and I hope it was a token for good. The hurry in the streets was quashed at once; some of the bonfires indeed remained: but scarce anyone was to be seen about them, but a few children warming their hands.[84]

News from the North became increasingly gloomy and by 22 November the Scots had reached Kendal. On this day some of the most important men in the West Riding met in the town to form 'the Leeds Parliament'. They argued that 'the forces now raised for the Defence of this County cannot act with effect against the Rebel Army in separate bodys' and stressed that Leeds was the natural gathering place for the men. Their views were forwarded to the lord lieutenants of the Riding and the Archbishop of York.[85] People were beginning to panic, trade links with Lancashire were already disrupted and merchants were extremely concerned about the effect on trade. On Sunday 8 December a band of citizens assembled and proposed to arm themselves and march to deal with the Jacobites. They were swiftly dissuaded from doing so when it was pointed out that 'should they be rash enough to encounter the Stuart prince & his host, they would sustain enormous loss of life & the clamour would certainly come to Leeds to burn it down in retaliation'.[86] The danger passed, however, as the Highlanders, having reached Derby, began to retreat, avoiding the town. Nevertheless, General Wade brought his men to Leeds and set up an encampment on Woodhouse Moor.

Soon the threat of invasion was over and the fortunes of the Jacobite cause died forever at the Battle of Culloden. For the merchants of Leeds it was to be a return to business as usual. At the corporation's meeting on 22 May 1746 it was agreed and ordered that:

> A meeting of this Corporation be had on Monday next, at the [public] house of John Newsham in Leeds, at the expense of this Corporation, to drink

The house of Ralph Thoresby in Kirkgate Originally built by his grandfather c. 1610, it was enlarged to become one of the biggest houses in the town, having 5 hearths by 1672. It housed his famous museum. Shown here long after Thoresby's day, the house included the four-storey building and the buildings to the left. The Earl of Oxford visiting it in 1725 commented rather uncharitably: 'the poor man [Thoresby] was now so old, so decayed, infirm, and decrepid, and, indeed, in a manner so superannuated, that he was the only piece of antiquity in the collection that one could have been contented not to have seen'.

his Majesty's Health, & to express their Joy upon the late glorious Victory obtained by his Royall Highness the Duke of Cumberland over the Rebells.[87]

Leeds had come quite close to the action. Thereafter, concern about the vulnerability of the town and the lack of regular troops in the area led to forces being stationed locally. The quality of the men enlisted must have been very variable resulting in constant problems. Ensign Storr's entry in his orderly book for 11 May 1761 gives an enlightening glimpse into the life of these *brave* men!

Leeds: Parole Aygsborough

The Battallion to March to Morrow Morning (to Knaresb.) the General to Beat at Five O'clock the Troop at half an hour after and March off Immediately 1 Serjt 1 Corpll & 12 men for the Baggage Guard. For the Rear Guard Lieut Watson 1 serjt 1 Corpll 20 Men. The Baggage Waggon to keep in the Rear of the Regt in order to take up any Soldier who may fall Sick or happen any accident upon the March. Any Soldier who appears Drunk on the parade to Morrow Morning will be March'd prisoner Try'd by a Court Martial & severly punished. The Sejts are order'd to see the Mens Quarters are Clear'd and report those that are not paid off at Evening parade.[88]

Merchants at Leisure

The front of a merchant's house was a statement of the success of its occupier. Early in the eighteenth century, as the borders of Cossins' Plan show, stone and the increasingly popular brick set a new standard of safety and fashion. Architects were now employed such as William Etty of York and John Carr, who designed a fine house on Boar Lane for Jeremiah Dixon in 1750.[89] If the exterior of a mansion or town house was built to impress, the interiors could be equally extravagant. Richard Wilson, Robert Denison and John Atkinson all employed the distinguished French artist Jacques Parmentier (1658-1730) who had executed work for William III. In Robert Denison's house, he decorated the walls of the hall with paintings of Andromeda, Perseus, Bacchus and Ariadne and covered the ceiling with 'The Four Seasons'.[90] There was an increasing use of wall hangings and wallpapers instead of heavy panelling, and carpet became popular and more readily available.

Some idea of the contents of merchants' houses can be gleaned from their wills and inventories. William Cookson, whose magnificent mansion is clearly shown on Cossins' Plan, in 1743 left, among other things, a fine library and 'the five pictures in the great dining Room of his Grandfather, Grandmother, Father, Mother and Uncle done by Mr. Partmentier.'[91] By far the most detailed early inventory is for Croft Preston's house.[92]

Only after 1780 with the building of squares and terraces on the Park Estate was there any tendency to separate the dwelling house from the warehouse and dressing shop. Before 1780 a merchant had to be prepared to pay from £1000 to £5000 to obtain a decent house with good facilities for his business. Even without them prices were high. In 1796 Mrs. Arthington sold a pair of houses in Park Place for £3,000.[93] Compare this with the £50 that a typical worker's cottage cost. In the mid-eighteenth century it was reckoned that about two-

Robert Denison's House built c. 1715, Later known as Sheepshanks House, North Street. This fine merchant's house represents the new fashion for brick buildings with stone dressings, using classical detail.

thirds of the Leeds merchants had incomes of about £200 to £600 per annum, and the remaining third had incomes well over £600. When it is realised that even by 1790, £400 a year would permit a household with five servants and a princely table, we see just how well off these men were. A clothier would be doing very well if the income of his family exceeded £50 a year.

If the contents of the houses were becoming increasingly refined and sophisticated, so too were the gardens of the town planted with a wider variety of trees, shrubs and plants. Sometimes these proved tempting to the light fingered passer-by as a notice in the *Leeds Mercury* revealed:

> Tues. Aug 22 1738
> Whereas Ald. Cookson's garden, joining upon the River, was robb'd on Sunday Night the 20th Instant., and great Numbers of Peaches, Nectarines, and Pears taken away, supposed to be done by Persons coming from Halton Feast. If any one will give Information thereof, that one or more Persons may be convicted he shall receive a Guinea Reward, and if the Informer be a Party, shall over & above the Guinea have his Pardon.[95]

Both a luxury and a necessity for a merchant was an education for his sons. Certainly in the first half of the eighteenth century the most prestigious school in Leeds was the Grammar School. Though a charitable foundation and often referred to as the 'Free School', its

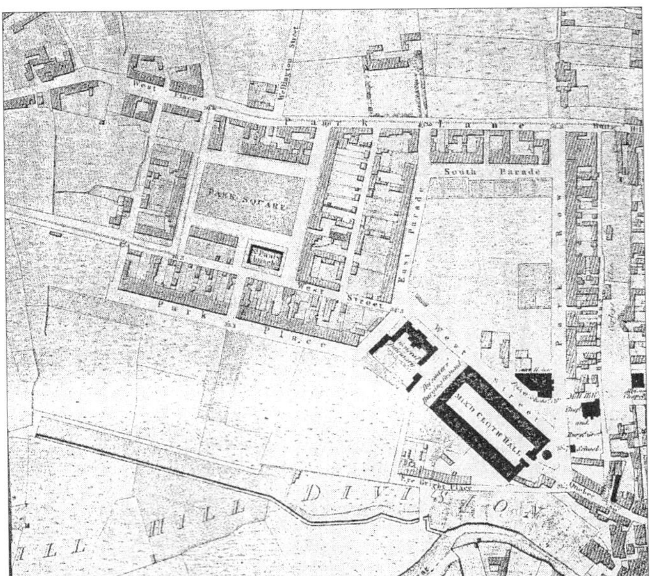

The Park Estate, the new haven of the Leeds élite, shown on Netlam and Francis Giles' Plan of 1815.

pupils were not paupers. Early in the century the sons of merchants and gentlemen, often living far from Leeds, attended. Thoresby commented in 1714 that the school 'now flourisheth under the learned and ingenious Thomas Dwyer who has at the same time committed to

Left: Park Square houses, part of the new high class estate built on land owned by the Wilson family.

Below: Denison Hall built for John Denison in 1786. The house and stables were insured for £2,600, the commercial and industrial premises behind for £500, and the contents for a staggering £3,000. Denison only occupied the house for a few years before moving to Ossington. It was then divided into two rented mansions.

his charge the sons of the Lord Archbishop and Lord Mayor of York with others of the Justices of Peace at large, besides those of the Corporation, etc.'.[96] With a far flung group of pupils, boarding was essential for many. To improve facilities, in 1780 a house for the headmaster with suitable accommodation for boarders was built. The school went into a temporary decline towards the end of the century with the number of pupils falling from 120 in 1760 to 40 in 1808. In part, this was due to the emphasis on a classical education and the absence of the commercial subjects essential to the training of a mercantile community.[97] Private schools such as Kemplay's Academy for Young Gentlemen (in St John's Place) and Joseph Tatham's Quaker School (at the Friends' Meeting House) rose to prominence, while other less illustrious schools sprang up, often providing merchants' sons with short courses in book-keeping, mathematics and languages.[98]

By far the most important part of a merchant's education, however, was his apprenticeship, which began when he was about fifteen years old and lasted on average for five years. The apprentice lived with his master's family, went daily into the counting house and finishing shops, and regularly visited the cloth markets of Leeds, Wakefield, and Halifax. If he was being trained with one of the large export firms he spent a year abroad visiting foreign correspondents and learning languages.[99] Social life could be quite hectic. A correspondent in the *Leeds Mercury* in 1742 noted 'that many of the merchants divide the week between their Pleasures & their Business & what they gather with one Hand scatter with the other'. Though Leeds had no formal 'season', 'taking the waters' and bathing took place at the many springs in the locality. Apart from the three on Quarry Hill there were others at Woodhouse, Weetwood, Potternewton and 'the Gipton Spa'.[101] Closeness to water even became a selling feature as an advertisement in the *Leeds Mercury* in 1728 indicated:

> To be sold, Two Messuages, a Croft containing half an Acre of Ground, three Gardens & a Gardenhouse, one of the Gardens joining to the River Air, with a convenience in that Garden for

Bathing in the River, without being exposed to publick View.

The town offered a variety of enjoyable evening activities for those who wished to mix in Leeds 'society'. From 1712 the facilities of the new cloth hall in Kirkgate were used for assemblies, and when the market functions of the hall were transferred to the second White Cloth Hall in Meadow Lane it became known as the 'Assembly Rooms'. Here 'treats' were held, sometimes with gaming and dancing.[103] Dancing lessons were readily available, adverts regularly appearing in the paper.[104] Leeds 'society' became more sophisticated as the century progressed. By 1777 the old Assembly Rooms in the first White Cloth Hall were replaced by the much larger and extremely elegant new Assembly Rooms above the third White Cloth Hall. In that year, Sir George Savile and Lady Effingham opened the New Assembly Rooms where over two hundred gentlemen and ladies were 'very agreeably surprised at the neatness and elegance of the different apartments'.[105] Admission for one gentleman and two ladies was half a guinea, far more than the ordinary worker could afford. Regular card and dancing assemblies were organised and the rooms were also used for special events. This delightful description of the ball given by the Yorkshire Archers on 26 October 1790 shows how magnificent such occasions could be:

> The company consisted of 200 ladies and gentlemen of the first rank and fashion in the county. The Ladies appeared in white, with green ornaments, and afforded the greatest display of taste and elegance. The ball was opened at nine o'clock by a minuet danced by the Earl Fitzwilliam and the Countess of Mexborough (patron & patroness of the society), the superior gracefuleness of which was deservedly admired by the whole company. Country dances commenced at ten, and the supper room was opened at 12 o'clock. It would be impossible to describe the decorations of the table. We will only observe that the propriety and brilliancy with which they were ornamented reflect the highest credit on Mr. Vickars, of York, under whose direction the whole was conducted. The effect of the festoons of coloured lamps was particularly pleasing. Dancing continued till three o'clock in the morning, soon after which the company began to retire, highly gratified with their evening's amusement.[106]

Travelling players performed in the theatre on Vicar Lane or in the Concert Room of the Rose and Crown Yard. The theatre in Vicar Lane was referred to in 1767 in a poem by 'Mr McGeorge':

> To Other Objects now must Change my Strain;
> Just for to take one peep in Vicar Lane;
> Up rear'd a Building lik'd by Great and Small;
> For Reasons there now term'd a Concert hall;
> Where tragic Stories form'd to Mend the Mind;
> and Propogate Good Moral in Mankind;
> To lash the Vices that Mislead the Age;
> This is the Purpos'd Business of the Stage.[107]

Drama in such a provincial town was sometimes of a dubious nature. In October 1778 the old Assembly Rooms was the location for a unique performance by the 'Famous Italian Patagonian Performers' who acted in 'a new Comedy call'd "Circe & Atlas, The Rival Magicians", exhibiting a beautiful Transformation of a Shepherdess into a Flower-Pot, then into a Fountain. Harlequin is tranformed into an Ass – Diana descends from Heaven, to the Assistance of Harlequin & Clora, in the Great Illuminated Temple'.[108]

86.The New Assembly Rooms opened in 1777 above the north end of the third White Cloth Hall at a cost of £2,500.

The interior of the New Assembly Rooms beautifully drawn by Peter Brears.

The Vicar Lane theatre seems to have closed when in 1771 Tate Wilkinson, the famous 'Wandering Patentee', opened his purpose-built theatre in Hunslet Lane.[109] The town clerk, Thomas Barstow, was a regular visitor, and when Lady Fleming attended to watch the play 'The School for Wives', the audience was described as 'elegant'. Occasionally players of note performed there; when Jane Shore (Mrs Siddons) opened in Leeds on 1 June 1789, the house was full and the tickets six pence more! With ticket prices at between 1s. and 3s. the theatre was relatively expensive entertainment which was aimed at the more affluent members of the community. When attendance ebbed the performances veered towards more populist attractions. The people of

The Theatre, Hunslet Lane. In 1806 it was described as 'a plain brick building, the dimensions of which are small and its form inconvenient, utterly unworthy of the populous and flourishing place to which it belongs'. Performances were held on three nights a week for about six weeks each summer. The usual prices were: boxes 3s., pit 2s. and gallery 1s.

Tate Wilkinson, the proprietor of the Leeds Theatre, whose theatre circuit comprised York, Pontefract, Wakefield, Hull and Doncaster. He described his business at Leeds as very 'slack and cool' until 1784, after which it greatly improved.

Leeds seem to have enjoyed farce, comic opera, and pantomime. More serious pieces were 'doctored' to give them more general appeal.[110]

Music, too, was very popular in Leeds. The Waits played at civic functions, and bell ringing and organ recitals became commonplace at the parish church. Performances of Handel, Vivaldi, Bach and Haydn are all mentioned in the newspapers, with a huge variety of instrumentalists taking part. The most popular piece appears to have been Handel's 'Messiah' which was performed every Friday from September 9th 1768 throughout the winter; a grand total of eighteen nights.[111]

The élite also frequented the better class inns, and the coffee house became a meeting place where they could discuss business, read the paper, catch up on local gossip or even enjoy a game of billiards. For those who cared to mix in more intellectual circles, there was the company of such men as Ralph Thoresby and, later, Joseph Priestley. From 1768 onwards, the Leeds Library provided the avid reader with an excellent selection of books.[112]

For those who preferred sporting pursuits there were quite a number of opportunities. The Leeds Races remained one of the most important events in the social calendar. The horses and jockeys weighed in at the Talbot in Leeds and then rode out to Chapeltown Moor to the starting point.[113] Gambling, dancing and cockfighting events were organised to coincide with the races. Cockfighting was extremely popular and there were several 'rings'.[114] In 1767 Revd Joseph Ismay, visiting his friend Revd Tidswell, was much impressed by the lifestyle of the Leeds merchant families:

> The Gentlemen and Ladies from Leeds frequently make an Excursion, either on Horseback or in their Chaises, to Chapel Town, in order to enjoy fresh Air upon this Moor in ye Mornings, that they may eat their Dinner with a keener appetite, and a better Relish at ye return.
>
> This village may, I think be called the Montpelier of Yorkshire. There is a very good Inn at ye Bowling Green, and excellent Accomodations. Three Clubs are held at this place, viz. one for bowling, another for Cricket, and a third which is called Lascelles Club.
>
> We walked about the Town and Fields in the Forenoon, and after Dinner we went to the Markee pitched upon ye Green for ye use of a set of young Gentlemen in and about Leeds, who meet there in ye summer Season every Thursday to play at Cricket. My Friend was one of the number and therefore I spent most of the afternoon in smoaking a Pipe in ye Tent and seeing the Gentlemen play.[115]

Athletics or 'foot races' also took place regularly on the moor.[116] The Leeds Hunt began around 1740 and by 1790 was meeting three times a week. This proved a nuisance to landowners north of the town, who on 9 December 1777 protested in the *Leeds Mercury* that their 'Gardens, Pleasure Grounds, Plantations, & Woods' had been 'very much tresspassed upon, and materially injured by Hare-Hounds & persons attending them'. 'It is hoped', they added, 'that all Gentlemen who follow the diversion of Hunting in this Neighbourhood will see the impropriety of such conduct'.[117]

Leeds in the eighteenth century was an exciting place. The bustling town could offer a wide variety of diversion to the merchant and the guests he entertained. If the merchant wanted more he travelled on the Continent or enjoyed the waters of Scarborough and Bath.[118]

Lives of the Lower Orders

The merchant families, of course, were the élite of Leeds, the majority of its population – usually referred to as 'the lower orders' – lived much more humble lives. It was an increase in the birth rate and the substantial in-migration of workers in search of employment which accounted for the rapid increase in the population of the bustling market town in the eighteenth century. Some of the inflow of people was seasonal workers, hoping to earn money during the slack periods of the farming calendar, but many hoped for a more permanent employment.[119] The incomes of the 'lower orders' were not high. Arthur Young, on his tour of the north of England in the late

Cottages built for the working classes around 1790 in the Turk's Head Yard, off Briggate. Today they house Whitelock's Public House.

1760s, noted that in the Leeds area few men earned more than 12s. a week, some as little as 5s.; women spinning earned a mere 2s.-3s. By the early 1790s the range of earnings for male workers was about 9s.-18s. a week.[120]

Itinerant workers might find accommodation in the inns and lodging houses, but most permanent inhabitants lived in small cottages often in the yards and folds running off the main streets. By 1774 nearly 60 per cent of the houses in Leeds were occupied by artisans and labourers paying rents of less than £3 per year. A survey of 1790 revealed that a small room between 12 and 18 feet square let for 4d. a week. A cottage for four or five people, with a living room and a sleeping chamber above, 14 feet by 14 feet would let for 6d. a week, whilst the artisan would possibly extend himself to pay 9d. a week for rooms of approximately 20 feet square. On average a worker's rent probably took about 5-8 per cent of his income. This was low by modern standards but accommodation was small and very basic. These brick cottages lacked a decent water supply and had primitive sanitary facilities.[121]

Wills and inventories for the lower orders occasionally survive and provide fascinating details about their possessions. William Browne of Nether Mills, who died in 1707, left goods worth a mere £4 12s. 0d.. Given his apparent poverty, his house held a surprising amount of furniture – four beds with bedding, a cupboard, four chests, four tables and chairs, some pewter, two desks, a barrel, a salting kit and a cooking range with pans, plus equipment for making oatcakes.[122] Robert Dixon of Quarry Hill, who died in 1724, must have been at the more prosperous end of the lower orders, as he left an estate worth £99 13s. 0d. Even so, his house was sparsely furnished. He had a range for cooking on, two tables, some chairs, a bed, a chest and a cupboard. Inside his home were the tools of his trade, a spinning wheel and a loom, plus yarn, a quantity of cloth and a large amount of wool.[123] At times clothiers bought wool cheaply, hoping to sell it at a higher price at a later date. In contrast, in 1707 Mary Sheffield, who was of 'the middling sort' (that is in the tier of society between the 'lower orders' and the merchant élite), left an estate valued at £282 13s. 4d. She ran a hat shop with stock worth over £120. Her home had curtains at the windows, she had pewter plates, leather chairs, brass candlesticks, a Delft plate, two silver spoons, a mirror and half a dozen pictures on the wall. Her lengthy inventory showed that she had a cooking range, brewing facilities and a salting kit.[124]

The diet of the lower orders depended on the season, the results of the harvest, availability and cost. Many of the inventories list the facilities for making oatcakes, and it is accepted that for many this formed a basic part of their diet. Some idea of a basic diet can be gleaned from the weekly menu of the Leeds Workhouse for October 1726:

	Breakfast	*Dinner*	*Supper*
Sun	Bread & Beer	Beef & Broth	Milk Porridg
Mon	Beef Broth	Rice Milk	Milk Porridg
Tues	Milk Porridg	Plumb Puddings	Bread & Beer
Wed	Bread &Cheese	Beef & Broth	Milk Porridg
Thur	Beef Broth	Potatos	Bread & Cheese
Fri	Bread & Beer	Rice Milk	Milk Porridg
Sat	Water-Porridg & Treacle	Pease Porridg	Bread & Beer

Bread, milk and porridge formed the main backbone of the diet, with meat being served only twice a week.[125] Clearly, the more affluent workers had a more lively diet. In the late 1760s Arthur Young noted the prices of cheese, mutton, beef and pork at 4d. per pound, bacon 7d., butter 8d., milk ½d. a pint in summer and 1-1½d. in winter, and oat bread at 1d. for 10-11 ounces.[126]

At times, however, the poor could not even afford enough corn for bread. The Revd Henry Crooke, curate of Hunslet, noted in his diary for May 3 1757:

> About 10, I was alarmed by an uncommon Bustle in the Town, and being apprehensive that the Mob was rising upon account of the Dearness of the Corn I went out among Em, and prevailed upon several to return to their respective Homes, and returned to my study.[107]

In good times the incomes of working-class families were sufficient to keep body and soul together, but when illness, old age or unemployment befell them during trade depressions, they had few reserves of money. For many, parish poor relief was all they had to fall back on. Most paupers were given small amounts of money from the poor rates and remained in their homes. The remainder, primarily the sick, the aged, or the young, were placed in the workhouse. The seventeenth-century workhouse in Lady Lane closed in 1705 but re-opened in 1726 with the object of 'the more orderly and easily regulating and relieving the poor of the township'.[128]

Once again the idea of

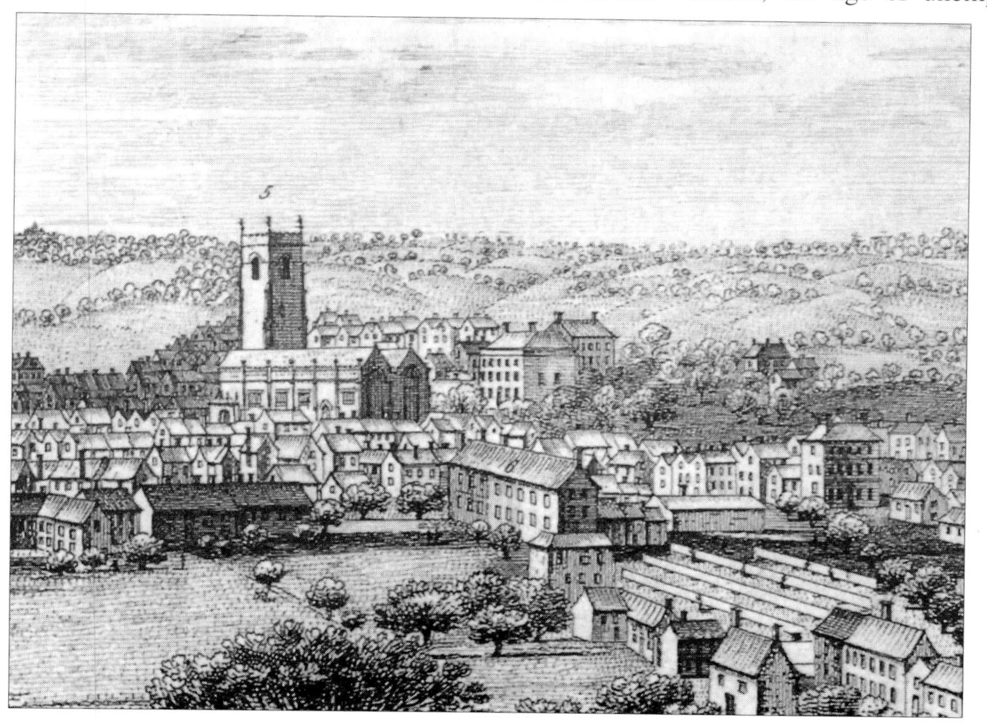

The Workhouse, Lady Lane, shown on Buck's panorama of 1745. The building has the number 6 on its roof. No. 5 is St. John's Church.

lowering the poor rate by making paupers earn their keep proved a failure. The workhouse closed in 1729 heavily in debt. Such establishments, however, were the only practical way of maintaining those genuinely unable to look after themselves and who had no relatives willing or able to support them. In 1738 the workhouse reopened. Efforts to make the inmates work for profit only resurfaced periodically when ratepayers clamoured loudly about the burden of the rates. Nevertheless, it remained a common practice to aid the blind in their begging by teaching them to play the violin.

Life in the workhouse cannot have been pleasant, but neither was it a brutal place of the kind Dickens depicted in the nineteenth century. There was no attempt to conceal the state of inmates from the public, for one of the duties of the master was to ensure that they were clean and well dressed, especially on Sundays when they attended the parish church. Indeed, shortly after the institution reopened in 1738, the workhouse committee was obliged to restrict public viewing of the building to the hours of two to four on Thursday afternoons. The emphasis on attempting to place only the 'deserving poor' in the workhouse suggests that the board believed it was offering something of merit. At the end of the century, Sir Frederick Eden (a national pioneer of social and economic investigation) found 'the dormitories and other departments kept with great neatness and the Poor well dressed, clean and orderly'. Likewise, if the diet sheet of the workhouse was adhered to, the food received by the inmates compared favourably with the fare offered by Leeds Infirmary.

Nevertheless, for the young and adults who refused to conform, the regime could be hard, humiliating and frightening. Those who stepped out of line might have a spell in the 'dungeon'. Young children rubbed shoulders with 'lunaticks'. People who told lies were 'to be set and stand upon a stool in the Dining-Room during Dinner-time with a Paper fixed on his or her Breast, whereupon shall be written, *Infamous Liar*, and also shall lose that meal'. All feared the periodic outbreaks of disease. Many of the sick entered the workhouse already suffering from smallpox or other contagious diseases. In January 1741 such an outbreak killed a quarter of the inmates. The workhouse was extended gradually during the century. In 1738 it accommodated 100 people; in January 1755 it housed 43 men, 60 women and 53 children. But even when trade and employment were in a healthy state, the building could only accommodate about one-fifth of the people being relieved from the poor rates. The workhouse board, therefore, was always anxious to apprentice out pauper children, and to return those poor who were not natives of Leeds to the parishes in which they were born.

An alternative to the workhouse much preferred by the elderly poor was the town's almshouses. Harrison's and Jenkinson's almshouses founded in the seventeenth century continued to offer places.[129] To these were added Potter's Almshouses in Wade Lane endowed by Mary Potter in 1736; two-roomed cottages for the widows of deceased tradesmen. Since the trustees and managers of these almshouses included the mayor and vicar of Leeds and members of the corporation, they can be regarded principally as semi-public institutions used to keep the middle classes, who had fallen on hard times, out of the workhouse. In addition to the almshouse, local charitable endowments also offered small grants of money or clothing for the poor.

For families outside the merchant group, education was a luxury which few received. Towards the end of the eighteenth century, growing numbers of the better off shopkeepers and manufacturers managed to obtain places for their sons at the Grammar School, but mainly they must have relied on the numerous teachers who established small private schools in the town. In 1781, for example, Mr Wray advertised the commencement of his school for twenty scholars in a room in Tinsdale's Yard (late the Angel), Briggate: Reading 7s. 6d. per Quarter; English Grammar 10s. 6d. per Quarter; and Latin, Greek, Writing and Arithmetic 10s. 6d. per Quarter.[130]

Concern about the lack of a school for pauper children produced the establishment of the Charity School (sometimes called the Blue Coat School) in 1705 in the old workhouse building. There were no aspirations to classical learning here. The school was financed by public subscription for the maintenance and education of 40 poor children in the principles of the Church of England, and instructing them in reading, writing and arithmetic, *to qualify them for trade*. Ralph Thoresby noted that there was a pew against 'the north wall of the Parish Church for the master and mistress of the Charity School with 40 poor boys and girls decently clad in blue'.[131]When the workhouse reopened in 1726 the school moved into the chapel belonging to Harrison's Almshouses. At the same time the practice of housing and feeding the scholars was discontinued and the charity was limited to clothing and educating the children. By mid-century the school taught the 3 R's to 70 boys and reading, writing and knitting to 50 girls, all in the age range 7-14 years. Boys were provided with a coat, waistcoat, breeches and cap of blue cloth, a pair of leather breeches, four shirts, two pairs of stockings and two pairs of shoes. Girls were given a gown and petticoat of blue cloth, a straw hat, a pair of leather stays ('which were to last the whole time they remained at school'), four shifts, two pairs of stockings and two pairs of shoes.[132] These were the lucky children. The bulk of working-class children received no formal education. In the 1780s almost two-thirds of the people marrying in Leeds were unable even to write their name in the parish register. By 1790 the situation was beginning to improve because of the founding of Sunday schools.[133]

Whilst the wealthier inhabitants of Leeds at times of ill health could consult and pay for the advice of the physicians and surgeons who had established themselves in growing numbers in the town during the eighteenth century, the labouring classes often relied on herbal remedies and 'quack' cures. Advertisements for the opium based 'Dr. Daffy's Elixir' regularly appeared in the papers, along with 'Dr. Bateman's Pectoral Drops' that claimed to be 'the safest & surest relief for the most acute Rheumatism ...Pains in the Breast, Limbs and Joints, Agues, slow and latent Fevers'. Against two diseases, in particular, such remedies could offer no hope. Smallpox was extremely frightening, and was no respecter of social status; even the Viscount Irwin of Temple Newsam died of the complaint in 1714.[135] As early as 1768 an advert appeared in the local paper, proudly announcing that 'Mr Faber proposes to inoculate for small pox at his own house at Shipscar; the situation is particularly healthy, airy and most commodious for this intention'.[136] Rabies was also a great problem. Infected animals were often publicly burnt, but in 1760 the situation had become so worrying that urgent action had to be taken. The magistrates informed everyone that their dogs had to be confined, and offered 12d. a head for every animal found in the streets. Over fifty were killed and their heads

The General Infirmary at Leeds. The building, designed by John Carr, was opened in 1771 on land behind the Coloured Cloth Hall. The cost of £4,599 was raised by the people of Leeds who either made donations, attended special concerts, or paid annual subscriptions. Initially, only 27 beds were available, but by 1792, as a result of extensions, the number had increased to 108.

William Hey (1736-1819). With a national reputation as a surgeon, Hey dominated Leeds Infirmary for 45 years until he resigned in 1812. He was mayor of Leeds in 1786/7 and 1801/2. In 1761 he married Alice Banks, 'an agreeable young lady with a handsome fortune' by whom he had 14 children. Note the Infirmary in the background.

brought to the constables. Despite such measures, the disease remained a threat throughout the century.[137]

Conscious of the lack of medical provision for the poorer inhabitants of Leeds, the merchants and doctors set up a project to build an infirmary. It was to be a charitable institution and those whose compassion was slow to reach their pockets were reminded of the benefits to be derived from the speedy return to work of sick servants and other employees. The scheme was initiated in May 1767 and subscriptions soon totalled over £1000. Temporary accommodation was found in Andrew Wilson's house off Kirkgate in the following October, but in 1771 'The General Infirmary at Leeds' opened its first purpose-built premises at the cost of £4,599. In 1788 John Howard, the prison reformer, described the hospital as 'one of the best ...in the Kingdom ...there is great attention to cleanliness' and added 'no bugs in the beds!' Leeds could be justly proud of this new institution.[138]

Limited financial means led to a restricted social life for the lower orders. Many frequented the numerous inns and alehouses where publicans organised cock-fights, and 'live' entertainment to lure people to their bars. On August 19th 1709 John Lucas, a local schoolmaster, went to the Queen's Arms Yard to see Thomas the Bold Welshman fight Thomas Pidgeon, Champion of the West. They fought with several sorts of weapons but, he noted, 'the performance proved to the Satisfaction of very few'. A week later, however, he returned to see 'one Fox, servant to Dr Green the Mountebank' perform 'wonderful exploits on the Slack rope'. This was more spectacular and was evidently well received.[139] These were relatively innocent pleasures; but the inns and alehouses were also places where many often gambled, sometimes too heavily. In 1757 the magistrates felt it necessary to try and dissuade publicans from allowing such activities on their premises. They issued the following declaration:

Publicans permitting Journeymen, Labourers, Servants, or Apprentices, to play at Cards, Dice, Draughts, Shuffleboards, Mississippi, or Billiard Tables, Skittles, Ninepins, or any other Implements of Gaming in their Houses, Alehouses, or Grounds, shall forfeit 40s. for the first offence, for every subsequent offence £10, to be levied by distress & sale; a quarter to the Informer, the rest to the Poor.[140]

The inns and alehouses continued to provide a place of recreation for the lower orders, but those higher up in the commmunity thought of them as a source of evil. In 1786 William Hey, the surgeon, formed an association to suppress 'immoral behaviour' especially 'the crime of drunkness and its never failing concomitants, sabbath breaking and lewdness'.[141] Nevertheless the church and chapels did have some influence. For many, bloodsports and gambling provided an exciting diversion. Bull baiting took place on Quarry Hill, sometimes with disastrous results. In September 1755 John Westerman, a labourer who lived in the Shambles, had his thigh gored by the bull. Within a few days the poor man expired.[142]

The races and the feasts and fairs seemed to be the highlights of the year. Mr. Isaac Tyson, a schoolmaster in Boar Lane, provided a wonderful description in verse of the Leeds Fair in November 1789:

Heighho! Drovers, bulldogs, oxen;
Butchers bragging, landlords coaxing,
Rapping, roaring, thumping, pricking
Poor dumb beasts – for only kicking!

Jockeys spurring, cursing, lying;
One-eyed horses – dirt a-flying-
Broken shins, and "– your blood, sir!"
"Clear the way! he's sound and good, sir!"

Pretty Pollies, Jacks, and Jennies,
Swindlers cheating simple ninnies;
Popping, thrusting, jerking, robbing –
Laughing this day, next day sobbing.

Waggons, cartmen; drums a-rattling,
Prudes in limbo, coquettes prattling;
Raree shows of short and long men,
Bears and wolves and weak and strong men.

Doxies dizzy, drunkards reeling,
Some quite down, and others keeling;
Town bloods dem-ming, blustering, puffing,
Homespun Johnnies rudely cuffing.

Pockets empty, bills unpaid, and
Rogues at dead of night afraid, and
Many a bargain – if you strike it –
This is Leeds Fair, how d'ye like it?[143]

Apart from the usual family celebrations, people appear to have used the news of foreign victories, the King's birthday and declarations of peace as an excuse for wild festivity. The Revd Henry Crooke, curate of Hunslet, wrote:

September 10th 1759:
I was disturbed in going two or three times to the Chapel to put a stop (if I could) to the strange Method some few of my People had of rejoicing for the small Victory lately gained over the French. They kept ringing the Bell and brought Ale to drink in the Chapel. I would have locked up the Doors had there not been a Person setting up a Monument in the Chapel.[144]

For many, this kind of event must have been a welcome relief from the normal daily worries of health, housing, employment and diet.

In many ways the period 1700-1790 represented a golden age for Leeds as a cloth-marketing town. Its merchants were at the height of their power and influence; the clothiers working on the domestic system were independent, free spirits with plenty of work and comparative affluence, if compared, for example, to agricultural workers. The town still had the feel of an extremely prosperous market town. The days of gross pollution of the river and the atmosphere, and the unpleasant conditions of the factories were yet to come. With the onset of the Industrial Revolution, this character was soon to be lost forever. A new style of life for both the working man and the merchant was about to dawn.

References

1. Daniel Defoe, *A Tour Through the Whole Island of Great Britain* (1724-6) (Penguin edition, ed. P.Rogers, 1971), pp. 500-05.
2. For a detailed analysis of these views and Cossins' Plan, and the background to their drawing, see: M.W.Beresford, 'East End, West End: The Face of Leeds During Urbanisation, 1684-1842', *Thoresby Soc.*, LX and LXI (1988), (hereafter *East End, West End*), pp. 22-61.
3. Traditionally the date of Cossins' Plan is given as 1725. However, its key refers to the 'New Prison' in Kirkgate. The borough quarter sessions minutes record a proposal to build a new prison in March 1726 (LDA, LC/QS (1725-36), fo. 16, March 1726), the drawing of the Plan therefore is likely to have taken place later in 1726. See also, Beresford, 'East End, West End', p. 38.
4. *Ducatus*, p. 76.
5. F.Beckwith, 'The Population of Leeds during the Industrial Revolution', *Thoresby Soc.*, XLI (1945).
6. See two chapters in D.Fraser, ed., *History of Modern Leeds* (Manchester, 1980), (hereafter, *Modern Leeds*): for population figures see: C.J.Morgan, 'Demographic Change, 1771-1911'; and for housing stock and building figures see M.W.Beresford, 'The Face of Leeds, 1780-1914'.
7. W.G.Rimmer, 'The Industrial Profile of Leeds, 1740-1840', *Thoresby Soc.*, L (1967).
8. *Ducatus*, p. 8.
9. Rimmer, 'Industrial Profile'.
10. *Ibid.*
11. R.Butler, *The History of Kirkstall Forge*, (Leeds, 1945).
12. H.Pemberton, 'Two Hundred Years of Banking in Leeds', *Thoresby Soc.*, XLVI (1963), pp. 54-86.
13. For excellent accounts of the development of the West Riding woollen and worsted industries over this period see: R.G.Wilson, *Gentlemen Merchants: The Merchant Community in Leeds, 1700-1830* (Manchester, 1971), (hereafter, *Gentlemen Merchants*), esp. chs 1, 3, 5; R.G.Wilson, 'The Supremacy of the Yorkshire Cloth Industry in the Eighteenth Century' in N.B.Harte and K.G.Pontings, eds., *Textile History and Economic History* (Manchester, 1973); H.Heaton, *The Yorkshire Woollen and Worsted Industries* (2nd edn, Oxford, 1965), (hereafter, *Woollen Industries*) chs. 8-12.
14. For details on output and Leeds' share of the market in the eighteenth century see: Wilson, *Gentlemen Merchants*, pp. 6-7, 47-52; Wilson, 'Supremacy of Yorkshire cloth', esp. pp. 225-35.
15. Defoe, *op. cit.*, pp. 501-2.
16. Wilson, *Gentlemen Merchants*, ch. 4.
17. The details about the White Cloth Halls given in this chapter are based on: *Ducatus*, p. 248; *Woollen Industries*, ch. 11; H.Heaton, 'The Leeds White Cloth Hall', *Thoresby Soc.*, XXII (1931), pp. 131-71; University of Leeds, Brotherton Library, Leeds White Cloth Hall Papers; LDA, FW/211, Leeds White Cloth Hall.
18. The details given about the Mixed or Coloured Cloth Hall given in this chapter are based on: Thoresby Society Library, Mss. Box IV, 29; P.Barfoot and J.Wilkes, *The Universal British Directory* (1790), p. 534; J.H.Leach, *A Walk Through Leeds or Stranger's Guide* (Leeds, 1806), pp. 10-1; E.Parsons, *History of Leeds* (1834), (hereafter, *Parsons' History*), II, p. 209; Leeds Mixed Cloth Hall subscription list.
19. *Leeds Intelligencer* 13 Jan. 1794, 16 Dec. 1811; E.Baines, *Directory, General and Commercial of the Town and Borough of Leeds for 1817*, p. 29.
20. Wilson, *Gentlemen Merchants*, pp. 17-9, 82.
21. *Ibid.*, pp. 76-80.
22. *Ibid.*, pp. 70-4.
23. *Ibid.*, pp. 64-75.
24. *Ibid.*, pp. 55-7, 74-5.
25. *Ibid.*, pp. 65-9.
26. *Ibid.*, ch. 3.
27. Wilson, 'Supremacy of Yorkshire Cloth Industry', pp. 244-6.
28. G.L.Turnbull, 'Provincial Road Carrying in England in the Eighteenth Century', *Journal of Transport History*, IV (1977-8).
29. *Leeds Mercury* 29 April 1729.
30. A.Young, *Six Months Tour Through the North of England* (1770), I, p. 136.
31. R.W.Unwin, 'Leeds Becomes a Transport Centre' in D.Fraser, ed., *History of Modern Leeds*, (Manchester, 1980), pp. 120-6; R.G.Wilson, 'Transport Dues as Indices of Economic Growth, 1775-1820', *Economic History Review*, XIX (1966).
32. *Parsons' History*, I, pp. 128-9.
33. H.C.Versey, 'The Postal History of Leeds', *Thoresby Soc.*, L (1968); T.Bradley, *Old Coaching Days in Yorkshire* (1889).
34. *Leeds Intelligencer* 17 Aug. 1756.
35. *Ibid.*, 2, 16 Sept. 1760.
36. *Ibid.*, 9 Sept. 1760.
37. *Ibid.*, 14 Jan. 1793.
38. For the history of the Aire and Calder Navigation, see: R.W.Unwin, 'The Aire and Calder Navigation: The Beginning of the Navigation' and 'The Navigation in the Pre-canal Age' *Bradford Antiquary* XLII (1964) and XLIII (1967); C.Hadfield, *The Canals of Yorkshire and North East England* (1972), I, ch. 1, 6, 7; B.F.Duckham, *The Yorkshire Ouse* (1967), ch. 5; G.Ramsden, 'Two Notes on the History of the Aire and Calder Navigation', *Thoresby Soc.*, XLI (1953); Wilson, 'Transport Dues'.
39. For the history of the Leeds and Liverpool Canal, see: C.Hadfield and G.Biddle, *The Canals of North West England* (2 vols., 1970), I, pp. 60-82, 149-81 and II, pp. 399-416; M.Clarke, *The Leeds and Liverpool Canal: A History and Guide* (1990).
40. J.Priestley, *Historical Account of the Navigable Rivers, Canals, and Railways of Great Britain* (1831), pp. 385-97.
41. W.G.Rimmer, 'Middleton Colliery, near Leeds, 1770-1830', *Yorkshire Bulletin of Economic and Social Research*, VII, No. 1 (1955), 41-57; Middleton Railway Trust, *A History of Middleton Colliery Railway, Leeds* (5th edn, 1973). 42. Versey, *op. cit.*.
43. For the history of the *Leeds Intelligencer* see: F.Beckwith, 'An Account of the Leeds Intelligencer, 1754-1866', *Thoresby Soc.*, XL (1953), and M.A.Gibb and F.Beckwith, *The Yorkshire Post: Two Centuries (1954). For the* Leeds Mercury see books about two of its editors: Edward Baines, jnr., *The Life of Edward Baines* (1851), ch. 3 onwards; S.J.Reid, *Memoirs of Sir Wemyss Reid, 1842-1885* (1905).
44. For a description of the composition and activities of the corporation see: R.G.Wilson, 'The Corporation of Leeds in the Eighteenth Century', *Thoresby Soc.*, LIV (1979), pp. 262-71. Its decisions are recorded in its Court Books, 1662-1835, LDA LC/M1-3. Regarding the rebuilding of the Moot Hall see these records and T.F.Friedman, 'A Noble and Magnificent Statue, *Leeds Arts Calendar*, No. 72 (1973).
45. The actvities of the corporation as magistrates are recorded in Leeds Borough Quarter Sessions Order and Indictment Books, 1662-1835, LDA LC/QS.
46. *Leeds Intelligencer* 9 Jan. 1770.
47. Leeds Parish Church Vestry Minute Books, 1716-1844.
48. 28 Geo. II, c. 41 (1755): An Act for Enlightening the Streets and Lanes, and Regulating the Pavements in the Town of Leeds.
49. For information about the significance and locations of the town bars see: Beresford, 'East End, West End', pp. 56-7; G.D.Lumb, York or East Bar Leeds', *Thoresby Soc.*, XXVI (1924).
50. 30 Geo. III, c. 68 (1790): An Act for Better Supplying the Town and Neighbourhood of Leeds with Water and for More Effectually Lighting and Cleansing the Streets. Unfortunately, the minutes of commissioners under the Leeds Improvements Acts before 1842 have not survived.
51. For a survey of the development of places of worship in Leeds in the eighteenthc century, see: K.Grady, 'The Georgian Public Buildings of Leeds and the West Riding', *Thoresby Soc.*, LXII (1989), esp. pp. 160-70.
52. *Ducatus*, p. 39.
53. T.F.Friedman, 'Jacques Parmentier in Leeds: A Newly Discovered Drawing', *Leeds Arts Calendar*, No. 94 (1984).
54. G.C.F.Forster, 'Holy Trinity Church in the History of Leeds, 1727-1977', *Thoresby Soc.*, LIV (1979); W.J.Connor, 'The Architect of Holy Trinity Church, Leeds', *Thoresby Soc.*, LIV (1979).
55. B.Greaves, 'Methodism 1740-1851' (unpublished Ph.D. thesis, University of Liverpool, 1968), p. 74.
56. LCR, L922.2 K639: A sketch of the late Samuel Kirshaw (1788); LDA, TN/LA/6: Papers relating to the Kirshaw-Scott dispute; R.G.Wood, 'Leeds Church Patronage in the Eighteenth Century', *Thoresby Soc.*, XLI (1954).
57. R.G.Wood, 'Leeds Church Patronage in the Eighteenth Century: A Further Note', *Thoresby Soc.*, L (1968).
58. LDA: Diary of the Revd Crooke.
59. See W.Allott, 'Leeds Quaker Meeting', *Thoresby Soc.*, L (1966).
60. LCR, Mss: J.Wray, 'A Compilation of facts illustrative of Methodism in Leeds, 1735-1833'; *Parsons' History*, p. 43.
61. B.Greaves, *op. cit.*, pp. 75-6; Parsons, *op. cit.*, II, pp.43-4.
62. N.Curnock, ed., *The Journal of the Revd John Wesley*, 8 vols (1909-16). For additional information relating to Methodism in Leeds, see: Leeds Local History Library: Extracts relating to Yorkshire from John Wesley's Journal transcribed by A.Mattison; J.Wray, A Compilation of facts illustrative of Methodism in Leeds, 1735-1835.
63. *Ibid.*
64. *Parsons' History*, II, pp. 47, 68-72, J.Ryley, *Leeds Guide* (1806), p. 40.
65. *Leeds 1817 D.*, p. 26; J.G.Miall, *Congregationalism in Yorkshire* (1868), pp. 304-6.
66. *Parsons' History*, II, p. 47; Ryley, *op. cit.*, p. 38; LCR, Mss: J.Wray, II, pp. 123, 247.
67. Greaves, *op. cit.*, p. 76.
68. J.Priestley, *Memoirs of Priestley to the year 1795* (1904), p. 39.
69. *Leeds Intelligencer*, 4 Aug. 1778.
70. *Parsons' History*, II, p. 38; J.W.Ashworth, *The Jubilee of South Parade Baptist Chapel (1877); Baines,* 1822 D., p. 26.
71. F.Beckwith, 'A Forgotten Eighteenth Century Baptist Chapel in Leeds', *Baptist Quarterly*, IX (1939); D.C.Dews, 'Two Eighteenth Century Baptist Chapels', in *Lantern Slide Leeds* (Thoresby Society Occasional Publication, 1984); D.C.Dews, 'Methodism in Leeds, 1791-1861', (unpublished M.Phil. thesis, University of Bradford, 1984), pp. 110-5.
72. J.Douglas, 'Catholic Churches in Leeds, 1783-1900', *Victorian Society: West Yorkshire Journal* (1983-4).
73. *Parsons' History*, II, pp. 1-80 provides a valuable and detailed contemporary account of the growth of Nonconformity in Leeds and its region.
74. C.Perrie, *The Jacobite Movement* (2nd edn, 1948), I, p. 157. For the background to the rebellion, see: J.Baynes, *The Jacobite Rising of 1715* (1970); B.Lenman, *The Jacobite Risings in Britain, 1689-1746* (1980).
75. Leeds Central Reference Library: LQP 942.75 LI, Letter to Revd Henry Plaxton from 'H.L.' dated 13 July 1715.
76. *Ibid.*.
77. W.T.Lancaster, ed., 'Letters to Ralph Thoresby', *Thoresby Soc.*, XXI, (1912), pp. 234-5.
78. LDA, TN/PO/3C/5: Lord Lieutenant's correspondence.
79. LDA, TN/PO/3C/7.
80. *Leeds Art Calendar*, No. 74 (1974).
81. For the local background to the '45, see: C.Collyer, 'The Leeds District and the Rebellion of 1745', *University of Leeds Review*, III, No. 2 (1952).
82. R.G.Wilson, 'Merchants and Land: The Ibbetsons of Leeds and Denton, 1650-1850', *Northern History*, Vol 24 (1988), pp. 88-92.
83. C.Collyer, 'Yorkshire and the '45', *Yorkshire Archaeological Journal*, XXXVIII (1952), pp. 78-9.
84. N.Curnock, *op. cit.*
85. LDA, TN/PO/3C/101.
86. F.J.McLynn, *The Jacobite Army in England: The Final Campaign, 1745* (Edinburgh, 1983), p. 147.
87. J.Wardell, *The Municipal History of the Borough of Leeds in the County of York* (Leeds, 1846), p. 47.
88. Yorkshire Archaeological Society Archives: Mss. 723, Ensign Storr's Orderly Book.
89. For Etty, see: Connor, *op. cit.*, p. 293-5. For Carr, see: D.Linstrum, *West Yorkshire, Architects and Architecture* (1978), pp. 373; Beresford, 'East End, West End', pp. 125, 274.
90. Friedman, *op. cit.* (Jacques Parmentier).
91. Wilson, *Gentlemen Merchants*, p. 213.
92. Borthwick Institute, York: Inventory of Croft Preston.
93. Wilson, *Gentlemen Merchants*, pp. 195-9.
94. *Ibid.*, pp. 85-7.
95. *Leeds Mercury*, 22 Aug. 1738.
96. *Ducatus*, pp. 83-4.
97. A.C.Price, *A History of Leeds Grammar School from its Foundation to the end of 1918* (Leeds, 1919), chs. 5 and 6.
98. J.E.Mortimer, 'Joseph Tatham's School, Leeds', *Thoresby Soc.*, 2nd ser., I (1991). For Kemplay's see: J.Sprittles, 'Links with Bygone Leeds', *Thoresby Soc.*, LII (1969), p. 48; *Leeds Intelligencer*, 14 Jan. 1805, 15 Jan. 1810.
99. Wilson, *Gentlemen Merchants*, pp. 23-5, 63-4, 209-10.
100. R.G.Wilson, 'Records for a Study of the Leeds Woollen Merchants, 1700-1830', *Archives*, VIII, No. 37 (1967), p. 15.
101. K.J.Bonser, 'Spas, Wells and Springs of Leeds', *Thoresby Soc.*, LIV (1974), pp. 29-50.

102. *Leeds Mercury*, 12 Mar. 1728
103. *Ducatus*, p. 38.
104. *Leeds Mercury*, 22 Jan. 1722.
105. *Leeds Intelligencer*, 17 June 1777. For additional details see: Brotherton Library, White Cloth Hall Papers, D7A, 9, 11; *Leeds 1817 D.*, p. 38.
106. *Leeds Intelligencer*, 26 Oct. 1790.
107. LCR, 'Leeds: a Poem by Mr. McGeorge' *c.*1760.
108. *Leeds Mercury*, 13 Oct. 1778.
109. Wilkinson, memoirs including many references to his experiences in Leeds, were published as: T.Wilkinson, *The Wandering Patentee: or A History of the Yorkshire Theatres from 1770 to the present time* (1795).
110. J.Copley, 'The Theatre in Hunslet Lane', *Thoresby Soc.*, LIV (1974).
111. E.Hargrave, 'Musical Leeds in the Eighteenth Century', *Thoresby Soc.*, XXVIII (1928).
112. F.Beckwith, 'The Beginnings of the Leeds Library', *Thoresby Soc.*, XXXVII (1939), pp. 145-161.
113. Hunter, ed., *Diary of Ralph Thoresby*, 17 July 1682; *Leeds Mercury*, 29 April 1729.
114. *Leeds Intelligencer*, 23 May 1758.
115. Revd J.Ismay, 'A Visit to Chapel Allerton and Harwood in 1767', transcribed in *Thoresby Soc.*, XXXVII (1945). For cricket see also: *Leeds Intelligencer*, 27 Aug. 1765.
116. D.H.Atkinson, *Ralph Thoresby the Topographer: His Town and Times* (Leeds, 1887), I, pp. 201-3.
117. *Leeds Mercury*, 15 April 1740, 9 Dec. 1777; *Leeds Intelligencer*, 23 May 1769.
118. *Leeds Mercury*, 10 Jan. 1737; *Leeds Intelligencer*, 12 Sept. 1769.
119. C.J.Morgan, *op. cit.*, pp. 48-51.
120. A.Young, *A Six Month Tour Through the North of England* (1770-1).
121. W.G.Rimmer, 'Workingmen's Cottages in Leeds, 1770-1840', *Thoresby Soc.*, XLVI (1960). Our knowledge of housing for the working classes in Leeds has been extended in minute detail by Professor Maurice Beresford, culminating in his exhaustive study of the central area in 'East End, West End'.
122. Borwick Institute, York
123. *Ibid.*
124. *Ibid.*
125. LDA, LO/M1-6: The Minutes and Order Books of the Workhouse Committee for Leeds, 1726-1826. For later diet sheets see: LO/M5 11 April 1764.
126. Young, *op. cit.*
127. LDA, Diary of Revd Henry Crooke.
128. The following account of the workhouse is based on: P.Anderson, 'The Leeds Workhouse under the Old Poor Law, 1726-1834', *Thoresby Soc.*, LVI (1980).
129. The following summary of the development of the almshouses in Leeds is based on survey appearing in the printed papers of the House of Commons, which was reprinted with the result of second major investigation in 1898: *Report on the Endowed Charities of the City of Leeds*, Parliamentary Papers, 1898, LXVI (hereafter *Endowed Charities Report, 1898*), pp. 6-8, 11-12.
130. *Leeds Intelligencer*, 9 Jan. 1781.
131. *Ducatus*, pp. 40, 107, 247.
132. J.H.Leach, printer, *A Walk Through Leeds, or, Stranger's Guide* (Leeds, 1806), pp. 32-3; 1826 Report on Leeds Charities, in *Endowed Charities Report, 1898*), pp. 9-10.
133. W.B.Stephens, 'Elementary Education and Literacy', in *Modern Leeds*.
134. *Leeds Intelligencer* 29 April 1760.
135. Leeds City Council Libraries and Arts Committee, *Temple Newsam House* (Leeds, 1951), p. 30.
136. *Leeds Intelligencer* 5 Jan., 9 Feb. 1768.
137. *Ibid.*, 16 Sept. 1760.
138. S.T.Anning, *The General Infirmary at Leeds* (1963); and, *The History of Medicine in Leeds* (Leeds, 1974).
139. LCR, J.Lucas, *The Diary of James Lucas – Master of the Charity School.*
140. Leeds Intelligencer, 1757.
141. S.T.Anning, *The History of Medicine in Leeds* (Leeds, 1980), p. 163; S.T.Anning, 'William Hey F.R.S.: The Father of Leeds Surgery', *Proceedings of the Leeds Philosophical and Literary Society*, XVII (1978-81), pp. 101-111.
142. *Leeds Intelligencer* 9 Sept. 1755.
143. Thoresby Society Library: R.V.Taylor's books of newspaper cuttings, No. 16.
144. LDA, Diary of the Revd Henry Crooke.

CHAPTER FOUR

The Industrial Revolution

The Age of Enterprise

I reached the great manufacturing town of Leeds just in the twilight. A transparent cloud of smoke was diffused over the whole space which it occupied, on and between several hills; a hundred red fires shot upwards into the sky, and as many towering chimneys poured forth columns of black smoke. The huge manufactories, five storeys high, in which every window was illuminated, had a grand and striking effect. Here the toiling artisan labours far into the night, and, that some romantic features might not be wanting in the whirl of business and illumination of industry, two ancient gothic churches reared their heads above the mass of houses and the moon poured her silver light upon their towers, and seemed to damp the hard glare of the busy crowd below, with serene majesty.

Herman von Puckler, Muskau Prince, *Tour in Germany, Holland and England 1826, 1827 and 1828* (1832).[1]

Between 1790 and 1840 the character and landscape of Leeds was transformed by the arrival of the factory age. It was one of the first towns in the world to experience an Industrial Revolution. It was an age both exciting and traumatic. Vast fortunes were made, and yet many livelihoods were ruined. While in one sense the streets of Leeds seemed almost paved with gold, the rustic charm of the market town was destroyed by the factories whose chimneys belched forth their noxious vapours. Leeds was never to be the same again.

The Transformation of the Woollen Industry

The first great entrepreneur of this mould-breaking period, a hero to some and a villain to others, was Benjamin Gott.[2] He had served his apprenticeship as a 'gentleman merchant' with Wormald, Fountaine and Gott, one of the five largest woollen cloth merchant firms in Leeds. By fortuitous circumstances in 1790, at the age of 27, he gained control of the firm. Being full of drive and energy, he was frustrated by his frequent inability to buy all the traditional Yorkshire broad and narrow cloths he required at the cloth halls. Equally, he was eager to obtain a local supply of the highly lucrative superfine cloth (usually made in the West Country), which was now much in demand, especially in the United States. To meet both requirements, in contravention of all that was sacred to his fellow gentlemen merchants, he launched out boldly upon the manufacture of woollen cloth. Over the next decade he built a massive mill complex on a 16 acre site at Bean Ing on the western edge of Leeds, and within another ten years he extended his operations to Armley Mills and Burley Mills higher up the Aire Valley, where water power was readily available. By 1797 he employed 1200 workers, and from 1800 to 1820 he was reckoned to be one of the ten or twelve largest employers in England.

Despite setting up his mill, the merchanting of cloth remained Gott's principal object. He continued to patronise the traditional domestic clothiers extensively, three-quarters of the cloth he handled being bought through the Leeds and Huddersfield cloth halls and by private purchase direct from clothiers. Park Mills (as the Bean Ing became known) enabled him to finish these very large quantities of cloth to a very high standard for resale, and to manufacture his own supply of superfines. By 1813 he had 133 looms and 253 workers engaged in spinning and weaving. The revolution he brought was primarily organisational rather than technological. His workers still used the traditional techniques of spinning and weaving, but these former domestic workers and their equipment were for the first time brought into a factory to work under close supervision. Indeed, he did not introduce water or steam-powered production for spinning and weaving for many years; their use was

Western Panoramic View of Leeds in 1831 by Joseph Rhodes. Gone is the genteel market town of 'Gentlemen Merchants', lost in a sea of huge mills, factories, foundries and dyeworks, where chimneys dominate the skyline and proclaim the triumph of the new industrialists and the Age of Steam.

restricted to the preparation of the wool and the finishing processes.

The quality of Gott's cloth was beyond reproach. When the Prince Regent visited Leeds in 1805 he declared that he would wear with pride the beautiful specimen of cloth manufactured at Park Mills, which he had accepted from the firm. In addition to superfines, Gott made blankets at Park Mills. With these, and cloth that he bought in, he was able to create a volume of sales way beyond the realms to which a traditional cloth merchant could have aspired. So vast was his capacity that he was able to build his success on supplying whole armies with uniforms and blankets, as well as capitalising on the British market and trade with North and South America, the Continent, and even the Orient. In 1808 he obtained British government contracts to supply the army, and later supplied the Swedish army. His success in the American trade was especially notable after 1814. In 1821 one firm alone in Boston ordered £28,000 worth of cloth from him. Gott was a millionaire when he died in 1840, at a time when £70 would have bought a back-to-back house.

It must be emphasised that Park Mills was a woollen mill of quite exceptional size, and it stood alone in the town for almost a decade or more. Perhaps there were only 20 factories of all types in Leeds by 1801.[3] Part of the explanation for the initial slowness in following Gott's example was that the potential emulators of the pioneer mills were deterred, particularly between 1800 and 1815, by limited demand due to war and the interruption of trade. Capital too was in short supply and high interest rates discouraged borrowing. Just as important, however, were the inherent technical difficulties of applying steam-power to spinning, and the strong opposition encountered from cloth workers, both of which were not significantly overcome until the 1820s. High profits, however, inevitably tempted other entrepreneurs into the field. By 1822 there were no less than 30 woollen merchant-manufacturers in Leeds plus 13 firms regarded as woollen cloth manufacturers. These 40 or so factories formed the lion's share of the 50 to 70 factories in the borough by this time. A particularly rapid

Benjamin Gott (1762-1840).

Park Mills, Bean Ing, begun by Benjamin Gott in 1792 — the world's first woollen mill.

phase of factory building began in the mid-1820s. With trade prosperous and interest rates down, woollen mills sprang up all over Leeds.[4]

The rise of the factory system hit the domestic system of woollen cloth manufacture very hard, though its decline was much more gradual than is often supposed. The traditional way of life, whereby the small independent clothier sold his cloth to the merchants of Leeds through the cloth halls, came increasingly under threat. Many of the skills learnt during a clothier's long apprenticeship became redundant as sophisticated factory-based machinery, predominantly worked by women and children rather than men, produced a better product at costs which came to substantially undercut those of domestic production. The first stages of this decline were gradual. Evidence given to Parliament's Commission on the Woollen Manufacture of England in 1806 suggested that of the 300,000 broad cloths and 166,000 narrow cloths manufactured in the West Riding in 1805, only 8,000 were produced in factories.[5] By 1822, however, Baines' *Directory of the County of York* revealed much more dramatic change: 'The whole number of master cloth-manufacturers in the West Riding of Yorkshire amounted, some years ago, to between 5 and 6,000, who employed, besides their wives and children, between 80 and 40,000 persons – latterly that number has been considerably diminished.'[6] The decline was reflected in the crash in the price of stands in the Leeds cloth halls. Those in the Coloured Cloth Hall had collapsed from £16-£24 in 1800 to no more than 50s. by 1822, while those in the White Cloth Hall had tumbled from £6-£8 to no more than £1. The number of independent clothiers attending the halls had halved to about 1,500.[7] Many clothiers were now either selling direct to the merchant-manufacturers, becoming factory hands, or simply going into other occupations.

Initially, it was the workers in the finishing stages of cloth manufacture who were most radically affected. William Hirst, a cropper-turned-manufacturer and former employee of Gott, sealed the fate of the croppers with techniques he perfected in 1816 at his mill on School Close, on the north side of the river, just west of Leeds Bridge. He not only introduced steam-powered hydraulic machinery, supplied by Fenton, Murray and Wood, to press cloth, but, more significantly, perfected the production of a new type of superfine yarn. The yarn's special characteristic was that when woven into high quality superfine cloth, the nap of the cloth could be raised with no ill-effect by a steam-powered gig mill and then cropped by a shearing frame. He had effectively broken the monopoly of the croppers. To attain this major achievement, he needed not only considerable technical skill, but also great physical bravery in face of the croppers' wrath and intimidation. He was obliged to place ten armed guards around his mill every night to protect it from attack. As his memoirs recalled: 'I never ventured out at night; and even when I went out at day time, I always had a brace of loaded pistols in my pocket'.[8] The obligation felt to Hirst by the Leeds merchant-manufacturers for pioneering and driving through these technical changes was considerable. When he went bankrupt in the commercial crash of 1825 and subsequently spent nine months in the debtors' gaol at Rothwell in 1837, the *West Riding Directory* called on the woollen manufacturers to purchase an annuity for the support of him and his family as a token of their gratitude.[9]

By the early 1820s the achievements of men like Gott and Hirst brought strong fears that the remaining 1500 clothiers and their workers would be totally overwhelmed by the factory system.[10] But these craftsmen were still to have considerable respite and it was not until the late 1840s and '50s that the crunch came. While powered machine spinning had been successfully adopted in many woollen mills by the late 1820s, the application of power to weaving remained a problem. In practice it was the weakness of woollen yarn, which made it unsuitable for use on power looms, which above all else saved the domestic system from collapse. The first power looms introduced could weave at no greater pace than the handloom because of the problems of snapping the yarn. It required many improvements in both spinning and weaving before the power loom could replace its predecessor. Except to obtain the higher grades of cloth, mill owners saw little point in paying the higher wages commanded by factory-based weavers when domestic clothiers would weave cloth for less.

As well as clinging on to the weaving stage of production, the independent clothier found ways of remaining competitive in costs in the other cloth-making processes. Edward Baines, junior, explained in 1858:

> Yet the domestic manufacture must have succumbed, had not the clothiers called machinery to their aid for those processes in which it has an indisputable superiority over hand-labour, that is, in the preparing and spinning. They combined to establish joint-stock mills, where each shareholder takes his own wool, and has it cleaned, dyed, carded, and spun; then taking the warp and weft to his own house or workshop, he has it woven by the hand-loom, often by members of his own family. The cloth is afterwards fulled at the mill, washed, and tentered; and then, in what is called the balk state, it is conveyed to Leeds and sold, and it is finished by the dressers under the orders of the merchant. The clothiers, by their industry and frugality, find themselves able to compete with the factory owners, whose great works and complicated machinery entail heavy expenses.[11]

The power loom was little used in the woollen industry until about 1832, and made very little progress during the next twenty years.[12]

But gradually the machinery was perfected, and from the 1850s the handloom steadily lost its hold on the woollen trade. The number of power-looms increased rapidly, the building of mills and the institution of steam plant became general, and weaving, the last of the cloth making processes, passed within the mill gates.[13]

The shift towards factory production of woollens reduced many once proud, skilled clothiers and craftsmen to mere factory hands who bitterly resented the decline in their status and independence, it also was accompanied by a dramatic decline in the gentleman merchant class.[14] The traditional woollen cloth merchants experienced great prosperity in the 1780s and '90s as the Yorkshire woollen industry expanded in an unprecedented manner. In spite of the outbreak of war with France, high prices and industrial unrest, there was no slackening in the foreign trade on which Leeds had always depended. Trade with the American colonies grew prodigiously to account for a full two-fifths of English woollen and worsted exports. Even exports to Portugal and Germany held up well. But in 1801 the bubble burst and 30 lean years followed. While the new breed of factory owner or merchant-manufacturer was obliged to go in search of markets in order to keep his factory employed, the wealthy merchant might simply buy less cloth to re-sell. The periodic closure of European markets during the Napoleonic Wars and the virtual prohibition of trade with the United States between 1808 and 1814 pushed the merchant-manufacturers into trade with South America and the satisfaction of the vast demand for army uniforms. But the majority of the gentlemen merchants were reluctant to risk capital in places such as Brazil and Argentina. Moreover, they were not prepared to commit their families to years spent abroad in these 'uncivilised' places, where merchant-manufacturers undercut their prices and offered better and more risky credit facilities. They preferred to invest their surplus earnings in land, government securities, and the occasional business venture. As for the option of taking up manufacturing – most thought it 'too troublesome'. Running a factory fifteen hours a day, six days a week, might be all very well for a former clothier, but it was no occupation for a gentleman. Though from 1815 the American market recovered to some degree, the European market remained weak. The demand for Yorkshire broad cloths, their staple trade, declined rapidly as it was replaced by a demand for a wide variety of 'fancy' cloths and light worsteds – goods which they were reluctant to handle.[15]

The net result of this inability and, often, unwillingness to adapt was that by 1830, of the 135 firms in Leeds engaged in the sale and manufacture of woollens, worsteds and blankets, only 21 had partners who could provide a direct link with the merchant firms of 1782. Thirty-seven firms were concerned solely with woollen merchanting and 46 were described as woollen merchant-manufacturers, and yet only 7 of these had been in existence half a century earlier as cloth merchants. Though some merchants had gone bankrupt, or retired, or failed to produce male heirs, the majority had defected from the industry. Instead of seeking a good apprenticeship for their sons, they now looked to the professions when they were unable to set their sons up with an independent income. It was thus that in Leeds the manufacturers replaced the merchants in the leadership of the woollen industry between 1783 and 1830.[16]

Before 1780 Leeds merchants had dealt in both woollen and worsted cloths. Specialisation was rare. In the two decades following 1783 there had been a rapid growth in the varieties of both woollen and worsted cloths, and after 1800 merchants tended to deal only in woollens or worsteds. As a result Leeds also had an important but small group of worsted merchants – the 1822 Directory lists 20 firms. Though there was some production of worsted goods (stuffs) in the town and its vicinity, worsteds were primarily made in and around Bradford and Halifax, as we have seen. Right up to the 1820s these merchants, by purchasing at the Piece Halls in Bradford, Halifax and Huddersfield, handled most of the output of these areas, and brought vast quantities of cloth back to Leeds to be finished and exported. In the 1830s and '40s, however, these merchants, too, left Leeds as Bradford, Huddersfield, and Dewsbury began to handle their own sales and exports.[16]

The rise of factory production in the woollen industry enhanced Leeds' position as 'the principal seat of the woollen manufacture in England'. Indeed, in 1842 the Parliamentary Gazetteer noted:

The great woollen manufacture, which extends its ramifications to the most distant extremities of the empire, is principally concentrated in Leeds and its vicinity, as its centre, or more properly its focus. In the clothing district of Leeds alone - a district which, though comprehending other parishes than that of Leeds, is intimately dependent on it as to commercial affairs - employment is afforded in the woollen manufacture, directly or indirectly, to at least 200,000 persons. The number of woollen mills in the parish of Leeds in 1838 was 106, employing 9,738 hands, 2,721 of whom were females. There are also hand-loom weavers engaged in the same branch of manufacture: in 1838 at 10,000 thoroughout the Leeds district; 541 of them being within the town.[17]

The Rise of New Industries

Great as the woollen industry was, the key to the future development and success of Leeds was the rise of other immensely important industries in the period around 1790-1840 and the diversification of the local economy. Gott's achievement was remarkable, but perhaps even more astonishing was the rise of John Marshall.[19] In 1781, at the age of 16, Marshall entered his father's linen drapers business in Mill Hill. When his father died in 1787 he became head of the business, and like Gott made the most of his opportunity. In 1788, in partnership with Samuel Fenton and Ralph Dearlove, he leased Scotland Mill, a water mill in Adel. There, with the assistance of Matthew Murray, a young engineer recently arrived from Stockton-on-Tees, he broke some difficult technical bottlenecks in using cotton spinning machinery to spin flax into linen yarn. He soon moved production to a site in Water Lane between the Leeds and Liverpool Canal and the Hol Beck, close to Leeds town centre, and between 1791 and 1792 erected a four-storey water-powered mill with a large warehouse, a counting house,

John Marshall (1765-1845).

Marshall's revolutionary flax spinning mills, Marshall Street, Holbeck, shown here in 1861.

Female workers in the dusty environment of one of Marshall's multi-storey mills.

Matthew Murray (1765-1826).

stables, a dry house, shops for smiths and joiners and several cottages. Significantly, he quickly abandoned water power, and substituted a 20 horse power Boulton and Watt steam engine. From 1793 to 1800, with new partners Thomas and Benjamin Benyon, the business grew prodigiously. Besides spinning and bleaching linen yarns for sale, the firm also produced coarse heavy linen cloth such as canvas, hessian and raven-duck. By 1798 half its yarn was woven on its own 150 hand looms, the remainder being put out to weavers in nearby villages. By 1804 it produced an extended line of heavy linens in bears and ships, and lighter cloths such as ducks and linens. The success was immense. By 1803 Marshall and his partners had a joint capital of over £80,000, and employed over 1,000 workers, with steam engines rated at over 150 horse-power driving nearly 7,000 spindles. No other flax spinner in the country approached this size.

Marshall, in contrast with Gott, used powered machinery from the start – first water power and then steam. Moreover, he actually pioneered the foundation of a major new industry in Leeds. 'Several manufactories', Baines observed in 1822, 'inferior in extent to very few in the kingdom', had been established for spinning flax for canvas, linen, sacking, thread, etc.[20] By 1821 there were 19 flax spinning firms in Leeds and by 1855 the number had risen to 37.[21]

Gott and Marshall and their emulators could only make their dramatic achievements with the aid of ingenious engineers and machine makers. One of the most brilliant inventive engineers, who pioneered the use of steam engines and flax hackling machinery, was Matthew Murray, the father of the Leeds engineering industry.[22] It is a great injustice that a statue of the engineer James Watt stands in City Square today, for most certainly that statue should be of Murray. The growth and prosperity of the textile industries in Leeds and its region generated a considerable demand for machinery and utensils. Hackles and gills, combs, gears and slays, steam engines and later machine tools, locomotives, cranes, boilers and a whole host of products were all eagerly sought. In 1795 Murray left John Marshall's employment and set up business nearby, where he pioneered large-scale organisation and new production methods in engineering. Fenton, Murray and Wood's Round Foundry became famed for the production of textile machinery, steam engines and locomotives. Indeed, so successful were they that Boulton and Watt, the pre-eminent steam engine manufacturers of the day at Soho Foundry in Birmingham, felt it necessary to buy land around Murray's works in an attempt to stop him expanding. In June 1802 they even contemplated purchasing an old malthouse that projected into the works, so that they could spy on Murray. James Watt, junior, commented that 'this would enable us to overlook their whole yard'. Watt even stooped to gaining access to the bedroom of one of Murray's workmen and used his key to open a trunk where 'we had complete examination of its contents, among which a roll of drawings of various parts of our Machinery and Engines deserves most conspicuous mention. The things are very indifferently done, but the dimensions are written upon the drawings, and upon separate slips of paper'.[23]

Watt had good reason to be concerned. A survey in 1824 showed that, far from Boulton and Watt dominating the market in Leeds, of the 129 steam engines installed in the town, 110 had been constructed by Leeds firms, two-thirds of them by Fenton, Murray and Wood.[24] The firm

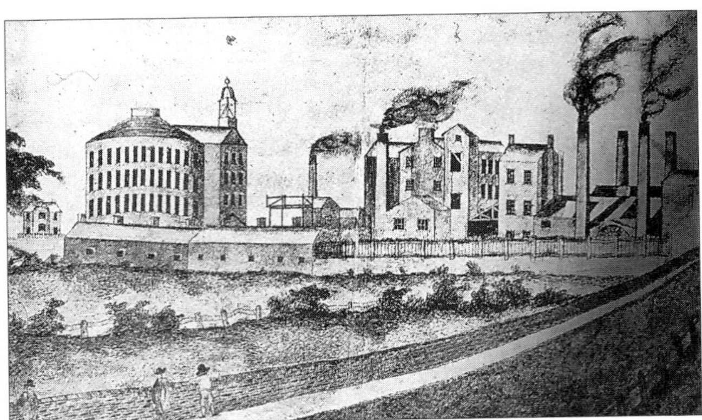

The Round Foundry, Water Lane, the works of Fenton, Murray and Wood. Blenkinsop's locomotive was built there.

became internationally famous and exported many of its products. One of its steam engines powered a tug boat on the Mississippi River, and in recognition of Murray's services the Emperor of Russia presented him with a valuable diamond ring and the king of Sweden gave him a gold snuff box!

Murray was not alone for long as a machine-maker. One year after he set up, Taylor, Wordsworth and Co. also began making textile machinery. They were emulated by two other prominent early nineteenth-century Leeds engineers, Samuel Lawson of Hope Foundry in Mabgate (1812) and Peter Fairbairn of Wellington Foundry (1826) on Wellington Street.[25]

There were at least 225 steam engines in use in Leeds by 1831 using 150,000 tons of coal each year (see Table 4.1).

Table 4.1

Steam engines in use in Leeds industries in 1831

	Number of Engines	Total Horse power
Manufacturing and finishing of woollen cloth	80	1,884
Dyeing, washing, and cleaning, cloth and stuffs	23	237
Flax Spinning	24	705
Grinding corn	17	282
Ware grinding	5	82
Seed crushing	5	160
Coal pits and locomotive engines	12	164
Iron foundries	11	145
Tobacco manufacturing	9	25
Machine making	8	68
Pumping water	7	18
Shear-making and grinding	2	12
Sawing wood	2	24
Paper manufacturing	2	42
Silk and cotton spinning	1	36
Worsted spinning	4	57
Carpet manufacturing	1	26
Other minor purposes	12	81
Total	225	4,048

[Source: *Parliamentary Gazetteer, 1842*, p.69]

The process of industrialisation in Leeds was accompanied and facilitated by an extraordinary increase in the size of both the town's population and its workforce. The population grew from around 25,000 in 1790 to what was by contemporary experience a massive 88,741 in 1841, while the numbers in the borough mushroomed from 53,276 in 1801 to 152,000 in 1841. The town's workforce, including female and child labour, trebled from around 12,000 in the 1790s to over 35,000 in 1841, while that of the borough reached 59,715.[26] For many years the stories of Gott, Marshall and Murray, supported by the figures for the amazing growth of Leeds between 1790 and 1840, and the travellers tales such as those of the German prince quoted at the start of this chapter, created the myth that in this period growth in Leeds was largely driven and dominated by large-scale factories. While it was true that the landscape became dominated by factories, for much of the late Georgian period most the growth of Leeds' industry and commerce was actually achieved by a spectacular increase in the number and diversity of small firms, often using traditional craft skills.[27] In 1841 only one out of every four or five occupied persons in Leeds worked in a factory and fewer than one firm in ten used steam power. By 1840 the average number of workers per firm was only 10. Leeds had no more than 20 factories in 1801, between 50 and 70 in 1817 and in the region of 150 to 200 in 1842.

Trade directories indicate that the number of 'firms' in the town (that is the number of individuals or partnerships listed in the directories as making or supplying goods or services) rose from around 1,000 in 1797, to about 2,500 in 1817, 4,500 in 1834, and over 7,000 in 1842. Many of these were no more than craft workshops, employing a handful of workers, or shops, or public houses; but the great increase in numbers reflected a dynamic and highly enterprising local economy which was expanding at an extraordinary rate. Importantly, this growth was accompanied by an increase in the range of trades and professions in the town which jumped from about 150 in the 1790s to just over 300 in the 1830s. In part this diversification reflected the subdivision of existing industries into more specialised branches, nevertheless there were many new industrial activities.

As early as the 1790s the woollen industry had begun to lose its overwhelmingly predominant position in the economy of Leeds. By that time, of the 12,000 workers in the town, perhaps less than half, around 5,000, were involved in woollen manufacture. Almost 2,000 were now working in other textile industries, notably flax spinning. Very significantly something in the region of 5,000 workers were in non-textile occupations. The relative decline continued. By 1841, out of a total of 59,715 workers in the whole borough, 13,338 were employed in the woollen industry – a large number, but now only one in five workers. The numbers in other textile industries (notably linens and worsteds) had leapt to 9,473, while those in non-textile occupations had grown to an astonishing 37,090, more than three out of every five workers.

The biggest areas of growth in non-textile employment were food supply, the making of clothes and footwear, building and engineering. The supply of food, drink, lodging (including trades ranging from butchers and bakers, to shops, beer houses, inns and hotels) and tobacco processing as a group employed one in five workers in the town by 1841. Tailoring, dressmaking and shoemaking establishments accounted for almost one in every ten entries in the trade directories. The several hundred small shoemaking concerns in the borough employed around 2,000 workers. Engineering and

The Leeds waterfront in 1827. The Aire and Calder Navigation warehouses on the north side of Leeds bridge had just been built.

building became very large employers indeed as a result of the growth of the textile industry and the huge number of buildings erected in the town. All these industries, except for engineering, were directly related to the need to feed, clothe and house the rapidly growing population not only of Leeds, but England as a whole. As the population of Leeds and its region soared, a sufficient local demand was created to make it worthwhile for new crafts and services to be provided. Insurance, furniture making, paper making, printing, plumbing, banking, and coffee houses are a just few examples. Kirkgate and its associated yards in the 1820s accommodated a fascinating sample of the town's trades.[28] In addition to inns and public houses, there were printers, booksellers, cobblers, bakers, feather merchants, brush makers, grocers, tea dealers, clothes dealers, painters and decorators, pawnbrokers, cabinet makers, tobacco and snuff manufacturers, drapers, confectioners, maltsters, glass and lead merchants, wine and spirit merchants, butchers, chemists, straw hat makers, clock makers – the list seems almost endless. Edward Baines, in 1822, after remarking on the achievements of Benjamin Gott, confirmed the range an importance of the trades and industries which in the previous thirty or forty years had grown up to complement Leeds' prodigious strength in textiles:

> In the immediate neigbourhood are some manufactories of crown and green glass, and the Leeds Pottery enjoys a considerable reputation in England, Scotland and Ireland, as well as in foreign countries. Several Iron Foundries have been erected around us, and there is a manufacture of Steam Engines, which, after Boulton and Watts', is perhaps equal to any in the kingdom, as well for its extent as for the skill and mechanical genius which presides over it. On the Aire and its tributary streams are numerous mills for grinding corn, dyers' wood, rape-seed, &c. as well as for fulling cloth, and turning, carding, and spinning machines. These works are, however, principally wrought by steam, the numerous furnaces of which contaminate the air, and impair the beauty and healthfulness of a well situated town. Beside the staple of cloth, linen, &c. the wholesale Tobacco Trade is carried on extensively in Leeds, and mills have been erected here for cutting this American production.[29]

The Foundations of Success

The successful expansion of Leeds as an industrial centre was underpinned by a number of key factors. The creation of mills for spinning cotton, flax, worsted and woollen yarns in the 1790s was partly due to the availability of cheap coal, a factor that was to encourage the production of bricks, pottery, soap, chemicals and sugar refining. Leeds was supplied with some of the cheapest coal in the country, transported to the town by waggonway. This was supplemented with coal from Halton and Rothwell.[30] The York Street Gas Works of 1818, revolutionised lighting in the town, but it too relied heavily on cheap coal supplies.[31] Sir George Head, visiting the town in 1835, commented:

> There is no manufacturing town in England, I should imagine, wherein more coal is consumed, in proportion to its extent, than Leeds: situated in the heart of a coalfield, and fed with an abundant daily supply, a single glance, whether by day or night is sufficient to verify the above conclusion. The sun himself is obscured by smoke, as by a natural mist; and no sooner does he descend below the horizon, than streams of brilliant gas burst forth from thousands of illuminated windows.[32]

Another major advantage was that transport links were constantly improving. The facilities of the Aire and Calder Navigation were frequently enlarged and, in 1816, the direct link to Liverpool via the Leeds and Liverpool Canal was at last completed.[33] These amenities were of great importance for the export of manufactured products and the importation of bulky raw materials such

The White Horse, Boar Lane was one of the busiest coaching inns in the town. In 1822 coaches left daily for London, Manchester, Hull and Ripon.

Blenkinsop's engine pulling coal waggons from Middleton Colliery to the coal staithes near Meadow Lane. Note Christ Church, the Million Act church, in the background.

as wool, flax, coal, iron ore and wood, as well as vital food supplies. The turnpike network did much to improve the quality of the roads. The coach journey to London which took three days in 1760, had been reduced to 21 hours by 1836.[34] Leeds developed as a major coaching centre based on the inns and yards of Briggate and Boar Lane. The growth was dramatic. In 1781 not more than half a dozen coaches ran from the town to London, Hull, York, Sheffield, Birmingham, Manchester and Carlisle, with additional seasonal coaches to Harrogate and Scarborough. By 1800 the number had risen to 40 coaches daily and this was to increase to a remarkable 130 departures by 1838, to destinations all over the country. This enhanced the position of the town as a social centre, creating further employment in the catering, brewing, tobacco and accommodation sectors. Freight transport boomed, despite being relatively expensive, with the number of carriers rising from 25 in 1781 to 108 by the 1820's.[35] These were centred on the inns and warehouses near the river. The search for more efficient forms of transport continued. The Revolutionary and Napoleonic Wars had created a dramatic rise in the price of fodder and horses. John Blenkinsop, manager of Middleton Colliery, sought ways of reducing his transport costs. He commissioned Matthew Murray to build a steam locomotive, the first

A Middleton Collier c.1814 with Blenkinsop's rack and pinion locomotive of 1812 in the background.

The view from Bishopgate Street to Park Row in 1826 engraved by J. Clark. To the left of centre is the magnificent frontage of the Court House, and partly hidden behind the trees is the Coloured Cloth Hall. In the centre is the Commercial Buildings built 1826-29.

trial of which was reported in the *Leeds Mercury* on 27 June 1812. This was the world's first successful commercial steam locomotive, though it was to be another 17 years before Leeds entered the age of the passenger railways.[36]

Another major asset to Leeds in its industrial and commercial expansion was the availability of excellent financial and legal services experienced in handling large foreign trade transactions.[37] As we have seen, the town's first bank, Lodge and Arthington, had been established in 1758. Subsequently, as Beckett's Bank, under the control of John Beckett, it became one of the country's leading banks. It was joined by Leeds New Bank in 1777 and Leeds Commercial Bank in 1792. The Commercial Bank failed in 1812 but the gap was soon filled by the foundation of the Union Bank in 1813. The Leeds banks tended to be a good deal larger than the average provincial banks. The economic boom and crash of the mid-1820s hit financial institutions hard and nationally 63 provincial banks failed, but most of the Leeds banks weathered the storm. The townspeople were so gratified by their performance that during the procession to the foundation ceremony of the town's new merchant exchange in 1826, the party halted twice to sing 'God Save the King' and give three cheers in honour of the banks of the town.[38] The New Bank failed in 1827 but no more succumbed in the next few years. The one newcomer was a branch of the Bank of England; its opening in 1827 causing considerable controversy in local financial and business circles. Between 1832 and 1836 these banks were joined by six new joint stock banks.

Underpinning all else in Leeds' ability to rapidly develop its industry and commerce was the plentiful supply of labour which eagerly flooded into the town, the sizeable local market created by its own population and that of its large hinterland, and its propensity to attract men with entrepreneurial skill and great energy. With these advantages, while neighbouring towns like Wakefield and Halifax tinkered with industrialisation, Leeds forged ahead decisively.

The Boom Town

> There is perhaps hardly a town in England in which the passion for improvement is so strong as it is in Leeds. Scarcely a week elapses that we have not the pleasure to announce some project for improving and adorning the town ...It is a rather curious coincidence that we have now erected or in contemplation three churches, three dissenting meeting houses, three markets, three bridges, and streets innumerable.
>
> *Leeds Intelligencer*, 2 December 1824

The huge increase in its population between 1790 and 1840 and the dramatic expansion of its industry and commerce changed the face of Leeds for ever. It confirmed its place as one of the largest towns in England, at a time of prolific urban growth nationwide. Its population of 17,117 in 1775 had mushroomed to 30,669 by 1801. By 1811 another 5,000 had been added, and in 1821 the total had reached 48,603. This rate of growth, which hit its high point in the 1820s with an

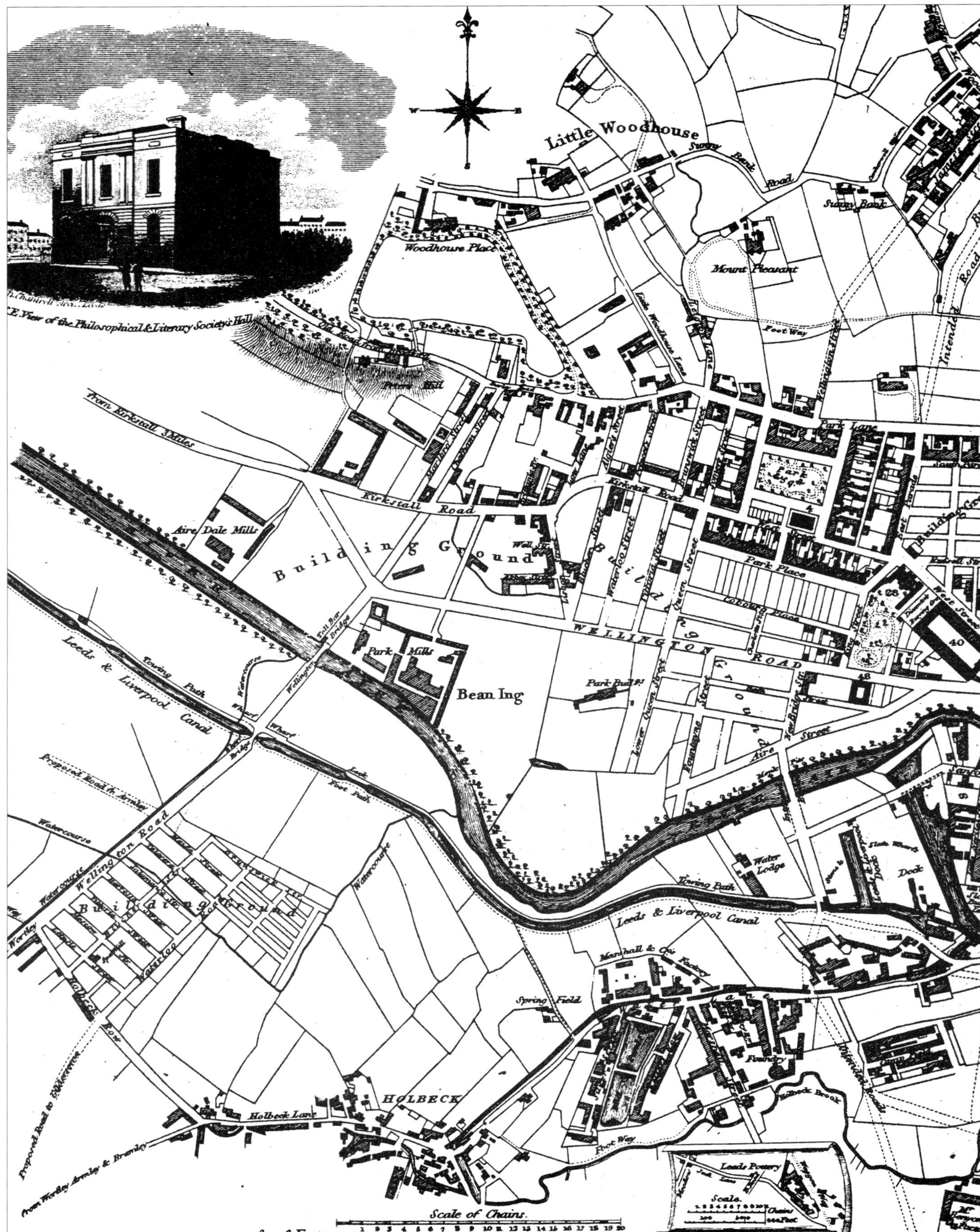

Fowler's Plan of Leeds, 1821. This splendid plan shows Leeds just as it is about to experience perhaps the biggest building boom of the nineteenth century. Many areas of land are designated as 'Building Ground' with the street grids laid out, and sometimes named, but with the houses yet to be built. Of particular interest are the streets immediately to the east of Vicar Lane — Union Street, Ebenezer Street and St George Street — the first streets of back-to-back houses built in Leeds. Note also the Bank, the area on the right of the map between Marsh Lane and the north side of the river, effectively the slopes and foot of Richmond Hill. Here Robert Baker and his contemporaries were to find the most squalid housing in Leeds. Note too the area behind St Peter's Square, between Quarry Hill and Marsh Lane. This district was soon to be crammed with houses, which were to become notorious for their insanitary condition. The plan also shows clearly the intended developments in the Park Estate, and the genteel terraces and individual properties created on the north west edge of the town in recent decades. The canal basin is prominent as are Park Mills at Bean Ing and Marshall's mills down Water Lane. Fowler proudly draws attention to the public buildings of the town. Fowler's plan of 1826 shows the same area with many additional buildings.

ference to Public Buildings
urches: 1. St Peter's or Parish Church, Kirkgate. 2. St John's Church, above Upper Head Row. 3. Trinity Church, Boar Lane. 4. St Paul's Church, Park Square. 5. St James's Church, York Street. 6. New Church, Meadow ne. 7. New Church, Quarry Hill. **Chapels:** 8. Albion Chapel, Albion Street. 9. Bank Chapel, Richmond Hill. 10. Baptist Chapel, St Ann's Street, St Peter's. 11. Bethel Chapel, St George's Street, Vicar Lane. 12. Call ne Chapel, Call Lane. 13. Ebenezer Chapel, Ebenezer Street, Vicar Lane. 14. Friends' Meeting House, Water Lane. 15. Inghamite Chapel, Duke Street, St Peter's. 16. Old Methodist Chapel, St Ann's Street, St Peter's. . Old White Chapel, Hunslet Lane. 18. New Methodist Chapel, Albion Street. 19. Mill Hill Chapel, Park Row. 20. Roman Catholic Chapel, Lady Lane. 21. Salem Chapel, Hunslet Lane. 22. Wesleyan Chapel, Meadow ne. **Charitable Buildings:** 23. Harrison's Alms Houses, Wade Lane. 24. Jenkinson's Alms Houses, Quebec. 25. Potter's Alms Houses, Wade Lane. 26. Charity School, St John's Church. 27. Free Grammar School, rth Street. 28. General Infirmary, West Street. 29. House of Recovery, Vicar Lane. 30. Lancastrian School, Alfred Street. 31. National School, High Court Lane, Kirkgate. 32. Workhouse, North Street. **Law, Commercial d Other Buildings:** 33. Assembly Rooms, White Cloth Hall. 34. Commercial Bank, Briggate. 35. Court House Rotation Office and Prison, Park Row. 36. Cross, Market Place. 37. Gas Works, York Street. 38. King's lls, Swinegate. 39. The Library, Commercial Street. 40. Mixed Cloth Hall, West Street. 41. Moot Hall, Briggate. 42. Music Hall, Albion Street. 43. New Bank, Bank Street, Boar Lane. 44. New Library, Albion Street. . News Rooms, Briggate. 46. Old Bank, Briggate. 47. Philosophical and Literary Society's Hall, Park Row. 48. Public Baths, Wellington Road. 49. Post Office, Call Lane. 50. Riding School, York Road. 51. Theatre, nslet Lane. 52. Vicarage, Kirkgate. 53. Union Bank, Commercial Street. 54. White Cloth Hall, White Cloth Hall Street.

St. Paul's Church, Park Square (architect, W. Johnson). Consecrated in 1793 on a site given by Christopher Wilson, Bishop of Bristol, and erected at the expense of its first minister, Miles Atkinson. (demolished 1905).

Wesley Chapel, Meadow Lane (built 1816).

Brunswick Chapel, Brunswick Street, built 1824-5 (architect, J. Botham).

An engraving of the junction of Infirmary Street and Park Row in the mid-1820s, from a drawing by R. D. Chantrell. On the far left is the Coloured Cloth Hall and, just beyond it is the Infirmary. To the right is the Court House with the elegant residences of Park Row stretching up to the new Philosophical Hall.

The Central Market and Duncan Street in 1830. The market, which was built in 1824-7, had 67 shops and a covered central hall with 56 stalls, and a bazaar on its balcony.

increase of over 4 per cent per year, was sustained by a massive influx of people from other areas. Between the 1790s and 1841 approximately 50 to 60 per cent of the population increase resulted from in-migration.[39] The 1835 Guide to Leeds noted that 'since the last census, the town has risen from the sixth to the fifth magnitude in England: for in 1831 it was found to have passed Bristol in the number of inhabitants, and to possess 71,602.'[40] Its population was exceeded only by London, Liverpool, Manchester and Birmingham.[41] By 1841 the total had reached 88,741.

Park Place. For a time one of the most desirable residential locations in Leeds, with wonderful views across to the Aire and beyond.

Public Buildings with Style

The rise in numbers created a demand for larger and new types of public amenities. Quite often the town's increased wealth allowed such amenities to be housed in buildings of an architectural elegance and style not hitherto attained. The 1790s brought a flurry of church and chapel building with Salem Chapel, Hunslet Lane, for the Independent dissenters (1791), and St Paul's Church, Park Square (1791-4), St James' Church, off Kirkgate (1794), and Albion Chapel, Albion Street (1796) for the Anglicans. For social purposes the Music Hall was built in Albion Street in 1790, financed at a cost of £1000 by a private company. Its music saloon was the biggest public room in Leeds (until the town hall was opened in 1858), and its other facilities included an art gallery and exhibition rooms.

The provision of new amenities was relatively slow between 1800 and 1819. No doubt the hardships experienced in the cloth trade and the frequent disruption of trade with the Continent and America, which also discouraged the building of mills, made civic leaders cautious. The emphasis was on extensions where possible: the workhouse was enlarged, as was the Mixed Cloth Hall, while the parish church was substantially renovated and the Charity School rebuilt. Some parties, however, were not deterred. A Methodist chapel was built in Albion Street in 1802, and the proprietors of the Leeds Library erected a magnificent new building in Commercial Street in 1808.[43] Indeed, there were some bold initiatives. The medical facilities of the Infirmary were complemented by the building of the House of Recovery (a fever hospital) in Vicar Lane in 1802-04. Two important new schools also were founded: the Lancasterian School (1812) in Alfred Street off Boar Lane and the National School (1813) just off Kirkgate. The most imposing new building of the period was the Court House erected in Park Row (1811-13) at a cost of over £10,000.[44]

Despite the erection of mills on the fringes of the town, already a picture was beginning to emerge of a town whose principal central streets were lined with imposing public buildings. The 1820s were to make this a reality. In 1827 John Cawood, when laying the foundation of the town's new corn exchange at the top of Briggate, commented: 'We are met here today to lay the last foundation stone of a series of public buildings, in this town, having their origin during the most unexampled tide of prosperity ever remembered.'[45] By 1819 the caution and restraint of the early years of the century had begun to dissipate. A report on the outlook for Leeds noted a new mood afoot: 'There is an evident alteration taking place in the character of the people of Leeds. They are putting off in some degree that rudeness which is peculiar to them, enlightened pursuits are more cultivated, and the elegancies and comforts of life are more sought after.'[46] The new mood was reflected in the building of the imposing Philosophical Hall (1819-22) in Park Row as the home for the town's new Philosophical and Literary Society, and the Public Baths (1819-20) in Wellington Street, a luxurious suite of Turkish and spa baths, 'public' only if you were very affluent.[47] The building boom took off in 1823 and 1824. The church and chapel building was remarkable. First the 'Million Act Churches' – St Mary's, Quarry Hill, Christ Church, Meadow Lane, and St Mark's, Woodhouse – were built between 1823 and 1826, in areas of working-class housing, with grants from Parliament's million-pound fund.[48] Then came the Nonconformist chapels - Queen Street Independent Chapel (1823-25), Brunswick Methodist Chapel (1824-25), South Parade Baptist Chapel (1824-25)[49], and a handful more of chapels belonging to smaller sects.

The most striking feature of the mid-1820s was the absolute mania for building markets and commercial facilities.[50] By the 1820s, as we shall see, Briggate's role as the main north-south route through Leeds made it unsuitable as the town's market place. Influential townspeople wanted to take the market stalls off the street and place them in a covered market. A combination of the failure to find a site all could agree on, and over-optimism about commercial prospects, produced a very surprising result – not one new market but five, and a merchants' exchange thrown in for good measure. Between 1823 and 1839 private enterprise financed and built the South Market, Meadow Lane, the Central Market, Duncan Street, the Corn Exchange, the Bazaar and Shambles, (between Briggate and Vicar Lane) and the Commercial Buildings. The South and Central Markets were genuine retail markets, but neither was sufficiently large to accommodate the Briggate market stalls, nor did they address the problems of the cattle market, still held in Vicar Lane, or the wholesale fruit and vegetable market in Briggate. As we shall see, the Improvement Commissioners were to solve this problem by the creation of the Free Market.

The shocking nature of the commercial crash at the tail-end of 1825, and the sheer extensiveness of the public building provision leading up to it, suppressed enthusiasm for new amenities in the 1830s. Notable exceptions were the Waterloo Swimming Baths (1833-34) erected beside the Leeds and Liverpool Canal Basin, and the establishment of the Zoological and Botanical Gardens (1837-40) at Headingley. Religious fervour, however, overcame caution and numerous churches and chapels were built, most notably St Patrick's Church Roman Catholic Chapel, York Road (1831-32), St Peter's Wesleyan Chapel, St Peter's Street (1834), Lady Lane Wesleyan Chapel (1835); St

George's Anglican Church (1836-38), Mount Pleasant (now Great George Street), St Ann's Roman Catholic Church, Park Terrace (1837-38), and Oxford Place Associationist Methodist Chapel (1840).[51]

With the exception of the Court House and the Free Market all these buildings and amenities were privately financed. The benevolent and charitable institutions were funded by subscriptions and donations, the more commercial ventures and those giving direct benefit to the middle classes, such as the Philosophical Hall, the Leeds Library and the Baths, by money raised by the issue of shares. The people who enthusiastically stumped up the £50 (the price of a back-to-back) or even £100 to buy a share in these undertakings were tempted by the high rates of dividend predicted, but as Earl Cowper's land agent noted there was also a strong desire to improve the town for social as well as commercial reasons. Urban rivalry, emulation and civic pride were strong incentives.

A correspondent to the *Leeds Mercury* in 1818 recommending the building of the Philosophical Hall commented: 'There are few large towns where such institutions do not exist or flourish, and they are patronised in many places, much less considerable in extent and much less respectable in the character of the inhabitants, than the town of Leeds.'[52] Similarly, a correspondent to the *Leeds Intelligencer* in 1822 looking forward to the replacement of the old butchers' shambles hoped that this would soon be followed:

> ...by other improvements consistent with the opulence and commercial importance of the town of Leeds, and no longer subject us to the scorn of visitors, who wonder that, with the advance of intelligence and general science, we have been negligent of those matters, by which other large commercial towns have facilitated the intercourse of strangers with their merchants ...I am for improving wholesale ...I must confess, because I have seen, for many years past, to my great mortification, that when any designs for public improvement have been suggested by my respectable townsmen in a *Retail* way, they have not been attended to.[53]

Housing the Multitude

So much for the civic face of Leeds, what about its domestic face? The growing numbers needed to be housed.[54] In 1790 the prestigious housing development on the Wilson's Park Estate provided a haven for many members of the Leeds élite. The most impressive houses on Park Row (1767-76), East Parade (1779-89) and South Parade (1776-78) were now complete and occupied. From the late 1780s more houses came on-stream. The houses in Park Place, 'a very elegant range of buildings' with one of the most pleasing outlooks in the town, were erected between 1788 and 1800. As the 1806 Guide put it 'all the houses are in a very superior style and principally inhabited by affluent merchants or gentlemen retired from business'.[55] Park Square too was laid out in 1788 and its houses completed by 1810. The guide remarked that 'though the houses are not equal to those of Park Place, they are all well built in the modern style'.[56] The estate marked an important break with tradition. Merchants, bankers, attorneys and surgeons who had formerly lived on the main thoroughfares of the town, often next door to people of lower rank, abandoned their houses. The fine merchant houses of Briggate were often subdivided, with the creation of shops on the ground floor, while the upper floors provided residential accommodation for the lower middle classes.

Lyddon Terrace, a fashionable middle-class terrace with large houses on the southern edge of Woodhouse Moor. The estate was laid out by the surveyor Henry Teal in 1825 at the instigation of Julia Lyddon, but the street was not completed until 1906.

The increase in traffic, the changing character of the yards, the noise in the streets at night, and rising crime encouraged many to move. The exclusive Park Estate combined wide roads, open spaces, pleasing views and genteel neighbours, with the advantage of being near the heart of commercial and social life. Many houses were insured for over £1,000 and yet even here home could still be combined with business, for the yards behind the houses often contained dressing shops, warehouses and consulting rooms. The opulent population of the Park Estate enjoyed their new environment, protected by restricted covenants on the leasehold plots. But their sanctuary was to be short lived. The estate was slow to develop. In 1792 Christopher Wilson, Bishop of Bristol, inherited the estate, and he and his heirs, being absentee landlords, displayed an indifferent attitude, simply wishing to increase their income. In 1805 the family sold for building development the large, pleasant, open space on to which Park Row, South Parade, East Parade and West Street (now Infirmary Street) faced. In 1806 even the beautiful central grounds in Park Square only narrowly escaped sale for building when the residents snapped it up. Other nuisances, which were to be a constant irritation to residents, ranged from the smoke emitted from Park Mills, to the increased traffic due to the construction of the new turnpike road to Bradford which started at the south-western end of Park Square. The occupants of the estate, nevertheless, faired better than residents south of the river, where the rapid spread of new mills and factories led to a rapid deterioration of the surroundings.

Despite some environmental drawbacks, the majority of townspeople still found living in a central location an attractive proposition. In 1792 freehold building plots were offered for sale in Albion Street. One of the most eminent men in the town, Dr. William Hey, purchased a plot on which the architect, Thomas Johnson, erected for him a fine residence, named Albion Place.[57] This locality, however, had never been envisaged as a purely residential area since the Music Hall and two chapels were soon constructed in the locality.

Fashion, however, began to change. Increasing numbers of the most opulent began to tire of the noise, smoke and close proximity of neighbours and chose instead to build detached villas surrounded by their own landscaped grounds. A new West End was created on the slopes of

Rose and Crown Yard, Briggate in 1887. Typical of the yards of Briggate with a mixture of bars, dining rooms, lodging houses, shops and rented accommodation. Today its site is occupied by the Queen's Arcade.

Little Woodhouse, where villas like Springfield House (1792) and Beech Grove (1796) occupied one field or more. Surprisingly, perhaps, merchants who moved still retained their workshops and warehouses at the back of these impressive residences. Building land was in plentiful supply. Small genteel houses were built in Queen's Square (c. 1806), St James's Street and Providence Row. Attempts were made to develop Woodhouse Square and Hanover Square in the 1820s and 1830s. Other streets on the north-western fringes of the town were begun in the 1820s: Blenheim Terrace began in 1824, Lyddon Terrace in 1825, and Kingston Terrace in 1826.

A few families chose to move even further away to the smoke-free plateaux to the north. The road improvements, since the turnpiking of the Leeds-Harrogate route in 1752 and the road to Otley in 1755, had increased the residential potential of the area immediately beyond Leeds township for those who could commute on horseback or by horse and carriage. The new turnpike routes to Kirkstall (1806), through Potternewton to Roundhay (1808), and to Meanwoodside in Chapel Allerton (1829), completed the basic network of links to the north Leeds communities of the later years of the nineteenth century.[58] Chapel Allerton, Headingley and Potternewton attracted a more mobile élite. Not all ventures were a success. The bid begun in 1828 to create a 'New Leeds' on Earl Cowper's land in what today we refer to as Chapeltown, by laying out the streets including and bounded by Chapeltown Road, Leopold Street, Spencer Place and Cowper Street, then more properly known as Potternewton, ended in disaster for the investors.[59]

The prime need, however, was to house the rapidly swelling ranks of the working classes. Leeds had no physical barriers to expansion, freehold land for development was plentiful, and yet even in 1837 the town measured little more than a mile from West to East. Lack of urban transport, low wages and the long hours of work, ensured that members of the working classes lived close to their place of employment.[60]

When the crowded yards at the back of Briggate, Kirkgate, Vicar Lane, Boar Lane and the Headrow, became increasingly sought after for commercial purposes, rents soared. Some of the workers moved to nearby villages, like Armley and Holbeck, but what was needed was large quantities of low cost housing in or near the central area. In 1793 the township had less than 7,000 houses, 48 years later it could boast of nearly 20,000. Because few speculative builders erected cottage property for sale to single purchasers, and land was normally sold in large plots, as early as 1786 terminating building societies were formed to meet the housing needs of some of the lower-middle classes and the more affluent workers. The pooled savings of members meant that land could be purchased and plots developed, and in this way individuals of moderate means were housed or became landlords. This produced the first rows of back-to-back houses in central Leeds namely, Union Street, Ebeneezer Street, and George Street just to the north of where Kirkgate Market now stands. The subscription to these clubs was beyond the reach of the ordinary working man; it was the craftsmen, artisans and retailers who took advantage of the schemes. In the 1820s several clubs had problems with dishonest treasurers, and as a result the popularity of the schemes waned.

With respect to the needs of the great mass of workers, in some towns mill owners built cottages for their workers, but in Leeds the demand for housing was met by the speculative building of large numbers of back-to-back houses which were rented out by a considerable array of landlords. The majority of these houses were located in the districts of The Bank, Far Bank, Quarry

Tunstall's Fold, north side of Mabgate, adjacent to Quarry Hill. Two-storey blind-back houses developed piecemeal from 1790. The road remained unpaved into the twentieth century.

Hill, Mabgate and the Leylands. Investing in working-class housing was a hazardous business, and growth was erratic, with periods of high activity being followed by slump. The first half of the 1820s was particularly hectic, with rapid development taking place even in the fields to the West of the prestigious Park Estate. Dr. John Simpson of Bradford in his diary for June 1825 noted a meeting with Mr Oastler, 'the old miser from Knaresborough' whom he found a 'shrewd old man'. Oastler told him that 'the people of Leeds are building houses and streets on speculation, and have to borrow money from such men as himself, and that if trade becomes bad they will all be ruined'.[61] This was the voice of experience! In 1805, forty-eight landlords owned just over a thousand properties, most of which were a mixture of one-room cottages and two-room back-to-backs. The greatest developer was Richard Paley. He arrived in Leeds in 1771 and by 1803 was the largest private landlord in the town, owning over 150 dwellings rated at £1 or less. His spectacular bankruptcy in that year overshadowed the housing market for nearly 20 years.

The cost of building a workman's cottage stood at about £40 in the early 1790s and rose to around £70-£80 in the late 1830s. The thirst for profit, coupled with the erratic and individualistic nature of the process and the pressure on the existing housing stock, led to a chaotic situation and low environmental quality. Since there was no return on land devoted to roads and pavements, these were kept to a minimum. Development was uncoordinated. Incomplete streets became a feature of the townscape in the East End, and high density housing often abutted open fields.

While some of the central streets became more elegant in appearance, the character and quality of other parts of the town, notably to the east and on the south side of the river, declined significantly. Kirkgate, for example, once one of the most important streets in the town and the residence of wealthy people, witnessed a radical change in fortunes. The 1806 Guide observed: 'It is extremely popular. But as fashionable people, and with them fashionable tradesmen, have deserted it, this street has fallen into some kind of disrepute, and if it did not happen to be the road to the Church, it would be a place, to adopt a fashionable phrase, which nobody knows.'[62] G. A.Cooke's description of Leeds in 1819 drew attention to other areas which had deteriorated:

> The town of Leeds is in general well-built, almost entirely of brick; but its different quarters form one with another a striking contrast. The houses upon the rivulet [Sheepscar Beck] are mean, and the streets and lanes, dirty, crooked, and irregular, emitting disagreeable smells form the dyeing-houses and the different manufactures. The southern edge of the town is almost as disagreeable; and though it has some good houses, it has to be said in great measure to have the appearance of a prison.[63]

While the pleasant northern slopes above Leeds were becoming the happy haven of the upper-middle classes, the townships to the south were being scarred by the onset of industrialisation. The historian Parsons in 1834 gave a vivid description of such a transformation:

> Holbeck was formerly a pleasant village, possessed of no claims to rural seclusion, yet still surrounded with verdant fields and thriving popular plantations, and enjoying an atmosphere uncontaminated and salubrious. Only one habitation interrupted the continuity of the prospect between the village properly so called, and Leeds. But now the scene is completely reversed. Holbeck is one of the most crowded, one of the most filthy, one of the most unpleasant, and one of the most unhealthy villages in the county of York. Numerous lanes swarming with a vast population now unite it with Leeds, the trees have been cut down, the meadows have disappeared, and the air is loaded with black vapours which issue from its immense manufactories.[64]

Governing the Town

The task of governing a town whose population, buildings, and industry were expanding at such a phenomenal rate was formidable. There were no provincial precedents and the rulers of Leeds observed the similar plights of Manchester, Birmingham and Liverpool with sympathy and great interest. Where would it all end? How should such novel problems of urban growth be tackled? The archaic and fragmented machinery of local government creaked under the strain. Townspeople attempted to cope with each new problem and situation by adapting the existing machinery of local

The Court House, Park Row, built 1811-13 (architect, Thomas Taylor).

government or, more often, introducing measures specially designed to deal with individual matters. The rulers of Leeds had to respond to two principal challenges. The first was the need to bring some semblance of order to the physical environment of the town, whose unrestrained and chaotic growth was seriously threatening its ability to function. The second was to maintain law and order, in a situation where the existing system appeared on the verge of collapse under the strain of the huge increase in the population.

Regulating the Streets

To meet the challenge of the rapidly changing physical environment townsmen looked to the improvement commission which, as we have seen, had been set up in 1755. In 1809 a new Improvement Act recognised the growth of the built-up area by extending the commissioners' powers of lighting, paving and cleaning the streets to one mile beyond the town bars.[65] It also addressed the growing congestion of the streets. For the first time, the commissioners were empowered to buy up and demolish property for the widening of the streets, provided the owners were in agreement, and three-quarters of the rate payers approved. The special rate levied for the purpose was not to exceed five pence in the pound in any year. The provisions of earlier Acts to clear the pavements of animals, carts, barrels and workers making and repairing goods were also strengthened. The disruption and danger caused by the heightened building activity was met with regulations making it compulsory to put hoardings or fences around buildings being erected or repaired, and lights around temporary holes in the roads and pavements. The increase in the number of public buildings was also dealt with by giving their trustees the responsibility for having their street frontages swept and cleansed. Pressure on the town's water supply was reflected in additional powers for the waterworks commissioners to reduce wastage of water from the system. Loopholes in the 1790 Improvement Act were closed by miscellaneous provisions ranging from the most earthy aspects of life to the most frolicsome. In future, 'no Necessary House or Bog House, Dunghill or Midden' was to be emptied except between 10.00 at night and 5.00 in the morning, while people were to be fined if 'they shall make Bonfires, or shall set fire to or let off any Gun, Pistol or cracker, or throw any Squib, Serpent, Rocket or Firework whatsoever within any of the said Streets, Lanes, Entries, public Passages or Places.'

When the problem of congestion in the central streets became acute, townsmen were obliged to overcome their instinctive abhorrence of taxation and interference with private property rights. Under a new Improvement Act in 1824 the commissioners were given what many must have regarded as draconian powers.[66] The effective strangulation of Briggate could not be allowed to continue. The Moot Hall and the block of buildings behind it, known collectively as Middle Row, had long been considered a public disgrace and half-blocked the street. Briggate was 63 feet wide at the front of the Moot Hall and, after deducting the hall's 26 feet frontage, a mere 23 feet and 14 feet respectively remained on either side for the roadway, known as Back Shambles, and the alleyway through the Shambles. Demolition had been delayed for years by the absence of alternative accommodation for judicial business and the butchers' shambles, and the lack of public funds to buy out the property owners and provide replacement facilities. The erection of the Court House (1809-13) and the Bazaar and Shambles (1823-25), at long last, resolved the accommodation problem. The 1824 Act gave the commissioners the powers to compulsorily purchase Middle Row with money raised by a special 'Middle Row Rate' levied between 1825 and 1833. The great achievement of removing Middle Row was completed in 1825 at a cost of £15,000.[67]

The Act empowered the commissioners to raise still larger sums of money and this enabled them to tackle another scheme much advocated during the market mania of the 1820s – the removal of the cattle and wholesale fruit and vegetable markets from the central streets. The commissioners eyed the site of the vicarage and its field in Vicar Lane with great interest. In 1822 most of the fruit and vegetable sellers moved from Briggate to the Vicar's Croft on an informal basis, but in 1825, with their new powers, the commissioners were able to purchase the land. In 1826 the commissioners took over the running of the site and one of Leeds' greatest institutions, Kirkgate Market, was born. Edward Parsons commenting in 1834 was unrestrained in his approval:

> The Vicar's Croft, as the plot of ground was called, which is now occupied by the market, was a field immediately adjoining the Vicarage on the West side, overgrown with weeds, and the common receptacle of every abomination. How such a place was ever suffered to exist in the centre of a large town, is indeed astounding.[68]

The new market he said was 'one of the most signal and beneficial improvements ever accomplished in the town of Leeds.' The Vicar too had good reason to feel pleased, for his parishioners used part of the £8,000 sale receipts to buy him an excellent mansion – 6 Park Place. To use Parsons' words, the future Vicars of Leeds 'were thus removed from the midst of smoke, and filth, and noise, to one of the best, one of the most respectable, and one of the most salubrious situations in the town.'[69]

Another of the major objectives of the 1824 Act was to repeal the 1755 Improvement Act and those parts of the 1790 and 1809 Acts relating to lighting, cleansing, improving and widening the streets, and to consolidate and extend these powers in a single Act. New clauses showed a gradual edging towards more of the town planning and development powers and controls of a modern local authority. From now on the commissioners were empowered not only to widen roads but create new ones. In future they could negotiate with people erecting new buildings about 'the line, direction or mode of building' and offer them financial inducements to improve the line of the street. All buildings were now to be built perpendicular from their foundations.

A host of miscellaneous matters were covered. In future the commissioners were empowered to contract with the gas companies for gas lights, they could fine people who annoyed others by exercising 'ferocious dogs' without muzzles, or playing football or cricket in the street. Such miscellaneous offences as throwing rubbish in the River Aire, placing unsecured plant pots on window ledges, and fly-posting, were added to the existing list of prohibited activities subject to fines. The commissioners were to be responsible for putting up street names and numbering every house and building within one mile of the bars. Finally, the Act created the basis of the modern Leeds taxi service: the commissioners were empowered to license a controlled number of hackney coaches, chaises, cars, gigs and sedan chairs to ply for hire in the town and borough. These were strictly regulated with their charges and manner of operation set out much in the way they are today.

During these years there were significant improvements to the town's central streets in addition to the removal of Middle Row. The clearing of Briggate greatly improved the north-south flow of traffic through the town, but the east-west flow was also a great problem because of the narrowness of Boar Lane. The critical improvement needed was the creation of a good route through from Kirkgate to the west side of the town. This process began with the creation in 1806 of Commercial Street on the west side of Briggate directly opposite Kirkgate. This elegant street, 'one of the most commodious avenues into Briggate', was initially known as Bond Street. The east-west route effectively was completed when the old prison half-blocking the Briggate end of Kirkgate was demolished, and Commercial Street was extended futher east by the addition of Bond Street, running across Park Row past the Philosophical Hall into Infirmary Street and West Street. When all this was achieved, Parsons commented enthusiastically that Boar Lane, 'always incommodious and narrow' was relieved of a large proportion of the carriages and passengers by which it was formerly crowded, and the convenience and appearance of the town was much improved.[70]

The Improvement Commissioners were involved in street widening schemes in Duncan Street, Quebec Street, Mabgate, Swinegate, Vicar Lane and Water Lane, and created Market Street in 1833.[71] The new turnpike roads made the town much more accessible from afar, as we have seen, but a key associated physical benefit to the town centre itself was their toll bridges. The river, though so vital to the town's commercial success, was also a handicap because it was a barrier between the north and south of the town. Until 1812, those wishing to bring vehicles across had to use Leeds Bridge, or go to Kirkstall Bridge two miles to the west, or Swillington Bridge five miles to the east. Parsons praised the opening of the Wellington Road, a venture which afforded 'a new entrance to the town from the West, and soon became the great avenue for carriages and passengers from Bradford, Halifax and Manchester'.[72] At the same time he admired the elegance and usefulness of Wellington Bridge (1818-19). Monk Bridge built in 1827, however, he noted, though 'intended to be the commencement of a new line of road to Halifax, has not yet produced any revenue to its projectors, nor yet has it involved any advantage to the public.' In contrast, he revealed the physical problems posed by the river in the central area and how one 'far humbler and meaner' footbridge had produced a dramatic improvement:

> The whole district known under the general name of School Close [the area between the large bend in the river and Swinegate] was formerly a confused labyrinth of scattered buildings, through which the numerous passengers proceeding to Holbeck from the western parts of the town, threaded their way to an inconvenient and sometimes dangerous ferry. A wide street [Neville Street], however, was opened from Mill Hill to the river, materially increasing the value of property in the neighbourhood, while a footbridge over the river, opened in 1829, formed the long awaited communication with the vast population on the southern side of the Aire.

The Struggle for Law and Order

The important task of controlling and governing the people of Leeds remained in the hands of the members of Leeds Corporation in their capacities as Justices of the Peace. As the town grew the amount of business for the magistrates' attention multiplied. In 1775 to better facilitate their work the Rotation Office had been established in Call Lane, where the magistrates could meet in 'rotation' to hold petty sessions to deal with fairly routine matters of town administration and dispense justice concerning less serious offences.[73] By 1796 the volume of business was such that the corporation established a new Rotation Office in the upper storey of a building in a yard off Kirkgate. The ground floor accommodated the Leeds Library, and alongside were dwellings for the chief constable and the librarian.[74]

By 1806 petty sessions were held there every Tuesday and Friday. The prison which had been erected at the top of Kirkgate in 1726 remained the sole place of confinement for criminals, and an unpleasant one at that. The 1806 *Leeds Guide* observed that it 'contains five or six dark and miserable apartments, without so much as a sewer or a fire place in the whole prison; none of the windows of this gloomy mansion are glazed, so that in winter, the unhappy wretches who lodge in it must be perished with cold'.[76] In practice, prisoners were rarely held there for more than one or two days, long stay persons being despatched to the West Riding House of Correction at Wakefield.

Accommodation for dispensing justice was very inadequate. The Moot Hall, where both the West Riding and the borough quarter sessions were held, was in a ruinous state, and the Rotation Office and prison were inconvenient. But with the corporation having very little money, what could be done? It was the threat of the permanent removal of the West Riding quarter sessions from Leeds, because of the poor accommodation, which seems to have tipped the balance.[77] In 1809 powers were obtained within the Leeds Improvement Act of that year to finance the building of a court house and prison. The building was financed by levying a 'Court House Rate' and a grant from the West Riding magistrates. The Court House, built in Park Row in 1811-13 at a cost of over £10,000, was designed by Thomas Taylor the noted northern architect, and in its day was the most handsome secular building in Leeds. The main court room could hold 800 people and in the basement was the prison with 13 cells and space for four fire engines. The Court House

Mary Bateman, the Yorkshire Witch. On the table is the bottle of poison used to kill Rebecca Perigo.

became the centre of public administration in Leeds being used not only for judicial business, but also for the meetings of the Improvement Commission, the Watch Committee, the Bankruptcy Commissioners, Turnpike Commissioners, and a range of public meetings.[78] Its cost proved higher than anticipated and in 1815 powers were obtained in another Act to raise more funds.[79] This Act, however, had a much greater significance for the future of law and order.

During the eighteenth century the town was 'policed' by a handful of constables, who were unpaid townsmen selected annually to assist the Justices in their spare time, supplemented by a night watch. In 1798 the police consisted of a chief constable and nine others.[80] By 1815, however, several notorious cases and a rising tide of crime had convinced leading townsmen that a much more effective system for the apprehension and conviction of criminals was required. Perhaps the most infamous Leeds criminal was Mary Bateman, 'the Yorkshire Witch'.[81] After a successful career in petty crime, she attracted fame as a fortune teller, charging people to see her remarkable hen which had allegedly laid an egg with the inscription on it – 'Christ is coming'! But her wickedness knew no bounds. In 1803 she poisoned three people living in a draper's shop near St Peter's Square. As soon as they were dead, she plundered the house and shop. Her evil career came to an end in 1809 when she was hanged at York for the murder of Rebecca Perigo, the wife of a Bramley clothier. The case is particularly interesting because she was convicted on forensic evidence – that of Thomas Chorley, a Leeds surgeon. He revealed not only that Rebecca Perigo had been poisoned, but that a bottle found in Mary's possession and the pudding which she made for Rebecca contained rum, oatmeal and arsenic. Mary Bateman's body was dissected in public to raise funds for Leeds Infirmary! Her skin was tanned and small pieces were given to applicants.

Crime was rife, and even some of the élite were tempted by the prospect of easy profit. In 1815 Joseph Blackburn, one of the most respected attorneys in the town, was found guilty of forging a £2 stamp on a mortgage deed. For this he was hanged at York, dying in absolute agony as the noose slipped from its normal position.[82]

The major importance of the 1815 Act was that it authorised the Justices to use the Court House Rate to meet the expenses of people who brought criminal prosecutions and served as witnesses. It also allowed them to pay reward money to people 'discovering, apprehending, prosecuting or convicting offenders'. Above all it put the police on a professional basis. The magistrates were empowered to appoint and to pay 'such reasonable salaries' as they thought proper to a Chief Constable, and other 'persons as they shall judge necessary or proper to be Deputy Constables, Assistant Constables, and Constables' within the borough. In addition they were to employ 'such able-bodied men as they shall judge necessary, to be employed as Watchmen or Patrollers within the Town of Leeds, and within One Mile of the Bars there of' and to provide them with 'all manner of 'Watch-houses, Watch-boxes, Places, Materials, Apparatus, and Arms'. Special constables could also be appointed from time to time as a back up. The watchmen, patrollers and special constables were authorised to arrest disorderly people.

Baines commented in 1822 that 'The Police of the Borough, without an undue exercise of rigour, or any ostentatious display of authority, is efficient and well regulated ...A Nightly Watch and Patrol has been established which are very vigilant in protecting the persons and property of the inhabitants'.[83] To modern eyes, in spite of Baines' praise, the full complement looks exceptionally puny – three salaried officers: the Chief Constable, the Deputy Constable, and Beadle/Assistant Constable, 10 part-time unpaid constables for the town and another 10 for the out-townships. In 1826-7 the constables for the town consisted of a bricklayer, 2 joiners, 2 maltsters, a butcher, a baker, a tailor, a shoemaker and an auctioneer.[84] It was no doubt the paid daytime Patrol of 16 men and the Night Watch of 38 men, which gave the feeling of security.

Periodically, however, the watchmen were a source of complaint. In 1825 the *Leeds Intelligencer*, in rebutting an attack on its criticism of the watch, replied:

> We did not complain of the watchmen *patrolling* the streets [in winter they were stationary], but for giving way to their gregarious tendencies and becoming *stationary* in groups of three or four for hours together in *one* street ...Lately four or five of these peripatetic guardians were found sitting in the middle of the night on the steps of a single house.[85]

The efficiency of the night watchmen was very poor and many had to be discharged because of old age and feebleness.

The townspeople of Leeds were horrified by the antics of bodysnatchers who sold bodies to 'medical gentlemen' for dissection. In May 1826 a regular watch had to be kept on the parish church burial ground in an attempt to deter 'the men with spades'. In November 1831 police seized as suspicious package that had been placed on a coach waiting in the Rose and Crown Yard, Briggate. Inside the box, addressed to 'Mr. Ben Thompson, Mail Office, Edinburgh', was the body of a young man, later identified as Robert Hudson. One of the grave robbers turned King's evidence and John Hodgson the ringleader was imprisoned.[86]

Criminal statistics show a rising tide of crime in the town between 1830 and 1835. In 1835 2,025 males and 391 females were brought before the borough magistrates, one-third of the offenders being between 15 and 21 years of age and another third between 22 and 31 years old. The offences consisted of 604 felonies (stealing), 751 drunk and disorderly, 515 vagrants, 391 assaults, and 155 other offences.[87] Robert Baker, the Leeds doctor, observed that:

> The classes of persons who stand prominent as violaters of the law are butchers, blacksmiths, bricklayers, clothiers, woolcombers, dyers, joiners, masons, machine makers, tailors, watermen and weavers. It is true, however, that these trades are the most numerous ...but it seems that certain classes, and especially those above named, are more addicted to intemperance and dissipation than the others.[88]

Undoubtedly, the feelings of insecurity suggested by the efforts to provide a better organised police force were partly associated with the large-scale migration of people into the town. Of the increase in population between 1801 and 1841 from 30,669 to 88,741, approximately two-thirds was the result of in-migration.[89] As far as the ruling élite was concerned the town was becoming full of strange faces. There was also the problem of beggars or 'vagrants' as they were termed. Baines noted in 1822 that a 'Vagrancy Office' had been established in Vicar Lane in 1818, as an appendage to the police, to suppress vagrancy. All vagrants found begging in the streets were sent to the establishment where they were lodged overnight and the next morning sent out of town to the place of their destination. Baines felt the 'office' was very beneficial to the town: 'The number of street beggars has, in consequence, greatly diminished, the common lodging-houses are no longer crowded haunts of vice and infection, and the number of crimes has probably decreased.'[90] Later evidence will suggest that Baines was very over optimistic about the state of the lodging houses, but undoubtedly the Vagrancy Office did have some impact. In October 1823 the *Leeds Intelligencer* noted that over the previous three months 315 vagrants had been lodged and relieved at the office, and 17 lodged and not relieved, at the expense of £8 1s. 6d.[91]

The Battle for Political Power

Outside the corporation and the magistracy, the other centre of administrative power in late Georgian Leeds was the parish vestry – the meeting of the ratepayers of the parish, which appointed the Improvement Commissioners, the churchwardens, the highway surveyors, and the workhouse trustees. The spheres of influence of the corporation and the vestry overlapped. The mayor, recorder and Justices of the Peace for the borough were automatically members of the improvement commission in addition to the members elected by the vestry. Similarly, the membership of the Workhouse Board, which administered poor relief in the parish, was made up of the overseers (chosen by the corporation in its capacity as borough magistrates) and the churchwardens and workhouse trustees (elected by the vestry). At the same time the members of the corporation as magistrates supervised the work of parish officials such as the highway surveyors and the constables.[92]

These potentially confusing and conflicting arrangements caused few difficulties while the Tory-Anglican merchant community dominated all aspects of local government. But, as we have seen, local industry diversified in this period and wealth spread well beyond the close knit ranks of the Tory-Anglican corporation. Whig-Dissenters, like John Marshall, were debarred from public office by their religion and the Tory-Anglican stranglehold on positions of power. Until the 1820s the Whig/Liberal Dissenters seemed to be resigned to their exclusion from the corporation, perhaps because its members acquiesced in them becoming Improvement Commissioners, Waterworks Commissioners and members of the Workhouse Board. Certainly, the names that were to dominate Liberal politics for a generation – Baines, Clapham, Rawson, Pease, Bower, Lupton – can be found in the lists of Improvement Commissioners who were elected by the vestry, without Tory opposition, each January. The usual pattern from around 1815 onwards was for 15 out of the 18 vacancies to be filled by Liberals.[93] In the 1820s, however, amidst the mounting national agitation for the reform of both local and national government, the attitude of the Whig-Dissenters changed. They became determined that they would have an effective voice in local affairs by right, and that Tory dominance would become a thing of the past. Heated political rivalry developed for control of the bodies and offices appointed by the vestry because these appointments were made by the votes of the ratepayers, in contrast to the self-electing nature of the corporation and the magistracy.

The election of the eight churchwardens for Leeds township generated quite amazing political controversy in the 1820s and '30s. The post of churchwarden was one of high social status and carried considerable power over parish affairs. The churchwardens held the balance of power on the Workhouse Board, and significantly were responsible for levying church rates. These rates were used to maintain the fabric of the parish church, and to finance church expenditure on items such as ecclesiastical dues, running costs such as wine, bread, gas and printing, and capital costs such as the purchase of equipment and the enclosure of burial grounds. Quite naturally Dissenters baulked at having to pay for the support of the Anglican church and in 1819 a concerted attack on church rates was begun by Edward Baines. The ensuing battle was remarkable.[94] From 1828 the Liberal Dissenters took control of church finances by voting in a majority of Liberal churchwardens, and between 1828 and 1833 never fewer than five of the eight wardens were Liberals. The annual elections became riotous occasions. In 1834 four thousand people attended the vestry led, according to the *Intelligencer*, by 'Marshall's mill people in full array under the command of their overlookers'.[95] The end result was that after 1835 a church rate was never again levied in Leeds.

The battle for the control of the Workhouse Board was perhaps of much greater importance than that for the offices of churchwarden because the cost of the Poor Law for Leeds township was the largest single item of expenditure in local affairs. The poor rates exceeded £34,000 in 1832 compared with church rates of less than £2,000.[96] During the eighteenth century, the Workhouse Board, composed of the Overseers of the Poor, the Workhouse Trustees and the churchwardens, had evolved a structure which unconsciously recognised the informal balance of political forces within the township. The 13 overseers were appointed by the magistrates and all but two or three were invariably Tory. The 12 trustees of the workhouse were elected by the vestry, and were invariably Liberal. The balance of power on the board was held by the eight churchwardens of Leeds township, who, as we have seen, until 1827 were all Tory. From 1828, as a result of the Liberals' success in electing the churchwardens, the Tories lost control of the board. In law the control of the administration of the Poor Law lay in the hands of the overseers alone, and therefore in 1835 the Tory overseers attempted to win back control by excluding the trustees and churchwardens from the administration of Poor Law affairs. The 2,000 ratepayers who turned up at the vestry were extremely angry for as they saw it, the old system had for 100 years 'contained the Intelligence and philanthropy of men of all parties in the service of the town and has given the ratepayers a wholesome influence over the expenditure of their money.'[97] The Tories were temporarily victorious, but their joy proved very short-lived, for the reform of the corporation in 1835 was to change the balance of power once again.

The King's Mills, Swinegate. In 1839, the Corporation bought up the feudal rights for £13,000, at last freeing householders from having to bring their corn to be ground at the mill.

Tithes and Tolls

The 1820s and '30s saw an end to two residual medieval obligations on Leeds townspeople. In 1823 the practice of the vicar levying tithes on the townspeople ended when they were commuted in return for an annuity of £500 per annum purchased with £14,000 raised by subscription and the magnificent gift of £7,000 from Richard Fountayne Wilson.[98] The other medieval obligation related to the manor of Leeds. The manor, was almost an irrelevance in late Georgian Leeds though the shares in the lordship held social prestige. Robert Sangster purchased his by auction in 1837 for £695, regardless of the fact that each share only yielded £17 per annum. At this time four of the nine shares belonged to Christopher Wilson of Ledstone, and one each to Lady Francis Gordon, Revd F.T.Cookson, Christopher Beckett, the Executors of the late Christopher Bolland, and Robert Sangster.[99] The one contentious matter was the survival of the soke of the manorial mill. In 1815 the lessees of the mills, Sandford Nevile and John Sowden, went bankrupt and the business was taken over by a proprietor who was determined to enforce the letter of the law. The *Leeds Intelligencer* carried a notice warning that:

> Whereas divers resiants and inhabitants of the Town of Leeds within the SOKE OF LEEDS OLD MILLS have from time to time neglected to bring their Wheat, Oats, Barley, Peas, Beans, Malt, Pulse etc. to the said Mills to be ground ...and also have used flour, oatmeal, malt etc. not ground at the said mills. Notice is hereby given that [anyone] found evading the soke ...will have Actions commenced against them. N.B. Any persons using hand mills or querns for the grinding of Corn, crushing of Oats, splitting of beans, peas etc. will be proceeded against.[100]

There seemed to be no escape even for small domestic users of flour. The *Leeds Intelligencer* advised: 'we would offer one hint which may save many from incurring penalties. It is that they be cautious in knowing that their servants, who may be sent to buy flour, buy such as has been ground at these mills.'[101]

This feudal obligation persisted right into the 1830s[102], but at long last in 1839 it abolished by the corporation's purchase of the soke for £13,000 under an Act of Parliament.[103]

Working-Class Lives

Incomes and Expenditures

Between 1790 and 1840 there was an enormous expansion in the ranks of the lower orders or those who now became known as the working classes. Particularly for those working in factories, life was very hard. Working hours of twelve hours or more a day, six days a week, were common. In the 1790s wages varied from around 9s. a week for unskilled labourers to 18s. for a skilled craftsman. By the end of the 1830s these had risen to around 11s. and 26s. respectively, but much if not all of these increases had been gobbled up by rising prices. Perhaps just over a quarter of male workers earned over £1 per week by the late 1830s. These were mainly the skilled workers chiefly in the expanding industries, such as mechanics, iron moulders, and mill-wrights, earning 20s. to 26s. Below them, just under a third of men, including wool-sorters, bricklayers, dyers, hatters and coopers, earned 15s. to 20s. The lower half of the male workforce, including handicraft workers, such as shoemakers, tailors, weavers, woolcombers, and labourers earned around 11s. to 15s. It is difficult to estimate family income from these figures, for women and children often worked. For a brief period of the family cycle, with a wife and two children at work, the family income might be increased by up to £1 per week; though, of course, family members added to family expenses.

Housing took quite a low proportion of income compared with today. In the 1790s two-thirds of the dwellings in the town were rented for less than £3 a year or 1s. 2d. a week. Most cottages were let for 6d. a week, while larger dwellings might be had for 9¼d., and single rooms for 3d. or 4d. A skilled weaver or craftsman, such as a stone mason or carpenter, receiving 15s. to 18s. who paid 9¼d. for a cottage, spent no more than 5 per cent of his income on accommodation. By 1839 housing had become significantly more expensive with rents having doubled or trebled. Two-fifths of cottages were rented for less than 2s. a week, but three-fifths now commanded between 2s. and 4s. In 1842 it was reckoned that 'the rates and rent of a house ...absorb ...perhaps a fifth or sixth upon the average wage of all classes of artisans, and labourers of all descriptions'.[104]

Accommodation was very cramped by modern standards. The cheapest dwelling house was single storey from three to six yards square, while the typical cottage had two rooms, one up, one down, around 14 feet square. The more prosperous artisan's cottage had larger rooms at around 20 feet square. Many houses had cellars which, as single room dwellings, were to become notorious for their squalor in the 1830s and '40s. The back-halves of these famous Leeds back-to-backs were reached by a narrow tunnel, to avoid the 'waste' of space involved in running a back alley behind a whole terrace.[105] Life was primitive. Most houses lacked a decent supply of clean water, being dependent on distant wells, standpipes or on costly water purchased from vendors, whose dawdling carts toured the streets touting for trade. The very alkaline, soft bore hole water which was dispensed from the carts was known locally as 'Spa water' and was much

Waterloo Court, Quarry Hill. Typical of the maze of alleyways and courtyards in the area. Note the woman looking out of the window of her cellar dwelling.

used for making tea.[106] The 'necessary' was often little more than a wooden screen round a bucket or pit, and some neighbourhoods completely lacked 'out-offices'.

The experience of living in these houses, however, varied considerably. The essential factor was location. The early houses, as we have seen, were crammed into the central parts of Leeds and the 'East End' of the town, where high densities produced ghastly conditions. Elsewhere on the outskirts of the town

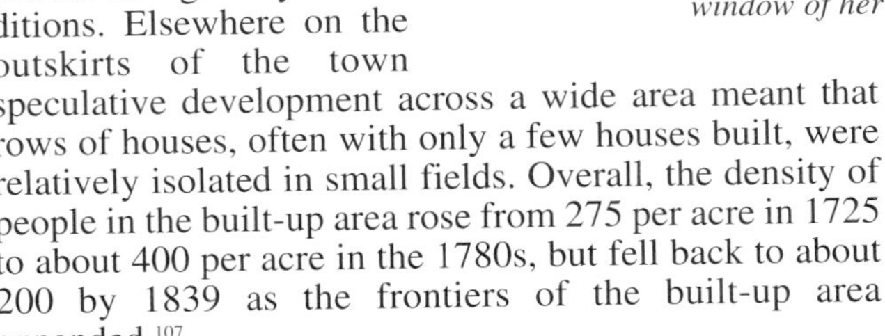

speculative development across a wide area meant that rows of houses, often with only a few houses built, were relatively isolated in small fields. Overall, the density of people in the built-up area rose from 275 per acre in 1725 to about 400 per acre in the 1780s, but fell back to about 200 by 1839 as the frontiers of the built-up area expanded.[107]

After paying rent, how far did a working-class family's income go? An estimate of the minimum necessary household budget of a family of five was made by Humphrey Boyle, a Meadow Lane shopkeeper in 1832:

	£	s.	d.
Rent 2/-, fuel 9d., candle 3d.		3	0
Soap 3d., soda 1d. blue & starch 1½d			5½
Sand, black lead, bees wax &c.			2
Whitewashing a cottage twice a year			½
1½ stone flour for bread – 2/6d.		3	9
¼ stone flour for puddings – 2/8d. st.			8
Eggs 2d., yeast 1½d.			3½
1½ pints milk per day at 1¼d.		1	1
¼ stone oatmeal 2/2d.			6½
1lb. treacle 3½d., 1½lb. sugar at 7d. lb.		1	2
1½oz. tea at 5d., 2oz. coffee 1½d.			10½
5lb. meat 6d.		2	6
Vegetables 1d. per day			7
salt, pepper, mustard, vinegar			2
7pts. beer 1½d.			10½
Water			1
Schooling for 2 children			6
Reading			2
Wear & tear in beds, bedding, brushes, pots, pans, & other household furniture			6
Clothing: husband 1/2d., wife 8d.		1	10
each child 4d.		1	0
TOTAL	£1	0s	3d

At a total of £1 0s. 3d. weekly expenditure at a time when about half the working men of Leeds earned 11s. to 15s. per week, not surprisingly he concluded that 'the earnings of workmen are not sufficient for the proper support of their families.'[108] He took no account, however, of the wages of other members of the family, nor of the possible contribution of lodgers. But on the other hand he took no account of spending on drink and entertainment. Without the wages of wives and offspring, the majority would not have had sufficient to support their families even in this austere way. For those with less, it is not difficult to imagine the priority of sacrifices - clothing, schooling, furniture, household utensils and maintenance. The skilled worker earning 20s. to 26s., on the other hand, might have significant room for manoeuvre.

For all, the threat of unemployment created severe feelings of insecurity. The economic crash of 1825/26 wreaked havoc. The town's Committee for the Relief of the Unemployed Poor reported in July 1826 that early in May one-quarter of the working population of the town had been wholly unemployed, and one quarter were employed from one to three days per week. Only half were 'so employed as not to require assistance'. They concluded that:

> Since that time the condition of the Poor is not at all improved, but on the contrary, the long period during which many of them have been unemployed has generally exhausted their little savings and in too many cases transferred their clothes and furniture from their own dwelling to the hands of the clothes-dealer, or the shop of the Pawnbroker.[109]

Similarly, in the period of depression from December 1831 to mid-March 1832, 2,548 Leeds families received poor relief.[110]

Given the uncertainties of life the prudent skilled worker might save money and make provision in a variety of ways for such events as sickness and death. Friendly Societies flourished in the town. The 1837 *West Riding Directory* noted that:

> Among the *Provident Institutions* in Leeds are ...many BENEFIT SOCIETIES, and SECRET ORDERS; including Lodges of *Free Masons, Druids, Odd Fellows, Ancient Romans, Foresters,* &c. These institutions for mutual aid in cases of sickness, infirmity and death, amount to nearly 300 in the town and surrounding villages, and are the means of keeping many families from the workhouse, and of materially reducing the amount of human misery.[111]

Typical was the Philanthropic Society founded in 1796. A subscriber paid 1s. entrance fee followed by 18 monthly payments of 1s. 3d., at which point he was deemed to be a 'free member' and entitled to benefit. He received 9s. a week when sick and confined to his room, 6s. when able to walk out, £3 should his wife die, or should he expire his wife would receive £9. Special rates had to be paid by those aged 35 to 40, and once over 40 the risk of death was regarded as so high that people were ineligible for membership.[112] Many Friendly Societies organised free medical treatment for members. Of course many working people either could not afford to join the societies or did not feel inclined to do so.

The Leeds Savings Bank was established in 1818 'for the beneficial investment of the savings of the humbler classes of society'. It did well. In 1834-35 from its profits it was able to erect a handsome building in Bond Street,

No. 74, Kirkgate, near the junction with Wharf Street. The Ancient Order of Foresters Court No. 1 was established here in 1790.

and by November 1836 it held £202,143 belonging to 5,019 individuals, 11 Charitable Societies and 33 Friendly Societies.[113] For some, insurance was the thing. By 1837, 35 fire and life insurance companies had offices in the town.[114]

Destitution and Ill-health

But so far we have been dealing with the provision for hard times made by the better off workers. For the poorer paid workers at times of unemployment and destitution, poor relief was their recourse. Contrary to today's popular myth, however, in the late-Georgian period it was highly unlikely that they would end up in the workhouse. The Leeds overseers' minute books show that between 1784 and 1795 the workhouse in Lady Lane accommodated on average only 150 people when it was at full stretch and, though it was extended a little before 1806, it could still only accommodate 250 in 1837. Until the close of the eighteenth century the workhouse population consisted of the old, the sick and the very young, and the overriding popular opinion was that these unfortunates deserved a certain measure of comfort and care.[115]

Attitudes seemed to harden considerably over the next thirty years as the population rose and the mass unemployment experienced in the 1820s began to weigh heavily on the pockets of the middle classes. New ideas and additional institutions came into being. While the middle classes accepted that temporary unemployment had become a permanent feature of the town, increasing distrust and hostility were shown to workhouse inmates who required aid for extended periods. Once more the idea that the workhouse gave shelter to many who would not work rather than could not work gained prominence. In 1831 a correspondent to the *Leeds Intelligencer* called for 'the separation of the deserving from the undeserving, of those who have been driven to this last refuge, save one, of suffering humanity by unavoidable misfortune, from those whose pauperism is the deserved termination of a life of idleness and profligacy'.[116] In 1833 the inmates of the workhouse were referred to in the *Leeds Mercury* as 'impudent, lying, revengeful and intolerably lazy'.[117]

The Leeds Workhouse at the junction of Vicar Lane and Lady Lane, painted by John O'Rourke in 1832.

The House of Recovery, Vicar Lane, built 1802-4.

The typical experience of the poor was 'out-relief' administered by the Workhouse Board. Eden's figures in his *The State of the Poor* show that in 1795 while there were 154 people in the workhouse, out-relief was being given to 415 regular and 251 casual, outdoor poor.[118] Since the cost of supporting a person in the workhouse was around 50 per cent higher than giving outdoor relief, there was no financial advantage in increasing its population. The board did its best to apprentice out pauper children who came to the workhouse, but inhabitants seemed very reluctant to take them.[119] Individual out-relief payments were incredibly small. In the mid-1820s a man or woman of 66 years or more received 3s. a week, and those aged 54-65 years received a mere 2s. If people had some other means of support payment could be as low as 1s. 6d. Even in cases of the most acute distress, payments never exceeded 3s. 6d.[120]

Relief might come in other forms. In 1822 Baines drew his readers attention to 'the Benevolent, or Strangers' Friend Society for the relief of the distressed of all religious denominations and especially those who have no other helper', which had been formed by the Wesleyan Methodists in 1790. Likewise, he noted the Soup Establishment which was 'in active operation only in times of peculiar stress'. At the same time there were also 'two or three Clothing Societies, by which benevolent females of the more opulent and middle classes supply their poor neighbours with garments, which these fair Samaritans make with their own hands'.[121] Harrison's, Potter's and Jenkinson's almshouses continued to flourish but between them they accommodated only 82 women from the most 'respectable' poor.[122]

At times of illness, by the standards of the day, the Infirmary continued to provide good medical care for a small section of the needy, but since its foundation it had refused admittance to those suffering from infectious diseases. In 1801 an alarming fever epidemic spread through the town. Hundreds were affected and some medical personnel died. In December attempts were made to establish a House of Recovery, based on similar lines to the successful venture in Manchester. Eventually land was made available in Vicar Lane and a spacious house, capable of holding 50 patients, was constructed. It opened in November 1804 with three physicians, three surgeons, an apothecary and an inspector, the latter gentleman's responsibilities ranging from the swift removal of victims, to supervising the fumigation of the patient's lodgings. The Revd T.D.Whitaker was impressed by the effectiveness of the institution, noting that:

> In 1802 whole streets were infected nearly house by house: in one court of crowded population typhus raged for four months successively; whereas in 1814 thirty different streets produced no more than 60 cases of typhus and scarlatina conjointly. There rarely occurs an instance of a second person being infected when the first has been removed.[123]

Such optimism was to be short lived, for in 1826, and more seriously in 1832, cholera visited the town. The House of Recovery could not cope with the magnitude of the 1832 outbreak. A Board of Health offered free medical care for all, and a specialist cholera hospital was created in St Peter's Square. Of nearly 2,000 cases, just over 700 died. Dr. Baker produced an excellent report highlighting the fact that the disease was most prevalent in the squalid areas where there was inadequate drainage, sewerage and paving.[124]

In the 1820s the Infirmary and the House of Recovery were complemented by a number of institutions. In 1821 a small General Eye and Ear Infirmary was established in St Peter's Square (where the West Yorkshire Playhouse now stands), and in 1824 the Lying-in Hospital for 'poor married women' was founded in the same square. In no way could the Infirmary cope with the huge growth of this population, and so emphasis was placed on the treatment of people as outpatients.[125] In 1824 Leeds Public Dispensary opened its doors for business in part of the House of Recovery. Only the sick received free treatment and one of the trustees had to vouch for the patient, except in cases of emergency. In 1828 it moved to North Street and by 1837 it was treating 3,000 patients a year.[126]

An increasing population, poor environmental conditions, the lack of a balanced diet and dangerous working conditions combined to create an ailing population. Huge demands were placed on the members of the medical profession. Training was inadequate, and courses in anatomy and physiology were infrequent and of variable quality. Dr. Baker, in his 'Remarks on the Abuses in the Infirmary at Leeds' (1827) drew attention to the scandalously high apprenticeship fees charged by medical gentlemen, who frequently neglected their pupils. In 1826 C.T.Thackrah established an excellent private school of anatomy at 9, South Parade, but petty jealousy ensured that it never received official recognition. Finally, in 1831, an enthusiastic group of doctors and surgeons founded the Leeds School of Medicine. To begin with they hired rooms in the Dispensary, but such was the success of the venture that in 1834 it moved to a fine house in East Parade close to the Infirmary.[127]

Education and Belief

So far attention has been given only to the physical needs of the working classes. What of their cultural and intellectual needs? In particular what of their education? The moral and cultural improvement of the working classes was a subject dear to the hearts of the middle classes and many of the working classes were eager to better their lot in life. The first significant breakthrough for the working classes was the rise of Sunday Schools, first introduced in Leeds in 1784. Rapid growth followed. By 1817 few churches or chapels were without Sunday Schools and in all they catered for some 5,000 pupils. While the principal impetus probably came from middle-class enthusiasm to impose morality and good behaviour on potentially 'dangerous' working-class communities, large numbers of working-class parents regarded the schools as important aids to the improvement of their children. Unlike today, Sunday Schools provided a full day's teaching and concentrated on giving instruction in reading, writing and arithmetic rather than scripture to children aged 8-14 years. Indeed, there was great opposition from pupils, teachers, and parents when attempts were made to stop secular instruction in Wesleyan Sunday schools in the late 1820s.[128] By 1837 there were more than 50 Sunday Schools in the town. The Sunday School Union established in 1816 comprised 20 schools and 4,000 scholars belonging to the Independents, the Baptists, the New Connexion Methodists, and the Revivalists; the Church of England had 13 schools with 3,400 scholars; the Wesleyan had 11 schools with 2,700 scholars; and the Associationist Methodists had 10 schools with 1,900 scholars – in all, an impressive total of 12,000 pupils.[129]

The next significant advance was the establishment of a modicum of elementary day school education through the founding of the Royal Lancasterian School in 1811 and the National School in 1813. These schools for children from the age of 8 years old to 11 or 12 taught reading, writing and arithmetic on the 'Madras System' whereby the teacher taught monitors (older children, usually aged 10 to 12 years), who then taught the younger children. The Lancasterian School, named after the educational pioneer Joseph Lancaster, began in the old Assembly Rooms in Kirkgate in 1811 and moved into a purpose-built school room in Alfred Street in 1812. The school taught 500 boys and, as an interdenominational institution, soon became linked to the British and Foreign School Society founded in 1814. The National School, on the other hand, was a Church of England school opened in 1813 in 'a handsome and convenient' building just off Kirkgate in Wharf Street on the site of the Tythe Barn.[130] Here 320 poor boys and 180 girls were taught. The establishment of the National School in some respects made the Charity School redundant and in 1815 its trustees converted it to an institution for clothing and bringing up girls of not less than 12 years of age, as household servants. The old building was demolished and the present building in St John's churchyard erected.[131]

The foundation of the Lancasterian and National schools was the start of an intense rivalry between the religious denominations in Leeds for the hearts and minds of the working classes. By 1837 there were an additional three Lancasterian schools in the town, another National school at Woodhouse, and four Wesleyan day schools. In 1826 the Leeds Infant School Society was established and by 1837 this had provided three schools for children from around two to seven years old.[132] The principal intent behind all these schools was philanthropic and their middle-class supporters aimed to provide instruction either free or at very low fees. The *West Riding Directory* commented in 1837:

> Ample provision is made in the town by posthumous charity and the annual contributions of the benevolent, for the instruction of the children of the poor in PUBLIC DAY SCHOOLS, conducted on the *Lancasterian*, *National* and *Infant systems*, besides which, here is a richly endowed *Grammar School*. These institutions now afford instruction to upwards of 1,400 children, exclusive of those who attend four large *Wesleyan Day Schools*, in School Street, Sweet Street, and at the Bank, where they each pay weekly, 2d. for reading and writing upon a slate, 3d. for accounts and writing on paper; and 4d. when instructed in grammar.[133]

But these respectable day schools educated at the very most only one-fifth of the town's working-class children of school age, and for only a short period in their lives. Many children from working-class families appear to have received no day school education at all. The Corporation's Statistical Committee Report in 1839 reckoned that 4,670 of these children of school age (school age apparently being regarded as between 4 and 9 years old) were not attending school, while, 6,759 of them (from whom we must deduct those in the schools already mentioned) were in private fee-paying schools, often of very low quality. Commenting on the 154 day schools in the town the committee noted that 112 were kept by females; knitting and sewing were taught in 107, and writing and accounts in only 74, though reading was taught in all of them. 'Many of those in which the charge is under 3d. a week', it warned, 'bear the character of dame schools only, and are in fact more for keeping children out of danger during the employment of the mother, than for the purpose of real education. In very few is anything taught beyond the elements of the English language, by persons more fitted to be scholars than teachers'. The committee reckoned that 82 of the schools charged less than 3d. per week, 27 – 3d. to 6d., and 45 – 6d. and above per week. On its estimate that those charging 6d. and above served the middle classes, this suggested that there were 109 schools, plus 20 factory schools, to provide for the education of approximately 11,500 working-class children between the ages of 4 and 9.[134] This grossly inadequate provision emphasised the importance of the Sunday Schools to working-class education.

The contribution of factory schools was very limited. The Factory Act of 1833 controlled the hours of textile workers of between 9 and 18 years. Children of between 9 and 13 years had to provide evidence that they had attended school part time in the previous week. No child who was 8 years old or under was allowed to be employed. The restrictions in the Act encouraged the establishment of factory schools. John Marshall's factory school was thought exemplary by contemporaries, but in 1839 the 20 factory schools in the town educated only 360 children and this on a half-time basis. Moreover, evidence of a mere two hours schooling per day was sufficient to meet the requirements of the Act.[135] The town had areas of depravity and destitution which seemed almost impossible for any school to reach. Indeed, many paupers on poor relief staunchly resisted the provision of education for their children. In response a couple of 'Schools of Industry' had been established at the turn of the eighteenth century, off Briggate and at Quarry Hill. One survived into the 1830s.[136] Without doubt, the effectiveness of all the town's schools was much reduced by low and irregular attendance, poor teaching, and very large class sizes.

Attempts to provide a modicum of education for adults were of very limited success. In addition to a few Adult Schools giving instruction on Sunday evenings, the most prominent initiative was the Mechanics Institute established in a large house in Park Row in 1825. Its object was to supply 'at a cheap rate, to the different classes of the community, the advantages of instruction in the various branches of science which are of practical application to their several trades or occupations'.[137] Though it built up a good library and its accommodation included a lecture room and class rooms, it was not a success. In 1837 it was commented that 'it has not received that liberal support from the rich, nor that general countenance from the mechanics it justly merits'.[138]

Attendance at Sunday Schools gives some indication of the importance of religion in the lives of a significant section of the working classes. Without doubt the impact of the Anglican Church on the lives of the working classes declined in late-Georgian Leeds. Even out of its pitifully low addition of seven new churches only three were in working-class areas. In 1837 the new vicar of Leeds commented that in practice the established religion in Leeds was Methodism.[139] In 1839 the township's 17 Methodist chapels accommodated 16,340 sittings, whilst the 9 Anglican churches could only hold 13,235 sittings, many of which were empty on Sundays. The other denominations between them came close to surpassing the Church of England, the 6 Independent chapels had 6,030 sittings, the 3 Catholic chapels had 1,970, and the 5 belonging to other sects contained 3,876. On a day-to-day basis, however, religion must have figured only in the margins of the lives of many working-class people. In 1839 the North, North-east and East Wards of the town, which were inhabited chiefly by the labouring classes, had only 11,850 sittings for a population of 43,046.[140]

Children and the Mills

No matter how much the middle classes might wish to 'civilise' the working classes through education and religion, the fact remained that for those who worked in the factories, daily life offered the prospect of brutality, horrific accidents and excessive hours of labour. Where possible, women and children were employed because they were cheaper and more submissive. Marshall and Co. preferred children of 11 or 12 years old to those of 9 or 10 because 'they do more work and require less superintendance', and made no apology for the 69 hours a week worked by these youngsters.[141] To maintain production targets and high productivity, overseers quite often resorted to violence. The frightening atmosphere for children in the mills was revealed by evidence given to Parliamentary inquiries. John Marshall, celebrated for his factory school, came in for severe criticism in evidence given to a Parliamentary Committee looking at working hours in 1832. The following year Mark Best, an overlooker, repeated his claims to a Royal Commission, telling the commissioners that there was a good deal of beating at Marshall's:

> They were beat with a strap. We had them of all ages in our room ...I think that those who strapped them most were best liked [by the employers]. I mean they were like to get more work done that way ...There has been many a one badly beat with strapping in my room. I have seen them flogged while they had marks on them, boys and girls both.[142]

One of the most notorious cases was that of David Trenham a young boy who worked as a screwer at Hives and Atkinson's Bank Mills in 1832 and died shortly after being refused permission to visit 'the necessary'. An older youth, John Fawcett, who was in charge of Trenham, described how the boys were only allowed to go to the privy in rotation and how they were strapped if their work was not up to scratch:

> I've seen it once or twice, where a spare hand had a spite against a boy, that he would not let him go [to the privy] in his turn. There were always buckets in the room at that time. I have never had much of Anthony's [the overseer's] strap ...I've seen Anthony strap the other boys, when they would not do as he telled them. If the boy's not up to time, the machine-minder would shout 'Stricks', and then the screwer would get strapped sometimes, or be telled to look sharp. It makes the machine-minders mad, if they are not up with their work: it makes bad work and has to come back again, and then he cries 'Stricks' and the overseer comes up and straps the screwer.[143]

Factory owners denied maltreatment of employees. Indeed, following the Trenham incident it was claimed that the strap was no longer used in Bank Mills, but a

Dr Robert Baker meeting the mill girls.

grim picture emerged of badly ventilated buildings filled with dangerous unboxed machinery, where people were expected to work excessive hours for poor pay. Not surprisingly, overworked children were often involved in horrific accidents. A doctor working at Leeds Infirmary in 1823 related the fate of one such unfortunate in his notebook:

> CASE 31: H. P. female aged 11 admitted 2nd January at 6 o'clock p.m. for a compound fracture of the Tibia and Fibula of the left leg with simple fracture of the right leg. Accident happened by the Girl's leg being caught in a revolving part of the machinery ...Under all these circumstances it seemed quite impossible that the Girl should recover exempting by amputating the left limb above the knee. The mother obstinately refused Amputation. The feet and legs were wrapped up with warm flannels and bladder bottles of hot water applied and frequently renewed. The child had a partly comfortable night and seemed a good deal revived. Amputation was therefore performed.[144]

A fortnight later the girl died from gangrene. Not surprisingly, these experiences had a brutalising effect on the character of significant sections of the working classes.

Robert Baker, a factory inspector as well as a doctor, felt that the massing of workers in towns, especially in company with those types of workers who ranked high in the criminal statistics, had a very bad effect on adults and particularly young people. He contrasted the life and manners of the mill girls who lived in the country with those of the mill girls living in the town:

> The mill girl from the country, within three or four miles of Leeds, is seemly in her person, and generally decorous in her deportment. If the question is asked where she lives, she tells you with civility; and if enquiry be made about the habits of her parents, they are found to be poor but industrious persons, living upon low wages, coming into the market together, and leaving it again so as to be home not later than eight at night. Take on the other hand, a mill girl from the town; she leaves her work and hastens to her associates, with whom during the day she has planned some project for the evening; her father is at the public house; her mother, thus left alone for months, has herself become careless in her person, and almost reckless in her habits; the daughter thus has no one to guide her; her associates at home and abroad are abandoned [i.e. given up to vice]; eventually she becomes so herself and is lost to all sense of decency. Many thus become independent and ungovernable and are avoided by those overlookers who have the sense to notice this difference and the courage to apply their wisdom.[145]

Working-class leisure and pastimes

Evenings and weekends (though most people worked on Saturdays) provided the working classes with a little time to relax and escape from the rigours of everyday life. The pleasures of the working classes were often ones of which the middle classes gravely disapproved. Inns and alehouses were much frequented by the working classes, though middle-class people like Humphrey Boyle viewed them with distaste. 'If less was spent at the public house', he observed, 'there would be a much greater degree of comfort in the workman's cottage than is to be met with at present.'[146] James Atkinson's apprenticeship indenture of 1823 clearly stated that 'Taverns or Alehouses he shall not frequent, unless it be about his said Master's business', adding 'At Dice, Cards, Tables, Bowls or any other unlawful games he shall not play.'[147] Despite such opinions the number of alehouses in Leeds almost doubled between 1826 and 1836. The relaxation of the duty on spirits had led to major problems of drunkenness and the Beerhouse Act of 1830, designed to lure the drinker away from the consumption of spirits, simply eased the availability of alcohol through more relaxed licensing regulations. The Temperance Movement tried to help the ordinary citizen cope with an alcohol free life. Many of the worst cases of abuse in society were blamed on the demon drink. Physically too the public houses and beer houses often were disgusting places. Robert Baker complained in 1839 that 'the offensive practice which prevails, of allowing the conveniences outside public houses to remain exposed to view cannot have escaped even the most casual observer'.[148]

Brothels too provided a particularly unsavoury aspect of both working-class and middle-class 'recreation'. Prostitutes plied for trade, notably in the North-West Ward of the town, where Baker noted that there were 37 houses of ill fame, three of which were 'dens of the most infamous description'.[149] The efforts of the Guardian Society established in 1821 to 'reclaim females who had departed from the path of virtue' were of limited effect, but its work was much encouraged by William Hey's provision of 'commodious accommodation' in St James' Street.[150] Baker counted 98 houses of ill fame as a whole in the town, 72 in the North, North-East and East Wards (see p151 for plan of ward boundaries). He considered this number quite low compared with other towns of comparable size, but he thought it was on the increase. 'No doubt a great deal of this arises from the congregations that exist in those filthy streets' he remarked.

For many working-class people gambling remained a great passion, but one which the authorities wished to discourage. Despite the efforts of many notable townsmen, a new race course was established in 1824 at Haigh Park (on the south side of the River Aire, opposite where Skelton Grange Power Station now stands). In July 1823 the *Leeds Intelligencer* had been 'happy to announce' that a race course would soon be open, but by February 1824 it changed its tone when the magistrates and around 200 prominent townsmen publicly condemned such races as 'a most serious evil and highly injurious to the morals and industry of the people'.[151]

Boyne later reflected that the races were 'only attended by the veriest scum of society' but this was not the case.[152] When the first races took place in June 1824 the *Intelligencer* was obliged to admit that 'several highly respectable gentlemen, though a very small proportion of the genteel population of Leeds', were present in the crowd of 15-20,000 people. Even Mr. Lepton Dobson, the mayor three years earlier, had been present. A ball was held on the opening evening and the theatre was specially open during the event.[153] The *Leeds Mercury* commented:

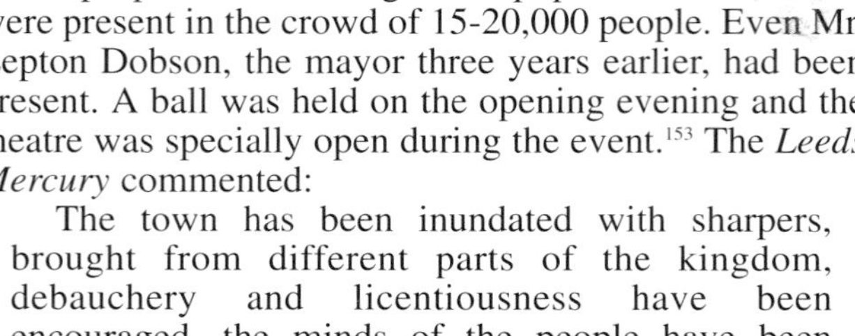

A woodcut from the top of the race list for the Haigh Park Races in 1824.

> The town has been inundated with sharpers, brought from different parts of the kingdom, debauchery and licentiousness have been encouraged, the minds of the people have been unsettled and their morals are in a fair way to being contaminated. A disposition for gambling, so foreign to the prevailing habits of the people of Leeds, has already begun to display itself, and the industry of the labouring classes has suffered a shock from which it will not speedily recover.[154]

The *Intelligencer* was shocked by 'the extensive sale of the most loathsome and obscene prints by the fellows who are employed in vending the Race Lists'.[155] Despite the addition of further attractions like wrestling, the races foundered through lack of support and finished for good in 1830. It must, nevertheless, have been a hard choice for members of the middle classes whose consciences struggled between the religious demands of living a highly moral life and the wish for gaiety and entertainment.

Bathing in the river was a pastime which children and youths enjoyed even if it could hardly be described as 'harmless' in view of the polluted state of the water. A contemporary recalled bathing in the early 1830s at Monk Pits, where the Dark Arches now stand, and at 'Sand Pits', Crown Point, before the building of the bridge, and at Aire Street. Monk Pits he recalled was the favourite spot for boys who could not swim because there were stepping stones across the river.[156]

The circuses, travelling zoos and 'curiosity' shows which regularly visited the town were a major attraction for the working classes, and no doubt some of the middle classes too. Wombwell's Menagerie was very popular though its visits were often tainted by the death of some of its exhibits or other unfortunate mishaps. In November 1823 the black bear escaped and entered the Union Inn on Briggate, where it proceeded to ransack the bar and kitchen. The customers barricaded themselves in the next room until help arrived.[157] Circuses became more sophisticated during the period. In 1807 they used the open ground at the bottom of Commercial Street, where the public were invited to view 'a great Variety of amusements ...by a troup of Equestrians not excelled by any other in the World.' Mr. Kite demonstrated the art of tight rope dancing, whilst Miss Buckley performed on the slack wire. Mr Harris was to 'exert himself in a particular manner on a single horse with whips, handkerchiefs etc.'[158] Artistry of a different kind was provided in September 1812 by Madame Tussaud, whose collection of 'The Grand European Cabinet of Figures ...Modelled from Life' occupied rooms in the house opposite the Royal Hotel.[159]

Circus poster for a performance in Alfred Street, Boar Lane, 20 July 1813. Boxes were 2s., Pit 1s. and Gallery 6d.

Balloon ascents proved a popular diversion which all classes of society could enjoy. In September 1823 two rival 'astronauts' arrived in the town. W.W.Sadler was to make his ascent from the Coloured Cloth Hall, while Mr Green was to set off from the White Cloth Hall. Mr Green had arranged with the gas company to fill his balloon first, much to the annoyance of his opponent, who attempted to inflate his balloon with experimental equipment. The inflated balloon had a 'mean and miserable appearance' and the ascent was not spectacular, unlike Mr. Green's which was hailed as 'one of the most splendid sights ever witnessed'. Mr Green eventually alighted in a field near Gainsborough, but unfortunately a strong wind blew the costly balloon across the Channel to Belgium![160] The White Cloth Hall yard was also used for firework displays and in August 1815 Signor de Montfort, the Prince Regent's Pyrotechnical adviser organised a magnificent exhibition of Chinese fireworks.[161]

The King's birthday, news of foreign victories and declarations of peace continued to be excuses for wild festivity. There was a whole week of rejoicing in early April 1814 'in consequence of the present happy change in the state of affairs, and the prospect of a general Peace.' Several processions took place but by far the best consisted of the workmen in the employ of Messrs. Gott and Wormald, at Bean Ing, 'who paraded the streets with a fleece and other emblems of their manufacture, after regaling plentifully on roast beef and ale, by the liberality of those gentlemen, who caused an ox to be roasted whole'. In the meantime, the London Royal Mail coach drove out of town with 'lighted flambeaux', and the guard was decorated with 'ribbands'. At eight in the evening the whole town was illuminated with special lamps, the most spectacular display being at Denison Hall, the home of H. Wormald, where 6,000 were hung in festoons and arches. At Bean Ing the latest gas lamps were used to make the shape of a Crown and Anchor, and all this because of the prospect of peace![162]

Middle-Class Comfort

The Industrial Revolution in Leeds not only produced a more distinctive 'working class', but greatly increased the number and diversity of the townspeople who could be regarded as 'middle class'. The useful, but at times simplistic, approach used in earlier chapters of dividing Leeds society into a ruling élite of merchants, bankers, lawyers, surgeons and other professionals, on the one hand, and clothiers and associated cloth workers on the other, can no longer be sustained. Throughout the seventeenth and eighteenth centuries there had always been in between these two groups a range of town-based independent craftsmen, shopkeepers, publicans and providers of urban services, not to mention people of independent means. Between 1790 and 1840, as a result of the growth of the town and its industry and commerce, their ranks were swelled by the host of individuals involved in trade and commerce, retailing, property letting, and above all manufacturing, noted at the start of this chapter. Some, as we have seen, came to challenge and, at times, to overhaul in wealth even the most prosperous woollen merchant.

By the 1830s the town's trade directories, in practice a catalogue of townspeople with some measure of independent economic status, encompassed around one-quarter of heads of households in the town.[163] But if the list is limited to professionals, proprietors of businesses, and self-employed retailers, the 'middle class' constituted at the very most one-fifth of the population. The more restricted group denominated by contemporaries as 'the opulent and influential inhabitants', or 'the leading inhabitants' – the very affluent upper middle class who ran local affairs – constituted perhaps only one-twentieth of the town's population.[164] It is virtually impossible to draw a precise boundary between the middle classes and the working classes for there was a great no man's land between those firmly identified as either middle- or working-class.

Middle-Class Homes

The lifestyle to which the upper middle classes of Leeds aspired is epitomised by the homes and domestic habits of Benjamin Gott and John Marshall; though none could match their very great wealth. Both men sought physical statements of their new found riches and importance in the community. Traditionally, the most successful merchants had tried to emulate the lifestyle of the local gentry and thus purchased land away from the township, often becoming 'Lords of the Manor'. In 1804 Gott purchased the Armley House Estate, ideally situated near the heart of his business empire with imposing views over the Kirkstall Valley and the burgeoning town of Leeds.[165] The house was old fashioned and too small for a large family with ten children, and the grounds comparatively small and unprepossessing. In 1810 he employed Humphrey Repton, the country's leading architect and landscape gardener, to submit plans for extending the house and landscaping the grounds. Repton skilfully made use of the magnificent views and suggested the prospect 'as a picture seen from the inside of a house.' Trees were planted accordingly, so that Armley Mills formed part of the view stretching out to the busy town of Leeds 'softened by its misty vapours.'

Robert Smirke, the architect of the British Museum, was employed to transform the homely Armley House into a magnificent Greek Revival villa. Noting Repton's advice that 'the great world of London must be copied at a distance of two hundred miles', the interior decorations and furniture were ultra modern. Gott now had the perfect environment in which to display his sculptures, paintings, prints and books. He commissioned important works of sculpture by Joseph Gott and Francis Chantrey, his portrait was painted by the influential artist Sir Thomas Lawrence, and he became a founder member of the Northern Society for the Encouragement of Fine Arts, one of the country's most important commercial outlets for contemporary artists. The county élite, leading members of the local community, internationally renowned artists, sculptors, industrialists as well as dignitaries from home and abroad, were all entertained in his magnificent home.

Armley House, the home of Benjamin Gott. The core of the house was built in 1781 for Thomas Woolrich. Gott purchase it in 1804, and employed Sir Robert Smirke to convert the house into a splendid Greek Revival villa. Today it is better known as Gott's Park Mansion.

As John Marshall's wealth grew he moved his family from Meadow Lane to New Grange in Headingley, which he leased in 1795.[166] Here he set about improving the grounds. He spent lavishly on paintings and books. John Russell, the famous portrait painter, had painted two portraits of John and his wife in 1802. Marshall's 12 children born between 1796 and 1815 were all given first class educations. The new house had 12 servants to cater for the needs of the family. His wife had been a school friend of Dorothy Wordsworth, the sister of the famous poet. They regularly visited each other and John soon appreciated the beauties of the Lake District. Fond of solitude and walking, he decided that the Lake District not only provided a healthy environment in which to bring up his family, but also granted him instant social acceptance, something denied his family in Leeds. He purchased large tracts of land in the area and moved into his new home, Hallsteads. In Leeds he bought Headingley House in 1819 as a winter residence, but he spent an increasing amount of his time away from the town. In 1825 he bought a house in Grosvenor Square so that he had a London base, and after 1830, because of ill health, he frequently visited the resorts of Bath and Leamington Spa.

Gott and Marshall, of course, represented the pinnacle of Leeds wealth and lifestyle. In the next tier down, as we have seen, smoke pollution and fear of infectious disease in the town prompted other wealthy inhabitants to move

St Peter's Square, Quarry Hill. These houses for the middle classes were financed by a terminating building club. Each house had a small, railed front garden. Today its site is occupied by the West Yorkshire Playhouse.

to the delights of the leafier suburbs to the north, though throughout the period 1790-1840 the Park Estate remained an upper-middle-class stronghold, its fine brick houses accommodating merchants, manufacturers and professional men. Land in the suburbs was relatively cheap and plentiful, allowing for the construction of large detached villas with impressive grounds, or stylish terraces with more modest gardens. In 1814 the Commercial Directory listed only four architects, by 1837 there were ten practising in the town.[167] They designed residences for the wealthy which could be elegantly furnished. An advert in the *Leeds Mercury* in 1822 revealed the vast array of furniture, china, glass and carpets to be found in the homes of the middle classes:

> PRESTON PLACE, WOODHOUSE-BAR
> VALUABLE & MODERN FURNITURE,
> CHINA GLASS &c. &c.
>
> Messrs Lumb respectfully announce that they are instructed to offer for SALE by AUCTION (by order of the Proprietor, Mr, Hernaman, who is Removing his Private Residence) on the Premises of No 2, Preston Place, near Woodhouse Toll Bar, on Monday and Tuesday, the 28th and 29th June, the elegant, Modern and Valuable DRAWING and DINING ROOM FURNITURE, comprising Twelve handsome Rose Wood Chairs with loose Cushions, Elegant Sofa; a Pair of beautiful Rose Wood Card Tables; Rose Wood Sofa Table; Pair of Foot Stools; Window Curtains, with Gilt Cornices, elegantly fitted up with Drab Moreen and Light Blue Silk Borders and Fringe; Ten and Two Armed handsome Mahogany Patent Dining Chairs and a Table, with Three Leaves; Elegant Mahogany Side Board; Mahogany Loo Table with Claw Feet; beautiful Mahogany Cabinet Book Case; Fire Screen; Brussels Carpets; Fenders; Fire Irons; Hearth Rugs; Window Curtains elegantly fitted up with Crimson Moreen and Silk Fringe; Foot Stools, &c. &c.
>
> Also the excellent BED ROOM FURNITURE, including handsome Mahogany Four Post and other Bedsteads, with Hangings and Window Curtains to match; Prime Feather Beds; Hair, Flock and Wool Mattresses; Carpets; Mahogany Ward-Robe; Pier, Swing and other Glasses; Painted Wash Stands, Dressing Tables and Chamber Services; Mahogany and Painted Chest of Drawers, &c. &c. Various Rich Cut Glass; beautiful China and Earthenware in Dinner, Desert and Tea Services; Vases; Ornaments, &c. Hat Stand; Passage Lamp, various Kitchen and Brewing Utensils, &c.
>
> The sale to commence each day at Eleven o'Clock and Catalogues, which may be had of the auctioneers, 19 Cheapside, Leeds, will be ready for Delivery on Friday the 25th instant.
>
> Messrs LUMB respectfully inform their Friends and the Public, that the above furniture having been supplied by the first Manufacturers in the Country, is of a very superior Description – is in the best possible condition; – and the Whole is the genuine Property of the Vendor.[168]

The vast majority of the middle classes did not join the upper middle classes in their move to the Park Estate or Little Woodhouse, and indeed, during this period, though the north-western area of the town had a high concentration of middle-class families, a scattering of all tiers within the middle classes could be found in all districts of the town. Men like James Green of Musgrave Fold and Eli Whiteley of Prospect Terrace off York Road, a handloom weaving master, needed to remain at the hub of their business, and could not move to the suburbs.[169] Shopkeepers, who had nearly always lived over the shop, did begin to abandon the rooms above and move to more select accommodation that was to be found nearby in places like St Peter's Square, but some stubbornly remained residents of the central streets. A good example was John Heaton, bookseller and stationer, who in 1815 resided in the house attached to his shop and warehouses at number 7 Briggate. His son's biographer noted:

> The parlour, or common sitting-room, was on the ground floor, at the side of the shop, and looked out upon the busy main thoroughfare of Leeds. This little sitting room was the last room of the kind in Briggate. It was not converted into a shop until after the death of Mr. Heaton; long before which time every other ground-floor apartment fronting Briggate had undergone that change. Behind the little sitting-room was the kitchen, and over these two rooms were two bedrooms. Over the front shop was a large apartment, which in the time of the Binnses had been the pride of the house, and had been a really handsome drawing-room. John Heaton, however, had no occasion for a drawing-room, and no desire in this matter to follow the example of his predecessor. So the room stood empty during the

whole of his occupancy of the premises, and was used as a play-room by his children. Behind this apartment was the spare bed-room, appropriated to visitors, whilst the whole of the upper floors, with the exception of certain small rooms devoted to servants, were employed for business purposes. One large room was filled with an immense number of second-hand books, of which Mr. Heaton had now a very valuable stock; another was used as a store-room for paper. At the back of the house was a pleasant little garden, where seventy years ago [c. 1815] the lilacs bloomed luxuriantly and flowers could be reared. Though in the very centre of the town, the home was not an unpleasant one; and it is worth being described, as it was undoubtedly a type of the house of the prosperous tradesman at the beginning of the present century. Nobody then was ashamed of 'the shop', and John Heaton, like thousands of other men whose children have risen in social rank, had duly mastered the old proverb 'Keep to the shop and the shop will keep you'.[170]

Kemplay's Academy for Young Gentlemen, St John's Place. Originally built for Matthew Wilson in 1720, today it is Nash's Fish Restaurant.

Education and Culture

Education and culture set the middle classes apart from the working classes. The Leeds élite became increasingly frustrated by the inability of Leeds Grammar School to give their sons an appropriate education. The decline of pupil numbers at the school by the early years of the nineteenth century was in some degree a reflection of poor teaching and discipline – the school minutes refer to the assistant master (the usher) employing a substitute, and to 'great insubordination' amongst the boys primarily in the upper school around 1796-1806, but the chief reason was the restriction of the school curriculum to Latin, Greek and divinity.

An attempt by the Pious Uses Committee (as the school trustees) to remedy the situation in the interests of the merchant community brought the school to national prominence with the famous Leeds Grammar School case. The intention of the committee to employ additional teaching staff to teach writing, accounts, French and German, in the face of opposition from the headmaster, Mr Whiteley, led to protracted wrangling. This was eventually resolved by a landmark judgement in the High Court of Chancery by Lord Eldon in 1805 which hindered the progress of similar schools all over the country. He ruled that such action was illegal because it ran in the face of the founder's intention that the school should be devoted to 'teaching grammatically the learned languages'. He noted:

> This is a scheme to promote the benefits of the Merchants of Leeds. It is not that the poor Inhabitants are to be taught reading and writing English, but the Clerks and Riders of the Merchants are to be taught French and German to carry on a Trade. I fear the effects would be to turn out the poor Latin and Greek scholars altogether.

In spite of the judgement the curriculum was slowly improved by the addition of maths. Writing and maths began to be taught on a limited basis but for other subjects most gentlemen's sons had private tuition. In those days Leeds Grammar School boys rose early. From March to November school ran from 6.30 a.m. to 5.00 p.m., with a one hour break at 8.00 a.m. and a two-hour break at noon. In winter, school started at 8.30 a.m. Boys were admitted at age 8. By 1816 numbers were back up to 99, and stood at 97 in 1830.[171]

The Leeds Philosophical Hall, Park Row, built 1819-22 (architect, R.D.Chantrell).

But the instruction of 100 boys was a drop in the ocean. The majority of the middle classes had recourse to a host of private schools, such as Kemplay's Academy, and private tutors. The Corporation's Statistical Committee Report of 1839, as we saw earlier, identified 45 middle-class day schools in the town, charging 6d. a week or more. Four of these were in the Mill Hill Ward, 9 in the North-West Ward and and 21 in the West Ward; the areas where the middle classes congregated in large numbers.[172]

The opening of the Music Hall in Albion Street in 1792 provided a venue for a range of cultural as well as social activities. Internationally renowned artistes visited the town, perhaps the most famous being the violinist Paganini who, in January 1832, performed for two nights; the *Leeds Intelligencer* stating euphorically: 'He can make it squeak, squall, and laugh and cry, and nearly speak; he can express mirth and sorrow; tragedy, comedy or farce'. The élite nature of the audience was reflected in the price of the tickets which were a staggering ten shillings each – over half a week's wage for many of the working classes.[173]

The establishment of the elitist Leeds Philosophical and Literary Society in 1819 provided a major filip for the cultural life of the upper middle classes, answering dissatisfaction with the town's narrow cultural experience and the fear of social inferiority to the élite of other towns. As one advocate put it in 1818:

> It has long been the subject of surprise to me and

> I believe to many others, that although the town of Leeds is justly celebrated for the number of its benevolent and humane institutions, it can boast of no society for the promotion of intellectual and literary improvement ...There are few large towns where such institutions do not exist or flourish, and they are patronised in many places, much less considerable in extent and much less respectable in the character of the inhabitants, than the town of Leeds.[174]

By 1829 its honorary members could be found in Paris, Cincinnati, London and Edinburgh. Leeds was gaining an international reputation. Its lectures ranged from comment on contemporary issues to geology and the history of Egypt. It provided inspiration and support for Dr Baker's pamphlets which did so much to shape people's understanding of Leeds. Its museum, which forms the basis of today's Leeds City Museum collection, could boast of thousands of natural history specimens, numerous coins, antiquities, busts, ethnographic material from India, North America, the South Seas and New Zealand, as well as cave deposits from Kirkdale and a Prussian wild boar. Perhaps the most prized possession was the magnificent mummy of the priest Nesy Amun, whose 40 layers of bandage were removed by local surgeon Thomas Pridgin Teale, who then carried out a thorough examination. Edward Sanderson George identified the spices and gums used in embalming, and Henry Denny completed a series of five drawings of the mummy. Their activities were recorded for posterity in William Osburn's *Account of an Egyptian Mummy* published by the society in 1828, an astonishing piece of research work.

Yet the society moved away from science, and only a small number of lectures were devoted to the subject. Increasingly, the educational element declined and the society became an aspect of the upper middle class's leisure pursuits. As members moved to the suburbs, lectures were not as well attended.[175] The society's museum was a welcome addition to one established by John Calvert around 1795. Such was the popularity of his exhibition that he moved into new premises in Commercial Street in 1827, where the public could view his collection of over 15,000 specimens imaginatively and skilfully displayed in cases, some of which had backgrounds painted by the celebrated Leeds artist Joseph Rhodes.[176]

Middle-Class Benevolence

Much of the spare time of the middle classes was taken up with town affairs and voluntary organisations. Though numerically small, the affluent group of upper-middle-class families, who lived in the Park Estate, Little Woodhouse and the suburban villages to the north, took most of the initiatives in the political, cultural and philanthropic affairs of the town. Unlike members of the working classes, they had time to devote to occupational, religious, charitable, leisure and political societies where the middle class could be seen to be playing an important role in local affairs, thus boosting their own status in the community.[177]

Those interested in the well-being of the working classes could busy themselves raising funds for Leeds General Infirmary, the House of Recovery, the Lying-in Hospital, the Dispensary of the Child Bed Relief Society. The unpredictability of the local economy, with its fluctuations between prosperity and depression, brought poverty with which many of the middle classes could sympathize. By 1830 there were 14 voluntary bodies collecting money, clothing and food for the needy.[178]

As we have seen, many members of the middle classes took a great interest in education, supporting everything from Sunday Schools and the National and Lancasterian Schools to provision for the Blind, Deaf and Dumb. One of the most noteworthy developments was the creation of the Mechanics' Institute, which despite its title remained very much the preserve of the monied class. As one observer noted: 'One regret needs expression in reference to the Mechanics' Institute, and that is, that the mechanics themselves so much neglect its beneficial uses.'[179]

Charitable giving by the middle classes was extensive. The *West Riding Directory* noted in 1837:

> The stream which flows from the fountain of benevolence in Leeds for the education of poor children, and the solace, poverty, and sickness, yields more than £11,000 per annum, exclusive of nearly twice that amount collected in poor rates ...*The yearly income* of the *Pious Use Property* amounts to upwards of £2,760; the three sets of *Almshouses* to £1,008; the Girl's Charity School to £397; and the Benefactors of Leighton, Baynes, Milner, and Dixon, to £352; making a total of £4,457 arising yearly from these sources of posthumous charity. Other schools and charitable institutes in the town, supported chiefly by subscriptions and collections, and partly by benefactors and legacies, disperse more than £6,500 per annum; of which about £3,200 is expended by the *General Infirmary*; £800 by the *House of Recovery*; £500 by the *Dispensary*, £350 by the *Benevolent Society*; £170 by the *Lying-in-Hospital*; and £60 by the *Eye Infirmary*.[180]

Middle-Class Frivolity

After the seriousness of town affairs and the philanthropic and cultural institutions, there was time for pure pleasure. Less cultured performers than Paganini visited the Music Hall. In June 1824 Monsieur Barnett advertised a 'Performance of the Celebrated Magical Illusion' in which he would 'introduce many novel and extraordinary experiments'. The support act was Monsieur Felix Testot who would perform 'some amazing Evolutions ...with brass hoops, daggers and golden balls'.[181] The Assembly Rooms continued as a major venue for drama, concerts and card playing, but the small ageing Leeds Theatre in Hunslet Lane struggled to retain custom. Plays, documentaries, pantomimes and operatic performances provided a varied programme. In November 1812 the pantomime 'Mother Goose' proved a success. The *Leeds Mercury* review was extremely complimentary. 'The manager promised the public that no trouble or expense should be spared in the production of this piece, and he has in every respect kept his word, for we have seldom seen so much splendour of Scenery, ingenuity of Mechanism, or correctness of acting.'[182] Despite such triumphs, the future of the Theatre remained precarious.[183] The strongly religious members of the middle classes had grave reservations about the theatre. In his book *Loidis and Elmete* written in 1816 the Revd T.D.Whitaker expressed great pleasure that the town 'for the space of four years by gradual dereliction and neglect had suffered its theatre to be shut up'. He proceeded to expand on the wickedness of the theatre and suggested that theatrical entertainment while being 'elegant and fascinating' tended 'to corrupt the principles, to debauch the heart, and above all to dishonour the Almighty'.[184] In 1834 Parsons expressed similar sentiments, declaring that the inhabitants of Leeds drew great credit for the fact that 'although the most splendid theatrical "stars" have been brought to emit their beams within [the Theatre's] walls, it has never exhibited anything like prosperity, and has occasionally been closed for considerable periods'.[185]

Tea gardens became fashionable places of resort. One of the most ambitious ventures was based at Knostrop Hall where the visitor could enjoy 'Tea, Harrogate water, ginger beer, cheese cakes, etc.' in the house's gardens in which 'antique curiosities' proliferated. The more discerning customers could arrive on a barge, accompanied by a military band, and enjoy their tea while listening to the Glee Singers perform 'Here in the Cool Grot and Mossy Cell'.[186] In contrast certain pursuits declined in respectability, with the local newspapers actively discouraging cock fighting and bull baiting. The Leeds Hunt, once a flourishing organisation, was desperate for members by 1810 when a meeting was held 'to determine whether the hounds shall continue'.[187] Innocent pleasures were encouraged and the *1806 Guide* commented that on Sundays the footpath from Leeds to Kirkstall was crowded with well-dressed people.[188] Sunday school outings, chapel meetings and musical evenings were enjoyed by many, while the increasing number of libraries ensured that books were available to an eager audience. The construction of the purpose-built spa baths in Wellington Street in 1819[189] and the Waterloo Swimming Baths, just north of the canal basin, in 1833 enabled the shareholders and subscribers to bathe in luxury.[190] The much improved transport network facilitated travel for leisure. Thomas Butler of Kirkstall Forge, for example, enjoyed the pleasures of the Lake District, Blackpool and Scarborough.[191]

Leeds was certainly a lively place and social facilities were constantly improving. Even a young solicitor's clerk, articled to Bloome and Gatcliffe in Commercial Street, found plenty to occupy his leisure hours in the 1830s. His pursuits included fencing, boxing, dancing, riding and shooting, along with regular visits to the inns, theatre and Literary Institution. He particularly enjoyed 'a most sumptuous dinner' the main courses of which were followed by 'pineapples, grapes, melons, almonds, raisins, walnuts, etc.'.[192] For someone of limited financial means this was an enviable lifestyle and reflects the variety of activities available to the 'middling sort'. Dining out seemed to afford a great deal of pleasure to the affluent middle classes. Certainly, in the 1820s, an opportunity seemed rarely to be missed for a good dinner, particularly where new public buildings were concerned. On the eve of the opening of Leeds Commercial Buildings in 1829 the *Leeds Monthly Magazine* remarked: 'The avidity of the English people for guzzling in public, must be perfectly astonishing to other nations; nothing at all can be done without it. Of course, a public dinner is absolutely necessary to give the opening of these Commercial Buildings proper *éclat*; and accordingly, we see one is announced.'[193]

One wonders how the participants at the Leeds Pitt Club Anniversary Meeting at the Music Hall in 1825 – all the leading Tories of the town, presided over by the Earl of Harewood – managed to walk out of the hall upright after the 32 toasts interspersed by 32 songs and glees![194]

Leeds and National Affairs

Leeds townsmen took a lively interest in the affairs of the nation. The pages of the *Leeds Intelligencer* and the *Leeds Mercury* kept them well informed about national issues. The two Leeds papers in the later years of the eighteenth century were not dissimilar in their content and the political leanings. The *Leeds Intelligencer* in the hands of the Wright family was an arch-Tory paper. It frequently contained paragraphs denouncing the advocates of the reform Parliament and the system of government, and the champions of civil and religious liberty. Towards Reformers and Dissenters it was contemptuous, violent and insulting. The *Mercury* was much milder in its tone but, as Edward Baines, junior, explained, at the end of the century when it was under the control of Messrs. Binns and Brown 'it was felt by the leading men of liberal politics in Leeds to be no representative of their party, but rather more Tory than Whig'.[195] This had changed when Edward Baines, senior, became its proprietor in 1801 with the financial backing of prominent Whigs and of Dissenting townsmen including John Marshall. Thereafter Baines strongly championed causes espoused by the Whig Reformers, thereby stoking up a very lively local debate on important national issues.

It is important for the understanding of what follows to explain that by the 1830s the reformers felt that, although they still supported the free trade views of Adam Smith, the championing of reform and civil

Edward Baines, senior (1774-1848). The famous editor of the Leeds Mercury.

liberties, and the freedom of the individual advocated by Charles James Fox, the term 'Whig' was too closely associated with the aristocracy to be appropriate in the new democratic age. They therefore began to refer to themselves as 'Liberals', a term already in use on the Continent, though it was not until 1868 that the first distinctively Liberal government was formed when Gladstone became Prime Minister.

When Baines took over the *Mercury* its circulation was around 700 copies each week, but by 1804 it had doubled to 1,500. It soon became the leading provincial journal proclaiming Whig-Liberal opinion and by 1829 it was selling up to 5,200 per week. The content was much increased: in 1801 the paper contained around 21,000 words, by the 1840s it was up to 180,000.[196] The bitter political and personalised rivalry between the *Intelligencer* and the *Mercury* was at its height between 1822 to 1833. Indeed in 1824 Alaric Watts, the editor of the *Intelligencer*, sued Edward Baines for libel. When further trouble flared in 1827 Watts gave as good as he got:

> As well might we say that the portly proprietor of the Mercury – the Sexagenarian dandy of Briggate – the Solon of the Leeds Workhouse – the Demosthene of the Hunslet rabble …is still the same poverty stricken adventurer that he was thirty years ago, when he wandered into Leeds, his whole future centred in a "composing stick" and his head as empty of learning as his back was bare of clothes.[197]

The War with France

As a town heavily dependent on foreign trade, few towns in England can have been more concerned about the threat to the nation from France. First came the horrors of the aftermath of the French Revolution, and then the very real need to prepare to defend the country, and the West Riding in particular, against the rampaging French armies. This was undoubtedly the most important national issue to affect the lives of Leeds people for almost a quarter of a century. In February 1793 the French National Convention declared war on Britain. The country was ill-prepared for such a conflict as reduced defence spending had left the army and the navy chronically undermanned. French successes made an invasion of England a distinct possibility and in response central government actively encouraged the formation of local Volunteer Corps. The atmosphere was very tense. The government feared not only an invasion but an insurrection of the working classes who seizing the moment, in imitation of the French lower classes might attempt to overthrow the ruling élite. The Leeds magistrates, in practice the Tory corporation, enthusiastically supported the creation of a group of loyal, armed townsmen who would support them should the lower orders rise up.

By the end of April 1794 two hundred gentlemen had enrolled as members of the Leeds Volunteers.[198] Thomas Lloyd, a popular merchant with experience of Volunteer organisations, was the obvious choice as Commander in Chief. The colours were consecrated and presented on Chapeltown Moor, where the Volunteers went through their manoeuvres and fired three volleys in a manner 'that would have done honour to a veteran regiment.' Under Lloyd's command the corps quickly gained a fine reputation, and the town was lavish in its support. Special dinners, concerts and theatre performances were arranged to coincide with military activity. One of the most spectacular gatherings was in May 1795, when the Volunteers from Leeds, Bradford, Halifax, Huddersfield and Wakefield assembled for three days of combined activity, culminating in the review on Chapeltown Moor. This attracted an estimated crowd of 60,000 spectators. Though not called upon to fight, the Volunteers were often called upon to help extinguish major fires. One of the most dramatic occurred in 1796, when Messrs Marshall and Benyon's mill burnt for three days, with 8 people killed and over 30 injured.

Austria's defeat in Italy and subsequent peace with France in 1797 left Britain feeling isolated and even more threatened. Early attempts to enrol a troop of cavalry from the town had met with little success, but the worsening situation led to a change of heart. In July a 'Riding School' was erected where ladies and gentlemen could be instructed in the exercise of riding by Sgt. Lamb on Tuesdays, Wednesdays and Saturdays, while the other days were reserved for the training of the Volunteer Cavalry.[199] Had the Volunteer Infantry and Cavalry been called away in the event of invasion, the area would have been left undefended, so another group of men formed into an Armed Association. Thomas Butler of Kirkstall Forge offered his services and noted in his diary of 29 June 1798 'Our uniform is to be Scarlet Coat faced with Black Velvet – White Waistcoat – White Linen Pantaloons – Gaiters – Black Stock and a Round Hat.'[200] Benjamin Gott also played a prominent role in this organisation.

By 1802 France dominated Europe, but the British navy controlled the seas, thus limiting French ambitions outside the Continent. Neither side could defeat the other and so a lull in hostilities suited both parties. The Treaty of Amiens was welcomed in the town. Special dinners, balls and concerts were organised, along with a general thanksgiving service at the parish church. The Volunteers, both the cavalry and the infantry, attended the service; the infantry depositing its colours in the church, before handing in their weapons on the assumption that its services would no longer be required. Peace, however, was to be short-lived and in 1803 war resumed with only the Volunteer Cavalry available for duty in Leeds. Members of the Volunteer Infantry were asked to re-enrol and by the end of August over 1,400 men had offered their services. The corps was formed into two battalions under the command of Lloyd. Training began immediately, but it was several weeks before arms (of Prussian manufacture) were available for use. News from the continent was grim. Napoleon had assembled an army at Boulogne and flat bottomed barges were ready to transport his troops across the channel. In November the Volunteers received orders to hold themselves in readiness and to provide 'shirts, shoes and brushes all packed up all ready to prevent any delay in the hour of danger'. The magistrates created 300 Special Constables for use in case of invasion. The immediate threat, however, quickly subsided.

In March 1804 the Volunteer Infantry were invited to offer their services to the War Office and be put on permanent duty until they 'acquired the necessary proficiency in military discipline'. 1,100 men agreed and in April the two battalions went for three weeks' training in York. All appears to have gone well. General Lee expressed his delight at the performance of the Leeds men, and when they marched home, they were met on the edge of the town by cheering crowds and proud civic dignitaries. Training continued on a regular basis until

October 1805, when much of the month was spent at Doncaster on military exercises and manoeuvres. Nelson's defeat of the Franco-Spanish Mediterranean fleet that month forced Napoleon to abandon serious preparations for invasion.[201]

In 1806 the French Emperor changed his tactics to the disruption of British trade. His decrees of 1806 and 1807, coupled with Britain's retaliatory Orders in Council, effectively disrupted trade with the Continent. America placed an embargo on British goods and the situation escalated, making life extremely difficult for the woollen industry. In 1808 the Volunteers were replaced by the Leeds Local Militia. The disruption to trade was so great that in 1808 Richard Bramley and William Cookson, two of the most successful Leeds merchants, both former mayors, went bankrupt. After a brief flurry of activity in 1809 the trading climate worsened. Widespread unemployment, short-time working and high food prices combined to make the lives of the lower orders extremely difficult. As we shall see later, these harsh conditions, especially in 1812, redirected the duties of the Militia from repelling Napoleon to preventing insurrection at home. Happily the progress of the British army under Arthur Wellesley (created Viscount Wellington in 1809), culminating in the Battle of Waterloo in 1815, totally removed the threat of invasion. The people of Leeds could now rest easy and the Leeds Local Militia was disbanded.[202]

Parliamentary Elections and Representation

Parliamentary representation was another matter of major importance to the ability of Leeds to play a part in the life of the nation and to have a say in the country's affairs. In spite of the townmen's deep interest in national political issues, the town had no Members of Parliament. The blatant unfairness and corrupt nature of the political system was demonstrated by the fact that in contrast to Leeds, Aldborough, seven miles from Ripon, with a population of a mere 484 in 1821 and 64 electors (all in the pocket of the Duke of Newcastle) returned two members to Parliament; Boroughbridge six miles from Ripon, with a population of 860 and 74 electors (also in the pocket of the Duke of Newcastle) also returned two MPs; Ripon itself with a population of 4,563 and 146 electors in 1821 also returned two members.[203] The reality of English political life was that in Yorkshire, as in other parts of the country, the aristocracy dominated the selection and choice of the country's representation in Parliament. If the people of Leeds wished to have a say in national affairs they had to do so by influencing the choice of the two MPs who represented the 750,000 people of Yorkshire. This would be no easy task for in the 1820s there were approximately 26,000 freeholders in the county who were entitled to vote, the vast majority of whom did not reside in Leeds.[204]

The first really significant influence Leeds gained in the selection of a county member came in the great contested election of 1807. Whereas in 1806 William Wilberforce and Walter Fawkes had been elected for Parliament without opposition, in 1807, while William Wilberforce was backed by all parties, the Whigs and Tories decided to fight it out over the second seat. The Whig Lord Milton, backed by Earl Fitzwilliam of Wentworth Woodhouse, fought against the Hon. Henry Lascelles, the son of the Earl of Harewood. The 15 days of the poll produced remarkable excitement:

> The county was in a state of the most violent agitation, party spirit being wound up to the highest pitch by the friends of the two noble families, and everything being done that money or personal exertion could accomplish; the roads in all directions were covered night and day with coaches, barouches, curricles, gigs, fly-waggons, and military cars with eight horses, conveying voters [to York] from the most remote corners of the county.[205]

It was reckoned that the election cost Earl Fitzwilliam and the Earl of Harewood upwards of £110,000 each. The Whig Lord Milton just crept in, the final tally of votes being : Wilberforce 11,808, Milton 11,177 and Mr Lascelles 10,990.[206] It was this election which first brought out Edward Baines and the *Leeds Mercury* as a political combatant.[207] The *Mercury* was the leading paper on the Whig side since it circulated in the manufacturing districts where Lord Milton's chief strength lay. The editors of the *Intelligencer* and the *Mercury* lambasted each other during the campaign. Baines took particular exception to an incident in York during the election when a Leeds magistrate, two Leeds merchants and three other well-dressed men, 'discharged a tremendous battery of hissing and hooting at him'. Tempers ran high. In Leeds the mayor Richard Bramley rather unwisely seized a boy who offended him by crying 'Milton for ever'. The populace rescued the lad and so 'hustled' the mayor, that he immediately read the Riot Act, called out a troop of horse soldiers, and ordered them to scour the streets.[208]

Apart from the reform of Parliament and municipal corporations, the major topics aired at public meetings and through the press in this period included the repeal of the Corn Laws, Catholic Emancipation (only from 1829 were Catholics allowed to sit in Parliament or hold public office), the repeal of the Test and Corporation Acts (which until their repeal in 1828 prevented Dissenters from holding public offices such as serving as members of municipal corporations or magistrates), and the wish to end slavery in the colonies.[209]

Baines through the pages of the *Mercury* became extremely influential in Yorkshire politics. In 1826 he successfully sponsored John Marshall as MP for the county – a major triumph for Leeds since Marshall was the first mill owner to sit in Parliament to represent the commercial interests of the West Riding. Likewise, such was his influence that in 1830 the county aristocracy allowed the talented Henry Brougham to stand as their Parliamentary candidate despite the fact that he was not a Yorkshireman. The Tory *Intelligencer* scoffed that: 'The Whig aristocracy of the great county of York have been compelled to succumb to the Bainesocracy of Leeds.'[210]

At the end of the General Election of 1830 the national issues of concern locally were clear. The *Mercury* concluded that:

> The freeholders had at this election most unequivocally expressed their opinions in favour of the following great measures: 1st, a speedy and entire abolition of negro slavery, 2nd, an abolition of the monopoly of the East India company, 3rd, freedom of trade especially in corn, 4th, an extensive and effectual reform in the representative of the people; and 5th, the most rigorous retrenchment and economy in the public expenditure.[211]

In 1821 Leeds, the fifth or sixth largest town in England, came close to gaining its first MPs and, at long last, having its interests directly represented in

Parliament. The electors of Grampound in Cornwall having been convicted of general bribery and corruption, a Bill was brought into Parliament by Lord John Russell to disenfranchise Grampound and to transfer its two seats to Leeds. When the Bill went to the Lords, however, it was modified so that instead of going to Leeds the two seats were allocated to Yorkshire as a whole, thus increasing its representation to four MPs.[212] In spite of this disappointment, the battle to gain Parliamentary representation for the town was now firmly joined. In 1830 a motion to give MPs to Manchester, Birmingham and Leeds was defeated in the House of Commons by a mere 188 to 140.

Leeds finally gained its first two Parliamentary seats in 1832 as part of the wider achievement of Parliamentary reform under the Great Reform Act of that year. Leeds had three groupings which joined in the extensive national agitation for reform between 1830 and 1832. The Leeds Association for Promoting within the County of York the Free Return of Fit Representation to Parliament, was dominated by the urban Whig élite, with Baines in the forefront. It organised petitions, called mass meetings and conducted negotiations with the aristocratic and county Whigs. Meanwhile, the Leeds Political Union, a carefully structured democratic organisation with 'middle-class' and 'operative' members each taking half the committee places, pressed for radical policies once Parliamentary reform had been achieved – abolition of titles, an end to taxes on knowledge, the repeal of the corn laws, and the reform of the corporation. At the same time, the Leeds Radical Political Union, the most aggressive organisation of the three, called for votes for the working classes. At a local level the campaign was seen as an attack on 'the present system of corruption and misgovernment'.[212]

The Reform Act of 1832 gave the borough of Leeds two MPs as well as the vote to all householders, tenants or owner-occupiers of houses rated at £10 or over (that is houses capable of being rented out at £10 per annum or more). The qualification to vote enfranchised the lower-middle classes but quite deliberately not the working classes. Lord John Russell wrote to Edward Baines to seek assurance that setting the qualification at £10 would not let in unsuitable voters. Baines asked canvassers to check whether the occupants of £10 houses would admit to the franchise 'a considerable number of persons who are not fitted by their station, intelligence, and state in society, to vote for members'. His canvassers responded unanimously that 'the £10 qualification did not admit …a single person who might not safely and wisely be enfranchised.' He reckoned that 'in the parts [of town] occupied chiefly by the working classes, not one householder in fifty would have a vote'. But 'in streets principally occupied by shops, almost every householder had a vote':

> In the township of Holbeck, containing 11,000 inhabitants, chiefly of the working classes, but containing several mills, dye houses, public houses, and respectable dwellings, there are only 150 voters. Out of 140 householders, heads of families, working in the mill of Messrs. Marshall and Co., there are *only two* who will have votes …out of about 100 householders in the employment of Messrs. Taylor and Wordsworth, machine-makers – the highest class of mechanics – *only one* has a vote.

Whig Reform Rally in the Mixed Cloth Hall, 14 May 1832. When the passing of the Reform Bill seemed in doubt, the Leeds Reform Association arranged this meeting to allow the public to vent their disgust.

He felt the mills referred to gave 'fair specimens of the proportion of the working classes who will be entitled to vote'. Calculations based on an actual survey of the borough made in May 1832 suggested that of the 5,547 people who would have the vote only 355 would be workmen and of these 143 would be 'clerks, warehousemen, overlookers, &c.'.[213]

The printed poll books and registers of electors of the period show that shopkeepers, manufacturers and craftsmen were numerically the most important group of voters. The 1832 register of electors has page after page dotted with shopkeepers, who constituted one-third of the voting population.[214] At the first borough election in December 1832 the voting was John Marshall, junior, 2,012, Thomas Babington Macaulay (later famous as a historian and poet) 1,984 and Michael Thomas Sadler 1,590. In this way two Whig-Liberals were elected as the first MPs for the borough. In those days there was no secret ballot. Indeed, as occurred in 1837, a Poll Book was printed listing all the electors and for whom they had voted. The 1832 election was marked by fighting both at the hustings and during the nomination meetings. Both sides recruited groups of toughs to police their campaigns. The Whigs complained that the wealthy Tories were threatening to boycott shops whose owners voted for the Whigs. The Earl of Cardigan was reported to have threatened his tenants with eviction if they did not vote Tory. But Baines felt that the voters were far too respectable to be bribed or intimidated into voting against their proper inclinations.[215]

Not only was there no secret ballot, but voting in elections took place over a number of days. This generated particular excitement. When Macaulay left for India in 1833, Edward Baines was nominated as a candidate to succeed him. Sir John Beckett, from the wealthy Leeds banking family, was his Tory opponent. The Tories spent great sums of money in engaging attorneys, inns, bands of music, flags etc. and leaned on the tenants of prominent Tories. The Whigs claimed to have used rigid economy in their campaigns. An enormous assemblage met on Woodhouse Moor for the nominations in February 1834. The poll commenced the following day. By 11 o'clock Beckett was ahead, by one o'clock his majority was reduced to 125, by the close of the day it was down to 70, with 1,663 votes for Beckett and 1,593 for Baines. The second day of polling was Saturday, market day and perhaps 'never had there been so high a degree of excitement' in the town as Baines recalled:

> The friends of Mr Baines, stung with shame at their position, made every possible exertion; whilst

those of Sir John Beckett, animated by unexpected success were scarcely less energetic. All business was at a stand. The clothiers left their places in the Cloth-hall and gathered round Mr Baines's Committee-room. The whole town was either in activity or in anxious suspense. At ten o'clock Mr Baines got ahead of his competitor; and the announcement made from the Committee-room, and sent round the town, of Baines 1,742, Beckett 1,741 produced an immense sensation. From this time the Reformers worked like men confident of victory, and the Tories left no effort untried to retrieve the day. At one o'clock the majority for Mr Baines was 30. On the close of the poll, at four o'clock the numbers were as follows:-

Mr Baines	1,951
Sir John Beckett	1,917
Mr Bower	24[216]

Leeds and the Ten Hours Movement

In national affairs, Leeds men dominated the early years of the campaign to reduce working hours in factories. This issue was very much intertwined with the run up to the 1832 Reform Bill and the first borough election in December 1832. In 1830 Richard Oastler, the son of a Leeds merchant and steward of the Yorkshire Thornhill Estates, sent a letter entitled 'Yorkshire Slavery' to Baines at the *Leeds Mercury* in which he attacked the hypocrisy of factory owners who condemned negro slavery and yet treated employees in a similar manner.[217] Baines was sympathetic, initially, but quickly tired of the hostile attacks on the 'masters' some of whom had enabled him to buy the *Mercury*. Nevertheless, Yorkshire workmen formed Short Time Committees to campaign for a marked reduction in hours. Oastler eventually headed the Ten Hour Movement, aided in Parliament by Michael Sadler, the Tory MP for Aldborough and a leading Leeds linen merchant and member of the corporation.[218] Dr Charles Turner Thackrah, whose influential book on occupational diseases in Leeds became an internationally famous work, expressed his support for a Ten Hour Bill stating 'the (factory) system tends to produce a weak, stunted and short-lived race ...I think ten hours is enough, and too much'.[219]

Richard Oastler (1789-1861). The Leeds-born champion of the Ten Hours Movement.

In March 1832 Sadler proposed his Ten Hour Bill but the Government refused to act without further enquiry. A Parliamentary Committee, under Sadler's chairmanship began to hear evidence. On Easter Tuesday 1832 the Short Time Committees organised a mass rally at York where a huge well disciplined crowd listened to the various speakers, including Sadler and Oastler. The *Leeds Mercury* reported that the marchers were 'badly behaved and disorganised'. This piece of inaccurate journalism created a storm of protest and on the following Saturday a mob gathered outside the *Mercury*'s office and burnt an effigy of Edward Baines carrying a placard 'The Great Liar of the North'.[220] The key to success was new legislation to limit the hours of work, but its progress was heavily dependent on the return of Michael Sadler to Parliament as one of the newly created MPs for Leeds, since his seat at Aldborough was to disappear under the Reform Act of 1832. As we have seen, the Whig-Liberals chose as their candidates, John Marshall, junior, and Thomas Babbington Macaulay, both of whom were hostile to factory reform and who favoured a laissez-faire approach to the question of hours and conditions. Throughout the exciting, bitterly fought campaign, Oastler made a valiant effort to keep the factory issue alive. But Sadler was defeated and the Ten Hour Movement was left without a voice in Parliament.[221]

During the election Sadler observed that the slave children in the West Indies worked only six hours per day, while John Marshall for his part claimed that 69 hours a week was acceptable and that the 65 hours worked by children in his own factories did them no harm! Throughout the campaign the Radical Reformers supported Sadler, but this perhaps alienated traditional Tories like Benjamin Gott, who abstained. Unfortunately, the operatives, who flocked in their thousands to hear Sadler speak, could not vote.[222]

Sadler's defeat marked the end of Leeds' period of dominance in the Yorkshire Ten Hour Movement; eventually Lord Ashley was persuaded to represent the cause in Parliament. In May 1833, members of a Royal Commission established to report on industrial labour arrived in Leeds to pursue their investigations. They were greeted with a mass demonstration outside their hotel. Three days later a huge rally, with over 3,000 children present, tried to influence the commissioners. Oastler arrived to voice his opinion, but the factory masters proved a powerful and articulate opposition. In July, a Bill, largely based on the commissioners' findings, suggested a 12 hour day for young persons aged 13 to 18. No child under 9 was to be employed and those aged 9 to 13 were to work no longer than nine hours, with an additional two hours for schooling. These proposals were accepted and this became the first Factory Act to affect the woollen industry. The most important innovation was the appointment of four factory inspectors with powers to prosecute offenders. Dr Baker, long a campaigner for better conditions, was eventually appointed a sub-inspector. The Short Time Committees, however, rapidly disintegrated and many masters joined in a campaign to prevent the implementation of the Act. Oastler became frustrated by the lack of fair prosecutions and suffered a nervous breakdown.[223]

The Reform of the Corporation

At the very end of the Georgian period a major national political reform occurred which was to have a most profound effect at local level – the reform of the country's municipal corporations.[224] The immense frustration of the Whig/Liberal Dissenters, some of the most dynamic and enterprising townsmen, at being totally excluded from holding office in Leeds corporation, has already been noted. The most critical problem, however, was that because the corporation was not elected by the people of Leeds, it lacked sufficient popular support to legitimise the raising of large sums by rates to tackle the really major problems of the town. This was a common dilemma throughout England; one-seventh of the population lived under the control of 246 municipal corporations. The rising problem of law and order, the religious and political exclusiveness of these self-electing corporations and the fact that towns like Manchester, Birmingham and Sheffield did not even have corporations, were the cause of calls nationwide for the reform of local government. Though the 1832 Parliamentary Reform Act had swept away many rotten boroughs, most of the corporate towns still returned MPs and corrupt corporations were often left with a great deal of political power. As *The Times* commented in 1833: 'the fact is that Parliamentary reform, if it were not to include Corporation reform likewise, would have been literally a dead letter.'

In July 1833 the Royal Commission on Municipal Corporations was set up to investigate the situation. The commission visited Leeds in December 1833.[225] A member of the corporation declared that the commissioners would find the corporation 'as pure as holy water' and, in the sense that they found no evidence of corruption, he was right. In particular, the commissioners commended the corporation for its administration of justice, noting that 'the great respectability of the present members of the corporation and their impartial conduct as justices were universally acknowledged'. But the major indictment of Leeds Corporation was its exclusiveness:

> The close constitution of the corporation is obvious; all vacancies in each branch of it being filled by the Select Body gives to that body absolute and uncontrolled self-election. Family influence is predominant. Father and sons and sons-in-law, brothers and brothers-in-law succeed to the offices of the corporation like matters of family settlement.[226]

The old corporation recorded a protest at its impending abolition in its Court Book on 12 June 1835:

> The Leeds Corporation has proved free from all taint of corruption and malversation and the magistracy appointed under its charter has ever performed its duties honestly, fearlessly and independently to the satisfaction of the inhabitants at large. Court therefore feels it a duty to record its sense of the unjust judgement by which this Corporation is included in the condemnation passed on Corporations generally.

The seal of the Reformed Leeds Corporation.

Unjust or not, in September 1835 the Municipal Corporation Act was passed and the old corporation, along with 177 others around the country, was abolished and replaced by a town council. One-third of the members of the reformed corporation or council were to be elected annually by all the householders actually paying rates, giving a total of 48 borough councillors, plus 16 aldermen who were elected by the councillors themselves for a tenure of six years.

Because the borough franchise was restricted to those house occupiers who *actually* paid poor rates, the practice of landlords compounding for poor rates on behalf of their tenants disqualified large numbers of potential voters. Nevertheless, twice as many people could vote in the municipal election in Leeds as could in the Parliamentary election, though this still excluded two-thirds of the working classes.[227] In the first municipal election in December 1835 the traditional governors of the town were routed, with the Liberals winning 42 of the 48 contested Council seats. Even after the victors charitably provided the Tories with four aldermanic seats the council was weighted 51-13 in favour of the Liberals. It was as Baines explained 'a transference of local power beyond all calculation'.[228] There was no great difference between the social composition of the corporation and the council. The fundamental difference lay in politics, religion and family history. The old corporation in 1835 was predominantly composed of cloth merchants (or wool staplers) and professional men. Indeed out of 38 members (three-quarters of the total) 16 were cloth merchants or wool staplers, 4 were bankers, 3 were doctors, 1 was a lawyer and 1 was a gentleman. The reformed corporation of 1836 included 15 cloth merchants or woolstaplers, 8 cloth merchant manufacturers, 5 bankers, 2 lawyers, 3 doctors, and 1 gentleman. It was as if the opposing team had gone into bat. The rival merchants, the rival bankers, lawyers and doctors, even the rival flax-spinners were now in charge.[229]

Trouble at' Mill

For much of the eighteenth century there was a harmony and balance to town life in Leeds, with the woollen merchant community as the natural leaders of local society and town affairs. The livelihoods of hundreds of independent clothiers relied on the skill of the merchants in finding markets for their cloth. As independent craftsmen the clothiers controlled their own pattern of work, and those that they employed outside their family circle had, by the system of seven year apprenticeship, the prospect of betterment and eventually becoming master clothiers themselves. When trade was bad they had their smallholdings to fall back on and in old age a system of family support to protect them. When they

Bank Mills on the River Aire by Leeds Lock.

took their cloth to market in the Leeds cloth halls, they met the merchants as customers rather than employers, and if these customers thrived by increasing the market for West Riding cloth, the clothiers thrived too. At the finishing end of cloth manufacture, the craftsmen were sometimes independent, sometimes employees of the merchants, but as highly skilled craftsmen were well paid for their work. Until the 1790s the town was small by the standards of half a century later and it was possible for the merchants or their appointed officials to know, or know of, most of the families of the town. In hard times there could be a personal touch in the relief of the poor and a genuine sense of paternalism. Indeed, as we have seen, until the development of the Park Estate from the late 1760s, the merchants and the lower orders lived side by side in the streets of the town.

From the 1790s, however, the domestic system and traditional pattern of the local economy and way of life began to decline. As the town's industries expanded and new factory-based industries developed, a much greater proportion of the vastly increased population of Leeds became a landless, wage-earning, manual working class. These workers were entirely without means of support other than their weekly wages, or poor relief, if they were unemployed. The clothiers and cloth workers, or at least their sons and daughters, became urban employees. The field with a cow and a few hens, which had accompanied their lives outside the town, was replaced by the rented cottage or back-to-back house, even though some, most notably the Irish, clung on to their rural roots by keeping pigs in their cellars. At the same time, literally thousands of workers without close local ties flooded into the town.

The shift for many of the lower orders to a master-servant relationship for the first time, and the fears induced by frequent bouts of unemployment and near destitution as the local economy became increasingly subject to severe economic fluctuations, brought discontentment and resentment amongst the lower orders – now more appropriately referred to as the 'working classes'. The massing together of workers in the town in such large numbers intimidated the middle classes at times of depression – they felt matters could easily get out of hand.

The Luddites and their Origins

In 1789 the French masses decided they were so unhappy with the distribution of power and wealth in France that they turned their system upside down by deposing the king and the aristocracy. The French Revolution sent shivers down the spines of the ruling classes of England, as we have already seen. Fears that the potentially unruly masses of England might decide to attempt to seize power for themselves was a strong undercurrent of everyday life. It is true that the lower orders of Leeds periodically saluted Tom Paine, the radical author of *The Rights of Man*, celebrated victories of the French Revolutionary Armies, and supported rallies for Parliamentary reform.[230] Nevertheless, the working-class disorder and conflict of the late Georgian period in Leeds was motivated primarily by economic distress and the threats to the traditional patterns of getting a living, rather than a desire to overthrow the existing order.

The large employers and the factory system generally stirred up profound hostility among thousands of small master clothiers. In 1795 they attempted to gain support by petitioning Parliament for a Bill to 'restore and preserve' the domestic system:

> Until lately, that system has been by cloth being manufactured by Persons residing in different villages in the County, and sold in the public Halls in Leeds to merchants who did not follow the manufacturing of cloth. Of late, several merchants have become manufacturers of cloth, and, for the better carrying on such manufacturing, have erected very large Buildings which are called Factories, wherein they intend to employ Clothiers as their Servants, so that persons, who, with their families, have been dispersed as before mentioned, will be associated together within, or near those Buildings in a dependant State.[231]

The principal industrial troubles centred around the croppers and cloth dressers – the highly skilled group of men who, often working in establishments of 40-60 men and apprentices, finished cloth supplied by the merchants by raising its nap, trimming it (with cropping shears), and then pressing it. This was a highly skilled occupation and if done well added greatly to the value of the cloth. Such was the industrial muscle of the croppers that they had for decades successfully prevented the introduction of labour saving machinery – the gig mill (a machine for raising the nap on cloth) and, much more significantly, the shearing frame, an eighteenth-century invention which, using a simple mechanism, made the principal skills of the cropper redundant.[232] The concentration of these workers in the town facilitated the organisation of an effective trade union. The 'Institution' ensured that those with a 'ticket' gained employment in the finishing shops of the district. Attempts to introduce the hated machinery were swiftly rebuffed, usually by threats of withdrawal of labour. However, in November 1799 when Messrs. Johnson of Beeston refused to give way and installed a gig mill, a riotous mob burnt down their mill. Rioters prevented lights from being brought near the scene and this made identification of the culprits impossible. Magistrates, worried about the possibility of further trouble, ordered Colonel Lloyd to have two drummers available during the night so that the Leeds Volunteer Corps could be speedily assembled. The outrage occurred at the time when the government feared that the working classes of England would co-operate with the French if they invaded the country, and it created alarm amongst the middle classes of Leeds. Nationally, the government passed the Combination Acts in 1799 and 1800 in an attempt to suppress trade unions, but as the inquiry into the Woollen Trade discovered in 1806 the 'Institution' continued to thrive.[233] Worries continued. In 1802 the Mayor of Leeds did his best to discourage merchant-manufacturers from adding gig mills or shearing frames to their works, being convinced that 'horrid outrages' would occur.[234]

During the early years of the nineteenth century all the legislation which at least historically had protected the traditional organisation of the woollen industry was whittled away by government – the seven year apprenticeship system, the banning of the gig mill and the restrictions on the number of looms which might be employed in one establishment. The road was now open for the factory, the gig mill, the shearing frame and the employment of unskilled and juvenile labour.[235] After several years of skirmishing, matters came to a head in 1812 with the Luddite outrages. The Leeds merchants and manufacturers must have read with anxiety the *Leeds Mercury's* reports on the Luddite machine-breaking outrages in Nottingham between March 1811 and February 1812. In mid-January 1812 the first signs that Luddism was spreading to Leeds occurred when a party of men with blackened faces were surprised on Leeds Bridge.[236] Messrs. Oates, Wood and Smithson had had the temerity to install a gig mill at Oatland Mill. On 19 January the mill was set alight. According to the *Leeds Intelligencer* 'thousands thronged to the spot, many lamenting the calamity, the multitude shouting and proclaiming it a blessing'. The next significant attack came in March with the destruction of 18 pieces of cloth belonging to Messrs. Dickenson, Carr and Co. The reward for information on the Luddites was raised to £1,000 but no one came forward.

The disturbances of this period were as much a response to the intense poverty of the working classes due to rocketing food prices and high unemployment, as they were for the installation of machinery. The atmosphere was very tense as outrages occurred throughout the West Riding. In March the insurrectionary tone of a leaflet distributed in the town must really have shaken the middle classes:

> **General Ludd, the Commander of the Army of Redressers.**
> To all Croppers, Weavers &c. & Public at large
> Generous countrymen,
> You are requested to come forward with Arms and help the Redressers to redress their Wrongs and shake off the hateful Yoke of a Silly Old Man [George III] and his Son more silly and their Roguish Ministers, all Nobles and Tyrants must be brought down. Come let us follow the Noble Example of the brave citizens of Paris who in the sight of 30,000 Tyrant Redcoats brought A Tyrant to the Ground, by so doing you will be best aiming at your own Interests. Above 40,000 Heroes are ready to break out, to crush the old Government and establish a new one.[237]

The repelling of the Luddite hammermen by William Cartwright at Rawfolds Mill in the Spen Valley in April 1812, with two people killed, was perhaps the high point of Luddism in the West Riding, but tension persisted and the local magistrates felt that the town was like a powder keg waiting to go off.[238] They feared the Leeds Local Militia was inadequate and so the Scots Greys, Queen's Bays and the West Kent Militia were garrisoned in Leeds during 1812. The *Leeds Mercury* of 14 April commented 'At night in particular, Leeds and Huddersfield have, with their picquets and military patrols, assumed more the appearance of Garrison Towns than of the peaceful abodes of trade and industry.' In August a woman calling herself 'Lady Ludd' headed a mob in Briggate. They heckled farmers, corn dealers, bakers and meal sellers, and there were several reports of people being physically assaulted. Many were on the brink of starvation. In August the Leeds soup house sold dried fish to the poor at 3d. per pound, but this did little to alleviate the misery of the masses.[239]

Improved trading conditions, a large military presence, better intelligence and well publicised arrests led to an easing of tension, though the painful reorganisation of industry continued apace, and, as we saw earlier in this chapter, in 1816 William Hirst successfully forced through the use of the gig mill and the shearing frame. Trade continued to be unpredictable and there was growing anxiety, at both local and national level, about the unruly urban masses. Many feared a breakdown of the social order. In 1819 Parliament voted £24,000 for the construction of a permanent military barracks at Buslingthorpe, between the roads to Roundhay and Chapel Allerton.[240]

In the final analysis the croppers had been proved right. Their skill was extinguished. In 1841 William Dodd in *The Factory System Illustrated* noted:

> In 1814, there were 1,733 croppers in Leeds, all in full employment; and now, since the introduction of machinery, the whole of the cloth …is dressed by a comparatively small number, chiefly boys, at from 5s. to 8s …and a few men at from 10s. to 14s. per week. The old croppers have turned themselves to any thing they can get to do: some acting as bailiffs, water-carriers, scavengers, or selling oranges, cakes, tapes and laces, gingerbread, blacking, &c, &c.[241]

This was a sad end to an honourable craft.

Turn-outs and Trade Unions

The violence of the second decade of the nineteenth century was not repeated in the 1820s and '30s, but the struggle between workers and employers continued. The Combination Acts had made 'unlawful combinations of workmen' illegal and attempted to suppress early forms of trade unionism. In 1824 a Select Committee of Parliament had concluded that the Acts had been ineffective in suppressing combinations, and recommended that, in matters of wages and hours, masters and workmen should be 'left at perfect liberty to make such agreements as they eventually think proper'. In 1824 the Acts were repealed, much to the chagrin of the town's employers, particularly those of building workers, just as the economic boom was coming into full swing in Leeds. The *Leeds Intelligencer* noted in April 1825:

> TURN OUTS
> The effects of the repeal of the Combination Laws are now beginning to be severely felt throughout the country. In the North of England, in particular, they have been especially obnoxious, although the annoyance, which such a measure was calculated to create, has been experienced all over the kingdom. Among the variety of instances of insubordination among the operatives during the last week, we are sorry to be obliged to include the Joiners of this town and neighbourhood, who have just turned out for an advance of wages, and thus the progress of nearly all the buildings now going forward will be impeded, to the injury and inconvenience of the proprietors and contractors. The journeymen joiners of Leeds have been earning twenty shillings a week. The advance they desire, or rather insist on, is to twenty-seven.

They moreover require their masters to make this the fixed rate of remuneration for all, a rule by the adoption of which the best and worst workmen in the town would be paid the same wages. Two or three hundred of these misguided people paraded our streets on Monday. One of the principal master joiners made his workmen an offer of twenty-six shillings a week, but the proposal was not relished by the select committee [the workers' leaders], and the men were consequently obliged to reject it. The Journeymen Bricklayers and Plasterers are, we believe, only waiting the result of this strike, to turn out themselves. The Masons have already announced their intention so to do. It is therefore of great importance that the people who are now trying the experiment should not be allowed to effect their object. The Stuff Weavers of Leeds struck on Monday last, to obtain 'an advance of one shilling on the thirty yards piece of worsted plaids, which was taken off three years ago, when provisions were low.' We are not so much disposed to quarrel with the operatives for desiring an increase in wages, as for the means they adopt for coercing their masters into a compliance with their wishes. The high price of provisions warrants, undoubtedly, some increase of their resources. But in the case of the Bricklayers, of this town in particular, they would, if they were capable of any feeling of gratitude, recollect that, from a kindly disposition towards them, their masters were induced to retain them through the winter.[242]

We have already seen the local battle over the length of working hours, which resulted in the 1833 Factory Act. Employers were determined to stem the growth of organised labour. In the wake of unsuccessful attempts in other parts of England, notably in Lancashire, to sustain the existence of general trade unions, in 1831 a 'Trade Union' was formed in Leeds. There was an element of secrecy about it and employers were hostile. In the summer of 1833, for example, one master dyer discharged all of his employees whom he knew to be unionists.[243] Matters came to a head in May 1834 when the manufacturers and cloth finishers, complaining of restrictive practices and inflated wage levels imposed by their workers, formed a 'Combination to Resist Trades' Unions.' They announced that from 12 May they would not employ any Union Labour and that those wishing to be employed should sign a declaration that they did not belong to the union. An estimated 3,000 men were locked out with 24 mills brought to a standstill. Mass meetings were held on Woodhouse Moor, and the magistrates, anticipating trouble, appointed around 500 special constables to deal with any possible disturbances. The *Mercury* commented 'We cannot foresee how long this struggle between the masters and the workmen will last; but it is obvious that the dull state of trade gives a prodigious advantage to the former.'[244] The words were prophetic. On Friday 13 June Simeon Pollard, secretary of the operative's trade union, sadly addressed the crowd, 'I come here today to recommend every man to sign if they can get a job by doing so'. Deprived of poor relief and with no money coming in, the end result was inevitable. Many of the more militant members remained unemployed and the bitterness of the dispute was to be long remembered.[245]

Keeping the Upper Hand

In spite of the emergence of the urban working classes, the upper-middle class élite managed to remain in control of the town, and through into the Victorian period there seems to have been remarkably little strong antagonism between the middle and working classes. The better-off skilled workers, the potential leaders of the working classes, apparently wished to be seen as moderate in politics and as respectable members of society. Indeed, political loyalties ran across class boundaries and there was virtually no division between the working class and middle class on political lines.[246] How was this achieved? In the eighteenth century the Tory-Anglican merchant and professional class had dominated Leeds as the controllers of its economy and as members of the corporation and its magistrates. In the early decades of the nineteenth century, this dominance was threatened on the one hand by the mass of urban workers and on the other by the burgeoning ranks of manufacturers and retailers. In order to retain control of affairs the élite needed to find a way to create a feeling of common interest and solidarity between themselves and the other elements of the middle classes, despite the differences in politics, religion, and social status which existed between them. They achieved this through the mechanism of the voluntary societies and the joint promotion of a range of public amenities, where differences of politics and religion were set on one side.[247] The coming together in this way was commented upon by the *Leeds Intelligencer* at the height of the building boom in Dec 1824:

> We cannot close this article without congratulating our fellow townsmen on the greatest of all improvements. A short time only has elapsed since war raged without, and party feuds within. Now one feeling seems to animate both Whigs and Tories, viz. an anxiety to improve the convenience of this ancient borough. We trust this spirit will remain undiminished until the town is susceptible of no further addition; either useful or ornamental.[248]

The voluntary societies were an excellent medium for tying the middle classes together. Through their hierarchies from patron, to president, to chairman, to committee member, to mere member or subscriber, they offered the opportunity for all the middle classes to be involved. The various titles and roles allowed the more well-to-do to mix with their social inferiors without losing self-esteem or social caché.

Organised in this way, the middle classes had strong cohesion, and the ruling élite, still primarily merchants and professional men, backed by this collective strength, were able to set about retaining their control of the town and keeping the working classes in check. The scale of paternalism required to maintain their credibility as still being truly concerned for the well-being of the working classes had vastly increased. It had outgrown the financial capabilities of individuals because of the growth of the town. Moreover, the huge increase in population made it impossible to maintain the personal knowledge of individuals which they had formerly used to advantage in the dispensing of charity. These needs were now met by collective action through the voluntary societies. It is debatable whether the provision of poor relief, education and religion for the working classes was primarily motivated by Christian piety and a desire for the betterment of the lower orders. No doubt for some there was a heart-felt desire to benefit the working classes, but the tenor of a great deal of the contemporary comment leads to the inevitable conclusion that keeping the working classes in a submissive condition was often

Cope's View of Leeds c. 1826. A truly industrial townscape with towering chimneys, a smoke filled sky, a river polluted by industrial and human effluent, and river traffic heading towards Leeds Lock. To the far right is Bank Mills.

of paramount concern. Poor relief seemed driven more by the desire to maintain social stability than welfare. The voluntary schools placed much more emphasis on inculcating orderliness and decency, than imparting knowledge. The medical institution operated on a system of working-class deference to the middle classes; those wishing to gain treatment normally having to receive the recommendation of a subscriber before being treated. And the power of religion to instill morality and submission to one's lot in life was a major driving force behind the provision of the Million Act churches.[249] All this said, the end product was that social relations remained remarkably calm during this period of dramatic change, and in consequence conditions prevailed in which the town prospered.

The Balance Sheet of Industrialisation

Between the early 1790s and the beginning of Victoria's reign, Leeds had undergone a phenomenal transformation. Its population had mushroomed from around 25,000 to over 85,000. The physical size of its built-up area had grown dramatically, indeed the out-township of Holbeck had almost merged with the town. Ribbon development along the roads and waterways had begun to tie in the industrial townships of Hunslet and Armley very closely to Leeds. The economic development of the town was also phenomenal, with the factories coming to the fore by the 1830s. For the middle classes the results were greater wealth, better urban amenities and in many respects a higher standard of living. For the working classes the benefits were more dubious. By the 1830s probably the more skilled workers were enjoying a higher standard of living, but for the majority the purchasing power of their incomes had probably stayed much the same.[250] What many of the working classes had lost was a way of life and an independence which they valued, even if, like wage-labouring, their former livelihoods had suffered from the irregularities and uncertainties of trade fluctuations.

Though the middle classes enjoyed distinct benefits from the economic growth of the period, there were major drawbacks which all classes experienced. The pollution of the atmosphere by smoke was one of the worst. The decline was epitomised by the blackening of the manor house with smoke. When the Winter family (tenants of the manor house, the former Wilson residence in Bishopgate Street) took the dyer, George Nussey to court in 1811, claiming that the smoke from his ten chimneys had changed an agreeable and handsome mansion into a 'place which was odious to inhabit', defence counsel pointed out that there were 450 chimneys in the immediate neighbourhood of the former manor house. Derisory damages of one shilling were awarded.[251]

In 1824 some of the residents of the West End of Leeds brought a prosecution against Benjamin Gott on the grounds that the smoke from his factory was a public nuisance. Witnesses attested that the smoke came in through their windows, that their washing was discoloured and the vegetables in their gardens blackened with soot. All this was true but, as the defence made clear, Gott's mill was only one of many in the area and it had been there before most of the houses had been built. In directing the jury, the judge observed that the indictment charged Gott with a public nuisance, 'yet an immense number of people had been building houses in the neighbourhood, which was a pretty strong evidence they did not consider it in that light.' 'Manufacturers', he observed, 'were of the greatest importance; if people chose to go and live where manufactures were carried on, which sent forth a great quantity of smoke, they chose to be annoyed by it, and had no right to complain ...In such a place as Leeds, which flourished in consequence of all this nuisance, some inconveniences were to be expected.' Gott was absolved of blame and the smoke was there to stay.[252] The most affluent middle classes could move north if they chose, and leave the smoke to others.

The great menace, however, was the extremely insanitary conditions in which many of the working classes lived. The full horror of the situation was revealed by the cholera epidemic of 1832 and the systematic investigation of working-class living conditions which followed in its wake. The cholera epidemic in Leeds (part of the national epidemic which started in Sunderland in 1831) began on 26 May 1832 in the person of a two year old child, of Irish parents living in Blue Bell Fold off East Street between the Bank and the river. Despite all the precautions of removing filth from the streets, whitewashing the dwellings of the poor, and the setting up of a cholera isolation hospital in St Peter's Square, the spread of the disease could not be prevented. By the time the epidemic ended six months later there had been nearly 2,000 cases and over 700

Dufton's Yard, off Somerset Street, near Lady Beck, was typical of the squalid conditions prevalent in the district around Lady Lane and Quarry Hill.

deaths. It was a frightening experience for all. Robert Baker's pioneering report on the cholera showed quite conclusively that the disease was prevalent in the unsewered, ill-ventilated, filthy, ill-paved and densely populated parts of the town – the streets, yards and folds where the working classes lived. The Boot and Shoe Yard, Kirkgate, Baxter's Yard, Quarry Hill, Cherry Tree Yard, Goulding's Buildings, Lemon Street, Marsh Lane, Fleece Lane, and Lee's Yard – the East End of Leeds – were the places where the biggest attacks of cholera occurred. The worst case occurred in the Boot and Shoe Yard which had 34 houses and 340 inhabitants but only three privies from one of which, during the cholera epidemic, 75 cart loads of 'soil' were removed.[253]

In 1833 a joint declaration by 6 physicians and 38 surgeons in the town asserted that the health of the population would be greatly improved by a general and efficient system of drainage, sewerage and paving, and the enforcement of better regulations regarding the cleanliness of the streets, and called for an Act of Parliament to permit, and no doubt enforce, such improvements.[254] But as the initial shock of the cholera diminished, no action was taken. Baker's Statistical Committee Report, prepared for the corporation in 1839, revealed a situation which, if anything, was even worse than had prevailed in 1832. Of the North-West Ward, for example, it observed: 'the streets become the receptacle for ashes, filth and refuse of every description, until they become far above their original level, and offensive beyond all measure at all times, and during all seasons.' The practice of keeping livestock to supplement the family diet compounded the problem. Baker gave a lurid example of such squalor: 'In one of these streets an expiring Irishwoman was found in a cellar-dwelling surrounded by her family and a number of pigs, the filth of which latter it would be necessary to remove into the street by hand.'[255] The houses were often unclean and ill-ventilated, and people often shared a bed. Baker expressed concern that brothers and sisters up to the age of adolescence were often sleeping in the same room and 'not infrequently in the same bed'.[256]

Apart from the problem of the lack of sewers and proper sanitation, the water supply was also in an appalling state. For the few who received water from the waterworks, the problem was that it was river water and by definition grossly polluted, but it could at least be used for washing and other domestic purposes. Baker vividly described the everyday problem for those without piped water of finding a decent supply of water. Describing the Boot and Shoe yard in 1839 he commented:

> There is no water within a quarter of a mile. Very few of the inhabitants possess a vessel in which to hold or fetch water. Those who have the means of fetching it can get it for about 2d. a week, but many of them pay from 4d. to 7d., and in some cases as much as two shillings.[257]

The effects of the poor sanitary conditions, combined with the poor diet of the working classes and the limited state of medical knowledge, were reflected in a high death rate. In the 1820s and '30s it is clear that Leeds was a very unhealthy place, but to what extent it was more unhealthy than other places is debatable. Certainly, by modern standards the death rate was high. In the 1820s and '30s up to 35 out of every 1,000 inhabitants died each year, compared to a rate today of around 12 in every

1,000. High as this was, the absolutely shocking figure was that probably over 200 of every 1,000 children died before the age of one, compared to a present-day figure of around 12 in every 1,000. Population growth was only sustained by a high birth rate of around 38 per 1,000 (compared to around 13 per 1,000 today), and a massive influx of people from the town's hinterland and other parts of the United Kingdom.[258]

By the beginning of Victoria's reign the people of Leeds had a number of challenges ahead of them in addition to the problems of health and sanitation. In the first place, if the town was to continue to grow and prosper, its infrastructure and amenities needed improving. Rapid growth meant that even comparatively new amenities quickly became inadequate. Thus, for example, in spite of the improvements to the market in the 1820s, by 1840 the *Leeds Mercury* was able to assert with confidence that 'it is notorious to all our readers, that for fair and market accommodation there is not a town in the Kingdom in so bad a condition as Leeds'.[259] The system of streets and lanes in the heart of the commercial and retailing centre were still those suited to a small market town rather than a large industrial city. The waterways and the turnpike roads had served the town extremely well, but the exciting new age of the railways was getting up steam.

Given the stresses and strains of the period from the 1790s to the 1830s, Leeds had really been remarkably stable in its class relations. Edward Baines, junior, writing to Sir Robert Peel in 1843 in outrage at allegations that there was 'a spirit of lawless insubordination' in Leeds commented:

> You will be relieved to hear that for more than forty years (and I know not how much longer) there has not been a riot of any kind in Leeds, except one, so called, after the Great Yorkshire election contest in 1807, when a hot-headed magistrate irritated by defeat, called forth the troops without the slightest necessity, and excepting also an insignificant brush at the turn-out of last autumn![260]

The middle classes, notably the ruling élite, perhaps would have looked back with considerable satisfaction at this stability. This in their view, no doubt, had been achieved by the sobering and restraining effects of education and religion, the benevolent and philanthropic works of the voluntary societies, the flexibility of the poor relief system, the presence of the police, and, in the last resort, the availability of the troops. Nevertheless, the system of local government in Leeds was creaking under the strain of the size of its responsibilities. Moreover, the scale of the town was reaching a level where the resources and motivation of private enterprise, which had been a key feature of the late Georgian period, might no longer be equal to many of the tasks. If Leeds was to continue to prosper and be a civilised town in which to live, all these problems would have to be tackled. Parliamentary reform in 1832 had given Leeds a voice in national debates and the 1835 Municipal Corporation Act at long last gave the Whig-Liberal Dissenters an opportunity to take centre stage in a potentially more assertive and more effective government of the town. It was for these men to attempt to solve the problems and meet the new challenges of continued rapid urban growth in the Victorian age.

References

1. Herman von Puckler, *Muskau Prince, Tour in Germany, Holland and England, 1826, 1827, 1828* (1832), IV, p. 210.
2. For Gott's industrial activities, see: W.B.Crump, ed., *The Leeds Woollen Industry, 1780-1820* (Thoresby Society Monograph, 1931), esp. chs. 1, 3, 4, 5; H.Heaton, 'Benjamin Gott and the Industrial Revolution in Yorkshire', *Economic History Review*, iii (1931).
3. For the development of factories in Leeds, see: E.J.Connell and M.Ward, 'Industrial Development, 1780-1914' in D.Fraser, ed., *History of Modern Leeds*, (Manchester, 1980), (hereafter, *Modern Leeds*); M.F.Ward, 'Industrial Development and Location in Leeds North of the River Aire, 1775-1914' (Unpublished Ph.D. thesis, University of Leeds, 1972); E.J.Connell, 'Industrial Development in South Leeds, 1790-1914' (Unpublished Ph.D. thesis, University of Leeds, 1975); D.T.Jenkins, *The West Riding Wool Textile Industry, 1770-1835: A Study in Fixed Capital Formation* (Pasold Research Fund Ltd, 1975).
4. Edward Baines, *History, Directory and Gazetteer of the County of York* (1822), (hereafter, Baines, *1822 Directory*), pp. 118-9, 129; R.G.Wilson, *Gentlemen Merchants: The Merchant Community in Leeds, 1700-1830*, (Manchester, 1971), (hereafter, *Gentlemen Merchants*), ch. 6.
5. Parliamentary Papers, 1806, III, Reports from the Select Committee ...[on] the State of the Woollen Manufacture in England, p. 12.
6. Baines, *1822 Directory*, p. 29.
7. *Ibid.*, p. 20.
8. Crump, *op. cit.*, pp. 48-51; Baines, *1822 Directory*, p. 30; J.Mayhall, *The Annals of Yorkshire* (1878), I, pp. 716-7.
9. W.White, *History, Gazetteer, and Directory of the West Riding of Yorkshire, with the City of York and the Port of Hull* (1837), p. 512.
10. *The Parliamentary Gazetteer for 1842*, pp. 69-70.
11. Edward Baines, *The Woollen Manufacture of England with special reference to the Leeds Clothing District, 1848* (K.G.Ponting, ed., Newton Abbot, 1970), pp. 98-100.
12. *The Parliamentary Gazetteer for 1842*, p. 70.
13. H.Heaton, *The Yorkshire Woollen and Worsted Industries* (2nd edn, Oxford, 1965), (hereafter *Woollen Industries*), pp. 356-8.
14. Wilson, *Gentlemen Merchants*., pp. 33, 107; 1806 Select Committee Report, p. 12.
15. This account of the decline of the traditional merchant community is based on Wilson, *Gentlemen Merchants*, p. 111-134.
16. *Ibid.*
17. White, *1837 Directory*, p. 512; *Gentlemen Merchants*, pp. 127-30.
18. *The Parliamentary Gazetteer for 1842*, p. 68.
19. For a detailed account of Marshall's industrial activities, see: W.G.Rimmer, *Marshall's of Leeds: Flax-spinners, 1788-1886* (Cambridge, 1960).
20. Baines, *1822 Directory*, p. 30.
21. *Ibid.*
22. For details of Murray's industrial activities, see: E.Kilburn Scott, *Matthew Murray, Pioneer Engineer: Records from 1765-1826* (Leeds, 1928).
23. *Ibid.*, pp. 36, 38.
24. W.Lindley, 'Number of Steam Engines ...in Leeds and its Immediate Vicinity ...March 1824', University of Leeds, Brotherton Library, MS No. 18.
25. Connell and Ward, *op. cit.*, p. 153.
26. *Census Reports of Great Britain*, 1801-1841; C.J.Morgan, 'Demographic Change, 1771-1911', in *Modern Leeds*.
27. The following analysis of industries and employment is based on: W.G.Rimmer, 'The Industrial Profile of Leeds, 1740-1840', *Thoresby Soc.*, L (1967); W.G.Rimmer, 'Occupations in Leeds, 1841-1951', *Thoresby Soc.*, L (1967).
28. Baines, *1822 Directory*, passim.
29. *Ibid.*, p. 30.
30. *Ibid.*, pp. 13-31; W.G.Rimmer, 'Middleton Colliery, near Leeds, 1770-1830', *Yorkshire Bulletin of Economic and Social Research*, VII, No. 1 (1955).
31. A.Lockwood, 'The Origins of Gas in Leeds: the Leeds Gas Light Company, 1817-35', *Thoresby Soc.*, LVI (1980).
32. Sir George Head, *A Home Tour through the Manufacturing Districts of England in the Summer of 1835* (1836), p. 172.
33. J.Priestley, *Historical Account of the Navigable Rivers, Canals, and Railways of Great Britain* (1831), pp. 385-97; and notes to Chapter 3.
34. T.Bradley, *Old Coaching Days in Yorkshire* (1889); R.W.Unwin, 'Leeds Becomes a Transport Centre', in *Modern Leeds*.
35. Unwin, *op. cit.*.
36. Kilburn Scott, *op. cit.*, pp. 62-77.
37. For the development of Leeds banks see: K.Grady, 'Commercial, Marketing and Retailing Amenities, 1700-1914' in *Modern Leeds*, pp. 177-99; H.Pemberton, 'Two Hundred Years of Banking in Leeds', *Thoresby Soc.*, XLVI (1963); W.C.E.Hartley, *Banking in Yorkshire* (1975), esp. pp. 132-7.
38. *Leeds Intelligencer*, 18 May 1826.
39. Morgan, *op. cit.*.
40. J.Heaton, publisher, *Walks Through Leeds* (Leeds, 1835), p. vi.
41. B.R.Mitchell and P.Deane, *Abstract of Historical Statistics* (Cambridge, 1962); C.W.Chalklin, *The Provincial Towns of Georgian England, 1740-1820* (1974); P.J.Corfield, *The Impact of English Towns, 1700-1800* (1982).
42. For an account of the provision of public buildings in this period, and details of the all the buildings, see: K.Grady, 'The Georgian Public Buildings of Leeds and the West Riding', *Thoresby Soc.*, LXII (1989).
43. F.Beckwith, 'The Beginnings of the Leeds Library', *Thoresby Soc.*, XXXVII (1941).
44. F.Beckwith, 'Thomas Taylor: Regency Architect', *Thoresby Soc.*, Monograph I (1949).
45. *Leeds Intelligencer*, 30 Aug. 1827.
46. Hertfordshire County Record Office, T4951, Report of surveyors to Earl Cowper on his Leeds estates, 1819.
47. E.Kitson Clark, *The History of 100 Years of Life of the Leeds Philosophical and Literary Society* (Leeds, 1924); *Byelaws of the Public Baths at Leeds* (Leeds, 1826).
48. M.H.Port, *Six Hundred New Churches: a Study of the Church Building Commission, 1818-1856* (1961).
49. J.J.Scottorn, *A Short History of South Parade Baptist Chapel, 1779-1979* (Leeds, 1979).
50. K.Grady, 'Profit, Property Interests and Public Spirit: The Provision of Markets and Commercial Amenities in Leeds, 1822-9', *Thoresby Soc.*, LIV (1976); K.Grady, 'Commercial, Marketing and Retailing Amenities' in *Modern Leeds*; S.Burt and K.Grady, *Kirkgate Market: An Illustrated History* (Leeds, 1992).
51. D.C.Dews, *Oxford Place Methodist Centre, Leeds, 1835-1985* (Leeds, 1985).
52. *Leeds Mercury*, 26 Sept. 1818.
53. *Leeds Intelligencer*, 15 July 1822.
54. For the development of housing in this period, see: M.W.Beresford's superb study, 'East End, West End: The Face of Leeds During Urbanisation, 1684-1842', *Thoresby Soc.* LX and LXI (1988), esp. chs. 6-8.
55. Anon., *The Leeds Guide; including A Sketch of the Environs, and Kirkstall Abbey* (Leeds, 1806), (hereafter, *Leeds Guide, 1806*), pp. 66-8.
56. *Ibid.*
57. Beresford, *East End: West End*, p. 168.
58. Unwin, *op. cit.*, p. 124.
59. C.Treen, 'Building and Estate Development in the Northern Out-townships of Leeds, 1781-1914' (Unpublished Ph.D thesis, University of Leeds, 1977). Treen's findings up to 1840 are summarised in M.W.Beresford, 'The Face of Leeds, 1780-1914' in *Modern Leeds*.
60. For the development of housing for the working classes, in addition to *East End: West End*, see the articles by M.W.Beresford, W.G.Rimmer and F.Trowell in the bibliography.
61. *Diary of Dr John Simpson of Bradford, 1825* (Bradford, 1981), p. 61.
62. *The Leeds Guide, 1806*, p. 75.
63. G.A.Cooke, *Topographical and Statistical Description of the County of York* (1819); J.Bigland, *The Beauties of England and Wales* (Yorkshire, 1819), pp. 775-796.
64. E.Parsons, *The Civil, Ecclesiastical, Literary, Commercial and Miscellaneous History of Leeds, Halifax, Huddersfield, Bradford, Wakefield, Dewsbury, Otley, and the Manufacturing Districts of Yorkshire*, (hereafter, *Parsons' History*) I, pp. 177-9.
65. 49 Geo. III, cap. 122 (1809).
66. 5 Geo. IV, cap. 124 (1824).
67. *Parsons' History*, I, pp. 140-2.
68. *Ibid.*, pp. 144-5.
69. *Ibid.*
70. *Ibid.*, pp. 137-8.
71. *Ibid.*, I, pp. 137-8, 140, 148, 150.
72. For this and subsequent Parsons quotes see: *Parsons' History*, I, p. 140.
73. *Leeds Intelligencer*, 14 March 1775.
74. Grady, *Georgian Public Buildings*, p. 163.
75. J.H.Leach, *A Walk Through Leeds or Stranger's Guide* (Leeds, 1806), p.35.
76. *Leeds Guide* (1806), p. 65.
77. *Leeds Intelligencer*, 8 Oct. 1810.
78. *Leeds 1817 Directory*, pp. 22-3.
79. 55 Geo. III, cap. 42 (1815).
80. E.W.Clay, *The Leeds Police, 1836-1974* (Leeds, 1975?), ch. 1.
81. E.Baines, *The Extraordinary Life and Character of Mary Bateman, the Yorkshire Witch* (Leeds, 1820).
82. S.Burt, *Criminal Leeds* (Leeds, 1985), pp. 20-1.
83. Baines, *1822 Directory*, pp. 16-7.
84. Clay, *op. cit.*, p. 10.
85. *Leeds Intelligencer*, 14 July 1825.
86. Burt, *Criminal Leeds*, pp. 22-6; *Leeds Intelligencer*, 18 May 1826.
87. Leeds Council, Statistical Committee, 'Report upon the Condition of the Town of Leeds', *Journal of the Royal Statistical Society*, (hereafter, *Statistical Committee Report, 1839*), II (1840), pp. 25-6.
88. *Ibid.*
89. Morgan, *op. cit.*, p. 53.
90. Baines, *1822 Directory*, p. 17.
91. *Leeds Intelligencer*, 9 October 1823.
92. D.Fraser, 'The Leeds Churchwardens, 1828-50', *Thoresby Soc.*, LIII (1971), p. 2.
93. D.Fraser, 'Improvement in Early Victorian Leeds', *Thoresby Soc.*, LIII (1971), pp. 71-81.
94. D.Fraser, 'The Leeds Churchwardens'.
95. *Leeds Intelligencer*, 5 April 1834.
96. D.Fraser, 'Poor Law Politics in Leeds, 1833-55', *Thoresby Soc.*, LIII, (1971).
97. Leeds Vestry Minutes, 1828-1844, p. 125.
98. *Parsons' History*, I, pp. 151-2.
99. White, *1837 Directory*, pp. 488-9.
100. *Leeds Intelligencer*, 16 Jan., 27 Feb. 1815.
101. *Ibid.*
102. White, *1837 Directory*, pp. 488-9.
103. *Leeds 1853 Directory*, p. 18.
104. Wages and rents, see: W.G.Rimmer, 'Working Men's Cottages in Leeds, 1770-1840', *Thoresby Soc.*, XLVI (1963); *Statistical Committee Report, 1839*, pp. 36-8; R.Baker, 'Report on the state and condition of the town of Leeds', in P.P. 1842, XXIX, Sanitary Inquiry, p. 13.
105. See works of Beresford and Rimmer.
106. P.P. 1867, XXXIII, Third Report of Commissioners appointed to Inquire into the best means of preventing the Pollution of Rivers. Rivers Aire and Calder, Evidence of Mr. Filliter, p. 182.
107. Rimmer, *Working Men's Cottages*, pp. 171-2.
108. *Ibid.*, p. 199.
109. *Leeds Intelligencer*, 6 July 1826.
110. *Leeds Mercury*, 31 Mar. 1831.
111. White, *1837 Directory*, p. 526.
112. *Leeds Intelligencer*, 22 Feb. 1796.
113. White, *1837 Directory*, p.526.
114. *Ibid.*, pp. 635-6.
115. *Leeds Guide, 1806*), p. 56; White, *1837 Directory*, p. 526; P.Anderson, 'The Leeds Workhouse under the Old Poor Law: 1726-1834', *Thoresby Soc.*, LVI (1980), pp. 110-2.
116. *Leeds Intelligencer*, 4 Aug. 1831.
117. *Leeds Mercury*, 1 June 1833.
118. Anderson, *op. cit.*, p. 91.
119. *Ibid.*, pp. 99-104.
120. *Ibid.*, p.105.
121. Baines, *1822 Directory*, pp. 27-28; White, *1837 Directory*, p. 526.
122. P.P. 1898, LXVI, *Report on the Endowed Charities of the City of Leeds*, pp. 6-8, 11-12.
123. *Leeds Guide 1806*, pp. 46-9; *Parsons' History*, II, p. 158; Whitaker, *op. cit.*, p.85.
124. R.Baker, *Report to Leeds Board of Health* (Leeds, 1833).
125. White, *1837 Directory*, p. 526; G.Black, 'The Leeds Eye Dispensary', *Thoresby Soc.*, LIV (1975).
126. S.T.Anning, 'The Leeds Public Dispensary', *Thoresby Soc.*, LIV (1975); White, *1837 Directory*, p. 526.
127. S.T.Anning and W.J.K.Walls, *A History of Leeds School of Medicine: One and a Half Centuries, 1831-1981* (Leeds, 1982).

128. W.B.Stephens, 'Elementary Education and Literacy' in *Modern Leeds*, pp. 226-9.
129. White, *1837 Directory*, p. 520.
130. *Leeds 1817 Directory*, p. 35; *Parsons' History*, II, pp. 105-6; White, *1837 Directory*, p. 521.
131. *Report on Endowed Charities*, pp. 9-10.
132. White, *1837 Directory*, p. 521.
133. *Ibid.*, p. 520.
134. *Statistical Committee Report, 1839*, pp. 31-2.
135. E.G.West, *Education in the Industrial Revolution* (1975), p. 78.
136. *Leeds Guide 1806*, pp. 53-4; *Leeds 1817 Directory*, pp. 28, 36.
137. J.Hole, *The Working Classes of Leeds: an Essay on the Present State of Education in Leeds* (Leeds, 1863), pp. 54-5; Baines, *1822 Directory*, p. 37.
138. White, *1837 Directory*, p. 527.
139. N.Yates, 'The Religious Life of Victorian Leeds', in Fraser, ed., *Modern Leeds*, p. 250.
140. *Statistical Committee Report, 1839*, pp. 28-9.
141. Queries Addressed by the Factory Commissioners for the Northern Districts to Mill Owners, 1 May 1833.
142. Royal Commission on Employment of Children in Factories, Report of 1834, Vol XIX (167), Minutes of Evidence, C1, pp. 75-7.
143. *Ibid.*, p. 107.
144. S.T.Anning, *The History of Medicine in Leeds* (Leeds, 1980), p. 115.
145. *Statistical Committee Report, 1839*, p. 26.
146. Rimmer, *Working Men's Cottages*, p. 199.
147. Author's collection: James Atkinson's apprenticeship indenture, 17 Nov. 1823.
148. *Statistical Committee Report, 1839*, p. 11.
149. *Ibid.*, pp. 27-8.
150. Baines, *1822 Directory*, p. 27; *Parsons' History*, II, p. 159.
151. *Leeds Intelligencer*, 31 July 1823, 5 Feb. 1824.
152. Leeds Central Reference Library: William Boyne's *History of Leeds* (a grangerized edition of works by Thoresby, Whitaker and other Leeds historians), Vol IV, p. 86. *Parsons' History*, I, p. 167.
153. Leeds Intelligencer, 24 June, 1 July 1824.
154. *Leeds Mercury*, 26 June 1824.
155. *Leeds Intelligencer*, 24 June 1824.
156. *Yorkshire Weekly Post*, 9 June 1894, Interview with John English.
157. *Leeds Intelligencer*, 13 Nov. 1823.
158. *Ibid.*, 6 July 1807.
159. *Leeds Mercury*, 26 Sept. 1812.
160. *Leeds Intelligencer*, 28 Aug. 1823.
161. *Leeds Mercury*, 5 Aug. 1815.
162. *Ibid.*, 13 April 1814.
163. R.J.Morris, *Class, Sect and Party: The Making of the British Middle Class, Leeds 1820-1850* (Manchester, 1990), p. 22.
164. D.Ward, 'Environs and neighbours in the "Two Nations": Residential Differentiation in Mid- Nineteenth Century Leeds', *Journal of Historical Geography, 6 (1980), pp. 144-6; Morris,* op. cit., pp. 8-12.
165. For Gott's lifestyle, see: V.M.E.Lovell, 'Benjamin Gott of Armley House, Leeds, 1762-1840: Patron of the Arts', *Thoresby Soc.*, LIX (1986).
166. For Marshall's lifestyle see: Rimmer, *Marshall's of Leeds*.
167. White, *1837 Directory*, p. 623.
168. *Leeds Mercury*, 6 May 1822, quoted in M.W.Beresford, *Walks Round Red Brick* (Leeds, 1980) (a study of the housing development on Leeds University's campus), p. 38.
169. Morris, *op. cit.*, p. 55.
170. T.Wemyss Reid, *Memoir of John Deakin Heaton, M.D.* (1883), pp. 50-5.
171. Foregoing account of Leeds Grammar School, see: A.C.Price, *A History of the Leeds Grammar School* (Leeds, 1919), chs. 6-8; *Report on Endowed Charities*, pp. 2-4; S.J.Curtis, *History of Education in Great Britain* (1967), pp. 123-6.
172. *Statistical Committee Report, 1839*, p. 30.
173. F.Dawson, 'Paganini in Leeds, January 1832', *Thoresby Soc.*, XXXIII (1935), pp. 447-59.
174. *Leeds Mercury*, 26 Sept. 1818.
175. For the society generally and its museum, see: E.Kitson Clark, *op. cit.*, passim; Morris, *op. cit.*, ch. 9; P.Brears, *Of Curiosities and Rare Things: The Story of the Leeds City Museums* (Leeds, 1989), pp. 7-11; W.Osburn, *An Account of the Egyptian Mummy preserved in the Museum of the Leeds Philosophical and Literary Society* (Leeds, 1828).
176. *Leeds 1830 Directory*, p. 215.
177. Morris, *op. cit.*, esp. chs. 7-12.
178. J.Myers Gardiner, *History of the Leeds Benevolent or Strangers' Friend Society, 1789-1889* (Leeds, 1890).
179. J.Sydney Curtis quoted in *Waddington's Guide to Leeds* (Leeds, 1894), p. 53.
180. White, *1837 Directory*, p. 525.
181. *Leeds Intelligencer*, 10 June 1824.
182. *Leeds Mercury*, 21 Nov. 1812.
183. J.Copley, 'The Theatre in Hunslet Lane', *Thoresby Soc.*, LIV (1975); and 'The Theatre in Hunslet Lane II', *Thoresby Soc.*, LIV (1976).
184. T.D.Whitaker, *The History of Loidis and Elmete* (1816), p. 86.
185. *Parsons' History*, I, p. 135.
186. *Leeds Mercury*, 27 July 1816.
187. *Leeds Intelligencer*, 16 July 1810.
188. *Leeds Guide 1806*, p. 67.
189. *Parsons' History*, I, p. 152.
190. *Leeds 1834 Directory*, p. 416; *Leeds Mercury*, 3 Mar. 1833.
191. T.Butler, *The Diary of Thomas Butler of Kirkstall Forge, Yorkshire, 1796-99* (1906), pp. 4-6, 55-65, 158-60.
192. LDA, Acc. 2720: Diaries of a law clerk articled with Bloome and Gatcliff of 15 Commercial Street, 1834-9.
193. *Leeds Monthly Magazine*, IX, Nov. 1829, pp. 429-30.
194. Pitt Club Dinner 1825: Printed programme (Thoresby Society Library, 22B6).
195. Quote and paragraph: Edward Baines, junior, *The Life of Edward Baines* (Leeds, 1851), pp. 44-7.
196. *Ibid.*, pp. 41, 50.
197. M.A.Gibb and F.Beckwith, *The Yorkshire Post: Two Centuries* (1954), pp.13-6.
198. For the history of the Leeds Volunteers, see: E.Hargrave, *'The Early Leeds Volunteers'*, Thoresby Soc., XXVIII (1928), pp. 255-84.
199. E.Hargrave, 'The Gentlemen Volunteer Cavalry, 1797', *Thoresby Soc.*, XXVII (1928), pp. 284-91.
200. T.Butler, *op. cit.*, pp. 233-4.
201. E.Hargrave, 'Leeds Volunteers, 1803-1808', *Thoresby Soc.*, XXVIII (1928), pp. 292-312.
202. E.Hargrave, 'Leeds Local Militia, 1808-1814', *Thoresby Soc.*, XXVII (1928), pp. 313-19.
203. Baines, *1822 Directory*, pp. 132-3, 145-47, 250-1.
204. *Ibid.*, p. vi.
205. J.Mayhall, ed., *The Annals of Yorkshire, From the Earliest Period to the Presents Time* (1878), I, p. 216.
206. *Ibid.*, pp. 215-7.
207. Baines, *The Life of Edward Baines*, pp. 63-5.
208. Mayhall, *op. cit.*, p. 217.
209. Baines, *The Life of Edward Baines*, passim.
210. D.Fraser, 'Fruits of Reform: Leeds Politics in the 1830s', *Northern History*, VII (1972), pp. 31-3.
211. Baines, *The Life of Edward Baines*, p. 151.
212. This and preceding paragraph: *Ibid.*, p. 116; Baines, *1822 Directory*, p. 15; Morris, *op. cit.*, pp. 124-7.
213. Baines, *The Life of Edward Baines*, pp. 156-9.
214. The Leeds Library Collection: *The List of Persons entitled to Vote in the Election of Members for the Borough of Leeds* (Leeds, 1832); *The Poll Book of the Leeds Borough Election, July 1837* (Leeds, 1837). For voting patterns, see: Morris, *op. cit.*, ch. 6.
215. Morris, *op. cit.*, pp. 127-8.
216. Baines, *The Life of Edward Baines*, pp. 179-188.
217. Ref to Oastler's letter to the Mercury; R.V.Taylor, *Biographia Leodiensis: Worthies of Leeds* (Leeds, 1865), pp. 499-503.
218. *Ibid.*, pp. 354-62.
219. C.T.Thackrah, *The Effects of the Principal Arts, Trades and Professions and of Civic States and Habits of Living on Health and Longevity: with particular reference to the Trades and Manufactures of Leeds* (Leeds, 1831; enlarged and amended version, 1832); A.Meiklejohn, *The Life, Work and Times of Charles Turner Thackrah: Surgeon and Apothecary of Leeds, 1795-1833* (1957).
220. R.Oastler, *A Well-seasoned Christmas Pie for 'the Great Liar of the North' Prepared, Cooked and Presented by Richard Oastler* (Bradford, 1834); C.Driver, *Tory Radical: The Life of Richard Oastler* (Oxford, 1946), pp. 160-5.
221. Driver, *op. cit.*, p. 202.
222. Morris, *op. cit.*, p. 128; M.T.Sadler, *Memoirs of the Life and Writings of M.T.Sadler* (1848), pp. 280-9.
223. Driver, *op. cit.*, p. 330.
224. For municipal reform in general and details regarding Leeds, see: D.Fraser, *Power and Authority in the Victorian City* (Oxford, 1979), chs. 1, 3.
225. Mayhall, *op. cit.*, I, p. 409.
226. P.P. 1835, XXIII, *Reports from Commissioners on Municipal Corporations in England and Wales*, pp. 1615-24.
227. Baines, *The Life of Edward Baines*, pp. 215-7.
228. Fraser, *Power and Authority*, p. 53.
229. E.P.Hennock, *Fit and Proper Persons* (1973).
230. The cloth hall under the Music Hall was known as the Tom Paine Hall. At times Paine was also vilified, see: E.P.Thompson, *The Making of the English Working Class* (1968), p. 113.
231. *Ibid.*, pp. 598-99.
232. *Ibid.*, pp. 570-1.
233. *Ibid.*, pp. 576-8.
234. *Ibid.*, pp. 573-4.
235. *Ibid.*, p. 578.
236. *Ibid.*, p. 608.
237. Crump, *op. cit.*, p. 229.
238. Thompson, *op. cit.*, p. 612.
239. *Leeds Intelligencer*, 24 Aug. 1812.
240. Baines, *1822 Directory*, p. 22; *Parsons' History*, I, p. 152.
241. W.Dodd, *The Factory System Illustrated*, p. 15, quoted in *Thompson,* op. cit., p. 602.
242. *Leeds Intelligencer*, 14 April 1825.
243. H.Pelling, *A History of Trade Unionism* (1963), p. 38.
244. *Leeds Mercury*, 17 May 1834.
245. *Leeds Intelligencer*, 14 June 1834.
246. D.Fraser, 'Politics and Society in the Nineteenth Century', in *Modern Leeds*, p. 354.
247. For a detailed discussion of this see Morris, *op. cit.*; and his article in *Modern Leeds*.
248. *Leeds Intelligencer*, 2 Dec. 1824.
249. Port, *op. cit.*, pp. 5-9.
250. Rimmer, *Working Men's Cottages*, pp. 192-6.
251. *Leeds Mercury*, 27 April 1811.
252. *Leeds Intelligencer*, 8 April 1824.
253. Baker, *Report to Leeds Board of Health* (Leeds, 1833); see also, Parsons, *History of Leeds*, I, pp. 155-9.
254. Parsons, *History of Leeds*, I, p. 158.
255. *Statistical Committee Report, 1839*, p. 10.
256. *Ibid.*, p. 17.
257. *Statistical Committee Report, 1839*, p. 9.
258. Morgan, *op. cit.*.
259. *Leeds Mercury*, 5 Sept. 1840.
260. E.Baines, junior, *The Social, Educational and Religious State of the Manufacturing Districts* (Leeds, 1843), pp. 10-1.

CHAPTER FIVE

The Victorian City

Monuments to Wealth

A town of the times is this great hive of workers, whose labours are for the welfare of mankind, and whose products have the whole wide world for their market. ...Though Leeds may lack the classic charm of Greece and Italy, or even the time-honoured dignity that reposes in our own ancient cathedral towns, she can place in the counterbalance her nine hundred factories and workshops, monuments of her wealth, industry and mercantile prestige.

London Printing and Engraving Co., *The Century's Progress: Yorkshire Industry and Commerce 1893*, p. 150.

While medieval Leeds is entirely remote to the present-day citizens and the Georgian period a distant past glimpsed through an elegant square or the remnants of a cloth hall, Victorian Leeds has left an indelible mark on the modern city. The city's great Victorian public buildings, the faded, but now often recently renovated, grandeur of its shops, public house and hotels, and its almost monumental factories and warehouses, convey an abiding impression of an age of great wealth.

A massive increase in the population of the town from 88,000 to 178,000 between 1841 and 1901, and of the borough from 152,000 to 428,000, provided a huge supply of labour for a rapid expansion of the town's industries.[1] Though the textile industry still employed two out of every five workers in the town in 1841, great changes were taking place.[2] The flax industry continued to expand and at its peak in the 1850s employed 9,500 workers, the majority of them female and Irish and including many children. It accounted for one-tenth of the gross output of British flax mills. Marshall's mills alone consumed one-tenth of the country's total imports of raw flax at one stage, an estimated 50,000 acres of land being needed to maintain their supply of raw materials.[3] But at no stage was flax able to challenge the supremacy of wool. In 1851 there were twice as many workers in woollens and worsteds as there were in flax. On the manufacturing side, the introduction into the woollen industry of steam-powered machinery for spinning, from the 1820s, and power looms, from the 1840s, finally drove all but a few domestic clothiers out of business.[4] For both woollens and worsteds Leeds remained the principal centre for dyeing, finishing and marketing until at least the middle of the nineteenth century and won many prizes at the Great Exhibition in London in 1851.[5]

From the mid-century, however, the textile industry went into decline as an employer. Having employed just over a third of the town's workforce in 1851, its

Panorama of Leeds from Beeston Hill in 1858. This view comes from the edition of the Illustrated London News which celebrated Queen Victoria's visit to Leeds to open the Town Hall. Note the scaffolding around the Town Hall's tower.

The Fourth White Cloth Hall, King Street, built in 1868 and demolished in 1895. Today it is the site is occupied by the Hotel Metropole on whose roof is the cupola of the cloth hall.

The interior of Marshall's Temple Mill built in 1838-40.

proportion fell to just under one-tenth by 1901. The numbers dropped from 29,000 to 18,000, in a period when the town's workforce more than doubled.[6] The really dramatic collapse was in the flax industry. In 1894 *White's Directory* noted that 'Belfast and Dundee now spin all they require and the chief portion of the linen manufacture has gone to these places'.[7] The decline was in part caused by a failure to adopt new machinery. By 1891 the great symbol of the Leeds flax industry, Marshall's loom shed, had become a clothing factory. The woollen and worsted industries, however, also faltered. Mills in Leeds had concentrated on producing coarse fabric, but the main growth area in textiles was the lightweight worsted trade, with its greater variety of cloths and patterns, which was primarily based in Bradford. In the 1840s and '50s most of the worsted firms remaining in Leeds defected to Bradford. At the same time the arrival of the railway gave the heavy woollen district around Dewsbury and Batley direct links to Hull, Manchester and Liverpool that by-passed Leeds, and released it from dependence on the town.[8] Employment in woollens in Leeds showed little prospect of growth from the 1870s, and by 1901 the industry ranked only fourth by size of workforce amongst the West Riding towns. By the end of the century exporting had ceased, the merchants as a class had disappeared, the cloth halls had closed, and firms produced mainly for the home market especially the clothing trades.[9] Nevertheless, the use of more efficient machinery permitted output to grow, and Leeds remained important for marketing. The 1901 *West Riding Directory* said of the town's woollen industry:

> Much of what is made in fancy cloths at Huddersfield, Dewsbury, Batley and Morley, passes through Leeds firms, and the tweed cloths, woven by power at Leeds, now form a very large branch of its manufacture. The cloth manufacture here embraces every description, so that the buyer can obtain at one mart all kinds of black and blue superfine cloths, Scotch camblets, coarse narrow cloths, ladies' cloths, shawls and blankets.[10]

The declining fortunes of the textile industry were in very sharp contrast to the experience of other Leeds industries. From the foundations laid by Matthew Murray and men like Peter Fairbairn, Leeds rapidly became one of the world's most important engineering centres. By 1861 engineering was the town's second largest employer and by the end of the century it had become the largest, employing one-fifth of the male workforce.[11] Following in the footsteps of Murray's Round Foundry, the town's steam engine making skills were brought to even greater prominence by James Kitson's Airedale Foundry, the Railway Foundry, the Hunslet Engine Company and Hudswell Clarke and Company. Leeds steam locomotives were exported to every part of the globe. John Fowler, whose magnificent steam plough became world famous, was drawn to Leeds because of these local engineering skills. His Steam Plough Works erected in 1859-64 at Leathley Road, Hunslet was close to Airedale Foundry.[12]

The Monk Bridge Iron and Steel Works in Whitehall Road was acquired by James Kitson and came to specialise in producing the best Yorkshire iron, crank and straight axles, boiler plates, bars, steel tyres, and the wheel centres for locomotives. Kirkstall Forge produced some of the finest axles in the world. Henry Berry and Co. founded in 1883, with premises in Balm Road,

Population of Leeds Townships, 1775-1901

	1775	1801	1811	1821	1831	1841	1851	1861	1871	1881	1891	1901
Leeds	17,121	30,669	35,951	48,603	71,602	88,741	101,343	117,566	139,362	160,109	177,523	177,920
Armley	1,715	2,695	2,941	4,273	5,159	5,676	6,190	6,734	9,224	12,737	18,992	27,521
Beeston	862	1,427	1,538	1,670	2,128	2,175	1,973	2,547	2,762	2,928	2,962	3,323
Bramley	1,378	2,562	3,484	4,921	7,039	8,875	8,949	8,690	9,882	11,055	14,787	17,299
Chapel Allerton	833	1,054	1,362	1,678	1,934	2,580	2,842	3,083	3,847	4,324	4,377	5,841
Farnley	540	943	1,164	1,332	1,591	1,530	1,722	3,064	2,964	3,608	3,590	4,351
Headingley-cum-Burley	667	1,313	1,670	2,154	3,849	4,768	6,105	9,674	13,942	19,138	29,911	41,561
Holbeck	2,055	4,196	5,124	7,151	11,210	13,346	14,152	15,824	17,165	19,150	20,630	28,249
Hunslet	3,825	5,799	6,393	8,171	12,074	15,852	19,466	25,763	37,289	46,942	58,164	69,064
Potternewton	419	509	571	664	863	1,241	1,385	1,878	3,457	5,107	9,269	26,004
Wortley	894	1,995	2,336	3,179	5,944	7,090	7,896	12,058	18,923	23,530	26,854	27,456
Coldcotes and Osmondthorpe		114	131	147	155	180	247	284	395	491	446	379
Totals	30,309	53,276	62,665	53,943	123,548	152,054	172,270	207,165	259,212	309,119	367,505	428,968

Source: C.J.Morgan, 'Demographic change' in D.Fraser, ed., *A History of Modern Leeds* (Manchester, 1980)

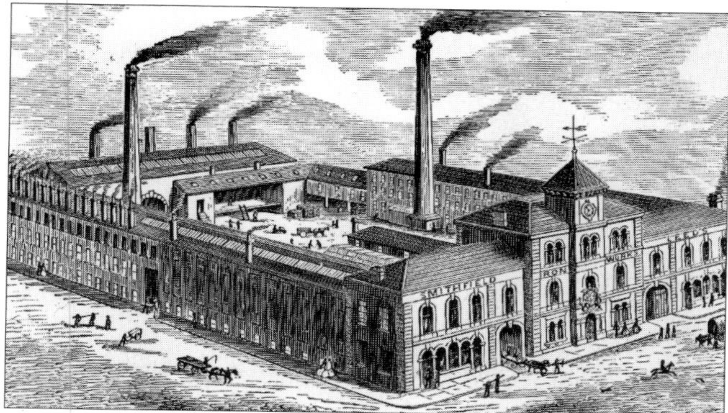

Thomas Green's Smithfield Ironworks, North Street, in 1892.

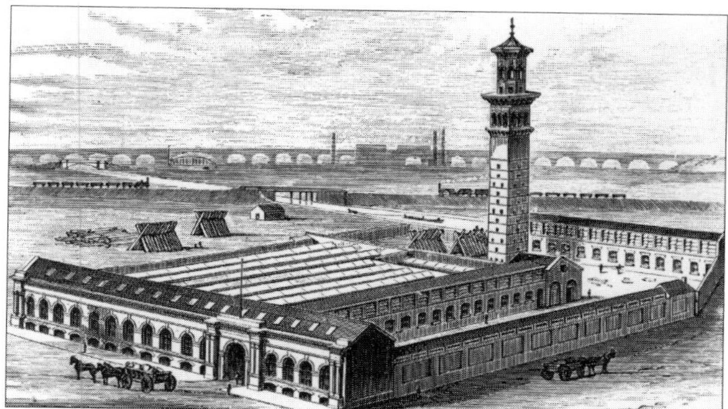

Tower Works, Globe Road, near the Leeds and Liverpool Canal Basin. Built to the design of Thomas Shaw in 1864. Its chimney is a copy of the Lamberti Tower in Verona. The factory made pins used in carding and combing processes. Its owner was Colonel Harding who was responsible for the creation of City Square.

manufactured hydraulic machinery and machine tools such as hydraulic presses, key machines for the mass production of rolling stock, wheels and sleepers, and many other iron and steel products for railways, bridges, and shipbuilding. Clayton, Son and Co. of Hunslet founded in 1868 specialised in making gasholders, reservoirs and oil tanks. Hathorn Davey produced pumping machines of all sizes and types, essential equipment for collieries.[13]

Leeds engineers pioneered the latest technology, constantly developing exciting products, and this inventiveness and originality made the industry prosper. In an age of gas lighting, George Bray produced non-corrosive burners that sold for 2d., and yet were superior to those selling at 18s. Later, faced with competition from electricity, he adapted the burners for street lanterns, which were first exhibited in front of Leeds Town Hall in 1879, and then in the streets of Edinburgh, Manchester, Birmingham, Belfast and Nottingham.[14] Thomas Green's North Street Works established in 1848 produced everything from sausage chopping machines and lawn mowers to early washing machines and guns. His vertical steam engines with unique applications were to be found across the world from Brazilian coffee plantations to Australia and New Zealand.[15] Greenwood and Batley on Armley Road supplied the war departments of Britain, Germany, Russia, Switzerland, Italy, China, Japan, and Turkey with guns, shells, bullets and machinery for bullet making.[16]

Another hugely important industry which developed and rapidly became one the the mainstays of the Leeds economy was the mass-production clothing industry, which was pioneered in Leeds by John Barran. Up to 1850 clothes were still made without the use of any kind

John Barran (1821-1905), the pioneer of the ready-made clothing industry.

of machinery. The middle classes's requirements were met by tailors, whilst the working man wore linen, fustians and moleskins often made at home or by a local seamstress. Barran set up as a tailor and clothes dealer at Bridge End in 1842. Instead of simply making made-to-measure clothes for individual customers, as was then the custom, he began to produce ready-made clothes for wholesale distribution to other clothes dealers and outfitters, as well as for sale in his own shop. In the early 1850s he speeded up production and productivity by installing the revolutionary Singer sewing machines in a small factory in Alfred Street (off Boar Lane). Soon after, he introduced Greenwood and Batley's band-knife, which for the first time allowed many layers of cloth to be cut at the same time. Specialisation was introduced so that workers became proficient at a particular task, and the production of garments was speeded up. The mass-production ready-made clothing industry was born! The town was ideally suited for the growth of this trade because of its strategic position in the cloth producing area, its large market, its engineering skills, its excellent transport facilities and its large supply of female workers used to handling cloth. Moreover, the decline of the textile industry made available old industrial premises for rent at low rates. Initially the town specialised in outwear for men and boys, producing clothes that were both cheap and good. Suits and coats 'off the peg' and boys' fancy suits were common products. By 1881 there were 21 wholesale clothiers listed in the town's trade directory, nearly all concentrated in the area bounded by Park Lane, Westgate, Park Row and Wellington Street.[17]

In addition to the factories and large workshops, the rapid expansion of the clothing trade was facilitated by the growth of a multitude of small workshops and homeworkers. Jewish immigrants driven from Russia and Poland, particularly after 1881, provided a stream of cheap labour. Many became highly skilled tailors with famed business acumen. By 1901 over 20,000 people were involved in the clothing trade as a whole, but conditions were often grim. The Jewish sweatshops, mainly concentrated in the Leylands district between North Street and Regent Street, became notorious.[18] By 1911 clothing accounted for one in four jobs for female workers in Leeds, and the total labour force in the industry had increased to a remarkable 30,000.[19]

John Barran's warehouse and clothing factory, Park Square, built in 1879 (architect, Thomas Ambler).

J.Hepworth & Son, Wholesale Clothiers. At the time this view was drawn in 1888 this impressive factory at 25 Wellington Street had just been 'reconstructed and enlarged'.

The interior of Meanwood Tanneries in 1891. Completed in 1857, it had 300 pits capable of processing 70,000 hides.

Another remarkable feature of the Victorian period was the rapid growth of the local leather industry. As the population had grown in the late Georgian period, the demand for footwear had risen. Skins and hides had been eagerly purchased from the butchers of the town, but the demand for leather had been so great that supplies had needed to be supplemented from India. From these small beginnings the Leeds leather industry grew rapidly between 1850 and 1880. Production was concentrated in the Buslingthorpe, Meanwood and Kirkstall districts. By 1868 the South Market Leather Fair had become the largest leather market outside London. In 1871, 23 tanneries and 60 curriers employed nearly 2000 people. One of the best known tanneries was the 'Joppa' tannery on Kirkstall Road, operated by the Nichols family. In 1858 it covered four acres and had 500 covered pits as well as drying sheds for 15,000 hides. It produced leather for the British government, and became famous for its army leather used in the making of British army boots. Allied to the leather industry, the Leeds shoemaking industry expanded in an astonishing manner. In 1858 two wholesale manufacturers turned out two-thirds of the shoes made in Leeds. Stead and Simpson employed over 1,000 people and made around 7,000 pairs of boots a week. Conyers of Boar Lane employed 600 and produced 4,000 pairs. These were supplemented by boots made in the southern out-townships, where clothiers, unable to compete with the factories, had turned to boot production. At its height in the 1890s Leeds produced 100,000 pairs of boots a week.[20]

Overall, it was the sheer diversity of Leeds industry which amazed and fascinated contemporaries by the end of the Victorian period. In addition to the industries already mentioned, the town had become a centre for printing, paper manufacture, glass production, dyeing, drugs and pharmaceutical products. It had a lucrative timber trade with sawing, planing and moulding mills. Its

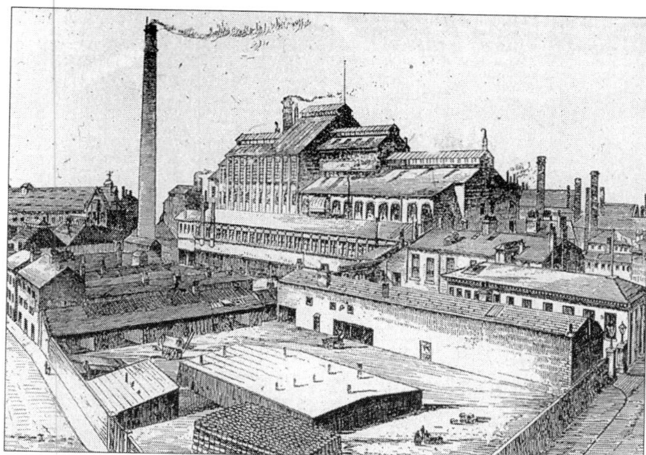

Tetley's Brewery, founded in 1822 when Joshua Tetley (1778-1839) took over William Sykes' brewery in Salem Place, Hunslet. Today Tetley's continue to manufacture ale of the highest standard.

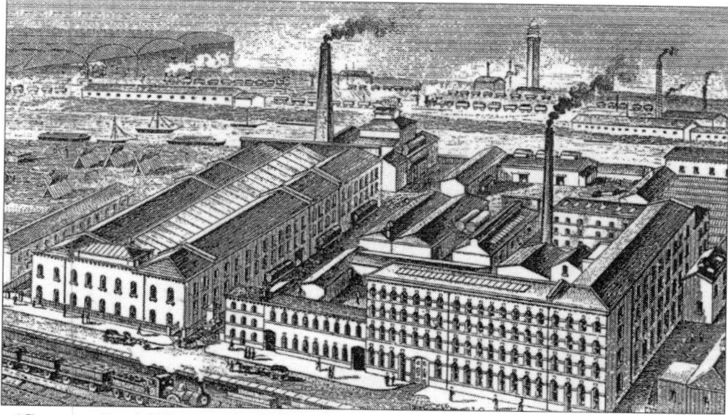

'Soapy Joe' Watson's Whitehall Soap Works, Whitehall Road in 1893.

furniture industry blossomed and by the 1870s there were over 100 manufacturers and 200 cabinet-makers in Leeds, figures which were to have doubled by 1900. The Co-operative Society, started in Benyon's flax mill in 1847, was now one of the biggest concerns in the country, owning its own stores, flour mills, farms, mills and factories. Local brickworks prospered and at Burmantofts beautiful architectural terracotta bricks were produced, not just for the home market but for export to Australia, Hong Kong, Singapore and even Brazil, where they were used on the front of the opera house at Manaos in the heart of the Amazonian jungle. Leeds produced everything from nails to chemicals, printing machines to electric motors and guns to babies' bottles. Many of the firms and their products became household names – Tetley's Bitter, E.J.Arnold's educational printers and suppliers, Moorhouse's Jam, Thorne's toffee, 'Soapy Joe' Watson's Venus soap, and Goodall and Backhouse's 'Yorkshire Relish', which in the 1880s sold six million bottles a year, the largest sale of any sauce in the world![21]

At a time when Britain was the most powerful nation on earth, when its colonies could be found in every corner of the world, Leeds had grown into the fourth largest city in England. Its products were internationally renowned. It had one of the most balanced economies in the country, with a huge diversity of jobs and firms, and at the same time it retained and enhanced its importance as a regional centre. It could justly claim to be 'The Capital of the North'.

Financial and Commercial Capital

A vital part of the growth and increased diversity of the economy of Victorian Leeds was financial, commercial, and legal services. Banking was a highly important, though at first very unstable, part of this sphere. All but one of the five joint-stock banks that had survived the collapse of 1837 went under in the 1840s. The Yorkshire Agricultural and Commercial Bank failed in 1842, and the Yorkshire District Bank in 1843. The others were sheltered for a while by the mid-1840s boom, but depression brought the failure of the Leeds and West Riding Joint Stock Banking Company in 1846 and the Leeds Commercial Joint Stock Bank the following year. Six banks withstood the crisis, above all Beckett's and the Union Bank. In 1859 a new wave of growth was ushered in by the formation of the Yorkshire Penny Savings Bank (today the Yorkshire Bank), and nine new banks or branches of non-Leeds banks were established by 1869. Between 1870 and 1900 the numbers of banks stabilised at about a dozen, despite periodic entries and exits, and thereafter numbers rose sharply as branch banking underwent rapid growth.[22]

A most striking feature of the period was the establishment of the Leeds Stock Exchange. In 1836 there were only two share brokers in Leeds but, as a result of the glut of railway company promotions, the number rose to over a hundred by 1845. In response, in December 1844 the Leeds Stock Exchange Association was formed. The *Leeds Intelligencer* greeted the event with great optimism and pride:

> There can be no doubt that this establishment will tend to increase the importance of the Leeds share business, by facilitating transactions, and thus centring in Leeds that portion of the share trade which the opulence and situation of the town have a right to claim, but which hitherto has (for want of an Exchange in Leeds) been transacted in other marts.[23]

The institution was rather more status-conscious than its provincial counterparts, and in 1846-47 erected its own premises in Albion Street at a cost of £12,500. For many years Leeds was the only provincial town with a purpose-built stock exchange. When the association began trading it had two rival groupings of brokers, but these quickly disappeared as share prices tumbled in the financial and commercial crisis of 1846. By 1850 the shake out left the stock exchange with about 50 brokers, a level of membership which remained stable for many years.[24]

Insurance companies were also strongly represented in Leeds. The premier companies in the town were the Leeds and Yorkshire Fire and Life Insurance established in 1824 with a capital of £1 million, the Norwich Union, and the Sun, all three of which in 1837 maintained fire engines to protect their interests. By then, 35 insurance companies in all had branches or representatives in Leeds. By 1858 the number of companies had risen to over 70. The bigger companies wished to demonstrate their financial stability by erecting impressive buildings. The Leeds and Yorkshire in 1852-55 built offices at the junction of Commercial Street and Albion Street, designed by W.B.Gingell at a cost of £6,000, which even today is one of the city centre's most ornate office buildings.[25] Other striking buildings were to follow, some of which still grace the city centre: the Scottish Widows' Assurance Society building by George Corson built in

Park Row in 1869: the Prudential Assurance Offices also in Park Row designed by Alfred Waterhouse in 1894, and the Standard Life Assurance Company's fire building erected in City Square in 1901.[26] The cluster of impressive banks and insurance company buildings on Park Row by the 1890s led *The Builder* magazine to describe it as the Pall Mall of Leeds. It discussed in detail the architecture of the National Provincial Bank, the Leeds Joint Stock Bank, the Midland Bank, Beckett's Bank, the Royal Assurance Offices (another Waterhouse building), the Sun Fire Office, the Prudential Assurance Office, the Scottish Widows, the Bank of England, and the York City and County Bank. *The Builder* concluded, 'Park Row, taken as a whole, is in an architectural sense no ordinary street; in fact it is not often that one meets with a modern city street which can show so large a proportion of buildings that are worth notice'.[27]

Top: Park Row in 1879 showing the Philosophical Hall on the left, Beckett's Bank on the right, and St Anne's Roman Catholic Cathedral in the distance.

Right: Leeds Stock Exchange built in 1846-7 at the junction of Albion Street and Albion Place.

Banking and insurance apart, the businesses and people of Leeds required other financial and legal services. By 1858, for example, the town had 22 firms of accountants, and by 1899 this had risen to 81. In 1837, 61 attorneys were listed in the trade directories and by mid-century the number had risen to 76 attorneys and solicitors and 4 barristers. By this time the geographical concentration of such talent was remarkable. Albion Street accommodated the offices of 20 solicitors and 7 sharebrokers; Park Row had 6 solicitors and 17 sharebrokers; and Bank Street, close by, was home to 9 solicitors and 1 sharebroker.[28]

Building societies also came to the fore in the Victorian period. Terminating building clubs or societies had first appeared in Leeds in the late eighteenth century, but the permanent building societies of the kind familiar to us today were a mid-nineteenth century phenomenon in Leeds. The Leeds and Holbeck Permanent Building Society was founded in Holbeck in 1875, though it had its origins in a series of terminating societies which commenced in Holbeck in 1845. The society moved its office to Albion Street in 1886. The 1901 directory noted that the society's chief offices in Albion Street occupied a large handsome edifice.[29] The Leeds Permanent Building Society was of marginally shorter lineage being founded in 1848, though by 1900 it was significantly larger than the Leeds and Holbeck.[30]

Leeds Chamber of Commerce was established in 1851 under the stimulus of the Great Exhibition. Its objects, an annual report pointed out, were 'finding new markets,

The Royal Exchange built in 1872-5 on part of the site of the Commercial Buildings on the corner of Park Row and Boar Lane (architect, Thomas Healey).

resisting encroachments upon us from all sides, and agitating for laws to protect us from dishonesty, and removing restrictions in the way of our business'. Delegations were sent to foreign exhibitions, and lectures on commercial and economic subjects were frequently arranged. Among the speakers on opportunities abroad was the 'intrepid African explorer', the Revd Dr Livingstone, who in 1857 addressed the members on 'the commercial bearing of his recent discoveries in Africa'. The chamber also provided a commercial and business information service specifically for local needs. In essence, it represented the collective voice of commerce and industry, the town's leading merchants, manufacturers, lawyers and bankers. Membership rose from 87 in 1851 to 228 in 1898, and it still thrives today.[31]

Facilities for the meeting of the business community were threatened by the demolition of the Commercial Buildings. But it was immediately replaced by the Royal Exchange which was erected on the same site in 1872-5. Costing £61,000, it incorporated an exchange room, a newsroom, shops, a club, a restaurant, and offices.[32]

The Press

The circulation of commercial, political and general information in the town was greatly facilitated by the town's two great newspapers, the *Leeds Mercury* and the *Leeds Intelligencer*. Both papers went from strength to strength in the nineteenth century. The presence of these newspapers, whose presses were used to print books and pamphlets as well, combined with the large number of booksellers in the town (52 by 1858), made Leeds a mecca of the printing industry in the Victorian era. The press provided vital commercial information as well as detailed accounts of national and local current affairs. From 1842 the *Intelligencer* was edited by Christopher Kemplay (the son of Richard Kemplay, the schoolmaster) who became its proprietor in 1849. It had a wide circulation, not merely in the West Riding but also in the principal towns of the North and East Ridings. By 1858 this weekly paper was printed with a four-page 'Supplement' and was sold at 4d. unstamped and 5d. stamped. It was then noted that:

> Its reports of local proceedings, especially those connected with the Church and Conservative party, are given with great fulness and care. As a commercial, family, and general weekly newspaper, the *Intelligencer* has obtained a high position amongst the provincial journals of this kingdom.

The *Intelligencer*, however, was surpassed in the nineteenth century by the *Leeds Mercury*. By 1858 the *Mercury* now run by Edward Baines, junior, and Frederick Baines (the sons of Edward Baines), was printed three times a week – on Tuesdays, Thursdays and Saturdays. It was by then the biggest circulation provincial journal in the country, and had an influence nationwide rather similar to that of the *Manchester Guardian* in the twentieth century.[33]

Such was the avidity for the consumption of news and information in Leeds that three more newspapers were established in Leeds by 1858. The *Leeds Times*, a Radical/Liberal newspaper, was established in 1833. From small beginnings this weekly paper, published on Saturdays, had reached a circulation of 12,000 copies a week by 1858. Between 1838 and 1842 it was edited by Dr Samuel Smiles, who later became one of the best known figures of the Victorian age with his classic best selling books, such as *Self-Help* and *Lives of the Engineers*, which extolled the Victorian values of self-reliance and self-betterment through individual effort and perseverance.[34]

In 1857 another Saturday paper, the *Leeds Express*, was established. It proudly proclaimed itself to be 'Liberal and Independent: unfettered by ties that might impede its free action, it strenuously advocates the cause of civil and religious liberty, and all measures tending to ameliorate the social and political condition of the working classes'.[35] The *West Riding Penny Post* advocating Liberal principles was also published in Leeds at this time.[36]

In 1861 the *Leeds Mercury* became a daily newspaper, and the *Intelligencer* followed suit in 1866 under the new title of the *Yorkshire Post and Leeds Intelligencer*.[37] Both the *Mercury* and what gradually became best known as the *Yorkshire Post* produced weekly supplements, the latter's, *The Yorkshire Weekly Post*, being a full-blown paper with a magazine style content. The *Leeds Express* remained a weekly paper throughout the Victorian period, but a new daily evening paper the *Leeds Daily News* was established in 1872. By 1901 to these papers published in Leeds could be added *The Magnet* (weekly), the *Sporting Chronicle* (daily), the *Sunday Chronicle* (weekly), the *Sunday Guardian* (weekly), the *Leeds Saturday Journal*, and *The Skyrack Courier* (weekly).[38]

Hotels

As a great commercial and industrial capital Leeds needed many hotels. Since the trade directories grouped hotels, inns and taverns together, it is difficult to distinguish the number of establishments offering good quality overnight accommodation. However, the 1858 *Leeds Guide* gives a selective list of the better quality establishments, some of whose names are still familiar to us today. For the 'principal hotels' it listed the Golden Lion and the Bull and Mouth, both in Briggate, describing them as 'old established commercial hotels'. To these it added as 'good' or 'convenient' commercial hotels: the Albion Hotel and the Royal Hotel, Briggate; the Griffin, West Bar; the Great Northern, Wellington Street; the Peel Hotel, and the White Horse, Boar Lane; and the Scarborough Hotel, Bishopgate Street. In the lesser category of 'highly respectable family and commercial boarding houses' it listed Andrew's and Beecroft's, both in Bishopgate Street, indicating that they were temperance hotels. To these were added Brown's,

The first Queen's Hotel, built in 1863, occupied the same site as the present hotel on the south side of City Square (architect, William Perkin).

Butler's, and Stanwix's, all in Briggate, and Oates's at West Bar, all with dining rooms and 'moderate charges'.[39]

By 1879 there had been extremely important additions to these facilities, most notably the Queen's Hotel, adjoining the New Station, Wellington Street; the Trevelyan Temperance Hotel, Boar Lane; the rebuilt Griffin Hotel; The Green Dragon Hotel, Guildford Street (now the Guildford); The Commercial, Albion Street; the Victoria Hotel, Great George Street; and the Wheatsheaf, on the Upperhead Row.[40] Perhaps the most impressive late Victorian addition was the splendid terracotta Hotel Metropole in King Street, opened in 1899. In one of the last flings of Victorian eccentricity, its proprietors had the audacity to mount the cupola of the fourth White Cloth Hall, on whose site the hotel was built, on its roof.[41]

The Post Office

Efficient postal communications were extremely important to the trade and industry of Leeds. By the 1830s the service was really quite sophisticated and surprisingly speedy considering the state of communications. The Revd Edward Parsons, who was not slow to criticise things he found fault with, in 1834 described the Post Office establishment in Leeds as 'an admirably conducted establishment [which] by its punctuality and propriety of arrangement, materially conduces to the commercial advantage and prosperity of the town'. He considered it a 'wonderful system'. A letter posted in Leeds at 9 p.m. would be in London by teatime the following day. Letters to most of the principal towns in the north of England would arrive within 24 hours. Letters to most major European countries could be dispatched once or twice a week. The fact that letters to other parts of the world could only be dispatched on one specified day each month says much about the long and uncertain delivery times. It is nevertheless impressive that in the 1830s someone could stroll into the Leeds Post Office and send off letters to such seemingly remote and exotic places as Madeira, Brazil, Jamaica, China, Australia, and America. Parsons marvelled that such was the magnitude of transactions that, at a time when inland postage cost around 4d. per half-ounce, the postage collected in Leeds during the year ending 5 January 1834 was £21,331.[42]

In 1834 the post office was in Mill Hill. When, in January 1840, the government introduced the uniform postal rate of one penny per half-ounce for any distance – Rowland Hill's Penny Post – the postal service was revolutionised. Requiring much larger accommodation, a big warehouse was taken in the lower part of Albion Street. By 1858 the post office staff numbered 25 clerks and 26 letter carriers, with three town and suburban deliveries each day! There were ten pillar boxes and 19 'receiving houses' in different parts of the town and suburbs.[43] In 1861 the Court House in Park Row was purchased by the government and converted to serve as the main post office and in 1872 another storey was added for the purposes of the postal telegraph. By 1879 the postal staff numbered 385 and postal deliveries were now made four times a day.[44] The ever increasing demand for postal and money order services was reflected in the building of the fine new General Post Office in City Square, on the site of the Coloured Cloth Hall, opened in April 1896 to the design of Henry Tanner, at a cost of £75,000.[45]

The Coming of the Railways

The economic success of Georgian Leeds had been strongly underpinned by its excellent transport facilities. The ability to transport raw materials, goods and people locally, nationally and internationally, better than rival towns, was critical to the town's prosperity. The coming of the railways, which were more footloose than water transport and much faster, would have led to a major challenge to the town's regional supremacy if it had not taken them up with alacrity. In the event, it became one the great railway centres of the Victorian age.

The advantages of the new form of transport caught the popular imagination and by the mid-1820s Leeds was in the grip of 'railway mania'. By early 1825 railways from Leeds to Selby, Leeds to Hull, and Leeds to Manchester were under enthusiastic consideration, but all three were quashed by the commercial crash of 1825/26.[46] The most important project, the Leeds to Selby line, was revived in 1829 and a company was formed by Act of Parliament in 1830 to build the railway. Transport to Hull was of vital importance to industry and commerce in Leeds, and the leading businessmen of the town were determined to break the stranglehold of the Aire and Calder Navigation whose proprietors were now enjoying annual dividends of over 250 per cent. The list of the holders of £100 shares reads like a roll call of the most prosperous entrepreneurs in Leeds. By taking goods to Selby by train, they could be loaded on to boats on the Ouse, and reach Hull totally avoiding the Aire and Calder. The line opened in 1834. The historian, Edward Parsons, was so impressed that he devoted seven pages of his book to it and included a plan of the railway. He noted:

> The railway sets out from the upper end of Marsh Lane, one of the most unpleasant and dirty, but likely soon to become one of the most improving parts of the town of Leeds. The Company's warehouses are admirably arranged, they are vastly extensive, and afford every possible convenience for the reception and transmission of passengers and goods.[47]

Though the railway was a great success, the day of its opening, 22 September 1834, was memorable for all the wrong reasons. The engine, the 'Nelson', pulled three first-class carriages – 'Juno', 'Dizina' and 'Vesta', all painted yellow, and six second-class carriages, open to the elements. The guards, dressed in fine green liveries, ensured that the 156 passengers were safely seated, and at 6.30 am the train set out from Leeds. Thousands lined the route to watch the spectacle. Unfortunately the track was wet with rain and the load proved too heavy for the engine, the wheels began to spin and ashes had to be strewn on the rails. In desperation, to the accompanying jeers of the crowd, the guards detached a second-class coach and redistributed the passengers among the remaining five. Slowly the train began to move, but after an hour and ten minutes it was still less than five miles from Leeds! These teething troubles, however, were resolved and the line operated well, carrying a great deal of freight and 3,500 passengers a week in the summer months.[48]

In 1835 the North Midland Railway Company was formed to build a line from Derby to Leeds. This opened in July 1840, with its station just south of Hunslet Lane, and linked Leeds directly with the Midlands and London. The company provided for three classes of passenger, but

Holbeck Junction in 1868.

clearly had a vested interest in travellers occupying the more expensive seats. Some claimed that chimney sweeps were being paid to travel in third-class carriages to encourage anyone who valued the appearance of their clothes to travel first or second class. Indeed, pigs were sometimes carried in the third-class car![49] In 1836-41 the Manchester to Leeds line was built. Though a great boon for freight carriage, it too offered little comfort for passengers paying the lower fares, as the *Leeds Mercury* noted:

> A passenger by the second-class carriages on the Manchester and Leeds complains that himself and a female relative have caught a severe cold from the holes in the floors of the carriages, which admit currents of air to the legs of passengers; he asks if there is any use or object in these holes, except to drive passengers into the first-class carriages. We cannot answer him.[50]

The amalgamation in 1844 of the North Midland Company with the Midland Counties and Birmingham & Derby Junction Railways created the Midland Railway Company which thereby became the largest railway in the country under a single management. The company's Hunslet Lane Station, however, was not ideally situated. When the Leeds and Bradford Railway opened in 1846, it built 'Wellington Station', between the river and canal basin, the first town centre passenger station, with its entrance on to Quebec by the Coloured Cloth Hall. The Midland quickly obtained powers to run into the station and transferred its passenger services to the Wellington site, constructing additional platforms which opened on 1 October 1850.[51]

The Leeds-Thirsk Railway was established in 1845-49 and ran trains into its own station (subsequently known as 'Central Station') on Wellington Street, just to the west of Wellington Station.[52] These two stations were soon to be supplemented by the Great Northern. *White's 1853 Directory* noted:

> During the last six years, the railway accommodation in Leeds has been greatly improved and extended by the formation of the *Wellington*, *Central*, and *Great Northern Stations* which extend about 700 yards along the south side of Wellington Street, and from which all the *Passenger trains* now depart, except those which leave *Marsh Lane Station*, for Milford Junction, to meet the York and Hull trains. There are two stations near Kirkstall, one on the Leeds and Bradford, and the other on the Leeds Northern Railway. The latter is called Headingley and Kirkstall Station.[53]

It reckoned that six to ten trains left Wellington Station each day, eight from Central Station, six from the Great Northern Station, and six from Marsh Lane.

By 1864 many of the smaller railway companies had merged into larger companies. The North Eastern had for some time realised that the isolated position of its Marsh Lane station was very detrimental to its share of the passenger market and its future profitability required improved interchange facilities with other railways. In response, in conjunction with the London and North Western, it decided to build a station adjacent to the south side of Wellington Station and extend its line from Marsh Lane across the town centre to this new terminus. The scheme was to have a dramatic impact on both the appearance and the physical development of the town centre for many years – an impact which is still strongly felt even today. Construction commenced in 1866. The route of the line, which had been fiercely debated, cut through the burial ground of the parish church, crossed the quadrangle of the Third White Cloth Hall, and ran across Briggate to the site abutting the Wellington Station. To prevent desecration of the graveyard, the enabling Act of Parliament stipulated that the railway should pass on a solid embankment so as not to interfere with the graves. The gravestones from the graves under the embankment were to be placed in corresponding positions on its slopes. The proprietors of the old White Cloth Hall were compensated with a new cloth hall on the east side of King Street. Once details had been finalised, work started on the extension, a quite remarkable engineering achievement, with the arches alone using over 18 million bricks. The 1,500 yard extension opened on 1 April 1869. It had cost an estimated £500,000 and, apart from 90 yards of embankment, it was carried on brick arches.[54] The press conveyed the wonderment of the whole feat:

> A small proportion of the thousands who pass in and out of the Wellington Station in the course of a day, never realise that the station itself is reared upon arches which bridge the Leeds and Liverpool Canal and a weir from the Aire; and in building the new station, which stands in parallel position to the Wellington, similar difficulties had to be encountered, and those who have not penetrated to the cavernous regions which constitute its basement, can hardly picture to themselves the magnitude of the enterprise, and the vast labour and skill which had been exerted in its completion.[55]

The building of the station created the Dark Arches. The novelty of the whole enterprise was conveyed by a newspaper report on 4 March 1869 which described the passage of the first trains:

> Although the inhabitants of Leeds had for the last two or three years been watching with increasing

interest the steady progress of these extensive works ...they were scarcely prepared for the scene that was witnessed this day. Railways through large towns are common enough now, but the sight of a locomotive steaming across some of the principal streets in Leeds was so entirely novel that the spectacle caused no small amount of amazement. Passers-by in the leading thoroughfares gazed in wonderment and admiration, and trades people hastened to the doors of their business premises, only to join in the expressions of astonishment. The moving locomotive was best seen from Briggate. As it crossed the girder bridge at the foot of that busy thoroughfare, the passengers gave a hearty cheer, and as the sound died away those who had heard it became fully alive to the fact that the undertaking was rapidly approaching completion, and that in reality the enormous traffic of a giant company would, ere long, be carried across the streets and amongst the house-tops.[56]

There could be little doubt that the opening of this line centralised passenger facilities in the town. Long distance rail links rapidly destroyed the coaching firms, yet the railways and industry grew hand in hand. Early railways were gradually absorbed to form larger units so that by the end of the First World War the city was directly served by only four companies – the North Eastern, the London and North Western, the Midland and the Great Northern, though the Lancashire and Yorkshire and the Great Central had running powers into the city using other companies' lines. The trend towards amalgamation and the decline of competition was deplored by Victorian businessmen, who objected to railway monopolies in the same manner as Gott, Marshall and Baines, before them, had objected to the monopoly of the Aire and Calder Navigation Company.[57]

An unusual feature in the case of Leeds, however, was that the coming of the railways did not wipe out the local waterways as competitors. When asked about this remarkable position by the River Pollution commissioners in 1866, Mr Bartholomew, the engineer of the Aire and Calder Navigation confirmed that the volume of traffic on the navigation had continued to rise, and the only decline had been in 'some articles of a higher class'. The staple goods carried were coal and corn. Stone flags and building stone also were still carried in considerable quantities, as were manure, limestone, lime and salt. He noted the carriage of 'pottery ware and a considerable amount of high class goods, bales and merchandise traffic'. One of the major reasons for the continued success, he reckoned, was the ready means of shipment at the port direct from the navigation's boats to the steamers. Goods could be being loaded on steamers at Goole within 9-10 hours of leaving Leeds or 13 hours if they were going to Hull, so they could compete with railways on time, convenience and cost.[58]

Early in the Victorian period the company had given up using horses to tow barges. Bartholomew noted that by 1866 it cost 2½d. per mile to tow by steam compared to 7½d. by horse. The cost of towing by steam tug had dropped considerably over the previous two or three decades. When the company had first introduced steam paddle tugs about thirty years before, it had cost 10½d per mile, but they now used screws as opposed to paddles. They towed at around 4½-6 miles per hour on the river. At one point in an attempt to encourage or perhaps retain passenger traffic, they had run fast boats towed by horses running at 9 miles per hour, but they soon gave them up because there was not enough passenger traffic to make them profitable.[59]

The view from Victoria Bridge c. 1868. In the middle distance is the chimney of Soapy Joe's Soap Works, to the right, beyond the bridge, is Victoria Coal Wharf, and across the river is Teal's boatyard. The lock used to enter the Leeds and Liverpool canal can be clearly seen to the left of centre and beside it is the Leeds and Liverpool Canal warehouse.

The Polluted Environment

The great drawback to continued rapid growth of industry and population in Leeds – and to its impressively growing wealth – was dramatically increased levels of pollution and squalor. Robert Baker, the influential Leeds doctor, councillor and factory inspector, in his 1842 report ranked smoke as one of the major nuisances in Leeds. He railed at the smoke emitted by the town's 362 steam engines, but drew attention also to the impact of the dye-house pans, 'whose chimneys are very low, and generally built alongside the brooks and rivulets, and contiguous to the dwellings of the poor, [and] pour out their dense volumes of unconsumed carbon, which traverses the streets and fills the houses'.[60] Smoke from factories, foundries, mills, dye works and domestic fires filled the air, but little effective action was taken.

The River Aire was in a disgraceful state too. Robert Baker, commented in 1858: 'Though a trout stream within the last seventy years having footpaths clothed with avenues of trees, [it] is now nothing but an open sewer, containing first the sewerage of Bradford, of Shipley, and lastly of all the Mills, Houses Dyehouses, Tanneries and Workshops which crowd its western banks.'[61] The mills and factories which had initially been drawn to the river for water power, now crammed the banks because of the access to both ready transport and, perhaps most important of all, the availability of large quantities of water. When taking evidence in Leeds in November 1866, the Royal Commission on the Pollution of Rivers heard graphic evidence of how the river was polluted:

> The river Aire and its tributaries are abused by passing into it hundreds and thousands of tons per annum of ashes, slag, and cinders from steam-boiler furnaces, ironworks, and domestic fires; by their being made the receptacle to a vast extent of broken pottery and worn-out utensils of metal, refuse brick from brick-yards and old buildings, earth, stone, and

Leeds Bridge in 1849. A grim scene showing bargees trying to steer their vessels through narrow arches that cross a river polluted with sewage, dye waste, rubbish from the Infirmary and the filth from mills and towns upstream. Heavy waggons cross the bridge towards the elegant Georgian buildings on Briggate, now defaced and covered with grime from the traffic and the smoke polluted sky.

clay from quarries and excavations, food scrapings, street sweeps, &c.; by spent dyewoods and other solids used in the treatment of worsteds and woollens; ...and by flowing in, to the amount of very many millions of gallons per day, of water poisoned, corrupted, and clogged by refuse from mines, chemical works, dyeing, scouring, and fulling worsted and woollen stuffs, skin-cleaning and tanning, slaughter house garbage and the sewerage of towns and houses.[62]

In particular they noted the way the owners of steam engines threw the cinder and ash from the furnaces (around one-eighth of the volume of the coal originally used) into the river:

> In dry weather periods the greater proportion of the bed of the river opposite such mills or works is filled by the 'cinder tip'. A stranger to the district, looking upon such a state of things for the first time, thinks it must be the deliberate intention of the manufacturer for some trade purpose or other, entirely to block the river at this point.

The report highlighted the vast quantities of river water used by the Leeds tanneries. All this water with its impurities was flushed back into the river. Richard Nichols, owner of Joppa Tannery on Kirkstall Road, with 300 workers and 320 tan pits which tanned about 12,000 skins of horned cattle, calfskins, horse hides, cowhides and sheepskins per week, used 120,000 gallons of water each week to wash 4,000-5,000 sheepskins.[64] Mr Reffitt's dye-works in Kirkstall Road was another typical offender using half a million gallons of water a day, (mainly from the river) the liquid refuse going first into a sewer and then into the river.[65] At Bank Mills, one of the town's principal flax mills, just beyond Crown Point Bridge, river water was used at a rate of 1,000 gallons per minute (600,000 gallons per day). It was reckoned that, before it re-entered the river, half the water was polluted by the machinery or the lavatories. The stench of the river at this point was so great that Mr Tenant, a partner in Hives and Atkinson's Bank Mills, had to keep his window shut in the summer.[66] Dead animals in the river were another nuisance: Mr Swale, the Inspector of Nuisances for the borough, reckoned that 50 dead animals came out of the river each day. He noted in particular 'a large accumulation of dead animals between Leeds Bridge and the Leeds and Liverpool Canal'.[67]

Sewage in the river water was the other major problem. When cattle plague broke out at Thorpe Hall pasture (on the banks of the Aire about one mile down river from Leeds) in August 1865, the chairman of the West Riding bench of magistrates, Francis Darwin, went down to investigate accompanied by the superintendent of police, having been advised to have his lunch first and not take it with him: 'On arriving at the place where the sewerage of Leeds is cast into the river, I certainly was very much astonished. I observed human excrement and carcasses of dogs and cats, and I may say I never saw anything so frightful in my life; every eddy of the stream was manifestly full of human excrement of the most terrible kind.' He estimated that eight to ten million gallons of raw sewerage was being passed into the Aire at this point every day.[68]

By the 1890s the level of environmental pollution was little better. In 1894 Alfred Orage, a schoolteacher, living in Chapel Allerton, presented a dismal picture:

> The view of the town from some outlying hill is like a peep from Abraham's bosom into the abode of Dives. Here on the height the air is fresh to the lungs ...But yonder, down there, the infernal pot is boiling, and the steam hangs like a nightmare over the city. Dantes need no Virgil to show them Hell; and Miltons need not to be blind. There, night and day, thousands of chimneys are allowed to belch out their poisonous breaths to be inhaled by human lungs below.
>
> The Aire is simply a huge sewer; it has the filth of Leeds in suspension. Unlike the Jordan seven dips therein would cause, not cure leprosy ...it has been transformed into the oily-flowing mud stream, into whose waters no fish dare venture, on whose banks no leaves can breathe, no trees may grow.[69]

As we shall see, these appalling environmental conditions had a major impact on the lives of the townspeople of Leeds.

Middle-class Domesticity

What were the townspeople of Victorian Leeds like? How did they live? Broadly speaking the population could be divided into two social groups – the middle class and the working class – though there were many subtle gradations within these classes. Let us turn first to the middle classes; the group in whose higher ranks were to be found the people who effectively controlled town

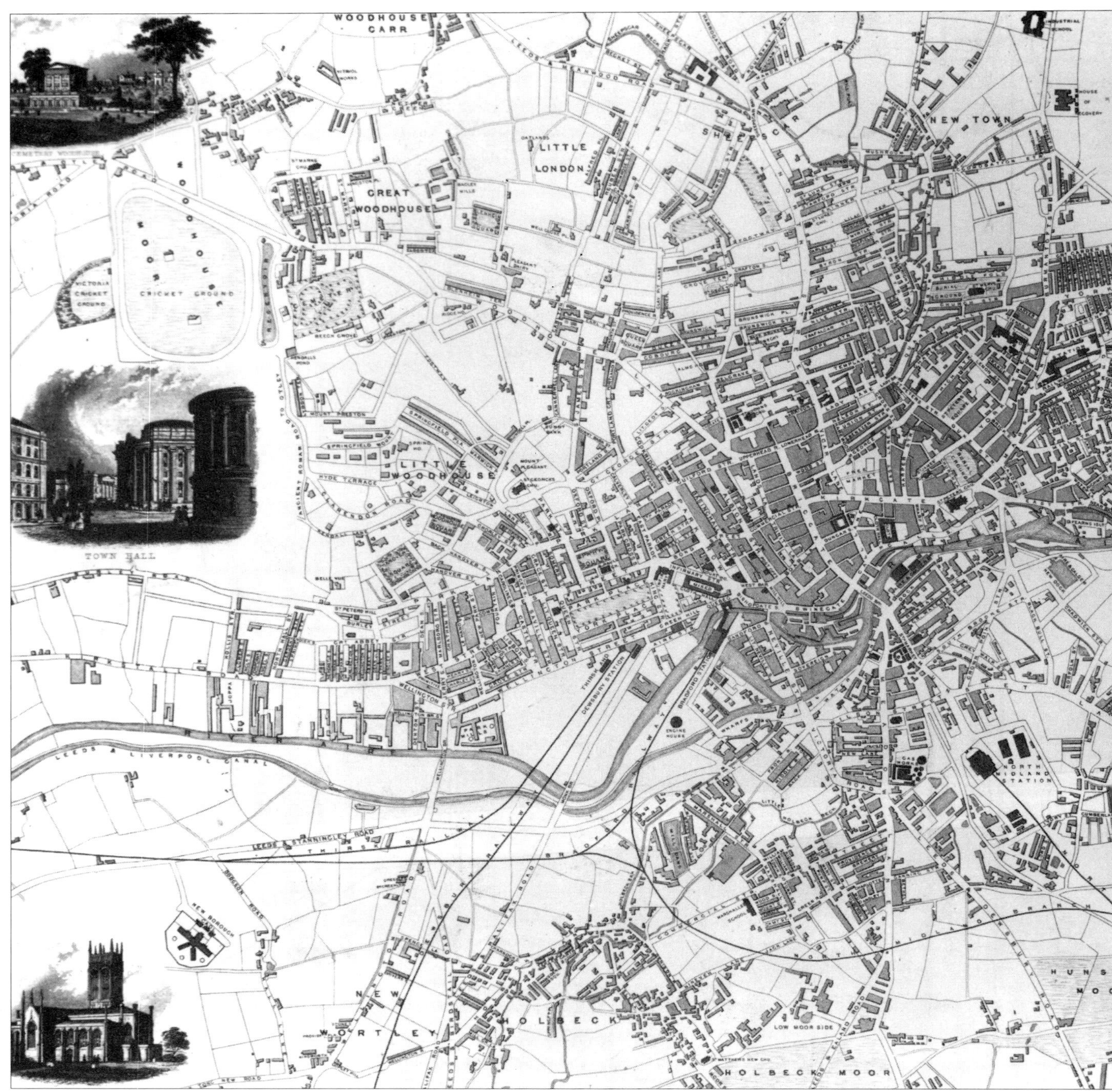

life. The middle classes were the providers of the capital for the industrial and commercial development of Leeds and the principal beneficiaries from it. In the 1820s and '30s a more distinct and coherent middle class had been created. Middle class status was attained by a variety of attributes of which income level on its own was not a sufficient qualification. In 1865 the journalist, J. Tomlinson, observing a large number of men leaving a Leeds locomotive works, was struck by the paradox that the weekly earnings of these men 'in grimy moleskin clothes' (clothes made of coarse, twilled cotton fabric) was on average far more than that commanded by a 'genteel clerk', probably the lowest rank within the middle classes, 'who must appear in fine broad cloth and immaculate shirt collars and contrive, out of his slender income, to keep up a respectable appearance, and yet to make some provision for his family or his old age.'[70] Indeed, to be middle class required a certain style of manners, dress, and social behaviour.

By common convention to be indisputably middle class in the first half of the nineteenth century an income was required of at least £150 a year; more, that is, than the wage of all but a handful of highly-skilled workers and an amount which would normally allow the employment of some domestic help.[71] There were, nevertheless, many people on lesser incomes who might through education, occupation, manner, and social and cultural aspiration, be grouped with the lower middle classes. It is not easy to ascertain the incomes from middle-class occupations, but here are a few examples of the remuneration of Leeds people receiving salaries as opposed to living on profits from business. In 1836 the Chief Constable received £250 per annum, while his superintendent received £100, and the inspectors £75. The Vicar of St John's, Briggate in the 1840s received a salary of £380 per annum. The matron of Leeds Infirmary earned only 50 guineas in 1862, though this was three times the salary of the nurses. In 1862 the

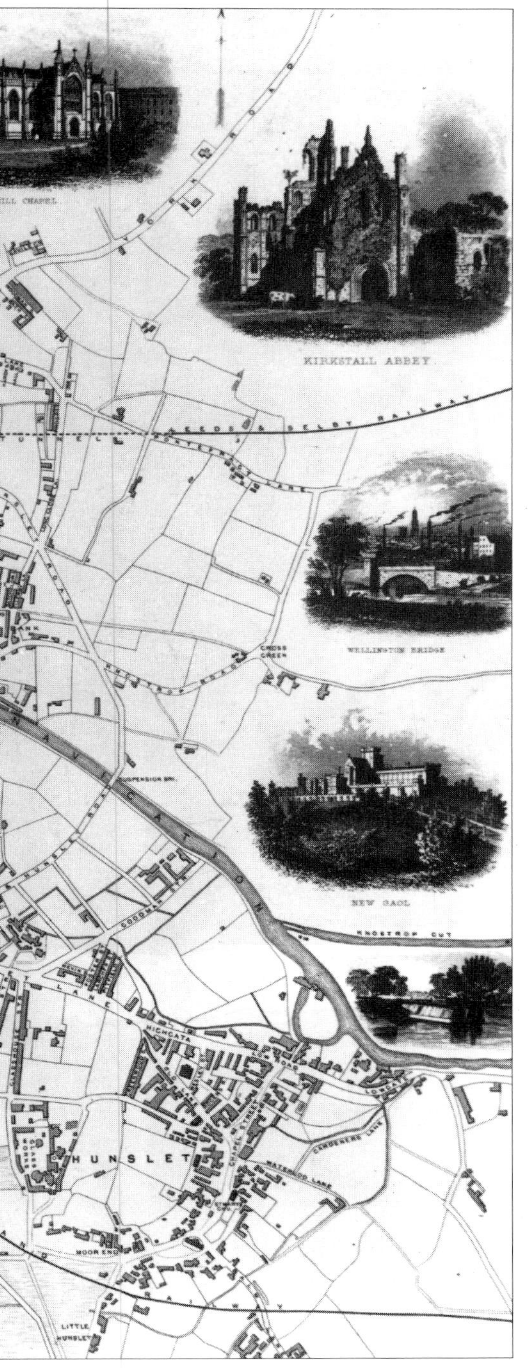

Rapkin's Map of Leeds in 1850. In its way this map is as much an essay in civic pride as was Cossins' plan of 1726. The vignettes include the private General Cemetery near Woodhouse Moor, the new Mill Hill Chapel, the recently built Armley Gaol, and Wellington Bridge, with Park Mills behind it and St Paul's Church, Park Square, and St. John's Church in the distance. The arrival of the railways is highly conspicuous.

Right: Woodbine Terrace, Headingley, genteel stone terrace houses for the middle classes.

headmaster of Leeds Grammar School had a salary of £500 per annum plus a quarter of the school tuition fees, a further £300. In 1895 the salaries of the assistant masters ranged from £150-£250.[72]

As the environmental conditions of the town grew worse, the trend for the wealthier middle classes to desert the central area accelerated. In the first half of the nineteenth century it was taken for granted that the middle classes would rent their houses, so it was relatively easy for people to change homes if they wished. John Atkinson of Little Woodhouse, giving evidence to the Select Committee on Smoke Prevention in 1845, stated:

> Park Place and Park Square, which used to be the residences of the best families in Leeds, have been gradually desecrated for several years past in consequence of the increasing smoke ...The houses there are too large for persons of moderate means, and are too smoky for those who could live in them. They are in the best part of Leeds but the parties are driven out of town; they live a mile or two out of town now; and as they have means of omnibuses they can do it. They used to live near their businesses.[73]

Darnton Lupton, mayor, added: 'Home property is much lessened in Leeds by the smoke; almost 25 to 30 per cent because everyone does as I did a few years ago. I went out, I could not bear it any longer; and everyone who can is going out of town.'[74] In the 1840s 'everyone who can' meant the upper middle class – the most affluent four per cent of the population.

As we saw in the previous chapter, up to the 1820s most of the middle classes, who could afford to move, limited their moves to the northern fringes of the township, but many of the wealthy merchants, bankers and new industrialists went further afield, taking leases on properties in the villages of Headingley or Chapel Allerton and Potternewton or on farmhouses with potential for improvement.[75] At the begining of Victoria's reign more than half of Headingley was still owned by the Earl of Cardigan, and over half of Potternewton (the area more commonly referred to as Chapeltown today) was accounted for by the combined estates of the Earl of Mexborough and Earl Cowper. These aristocratic landowners became increasingly keen to exploit their estates. The low density residential development of Headingley Hill had begun in the late 1820s with the building of mansions and villas of a superior class, but the large excess supply of building land had led by 1850 to a lowering of the landowners' and builders' aspirations resulting in 'commodious and respectable dwelling houses' on much smaller plots. Though smaller, these were still extremely desirable houses with large gardens and annual rentals in the region of £30. Since the norm was for the middle classes to spend between one-tenth and one-eighth of their income on housing, this implied tenants with income of £240-£300 per annum. It was still only the more well-to-do middle classes who had made the move.

From 1850-70, however, large numbers of the middle classes managed to move out. 'Respectable terraces' with accommodation for one or two servants, though rarely with provision for a stable or carriage house began to be built. Such dwelling houses in the Hyde Park area just beyond Woodhouse Moor, for example, at £20-£40 annual rent, were taken mostly by tradesmen who had businesses in Leeds, or professional men, who 'transacted business at offices in Leeds during the day and hoped to return home at night to quietness and peace'.[76] The developments were projected by quite a number of competing landowners and builders and initiatives were both encouraged and buffeted by swings in local prosperity. As a result the process of developing the suburbs was often one of misjudged opportunities, abortive schemes and long drawn out projects. Nevertheless, the population of the northern out-townships (or suburbs) began to grow rapidly. The census report for 1861 found it necessary to explain the 50 per cent increase in Burley and Headingley since 1851 by the presence of 'a large part of the mercantile community of Leeds'. The availability of the omnibuses from the town centre to Headingley and Potternewton and Chapel Allerton from 1838 facilitated the move to the suburbs.

An idyllic suburban street scene in peaceful Chapel Allerton, a haven for the monied classes.

Despite such moves, it would be a mistake to imagine that the middle classes became physically segregated from the working classes in this period, for all the wards of the town continued to have a mixture of working-class and middle-class residents. Indeed, between the mid-century and the early 1870s the degree of residential segregation of the less affluent members of the middle classes actually declined. Most middle-class families would have had working-class families living close by. Even as far north as the community of Far Headingley, created in 1831 by the selling of building plots as a by-product of the enclosure of Headingley Moor, magnificent houses such as Castle Grove might be found just a stones throw from the the new four-roomed working-class dwellings of Cottage Road. About half of the upper middle class (around two per cent of the population) were settled in the north-western district of Leeds by 1871, constituting perhaps half of its population and thus forming a superior middle-class suburb. But this still left half of the upper middle class living in other parts of the town, and perhaps another ten per cent of the population, who might be regarded as middle class, residing in other areas of Leeds.[77] What was significant about the small, wealthy middle-class group who lived in Mill Hill, Headingley and the suburban villages to the north, was that they spent their domestic life in the most exclusive social setting in Leeds, while being the most influential people in the town. It was these people, whose familiarity with the conditions of working-class life might be much more limited than that of the middle classes as a whole, who took most of the initiative in political, cultural and philanthropic affairs.

The arrival of the 'respectable' terraces in Headingley drove the most affluent of the upper middle class still further afield in search of the genuine social seclusion of a mansion. In 1861, for example, William Brown built Bardon Grange in Weetwood Lane, and the banker Henry Oxley built 'The Elms' (now Oxley Hall). The following

The Elms, Weetwood, built in 1861 for the banker Henry Oxley. One of the many grand houses set in their own grounds, built for the upper middle classes in the northern suburbs of Leeds. Today the house is known as Oxley Hall and is a university hall of residence.

The impressive study in Gledhow Hall, the home of James Kitson.

year, the brewer F.W.Tetley, commissioned George Corson to design 'Foxhill'. 'Spenfield', near the reservoirs on the Otley Road, was designed in 1875 for another member of the Oxley family. Others went beyond the northern fringes of the borough into Roundhay and Adel.

One of the major factors which distinguished the middle classes from the working classes was the employment of domestic help. At the start of Victoria's reign an income of £150 might make possible a servant for occasional charing at £3 a year. On £200 a year there might be a young resident maid-servant at £9 a year, and at £250 the 'wife' could be promoted to a 'lady' and have an experienced maid-servant at £16 a year.[78] Generally, a greater income brought a larger domestic staff. At the most affluent level of the middle classes in Leeds in 1851, the Nicholson family of the Mansion, Roundhay Park, had nine servants ranging from scullery maid to butler.[79]

The superior incomes of the middle classes meant that they could consume a much greater range of goods than the working classes. There was great competition for their custom amongst the grocers, butchers, tea dealers, bakers, high class confectioners, booksellers and specialist dealers of Briggate, the Headrow, Commercial Street, Call Lane, Kirkgate, Vicar Lane, and Woodhouse Lane.

As the century wore on, the domestic expenditures of the middle classes were pushed up by the growth in the 'paraphernalia of gentility'. These increasingly elaborate and ostentatious consumption habits were reflected in the growing elegance of Leeds shops and the range of goods they sold. In the 1850s Joseph Smith and Son of Commercial Street respectfully informed 'the Nobility, Gentry and Public generally' of their ability to supply hats, hosiery, coats, shirts, ties, etc. of all descriptions. While 'the Misses Taylor of the Lower Head Row (successors to Miss Harrison)' supplied fashionable head dresses, dress caps, widows' caps, ribbons, flowers, feathers, etc. Ladies and gentlemen 'wishing to procure boots and shoes with perfect ease and comfort in fitting combined with elegance and first-rate quality' need go no further than Mr Paley's 'Boot and Shoe Establishment' in Briggate. Furs in the newest Parisian and London fashions might be bought at the 'Fur

Shopping in Briggate c.1875. Until the redevelopment of Boar Lane, Briggate was almost unchallenged as one of the finest shopping streets in Yorkshire. Its shops pandered to the needs of the middle-class clientelle.

Establishment' in Commercial Street. Damasks, moreens, tournays, window cornices, table covers, blankets, sheetings, linens and Hollands could be purchased at Denby and Co. at the Exchange Rooms, Albion Street.[80]

Clocks, watches, jewelry and silverplate could be bought at Hirst Brothers in Briggate; furniture, carpets and wall paper from G.W.England of Commercial Street. Ironmongery and hardware of all descriptions ranging from stoves, fenders, and fire irons to papier-mache tea trays and silver-plate cutlery could be bought from John Wright of Boar Lane – ironmonger to the nobility and gentry. Piano fortes could be bought from many establishments; the instruments made by Smith and Whinkup of Woodhouse and Wade Lanes 'united power, purity and justness of tone'. Carriages and gigs of all descriptions could be bought from the 'West Riding Carriage Manufactory' in Great George Street which claimed to have on display the largest stock of carriages in the country.[81]

Having acquired the trappings of middle-class gentility, the middle classes – at least the most affluent of them – wasted no time in showing them off by entertaining friends at home. In the 1840s and '50s, because the middle classes dined at two o'clock in the afternoon, they had the benefit of a long evening for entertaining. T. Wemyss Reid, the editor of the *Leeds Mercury* and a leading Liberal, observed approvingly:

> Tea at six or half-past six o'clock was the customary meal for which invitations were issued; then came three or four hours for pleasant talk or amusement. Everybody was in the best of possible humours for occupation of this kind. Nobody had been made drowsy or listless by partaking of a heavy meal and of a variety of wines, more or less pure; there was no separation of the sexes at the very time when mutual conversation ought to be most enjoyable to both; and it need hardly be said that, in provincial towns at least, there was not the faintest suspicion that a time would come when tobacco would compete successfully with the fair sex for the attention of gentlemen. At the close of the evening thus pleasantly spent, came a meal which gave completeness to the entertainment – supper. It was the custom in Leeds in those days, in the houses of the fashionable, to serve this meal about ten o'clock at a buffet. It was not a heavy meal, and though I am aware of the horror in which the present generation professes to hold the very idea of supper, [he was writing in 1883] I am prepared to maintain that a light meal of two courses under this name at ten o'clock is not necessarily more injurious to the digestion than a heavy meal of ten or twelve courses, under the name of dinner, at eight or nine o'clock.
>
> It was one of the most fortunate results of the custom then prevailing in Leeds of having early dinners, that social gatherings at the houses of friends were then both more numerous and more largely attended than is now the case.[82]

Outside the home it is difficult to say where 'improvement' stopped and leisure began for the middle classes. As we shall see, so much of their time seemed to be devoted to membership of 'self-improvement' societies or running societies and institutions which aimed to 'improve' the lot of the less well off members of Leeds society.

Music, as today, was one of the pre-occupations of the middle classes. It was bragged in 1858 that there were so many good musicians in the town that an orchestra of upwards of 300 could be raised within the borough at a few hours' notice, 'which would delight the most fastidious' and would be headed by the 'Yorkshire Queen of Song' – the celebrated Mrs. Sutherland, the greatest female singer Yorkshire produced in the nineteenth century.[83] There was the Leeds Madrigal and Motet Society, founded in 1850, whose members had sung in the Grand Handel Festival at the Crystal Palace in 1857. Then there was the Leeds Choral Society founded in 1832 for 'the practice and cultivation of vocal and instrumental music'. The members of this society had become 'celebrated throughout the West Riding for their excellent oratorial performances'. Change was in the wind in 1858 for *Fenteman's Guide* noted that these musical societies would probably be merged into one grand society called the 'Leeds Festival Choral Society'.[84]

The finest musicians in the country could be heard playing in the musical festival in Leeds Town Hall. The first had been held there in 1858 to raise funds for Leeds General Infirmary. Before this there had been no suitable venue. The 96-piece orchestra and full chorus performed a varied programme ranging from Mendelssohn, Mozart, Rossini and Beethoven to the premiere of the 'May Queen' by the renowned Dr Sterndale Bennett, professor of music at Cambridge. Unfortunately, petty squabbling between the Choral Society and the Madrigal Society delayed the second music festival, nevertheless, there were nine more before the end of the century.[85]

In the early and mid-Victorian period the theatre was little patronised by the middle classes. Indeed, many considered it immoral. James Hole, the secretary of the Yorkshire Union of Mechanics' Institutes, writing in 1860, commented:

> The drama in Leeds is very inferior, and such as would not be tolerated in the smallest continental town; and the associations connected with the theatre generally are, it might almost be said, so incurably bad that it is in vain to speculate upon what might be done to it under better management ...A new theatre ought to be erected in Leeds, and if the middle and upper classes supported it, it would be commercially remunerative, and thus enable it to dispense with the representation of pieces of an improper character, and to remove the grosser associations connected with it.[86]

Right up to the 1880s the Baines family refused on moral grounds to allow any adverts or reviews for the Leeds theatres to appear in the *Leeds Mercury*. Wemyss Reid, the paper's editor from 1870, conscious of the much greater respectability of the theatre by his day and the annoyance caused to readers by the lack of such information, approached Edward Baines, junior (then in his 70s), to reverse the policy. He met with a strong rebuff from Baines who said, 'I am sorry to say that between the years 1819 and 1822 I attended the theatre frequently in London, and I can never forget the shocking immorality I witnessed both on the stage and among the audience.'[87]

As if in answer to Hole's call, the theatre began to improve in the 1860s and to draw all classes in more substantial numbers. The arrival of John Coleman in Leeds in 1863 saw the revival of the fortunes of the old theatre in Hunslet, where audiences could enjoy everything from the 'Gorgeous Christmas Pantomine of

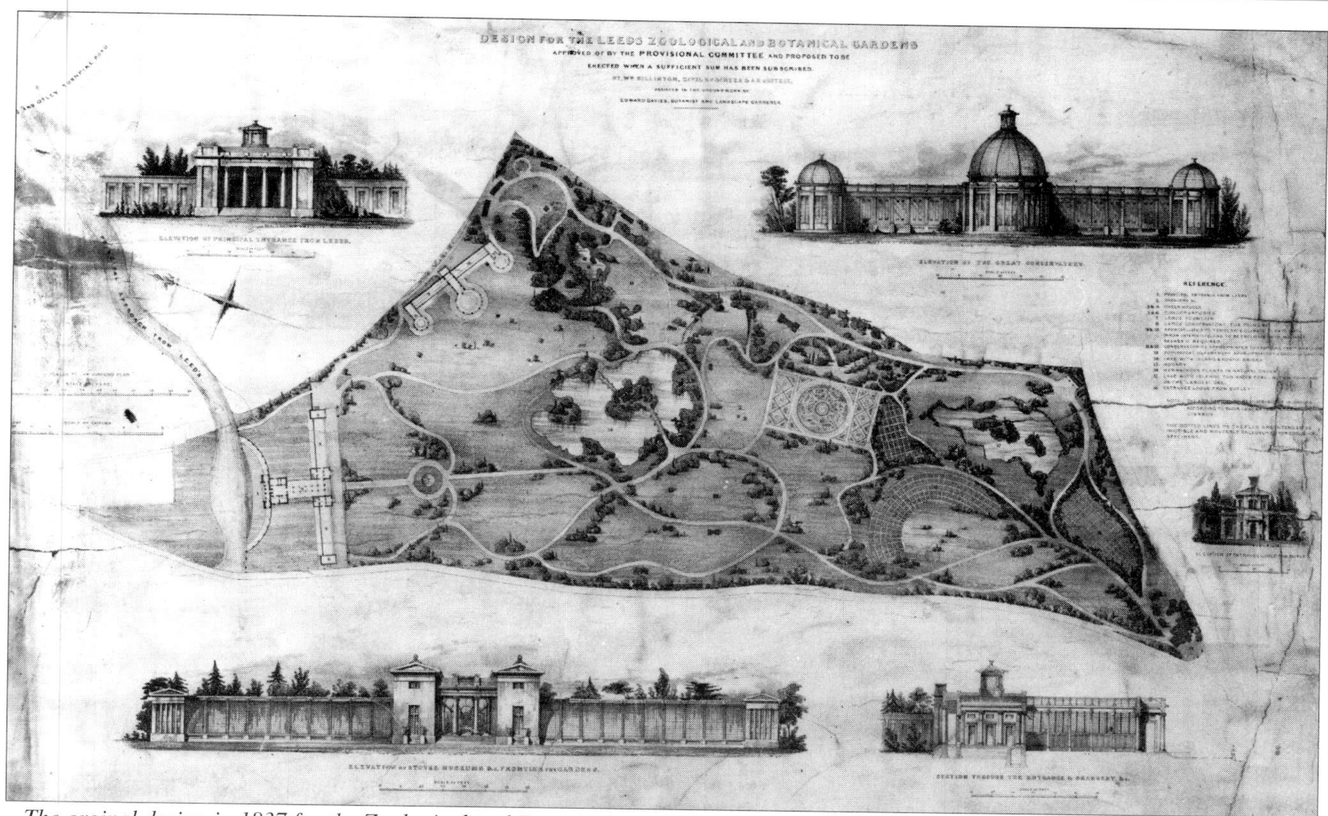

The orginal design in 1837 for the Zoological and Botanical Gardens, Headingley. Though all the land was purchased, some of the more elaborate aspects of the scheme were never completed.

the Yellow Dwarf' to Shakespeare's *Richard III.* The success in 1865 of Charles Reade's famous Victorian melodrama 'It's Never Too Late to Mend' highlighted the inadequacies of the old building, which Coleman decided to rebuild. The new, greatly enlarged theatre opened in September 1867. The performances became more elaborate and Cinderella which opened on Christmas Eve 1872 could boast of its 'Dazzling Transformation Scene and two hundred auxiliaries'. Unfortunately, fire completely destroyed the theatre on the night of 28 May 1875. Due to a poor insurance settlement the theatre was not rebuilt and Coleman left Leeds.[88] As we shall see later, however, this had a fortuitous outcome which was to be the making of theatre in Leeds.

For the Victorian gentleman who wished for a quiet evening away from the family or somewhere to have a good midday meal or a nightcap after an evening meeting, there was the Leeds Club in Albion Place. With its handsome coffee, smoking and dining rooms, its drawing, reading and writing rooms, spacious billiard room and excellent overnight accommodation, it was, and still is today, a very comfortable haven. Fenteman's 1858 Guide noted:

> It has an air of domestic comfort, whilst it may almost vie with any club house out of London. This institution is found to be very convenient to the gentry of the neighbourhood who have occasion to visit Leeds, and is also much frequented by the merchants, and professional gentlemen of the town.[89]

With a joining fee of 20 guineas and an annual subcription of 5 guineas, in the 1860s, this was an exclusive club.[90]

With respect to outdoor pursuits, a major venture which was never entirely successful was the Leeds Zoological and Botanical Gardens in Headingley opened as a commercial venture in 1840 with entrance fees of 6d. for adults and 3d. for children. Religious groups campaigned hard for the gardens to be closed on Sundays, but for many this was the only day they could visit. In 1841 a compromise was reached whereby, to avoid clashes with church and chapel services, opening on Sundays was from 4 p.m. to sunset, with admittance only for those who had purchased their tickets the day before.[91] In part, this seems to have been a measure to restrict the entry of the working classes. Whilst enlightened figures like Robert Baker advocated free entry for the poor once a week, paid for by an annual subscription from the rates,[92] Edward Baines revealed a typical middle-class attitude in a complaint about the working classes descending on Headingley:

> You bring together a crowd of people, of both sexes and all ages, without any means of rendering the company select. I need not say that the vilest characters as well as the most frivolous, worldly and worthless are more abroad on the Sabbath than any other day. Here you offer a public attraction which concentrates them in one place. You gather them out of the street, out of the highways and hedges, and bring them to a focus. If they shall have bought tickets you cannot refuse them admission. I do not even know that you can exclude abandoned females ...See then the kind of company into which our youth are likely to be thrown on the afternoon of the Sabbath as a means of improving their morals and cultivating their piety.[93]

Describing the gardens in 1840 the *Leeds Mercury* noted:

> The gardens are surrounded by a high wall within which on the west, south and east, is a plantation of trees in proper botanical arrangement, and on the north are fruit trees trained against the wall. The interior of the Gardens is varied by undulating

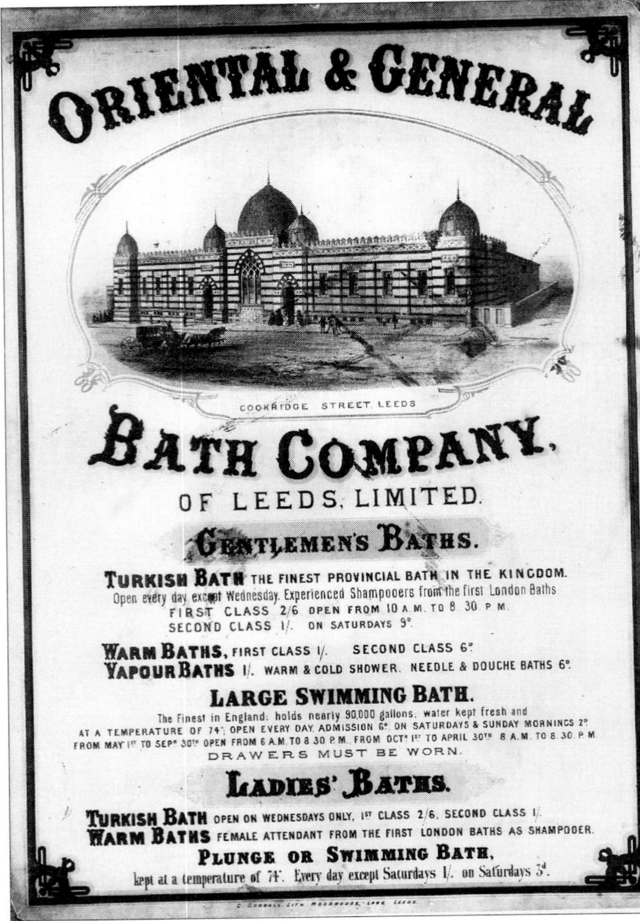

The Oriental Baths, Cookridge Street, built 1866-7 (architect, Cuthbert Brodrick). As this poster shows, the middle classes could relax in great comfort and style.

ground and laid out in beautiful slopes of grass plots, tasteful parterres and shrubberies, with winding walks, two very handsome ponds with islands and a beautiful fountain. A profusion of flowers …adorn the Garden, and especially a circular plot below the upper pond. Near the entrance to the grounds from Headingley is a conservatory, containing a beautiful collection of geraniums and a variety of exotic plants and flowers. The zoological department as yet is confined to a fine pair of swans and some fowl, an eagle, a racoon, a fox, some monkeys and tortoises.[94]

Today Cardigan Road slices straight through the middle of the site of the former gardens, almost the only surviving feature being the castellated bear pit. The gardens struggled to reach profitability despite band concerts, firework displays, exhibitions and balloon ascents. They were sold in 1848 and came under the management of the resourceful entrepreneur Thomas Clapham, but were sold as building ground in 1858. Clapham immediately transferred his attention to the Victoria Cricket Ground on the north-west side of Woodhouse Moor, where he established a large pleasure ground which became known as the Royal Park. Over the next decade or so, the park, with its skating rink, bandstand, green houses and other attractions, experienced fluctuating commercial fortunes.[95]

One of the most interesting features of the period was the Archery Ground in Blackman Lane adjoining Blenheim Square. Here in spring and summer the middle-class members of the Leeds Archery Society founded in 1848 practised their skills whilst donning dark green uniforms.[96]

With the advent of the railway came the excursion, a most successful innovation of the period. The Mechanics' Institute went to Castle Howard, Chatsworth and York. Holidays at the coast became fashionable and excursion agents began to operate in the town. Trips from Leeds to Scarborough in 1851 were organised by Clapham. Rail travel brought new and more distant resorts within reach of the middle classes. Cheap fares meant that in 1853 even a solicitor's clerk could afford to take his wife to Morecambe for a week, with a steamer trip to Belfast adding extra interest to the holiday. A branch of Thomas Cook catered for the more affluent and ambitious.[97]

The prestigious Royal Agricultural Show held at Cardigan Fields, Kirkstall Road in August 1861 provided an event of great interest to the middle classes in particular. To the left can be seen the chimneys of Fowler's revolutionary steam ploughs.

The Working Classes

Cottages and Lodging Houses

'There's no place like home' declared the words of the Victorians' favourite song. Indeed, still today it reminds us of the Victorians' concept of the virtue of life at the family's fireside. For only a few working-class homes in Leeds, however, was this image a reality. Writing in 1865 the journalist, J. Tomlinson, described in almost idyllic terms the homes to which the most affluent and respectable Leeds working men returned after their day's labours:

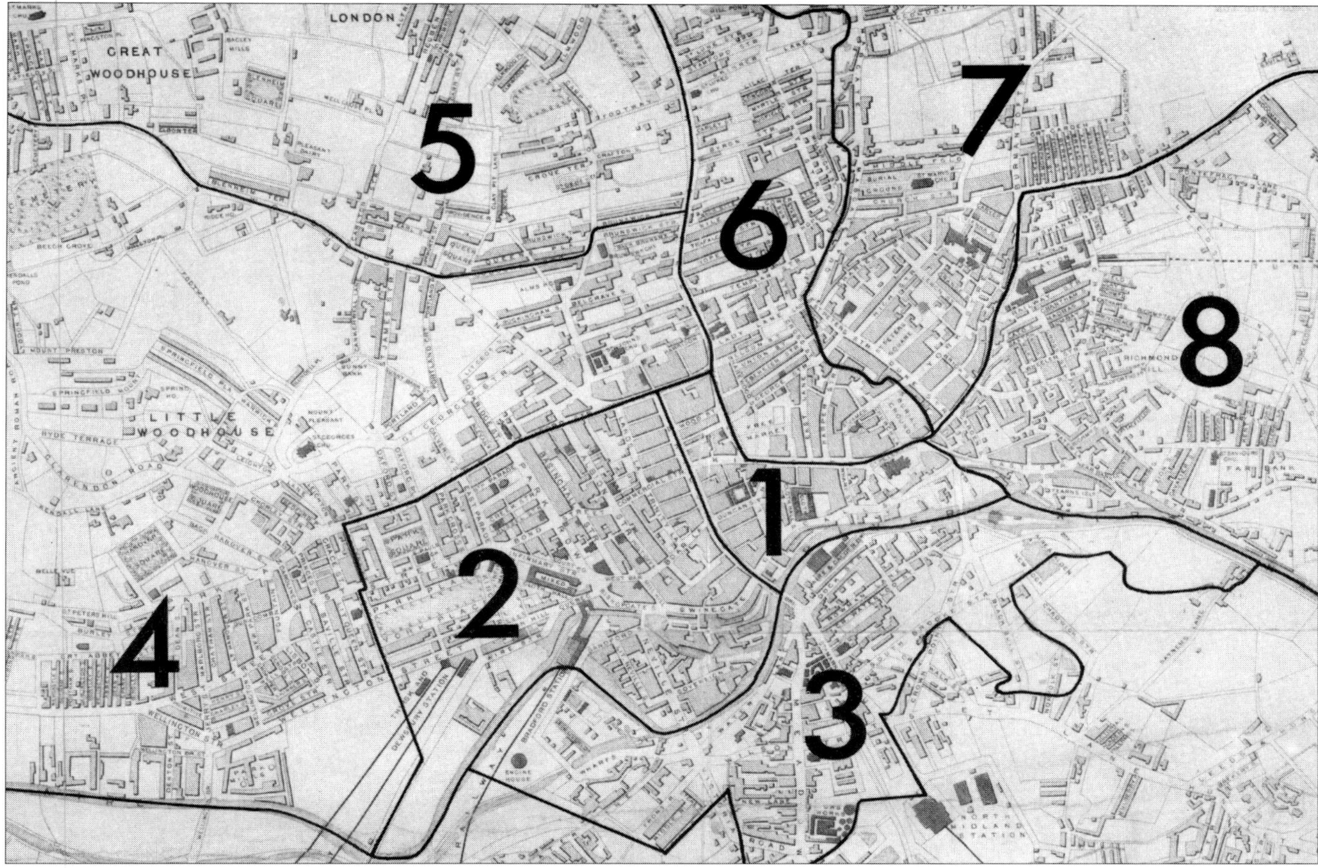

The ward boundaries of Leeds township, 1835-81: 1 Kirkgate ward, 2 Mill Hill ward, 3 South ward, 4 West ward, 5 North West ward, 6 North ward, 7 North East ward, 8 East ward.

A few have model homes, and home pleasures are the great enjoyment of their life. Look in upon one of these firesides – a pleasanter picture there is not in the whole world. The wife is a tidy, cheerful little body, the house is scrupulously clean, and, having washed himself, and taken little Teddy on his knee, the tired artisan sits down to a comfortable supper, with a heart imbued with thankfulness for all these mercies. All night long he will not give up his corner chair, either for the Casino or the public-house, or even for the reading room, but takes his pipe and the newspaper or magazine (very likely next week he will be reading to his wife the very remarks which I am penning), and feels as a man ought to feel who does his duty in the sphere which Providence has assigned him. It is really surprising, what comforts a working-man may furnish when he does not fritter away his money in foolish recreations or mere selfish indulgences.[98]

Of course significant numbers of the working classes lived in reasonable conditions by the standards of the day. In 1842 none other than Robert Baker, the greatest publicist of the horrors of the Leeds slums, reminded his readers that even in the notorious Bank area, on the higher ground to the east where good drainage could be effected, the back-to-backs could provide good housing and a good 'moral and social' environment:

In the Bank, a part of the East ward in which there is every size and order of cottage dwelling, there is a large population located under a good landlord, who has erected his houses upon a good plan, with a due regard to the wants and requirements of his tenantry, with a due share of out-offices, and other accommodation; and with streets well paved and sewered; he has very rarely any houses to let. The whole estate bears upon the face of it comfort and enjoyment. Every house is clean and neat, and tenanted by a respectable occupier ...There are no violations of decency to be seen here, and no disturbances nor assemblies of Sabbath-breakers.[99]

Inevitably, the major determinant of the quality of life for working-class families was their level of income, and the regularity with which this income was received. If we set aside the way in which some families squandered their income on low living and drink, it was the basic level of income which determined the type of dwelling a family might rent, the quality of diet, and the ability to afford some of the comforts of life. In considering wage levels in Leeds, it is important to remember that because many working-class women and children worked, the family income was often swelled to a level significantly in excess of the man's weekly wage. Between the beginning of Victoria's reign and the 1850s there was perhaps a small increase in the nominal wages of workers, but it is unlikely that this resulted in a notable rise in real incomes.

In 1858 Robert Baker and Edward Baines between them provided useful figures on wage levels in the industrial sector of the Leeds economy.[100] In the woollen industry, girls and boys earned weekly 5s.-6s., women 6s.-12s., the best paid being the operators of the power looms. Men's wages averaged around 22s., with large numbers earning 15s.-22s., but the skilled workers, the drawers, tenterers, press setters, dyers, and foremen and overseers earned from 30s.-40s., even 60s. in the case of dyer foremen. Handloom weavers both in woollens and worsteds at this time might earn around 15s. a week. In the flax industry wages were lower. An overseer might get 21s., a general labourer, 15s., women, 6s. 6d., lads around 5s., and weavers from 10s. to 15s. As in woollens, the mechanics and enginemen were the best paid workers, receiving around 29s. a week.

Dyeing was a very important trade and very skilled workmen might receive as much as 120s. a week. The iron and machine making trades were very clearly the best paid sector of Leeds industry. The makers of flax and tow machinery, tool engineers and machine tool makers, engineers, millwrights, boiler makers (including locomotive makers) and those working in foundries earned in the region of 25s.-32s. per week. Baker noted that the railway termini employed just over one thousand workers at an average wage of 21s.

Such wage levels suggest quite a range of family incomes hovering principally around the 22s. level, but in instances where the husband was a highly skilled workers reaching 30s. to £2, occasionally even more. But of course not all trades worked twelve months a year. Outdoor non-industrial employments, particularly associated with building, might only be carried on for 9-10 months a year. Likewise, a depression could bring longish periods of unemployment. A very approximate rule of thumb is that in good years the families of the better-paid skilled workers might have annual incomes of around £75-£100, those of lesser-skilled workers around £60, and those of unskilled general labourers around £50 per annum. Compare these to the minimum £150 a year income which indisputably middle-class families enjoyed.

In the early 1840s Baker felt that a working-class family, if it spent its money wisely, should be able to live perfectly well on just over £50 a year and 'with economy, to lay by something for the decline of life'.[101] But large numbers of the working classes found themselves unable to live up to Baker's ideal. Spending on drink and gambling, the desire for more gaiety, and the very narrow margin of income between sufficiency and poverty – these, combined with irregularity of employment, conspired against the achievement of his model lifestyle. Moreover, to set against the well-built houses and amply drained and laid-out streets noted by Tomlinson and Baker were the notorious back-to-backs and common lodging houses for which Leeds became infamous. The doubling of the town's population to 177,920 between 1841 and 1901 was accommodated by an almost exact doubling of the number of houses to just over 40,000.[102] The town became dominated by row after row of back-to-backs, which constituted two-thirds of its houses by the end of the century. To the south of the river in Hunslet and Holbeck, back-to-backs surrounded the mills, factories, foundries, gasworks and brickyards. Most of the working-class streets condemned as insanitary by Robert Baker's report in 1839 survived virtually untouched throughout Victoria's reign.

Baker's assessment of the living conditions of the working classes in the early Victorian period was complemented by a report by James Smith in 1845 to the Select Committee on the State of Large Towns and Populous Districts:

> By far the most unhealthy localities of Leeds are close squares of houses, or yards, as they are called, which have been erected for the accommodation of working people. Some of these, though situated in comparatively high ground, are airless from the enclosed structure, and being wholly unprovided with any form of under-drainage, or convenience, or arrangements for cleansing, are one mass of damp and filth ...The ashes, garbage, and filth of all kinds are thrown from the doors and windows of the houses upon the surface of the streets and courts ...The privies are few in proportion to the number of inhabitants. They are open to view both in front and rear, are invariably in a filthy condition, and often remain without the removal of any portion of the filth for six months. The feelings of the people are blunted to all seeming decency, and from the constantly contaminated state of the atmosphere, a vast amount of ill-health prevails, leading to listlessness, and including a desire for spirits and opiates; the combined influence of the whole condition causing much loss of time, increasing poverty, and terminating the existence of many in premature death.[103]

The Briggate entrance to the Smithfield Meat Market, one of 7 slaughter houses which created appalling conditions down the yards on the east side of Briggate in the Victorian period. Note the frontages of the butchers' shops on either side, and the illuminated sign advertising the Temperance and Commercial Hotel upstairs.

Writer after writer highlighted the moral debasement which they felt resulted from working-class houses having only one bedroom. J.C.Symons, inspecting Leeds on behalf of the Children's Employment Commissioners, remarked in 1843:

> Not one half of the working classes in Leeds occupy, I am told, above two rooms, one for living in, and one for sleeping in, called 'the lodging room'; occasionally if there is a large family the man and his wife will sleep down stairs, but generally one room serves for all. Hence an early initiation in scenes which blunt all pure feeling and open the road to every licence and debauchery.[104]

James Hole describing housing in Leeds in 1866

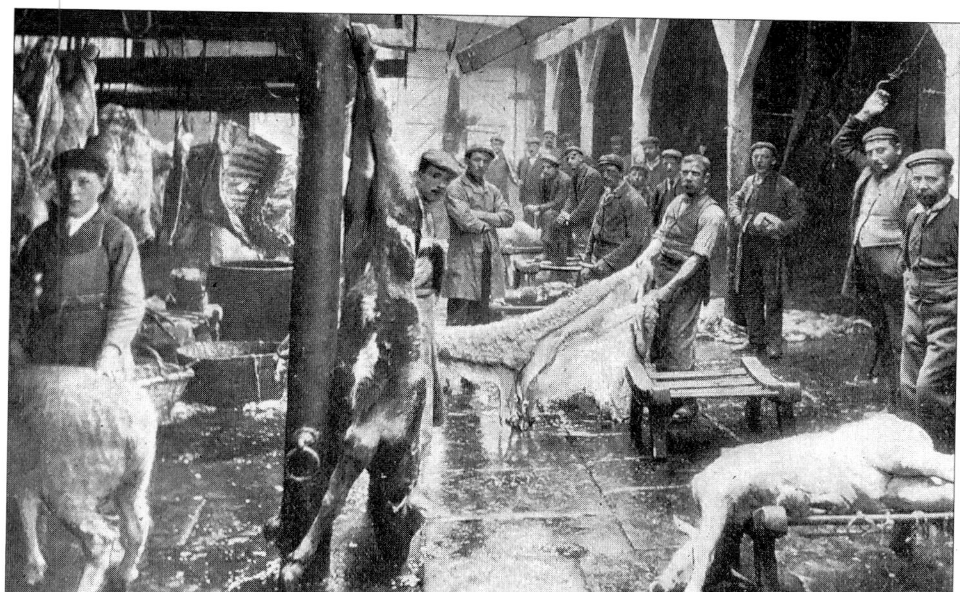

The Leadenhall Slaughter House on the north side of Leadenhall Street c.1880, looking towards the entrance from Vicar Lane.

reached very similar conclusions to those of Baker and Smith.[105] Defenders of back-to-back houses, as the council was throughout the nineteenth century, always argued that there was nothing intrinsically wrong with the houses themselves provided they were in an airy situation, had good sanitation, and were not overcrowded with people, but frequently this was not the case.[106] The continued building of such insanitary property for most of the century in such a haphazard and unplanned manner was guaranteed by the economics of the property market. Baker noted in 1842:

> In periods of great prosperity, no property is more valuable than what is called cottage property in towns; for the demand for labour enables the operative to pay a high rent, which, for the most part, is collected weekly or quarterly, according to the character of the tenantry. Thus whole streets of houses have arisen in Leeds, in an inconceivably short space of time, and in many instances evidently for the sole end of speculation, without regard to the absolute wants of the tenants.

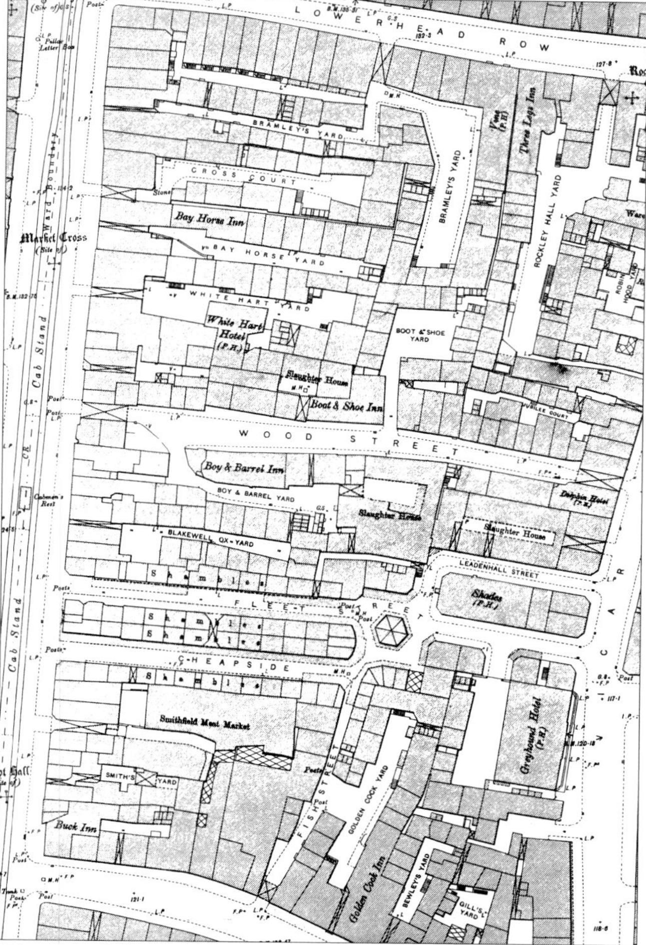

The crowded courts and yards between Briggate and Vicar Lane shown on the large- scale Ordnance Survey map of 1890. They contained a mixture of slaughterhouses, pubs, warehouses, shops, cottages and common lodging houses. The area from the Bay Horse Yard to Cheapside was to be completely redeveloped by the Leeds Estate Company between 1898 and 1902.

A pair of back-to-backs would cost about £130-£140 to build, he noted, plus £20 for the site, making the cost of each house about £80. When new, each house would let for £12 a year, and continue to be let at this rent for a considerable period.[108] The predicament of the working classes was that the most awful older property paid the highest return because a landlord could buy it cheaply and obtain a disproportionately high rent. Alderman Robert Carter commented in 1866:

> Cottage property has increased very much in value in Leeds in the last five or six years …I know that the cottage property in Leeds at present, or the majority of it, pays from 7 to 12 per cent and the worst cottages and the cellar dwellings pay the highest interest of almost any in the whole lot. The best class of cottage property pays the lowest percentage, and the worst pays the highest.[109]

The working classes who could not afford to rent a house or cellar dwelling, usually single men but at times whole families, lived in the common lodging houses. There were literally hundreds of them in mid-nineteenth century Leeds. In 1851 there were 222 lodging houses near the parish church with 536 rooms, 1035 beds, and 2429 inhabitants.[110] They were notorious for their cramped and insanitary conditions, Baker in 1842 noted one with rooms 10 feet square each sleeping 18 people, three to a bed.[111] In 1843 J.C.Symons visited some of the worst examples in the town:

> The lodging-houses we visited were situated chiefly up narrow alleys running out of the Kirkgate, and are intermixed with working-class brothels. These alleys are wholly without sewerage; there is a gutter down the middle, but no underground channel whatever; they are in a filthy state. Some of the lodging-houses were wretched places – mere dens with no sort of comfort save a good fire: they had all, however, beds of some description, though in some I saw bundles of straw for the accommodation of an occasional surplus of 'company'. With the exception

Wood Street looking towards Vicar Lane. The 'street' was entered by passageways on Briggate and Vicar Lane.

of Glasgow I have seen nothing more wretched than these places …

The most motley crew are usually assembled downstairs. In one we found a party having tea. A shabby-genteel youth in a frock coat, who looked like a broken-down swindler, was standing at the fire frying his supper with a frying-pan in his hand. In another corner a woman was industriously frilling a cap at a German heater, which she had first been washing and ironing. Three very young dirty children were crouching round the fire; three rough-looking fellows were getting their supper in a corner; one old woman half-drunk abused the police, and another [woman] was suckling her child.

In nearly all we found some young children up at half-past ten o'clock; and in one room we found a girl with another in her lap, and two more sitting by themselves, all four fast asleep; the mother was not with them.[112]

Inevitably, campaigners for improved living conditions for the working classes highlighted the worst examples of bad conditions, but they did not have to look far to find them.

Diet, Domestic Manners and the Factory

The diet of the working classes was poor. Oatmeal porridge sweetened with treacle, oatcakes, boiled potatoes and fried bacon formed the basis of the working man's diet. Workers rose at around 5 am, made a pot of tea, walked to work and after working two hours, usually had time to eat breakfast, which comprised of bread with dripping, treacle or jam, washed down with a pot of tea. Dinner often took a similar form, although the better off ate sheep's head broth or potatoes and vegetables, perhaps with meat and Yorkshire pudding. Tea time at the mill was identical to breakfast, but, if it were taken at home, a prosperous family could enjoy broth with dumplings, rabbit stew, fish or corned beef hash.[113]

For the more affluent workers, dining rooms were provided by Working Men's Institutes. A visitor to the Leeds Institute, housed in the former Assembly Rooms above the Third White Cloth Hall, observed over 150 men and youths, 'a number of them doing justice to sundry steaks, chops and savoury rashers of bacon, which viands were supplied to them through a trap-door from the kitchen, the recipients paying one half-penny each for the cooking'. No intoxicating drinks were allowed on the premises, but any of the members could have tea or coffee on payment of one penny per cup, and bread and butter or muffins at equally reasonable rates.[114]

For those who were unemployed or who could only obtain temporary employment, their diet was much worse. Robert Baker noted that Irish factory children survived on coffee, bread and tea, and occasionally meat.[115] Even at the end of the century Leeds slipper makers relied on home-made bread and tea, with three pence worth of meat some weeks and plenty of onions for sustenance. Street hawkers sold pie and peas, cockles, muffins, and roasted potatoes for those that could afford them.[116]

As a factory inspector, Robert Baker was particularly interested in the impact of the factory system on working-class lifestyles and morality. He was absolutely convinced that the large-scale employment of young girls

Factory hands leaving Marshall's Temple Mill for dinner in 1885.

and women in the mills (half the workforce he estimated) was destroying the fabric of family life and the prospects of an orderly and respectable working class. He objected in particular to the early loss of parental control over girls due to their earning of wages; the employment of women when men were unemployed which he considered 'reversed the order of nature', and 'the utter inability of the wives of the operatives to obtain requisite domestic acquirements by which the homes of future husbands may be made more attractive than society abroad'. He lamented

> the inability to make home desirable, by the entire want of domestic education, which is consequent upon the early and continuous employment of females in factories. The charm which makes home so desirable to every heart, making a man's own fire-side more agreeable than the public-house, and the step by step encroachment of society abroad to be so much dreaded, is unknown; the principles of good management have neither been learned nor cultivated, the basis of all human happiness is unappreciated.[117]

Revd Pollen, who was a curate at St Saviour's in the Bank in the late 1840s, left a lurid description of life there and echoed a view common amongst the middle classes that the congregation of the working classes in large numbers in mills promoted their moral debasement. He vehemently attacked the propagandists of the socialist movement, begun by Robert Owen, who he felt led the working classes astray by mocking religion and calling for a new society based on 'co-operation' rather than competition:

> If it be noon, the factory bell will be sounding, and troops of women and girls defiling along the streets, clothed in long canvass aprons, their heads covered with a loose handkerchief – the neck and arms uncovered, and adorned with gaudy trinkets – coarse and immodest in voice, looks, and expression.
>
> In the short days, after dark and before the light, a crowd of young persons of both sexes, some of them never baptized, return to their homes in these narrow lanes and passages. In a back street or lane, not many hundred yards removed, is a large upper room lighted most nights. This is a place for balls, where a band plays, and socialists invite the labouring young to come and enjoy themselves. Further on is a larger building still. It is a Socialist Hall, and there are places in plenty, worse, if that is possible, than these. In the summer months a band parades the streets from the socialists, to lure them to these attractive haunts, where the restraints of 'society' have no hold, and are not known. It will be wondered at that education, that is, instruction in reading and writing, narrow as its sphere has been, has not still some whom it has raised to higher employments and tastes less fearfully debased.
>
> At a later hour coarse oaths and blasphemies, and other revolting sounds and sights, break the solemnity which, in this place of remorseless toil, is known only to the dead of night.
>
> But a worse element of evil is the early inculcation of the knowledge of what is bad. A familiarity with corruption begins in early youth. The great numbers of each sex so constantly together, either during work or on the way to and fro, are a guarantee, per se, of the loss of simplicity and purity of life, supposing even that the sexes are, in general, separate; but where, besides this corrupting collection of numbers, society is without restraints at home, the evil is complete.[118]

The Immigrants: the Irish and the Jews

The most distinctive groups amongst the working classes of Leeds in the Victorian period were the immigrants. From the seventeenth century, because of trading links with the Continent, Leeds had always been home to a smattering of foreigners. In the nineteenth century, however, there was large-scale immigration, first by the Irish and then by the Jews. According to Baker's calculations, of the town's total population of 87,613 in 1841, 5,196 residents had not been born in England: 611 were Scottish, 275 were 'foreigners' and 4,310, five per cent of the population, were Irish. Baker reckoned that:

> Of these emigrants, the Scotch appear to be scattered through every branch of occupation, and confined to no one in particular. The Irish are almost exclusively limited to plaid weaving, flax spinning, and bricklayers' labourers. The foreigners are wool-merchants, or agents having commissions in manufacture, with here and there Italian dealers in picture frames, looking-glasses, small wares, and plaster-of-Paris figures.[119]

Flooding into England to escape the famines at home, the Irish arrived virtually penniless. In particular, the potato famine of 1846-7 brought large numbers of them into the already overcrowded yards and alleyways off Kirkgate and around St James' Church behind the market. Desperate for shelter, they resorted to erecting shanties, copies of the turf cabins they had left behind, among the courts and alleys. The Revd Edward Jackson vividly recalled their plight in June 1847:

> Tall men, with long coats and hats without crowns, and women, wild and haggard, with numbers of unearthly looking children – strange beings that ran alongside of the men and women, and looked at you out of the corner of their eyes, with a sort of half-frightened, half-savage expression. The usual low lodging-houses for this class of people were soon more than full, and they extemporized for themselves dwellings such as none but they would have occupied. Why the Poor Law Authorities did not bestir themselves in time, and open proper places for the reception of these wretched exiles, seems now a strange blunder. Being Irish, I suppose they were not legally chargeable to the township. But it was a great mistake and a woeful economy; for the emigrants brought with them not only hunger, but

Shops on the east side of Bridge Street in the Leylands, between North Street and Regent Street, towards the end of the century. As the shop names, Cohen and Kelly, indicate, though this was predominantly a Jewish area, the Irish were also present.

death. In a very short time the frightful Irish fever [typhus] was epidemic in all the lower parts of the town.[120]

The Irish population of Leeds township numbered just over 5,000 in 1841, and rose rapidly to 10,000 in 1851, and almost 15,000 in 1861 – over 12 per cent of the town's population.[121] Certainly, in prosperous times their labour was much in demand, for Baker noted that in 1835 and 1836 many of the flax mills would have been forced to stand idle for want of workers but for the influx of Irish labourers at that time. But their incomes were pitifully low. Baker reckoned that Irish families in which the wife and children worked would have a weekly income of about £1, the husbands earning around 12s. per week. In a bad year a family's income would average about 14s. 3d. per week and in a good year around £1 1s. 7½d.[122] Irish female labour came to dominate the labour force in the unpleasant conditions of the flax industry. In 1866 it was noted that:

> English girls have had facilities for the last few years of getting to the power-looms in connection with the Worsted business and with the Cloth business, and they are getting to be employed with the sewing machines in large towns like Leeds. English girls have almost entirely got into better occupations, and those flax mills, where there is such a large amount of dust and heat and steam, are filled almost entirely with the children of the lowest class of people – they are nearly all Irish now.[123]

The poverty of the Irish took them to the worst housing in Leeds. While the area around Kirkgate Market to the east of Vicar Lane was their principal town centre home, most lived at the Bank, in the area between York Street, York Road, East Street and Ellerby Lane. Between 1841 and 1861 around one-quarter to one-third of the population of the North, North-east, and East wards of Leeds township were Irish.[124] The lifestyle of the Irish did nothing to improve their already terrible accommodation. In 1842 Baker noted:

> In the houses of the Irish poor ...there is a general state of desolation and misery. Whether it is the improvidence of the Irish character, or that their natural habits are filthy, or both, or whether there exists the real destitution which is apparent in their dwellings, I know not; but in them is more penury, and starvation, and dirt, than in any class of people which I have ever seen.[125]

He described a typical home in detail:

> An [Irish] plaid-weaver, for instance, of industrious habits, will rent a small house, consisting of a kitchen and chamber, at an annual cost of about £4, or a cellar at £2 10s. In the former case, the kitchen is not only appropriated to culinary purposes, but is the house, the sleeping-room, the hen-house, and the piggery; whilst upstairs are three or four looms, all but touching each other; and perhaps, in a corner, a bed on the floor for one of the owners of those looms, which are employed as follows: one by the occupier of the house, the others by persons to whom they are either sub-let at a

weekly rent, or who are relatives, friends of, or labourers for, the owner, who work either for weekly wages, or for the common maintenance of the family. In a cellar, a single loom for the weaver is all that it will contain.[126]

Angus Reach, a journalist with the *Morning Chronicle*, was shocked by the plight of the Irish in the east and north-east wards in 1849. He was morbidly fascinated by the way some eked out an existence picking oakum – the unpicking of old ropes to prepare the fibres (the oakum) for grinding up and making into shoddy, canvas and sacking.[127]

Without doubt the Irish became a distinctive and colourful aspect of local life. When the Prince of Wales processed through Leeds in 1868 to open the National Fine Arts Exnibition at the new Infirmary in Great George Street, the press remarked on the presence of the Irish in the crowds who greeted him as his carriage passed by:

> Even the supposed Fenian sympathisers in Kirkgate, who but a short time before had shown some ill-feeling to the Corporation, forgot to hiss. They cheered and cheered again – old hats that no one but an Irishman would wear, brilliantly-coloured handkerchiefs that only an Irish woman would delight in, were waved over and over again in the breeze, and the Prince graciously and smilingly acknowledged the greeting.[128]

On this occasion the Irish were regarded as colourful characters, but, as we will see, many people in Leeds regarded them as anti-social, work-shy, and worthless scroungers who periodically posed a major threat to public order.

The second major wave of immigration into Leeds in the nineteenth century was that of the Jews. In the early 1860s Leeds had only a handful of Jews, but the assassination of the Tsar in 1881 and subsequent pogroms forced many Russian and Polish Jews to seek safety in Britain and America. The clothing industry of Leeds made use of the talents of these refugees, many of whom were willing to work for extremely low wages. By the end of the Victorian period Leeds had some 15,000 Jews, the second largest community outside London.[129] The vast majority lived in an enclave known as the Leylands and around Camp Road – the Leeds ghetto. They congregated together for safety, help and comfort. Their religion, dress, Yiddish language and subsequent success led to anti-semitism. Like the Irish before them, they were branded as a filthy people. It was left to the *Lancet* to give a more informed view:

> We do not find that the interiors of the Jews' houses are particularly dirty. Some are dirty but some are particularly remarkably clean, and they are much more careful in respect of their food than their neighbours. They are a remarkably intelligent race, and they would never dream of resisting pressure from properly constituted sanitary authorities. There is a tendency, however, to leave them alone, under the pretext that they are foreigners and that nothing decent can be expected from them. This is at once a shortsighted and ungenerous policy.[130]

The reputation of the Jews in this period was not enhanced by the tales of the long hours and the grim conditions in their tailoring sweat shops which were mainly concentrated in the Leylands. Indeed, when the Jewish Tailors Union went on strike in 1888, apart from seeking higher pay, its principal aim was to secure a reduction in working hours to 58 hours a week! Almost inevitably, such was the vulnerable position of the workers that the union soon collapsed.[131] Robert Sheracy visiting the sweating dens in 1896 was appalled by the plight of the workers:

> I am convinced that their circumstances are at least as bad as those of the sweated tailors in London. They all work on a weekly wage, and from twelve to seventeen hours a day. Here may be seen, in some filthy room in an old dilapidated factory in the Leylands, fifty people (men, women, boys and girls), all huddled together, sewing as though for dear life. A girl may be earning 6s. a week, a man from 22s. to 30s. The stench in the room, its uncleanliness, surpass description. The finished garments are lying pell-mell on the floor in the filth and vermin. They are 'flogged into their work' as one said, for all the time the gaunt sweater stalks about, scolding, inspecting, while now and then he will snatch a garment from some worker's hand, and set himself to work upon it, whilst a stream of vituperation pours from his lips. He is usually a haggard and starving man, himself a victim of inhuman competition. There are weeks when he does not earn a penny himself. In a good week he may earn £10.
>
> A girl whom I interviewed at the office of the Wholesale Clothiers' Operative Union, told me that she had often spent 10d. on sewings out of a weekly earnings of 2s. 7d. She remembered one week when she had only earned a shilling, and had had to pay 8d. She could not make a living at it. She had been in a 'punishing house', and had often been so weak from want of food that she had fainted over her machine. Many of her fellow workers used to beg food off the men in the factory, but she had never cared to do this as it led to things.[132]

Pubs, Beerhouses and Singing Rooms

The contrast between the living conditions of the affluent middle classes and those of the mass of the working classes was stark. The difference was equally great with respect to leisure activities. The long hours worked by the working classes meant that only a short time in the evenings plus Sunday was available for relaxation. A significant improvement was achieved when the 1847 Ten Hours Act and the Factory Act of 1850 brought release from Saturday afternoon work, but, apart from public holidays, holidays remained out of the question for the majority of people because they received no paid leave.[133]

The middle classes were perpetually worried by the way the working classes spent their free time and condemned it as morally debasing. The middle classes shunned public houses, whereas for the working man the public house or beerhouse was a place of frequent resort. At worst they were places of refuge from the squalor and claustrophobia of a worker's home, at their best they were places for social gatherings with friends and bases for the activities of friendly societies, benefit clubs, and a variety of other clubs. James Hole, writing about the condition of the workings classes in Leeds in 1863, emphasised that a distinction must be drawn between:

> some public houses and a few more respectable beerhouses, generally well conducted, and the dramshops and lower class beerhouses. Apart from the besotting influence of the drink, the low

beerhouse is too often the focus of depravity for a whole neighbourhood, a place where gambling and card playing constitute quite as great attractions as drinking, and where prostitutes are regularly kept.[134]

After the Beerhouse Act of 1830 permitted virtually any householder who paid a small fee to sell beer upon his premises, the number of inns, beerhouses and gin shops increased rapidly. The town had 450 by the end of the 1830s.[135] It was estimated by temperance workers that nationally the total expenditure on drink rose from over £67 million in 1830 to nearly £81 million in 1850. This averaged almost £3 per person per year, which in a working-class family of five or six amounted to perhaps double the sum they paid in rent.[136] As the public houses increased, a drink with friends at one of these establishments became the highlight of a man's day. This habit, viewed by the middle classes as the root of many families' financial difficulties, often resulted in drunkeness and fighting, which became a feature of life in working-class districts.

In 1843 J.C.Symons' Saturday night tour of the low places of resort of the working classes included a score of beerhouses and public houses. Starting at 9 o'clock in the evening, these he found were:

> crowded with lads and girls – a motley assemblage of thieves and youths of both sexes from the factories.
>
> There were, on an average, about thirty in each house, and in each case ranged on the benches round the walls of the room, with a blazing fire, and well-lighted. I am confident that, of the 600 persons I saw in these places, not above one quarter, if so many, were turned of 25 years of age, and at least two-thirds were under age. In the beerhouses there were several more children. In almost all there was a sprinkling of professed prostitutes. In some, perhaps a third of them, several men and boys were pointed out to me as professed thieves. In some of these houses there was a speedy clearance of the company out of one room as we entered another, so that we saw only a part of the inmates ...
>
> A boy of 14 was sitting in one of the more decent houses by the side of his father, who told me he was his son, and that he worked all the week at the factory. This was at half-past ten at night, and yet his father seemed to be wholly unaware that there was anything wrong in bringing his child to a beer-house and keeping him up to that hour after a week's work in the factory. Now this man was to all appearance not below the average of the working classes in Leeds in point of character.
>
> In some of these places we found a fiddle or some other instrument being played: these places were thronged as full as they could hold. In another dancing was going on in a good-sized room upstairs, where I found a dozen couples performing a country-dance; the females were all factory-girls and prostitutes; obscene attitudes and language accompany and form the chief zest to this amusement.
>
> Not one of these dancers, boys or girls, was above 20 or 21 years of age, and most of them 16 and 17. The prostitutes were easily distinguished from the factory-girls by their tawdry finery and the bareness of their necks, although the costume and head-dress of the factory-girls is not altogether dissimilar. In many of these places there was convenience upstairs for the cohabitation of the company below.[137]

It was this description of the public houses and brothels of Leeds which was seized upon by Lord Ashley (later Lord Shaftesbury) as evidence to support his campaign for factory reform, and led the national Bible Society to dub Leeds the 'modern Sodom'.[138] Edward Baines reacted angrily pointing out that such investigations were attempting to prove a case and sought out the worst examples of squalor and depravity they could find. Vice in Leeds as a whole, he considered, was probably no worse than in any manufacturing town – at Manchester, Birmingham, Sheffield, Wolverhampton, Willenhall, Bilston, Sedgley, the Potteries and Nottingham.[139]

Quite a number of the central pubs had singing rooms of a respectable nature. J.Tomlinson has left an atmospheric account of an evening exploring one of them, probably in Briggate or Kirkgate, in the 1860s:

> I followed a pair of decent looking folk through the dram shop, and up a long flight of stairs. To the left of the landing was a little snug, in which about twelve or fourteen individuals, of both sexes, were enjoying a quiet glass and chat. On the right was a large well-lighted room, in which were assembled from one hundred to a hundred and fifty people. Next to the walls were long rows of Windsor chairs, nearly all of them occupied, and across the room I counted seven narrow tables, with a passage between each, and wooden benches on one side only, so that the whole company faced a small platform at one end of the room, now occupied solely by the pianist and his 'box of sounds'. The walls of this saloon were plentifully embellished with highly coloured prints. Here was the pugilistic encounter between Tom Sayers and the Benecia Boy, closely adjoining a pensive-looking nymph, with sunny ringlets, and a great amplitude of bare arms and bosom. On a conspicuous part of the wall a notice was posted stating that no smoking is allowed. No doubt this prohibition was felt by many to be an encroachment on true English liberty; to revenge which some of the company present evidently resolved to imbibe an extra quantity of fluids; certainly the waiters had abundant occupation.
>
> "Here *garcon*", called out a bluff looking personage (for during the *entente cordiale* we have picked up a smattering of French), "fill these three pints".
>
> A young man on the same form whispered to his companion – "Drink up, Susan, and hev summit short."
>
> "Noa, Jim," replied she, "I should prefer another bottle o' pop."
>
> "Silence gentlemen, for Mr. Mackinnon's song," bawled out a voice at the far end of the room, and presently the singer took his place by the side of the pianoforte. Mr. Mackinnon was a very stout man, and when he gave the introductory "Hem!" the fact became apparent that he had a very stout voice. The stalwart Scotchman excited scarcely any sympathy however, amongst his audience, and when he resumed his seat the applause was exceedingly limited. It was a song little adapted to the popular mind, being neither comic nor sentimental, but rather abstruse. It provoked the silence of discontent. It was a dry song, and the people supped. Bye and bye, a puny, pale faced youth advanced to the rostrum

without any introduction, and, dispensing with musical accompaniments, began his song. At the first few notes, slow and plaintive, the attention of every one was riveted; for, dwarf-like as was his appearance, the singer became master of all their sympathies. His was one of those popular melodies which appeal to the truest impulses of our nature; and when he warbled the refrain–

"Why did she leave him?
Because he was poor,"

the countenances of the gentler sex, in particular, betrayed emotions of pity and indignation. They would never have left him when he needed help and comfort they would have lightened his poverty with a smile. This song, thought I, has done the lasses good. Then, having finished my glass, I walked out again into the streets.[140]

The establishment which drew a torrent of abuse from the middle classes was the Leeds Casino and Concert Hall – a ramshackle wooden building in Lands Lane which was opened by a publican, Joseph Hobson, in 1849. It was one of the first music halls to be opened in Britain. When its opponents visited it in November 1851, with the intention of distributing religious literature, they were horrified to find an audience of some seven to eight hundred 'gazing with zest on scenes, and listening with delight to sounds, which to us, at least, were both humiliating and appalling'. Unfortunately, the Reverend Stalker and Samuel Barbour never enlarged on the exact nature of the entertainment they witnessed. However, over the following months they interviewed both prostitutes and juvenile offenders in Armley Gaol, all of whom admitted to frequenting the Casino, leading to their conclusion that 'nothing is learned there but wickedness'.[141]

In 1863 James Hole provided a description of an establishment which almost certainly must have been the Casino. After condemning the dram shops and low beer houses, he remarked:

> There are other places where the attractions are perhaps less coarse, but not less seductive, nor ultimately less pernicious – the casino and singing rooms. Comic songs of a more than doubtful character, recitations spiced with *double entendre*, dancing, semi-dramatic performances, and mere buffoonery, accompanied by tobacco smoking and drinking, are the ordinary attractions of such places. One place of the kind in Leeds has a larger nightly attendance than the evening classes of all its 17 Mechanics' Institutes put together![142]

The response of the middle classes to such evils was to promote 'rational recreation' for the working classes. Directly in response to the opening of the Casino, the Leeds Rational Recreation Society was founded in 1852 with the rather ambitious object of entertaining and improving the working classes by providing:

> a counteracting agency to the attractions of objectionable places of amusement, and by giving very cheap musical entertainments, to promote a wide diffusion of musical science and taste, the effects of which are not confined to the concert room, but are likewise observable in the home of the mechanic.[143]

The society sponsored 124 concerts at the Music Hall in Albion Street (a cultural venue) between 1852 and '59. Admission prices were set at 3d., 6d., and 1s. The concerts were almost entirely a mixture of opera, glees, ballads and a considerable amount of comic song. The concerts were a success, with average attendances of around 700 people of whom at least a quarter were working class – though these may have been mainly skilled artisans.[144] Undoubtedly, the middle classes viewed the concerts as an opportunity to teach the working classes good manners and greater refinement. At speeches at the end of the concerts the middle classes quite overtly patronised the working class section of the audience though it did not stop them coming. In 1857 Alderman John Botterill commented: 'No workman could attend these concerts without having his taste refined, for no one could mingle amongst those moving in a higher sphere to himself, without such results, and without his ambition being excited to attain a position no less elevated and respected.'[145] John Hope Shaw, the solicitor who was three times mayor of Leeds, was much more diplomatic: 'It was impossible', he said, 'that all classes of society could mingle with each other week after week, as at these concerts, without feeling their mutual regard for each other strengthened and confirmed'.[146]

The concerts were very successful, but they were a drop in the ocean in the middle classes' battle against popular working-class entertainment. By the mid-1860s Leeds had at least three music halls of the Casino variety. By 1865 the Leeds public could attend the Casino under its new name, the Amphitheatre (the Casino had burned down); the Princess Palace, opened in 1864; and the White Swan Varieties, which, as the City Varieties, still operates today.[147]

For the more respectable workman the Working Men's Institute, established in the Assembly Rooms in 1861, offered 'innocent amusement free from the contamination and ruinous cost of the beer house'. It was a great success and by 1863 attracted between 1,800 and 2,000 men each week to use its facilities. In the reading room, well supplied with newspapers and periodicals, he could relax and enjoy a

Top: A token showing the Casino, the infamous singing room and music hall, in King Charles Croft, off Lands Lane. Bottom: Poster advertising the Leeds Regatta Fetes at Kirkstall Abbey, 10 and 11 July 1867. Brass bands played popular tunes as immense crowds watched spectacles ranging from people trying to cross the river on perilously positioned slippery poles, to boating and dancing competitions. Sadly, the weather was too bad for Eurado to perform!

quiet moment, or, should he feel more sociable, the adjoining room had over forty chess or draught boards and at the far end a dining area where a meal could be eaten with friends. Its weekly Discussion Class, weekly Lecture, Outdoor Games, and Musical Entertainment each attracted well over 700 people.[148]

The Nonconformists, particularly the Baptists and Methodists, promoted the Temperance movement in an attempt to lure the working-classes away from the demon of drink. The Leeds Temperance Society founded by Edward Baines, the elder, in 1830, was one of the first in the country. As the century progressed, numerous temperance organisations in the town offered a range of amusements for the whole family in an abstemious atmosphere, in stark contrast to the male dominated pubs. The Revd Jabez Tunnicliff (1809-1865) founded the Band of Hope in 1847 to 'prevent the youth of our land from becoming victims to the drinking vices of the age'. He spent a great deal of time composing popular songs, visiting schools and holding weekly meetings to highlight the evils of drink. The Leeds Band of Hope League continued to prosper after his death, and on Good Friday 1870, 38 Bands of Hope, numbering 8,871, met in front of the Town Hall, where, after singing a number of melodies, they marched through the streets, with colourful flags and banners, accompanied by a number of bands.[149]

Zealous though the work of the Temperance movement was, the draw of the lights streaming from the gin shops such as that at the top of Briggate in 1865 was formidable. As Tomlinson passed by, he debated whether to go in:

> Curiosity conquered propriety, therefore I went in. Immediately behind the door were stationed a harper and a fiddler, with their instruments lying carelessly beside them, while they partook of rum-and-water, hot, which had been paid for by one of the fast young gents in the company. I called for a glass of sherry. By my side was a nervous, modest-looking young man, whose eyes sparkled too brilliantly as he sipped his glass in silence. Ranged along the counter were five or six nymphs, some with very pink cheeks, others with very black lustrous eyes, and all gaudily if not expensively dressed. One of them shewed a disposition to be on affable and familiar terms with the youth alluded to, enquiring in a very bewitching manner – 'Well, my dear, and how are you tonight?' He appeared nonplussed, and, for the moment, unable to utter a word. A gentleman present, remarking, no doubt, his trepidation, was considerate enough to answer for him – 'O, pretty bobbish; it was very kind of you, Sall, to inquire after my health'; upon which the company set up a great laugh.
>
> After a while one of the other girls made some remark to the aforesaid nymph, which bore a disparaging insinuation. The countenance, which so lately wore a bewitching smile, was now so distorted by anger, while oaths and curses were dispensed with an awful facility, and the bar-keepers had much trouble in preventing a fight. The music struck up in the midst of this altercation, and, strange anomaly of human character! before five minutes were passed, the two belligerents were ogling a new set of visitors, and laughing as loudly as if nothing had occurred. Ah, thought I, but this is not like the light-heartedness of innocence. It seemed to me that those bursts of wild laughter were the utterances of a deeper misery than could find vent in tears. That condition is not altogether irremediable which is associated with remorse, but these poor outcasts dare not reflect, for there is nothing but the grave which can protect them from the world's scorn.[150]

References

1. J.Morgan, 'Demographic Change' in *Modern Leeds*.
2. W.G.Rimmer, 'Occupations in Leeds', *Thoresby Soc.*, L (1967).
3. W.G.Rimmer, *Marshall's of Leeds* (Cambridge, 1960) esp. ch. 5; E.J.Connell and M.Ward, 'Industrial Development, 1780-1914' in *Modern Leeds*, p. 150.
4. McCorquodale, *Leeds Directory, 1876*, p. 47; White, *Leeds Directory, 1894*, pp. 581-2.
5. R.J.Morris, 'Leeds and the Crystal Palace', *Victorian Studies*, 13 (1970).
6. Occupational Census Statistics given in Rimmer, 'Occupations in Leeds'.
7. *White's Directory of Leeds,1894*, p. 582.
8. W.G.Rimmer, 'The Woollen Industry in the Nineteenth Century', *Leeds Journal*, 30 (Leeds, 1959).
9. Rimmer, 'Woollen Industry in the Nineteenth Century'.
10. *Kelly's Directory of Leeds, 1901*, p. 4.
11. Rimmer, 'Occupations in Leeds', p. 166.
12. E.Kitson Clark, *Kitsons of Leeds, 1837-1937* (1938); *Empire Mail*, July 1926, p. 431; M.R.Lane, *The Story of the Steam Plough Works: Fowlers of Leeds* (1980).
13. *Imperial Review*, October 1936, pp. 14-5; *Leeds Sketches and Reviews* (Leeds, 1902), pp. 30-3; Historical Publishing Company, *England's Great Manufacturing Centres: Yorkshire – Leeds and Bradford* (1888), p. 141.
14. M.W.Beresford and G.R.Jones, eds., *Leeds and Its Region*, (Leeds, 1967), p. 161.
15. *Leeds Illustrated* (1892), p. 52.
16. London Printing & Engraving Company, *The Century's Progress: Yorkshire Industry and Commerce* (1893), p. 157.
17. J.Thomas, 'The Leeds Clothing Industry', *Yorkshire Bulletin of Economic and Social Research*, Occasional Paper No. 1 (1955).
18. R.Sheracy, 'The White Slaves of England: The Slipper Makers and Tailors of Leeds', *Pearson's Magazine*, II (1896), pp. 263-8; M.Freeman, *Leeds Jews: The First Hundred Years* (Leeds, 1992).
19. Rimmer, 'Occupations in Leeds', passim.
20. W.G.Rimmer, 'Leeds Leather Industry in the Nineteenth Century', *Thoresby Soc.*, XLVI (1961).
21. C.Lackey, *Quality Pays: The Story of Joshua Tetley and Son* (1985); J.Chartres, 'Joshua Tetley & Son, 1890s to 1990s: a century in the tied trade' in J.Chartres and K.Honeyman, eds., *Leeds City Business, 1893-1993* (Leeds, 1993); Anon, '100 Years of School Printing: Arnolds of Leeds', *British Printer*, Vol 76, No. 4 (April, 1963), pp. 84-8; 'William Moorhouse and Sons Ltd', *The Leeds Graphic*, Vol 1, No. 3, August 1958, pp. 18-9; Joseph Watson's Whitehall Works' in *The Century's Progress*, p. 151; K. Honeyman, 'Soapy Joe's: the History of Joseph Watson and Sons Ltd, 1893-1993' in Chartres and Honeyman, *op. cit.*.
22. K.Grady, 'Commercial, Marketing and Retailing Amenities, 1700-1914' in *Modern Leeds*, pp. 187-195; H.Pemberton, 'Two Hundred Years of Banking in Leeds', *Thoresby Soc.*, XLVI (1963).
23. *Leeds Intelligencer*, 18 Jan. 1845.
24. W.A.Thomas, *The Provincial Stock Exchanges* (1973); J.R.Killick and W.A.Thomas, 'The Provincial Stock Exchanges, 1830-70', *Economic History Review*, XXIII (1970).
25. White, *1837 Directory*, pp. 508, 635-6; T.Fenteman, *An Historical Guide to Leeds and its Environs* (Leeds, 1858), (hereafter *Fenteman's Guide* (1858), p. 48.
26. *Kelly's Directory of Leeds, 1914*, p. xxxv.
27. *The Builder*, 19 Dec. 1896, pp. 510-2.
28. White, *1837 Directory*, pp. 623-4; Charlton and Archdeacon's, *Directory of the Borough and Neighbourhood of Leeds, 1849-50*, pp. 419-28; *Fenteman's Guide* (1858), p. 49; *Kelly's Directory of Leeds, 1899*.
29. Leeds and Holbeck Building Society, *One Hundred Years of Progress and Service*; *Kelly's Directory of Leeds, 1901*, p. 21.
30. K.J.Bonser, *The Leeds Permanent Building Society: A Centenary Booklet* (Leeds, 1948); M.Collins, 'The History of the Leeds Permanent Building Society, 1893-1993', in Chartres and Honeyman, *op. cit.*
31. M.W.Beresford, The Leeds Chambers of Commerce (1951).
32. H.H.Sales, *A Description of the Royal Exchange in Leeds* (Leeds, *c.*1872).
33. For both papers, see: *Fenteman's Guide* (1858), pp. 39, 124-6.
34. *Ibid.*, p. 125; S.Smiles, *The Autobiography of Samuel Smiles* (edited by Thomas Mackay, 1905).
35. *Fenteman's Guide* (1858), p. 125.
36. *Ibid.*
37. J.Dodgson, *Historical and Descriptive Guide to the Borough of Leeds* (Leeds, 1879) (hereafter *Dodgson's Guide* (1879), pp. 117-8. For its subsequent history, see: S.Caunce, 'Yorkshire Post Newspapers Ltd.: Perseverance Rewarded', in Chartres and Honeyman, *op. cit.*
38. Kelly's Directory of Leeds, 1901, p. 21.
39. *Fenteman's Guide* (1858), pp. 126-7.
40. *Dodgson's Guide* (1879), p. 118.
41. *The Builder*, 15 July 1899.
42. *Parsons' History*, II, pp. 258-63; H.C.Versey, 'The Postal History of Leeds', *Thoresby Soc.*, L (1968), pp. 181-92.
43. *Fenteman's Guide* (1858), pp. 114-5.
44. *Dodgson's Guide* (1879), pp. 105-7.
45. *Kelly's Directory of Leeds, 1901*, p. 21.
46. *Leeds Intelligencer*, 1, 6 Jan. 1825, 21 Oct. 1830.
47. *Parsons' History*, II, pp. 221-7.
48. *Leeds Mercury*, 23 Sept. 1834.
49. H.Parris, 'Leeds and its Industrial Growth, No. 11: Leeds and its Railways', *The Leeds Journal*, Vol. 26 (1955), p. 158.
50. *Ibid.*, p. 159.
51. R.Oliver, *Leeds-Holbeck: The First Wisp of Steam* (Leeds, 1980), pp. 8-13.
52. R.Unwin, 'Leeds Becomes a Transport Centre', in *Modern Leeds*, pp. 132-3.
53. *Leeds 1853 Directory*, p. 290.
54. For background see: 28 & 29 Victoria, cap. 251 (1865): The North-eastern Railway (Leeds Extension) Act; Mayhall, *Annals*, III, 54-5, 242-3, 246-50; W.W.Tomlinson, *The North Eastern Railway* (1914), pp. 634-5.
55. Mayhall, *Annals*, III, p. 247.
56. *Ibid.*, p. 240.
57. *The New Leeds City Station* (brochure, 1967).
58. P.P. 1867, XXXIII, Third Report of the Commissioners appointed to Inquire into the Best Means of Preventing the Pollution of Rivers (Rivers Aire and Calder), pp. 228-31, evidence of W. H. Bartholomew.
59. *Ibid.*
60. R.Baker, 'Report on the State and Condition of the Town of Leeds', in P.P. 1842, XXIX, Sanitary Inquiry, p. 59.
61. R.Baker, 'The Industrial and Sanitary Economy of the Borough of Leeds in 1858', *Journal of the Statistical Society of London* (1858), pp. 5-6.
62. *River Pollution Commission 1867*, p. xi.
63. *Ibid.*, p. 188.
64. *Ibid.*, p. 202-3.
65. *Ibid.*, p. 258.
66. *Ibid.*, pp. 216-9.
67. *Ibid.*, p.208.
68. *Ibid.*, pp. 170-1.
69. T.Steele, *Alfred Orage and the Leeds Arts Club, 1893-1923* (1990); A.R.Orage, 'A Study in Mud' in A.T.Marks, ed., *Hypnotic Leeds* (Leeds, 1894), p. 17.
70. J.Tomlinson, *Some Interesting Yorkshire Scenes* (1865), p. 22.
71. J.Burnett, *A Social History of Housing, 1815-1970* (1978), pp. 94-100.
72. E.W.Clay, *The Leeds Police, 1836-1974*, (Leeds, 1975), p. 12; P. P. 1898, LXVI, *Report on the Endowed Charities of the City of Leeds*, pp. 137 and others; S.T.Anning, *The General Infirmary at Leeds* (1963), I, pp. 65-6, 78.
73. P.P. 1845, XIII, *Select Committee on Smoke Prevention*, p. 560.
74. *Ibid.*, pp. 560, 577.
75. For further details about the developments described in the following section on middle-class housing, see C.Treen, 'The Process of Suburban Development in North Leeds, 1870-1914' in F.M.L.Thompson, ed., *The Rise of Suburbia* (Leicester, 1982), pp. 160-87.
76. *Ibid.*, pp. 168-9.
77. D.Ward, 'Environs and Neighbours in the "Two Nations": Residential Differentiation in Mid-Nineteenth-Century Leeds', *Journal of Historical Geography*, 6, 2 (1980), pp. 133-162; R.J.Morris, *Class, Sect and Party: The Making of the British Middle Class: Leeds, 1820-50* (Manchester, 1990), pp. 54-6.
78. Burnett, *op. cit.*, pp. 94-100.
79. Census Enumerators Returns for Leeds, 1851.
80. *Leeds 1849-50 Directory*, pp. 16, 23, 50; White's 1853 Leeds Directory, pp. 9, 16.
81. *Leeds 1849-50 Directory*, pp. 7, 11, 12; White's 1853 Leeds Directory, pp. 8, 99.
82. T.Wemyss Reid, *Memoir of John Deakin Heaton, M.D.* (1883), pp. 101-4.
83. *Fenteman's Guide* (1858), p. 7; D.Russell, 'The Leeds Rational Recreation Society, 1852-9: "Music for the People" in a mid-Victorian City', *Thoresby Soc.*, LVI (1981), p. 147.
84. *Fenteman's Guide* (1858), pp. 121-2.
85. J.Sprittles, 'Leeds Music Festivals', *Thoresby Soc.*, XLVI (1961), pp. 200-70.
86. J.Hole, *The Working Classes of Leeds: An Essay on the Present State of Education in Leeds, and the Best Means of Improving It* (1863), p. 120.
87. S.J.Reid, *Memoirs of Sir Wemyss Reid, 1842-1885* (1905), pp. 100-1.
88. J.Copley, 'The Theatre in Hunslet Lane, II', *Thoresby Soc.*, LIV (1976), pp. 196-208.
89. *Fenteman's Guide* (1858), p. 115.
90. *Jones's Mercantile Directory of Leeds, 1863*, p. 14.
91. F.Trowell, 'Speculative Housing Development in the Suburb of Headingley', *Thoresby Soc.*, LIX (1985).
92. Baker, *op. cit.* (1842), p. 56.
93. *Leeds Mercury*, 1 Aug. 1841.
94. *Leeds Mercury* 11 July 1840.
95. Trowell, *op. cit.*, pp. 62-71.
96. *Fenteman's Guide* (1858), p. 123; G.D.Gaunt and D.H.C.Sillers, 'The Leeds Archers Society (1848-1892)', *Journal of the Society of Archer-Antiquaries* (1980), Vol. 23, pp. 3-11.
97. J.K.Walton, *The English Seaside Resort: A Social History, 1750-1914* (Leicester, 1983), pp. 29-30.
98. Tomlinson, *op. cit.*, p. 24
99. Baker, *op. cit.* (1842), p. 14.
100. E.Baines, *The Woollen Manufacture of England: With Special Reference to the Leeds Clothing District* (Leeds, 1858), pp. 93-8; Baker, *op. cit.* (1858), pp. 10-17.
101. Baker, *op. cit.* (1842), pp. 16-9.
102. M.W.Beresford, 'The Face of Leeds', in Fraser, ed., *Modern Leeds*, p. 73.
103. P.P. 1845, XVIII, pp. 312-3.
104. P.P. 1843, XIV: *Children's Employment Commission (Trades & Manufacture)*, Report by J.C.Symons, pp. E 37-9.
105. J.Hole, *The Homes of the Working Classes* (Leeds, 1866).
106. M.W.Beresford, 'The Back-to-Back House in Leeds, 1787-1937', in S.D.Chapman, ed., *The History of Working-Class Housing: A Symposium* (Newton Abbot, 1971).
107. Baker, *op. cit.* (1842), p. 11.
108. *Ibid.*
109. *River Pollution Commission 1867*, p. 220.
110. *Leeds Mercury* 15 Feb. 1851; *Leeds Intelligencer* 15 Feb. 1851.
111. Baker, *op. cit.* (1842), p. 12.
112. P.P. 1843, XIV, pp. E 37-9.
113. P.Brears, *Yorkshire Food and Tradition* (Edinburgh, 1987), pp. 9-16, 35-41.
114. Tomlinson, *op. cit.*, pp. 25-6.
115. Baker, *op. cit.* (1842), pp. 45-6.
116. Sheracy, *op. cit.*, pp. 263-8.
117. Baker, *op. cit.* (1842), pp. 46-8.
118. Pollen, *op. cit.*, p. 17. For the activities of the Socialists, see: Smiles, *op. cit.*, pp. 105-7.
119. Baker, *op. cit.* (1842), pp. 23-4.
120. E.Jackson, *A Pastor's Recollections* (Leeds, 1890), No. 5, p. 10.
121. T.Dillon, 'The Irish in Leeds, 1851-1861', *Thoresby Soc.*, LIV (1973).
122. Baker, *op. cit.* (1842), pp. 15-7.
123. *River Pollution Commission 1867*, p. 223, evidence of Alderman Carter.
124. Dillon, *op. cit.*, pp. 9-10.
125. Baker, *op. cit.* (1842), p. 15.
126. *Ibid.*, p. 17.
127. A.Reach, 'Labour and the Poor', *The Morning Chronicle*, 10, 13 Dec. 1849.
128. Mayhall, *op. cit.*, II, pp. 194-201.
129. J.Buckman, *Immigrants and the Class Struggle: The Jewish Immigrant in Leeds, 1880-1914* (Manchester, 19830; E.Krausz, *Leeds Jewry: its History and Social Structure* (Cambridge, 1964); E.Sterne, *Leeds Jewry, 1919-29* (Leeds, 1989).
130. 'The Sweating System in Leeds', *The Lancet* (1988).
131. Leeds Central Reference Library, LQ 331.892 LS17: newspaper cuttings about the Leeds Jewish tailors' strike, 7-23 May 1888.
132. Sheracy, *op. cit.*, pp. 263-8.
133. F.M.L.Thompson, *The Rise of Respectable Society: A Social History of Victorian Britain, 1830-1900* (1988), pp. 274-6.
134. Hole, *op. cit.* (1863), p. 115.
135. *Statistical Committee Report, 1839*, p. 27;E.M.Sigsworth, 'The Brewery Trade During the Industrial Revolution: The Case of Yorkshire', *Borthwick Papers*, No. 31 (York, 1967).
136. J.F.C.Harrison, *Early Victorian Britain, 1832-51* (1979), pp. 96-7.
137. P.P. 1843, XIV, pp. E 37-9.
138. E.Baines, *The Social, Educational and Religious State of the Manufacturing Districts* (1843), p. 8.
139. *Ibid.*, p. 7.
140. Tomlinson, *op. cit.*, pp. 27-8.
141. Russell, *op. cit.*, p. 142.
142. Hole, *op. cit.*, p. 116.
143. *Fenteman's Guide 1858*), p. 122.
144. Russell, *op. cit.*, p. 146.
145. *Ibid.*, p. 149-50.
146. *Ibid.*
147. *Ibid.*, pp. 152-3.
148. Hole, *op. cit.* (1863), pp. 160-2.
149. Leeds Band of Hope League, *Annual Report* (Leeds, 1870), pp. 6-9.
150. Tomlinson, *op. cit.*, pp. 28-9.

CHAPTER SIX

The Pillars of Victorian Society

Governing Victorian Leeds

When the reformed Leeds Corporation or council met for the first time in December 1835 it had responsibility for little more than the finance and management of the police. When Parliament reformed the municipal corporations in 1835 it had no intention of establishing authorities equipped to govern rapidly evolving towns like Leeds. After all, as we will see, it had just reformed the Poor Law to set up boards of guardians to deal with the poor; and it had passed numerous Improvement Acts to enable improvement commissioners to regulate the built environment of growing towns. Municipal corporations in the past had played their principal role in the administration of justice and law and order, and the principal aim of reform was to ensure that from now on this was done on a democratically elected basis. Few could have had the notion that during the Victorian heyday of freedom of enterprise and individualism, a town council like Leeds would come to widen the range of its activities until it had achieved a major influence over many facets the town's life. By the end of Victoria's reign the council provided gas, water, electricity supply and trams. It had responsibility for environmental health; it had created parks, libraries, markets and other amenities, and it had begun to tackle the problems of the slums.[1]

Public Health

The council's Statistical Committee Report of 1839 laid bare the problems of the insanitary housing of the working classes, the ill-paving, the lack of sewers, and the inadequate water supply. The major response to this and subsequent investigations was the Leeds Improvement Act of 1842.[2] The Act transferred the functions of the improvement commission to the council along with major new powers to improve public health. At that time it was one of the most complete and comprehensive Acts obtained by a local authority, and it gave great hope for a rapid improvement in the sanitary and housing conditions in Leeds. These hopes, however, were slow to be fulfilled. One of the most important provisions of the Act was to empower the council to construct a comprehensive sewerage system for the central urban area in the townships of Leeds, Holbeck, and Hunslet. Unfortunately for the working classes of Leeds, technical, legal and financial obstacles, and the economic uncertainties of the early 1840s, prevented the council from taking immediate positive action.[3] The Act also gave the council power to enforce minimum standards in the construction of new houses and new streets, but to its shame these were not enforced. In part this was because the only penalty for non-compliance with the regulations was the draconian one of having the offending houses demolished, but the fact that many councillors came from the landlord class must also have influenced their attitude. The penalty clause was not amended until the Leeds Improvement Act of 1866 by which time a further 12,000 houses had been built.[4]

The problems caused by the council's reluctance to enforce minimum building standards and its slowness to build a comprehensive central network of sewers were compounded by its failure to compel landlords to connect their properties to the sewers when they were provided. In the light of the housing conditions of the working classes described earlier, this seems like nothing short of cruel neglect by the middle classes who, while regularly attempting to indoctrinate the working classes with high-flown moral principles and behaviour, chose to protect their vested interests and deny vital help to their less fortunate fellow townspeople. Perhaps more charitably, James Hole felt that the segregation of the upper-middle-class decision takers in the north-western sections of the town or in the remoter northern suburbs had deprived them of direct knowledge of the appalling living conditions of the working classes.[5]

Be that as it may, in another important sphere affecting public health, the interment of the dead, the council acted with commendable speed. Almost all the burials which took place in Leeds were at the parish church graveyard. As the population of Leeds mushroomed, the graveyard was too small to accommodate all the bodies. In the early 1830s a piece of ground capable of taking a further 3,680 graves was added, but by 1841 that too was full.[6] It was then that the scandalous practices at the graveyard became common public knowledge. Robert Baker revealed that:

> The bodies, when interred in particular places selected by friends, were disinterred after the funeral and the retirement of the friends, and re-deposited in some other part of the ground; a practice which came before the magistrates of the town officially, and thus became of public notoriety.[7]

Worse still, family graves became so full that coffins were being buried only two feet six inches from the surface. When the next funeral took place, in order to make enough space, the coffins nearest the surface, and often those below, were dug out and smashed to pieces and the bones of their occupants thrown back into the grave. Robert Baker related the horror of one unfortunate man who arrived at his family grave prior to an interment to find the skulls and bones of his father and brother strewn alongside the grave. 'Look!', he said, 'these are the skulls of my Father and my Brother, and the bones of my relations, is not this a bad business? It cannot, I suppose, however, be helped; I must have a family grave'.[8] Baker condemned both the inhumanity of the situation and the danger to public health.

In an attempt to remedy this situation, at least for the middle classes, in 1835 the Leeds General Cemetery Company opened a large and well-appointed private cemetery. This burial ground, with its 12 feet high

Beckett Street Cemetery with the Leeds Union Workhouse in the distance.

boundary wall and imposing portico and mortuary chapel, was on ten acres of land, known as St George's Field, just south of Woodhouse Moor. Today it is surrounded by Leeds University. The £11,000 required was raised in £10 shares. The ground was not consecrated for church use, so it was only used by Dissenters.[9] Leeds desperately needed a burial ground which all religions would feel able to use, and which would accommodate the poor as well as the rich. In 1842 the council was successful in obtaining the Leeds Burial Act which permitted it to levy rates for the purposes of the interment of the dead.[10] Three years later Beckett Street Cemetery, or rather Burmantofts Cemetery as it was then known, was opened. The cemetery provided an almost perfect representation of Leeds society. It was divided into two sections, one for Anglicans and one for Dissenters, and each had its own chapel. Although the buildings were identical local custom referred to them for ever after as 'the Church' and 'the Chapel'. Not only religious division was recognised, for 'first-class' graves were placed on the top of the hill and 'fifth-class' or 'lowest' graves at each end; the 'two nations' rich and poor were divided in death as well as in life.[11]

The cholera epidemic of 1832 which killed over 700 people had prompted the first in-depth study of living conditions in Leeds. In 1849 a second epidemic which killed over 2,000 townspeople shook the rulers of Leeds to the roots. The council began to tackle the drainage, sanitation and water supply issues in real earnest. In 1850 it began to build new sewers and by 1862 it had spent £211,155 on a network through the town.[12] Worthy as this was, its continued failure to compel landlords to connect property to the sewers dramatically reduced their impact. In 1857 a council inspection sub-committee, after a tour of the drainage district, reported to the council with regret 'the very large number of streets either wholly or inefficiently drained, notwithstanding the excellent outlet which has in almost every instance been brought close to them by your main sewers'.[13] The majority of the population continued to rely upon the privy-and-ashpit for the disposal of human and household refuse.

The council also attempted to take the problem of inadequate water supply by the scruff of the neck. In 1837 the improvement commissioners had resigned the management of the waterworks, and it was vested in a joint stock company with a board composed of equal numbers of shareholders, directors and councillors. Under the terms of the 1837 Act the council had the right to buy out the company at any time after twelve years had elapsed. In 1852 Alderman John Hope Shaw, the Liberal solicitor convinced the council that its acquisition was the most effective and efficient way of obtaining an enlarged supply of pure water. The purchase was completed at a cost of £227,417. Disregarding warnings about the pollution of the River Wharfe, the council obtained Acts in 1856 and 1862 which permitted it to adopt the least costly option of pumping six million gallons of water out of the Wharfe everyday. By the 1860s, however, the predicted pollution was causing problems. The council was now forced to opt for the alternative proposed in the 1850s of taking water from the River Washburn and storing it in reservoirs. The Leeds Waterworks Act of 1867 permitted a three-stage scheme which resulted in the construction of reservoirs at Lindley Wood in 1869-75, Swinsty in 1871-77, and Fewston in 1874-79. At a cost of £508,173, this was a massive local authority capital expenditure. The council's acquisition and improvement of the waterworks produced major benefits for the people of Leeds. In 1842 less than 10 per cent of the total houses in Leeds were supplied with water from the mains, by the mid-1860s this had increased to 95 per cent.[14]

The provision of main sewers and an enlarged water supply encouraged the idea that public health was improving, and indeed, the death rate in Leeds township dipped from around 29 per thousand to 27 per thousand between 1853 and 1858.[15] Unfortunately, such optimism was soon overshadowed by events as the fall in the death rate was reversed by a sustained rise into the early 1870s. By the late 1850s the sanitary condition of Leeds was beginning to be a subject of national concern. Dr Hunter from the Privy Council's Medical Department arrived in Leeds in 1865 to see one sanitary problem at its height. As late as 1865 only 3,221 houses in the town had water closets, and consequently the majority of the population used middens. The emptying and cleansing of middens was therefore of vital importance to the health of the town. Before 1859 the removal of domestic waste was solely the householders' responsibility, but in that year the council decided to provide a cleansing service in the drainage district. At first the task was performed by council employees, but in 1862 it was put out to contract with disastrous results. Dr Hunter arrived to inspect Leeds just as the Leeds Economic Sanitary Company, which removed the midden filth, had gone bankrupt, leaving the council struggling to clear up the mess.[16] He graphically described the scene:

> Hundreds of people, long unable to use the privy because of the rising heap, were depositing on the floors. A few dawdling carts ...would after many applications relieve the midden of such inhabitants as could by peremptory manner or by influence obtain a hearing. Even then the relief was most imperfect ...Such carts as were employed only carried the midden filth to a deposit in the town, by the water side, except a few by which some railway trucks were loaded. At this deposit stood thousands of tons of midden filth needlessly waiting for removal by boat or cart for consumption ...Although not far from the centre of the town the deposit (as was alleged) was not in a very populous part, because a great part of the surrounding buildings were mills and factories. But people filled these places all day, and Mr Wheelhouse, F.R.C.S. informed your inspector that in whatever part of the town they lived fever followed those people who worked within scent of this obviously ill-placed and ill-managed deposit.[17]

Dr Hunter's report in 1865 branded Leeds as a filthy place. The Medical Department of the Privy Council visited Leeds in 1858, 1865, 1870, and 1874, and their findings prompted Sir John Simon to declare unequivocally that the administration of public health 'in

Kirkgate Covered Market (opened in 1857) on the eve of its demolition.

proportion to the importance of the town may perhaps be deemed the worst that has ever come to the attention of this department'.[18]

Markets and Fairs

Public health aside, one of the key areas of the council's activities was the provision of improved market facilities. Like the unreformed corporation before it, the council was unequivocally the lord of the town's market; an institution not only of great importance to the functioning of the town, but one of considerable profit to the public purse. Despite the building of the private markets in the 1820s, thousands of people still flocked on market days to the stalls which lined Briggate. The transfer of the cattle and fruit and vegetable markets to the 'Free Market' on Kirkgate had proved extremely beneficial, and in 1842, under the powers of the new Improvement Act, the council formed a market committee and took over the running of Kirkgate Market from the improvement commissioners.[19]

In 1842 the committee decided to enlarge Kirkgate Market by purchasing some adjoining land. The extended area would provide more room for the sale of livestock, and there were to be shops around the perimeter. As the committee pointed out, an additional merit of the scheme was that the redeveloped land included the most insanitary property in the town, notably the notorious Boot and Shoe Yard. The completion of the extension in 1846 now provided room for the normal livestock markets, but it was not intended to cope with the huge volume of business at the annual horse and cattle fairs held in July and November. In 1845, after an unsuccessful attempt to obtain the use of St Peter's Square, the market committee solved this second problem by establishing a fair-ground on a 1½ acre site in Woodhouse Lane, leased from the trustees of Potter's Almshouses.[20]

In the 1850s, however, discontent with the shortage of covered market accommodation in the centre became very vocal. In 1853 the proprietors of the Central Market, seeing the possibilities of the situation, applied to Parliament for an Act incorporating their company and permitting them to enlarge their building. The council, alarmed by the threat of interference with its rights, opposed the Bill. Although the legislation was rejected, the council received a sharp rap on the knuckles from the Commons committee, which agreed that a new covered market was urgently required, and implied that the council had better remedy the situation, or a renewed application by the Central Market proprietors might not be rejected. The committee's comments had their effect; in addition to embarking on a scheme to erect a covered market, the council decided to investigate the provision of improved accommodation for the sale of cattle. In 1853 the market committee purchased a site between Camp Road and North Street intending to lay it out as a cattle market. Smithfield Cattle Market, as it was known, opened in 1855 at a cost of approximately £14,000. Sales of cattle were removed from Kirkgate Market and the sale of horses in the streets was prohibited. A centuries-old practice, the sale of livestock in the streets, had been brought to an end.[21]

Meanwhile the plans for a covered market were under way. In December 1853 the council accepted the market committee's recommendation that a covered market should be erected on the Kirkgate Market site, and voted £14,000 for the purpose. The market was opened in May 1857. Its design was manifestly inspired by the Crystal Palace, in fact the plans were submitted to Sir Joseph Paxton for his comments.[22] The 1858 guide to Leeds described the new hall and its surroundings:

> The building is of iron and glass, covering an area of 4,040 yards, and is situated at the junction of Vicar Lane and Kirkgate. The style of architecture is Gothic …It has 44 convenient shops on the outside, and 35 inside, where there are also four rows of iron stalls. At night this beautiful crystal market hall is well illuminated by 200 gas lights, arranged round handsome cast iron pillars. Altogether it is the most complete structure of its kind in England …At the east side of this market there remains about 5,000 square yards of open market ground, where an extensive variety of fruit and vegetables are exposed for sale on Tuesday and Saturday; besides which there are several shops with fruit, poultry, fish, and other goods.[23]

Perhaps the covered market's greatest claim to fame is that it was the birthplace of Marks and Spencer, for in the 1880s it housed Michael Marks's first Penny Bazaar. From the 30 November 1857 the placing of stalls, benches, goods, wares or merchandise in Briggate was prohibited. The Briggate street market too had become a thing of the past.

By the 1850s, perhaps the most neglected of all Leeds

traders were the corn factors. There had been no improvement since the building of the corn exchange in 1825-27, and farmers selling grain in sacks were still trading in the open air in Kirkgate Market. In 1859, after repeated petitions, the council decided to erect a building to house both the sack market and the sale of corn by sample. This oval-shaped Corn Exchange, which still survives, was built in 1861-64 to the designs of Cuthbert Brodrick, at a total cost of £32,000. Although the council rejected the idea of an additional storey, the exchange was still substantial enough to accommodate 59 offices and an open area with space for 170 stands. The building is a reminder that although Leeds was a hive of industry it was still a major centre for the marketing of agricultural produce.[24]

Leeds Town Hall opened in 1858 (architect, Cuthbert Brodrick). This engraving, made before the tower was built, shows an early idea for its design.

Dr John Deakin Heaton (1817-80), a leader of Victorian society in Leeds and a major supporter of the Town Hall project.

Building the Town Hall

In spite of shortcomings in the sanitary sphere, the 1850s were years of great endeavour by the town council. The project which most symbolised the determination to improve both the image and the reality of Leeds was the building of the Town Hall. In the climate of the last decade of the twentieth century, when local government is short of funds, it seems almost inconceivable that the Victorian council, faced with the almost overwhelming problems already described, could justify spending £122,000 on building the country's most magnificent town hall. The answer is that it came about almost unintentionally. Throughout the 1830s and '40s the town's principal inhabitants felt conscious of the lack of a large hall for public meetings. At the same time, as the population of the town grew and the responsibilities of the council increased, the Court House became woefully inadequate for both judicial purposes and for council meetings and the conduct of local administrative affairs. In 1851 the council decided to meet all these needs by the erection of a town hall.[25] Its anticipated outlay, however, was £45,000 not £122,000. A long drawn out battle commenced between the economy and utility lobby and those councillors and leading townsmen who wanted an inspirational display of culture, elegance, and taste.

As Dr Heaton, one of the leading advocates of the scheme, explained it:

> If a noble municipal palace that might fairly vie with some of the best Town Halls of the Continent were to be erected in the middle of their hitherto squalid and unbeautiful town, it would become a practical admonition to the populace of the value of beauty and art, and in the course of time men would learn to live up to it.

The inspirationalists gradually won the battle. Cuthbert Brodrick won the architectural competition in June 1852, and in 1853 tenders were accepted which would have made the final cost of the building around £50,000. But in 1854 and 1855, as the building work progressed, lavish modifications were made to the scheme. The vestibule was extended, a gigantic organ was added at a cost of £6,000, and quite literally above all, purely for the sake of display, it was decided that a massive tower should be added to the building at a cost of over £5,000. The combination of under-estimates of building and material costs, and the lavish alterations to the original scheme sent the costs spiralling, and the council threw caution to the wind in the most remarkable fashion.

Beneath the classical magnificence of the structure the building satisfied a number of vital functions. The basement contained the police station and bridewell; on the ground floor at three corners were court rooms and at the fourth was the council chamber. These four corner rooms abutted the magnificent central concert hall, to each side of which were refreshment rooms, dressing rooms and retiring rooms. What remained of the ground floor was appropriated to the town clerk's office, the

Queen Victoria arrives to open Leeds Town Hall on 7 September 1858.

borough surveyor's office, the rate office, rooms for judges, barristers, magistrates and juries and waiting rooms. On the first floor there was the West Riding magistrates' court, the mayor's reception rooms, and the borough treasurer's offices. The building was thus a true centre of local government administration and justice, as well as a magnificent public hall.

The visit of Queen Victoria on 7 September 1858 to open the town hall was perhaps the most illustrious occasion in the history of Leeds. The decoration of the town was spectacular with numerous impressive floral arches. One chemist in Park Lane even perfumed the air outside his shop in honour of his monarch's visit. The Queen inspected 32,110 school children on Woodhouse Moor on her way to opening the town hall. The population and press were ecstatic. As the *Leeds Mercury* exclaimed with great pride: 'For a portion of two days, through the condescension of Her Majesty this old and busy seat of industry became the seat of the Empire.'[26]

Law and Disorder

The New Police Force and Gaol

The rulers of Leeds – the middle classes – had a strong vested interest in a stable society. The order of society which had brought them a comfortable position in life was worth defending and consolidating. While the rapidly growing ranks of the working classes enabled the middle classes to increase their wealth, their strength in numbers and periodic unruliness were a potential threat to middle-class power and property. The middle classes thought it essential that the working classes should 'know their place' and be taught to accept it. They hoped to achieve this by providing for the needs of the working classes in times of hardship through the Poor Law and philanthropic endeavours, and by imbuing them with appropriate moral values through education and religion. In the last resort, quite overt and direct methods of enforcing subservience were deemed necessary. It is to the police and the maintenance of law and order which we now turn.

When the reformed corporation was created, the only committee it was obliged to set up under the terms of the Municipal Corporation Act of 1835 was a Watch Committee.[27] It inherited a small salaried day police force consisting of a chief constable, two deputy chief constables, and five assistant constables. The officers' role was primarily that of apprehending felons, serving summonses and warrants, attendance on the magistrates and attendance at court. It was in no sense a crime prevention force. That function fell to the night watch which consisted of 85 men: a superintendent, a chief inspector, 12 inspectors and 71 watchmen. The council's first major decision, in April 1836, was to create a preventative police force modelled on the Metropolitan Police (the force set up in London by Robert Peel's Metropolitan Police Act of 1829).[28] While the existing night watch was strengthened, the council dismissed the day police. Twenty men were sought to form a new day police: a chief officer at £250 per year, a superintendent at £100 a year, four inspectors at £75, and fourteen constables at 18s. a week plus clothing. Applicants were expected to be between 21 and 35 years old, at least 5ft. 7ins. tall, and, as the advertisement put it, 'must be able to read and write with facility and must be well recommended for Command of Temper, Sobriety,

Armley Gaol, built 1846-7 (architects, Perkin and Backhouse).

Honesty, Activity and Intelligence by [their] last and present employers'.[29] In their new blue uniforms the police were the subject of frequent public comment. The daily surveillance of working-class areas was one of their prime functions. Only a fortnight after the force had begun operation the *Leeds Mercury* commented:

> We hear with great satisfaction from all quarters testimonials to the excellent work of the New Police in this town. The streets are now in a much better state, especially in Kirkgate and those streets contiguous to the haunts of vice. Persons of infamous character are not allowed to annoy the inhabitants as formerly, and scenes of low debauchery are prevented or checked. On Sunday the outskirts of the town are no longer allowed to be infested with gamblers, dog fighters etc., and the improvement is felt to be exceedingly great in this respect.[30]

The initial impact was perhaps to redistribute crime rather than reduce it, for the inhabitants of Headingley claimed that the efficiency of the police in the centre was driving delinquents to the outskirts of the town. The Tory *Leeds Intelligencer*, probably still smarting from the ousting of the Tories by the new Liberal council, could see no use for 'the day parades of dandy policemen':

> The streets have been studded with an idle day police the main performance of which is the payment of object homage to their Whig-Radical creators by the salute military as they pass along. On foolish frippery of this sort it is that the public money is squandered.[31]

For many years the police had responsibility for fire-fighting in the town and were complemented by the fire engine services provided by various insurance companies. Inefficiency in this role led to the dismissal of the first chief constable, William Heywood, who, at the height of a big fire in Hunslet, was engaged in 'drinking and tossing for "grog" with two inspectors at the Malt Shovel Inn, Meadow Lane, for upwards of two hours'.[32]

Shortly after the reorganisation of the police the first moves were made to establish a borough prison.[33] In part this was due to pressure from the Home Office and irritation at the size of the borough's contribution to the running costs of the county prison at Wakefield. It must also have irked people, however, that a town of the size and dignity of Leeds was entirely dependent upon the West Riding prison authorities at Wakefield for the custody of its long-stay prisoners. The council made the decision to erect a borough gaol in November 1837, but it was not until 1842, after five long years of wrangling over the expense, that the final go ahead was given.[34] The gaol was completed in July 1847 at a cost of £43,000 including land and buildings.[35] It was soon the object of civic pride, as a local newspaper demonstrated:

> It is pleasantly situated near Armley, on the south side of the picturesque valley of the Aire, about a mile and a half west of the town. It is a noble castellated stone structure presenting a massive pile of masonry, and is visible from many distant points. Messrs. Perkin and Backhouse of Leeds were the architects … The discipline of this gaol is that of the "Silent System". Each inmate has a separate cell (of which there are about 334), where he follows the occupation to which he may have been accustomed. Those who have no defined calling are employed in picking oakum, or making matting, the proceeds of which are applied in aid of the establishment.[36]

EXECUTION OF

JAMES SARGISSON For the Murder of John Cooper, Near Rotherham: also

JOSEPH MYERS FOR THE MURDER OF HIS WIFE At SHEFFIELD, June 10th, 1864.

JAMES SARGISSON was charged with the Murder of John Cooper, gardener, of Handsworth, on the night of the 9th of April. The Court was crowded, and a large number of persons were unable to obtain admission.

The main evidence against Sargisson resulted from his own confession. A few days after the Government had been induced to offer a reward of £100 for information of the murder, and a free pardon to an accomplice who did not strike the fatal blow, Sargisson, who had previously been suspected, began to talk unguardedly, and was then apprehended. He immediately confessed to having been present at the murder, but said Denton was the man who induced him to go, and who both murdered Cooper and robbed him. In proof of this he told the police that the watch and keys of the murdered man were hid in his (Sargisson's) pigstye, having been secreted there by Denton's directions.

Other witnesses were called, who spoke to having repeatedly seen Sargisson and Denton in company together, both before and after the murder; and also to their having seen Denton in the neighborhood of Laughton on the night of the murder. The two silk handkerchiefs which were found in Denton's possession, are stated to have belonged to the deceased.

The learned Judge then summed up at great length. The Jury found a verdict of Guilty, and sentence of Death was passed upon Sargisson, without any hope of mercy on this side the grave.

At a early hour this morning the Court was crowded to excess to get a sight of the prisoner; Joseph Myers, who was charged with the Murder of his wife, Elizabeth Myers, at Sheffield, the 10th day of June last.

George Jackson, police-constable, said: On Friday morning I was called to the house in which the murder had been commited. Deceased was then dying. Myers, whose throat was cut, was in Mrs. Hall's house. As soon as he saw me he said "Here, policeman, I want to say a few words to you. I have done it, and I hope the b—— will die. I stabbed her wih the scissors blade." (Sensation) He afterwards said, "Lend me a knife and let me finish myself off." I tied his throat up, and took him to the Infirmary. On the way he kept asking me whether she was dead. I replied I did not know. He said "I hope she will die; all I feel sorry for is the children." The knife produced I found on the table, near Myers, and when I was handing it to a surgeon at the Infirmary, Myers said, "Give it me, and let me finish myself." When we were carrying him from the cab he asked not to be laid on his back for fear of being choked.

The learned judge then summed up, and in a clear and explicit mannner went through the whole of the evidence. The jury then returned with a verdict of Guilty of Wilful Murder. His Lordship who appeared deeply affected, said the prisoner had been found guilty of one of the most heinous offences known to the laws of this country. The jury after a careful consideratioc of the case, had felt it to be their duty to fiud the prisoner guilty of wilful murder.

His Lordship then passed the usual seutence of death.

THE CONDEMNED SERMON.

On Saturday the Bishop of Ripon had interviews of an hour each with the two condemned men. The Condemned Sermon, preached by the Rev. Henry Tuckwell to about 380 Prisoners, 60 of them women, formed the congregation. Myers appeared to pay little attention: Sargisson displayed the utmost interest. The text was from Luke xxiii., 42,--"Lord remember me when thou comest into thy kingdom." "My Brethren, this is the last Lord's day which two of you can expect to spend on earth: when another Sabbath morn shall dawn, you will be numbered with the dead; you will be where there can be no repentance, no seeking for salvation. You will then be either saved or lost; with Christ in Paradise, or tormented in never-quenched flames. How all-important to you is it that a similar salvation to that which was sought and found by the condemned and dying thief, should be sought and found by you. In the way of repentance, in the way of confession, in the way of prayer, he obtained pardon and peace; his last moments were cheered by a most precious promise, and he died, condemned on earth, to be accepted and welcomed in Paradise and Heaven. No other path of safety lies open before you; there is no other Saviour than his Saviour. Do not delay, then, do not hesitate, do not neglect to seek Jesus. I solemnly, yet affectionately, ask each one of you to pray this day and every day of this week, to pray for yourselves, and for those condemned to die,---'Lord remember me, remember them, when Thou comest into Thy kingdom.' 'In the hour of death and in the day of judgment, good Lord, deliver me; good Lord, deliver them!'"

INTERVIEW BETWEEN MYERS AND HIS FAMILY.

On Monday last the members of Myers' family, consisting of his son-in-law, his son, and his two young children, were admitted to see him in prison. He asked his son pointedly, and with much eagerness, whether he thought the murder premeditated; the son answered that he thought it was. This answer took him aback, and visibly troubled him. His youngest child was asked, "Would you like to live with your father?" "Not here," said the child; "If father could fetch mother back, we'd go and live at home again." At this touching allusion Myers broke down, tears rolled down his face, and he was for some time convulsed with grief. The simple language of the child—simple as truth and innocence could make it, almost choked him with emotion. Turning to his son-in-law he said, "Can you forgive me?" The son-in-law, seeing his penitence, said he thought he could. Turning next to his son, he asked the same question. The son, moved by his contrition, replied that he also could now forgive him. He said, in a husky voice with feeling, "Now I can die content." The jailors, accustomed as they are to solemn scenes, were moved by this uncommon exhibition of passionate penitence, and they also were in tears.

THE EXECUTION.

This morning the crowd to witness the Execution was immense. The people flocked from all parts of Leeds, Bradford, Wakefield, Huddersfield, Sheffield, Rotherham, and other places. Even women with children in their arms were seen wending their way towards the vicinity of the jail. The concourse of spectators was so great, that it is estimated there has not been seen so great a number since the Queen's visit to Leeds; owing to this being the first execution ever witnessed at Armley Jail —Sept. 10th, 1864.

The worthy chaplain visited the cell of the condemned criminals, and administered to them for the last time the soothing consolation that there is a God both able and willing to save all true penitents. At the time announced, all the officials of the prison, with the executioner were in readiness, when the sombre toll of the death-bell was heard, which was the signal for the approach of the mournful procession: they were seen through the immense living mass below. All things being in readiness, the bolt was drawn, and they were launched into eternity.

Within a dark and dreary dungeon,
I for mercy now do cry,
For killing of my own dear Nancy
At Armley Jail I am doomed to die.
Cursed drink and aggravation
That have brought me to the tree;
I deprived of life my loving wife,
And I a wretch must hanged be.
CHORUS.
Oh! men, pray never let temptation
Lead you on to cursed drink;
That, and wicked aggravation
Have brought me to the gallows brink.
Twenty years with my dear Nancy,
We together struggled on through life.
Go drunken, dissipated husbands,
She a true and faithful wife.
We had many honest children,
And long we yet might happy be,
But I did kill my own dear Nancy,
And she was aged forty-three.
It was on the tenth of June that's over,
Alas! that was the fatal day,
In eighteen hundred and sixty-four,
In Sheffield I did Nancy slay.
Oh! tremble, brother malefactor,
Tremble on the fatal tree,
James Sargission who murdered Cooper,
Along with me is doomed to die.

James Sargission but aged twenty,
Is with Joseph Myers doomed to die,
At Laughton he did slay John Cooper,
And he must reach the gallows high.
One hundred pounds reward was offered,
Which when the murderer did read,
He laid the charge upon George Denton,
And swore he did commit the deed.

But Denton he was soon acquitted,
On the Murderer's lips was seen a lie,
Sargission was then committed,
– Tried and committed doomed to die.
Sargission and Myers die together,
Hurried from an early li e,
Sargisson for slaying his neighbour,
Myers for murdering of his wife.

Behold us two sad malefactors,
Which no power on earth can save,
Fast the moments are approaching,
We must lie in a murderer's grave.
Side by side we lie together,
Were our bodies will decay,
For killing of a wife and neighbour,
We must answer at the judgment day.

John Smith, Machine Printer, Briggate, Leeds.

This broadsheet details the crimes of James Sargisson and Joseph Myers, the only two people to have been publicly executed at Armley Gaol.

Crime, Prostitution and Dripping

During the Victorian period there was a big increase in the recorded numbers of serious crimes and petty offences in Leeds. There was certainly more for the police to do as the population rose, but to properly assess whether this represented a general increase in criminality, the crime statistics would need to be adjusted to take account of improved methods of recording crime and the rise in the population.[37] The Watch Committee reckoned that between 1858 and 1867, whilst the population had increased by 20 per cent, crime had increased 56 per cent and the number of criminals by 93 per cent. The greatest increase was in cases of drunkenness rising from 675 to 1340 per annum, and in larceny (stealing) rising from 129 to 300. Their explanation had a familiar ring about it: 'very lenient punishments'; 'a most comfortable prison'; and 'the temptation to sin caused by the excessive number of beer houses, dancing saloons, low theatres and other drinking establishments, which are found in nearly all our public places of resort and too often prove the ruin of our artisans'.[38]

By 1869 the cases of larceny in the borough were up to 840, but the numbers convicted of drunkenness or drunk and disorderly behaviour had fallen to 1,205 (including 208 women). Perhaps this was linked with the work of the temperance movement and the new Wine and Beer House Act which had enabled the magistrates to close down 46 beer houses on the grounds that they were 'frequented by thieves, prostitutes, or persons of bad character'.[39] Next to drunkenness and larceny, the most common offence was that of assault, for which 828 men and 106 women were convicted. Surprising to us in an age when house breaking seems endemic, there were only 109 cases of burglary recorded.

The first police station, other than the Court House, was opened in 1850 in Mill Street in an effort to combat increasing lawlessness on the eastern side of the town. By 1851 there were 33 day police and 100 night police, and within six years the number of police stations in the borough had reached sixteen.[40] The day and the night forces were amalgamated in 1859 under the resourceful leadership of Stephen English a Chief Constable who achieved early note when, by disguising himself in 'the garb of a collier' he managed to apprehend a murderer near Sheffield.[41]

Leeds was now a growing and powerful industrial centre, and the council decided to press a claim for it to be made into an assize town. In 1863 a commission from the Home Secretary visited Leeds to inquire into its suitability, and in 1864 the Privy Council decided that the whole of the West Riding Assizes should be held in Leeds. The first assizes were held in August 1864.[42]

Leeds Chief Constables frequently were anxious to increase the size of the police force. In 1892 the Chief Constable called for an additional 99 men. In support of his case he cited not only the growing size of the borough, but also the increase in criminals:

> In the Borough residing at present are 21 known convicts, 17 persons under police supervision, 335 suspected persons, i.e. persons who seldom or never work, but loaf about the streets, watching persons getting into or out of tramcars with a view to picking pockets, or frequently following women who are of loose repute, and who entice men into secluded spots where they are robbed and ill treated by the man or men and woman. Places to be most avoided are the Dark Arches, Swinegate, Whitehall Road, and anywhere behind the Queen's and Great Northern Hotels. If there were more police these places would soon be cleared.[43]

By 1900 the complement of the police force had increased to the Chief Constable, 8 superintendents, 17 inspectors, 57 sergeants and 417 constables – a total of 500.[44]

Prostitution was rampant in Victorian Leeds as Revd J.Slatter was shocked to find when he made an unfortunate choice of accommodation near St James' just off Kirkgate when he arrived in Leeds in the mid-1840s:

> The part immediately around St James's Church was inhabited, with a few exceptions, by the most wretched characters. I had given me by the police a list of the brothels in my district, and I was horrified to find that, in a circle of one hundred yards of which my room was the centre, there were no less than thirteen of such dens. The proceedings of the miserable creatures who tenanted them were so openly disgusting, that I was obliged to call in the aid of the law to abate the nuisance.[45]

Despite the attitudes of men like Slatter, many of the middle classes of Leeds took a pragmatic view of prostitution. They preferred to have brothels regulated and controlled by the police rather than banned. Their ambivalence towards this branch of immorality is reflected in the Borough Chief Constable's annual report in 1852:

> The plan adopted of keeping a classified and continually corrected register of the proprietors and inmates of brothels and low lodging houses has tended materially to check disorder and to aid the police in detecting crime and bringing offenders to justice. Any attempt at the removal of these places would answer no good for the sons and daughters of vice would find a resting place elsewhere and most likely would get into respectable neighbourhoods where their proximity would be deeply deplored.[46]

The accompanying statistics recorded 85 brothels in the borough of which 12 were thought to be well conducted, 18 indifferently conducted, and 55 were 'bad'. One wonders whether the authorities today would be happy to describe such establishments as 'well conducted'! These establishments had 150 resident prostitutes of whose general behaviour it was noted that 41 were good, 19 indifferent, and 90 bad. Visiting several brothels in 1843 Symons noted that they presented a far more cleanly aspect than the town's lodging houses.[47]

Apart from the day-to-day crime, the police periodically had to deal with major incidents of public disorder. A series of these provide graphic insights into the character of life in the town and the attitudes of the lower orders to the police and the civic authorities. Problems with the military establishment in the town were not uncommon. A major affray occurred in 1844 when on 8 January someone had the rashness to write on a table in the Green Man public house, York Street – 'No swaddy Irishmen or soldiers wanted here'. This prompted a group of soldiers from the 70th Infantry to make indiscriminate attacks on every person leaving the Green Man and to rampage up and down Kirkgate.[48] Tensions remained and in June later that year there were serious fights between the police and the military. On the evening of the 9th the police were called to a surgeon's shop in Kirkgate where they found a man seriously wounded. They arrested the two soldiers responsible at the Green Man, but other soldiers attempted to rescue their comrades, and a pitched battle ensued in Briggate. The police were eventually victorious, but the following evening, though the soldiers were confined to barracks in Woodhouse Lane, about fifty managed to sneak out and assemble at the Green Parrot in Harper Street. Armed with sticks and bludgeons they went in search of the police. Several of the police were very seriously injured in the vicious fighting which followed. Lack of public support for the officers of the law was revealed by a contemporary newspaper report: 'During the affray the streets and windows in Briggate, Kirkgate and Commercial Street were crowded with people. The populace generally seemed to sympathize with the military. They cheered them on through the streets, and in some instances assisted in the riot'. At length a piquet arrived to quell the disturbance. On the following evening the soldiers remained in their barracks but 'a rabble infested the streets, and about nine o'clock fell upon the police in Kirkgate, pelting them with stones, bottles &c.' Ultimately, a large force of police arrived with cutlasses and cleared the streets. As a result of the various arrests, four soldiers were imprisoned for 8-12 months, and three civilians received short prison sentences.[49]

Perhaps the oddest incident in the history of law and order in Leeds was the 'Dripping Riot'. In January 1865 Henry Chorley, surgeon and magistrate, had his cook committed to Armley Gaol for one month for stealing a small quantity of dripping from his kitchen. The imprisonment was met with howls of protest from the working classes who subjected Chorley to all sorts of annoyances including inscribing 'Chorley's Dripping' on walls all over the town, showering him with abusive letters, and avidly buying and reciting several street ballads including:

> Oh, if I was the doctor, I would let them see;
> I'd take an example from Victor Townley;
> If ever I dealt out such justice again;
> I'd jump from my seat and fracture my brain.

Thousands awaited Chorley's cook, Mrs Stafford at the gates of Armley Gaol on the day of her release, 22nd February, but, in the hope of avoiding trouble, the authorities spirited her away to Scarborough to stay with her daughter. The crowd were good humoured and when Mrs Stafford did not appear a tall man, dressed in women's clothes, issued from a house by the road side and announced 'herself' to be Mrs Stafford. The crowd dispersed, but by midday assembled again outside Mr Chorley's house in Park Square. It looked as though they were itching for a fight. A stone broke one of the windows and handfuls of sludge, dirty orange peel and sticks were hurled at a small party of police. Alarmed by the mounting tension, the mayor sent to Bradford for as many police as could be spared, and telegraphed the Lord Mayor of York, requesting that he would apply at the barracks for two troops of cavalry to be sent. Meanwhile, two men perambulated the street in front of Mr Chorley's house with a long pole at the top of which was suspended a 'physic bottle and a dripping pan'.

The police's efforts to disperse the crowd were unsuccessful, so a notice was issued from the Town Hall warning people to disperse from the Park Square and Town Hall area or suffer the legal consequences. This measure was successful temporarily, but in the evening while the mayor and magistrates were deliberating in the Town Hall, a crowd of about 2,000 assembled outside hooting and jeering. To the magistrates' immense relief, the crowd was largely dispersed by 30 policemen with staves, though there was considerable stone throwing – five of the offenders being a forgeman, a tailor, a joiner, a baker, and a shopman. A major riot seems to have been narrowly avoided. The magistrates clearly realised the error of their ways, and avoided further inflaming the situation by issuing very lenient sentences to those arrested. They remarked that 'considering the very silly excitement which was going on, [those arrested] might have been led into the disturbance unintentionally'.[50]

The 'Dripping Riot' conveyed the message to the middle classes that the working classes were not prepared to respect the law if its implementation was blatantly unjust. In that the missiles thrown at the police tended to be snowballs and orange peel rather than stones, and the protest was conducted with considerable wit; the impression is that the working classes wanted to make their point in an essentially peaceful way, while giving the middle classes a fright.

Troubles with the Irish

One of the major sources of problems for the police and the public authorities was the Irish. There were strong tensions between the Irish and English communities. A very serious affray, for instance, took place between the residents in the neighbourhood of York Street and Marsh Lane in November 1850 when one man was killed and several received severe injuries.[51] The biggest threats, however, were associated with the activities of the Fenian Brotherhood.

The issue of home rule for Ireland and the establishment of an independent republic was one of the great causes in nineteenth-century British politics. The Fenian Brotherhood, intensely committed to the republican cause, organised attacks on public and private property throughout England and Ireland, notably in 1866-7. With the large Irish population in Leeds, there was very obvious nervousness in the town, and the authorities were on their guard. In September 1865 James McCarthy, a workman at Messrs Lawson in Mabgate, was brought before the mayor, it being suspected that he was secretary of the Leeds Fenian Society. Fellow workers gave evidence that he had often expressed strong hatred of England and called for Ireland to assert her independence. Indeed, they claimed that he had said that he looked forward to seeing 'the streets running with Englishmen's blood'. The mayor cautioned McCarthy and passed on the evidence to 'the proper authorities'.[52]

In March 1866 worrying rumours circulated that the Fenians were planning an uprising in Leeds on St Patrick's Day. On the 16th the mayor stated that he had information of 'pike making and secret drilling being carried on in the town by the supporters of Fenianism, who were in constant communication with the friends of the movement in Ireland'. As a precaution, unnecessary as it turned out, the police force was supplemented by 40 members of the West Riding Constabulary and many members of the town's Volunteer Corps and 100 tradesmen were sworn in as special constables.[53]

In February 1867 the magistrates had a much more serious cause for concern. On the morning of the 11th, large numbers of Irishmen left Leeds, Bradford, Halifax, and Huddersfield apparently with the intention of meeting fellow Fenians in Chester with the object of raiding the large store of arms in the castle and starting an uprising. That day some 1,200 men 'of a very doubtful character' arrived in Chester, but dispersed at nightfall when the Home Secretary rushed police and troops into the town. Certainly there was cause for worry in Leeds as well, where that night the constable at Wellington Station saw a young man carrying a bulky parcel of 'suspicious appearance'. He followed him down Basinghall Street and challenged him. When the parcel was opened it consisted of 24 packages containing 140 ball cartridges all greased and ready for use.[54] Civil disorder in Ireland over the next few days confirmed the view that the Irishmen had been after the arms in Chester Castle. On the 13th packages of rifle cartridges were found in Morley railway tunnel, probably having been thrown from a train on the way back from Chester.[55]

The nationwide alarm in this period was heightened in September 1867 when a police sergeant was killed in Manchester while resisting an attempt to rescue some Fenian prisoners.[56] Four Irishmen were sentenced to death for the killing and several others to penal servitude. Three of them were hung in front of New Bailey Prison, Salford, on 23 November 1867. The atmosphere reached fever pitch in December when the wall of Clerkenwell Gaol in London was blown-up in an attempt to rescue two prominent Fenians. Seven people were killed and 41 badly wounded and several houses were damaged. On 13 December large placards with deep black borders were posted all over Leeds:

> GOD SAVE IRELAND! – A funeral procession in honour of the Irish patriots executed at Manchester on November 23rd 1867 will take place in Leeds on Sunday next, the 15th December. The procession will assemble at Vicar's Croft, and start at two o'clock p.m., and will parade the principal streets to St Patrick's Cemetery, York Road. All lovers of Ireland, men and women, are requested to attend and show their respects to the memory of their fellow-countrymen.

The Leeds magistrates banned the procession, fearing major civil disorder, but preparations for it proceeded and a proposed route was published. On Sunday 15th immense crowds gathered in Leeds, many no doubt curious to see how events unfolded. The authorities were ready with what must have been one of the biggest displays of force seen in the town for many years. The mounted special constables were present in large

Baxter's Yard, Quarry Hill, one of the notorious streets with a high concentration of Irish inhabitants in 1851.

numbers and the military came out in great strength in the neighbourhood of Kirkgate. Imagine the scene – 150 infantry men of the 70th Regiment waited in the Corn Exchange, a battery of Royal Artillery with field pieces were drawn up in front of the White Cloth Hall, guarded by a detachment of infantry with loaded rifles; the Leeds squadron of Yeomanry, commanded by the Earl of Harewood, were at the ready near by. The police took possession of Vicar's Croft and drew up in a double line at the entrances in Kirkgate, Ludgate Hill and George Street, while the magistrates stood ready at Vicar's Croft and the Corn Exchange, Darnton Lupton, the Liberal magistrate, on his horse. This great show of strength won the day. When the great bell at the Town Hall struck two o'clock no procession started. Instead the mounted artillery and yeomanry marched down Kirkgate and into York Road followed by an immense rush of people. As the local press noted: 'In York Road very few people were assembled, but here some of the better class of Irish were walking about. The whole proceedings passed off without any disturbance.'[57] This proved to be the height of the Fenian disturbances in nineteenth century Leeds, though the issue of 'Home Rule' for Ireland remained a political topic of major interest.

Fire-fighting

Throughout the nineteenth century, fire fighting remained the responsibility of the police. In 1846 a new council committee was formed, charged with duties, under the Leeds Improvement Act of 1842, including the formation of a fire brigade for the borough.[58] In 1861 the central fire station was transferred from the Court House to the basement of the new Corn Exchange. The fire brigade remained under the jurisdiction of the police, but in the 1870s there was considerable public disquiet about the way in which the town's brigade raced the insurance companies fire fighters to get to fires and how they repeatedly tried to impede each other's progress. One critic complained of 'engines rushing through the streets with their thundering steeds and crashing wheels, threatening death and destruction to all who cross their path'.[59] In 1883 the Central Fire Station was moved to Park Street where it remained for many years. By 1886 the brigade consisted of 30 men all of whom were policemen.[60] One of the biggest fires in Leeds history occurred on 13 January 1892 when the Dark Arches caught fire. The conflagration, which lasted twenty hours, was extinguished only with the assistance of firemen from Bradford, York and Derby. James Potter Schofield, a member of the Liverpool and London and Globe Insurance Brigade, was killed in the blaze. It is estimated that 100,000 people turned out for his funeral. A firemen's memorial was erected by public subscription over his grave at Woodhouse Cemetery.[61]

Workhouses and Infirmaries

The Poor Law

The low incomes of the working classes, combined with periodic bouts of high unemployment caused by sharp fluctuation in the economy, meant that large numbers of the working classes in Leeds were never far from the threat of destitution. The majority of the middle classes of the town accepted their social and moral duty to provide relief for the poor. Recurrent bouts of high unemployment in the first three or four decades of the nineteenth century led the Workhouse Board to place the emphasis on relieving the poor by out-door relief rather than attempting to place them in the workhouse. In the mid-1830s, however, they faced a dilemma. In national government circles there was strong pressure for the reform of the Poor Law. Recent sharp rises in poor rates nationwide were attributed to the prevalent system of out-door poor relief which, because it was paid according to family size and as a subsidy to low wages, was believed to be encouraging idleness and excessive population growth, and to be distorting the free operation of the labour market. The government's answer was the Poor Law Amendment Act of 1834. The Act aimed to drastically reduce the demand for poor relief by ending the practice of giving out-door relief and in future restricting relief to those people who revealed their genuine need by being sufficiently desperate to enter the workhouse. In addition, the Act aimed to make the Poor Law more cost-effective by replacing the parish as the basic unit of administration by Poor Law Unions, dealing with larger areas and numbers of people, which would be run by elected boards of guardians.

Leeds Moral and Industrial Training School, Beckett Street, built 1846-8 (architects, Perkin and Backhouse). Now the Lincoln Wing of St James's Hospital.

In those days, however, central government was not as powerful as it is today, and it was necessary to persuade and cajole local authorities to co-operate with such legislation. In the north of England both local government and the working classes vehemently opposed the legislation. The Anti-Poor Law agitation of this period was one of the most massive campaigns of early Victorian England.[62] To the middle-class ratepayers of Leeds, much as they might want to reduce the burden of the poor rates, which by 1832 had risen to £34,000 per annum, it was manifest that they would need an enormous workhouse if they were to accommodate the large numbers of unemployed people in times of depression. Experience showed clearly that it was cheaper to support a man and his family in his own home by a dole. The working classes, quite naturally, were terrified of being thrown into these 'Bastilles' with husbands and wives, and their families being separated.[63]

The Leeds Workhouse Board chose in effect to ignore the 1834 Act, believing its provisions to be inappropriate to a town like Leeds, and being far too absorbed in complex political wrangling between Liberals and Tories for supremacy in Poor Law affairs. An attempt to elect a board of guardians in 1837 proved to be a total fiasco and was abandoned.[64] The existing workhouse certainly was inadequate for the purposes of the Act. In 1835 the board started its own internal investigation and concluded that:

> The want of proper classification, the almost unrestrained intercourse [i.e. mixing of inmates] and the absence of suitable employment in the Workhouse: together with its liberal allowance of the best kinds of food have but too generally induced upon those whose circumstances have led to a temporary residence there, habits of idleness and improvidence: and in innumerable instances been the means of their eventually becoming, at no distant period, [permanent] residents in that establishment.[65]

Inspection in 1843 showed it to be overcrowded, with young and old, men and women, infirm and able being thrown together. The moral standards of the inmates were low and children of only 12 to 14 were found copulating in the privies. Charles Clements, a Poor Law inspector, condemned the conditions there as being 'altogether discreditable to a civilised society'.[66]

At the beginning of Victoria's reign, senior townsmen acknowledged that a new workhouse was needed, but

Leeds Union Workhouse, Beckett Street, built 1858-61 (architects, Perkin and Backhouse). Now the Ashley Wing of St. James's Hospital, and shortly to become the Thackray Medical Museum.

Leeds Union Infirmary — 'Able-bodied inmates'.

realised that its financing was unlikely to receive the necessary support of the parish ratepayers because of the large expense. They therefore decided on a partial implementation of the 1834 Act by the establishment of a board of guardians for Leeds township, which could then by-pass the parish vestry and secure a new workhouse. In December 1844 the first board was elected.[67] One of its first acts was to purchase land in Beckett Street, Burmantofts, for building the Moral and Industrial Training School. The school's purpose was to maintain and educate orphans and a few children of the 'deserving poor' who would otherwise end up in the workhouse. The contemporary description of the building as 'handsome and elegant' was no exaggeration, and this large Tudor Gothic building, accommodating 400 boys and girls in its spacious airy situation, brought a completely new degree of comfort and style to poor relief in Leeds.[68] This was an extremely enlightened and worthy venture. At the laying of the foundation stone on 14 October 1846 John Metcalfe, Chairman of the Board, explained the underlying aim of providing an education for those who 'might otherwise become the prey of the abandoned and the profligate', adding that it was their intention to 'cut the cord or connection between pauperism and degradation, and establish a feeling of independence in the rising generation'.[69] On completion in October 1848, the school could accommodate 499 children, who were to spend half their time on school work and the other half on industrial training: gardening, tailoring and shoemaking for the boys, domestic duties and sewing for the girls. This was one of the first workhouse schools in the country.

However handsome the buildings, institutional life could be a harsh environment for children, and they did not always react well to it. In 1867 a group of boys put lighted papers under the floorboards. The arson attempt failed and each child received ten strokes of the cane and then spent three days in the workhouse in solitary confinement. In 1879 the guardians became concerned about the sickly, pale and dejected appearance of the children. The industrial training aspect seemed inadequate with numerous boys and girls returned to the hands of the guardians as 'failures' who were shiftless, dull or unmanageable. Eventually the children were sent to local board schools and the space thus freed was converted into new hospital accommodation. Boarding out and emigration schemes reduced the numbers and in July 1902 a new home for the remaining children opened in Roundhay, allowing the whole of the original school building to become part of the workhouse infirmary.

Meanwhile the board of guardians struggled on with the old workhouse buildings in Lady Lane periodically extending its totally inadequate and unsuitable accommodation. Despite censure by the government's Poor Law Commissioners that the workhouse was 'highly discreditable to the township', in May 1845 the guardians resolved that there was no need for a new workhouse. The commissioners at least expected a major extension to the accommodation, but the guardians would only agree to partial alterations. In sheer frustration, Clements, the Poor Law inspector urged them:

> to render the Workhouse tolerably creditable where the aged and infirm can be accommodated with decent comfort, the sick properly attended to, the helpless idiot sufficiently protected and the unruly and shiftless able-bodied male pauper kept apart from the vicious and abandoned of the other sex.[70]

But the guardians remained unmoved. They still believed that out-door relief was the best method of dealing with short-term poverty. In the search for a mode of dealing with vagrant Irish, in 1847 Darnton Lupton offered the novel suggestion: 'that large rooms be provided by the Guardians at which rice pudding should be furnished to all comers to be consumed on the spot – the rice to be prepared according to a recipe which he would furnish if the plan was approved'. The guardians rejected the idea, but lest the Lupton patent rice pudding recipe be lost to the world they agreed to try it out on the paupers.[71]

Finally in the 1850s a decision was taken to build a new workhouse. On 5 April 1858 the foundation stone of the impressive new building alongside the Moral and Industrial Training School was laid. A workhouse chapel was erected between the two buildings. As *Fenteman's Guide* pointed out in 1858, the line of the buildings when complete would produce 'an architectural facade of great extent and beauty.'[72] The workhouse was built to accommodate 810 paupers, 360 males and 450 females. Its architects were Messrs. Perkin and Backhouse, and the final cost was £31,000.[73]

Combating Disease

The provision of poor relief in times of destitution was seen by the middle classes as both essential to the maintenance of public order and as a christian duty. This mixture of philanthropy and self-interest (some might say self-preservation) was, as we have already seen in earlier periods, extended into the sphere of medical assistance. The medical charities flourished in the Victorian period. Leeds General Infirmary, the House of Recovery and the Dispensary remained the mainstays of

Harrison's Almshouses and St John's Church c.1930. The orginal almshouses built in the mid-1630s were completely rebuilt in 1849.

medical provision for the working classes, and all three institutions were developed considerably. Throughout the nineteenth century the squalid and insanitary condition of many areas of the town meant that the outbreak of epidemics of infectious diseases was the perpetual fear of all classes of society. The battle to deal with the cholera – a dramatic killer – and the diseases which through their continuous presence were much more important killers – tuberculosis, typhus, typhoid and dysentery – was led by the House of Recovery. By the early 1840s it was felt that the House of Recovery in Vicar Lane was too close to both the areas in which various infectious diseases were endemic and to the dense centre of population. As a result a new building was opened in Beckett Street in 1846 almost opposite the Moral and Industrial Training School.[74] The great pressure on medical institutions at times of epidemics was demonstrated in 1847 when there was a major outbreak of typhus fever.[75] The Revd Edward Jackson recalled the horrors of the outbreak in the Bank area:

> 'Do go with me, and see a part of my district,' Mr. M---, the new curate, said to me one day; 'I don't think the workhouse authorities can know how bad things are.' I went with him. It was frightful indeed. Here, in this district, which was one of an especially Irish character, it was simply horrible. Every place above ground, and underground, was crammed with miserable, famished wretches, scarcely looking like human beings. In one cellar we counted thirty-one men, women and children, all lying on the damp, filthy floor, with only a few handfuls of straw under them; while the frightened neighbours, who would not venture inside the pestilential depth, were lowering water in buckets to allay the intolerable thirst of the miserable people. One young curate was excited to the last degree ...He himself would go down to them in their cellars, or climb up into their close, choking chamber, raise their heads, put fresh straw under them, give them the gruel with his own hands, and though they wanted not his religious ministrations, having their own priests, who, to their honour never shrank from their duty, and of whom several laid down their lives in the performance of it, yet his heart was continually going out in labours and benedictions for the wretched sufferers. And when, at last, temporary hospitals were opened, it was he who brought out the first that were removed, carried them in his own arms, and laid them gently down in the carts which were brought to remove them. It was indeed an anxious and alarming time, both on account of that which was every day taking place, and from the anticipation of what might yet be to come.[76]

At its height in June, the House of Recovery and a temporary fever hospital were full and the board of guardians were obliged to supplement this accommodation by erecting a wooden shed in Accommodation Road, Richmond Hill. So desperate was the situation that Victoria Mill in York Road was converted into a fever hospital, but neighbours complained about the stench from the privies and the smoke from the burning of dirty straw used on the floors.[77] The epidemic did not confine itself to the poor. The middle classes must have been shocked that, as Jackson recalled, between May and July five Catholic priests and one of the curates of the parish church who ministered to the poor died of the disease.[78]

No sooner had the typhus epidemic been overcome than the cholera returned again in 1848-9, killing 1,674 people in the town and 2,000 in the borough as a whole.[79] Once again the east end of Leeds was ravaged by the disease, in the thick of the infection were found many of the clergy, ministering to the needs of the sick, dying and needy. Revd Pollen related the true horrors of the epidemic:

> There was no great stock of knowledge about cholera any where in Leeds; they soon learnt what was known, and went always with calomel and cayenne pepper, spirit of camphor, and other remedies, in their girdles. The Clergy went in their cassocks.
>
> Not till late would friends, nor always even very

near relations, bear to wait on the patients. They sent off direct for a priest, and he had to minister to every one when he was stuck, both in temporal things and spiritual. He had to give calomel or what not with careful directions, then to deal as he best could with the poor sufferer's soul ...He returned again to commend the dying into the hands of God, and often to lay out the body, and burn carbonate of lime round the bed; then the house was shut up; afterwards the undertakers came with a cart and went in; at sight of them every body stopped short in the street: the window opened and the bedding and clothes of the dead were thrown out. Then at night the workhouse hearse went round and took away each to a distant burying ground.[80]

In 1865-6 there was another big outbreak of typhus. Six hundred patients were admitted to the House of Recovery. Several house-physicians died from the infection.[81] In 1882 a condemnatory report stated 'it is obvious that the Hospital does not fulfil its function as a means of isolation to any adequate degree'. The council bought the building in 1885, eventually replacing it with Seacroft Hospital (1893-1904) on the outskirts of Leeds.[82]

With regard to non-infectious disease and other medical conditions, throughout the Victorian era all the medical provision for the poor in Leeds, save that given in the workhouse, was funded by charities. The Leeds Public Dispensary, which had been founded in 1824, continued to provide valuable assistance. In 1867 it moved into new purpose-built premises in North Street. The scale of its activities can be judged by the fact that its waiting room accommodated 200 patients. But its medical services were not limited to patients who could attend its clinics. In 1878 it was reckoned that 2,558 patients had been under treatment, of which 2,213 had been visited in their own homes.[83]

When the new workhouse was erected at Burmantofts in the late 1850s, it too had a small infirmary behind the main buildings and 'an idiotic and fever ward'.[84] The standard of care was good, but it became apparent that the sick posed a threat to the health of the institution as a whole and greater isolation was required. On 26 November 1874 the Leeds Union Infirmary with 216 beds was opened for the first time, under the control of a resident medical superintendent, with eight nurses, a matron, steward and cook. Pauper inmates continued to be used as helpers in the care of up to 500 patients. It quickly gained a fine reputation, yet it was to be a long time before the pauper women attendants for the sick were finally replaced by trained and salaried nurses. It was this Leeds Workhouse Infirmary which in 1925 was to be renamed St James's.[85]

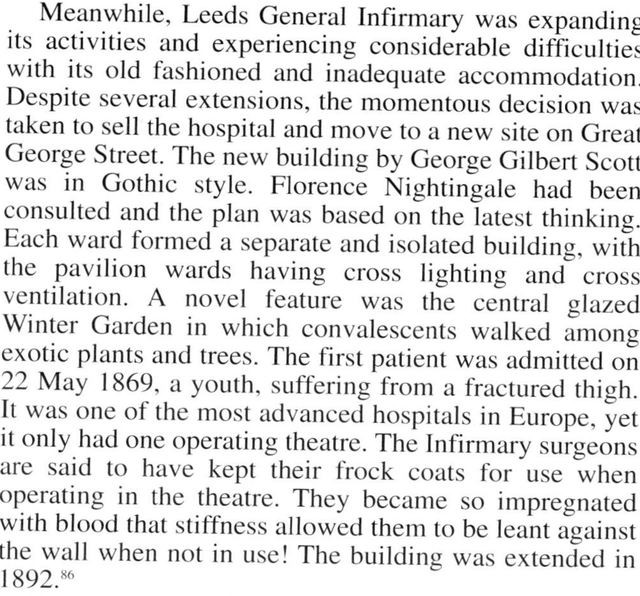

Meanwhile, Leeds General Infirmary was expanding its activities and experiencing considerable difficulties with its old fashioned and inadequate accommodation. Despite several extensions, the momentous decision was taken to sell the hospital and move to a new site on Great George Street. The new building by George Gilbert Scott was in Gothic style. Florence Nightingale had been consulted and the plan was based on the latest thinking. Each ward formed a separate and isolated building, with the pavilion wards having cross lighting and cross ventilation. A novel feature was the central glazed Winter Garden in which convalescents walked among exotic plants and trees. The first patient was admitted on 22 May 1869, a youth, suffering from a fractured thigh. It was one of the most advanced hospitals in Europe, yet it only had one operating theatre. The Infirmary surgeons are said to have kept their frock coats for use when operating in the theatre. They became so impregnated with blood that stiffness allowed them to be leant against the wall when not in use! The building was extended in 1892.[86]

Some of the smaller medical institutions established earlier in the century were amalgamated with the Infirmary. The Eye and Ear Infirmary, for example, was merged with it in 1869.[87] Other new independent medical institutions, however, were established. The Hospital for

Leeds General Infirmary, Great George Street, built 1862-8 (architect, George Gilbert Scott).

One of the wards at the Infirmary.

Women and Children opened at Springfield Lodge, Woodbine Place in 1861. The United Institution for the Blind and the Deaf and Dumb, which resulted from the amalgamation of two societies, opened purpose-built premises at the top of Albion Street in 1877. In 1865 the Little Sisters of the Poor established a house for the aged and infirm poor in Hanover Square. By the 1870s it had been transferred to newly-erected premises in Belle Vue Road, whose large and lofty day rooms, dormitories and sick wards accommodated 200 people.[88]

Given the extensive medical community in Leeds, the Leeds School of Medicine went from strength to strength at its premises in East Parade. It was here that the first trial of ether anaesthesia took place in Leeds. C.G. Wheelhouse, a student at the time, remembered their experiments in 1846-7:

> We soon rigged up a large glass vase, like a tea urn, filled it with sponges, attached an india rubber tube to the spout, saturated the sponges with ether and through the tube inhaled the vapour as through a Turkish hookah pipe, and we fell over one after another quite insensible and unconscious of anything that was done to us. I well remember how I, as an early volunteer to take it, was nearly suffocated in the attempt. Indeed how nearly we killed ourselves or each other we neither knew nor cared! Here was a demonstrated fact, and from the dissecting room at the school to the operating theatre over the way, the fact was speedily conveyed, and before many days we saw patients operated on in this insensible condition, and we found that they recovered quite as well as those who had borne the agony of the operation.[89]

The School of Medicine outgrew these premises and in 1865 moved to a purpose-built school on Park Street, but the pace of change and growth was such that in 1894 a new Medical School building was constructed in Thoresby Place. W.H.Thorp's design incorporated many advanced features, including the use of copper piping and electricity. The new building was not without its problems. The heating system proved faulty and smoke found its way into the dissecting rooms, and valves had to be introduced into the duct work to prevent odours from the anatomy cellars reaching the Physiology Department.[90]

Schools For All

Working-class Elementary Education

The desirable goal of providing the children of the working classes with a basic education, which had been recognised in the late Georgian period, was pursued with vigour in the Victorian era. The expansion of day school education from the 1830s was remarkable. The best education was provided in the denominational schools. By 1869 there were 54 Anglian church schools in the borough, with 15,364 pupils on the roll; 3 British schools and 22 Protestant Dissenting schools, with a combined role of 4,782 pupils; and 4 Roman Catholic schools with 1,729 pupils.[91]

From 1833 Parliament began to make grants to certain recognised religious schools, sometimes as subsidies for school buildings and their maintenance; by the 1860s State education grants amounted to around £1 million nationwide. As in other towns, there was great controversy in Leeds about the advisability of the State becoming involved in educational provision. The vicar, Dr Hook, was a tower of strength in raising large sums of money for school buildings in order to obtain a share of the government grants. Indeed, he was a strong advocate of a more fully state-provided school system. Some Leeds Nonconformists feared that the State might combine with the Anglian Church to promote rate-supported schools controlled by the Anglicans. Edward Baines, junior, opposed the introduction in 1846 of State grants for pupil teachers, but by 1867 even he admitted that a completely unaided voluntary system of education was not viable.

It is difficult to assess the educational impact of the schools. A sample of the children leaving the schools suggests the average leaving age was 9½ years and the average period at school was about 4½ years.[92] The temptation for parents to take their children out of school was great because on leaving they could earn from 3s. 2d. to 5s. a week. An investigation of parish registers has shown that between 1842 and 1869 the proportion of bridegrooms signing the register with their mark fell from 29 per cent to 19 per cent, while the equivalent figure for brides fell from 45 per cent to 28 per cent.[93] From the 1830s the combination of legal restrictions on child employment, a rise in working-class incomes, and the better provision of day schools, gradually decreased the need for Sunday schools as providers of general education. By 1860 no writing was taught in Anglican or Wesleyan Sunday Schools in Leeds, and only about a third of the Sunday School Union's pupils were being taught to write, and most of these in weekday evening classes.[94]

By the late 1860s there was no shortage of school places in Leeds for those seeking schooling, but this masked a serious problem. In the first place attendance was very irregular; the average attendance of the 20,000 children enrolled in the inspected schools was only 12,400. In the second place, many children were on the books of no school at all; there would have been a big deficiency of places had schooling from the age of 5-13 years been compulsory.[95] Given the age restrictions on child labour in factories it is clear that there was a large number of children that were neither in school nor at work. J.G.Fitch, investigating Leeds schools for the Schools Inquiry Commission of 1864 condemned Leeds as 'one of the most benighted towns educationally in the country'. He found that less than half the children of school age were under instruction, and during one morning he found 900 children playing in the streets.[96]

Additional educational facilities were provided for the children of the poor in this period. As we have seen, for children deprived of one or both parents, who required maintenance as well as education, the board of guardians built the Industrial School. Two Ragged Schools provided day school instruction and a humble midday meal for the 'outcasts of the streets', who could not be persuaded to attend the ordinary day schools. In an attempt to provide more humane treatment of juveniles convicted of crimes, a Juvenile Reformatory was established at Adel in 1857, where by firm discipline and a combination of school instruction with industrial training it was hoped to reform these lawbreakers.[97]

Nationally, pressure built up for more coherent provision of education by the State. The numbers of children neither in school nor work, the need for a better educated workforce to meet economic competition from abroad, and the view that the half of the urban working

The first Leeds Board School, Bewerley Street, Dewsbury Road, built 1872-3 (architect, George Corson).

A Leeds Board School classroom.

Leeds Central Higher Grade School, Woodhouse Lane, opened 1889.

classes given the vote by the 1867 Reform Act must be educated to vote wisely, were all factors which led to Forster's Education Act of 1870. In spite of the religious denominations' misgivings, the Act established a national system of elementary education. While it encouraged the voluntary schools to expand, it decreed that state schools should be provided to fill in the gaps. These would be known as 'board schools' because they were to be provided by locally elected school boards financed by local rates and governmental grants. The education was to be free, as it was now also to be in the voluntary schools. Initially the question of whether education should be compulsory was left to the discretion of the local boards, but in 1876 Parliament made attendance compulsory up to the age of ten, and between ten and thirteen for those without a certificate showing that they had obtained a certain standard in the 3 R's.[98]

Leeds adopted the Elementary Education Act in 1870 and its first School Board was elected on 28 November under the chairmanship of Sir Andrew Fairbairn. A census of children showed that 48,787 should be attending school, but there was accommodation for only 27,329. The School Board's response to the situation must be viewed as one of the great achievements of Victorian Leeds. Action was rapid. By November 1878, 31 large schools capable of accommodating 19,000 pupils had been erected in the borough at a cost of £177,000. The teaching staff consisted of 740 masters and mistresses.[99] Some people viewed this achievement with circumspection. *Dodgson's Guide* commented in 1879:

> The expenditure for the year ending 29th September 1878 was £94,724. £36,000 of this amount was raised by a rate of little more than 8d. in the pound of the rateable value of the whole Borough. The ratepayers generally have no idea of the extravagant expenditure of the School Board, as the rate is levied and collected with the Borough rate, so that the Corporation bears the onus of the heaviness of the rate; were it collected separately, it is probable that the matter would not be allowed to pass so quietly.[100]

The 1870 Education Act made no provision for secondary education and so it remained essentially privately financed, fee-paying, and the preserve of the middle and upper classes. Throughout the country, however, board schools began gradually to extend education to older children and provide teaching in technical and commercial subjects. In 1873 Leeds School Board opened 14 evening schools and 7 science and art classes. Post-elementary tuition was eventually formalised nationally by the establishment of what were known as Higher Grade Schools, the country's first being established in Bradford in 1875.[101] In 1885 Leeds School Board opened its first Higher Grade School in temporary premises. Four years later it moved into a magnificent new building in Woodhouse Lane, which opened on 4 November 1889 as the Central Higher Grade School. Many years later the school was renamed City of Leeds School, and remained in the premises until 1993. The school's prospectus makes remarkable reading from many points of view. The most astonishing was the numbers of children the board planned, without any hint of impropriety, to cram into the building: 'Ground floor – 542 Deaf Mute, and Blind children, and scholars taking Cookery Instruction; Physical Training, &c.; 1st floor – 752 boys; 2nd floor – 752 girls; 3rd floor – 454 Science and Art Students.' Parents were assured that: 'so far as excellence of accommodation is concerned, the School will rank as one of the foremost educational institutions in the kingdom. The instruction will thus be carried on under the most healthful conditions, calculated to aid thorough teaching without overstrain.'

The school was a 'City Technology College' of its day. The prospectus noted: 'The aim of the Board is to give the means of extended education to the most advanced and promising pupils from the ordinary elementary schools, whose parents are willing to prolong their children's school life. On a basis of elementary education it is intended to superadd a system of higher education which, at a moderate charge [1s. per week or 10s. per quarter] will train pupils for industrial, manufacturing and professional pursuits.' The school seems to have had a small Elementary Section which added French, elementary maths and sciences to the requirement of the Education Code, but its principal component was its Higher Section. This gave a three-year course of instruction offering a choice of subjects to be selected by parents and teachers, according to the child's likely future occupation. The seven subjects offered in each year were English, Latin, Mathematics, French, German, Science and Drawing. To promote the entrance from the borough's Elementary Schools of 'promising boys and girls' with parents of limited means, 180 scholarships giving free admission were awarded each year by competitive examination. Likewise, scholars who had passed 'Standard VI' at twelve years of age, in ordinary Elementary Schools (presumably regarded as bright pupils) were admitted at half the ordinary fee. The school hours were from 9 to 12 a.m. and 2 to 4.30 p.m.[102] Clearly, the school was regarded as a great success, for Cockburn High School was erected in 1902 to provide secondary education for children on the south side of the town.

The overall achievement of Leeds School Board was very impressive. When it was superseded in 1902, it handed over to its successor 157 Elementary Schools; 2 Higher Grade Schools; 4 Industrial Schools for children convicted of petty offences or in danger of degenerating into criminals; 5 schools of a special type – 3 being for mentally handicapped children, 1 for the blind, and 1 for the deaf; a Pupil Teacher Centre; and nearly 60 Evening Schools. On the registers of the day schools were 57,632 children (compared to 25,000 in Voluntary Schools) of which 16,687 were infants, the average attendance being 49,358. For the instruction of these children there were 157 head teachers, 800 certificated teachers, 272 uncertificated teachers, and 508 junior teachers (pupil teachers and candidates), 29 manual instructors, 19 cookery teachers, 27 teachers of special subjects at the Higher Grade Schools, 13 pupil teacher instructors, 8 swimming instructors, 3 physical exercise instructors, an instructor in drawing and an instructor in music – making a total staff of more than 1,900. The key personality in the advances made by the School Board in the 1880s and 1890s was George Cockburn, who as chairman of its Education and Management of Schools Committee for 18 years had largely guided policy and the administration of its affairs. His immense contribution was to be recognised in the naming of Cockburn Higher Grade School which opened in 1902.[103]

Middle-class Education

The middle classes primarily sought education for their children in fee-paying schools. The story of Leeds Grammar school in the Victorian period was one of consistent failure to adapt to the needs of the middle-class families of the town.[104] There were persistent wranglings between the trustees and the Charity Commissioners concerning schemes to modify the plan upon which the school was run, but no really fundamental change was made in the curriculum, and even by the mid-1890s almost two-thirds of the older pupils' tuition was in languages. Due to the deterioration of the environment in which the old school building was situated, and the inadequacy of its accommodation, it was decided to move the school to an 'airy situation'. In 1858 a splendid new school was erected beside Woodhouse Moor to the designs of Edward Barry, the son of the architect of the Houses of Parliament, at a cost of £15,000.

The new buildings only marginally revived the school's fortunes. While the headmasters hung on to their salary of £500 per annum, a house rent free and one-quarter of the tuition fees (around £300 in 1862), the number of pupils fluctuated between 150 and 200. In the 1860s the school fees ranged from 4 to 6 guineas for local boys ('foundationers') to 16 guineas for 'non-foundationers', while the salaries of the assistant masters (9 by 1895) ranged from £150-£250. By 1895 the number of boys (who were taken from the ages of 9 to 19 years) had declined to 161. The list of the occupations of their parents is instructive: professional classes (including 17 clergymen) 60; merchants and manufacturers 34; clerks (including managers, secretaries, and commercial travellers) 20; tradesmen and shopkeepers 37; farmers 3; and 'others' 7.

Leeds Grammar School built 1858-9 (architect, E.M.Barry).

The falling off in the number of boys was attributed by the headmaster partly to the development of the Yorkshire College, but mainly to the competition of the Central Higher Grade Board School. He noted that at long last a local authority financed secondary school had been created of a type to which the lower middle classes might send their children. The school had 'excellent buildings providing accommodation for 2,099 scholars' and had an attendance of 1,498 in 1894-5. By the 1890s the Gothic style buildings of the Grammar School were felt to fall very far short of the modern standards required for a school: 'the style is ill-adapted to the requirement of classrooms; there is much waste of space, and the rooms are difficult to arrange in respect of light, are for the most part cold and draughty, and are acoustically defective'.

Throughout the century the school had been managed by the Committee of Pious Uses. Due to its other functions being superceded by the council, the committee members saw their principal role as being the trustees of the school. At the very end of the century, the committee finally agreed to the Charity Commissioners' demand that the Grammar School charity should be modernised by a radical broadening of the composition of its trustees. This reorganisation effectively ended the role of the Committee of Pious Uses after almost 300 years, though it pursued minor poor relief functions in the twentieth century. For the Grammar School, on the other hand, the change offered a much brighter future.

The trustees of the Grammar School had steadfastly resisted the recommendations of the Charity Commissioners that they should consider the education of girls. However, in 1876 the Yorkshire Ladies' Council of Education and the Leeds Ladies' Educational Association were successful in filling the gap by forming Leeds Girls' High School Limited. Their purpose, they decided, was 'to establish and maintain a high class Day School for the girls of Leeds which shall be to them what the Grammar School is to their brothers'. The school opened in 1876 with 42 pupils aged from 8-16 years old. In 1906 the school moved to its present site in Headingley Lane. In 1895 its proprietors established a preparatory department for boys and girls, and in 1901 a branch school, initially for boys and girls aged 4-12, which very quickly extended its teaching to older girls, and became known as Chapel Allerton Girls' High School. In 1914 this was taken over by Leeds Education Committee and became Chapel Allerton Girls' High School.[105]

Faced with the inability of the Grammar School to meet their requirements, the middle classes needed to look elsewhere for the commercial and scientific education they desired for their children. In 1845 the Mechanics' Institute established its Mathematics and Commercial School for boys. By 1852 this fee-paying day school had 211 pupils who were taught arts and commercial subjects. In 1854 this initiative was extended by the foundation of 'Leeds Educational Institute for the Education of Girls', which for twenty years was the only 'public' secondary school for girls in Leeds, and eventually became Leeds Girls' Modern School. The middle class pupilage of these schools cannot be in doubt. Dr Fitch commented, whilst praising the schools, in the 1867 Taunton Commission Schools Report:

> It is well known that the name 'mechanics' does not fairly represent the social position of the persons who avail themselves of such institutions. It is the more intelligent shopkeepers, clerks, warehousemen, and travellers of a great town like Leeds, who compose the Mechanics' Institute. It is for the children of this class that the committee has made ample provision in their day schools. In them are the advanced studies which are proper for the Middle Class Day School.

By 1869 the boys' school had nearly 300 pupils. In 1889 it moved to new premises in Rossington Street and was charging boys annual fees of £5. By 1901, the school, now known as Leeds Boys' Modern School, was reckoned by the Board of Education inspectors to be the most important secondary school in Leeds.[106]

Another product of this trend was Leeds Parish Church Middle Class School. By 1869 the number of children in the upper class of the Parish Church School was almost one hundred, and this prompted the church authorities to establish another school. This school began in Basinghall Street in 1870. The *Yorkshire Post* noted:

> The schools are intended mainly for the children of the middle classes, and will be available for both boys and girls. Instruction will be imparted by competent masters, in the sciences and languages, in addition to the usual elementary branches of an English education, and it is intended to qualify the pupils for commercial and other professional pursuits.[108]

When the fees were sufficient to make the school self-supporting, its managers decided to erect purpose-built premises. These were opened in Vernon Road in 1876 at a cost of £10,000. From the start chemistry was given very special emphasis and the school was one of the first in the country to be properly equipped with a laboratory. Many of the pupils won scholarships to the Yorkshire College.

Technical and Adult Education

The provision of technical and adult education became an issue of increasing concern in Leeds during the Victorian period. As we have seen, the Mechanics' Institute failed to attract the working classes. Nor were its scientific classes popular. By 1839 they drew only 140 students and by 1859 the numbers were no higher. In 1842 the Institute merged with the Leeds Literary Society, with Edward Baines as its first president and James Kitson, the engineering magnate, as one of its secretaries. Despite the paucity of students, due to considerable middle-class patronage the Institute was able to attract sufficient funds to erect a magnificent Institute building in Cookridge Street in 1865, designed by Cuthbert Brodrick.[109]

Meanwhile, with the aid of government finance, in 1846 the Institute was able to establish Leeds Government School of Design. The government was keen to promote technical education for adults and in 1851 it established the government Department of Science and Art. This gave a great boost to the school in Leeds, which in 1852 changed its name to the Leeds School of Art and gradually became more scientifically and practically orientated in its instruction. In 1903 new premises for the school were erected beside the Mechanics' Institute.[110]

The Mechanics' Institute built 1860-5 (architect, Cuthbert Brodrick). Now the Civic Theatre.

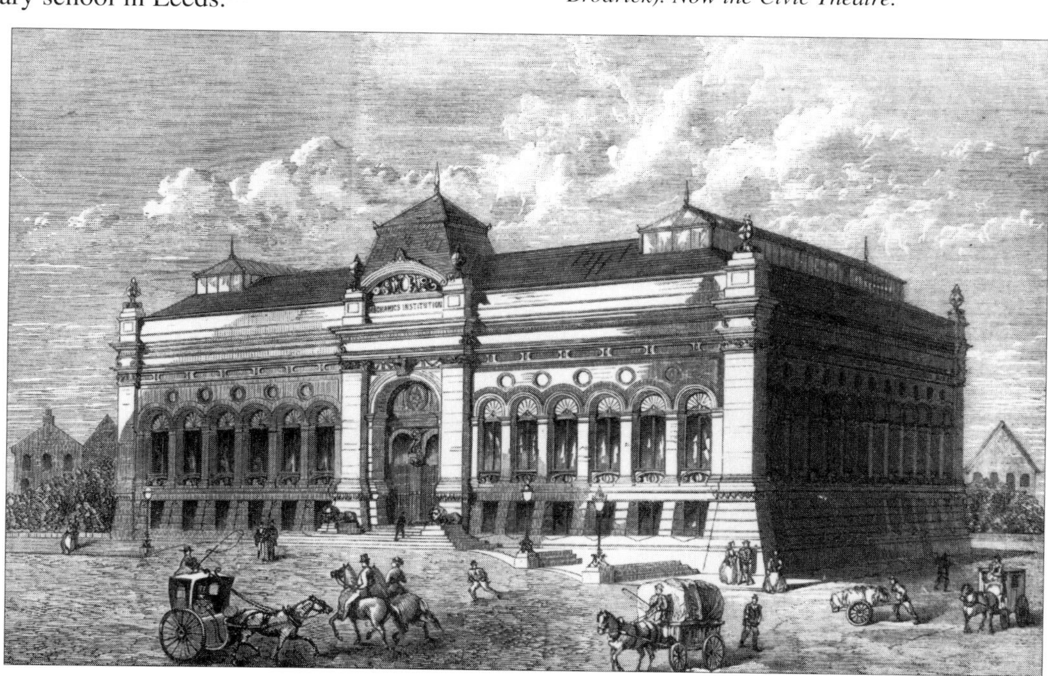

The Yorkshire College, College Road, built 1877 and later (architect, Alfred Waterhouse).

The provision of education on such an enlarged scale in Victorian Leeds would not have been possible without a great increase in the supply of teachers. In 1845 the system of monitors in the denominational schools was replaced by the pupil teacher system, whereby pupil teachers remained in these schools for five years, receiving extra tuition from their teacher. In 1870 pupil teachers taught for five hours a day in the schools, prepared lessons in the evening and attended school at 7.45 a.m. every morning for instruction from the headteacher. In 1895 the School Board decided to adopt a system of central day classes and in future pupil teachers spent half their time at the centre being trained and the other half with classes at school. In 1901 the Leeds Pupil Teacher College was opened on Great George Street in the purpose-built building which later was to be occupied by Thoresby High School.[111]

There was a need to produce well-trained teachers to teach cookery, laundry work, home management, needlework, and dressmaking, and it was felt that an institution was also needed for young women of good education who wished to qualify as housekeepers, cooks and matrons. As a result in 1874 the Leeds branch of the Yorkshire School of Cookery was established.[112]

In the field of adult and technical education the most notable landmark of the Victorian period was the establishment of the Yorkshire College. In 1867 George Henry Nussey and Arthur Nussey proposed the establishment of a 'Technical Institute' for Leeds, pointing out that Continental manufacturers were now equalling and in some cases surpassing English manufacturers. The principal cause was attributed to the great attention being paid by foreign governments to scientific improvement and sound scientific and technological education for work people and employers. The institution was to encompass all the trades in the district. It was to enhance mechanical engineering in all its branches, spinning, weaving, finishing, designing, and dyeing of woollen and worsted fabrics; spinning weaving, finishing and designing of linen fabrics; manufacture, finishing, dyeing and designing of leather; mining, metallurgy, pottery, brick-making and building, contracting, and furnishing trades. A School of Art and Design was to accompany it to afford art education to every trade in the district.[113]

There was no immediate response to their proposals, but it is clear that other citizens' minds were turning in the same direction. A group of local enthusiasts, the Yorkshire Board of Education, had encouraged the introduction of science into day schools and organised evening classes, the success of which led their thoughts towards a 'central college'. In 1874 the college came into being in a rented building in Cookridge Street with a staff of 3 professors and 24 students. Its purpose was 'to supply instruction in those sciences which are applicable to the manufacture, engineering, mining, and agriculture, of the county of Yorkshire, also in such arts and languages as are cognate to the foregoing purpose'. In 1878 the institution changed its name to the 'Yorkshire College', and in 1887 the Yorkshire College and the Leeds School of Medicine amalgamated and became part of the Victoria University in association with Owens College, Manchester, and University College, Liverpool. Following the dissolution of the Victoria University, in

1904 the college became independent once again and had the title of the University of Leeds conferred upon it. In 1880 the Textile Department moved to the present building, between Woodhouse Lane and what was then known as College Road, and the other departments followed four years later.[114]

No account of education in Victorian Leeds would be complete without a mention of the innumerable societies and clubs, which, in addition to the exclusive Leeds Philosophical and Literary Society, and the Leeds Library, were established primarily by the middle classes to encourage interest in artistic, cultural, and scientific matters. Many of these organisations or their successors still exist today. Foremost amongst them, for those interested in the history of Leeds, is the Thoresby Society which was founded in 1889. Its collection of books and archives and its quite outstanding series of publications are one of the great treasures of Leeds.[115] Other societies founded in the Victorian period included: Leeds Horticultural and Floral Society (which was re-established in 1837);[116] Leeds Photographic Society (founded in 1852);[117] Leeds Astronomical Society (founded in 1859);[118] Leeds Naturalists' Club and Scientific Association (founded in 1870);[119] and Leeds Arts Club (founded in 1893).[120]

In a non-academic way, the formation of cycling clubs made a significant contribution to broadening the experience of the working and lower-middle classes. The 1890s saw the formation of numerous clubs often with large memberships. The Potternewton Club had 140 members in 1893. Saturday afternoon proved ideal for cyclists who sometimes used the railways to take them as far afield as Bridlington and Ingleborough. Some of the rules for these early clubs seem farcical to us. The group of cyclists, complete with bugler, set off for their outings led by the captain, protocol dictating that no one should overtake him! The heyday of the cycling clubs was in the 1890s. By 1901 there were no less than 28 local bicycle manufacturers.[121]

The Battle for Souls

The Anglicans Fight Back

When Queen Victoria came to the throne Leeds was a noted centre of Nonconformity. The Church of England provided only 8 of the town's 35 places of worship.[122] As we have seen, the Anglicans had been ill-prepared to meet the challenge of urbanisation, and other religious denominations, above all Methodism, had proved popular alternatives. W. R. W. Stephens, the son-in-law of Dr Hook, Leeds' greatest nineteenth century vicar, observed that the 'excitable, impulsive, and emotional temperament' of the town's inhabitants 'supplied a peculiarly favourable soil for the reception of Wesley's doctrines'. 'Methodism', he noted, 'grew and flourished; Methodism alone kept pace with the rapid and enormous increase of population ...and stuck its roots deeper and deeper, year by year into the affections and understandings of the people.'[123] Astonishing as the growth of Methodism was, equally bewildering was the fragmentation which this rapid growth brought. By the mid-century the Methodists had divided into Wesleyan Methodists, Wesleyan Methodist Associationists, Wesleyan Reformers, New Connexion Methodists, Primitive Methodists and even a few smaller sects.[124]

This subdivision made new chapels necessary and, as if to demonstrate the righteousness of their cause, each sect confidently pursued ambitious building programmes. The Wesleyan Methodists could boast of Hanover Place Chapel, Park Lane, built in 1847 with seating for a 1,000, while the Methodist New Connexion was duly proud of Woodhouse Lane Chapel, 1857-8, with seating for 1,200. Old chapels were rebuilt, enlarged or renovated. The United Methodists rebuilt Park Chapel, off Park Lane in 1864, creating seating for 1,000 people, whilst four years later the Wesleyan Methodists renovated St Peter's Street Chapel, with accommodation for 2,000. In 1872 the Primitive Methodists enlarged Rehoboth Chapel, Park Lane, to seat 700. Conscious of the movement of people to the fashionable villages to the north, the Wesleyan Methodists built a chapel at Headingley in 1845, and in 1874 spent over £12,000 on another fine chapel at Chapel Allerton.[125]

Woodhouse Lane in 1858. The crowds await the arrival of Queen Victoria near two recently built places of worship. The chapel on the left, with the pediment, is the New Connexion Methodist Chapel built in 1857-8, and the church with the spire is St Columba's Presbyterian Church built in 1855-6.

Other Nonconformist groups were equally active. The aged Unitarian chapel at Mill Hill was demolished in 1847, when influential members of the congregation decided that it was unsuitable for modern forms of worship. It was replaced by the fine Gothic chapel familiar to us today, designed by Bowman and Crowther and opened in December 1848 at a cost over £7,300.[126] The Baptists built Blenheim Chapel, Woodhouse Lane, in 1863 and enlarged their premises on South Parade in 1886.[127] The Presbyterians erected St Columba's on Woodhouse Lane in 1855 and the Congregationalists built their Beeston Hill chapel in 1865.[128] The following year the Society of Friends began to construct fine new premises on Woodhouse Lane.[129] As a result of this extensive phase of chapel building, impressive places of worship could be found in prominent locations throughout the town centre. Their imposing frontages proclaimed the importance and continued success of Nonconformity.

Today's spirit of ecumenicalism makes it difficult to appreciate the acute rivalry between religious denominations in the Victorian period. The Anglican Church felt the need to counter-attack in the face of the Nonconformist onslaught. But how? Just in the nick of time the standard bearer arrived in the person of the charismatic and dynamic Walter Farquhar Hook. In 1837, on the death of Revd Richard Fawcett aged 77, Hook became Vicar of Leeds.[130] Fawcett and his fellow clergy had been overwhelmed by the huge growth in the

Left: Walter Farquhar Hook, Vicar of Leeds, 1837-59.

Right: The new Parish Church erected 1838-41 (architect, R. D. Chantrell).

population of the parish during his incumbency, eventually having pastoral responsibility for some 125,000 people. The vicar, one curate and a clerk in orders had spent most of their time at baptisms, marriages and funerals. They had been at the parish church from eight to half past eleven every morning for marriages, baptised twice every day and performed burials twice a day in winter, and three times a day in summer. Such demands left little time to forward the cause of the Established Church, and on Sundays fewer than 50 communicants attended the services.[131] From 1833, as we have seen, the parish church had been starved of resources by Nonconformist churchwardens. Something radical needed to be done.

Hook quickly grasped the enormity of the task before him. He was horrified to find the church structure in an appalling state, the surplices in rags and the service books in tatters. When the hostile churchwardens assembled in the church for vestry meetings they had the insolence to pile their hats and coats on the holy table and some even sat on it! He told them that he would take the keys off them and would hold no meetings there in future. Accepting the extreme unpopularity of church rates, he substituted collections at the end of services to raise funds.[132]

Hook was a great preacher and the congregations at the parish church soon became so large that regular worshippers asked for improvements. A subscription list was opened and the architect R. D. Chantrell was appointed to draw up plans. Unfortunately, the foundations of the old church were found to be rotten and he advised that a new church should be built. On 4 March 1838 the medieval church closed and over the next three years rebuilding progressed. The fine new church was consecrated on 2 September 1841, the cost of £28,000 being financed by voluntary contributions. Significantly, the new church had free pews for the poor.[133]

The population of Leeds was increasing so rapidly that the only way Hook could fulfil his desire to provide 'for every poor man a pastor and for every poor child a school' was to break up the ancient parish into smaller units. This he delivered with the Leeds Vicarage Act of 1844 which sub-divided the parish into smaller parishes, stimulated the building of churches, schools and parsonages, and actively encouraged the provision of free pews.[134] He was keenly aware that an organisation was needed to promote Anglicanism within the town. In January 1857 the Church Institute was formed and, such was the success of this new body, that on 29th October 1866 the foundation stone of a fine new building was laid in Albion Street. The Institute became a power house of new ideas. It adapted and changed over the years, providing everything from classes in English, French, Maths and Literature, to Prayer Book classes and courses of lectures. The Institute began to issue an annual selection of Whitsuntide hymns. Under its roof were housed a variety of organisations, ranging from the Missionary League, to the Leeds Church Extension Society.[135] The latter organisation, founded in January 1865, helped organise and finance the construction of new Anglican churches in the parish. Hook had been aided in his ambitious church building programme by generous grants from the Ripon Diocesan Church Building Society. Few had been financed by individuals, one notable exception being Meanwood Church, built in 1849 at the expense of Mary and Elizabeth Beckett.[136] In the period 1865 to 1901 the Leeds Church Extension Society continued this important work by building 25 new churches including St Clement's, Chapeltown Road in 1868, and St Augustine's, Wrangthorn, Hyde Park Corner, in 1870.[137] When Hook left Leeds for Chichester in 1859 there were 18 town churches, 18 suburban churches, 21 Anglican day schools and 69 clergy.[138] It was a remarkable achievement, though one which had not been accomplished without difficulties.

The Rise of Anglo-Catholicism and the Roman Catholics

One of the most distressing problems to confront Hook was that of St Saviour's Church, opened in 1845 at the expense of Dr E.B.Pusey. Pusey was one of the leading members of the Oxford Movement which began in 1833. Its proponents argued that though the Church of England was 'Protestant' in that it protested against Papal authority, it was still truly Catholic. Pusey's aim in financing St Saviour's was to put Anglo-Catholic teachings into practice in a poor working-class parish. Dr Hook had great sympathy with these High Church views, and was very taken aback when leading Anglicans began to express real concern about the 'Romish' practices encouraged by this Oxford clique. There was an outcry in the local press and Hook began to distance himself from the movement. Unfortunately, some of the new clergy at St Saviour's openly used the new forms of service, including the hearing of confession and bowing before the altar.

Dr. Hook became extremely frustrated at his inability to influence the situation, since under his own Act St Saviour's had become a separate parish. He openly expressed doubts about the clergy at St Saviour's and their 'Romish' practices, stating:

> When I had ascertained the character of the proceedings, I remonstrated with the patrons of the

St Saviour's Church built 1842-5 (architect, J.M.Derick). It was eventually given an impressive tower.

Cartoon depicting Hook trapped between the Nonconformists and the Liberal press on one side and the 'hornets' of St Saviour's with their Catholic leanings on the other.

living, but I was warned that I had no more to do with the parish of St Saviour's than I have with a parish in London, and when I ventured in reply to observe that I might justly complain when a hornet's nest was planted at my garden gate, the rejoinder was that what I took for a hornet's nest was a hive of sweet honey.[139] What the honey is, events have shown.

Things came to a head in 1851 when the first vicar and a curate of St Saviour's, who had carried out praiseworthy social work amongst the poor, joined the Roman Catholic Church. Other defections were to follow and it remained a thorn in Hook's side.[140]

While the Anglicans and the Nonconformists were fighting each other and amongst themselves, Roman Catholicism was making steady progress. At the beginning of the nineteenth century only a handful of Catholics worshipped in their chapel at the junction of Lady Lane and Templar Street, but by 1898 the life of Catholics in Leeds had been transformed. A Catholic population of over 30,000 was now served by 19 priests and 11 places of worship, and 5 convents housed over 60 nuns.[141] James Holdforth (1778-1861), a staunch campaigner for Catholic emancipation, became Mayor of Leeds in 1838 – reputedly the first Roman Catholic mayor in England since the Reformation.[142] The same year the new mother church of St Anne's, Guildford Street, now the Headrow, opened.[143] In 1820 Leeds had over 3,000 Irish Catholics, most congregated on the eastern side of the town. These numbers were further boosted in the 1840s with a huge influx of Irish migrants. St Patrick's Chapel, in York Road, erected in 1831,[144] proved totally inadequate for the needs of the district,

Tab Street at 'The Bank'. Mount St Mary's Roman Catholic Church, built in 1853-7 on Richmond Hill, dominated this area with its concentration of poor Catholic families.

and in 1857 the cathedral-proportioned Mount St Mary's, Richmond Hill, with seating for 2,000, opened at a cost of £20.000.[145] The importance of the town as a centre of Catholicism was formally recognised in 1878 with the formation of the Diocese of Leeds, and this new status was confirmed on 28 October 1879 when the first Bishop was installed in the episcopal throne in St Anne's, which now became a cathedral church.[146]

The Hold of Religion

Victorian Leeds was a town in which a great diversity of religious beliefs were practiced. On Sundays, Anglicans, Roman Catholics, Independents, Unitarians, Quakers, General Baptists, Particular Baptists, Methodists, Mormons and others made their way to worship. The townscape was peppered with churches and chapels. Nevertheless, appearances were deceptive. Had all the people of worshipping age wanted to go to a place of worship on a Sunday they could not have done so. The Religious Census of 1851 showed that the town's 57 places of worship provided only 47,000 sittings for a population of 101,345. By then these sittings were divided almost equally in three parts between the Anglicans, the Methodists, and the other religious denominations. More surprising, however, is that much of the church and chapel building seems to have been in vain. On the day of the census, Sunday 30 March, only 18,933 people attended morning service and 20,604 in the evening.[147] The plain truth was that at best, the town's places of worship, both Anglican and Nonconformist, were nearly half-empty. One major exception was the parish church where Hook's appeal was such that 350 people customarily stood through every service.[148]

Even if church and chapel attendances were smaller than might be expected from the plethora of buildings, the very powerful influence of religion on life in Leeds cannot be under-estimated. We have already seen how important it was in the sphere of education. It provided the standards for the moral behaviour expected of the middle and working classes. It supplied the spark behind a great deal of philanthropic work. The hold of religion on the society was immediately to be seen in the special character of Leeds on a Sunday. The Revd William Guest writing in 1857 observed:

> Oh, it is not easy to those who have never seen it to understand the difference between an English and a Continental Sunday. Walk through Leeds at noon on the Sabbath-day. In Briggate every shop is shut, and the young men are at liberty. In Park Lane every warehouse is fastened up, and the warehouse-men are with their families, or in the house of God. In Park Row every lawyer's office is closed, and the clerks call the day their own. At the public works the hammer is silent, and the masons and carpenters have suspended their labours. No loaded waggon is being dragged along to the railway. The carriers and the horses have rest. Blessed English Sabbath, of which all this may be said.[149]

Working-class attendance at church and chapel was very low. The *Leeds Mercury* asserted in December 1838 that out of the 60,000 working-class people of worshipping age in the borough, 40,000 never went to church or chapel.[150] But it was the attendance of the middle classes which proved critical. It would have been difficult to find a leading politician or businessman who did not attend worship. The leaders of Leeds society, almost to a man, professed Christian moral values.[151]

Missionaries in 'Darkest Leeds'

The desire to bring religion to the poorest of the working classes prompted the religious denominations to move into the working-class areas. St Saviour's and Mount St Mary's, in particular, were strategically sited to cater for the needs of those who struggled to live in the Bank area. The curates and priests who ministered to the needs of the poor, particularly at times of epidemics, were brave men, as we have seen.[152]

Considerable efforts began to be made to lure the working classes to church. Christians had always expressed concern about the poor within the township and in hard times soup kitchens, clothing and fuel were provided for the needy, but as clergy, priests and ministers became more numerous, greater effort could be devoted to those who lived in the squalid, insanitary dwellings that had engulfed the town. For some it was a bewildering journey into an evil, depressing environment. Revd J.Slatter, from the parish church, noted the improvements since the Church of England began to have an influence:

> What Leeds was before Dr. Hook came to it, and before the really noble exertions of himself and his first curates had told upon its heathenism, I only know, of course, by hearsay; but I have been told by a person on whom I can fully rely, that before the St Saviour's district had been placed under the charge of two zealous curates, it was quite impossible for any decent person to pass along East Street, when the factory people were in it, without encountering the grossest personal insults. That is now, of course, changed, but it is important to notice it, because, if vice is still found of the most enormous kind, it shews that the first operations, real and excellent as they were, did not prick to the bottom of the evil, which still remains as deep-seated as ever, curtailed only in its outward expressions.[153]

Appalling environmental conditions dogged every effort to improve the lifestyle of the poor. One brave attempt was the opening of The Good Shepherd Mission in the Quarry Hill district in 1882. T. H. Brameld worked in the area for 55 years and recalled with dismay the difficulties he encountered trying to open a youth club.

> The whole club was infested with vermin. Right through the whole fifty-five years this horror was more or less there, and at first it was dreadful. I was present at the reconstruction of a house, the next house to the Mission Buildings, and saw, as they removed the woodwork, these creatures, not in hundreds, but in thousands and thousands. I took two cottages and had them made into one for use as a club. We kept the place empty for six weeks and had it stoved for five nights a week during the whole time, and when we ventured to open it they simply swarmed, and we had to close it and begin all over again. On Sunday afternoons in summer, Sunday School work had to be stopped in some rooms while a great slaughter took place. I have had them crawling over the music as I played at service: I have had them crawling off me at home at supper on Sunday evenings. These facts are given to show the conditions under which Church work was carried on and what a hopeless outlook it was for the decent poor.[154]

Despite such difficulties he managed to organise a Sunday School, bible classes, and a youth club which provided cricket, football, swimming, athletics, trips to

The Good Shepherd Mission Chapel and School Room, opened in 1882 at the corner of St Peter's Square.

the seaside, whist drives and dances. Yet, even towards the end of the century the situation remained grim. As Revd Hugh Marks remembered:

> The beginning of the work at the Railway Arch in 1895 was a venture of faith. It was an attempt to bring spiritual help through the work of the Church to the people living in the very congested slum district which at that time lay between York Street and Marsh Lane. This district was then very largely made up of Common Lodging Houses, and it contained a great number of public houses with here and there a fried fish shop and a fringe of little shops along the boundary line of Marsh Lane. There were a great number of evil courts and mean streets. Drunkenness and fighting were very common and the system of furnished rooms was directly conducive to immorality. In many of the courts it was difficult to find a couple living in wedlock. None of the existing agencies of religion seemed to reach the people living in this district. The police on night duty always went in couples. When the City undertook the task of improvement, the Arch district formed the worst half of what was marked out on the map as "the condemned area". It was a district that was "full of darkness and cruel habitations". The only hope of bringing Light of Life to the people dwelling there, seemed to lie in placing at their doors some simple little Mission Room.[155]

There was no easy solution. Nevertheless, progress was made and by the end of the century in the town as a whole Sunday schools were flourishing, pews were nearly all free, and many more working people had become involved in the churches and chapels. Christians were more active in poor communities, and through the Temperance Movement and the Band of Hope, real efforts had been made to tackle the evils of alcohol abuse. The Salvation Army, founded by William Booth in 1878, continued to offer hope for the most unfortunate members of society.

The last fifty years of the century had brought mixed blessings for the Independents, Baptists and Methodists, who had seen both the continued revival of the Church of England and the decline of the Unitarians and Quakers. The Irish migration to Leeds had bolstered the position of the Roman Catholic Church. St Anne's Catholic Church, Guildford Street, which received cathedral status in 1878, was demolished at the turn of the century for road widening and replaced by a magnificent new cathedral church in Cookridge Street in 1904.[156] The other major group of migrants, the Jews, added a totally different perspective to the religious life of the town, their first synagogue being constructed in 1847 in Belgrave Street and more being added with the arrival of Jews fleeing from Russia and Poland in the 1880s.[157] For all religious denominations the closing years of the century were to pose new challenges. As the trend towards suburban living increased and the town centre population began to either decrease or relocate due to the demand for office and business accommodation and road widening, more churches and chapels were needed in the suburbs, and town centre churches found themselves under-subscribed and comparatively over-staffed.[158]

People and Politics

It is difficult to say which was the most influential factor in creating the fairly stable society which Leeds enjoyed during the Victorian period. Was it the restraining influence of the forces of law and order, the availability of poor relief and medical care, or a respect for the social order inculcated through better schooling and religious teaching? Perhaps more fundamental was the prosperity of the local economy which was so diverse that it was rare for all groups of workers to simultaneously feel the effects of difficult trading conditions. Whatever the reason, a climate existed in Leeds in which there was comparatively little public disorder to hamper the progress of the town. Nevertheless, at the political level there was very considerable conflict. This embraced the battle between the parties for control of local government; the battle over national issues played out in particular at parliamentary election time; and the developing and long-term aspirations of the working classes to both gain an effective voice in local and national government, and to become powerful in the battle between capital and labour.

After the humiliation of being thrown out of office in 1835, briefly in the late 1830s, the Tories came within sight of gaining control of the reformed corporation – the council. The 1839 election gave the Conservatives more councillors than the Liberals, but the Liberals held on to power by virtue of possessing a greater number of aldermanic seats. After the 1840 election the council was exactly divided between Conservative and Liberal members, and in practice better attendance by Tory councillors effectively weakened Liberal control. The Tories' success resulted from popular resentment at increased municipal expenditure, superior party organisation, and the local effects of a declining Whig/Liberal government. In 1841, however, the Liberals battled through to hold on to power, and, as if exhausted by their supreme effort, the Tories declined rapidly as a political force in the council elections thereafter. Not for another 30 years was there to be the prospect of a Tory town council. In contrast, when the New Poor Law came into force in 1844, the Tories won control of the board of guardians and retained control for the rest of the decade. In 1844-45 the three non-Tory guardians were Chartists. For most of the mid-Victorian years the board was the one bastion the Tories held against the Liberals.[159]

In the sphere of parliamentary politics a Whig-Radical alliance had returned Edward Baines and his radical partner, Sir William Molesworth, to Parliament in the 1837 election. During the next two or three years, however, inspired by the newly established *Leeds Times*

Leeds people took a great interest in the Crimean War. In August 1856 the Earl of Cardigan, the leader of the Charge of the Light Brigade, was entertained at a grand banquet in the hall of the Stock Exchange, where 'the people of Yorkshire' presented him with a splendid sword which had cost £250.

the radicals could hardly be contained within the Liberal fold. Over the next decade, of the great national political causes which dominated the period, Chartism and the campaign for the repeal of the Corn Laws were particularly notable in Leeds.

Chartism, the Plug Riots and the Corn Laws

Leeds was the most important centre of Chartism propaganda in the north of England, for Feargus O'Connor, the Chartist folk hero, published the *Northern Star* in Leeds.[160] When the People's Charter was launched in 1838, many of the radicals sprang to its support. Chartism was a nationwide movement primarily backed by handicraft workers and skilled artisans who were gravely unhappy about their lack of an effective voice in political matters and the uncaring attitude of Parliament to the working classes. This was reflected in the failure of the 1832 Reform Act to make Parliament representative of the working classes, the failure of the 1833 Factory Act to address the demand for a maximum ten hour working day, and the imposition of the noxious Poor Law Amendment Act of 1834. The People's Charter, the cornerstone of the Chartists' massive petition to Parliament in 1839, demanded votes for all men, annual parliaments, vote by ballot, equal electoral districts, the payment of MPs, and the abolition of property qualifications for candidates. Samuel Smiles recalled the disruption caused by the Leeds Chartists during this period in their efforts to force their campaign and objectives before the public. He recalled how they mustered at public meetings and demanded that the government implement the Charter. He related the events at a meeting of the British and Foreign Schools Society held in the Commercial Buildings on 4 September 1839 at which Feargus O'Connor and other Chartists were present:

> Mr Baines, M.P. was in the chair, but a motion was proposed that Joshua Hobson [a leading Chartist] should preside; and a vigorous contest took place. Mr Baines stood firmly to his post, though Hobson tried to push him out of the chair. The quiet Quaker ladies sat still and looked in amazement. Of course, nothing could be done. The members of the Society eventually retired. The gas was turned off, and the meeting broke up in disorder.[161]

In Leeds, Chartism was supported and led primarily by artisans and craftsmen, shopkeepers, teachers and writers, and had a fair number of lower-middle-class sympathisers. Elsewhere in Yorkshire, however, it was essentially a massive working-class movement. The years from 1839-42 were ones of severe depression in the local economy. The destitution and desperation this induced amongst the working classes rallied great support for Feargus O'Connor's calls for the use of 'Physical Force' to achieve the objects of the Charter.

The social composition of the supporters of Chartism in Leeds encouraged hopes that the Chartists might work closely with the middle-class radicals to achieve parliamentary reform. In 1840 the leading Leeds radicals – the cloth merchant Hamer Stansfield, the wealth flax spinner James Garth Marshall, and Samuel Smiles, the editor of the *Leeds Times* – formed the Leeds Parliamentary Reform Association (sometimes referred to as the Household Suffrage Association). In January 1841 the association, in a bid to bring about co-operation between middle and working-class radicals, organised a splendid festival in Marshall's new mill. It drew an audience of 7,000 including middle- and working-class radicals from all over the country. In Samuel Smiles' words 'the object was to have a friendly conference with the working people, and to exchange thoughts freely with them about the extension of the franchise'.[162] But this alliance soon withered away and the Leeds Chartists sought power independently. In the 1840s the Chartists were extremely influential in the vestry: in 1842 they temporarily captured the improvement commission, and for ten years they controlled the board of the highway surveyors. In addition, they sat on the first board of guardians. From 1842 Chartist councillors were elected, though they did not always designate themselves as 'Chartists', and clearly were not poor men since, to be eligible to be a councillor, ownership of property rated at £30 per annum or with a value of £1,000, was required.

In the harsh economic conditions of 1842, with no prospect of the demands of the People's Charter being attained, riots broke out in many parts of the country. Thousands of workers throughout Lancashire and the West Riding were unemployed. The disorder in which they took part was best known as the 'Plug Riots'. Crowds of men and women went from place to place, bringing mills to a standstill by pushing in the plugs of steam engine boilers. This caused the water to escape over the flames in the furnace, both extinguishing the fire and severely damaging the engines. By July 1842 the depression and unemployment in Leeds was so great that the town was ripe for trouble.[163] The council wrote to the government in alarm: 'Never in any former period in our recollection has this manufacturing district experienced distress so universal, so prolonged, so exhaustive and so ruinous.' The writing was on the wall as the Plug Riots swept through Lancashire and into Huddersfield, Halifax and Bradford. The council and magistrates made preparation to safeguard the town. Thirty thousand staves were provided for the Special Constables, the streets were cleared early in the evenings, and public houses were forced to close at 8 p.m. On 17 August riots broke out, mainly in Hunslet, Holbeck and on the western edge of the town. Sixteen hundred Special Constables were sworn in to assist the regular police; the 17th Lancers, under the command of Prince George of Cambridge, and the Yorkshire Regiment, under Lieutenant Colonel William Beckett, were also called out.

A large body of men had stopped mills at Farnley and Wortley, and it was reported that they had gone to Pudsey for reinforcements with the intention of moving on to attack mills at Armley. The forces of law and order set off from the Court House to intercept the mob. First came the police on foot, armed with cutlasses and heavy batons. Then came 1,200 Special Constables walking three and four abreast, and all carrying heavy batons. The armed forces brought up the rear – a troop of the 17th Lancers, 18 men of the 187th Infantry with fixed bayonets, a party of the Royal Horse Artillery with a mounted field piece, and, finally, the Ripon Troop of Yeomanry.

On the way, this formidable force received news that the mob had stopped a number of mills in the Holbeck area, and the column hastened to that neighbourhood. J.G.Marshall and his workmen stoutly defended the boiler house of Temple Mill, but could not prevent the mob breaking in. Fortunately for Marshall's, the mob could not locate the boiler plug. Prince George and his Lancers met the rioters in Water Lane, Holbeck, where the reading of the Riot Act and a line of artillery with field pieces was sufficient to disperse the mob. But the mob moved on to Messrs Maclea and Marsh's mill in Dewsbury Road. Only a few of them managed to get into the mill yard before the Chief Constable arrived on horseback, rushed into the yard and succeeded in having the doors closed. The Riot Act was read again and the mob was ordered to disperse. An urgent request for assistance was sent to the military, but before they could get there, the large force of Special Constables arrived and arrested 38 people. Thereafter the rioters dispersed. The prisoners were brought before a special commission at York and were given sentences varying from deportation for ten years to being bound over to keep the peace. Though the riots were linked with Chartism, there is no evidence that leading Chartists in Leeds were directly involved. Chartism was to fade from the national stage after its final big upsurge in 1848. Though there was fighting in Bradford and Bingley in 1848, there was none in Leeds, despite very large public meetings taking place in Vicar's Croft and on Woodhouse Moor.

Throughout the period 1838-46 there was great rivalry between the Chartists and the other great campaign of these years, the Anti-Corn Law League. The League, which had great support in Leeds, aimed for the repeal of the Corn Laws which it believed kept the price of grain, the staple diet of the poor, at artificially high levels. The Chartists felt that the Anti-Corn Law campaign would sap the strength of their movement. Samuel Smiles was intimately involved in the work of the League in Leeds and his autobiography chronicles the great fervour the movement generated in the town. The campaign leader, Richard Cobden, spoke often in Leeds and regularly corresponded with Smiles to discuss tactics. The success of the campaign for repeal in 1846 was greeted with delight by Smiles and his colleagues.[164]

Voluntary versus State Education

The issue of voluntary-provided versus State-provided education was the most divisive national political issue within Leeds. As we have seen, the religious denominations played a major role in the provision of schools at the start of Victoria's reign. As the State began to show a greater interest in education there were two major fears. On the one hand, all denominations were worried that the religious influence in education would be diminished if it were provided by the State; on the other hand, the Nonconformists feared that if there was a strong religious influence in State-provided schools, it would be predominantly that of the Church of England.

By the mid-1840s many Anglicans, including Dr Hook, had come to accept the need for State involvement in education, because of the scale of the problem, and had acknowledged that the Church of England had no moral claim to favoured treatment. Meanwhile, the influential Liberal Nonconformist, Edward Baines, junior, remained adamant that the State should not be involved. Some of his fellow Liberals, however, had become more receptive to the idea of increased State aid, if it was free from the taint of Church domination. The controversy caused major internal division within the Liberals; indeed, it led them to sacrifice county as well as borough parliamentary seats on two occasions.

The education debate raged through the council in the 1840s.[165] In the 1847 parliamentary election, since the Liberals were agreed on all issues except education, it seemed sensible for them to reach a compromise between themselves by nominating one Liberal candidate pro-state education and one pro-voluntaryism. In practice this is what happened, but only in the face of strong resistance from Baines. One of the two Liberal candidates was James Garth Marshall, the flaxspinner and radical free trader, who, as a supporter of State education, would draw the support of many Liberal state-educationalists, but was anathema to Baines. The second candidate was Joseph Sturge, a leading voluntaryist Liberal, who Baines insisted on bringing in from Birmingham. Baines made the whole election turn on the education issue, rather than general support for Liberal causes, and in consequence the outcome was disastrous for the Liberals. Marshall was elected with ease, but the quarter of the Liberal voters which favoured State involvement in education refused to vote for the outsider Sturge, and supported the local Tory and State-educationalist, William Beckett. As a result, Beckett was elected and a safe Liberal seat was sacrificed to Baines' principles. A similar process was repeated in the county election of 1848. In 1852, however, differences within the Leeds Liberals were patched up and two Liberal MPs were elected for the borough in 1852, 1859, 1865 and 1868.

Liberal Domination and Gladstone's Triumph

The Liberal domination of the council was not threatened again until the 1870s when large expenditure on the improvement of the borough brought accusations that the borough debt was more like a mini-national debt. Nevertheless, except for 1841-42 when the Liberals' 32 seats were matched by those of the Tories and 1873-74 when the Liberal majority was reduced to six seats, the Liberals had a majority on the council from 1835-36 to 1894. In 1895 the Tories finally returned to power with 38 seats to the Liberals' 26. It was not until 1904 that the Liberals regained power, but by then, as we shall see, 'Labour' had arrived on the scene as an electoral force to complicate the position.[166]

From 1870 the triennial elections for the School Board were another area for political activity, though in reality the religious rather than the political persuasion of its members is the most useful way of evaluating the board's composition. In three of the five elections between 1870 and 1882 members of a Liberal/Unsectarian outlook held a bare majority over the Church, Denominational, and Independent members. At the other two elections no group had an overall majority.[167]

'Stopped for furious driving'. This cartoon circulated during the General Election of 1880. The Liberals candidates, Gladstone and John Barran, grasping plans for domestic muddles and foreign messes, are stopped by the Conservatives candidates, Wheelhouse and Jackson, who state 'we can't allow you to go any further, such conduct is reckless'.

Mr Gladstone speaking to an adoring audience at the Coloured Cloth Hall in October 1881.

Leeds was essentially a Liberal town. The Conservatives won only one-third of the parliamentary seats contested between 1832 and 1880, and no more than one-third of the council seats between 1835 and 1880. The magnificent Liberal Club built in Quebec Street in 1890 is physical testimony to the strength of Liberalism in Victorian Leeds, but it was the visit of Mr Gladstone in 1881 which most vividly demonstrates its hold on the people. Gladstone and the Liberal Party lost office in 1874 and there followed six years of Conservative government under the premiership of Benjamin Disraeli, then Lord Beaconsfield. At the 1880 election, despite the plea of Leeds to Gladstone to stand with John Barran as their candidate, he chose to fight for the Tory stronghold of Midlothian. Remarkably, despite his candidature in the Scottish seat, the Leeds Liberals still nominated him as MP for Leeds in the hope that he would represent Leeds if he lost in Midlothian.[168] In fact, Gladstone scored great victories in both Midlothian and Leeds, and swept back to power. He chose to sit for Midlothian, and soon after, his 25 year old son, Herbert, was elected unopposed to the Leeds seat.

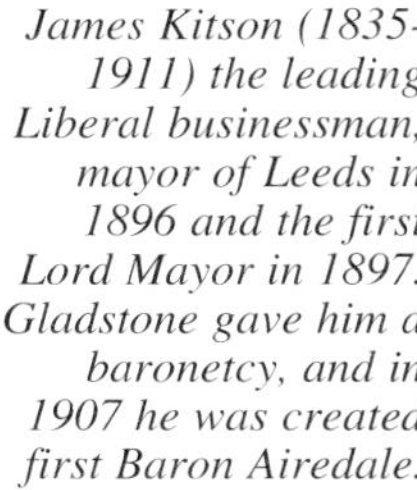

James Kitson (1835-1911) the leading Liberal businessman, mayor of Leeds in 1896 and the first Lord Mayor in 1897. Gladstone gave him a baronetcy, and in 1907 he was created first Baron Airedale.

In October 1881, Gladstone – 'the Grand Old Man' aged 71 – prime minister once again, rewarded Leeds with a two-day visit. It is almost impossible for us today to comprehend the reception this politician received – it was as if a god had come to Leeds. The town was decorated as though for a Royal visit. There was enormous competition for the 30,000 tickets for the special meetings during his visit. There were two great occasions. The first was the Friday evening banquet in the specially erected building in the Coloured Cloth Hall Yard, where he addressed 1,300 diners. He did not take his seat at the high table in the hall until dinner was over and the speeches were about to begin. After gazing with admiration upon the brilliant scene, he leant forward, and covered his face with both hands in prayer. Then he delivered one of his most famous speeches on the Irish Question. He was then taken across Woodhouse Moor to the home of Mr James Kitson, escorted by an immense torchlight procession. George Ratcliffe, a working-class lad who later became Lord Mayor of Leeds, recalled with great pride how at the age of 17 he had carried a torch in the procession.[169] The second great occasion was the following day when Mr Gladstone addressed thirty thousand people in the Coloured Cloth Hall Yard. The audience was tightly packed together in a sweltering mass, and in no condition to listen patiently to speeches. The noise and hubbub was little short of deafening. One eminent Liberal after another attempted to move the preliminary resolutions, but not a word could be heard beyond the limits of the platform. Weymss Reid recalled the Gladstone magic:

> It seemed that nothing could be done to reduce the vast audience to silence, and we were in despair at the thought that Mr Gladstone would have to face so severe an ordeal. When at last his turn came, and he stepped to the front of the platform, thirty thousand throats sent up such a shout that it seemed to shake the building. Again and again for a space of some minutes it was renewed, whilst the orator stood pale and motionless. What could one voice have done against thirty thousand? Then just as the cheering seemed to be subsiding, someone started "For he's a jolly good fellow", and the whole thirty thousand joined in the song. After that it took some minutes for them all to settle down again, and still there went on that under current of murmuring talk which seemed to make the attempt of anyone to address the gigantic meeting hopeless. But suddenly Mr Gladstone raised his hand, and it was almost as if a miracle had happened. In an instant there was a deathlike silence in the hall, and every man in it seemed to be holding his breath. The speaker's voice

rang out, clear and musical as of old, and it reached the furthest corners of the mighty apartment. But he had not got further than the conventional opening words when his audience seemed to go wild with delight. A frenzied burst of cheering, far exceeding that which had welcomed him on his first appearance, proclaimed the joy with which they had heard the voice of the man they adored.

The Rise of the Labour Movement

Class never became a powerful determinant of political behaviour in Victorian Leeds. In the competition for power and authority the main contenders could always call on rich and poor alike.[170] In the last two decades of the century, however, Labour began to established itself as a separate and independent political interest, and the seeds of the collapse of the Victorian political system in Leeds began to take root.

As we have seen, in the years from 1790 to around 1830 the emergent working classes were regarded by some contemporaries as a serious threat to the established political order. The espousal of Tom Paine's writings, periodic celebrations at the progress of Napoleon's armies, the activities of the Luddites, the organisation of early trade unions, and Chartism in its 'physical force' phase, had all in their day struck fear into the hearts of Leeds middle classes. But after the initial flirting with 'co-operation' and Chartism, the bulk of the working classes, instead of striking out to form an independent working-class political movement to represent their interests, in practice gave their support to the Liberals.[171] A 'respectable' upper tier of workers emerged who in mid-century Edward Baines believed could be safely given the vote. These were 'the better portion of the working classes …earning good wages …skilled and educated men', about one-tenth of the town's working classes, who had proved themselves by their participation in 'twenty-three mechanics institutes, the savings banks, friendly societies, temperance, building, and church and charitable societies'.[172]

Samuel Smiles noted some of these in the 1840s. He recalled in 1841:

> I became a member of the Manchester Unity of Oddfellows, and of the Ancient Order of Foresters. Although they have 'words' and 'signs', and are invested with some show of secrecy, they are really and truly societies for mutual benefit and support. Not fewer than 8,000 working men of Leeds belonged to the Manchester Unity; but there were many other societies – Independent Oddfellows, Gardeners, Foresters, Ancient Druids, Order of the Ark and the Peaceful Doves, the Knights Templar, the Ancient Romans, Knights of Malta, Loyal Ancient Shepherds and Shepherdesses, and even an Order of Ancient Buffaloes![173]

By the late 1860s the Leeds labour movement consisted largely of skilled trades organised in 28 small trade unions, with a total membership of around 3,500, all thought to be Liberals.[174] After the 1867 Parliamentary Reform Act gave the vote to around half the urban working classes, the number of voters on the Leeds electoral register soared from 8,480 to a little over 38,000. A Liberal Party report noted that 'this extraordinary addition is principally composed of mechanics and factory workers, or as they are termed here "mill hands". There has been no gauge taken of their opinion, but they are believed to be Liberal'.[175] 'They' were the working-class communities, notably south of river which came to be regarded as Liberal strongholds.

The workers' organisations were primarily concerned with bread and butter issues rather than political philosophy. The Leeds Trades Council was an important centre of the labour movement, but essentially was concerned with protecting the interests of working people organised in particular trade unions. By far the greatest part of its time was devoted to mutual aid and support in the almost endless series of local strikes and lock-outs; to the collection and publication of lists of local businesses which paid union rates; and to the protection of the legal position of trade unions.[176]

Pioneers of modern socialism in Leeds in the 1880s were frustrated by the persistent failure of their fellow workers to recognise the real issue at the heart of their position – the conflict of interests between the capitalist employers and the working man. Tom Maguire, an east Leeds Catholic of Irish extraction, felt that the workers' energies were wasted in identification with largely irrelevant Liberal causes, like reform of land ownership and the value of individualism, which they mistakenly saw as worthwhile battles to be fought out with the Tories. Against Liberal emphasis on individual advancement he counterposed the idea of collective action: 'We working men, although divided by politics and religion, are socially one …Can the political differences of Whig and Tory be really the political differences of a plasterer and a bricklayer?'[177] He was horrified by both trade union and working-class support for a Liberal council, many of whose members were the very employers with whom the workers should be in conflict. Moreover, he was appalled by his fellow workers' acquiescence for decades in a local government system where *working-class* interests were supposedly represented by *middle-class* councillors.

Maguire and fellow socialists called for workers to have their own political organisation. In September 1884 a branch of the Social Democratic Federation was formed in Leeds, with Maguire as its secretary.[178] In March 1885 it was decided to dissolve the branch and declare its members, members of the Socialist League. Initially, they were preoccupied with developing a vision of the future socialist society, but they seemed to tire of these purist revolutionary ideas, and in the late 1880s and early 1890s began leading a new political labour movement based on trade union support, and demands for reform in local and national government. Their activities were highlighted by an upsurge of strikes in Leeds between 1889 and 1892.

In June 1889 the Socialist League helped the builders' labourers organise a union and to increase their hourly rate by 1½d. In October 900 girls went out on strike at Arthur's tailoring shop, and in the New Year 3,000 tailors joined them. Each strike was followed by the formation of a new union – tramway workers, blue dyers, corporation workers and others. On May Day 6,000 workers marched through the town demanding an eight hour day, the overthrow of race hatred, and the emancipation of women. The climax to this unrest came with the Gas Strike of June and July 1890.[179] For the first time in many years there was a near breakdown in law and order, with confrontation between the strikers and the military. The Gas sub-committee of the council had decided to take advantage of the low summer demand for gas to claw back concessions they had made to the strikers the preceding winter, when public pressure had forced it to give in. Blacklegs were brought in from as far away as London to work in the gasworks. At the height of the strike, 260 blacklegs, the mayor, and other civic dignitaries, surrounded by 500 police and soldiers, left the Town Hall and pushed their way through a crowd estimated at 30,000. There was no sign of violence until the procession approached the railway bridge near New Wortley gasworks, then all hell broke loose. The blacklegs were pushed and battered as they went into the works. The following evening the crowd renewed its attack on the works and the mayor read the Riot Act. On the same day a great crowd attacked the Meadow Lane gasworks. Many blacklegs fled and the committee was obliged to back down. This had been a momentous victory for the workers, and had cost the council a small fortune.

The militant mood of workers nationwide was to lead to the formation of the Independent Labour Party in Bradford in January 1893, and the ILP in turn encouraged the emergence in 1900 of the Labour Representation Committee, which aimed to create a distinct Labour Group in Parliament, and eventually became the modern Labour Party. The Socialist League collapsed in 1890, but the labour movement in Leeds was set for a period of rapid development, and working-class support for the Liberals began to decline noticeably. The Leeds socialists had made contact with the wider working-class movement, and had been instrumental in the formation of the local branch of the Gas Workers' and General Labourers' Union. In 1892 the East Hunslet Independent Labour Club was set up and soon there were seven such clubs. In November of that year 40 delegates met and formed the Leeds Independent Labour Party, but for the rest of the decade it lacked strength because it excluded the Leeds Trades Council and the town's wider labour movement. If Leeds workers were to gain their own representatives on the council and in Parliament, what was required was an organisation which would unify them. In 1900 the Leeds Trades Council affiliated to the national Labour Representation Committee, initially seeing it as a body which would work in co-operation with the Liberal Party. But, after pushing from the Leeds Independent Labour Party, the newly established Leeds branch of the Labour Representation Committee established itself as an alliance which included all trade union and socialist organisations, but which specifically excluded the Liberal Party.

By 1903 the Leeds Labour Representation Committee had won the right to speak politically for the labour movement in Leeds, and in that year the first 'Labour' councillor was elected to the city council. By 1909, 47 different trade unions and 16 political associations (including ward Labour representation committees, the Independent Labour Party, socialist clubs, and Women's Labour League branches), representing a total membership of 11,232, were affiliated to the Leeds Labour Representation Committee.[180] The Labour movement was on the road to power in its own right.

Transforming the City 1870-1900

In many respects the second half of Victoria's reign brought a major transformation in the public face of Leeds; one wrought by the combined efforts of the local authority and private enterprise. The period brought increased elegance and style to the public streets, a much improved and wider range of public amenities, and considerable justification for the official designation of Leeds as a city by the charter granted by Queen Victoria in 1893. The role of the town council in all this was very considerable and represented a quite remarkable achievement. The progress made towards transforming the private face of Leeds, however, was much less laudable. Although very important measures were taken from the 1860s to improve essential services associated with private housing, it was not until the tail end of the nineteenth century that the problem of the slums was whole-heartedly addressed.

The Slums

When considering the private face of Leeds, it is important to remember that this was the great age of 'laissez-faire' and belief in leaving the market and private enterprise to solve problems. By the standards of the day, in providing a basic network of main sewers and a goodish water supply, not to mention new burial grounds, the council had by the 1860s already undertaken some quite radical and commendable ventures. On the other hand, its failure to intervene decisively in the sphere of private housing was a major shortcoming which continued throughout the nineteenth century.

In spite of the great expectations raised by the Leeds Improvement Act of 1842, it was a sad indictment that more than thirty years after Baker's Statistical Committee Report of 1839 had identified the problem of the slums, most still existed in 1870 and were still there in 1900. The extension of Kirkgate Market had by chance cleared a few slums,[181] as had the cutting of the railway viaduct across the town in 1868-9,[182] but there was no slum-clearance policy. In the late 1860s the council at last began to take the first tentative steps towards effective regulation of house building and housing conditions. These steps, however, were to remain tentative. Though the Leeds Improvement Act of 1866 permitted the formulation of a detailed code of building bye-laws, against the national trend the council refused to prohibit the building of back-to-back houses. It settled for introducing a slight departure from existing practice by insisting that they be built in blocks of no more than four pairs, with each block separated by a space 'free from any erection above the level of the ground, excepting privies'.[183] Later regulations increased the air space, but the 1866 standards remained essentially unmodified for over 40 years. The erection of mean streets of housing, with a high density of inhabitants per acre and the potential to become slums, was to persist. Right up to 1909 the council successfully resisted the efforts of national government to have the building of new back-to-backs banned in Leeds as they were in almost every other town in the country.[184]

Under the Leeds Improvement Act of 1870 the council first obtained powers of slum clearance, but its record of clearance was extremely poor over succeeding years. Between 1871 and 1885 only 247 houses and 67 cellar dwellings were demolished, most of these in the vicinity of Kirkgate Market. Not only were these clearances a drop in the ocean, but, since the council provided no alternative accommodation, the 1,700 or so people they displaced had little alternative but to seek refuge in the remaining already overcrowded slums in the neighbourhood. In the 1870s the board of guardians

Archetypal rows of Leeds '8 block' back-to-backs with occasional through terraces. This view has Carlton Street in the foreground and looks across to All Souls' Church, Blackman Lane.

claimed that the scarcity of working-class dwellings was forcing people to seek admission to the workhouse, and in response the town clerk recommended that cheap land on the outskirts of the town should be purchased to build houses for the 'very poor' – but nothing happened.[185]

Almost certainly the council was deterred from slum clearance by its high cost. The Victorians' fierce protection of private property rights ensured that the owners of compulsorily purchased property often received double its true value. In 1890, however, this changed when the Housing of the Working Classes Act permitted councils to buy up slum property at 'fair market values'. The Act allowed councils to discount valuations based on rentals which were artificially high because the properties were overcrowded with tenants, and to make deductions for defective sanitation and dilapidations.

The opportunity to buy property on these improved terms, coupled with the increasing electoral strength of the Conservatives and a more general acceptance of high council expenditures, led the Liberal council at long last to embark on two extensive slum clearance schemes. In 1895 the York Street insanitary area scheme, comprising 16 acres and the homes of 4,000 people, was launched, and the purchase, though not the demolition, was completed in 1900. Meanwhile, the Quarry Hill insanitary area scheme covering 50 acres with 9,000 residents was also canvassed. Property purchases began in 1902. Combined with the adjacent York Street area, the council soon owned 67 acres of the worst slums in Leeds comprising the area bounded by Quarry Hill on the north, Mabgate beck on the east, Marsh Lane on the south and St Peter's Street on the west.

The intention was to gradually demolish these slums over a number of years. By 1914 three-quarters of the York Street area and half the Quarry Hill area had been cleared. In certain respects it was just as well that the clearance was slow, for the council found it uneconomical to provide alternative accommodation at rent levels which this class of poor displaced tenants could afford. By 1900 the only accommodation built was houses for 906 people at the Ivy Lodge estate and two small blocks of tenements on the edge of York Street. The council pleaded with the government to give it permission to build the most economical housing it knew of – back-to-backs – on the York Street site, but it was refused.[186]

Despite the appalling inaction on the slums, the council undertook some highly commendable work associated with housing. Though it refused in the mid-1870s to create a bye-law prohibiting the provision of privy-and-ashpits as opposed to water closets in new properties (and it was not until 1899 that water closets were made compulsory), from the 1870s the sanitary committee began a systematic campaign against 'the abominable middenstead and cesspool'. This combined with rising standards of new housing led to a rapid increase in the number of houses, both new and old, with

W.C.s. In 1870 only 6,348 houses had them, but by 1884 the number had risen to 20,281, and by 1901 four-fifths of the town's houses had them. Very major progress too was made in the provision of sewers (nearly £600,000 was spent on sewers between 1877 and 1900) and the main system of sewers was gradually extended to the whole of the borough. In the 1880s and 1890s approximately 120 miles of sewers were built in each decade.[187]

New Markets and Public Utilities

The council made very important additions to the provision of public services and amenities in the late Victorian period, even if at times it was rather hesistant to act. Though Kirkgate Market had been extensively improved in the 1850s, the growth of demand was such that in 1875 a major new extension was built behind the market hall, known to contemporaries as Leeds New Market.[188] It included ninety shops, two blocks of wholesale shops, a market square, and a new fish market which replaced the old and inadequate premises near the Shambles. Likewise, increases in the livestock trade made the 5 acre Smithfield Cattle Market too small and in 1886 the council replaced it with the extensive new Victoria Cattle Market on a 16 acre site in Gelderd Road, south of the town centre, at a cost of £43,357.[189] The delapidated state of the Shambles and the squalor and public health risks associated with the five or six slaughter houses in the yards on the east side of Briggate was a cause of growing concern. The principal key to solving this problem was provided when the council built the fine Wholesale Meat Market and Abattoir in Harper Street, just behind the Kirkgate Market, in 1898-9 at a cost of £25,809. As the brochure celebrating the opening pointed out: 'Under these circumstances it was obvious that the provision of premises adequate in area, centrally situated, and conveniently constructed could not be delayed, if Leeds was to retain its position as the important meat centre of the North.' The new premises cost £25,809.[190]

Kirkgate Market in 1883, showing the general produce market and Block Shops of 1875 which stood behind the market hall.

The most spectacular addition of the period was the City Markets, built in 1902-04. In 1893 the Central Market had been severely damaged by fire and, although the building remained partly in use, it was resolved to demolish it in the near future. Around the same time the need for widening Vicar Lane had become urgent. This combination of circumstances, and an increasing volume of trade, resulted in a scheme for rebuilding Kirkgate Covered Market. In 1898 the council authorised the erection of a new market hall. The shops and 'open square' at the back of the existing hall were covered over, then in 1902 the hall was demolished and work began on its replacement. The City Markets were opened in 1904

Turn of the century view of the Corn Exchange, built 1860-3 (architect, Cuthbert Brodrick), and the recently widened Duncan Street, with a lady descending from one of the stylish new electric trams.

An artist's impression in 1901 of Leeming and Leeming's design for the new Borough Market.

and consisted of a hall with 18 shops fronting the main roads and an open area inside, occupied by stalls and surrounded by small shops. Its upper storeys housed a hotel, a restaurant and billiard, coffee and club rooms. The cost of the project was £116,750.[191]

Over the same period as these market improvements were undertaken, the council moved into the provision of public utilities in a big way. In 1870 the council was empowered to buy the town's two gas companies.[192] Since it had already absorbed the functions of the highway surveyors and was buying out the bridge and turnpike trusts in the borough, buying out the gas companies, which frequently dug up the roads to lay pipes, was a logical part of establishing absolute control over the highways. An even more tempting incentive, however, was the prospect of bringing to an end the collusion between the gas companies, which brought them a comfortable monopolist's profit. As a major consumer of gas for street lighting, the council might now obtain a cheap supply of gas and supply cheaper gas to the public, whilst receiving a healthy profit. The transaction cost the council £763,245 and, with occasional exceptions, did prove a profitable one.

In 1869 a private company announced its intention to promote an Act to allow it to operate a tramway in Leeds. The council's initial reaction was to consider opposing the bill and applying for powers to establish its own trams, but the government's Tramway Act of 1870 forbade councils to run their own trams. In 1872 a private tram company was established and the Leeds horse trams began operation. The council, nevertheless, was empowered to purchase the track and rolling stock after 21 years, and in response to damage to the town's road caused by the new steam trams, in 1894 it did so at a cost of £112,226.

Unable to find a suitable private operator, the council took on the permanent management of the trams. The result was cheaper fares, aided by electrification, and more passengers. In 1895, 10.5 million passengers were carried each year and this number increased to 93.7 million by 1914. By 1914, the track had increased from 22 miles to 114 miles and the total capital expended amounted to £1.5 million. The trams, however, were not cheap – they catered for the suburbanite rather than the working man. Even as late as 1914 only 7 per cent of passengers were taking advantage of early morning working men's fares.[193]

During the national boom in the promotion of electric lighting companies in the early 1880s, the council dithered over whether it might provide electricity and electric lighting itself. Instead, in 1891 the private Yorkshire House-to-House Electricity Company was established. The profitability of the company and the mess it made of the town's streets demonstrated the short-sightedness of the council, and in 1895 it bought out the company, thus taking on yet another municipal function.[194]

The council's prime motives in taking over the four major public utilities – water, gas, electricity and the trams – in the Victorian period were consistent: in each case there existed a local monopoly of supply, obvious or disguised; likewise all four utilities interfered with its statutory duty of maintaining the highways.

Creating the Shopping Centre of the North

One of the most startling achievements of the last three decades of the nineteenth century was the improvement of the appearance and the width of the town's streets. This was the result of the combined efforts of private enterprise and the council. As we noted in Chapter Five, the streets were dignified by the erection of premises for banks, insurance companies, and other commercial and financial institutions, as well as a number of hotels. At the same time they were greatly improved by new shopping facilities which were encouraged by road improvement schemes. The most important were associated with Boar Lane, Briggate and Vicar Lane. The first really major initiative came in 1868 with the Boar Lane Improvement Scheme, which widened the street from a mere 21 feet to 66 feet and produced the impressive street which is familiar to us today.[195].

Boar Lane had Leeds' finest and most fashionable shops. The middle classes, wishing to avoid the market,

Boar Lane at its junction with Briggate on Market Day in 1872. Despite the widening of Boar Lane it remained a bustling crossroads.

shopped at 'Mr Richard Boston's Great Fruit, Game and Fish Market' which occupied a prime site opposite Holy Trinity Church. In 1894 Waddington's Guide to Leeds waxed lyrically about the establishment.

> The sight of Mr Boston's stock is enough to shorten an epicure's breath and give an appetite to the most dyspeptic. Everyday needs and Sybaritic taste are alike provided for. Does the reader seek fish? Here he finds 50 varieties. Does he want birds? There is scarcely a wing that flutters in life that may not be found drooping here in its season. Does he need poultry? Let him ask and he can have. Thirty-six varieties of vegetables, one hundred sorts of fruit, a selection of luxuries too numerous to name and a business-like briskness in attention to the smallest order are within the customer's reach.

One of the most celebrated shops in Boar Lane was Alexander Monteith's Grand Pygmalion which, when it

R. Boston & Sons' shop on Boar Lane.

opened in the 1880s, heralded the arrival of a new concept in shopping – the department store. His 200 employees pandered to the needs of his middle-class customers who flocked to the store in droves. As an advertising feature of 1888 explained: 'The Grand Pygmalion contains four lofty and commodious floors, and these are replete with the various interesting and attractive features of a stock so extensive and so comprehensive that detailed description of it is quite impracticable.' The showrooms provided for the leading departments were 'of elegant appointment and careful arrangement', and everywhere the goods were displayed with 'consummate taste and effect'. A description of the stock reads like a catalogue of the Victorian middle classes' household requirements:

> Mantles, dolmans, and jackets, costumes, children's costumes, silks, millinery, prints, dress goods, heavy drapery, curtains, decorative upholstery and furnishing drapery, fancy drapery, ladies' hosiery, corsets, bags and purse bags, ladies' underclothing, baby linen, ladies' vests, ladies' boots, gloves and umbrellas, mourning goods, sunshades and parasols, art needlework, haberdashery and trimmings, gentlemen's hosiery, boys' sailor suits, carpets, bedding, bedsteads, and all house furniture. [Not forgetting to mention] the large and choice stock of earthenware reproductions of the beautiful old Dresden and Derby patterns. These are superb goods, comprising many fine table services, bread trays, vases and pedestal flower pots, tables, figures, plaques, cheese dishes, baskets, &c., &c.'[196]

The Grand Pygmalion, Boar Lane, one of the first department stores. Today the site is occupied by C & A.

From the late 1870s the middle classes could enjoy the novelty of shopping in arcades. Thornton's Arcade opened in 1878, and such was its success, it was followed by the Queen's Arcade (1888-9), the Grand Arcade (1896-8) and the Victoria Arcade (1898).[197] The most spectacular, however, resulted from the fortunate coincidence of the council's desire to build a new market hall and widen Vicar Lane, and a private company's desire to build a major complex of shops, including an

The Leeds Estate Company's stunning redevelopment of the area between Upper Briggate and Vicar Lane in 1898-1900. The scheme included the creation of the County Arcade, King Edward Street, Queen Victoria Street, and the Empire Theatre which opened in 1898 and was eventually demolished in 1962.

arcade and theatre on the site north of Kirkgate between Briggate and Vicar Lane. In 1897 Leeds Estates Company was formed to redevelop a large section of the west side of Vicar Lane and the east side of Briggate. The council assisted its progress by compulsorily purchasing all the Bazaar and Shambles estate and selling it on to the company, which, when this was added to its other land purchases, was able to build the sumptuous County Arcade with the adjacent Cross Arcade (1898-1903) and the splendid Empire Theatre. Their architect Frank Matcham had designed over a hundred theatres and music halls, including the London Palladium. The council for its part was able to open King Edward Street and Queen Victoria Street, around which the complex of buildings stood, and to widen Vicar Lane from 27 feet to 75 feet.[198] The effect was stunning. When these improvements were added to the development of Duncan Street and the magnificent new Leeds City Market, the 1909 Leeds Shopping Guide could comment with little exaggeration:

> No city in England can boast a more wonderful transformation than that witnessed in Leeds during the past two or three decades . . .The centre of Leeds has been practically re-carved and polished. Nearly the whole of the ramshackle property that skirted the east side of Briggate has been demolished, and on the site has been erected a class of shop property that would do credit to any city in the country. With the offices in Park Row, East Parade and South Parade almost equal improvements have been made, while for some time past there seems to have been a wholesome rivalry amongst the owners of shop property in Commercial Street to remodel their premises in the most up-to-date and withal artistic lines. Boar Lane, Duncan Street and Vicar Lane reveal equally amazing individual enterprise.[199]

Street widening was absolutely essential not only to increase the grandeur of the town but to deal with the major increase in the volume of traffic. From the late 1870s traffic control became necessary. In 1878 letters had been sent to the council complaining about the danger caused to pedestrians crossing the Briggate end of Boar Lane by the heavy traffic. It was suggested that a policeman should be stationed in the centre of that street to direct traffic and assist pedestrians. As a result, for the first time the Leeds police became involved in traffic duties.[200]

In his annual report in 1895 the Chief Constable pointed out the traffic problems on Commercial Street and Bond Street: 'There, on the very busiest days and at the very busiest hours, may be seen the heaviest traffic, including carts from the Sanitary Department, handcarts, carriages, and even cattle being driven, the consequence is that very often there is a complete block of traffic for some minutes.' In 1897 he recommended the exclusion of heavy vehicles from these streets between 12 noon and 3 p.m. – the first step towards the pedestrianisation which occurred 70 years later. In January 1898 a count of traffic was made on Briggate for a ten minute period from 8.20 p.m. to 8.30 p.m., the figures were 2,306 pedestrians, 3 omnibuses, 10 tramcars, 3 four-wheeled cabs, 6 hansoms and 2 post mail carts.[201]

Late Victorian Recreation and Culture

The council and private enterprise were to bring very considerable resources to a major enhancement of public recreation and culture in the city during the second half of the Victorian period. Leeds adopted the Public Libraries Act in 1869, and the lending department of the Central Library opened in April 1872.[202] The Public Library began to collect items of local interest. One of its most important purchases was William Boyne's 'History of Leeds'. Boyne (1813-93) had taken T. D. Whitaker's *Loidis and Elmete* and his second edition of Thoresby's *Ducatus*, both published in 1816, and had added to them illustrations by John and Joseph Rhodes, William Bowman, J. Greig and others, as well as 14 drawings and deeds once in Thoresby's museum. Formerly, expensive books and priceless paintings had been available only to the élite of the town. Now through the Public Libraries they were made available to all. Colonel Harding, owner of Tower Works, worked long and hard for the creation of the Leeds Art Gallery, which eventually opened in 1888.[203] The library's fine collection was soon to be housed in the imposing new Municipal Buildings erected in Calverley Street and opened in 1884 to the designs of George Corson. The new City Art Gallery was added to

George Corson's imaginative design for the Grand Theatre which opened in 1878.

The official opening of the Municipal Buildings, built 1878-84 to the designs of George Corson. The aim was to bring all the council administration under one roof.

Leeds Art Gallery, built 1887-8, as it appeared at its opening in 1888 (architect, W.H.Thorp).

the Municipal Buildings in 1887-8, this time with William Thorp as the architect. The *Illustrated London News* said of it: 'All the new rooms …are lighted from the roof, and their walls are in maroon of dead texture, which shows off the pictures and their gilt frames to best effect'.[204]

In the purely private sphere, the destruction by fire of the Hunslet Lane theatre in 1875 provided the opportunity for the formation of a company to build a theatre worthy of the town and of 'the support of the best people'. The Grand Theatre and Opera House, which opened in New Briggate in November 1878, was hailed as one of the finest and handsomest theatres outside London. With its pit and orchestra stalls, dress circle, upper box circle, amphitheatre, gallery, 8 stage boxes, and 22 private or family boxes, it could seat 3,150 people. Its auditorium was sumptuously decorated, as it is today, in a stunning crimson and gold. It was quickly hailed as a worthy companion to the Town Hall. Ordinary admission prices ranged from three guineas for the stage boxes to sixpence in the gallery. For the serious theatre-goer 'Much Ado About Nothing' was performed, whereas 'Bluebird the Grand', or Harlequin's 'The Amorous Ameer of Afghanistan' appealed to the family market, particularly appropriate and topical with the Afghan War still raging. The theatre was a success and in April 1898 two great music hall favourites, Marie Lloyd and Little Tich, graced its stage.[205] Competition came from the Empire, Briggate, which opened on 29 August 1898, and became a regular venue for many of the popular artists of the day.[206]

Meanwhile the Town Hall continued to provide the major venue for classical music. The Leeds Musical Festivals had the honour of Sir Arthur Sullivan as their conductor from 1880 to 1898. His melodramatic behaviour made a huge impact as one concert goer recalled:

> It was a thrilling experience – the excitement of going, the large Victoria Hall filling up with people elegantly dressed, the lovely flowers of the decorations, the Orchestra and the Chorus assembling all made a brilliant scene …After the conclusion of *The Golden Legend*, which Sir Arthur Sullivan had written specially for the festival of 1886, the audience applauded with the greatest enthusiasm. Madame Albani who had been singing, [was] smiling and clapping her little gloved hands. The chorus rose to their feet, waved, and gave round after round of applause. Sir Arthur turned and bowed his acknowledgement to the audience, then back again, bowed to the Orchestra and Chorus, and then just laid his head down on his desk and wept.[207]

Today one of the glories of Leeds is its parks and recreational facilities. The enlightened and far-sighted initiatives which have produced this wonderful endowment were largely undertaken in the mid- to late Victorian period by the combined efforts of the council and private enterprise. In 1855 the council had begun creating public parks when it purchased what contemporaries described as 'the lungs of Leeds' –

Woodhouse Moor.[208] This provided the working classes with facilities which hitherto they had lacked. Most houses had no garden and there were no parks or nearby open spaces for sport. On Sundays crowds of between eight and ten thousand people – often family groups – could be found strolling on the moor while the band played sacred music.[209] This enlightened purchase was complemented by the acquisition of Bramley Park in 1870, Woodhouse Ridge in 1876, part of Holbeck Moor in 1878, and Hunslet Moor in 1879. From the 1880s the council began to make regular purchases of land to create recreation grounds in all parts of the borough.[210]

These purchases were particularly beneficial because of the rapidly increasing popularity of organised sport. On 7 March 1864 an advert appeared in the *Leeds Mercury*: 'Football. Wanted a number of persons to form a football club for playing on Woodhouse Moor for a few days a week from 7 to 8 o'clock a.m.' There was an enthusiastic response, despite the hour, and it soon became necessary to arrange additional evening matches. The formation of the Football Association in 1863 had at least produced an attempt to sort out common rules. Little football, however, was played in Leeds. Instead by the 1880s, nearly every church ran its own rugby club.[211] The clergy were active in encouraging this pastime, luring the working man away from the temptation of drinking, gambling and dancing. In 1870 St John's Church (New Briggate) formed a club, playing first on cinders at the Militia barracks, and then on Cardigan Fields in Burley.

It was at this time that private enterprise, complementing the council's provisions, created perhaps its most important legacy to Leeds in the sphere of public recreation. Leeds lacked a sports ground for big events, in particular, the new national attractions, cricket test matches. Several leading business men, among them W.L.Jackson, MP, W.B.Nicholson, the builder, J.Watmough, the printer, and C.F.Tetley, the brewer, banded together in 1888 to purchase Lot 17A of the Cardigan Estates and resolved to transform it into one of the most magnificent cricket and football enclosures in the country. They formed the Leeds Cricket, Football and Athletics Company. The hallowed turf of Headingley had been created. The Leeds St John's rugby football club became the football section of the new company at the end of the 1889-90 season. The first match at the ground took place on 20 September 1890. Initially a Rugby Union club, the club changed to the Rugby League code in 1897-8. The Yorkshire County Cricket Club first played on their part of the ground in 1890, but it was to be another 13 years before Headingley became its headquarters.[212] Hunslet Rugby League Football Club had its roots in a cricket club started in 1856, and played at Woodhouse Hill. Holbeck, Headingley and Bramley all had clubs, but they played according to Rugby Union rules and were non-professional.[213]

The most popular commercial open space in Leeds was just to the west of Woodhouse Moor. Tommy Clapham's Royal Park had a huge dance floor for dancing parties, a well stocked conservatory with foreign birds and grounds to stroll through, but at Whitsuntide 1870 he organised a special gala:

> There will be balloon ascents each day, by Professor Jackson, the brothers Autoleon, from the Imperial Circus, at Paris, will go through some marvellous performances, Mr. Guy Linton, the celebrated vocalist, will be a host in himself in comic entertainments, and from the Sisters Rushbrook much graceful dancing may be expected. Miss Dalton, the London vocalist, has also been engaged. Then there is Professor Burniman, "the Man of Mystery and Necromantic Nondescript", and his educated dogs. Mr Norman's old Punch and Judy, Davis's Marionettes, and Professor Caldwell, the firework artiste. On Monday and Tuesday there will be horse and donkey races. The Royal Park, the Bramley, the Steam Plough, and the Leeds Operatic String bands having been engaged, there will be no lack of good music.[214]

This was a good outing for the whole family and broke the monotony of everyday life. But in 1875 half of the 20-acre site was sold for building ground, and the other half was bought by the Leeds Horticultural Gardens company, which provided an indoor skating rink, a bowling green, gymnasium, cricket pitch, lawns, a conservatory, vinery, brewery, refreshment rooms, and a concert hall and ballroom. But once again these gardens failed and were sold in 1884 and were soon covered by bricks and mortar.[215]

Whilst we might lament the loss of the Royal Park, in the early 1870s the council made a momentous decision which has benefitted Leeds to this day. In 1871 it made the very major purchase of the Nicholson family's 773 acre estate, at a cost of £127,000, to create Roundhay Park. The park remained essentially the playground of the middle classes until 1891 when the electric tram brought it within the reach of the masses. Before this, people had had to

Left: Badges worn by rugby club supporters.

Below: The Royal Park, situated on the north-west side of Woodhouse Moor.

Above: With the introduction of cheap tram travel in 1891, Roundhay Park could at last be reached by the working classes.

Right: 1882 cartoon of John Barran leading his 'White Elephant' (Roundhay Park). The caption read 'Little ixey, wixey Jumbo, did 'em naughty rate payers think they were going to get him for nothing?'

hire hansom cabs to take them out to enjoy the splendour of the lakes, woods, and open parkland. So few could afford the journey and so vast had been the expenditure that it was branded a 'white elephant' with one critic remarking that 'it would be just as sensible to buy Blubberhouses Moor as Roundhay Park'.[216] Another wit placed an advert in the press proclaiming: 'Lost: Eighty Thousand Pound and Upwards, at Roundhay Park by the Ratepayers of Leeds: Anyone finding the same please restore it to the purchaser of the park.'[217] John Barran, the key figure responsible for its acquisition, had a perceptive vision: 'Future generations will remember us with gratitude as they stroll along the pleasant walks and enjoy the ease and the shade of the trees.'[218] Another very important acquisition was the ruins and grounds of Kirkstall Abbey which in 1888 were purchased for £10,000 by Colonel North, who then returned the money to the town.[219].

By this period the Leeds temperance societies were well aware that to retain their following they must provide decent entertainment and they made good use of the town's recreational facilities. In 1892 the Sunday evening meetings of the Leeds United Men's Temperance League were held in the Grand Assembly Rooms, Briggate (presumably those attached to the Grand Theatre) and attracted audiences in the winter months of nearly 2,000 people. On Saturday nights, special Grand Concerts were organised to provide good amusement away from public houses and singing saloons. The 1892 Annual Report noted that the league had held 313 meetings with an estimated total attendance of over 200,000 people. But not all its events were successful. The Sports Day held on 2 July 1892 in the Hunslet Football Ground proved a disaster, perhaps in part because it coincided with the General Election and poor weather. The organisers commented 'we are not in the habit of having failures in our work, but to this we can write in capital letters - Nothing in our line in the future'.[220]

Clearly, the council wished to promote orderly public recreation and to discourage activities of which it disapproved. It regarded amusement fairs as centres of vice, and banned them on council-owned land. But the fairs survived! Indeed, in the 1880s they were held in greater numbers than they ever had been.[221] Leeds Fair and the feasts on Holbeck, Hunslet and Woodhouse Moor provided thrilling entertainment. People flocked in their thousands to go on the swing boats, roundabouts and flying boxes, try their luck in the boxing ring and shooting tents, or marvel at the weird and wonderful side shows where they could see the bearded lady, the giant rat, the harem girls and the like. Stalls selling fruit, nuts, brandy snaps, hot peas, gob stoppers, toffee apples and parkin pigs kept them well fed.[222] Travelling shows like Wombwell's Menagerie and Pablo Fanque's Circus often visited the town, though the visit of Buffalo Bill Cody's Wild West Show in 1903 was a spectacle many were to remember for the rest of their lives.[223]

Victorian Overview

The phenomenal success of Leeds as a centre of wealth creation in Victorian England is manifest. While in the early decades of the nineteenth century commentators on the town's economic progress focussed on the advent of the factory system, in the Victorian period their imagination was captured by the evolution of the town as a whole. It was a highly responsive organism continuously evolving and adapting to meet the economic demands and opportunities of the age. When railways became the thing, it invested in them. When more sophisticated financial institutions were required, it enthusiastically welcomed them. When new products or markets beckoned, its industry and commerce seized the openings. The introductory remarks made in the *Leeds Mercury*'s supplement of 1887 celebrating Queen Victoria's Golden Jubilee seem appropriate to the entire Victorian period:

> When the people of Leeds look back over the fifty years that have elapsed since Her Majesty ascended the throne, and take note of the progress which the town has made during the period, feelings of pride and gratitude must surely possess them. From whatever point we make the survey the advance has been remarkable ...The gratifying result is due to many causes. Like other West Riding communities we have had not a few natural advantages. We have cultivated a variety of industries which have had the world for a market. The management of these has been characterised by great enterprise and tenacity of purpose. The working people, inheriting the qualities of their fathers, and of their mothers, too, have been apt, skilful, and industrious. Like the nation at large, we have shared in the advantages of Free Trade, railways, improved ocean carriage, telegraphs, and the like. Our popular local self-government has been a powerful aid to industrial and social advancement; and while efforts are ever being made to achieve a higher civic life, there are few towns possessing institutions more calculated to promote the well-being of the community than are those of Leeds. The mainspring of the prosperity has unquestionably been our manufactures, with all the qualities and resources which have contributed to their success. All else has been subsidiary, and for the most part it is an industrial triumph that has to be recorded.[224]

Yet the press and writers of the day were above all addressing a middle-class readership, and the middle-class view of Victoria's reign was likely to put something of a rosy glow on the events of almost seven decades. How did the experience of the middle classes and working classes compare? Did all classes benefit from the vast wealth which the town generated? The great majority of the middle classes were by definition comfortably off. The increase in their numbers, and the great leap in the number of business concerns and properties from which they derived their incomes, were testament to their progressively enhanced prosperity. As the decades passed the increase in the numbers of luxurious shops, well-appointed houses, and high quality amenities to meet their needs demonstrated their increased purchasing power. There can be no doubt that up to the 1870s increased smoke pollution, sanitary problems and urban overcrowding adversely affected the quality of the daily lives of the large numbers of the middle classes who remained in the town centre, but thereafter even those of comparatively modest means had the opportunity to move out.

The standard of living of the working classes charted a less certain course. There was only a very modest increase in both their nominal and real wage levels over the period from around 1837 to the 1850s – perhaps 10-15 per cent for certain types of workers – though possibly the proportion of the population employed in the better-paid occupations grew.[225] Given the severity of the periodic slumps in the economy and the high levels of unemployment they brought, many of the working classes continued to live on the brink of disaster. The insanitary conditions of life in Leeds township and poor diet continued to be reflected in a high death rate which remained at around 29-30 per thousand from the beginning of the century up to 1870, with a short-lived dip to around 27 per thousand in the mid-1850s.[226] Contrast this with a death rate of around 11-12 per thousand today. These factors, combined with the perpetuation of appalling work-place experiences and squalid domestic living conditions, meant that for many of the working classes, life remained very unpleasant well beyond the middle of the century.

By the late-1850s, however, for significant sections of the working classes, there were signs of improvement in health, if they could escape the epidemics of cholera and typhus, and the ever present tuberculosis, typhoid and dysentery. Robert Baker in his 1858 report observed:

> There can be no doubt of the improved healthiness of Leeds ...Though much of this altered condition may be, and I believe is, attributable to sewerage which has wisely threaded these dense populations first, yet other causes operating within the same period may have also tended to the same result; such, for instance, as compulsory vaccination, the decrease of cellar occupancies, migration to better ventilated districts, better regulations as to hours of work, improved wages, temperance societies, a higher social and intellectual state, or a better knowledge of the general laws of life, disseminated by lectures, cheap publications, and Institutes for mutual improvement; all of which remedial elements Leeds possesses in an eminent degree.[227]

It was from the late-1860s onwards, however, that there was a much more distinct and sustained improvement in the condition of the broad mass of the working classes – an improvement which was both physical and cultural. The Jubilee Supplement of the *Leeds Mercury in 1887* commented:

> In the whole of our tolerably comprehensive review of the progress of Leeds during the half-century there is nothing more gratifying than the remarkable improvement that has taken place in the social condition of the working people. The lot of many at the present time may excite commiseration but that of even the poorest must be more endurable than the condition of the great mass when the Queen ascended the throne, and for many years afterwards ...During the last twenty years especially a remarkable advance has been made by the working class. Within that time they have acquired the franchise, educational advantages have been multiplied, wages have increased, dwellings have been improved, the cost of food, clothing, and almost all other necessaries of life have become less, the means of recreation have been increased, mills and workshops are better regulated – in nearly every respect there has been considerable amelioration. During the half-century wages have probably increased from 20 to 40 per cent. Butcher's meat is

dearer and house-rents higher, but in most other respects the circumstances have much improved. The provision which has been made for "the rainy day" proves this indisputably.[228]

The purchasing power of the working classes' wages increased by between around one-fifth and two-fifths over the period, principally in the second half of the century.[229] Moreover, the material, cultural and political gains from the late 1860s, noted by *Jubilee Supplement*, were genuine. Nevertheless, progress was being made from a very low base. The preceding pages have given ample evidence of the squalor, poverty, appallingly low pay, and terrible living conditions which significant sections of the working classes still endured at the close of Victoria's reign. By 1900 the death rate in Leeds township had fallen from the 29-30 per thousand of 1870 to around 23 per thousand.[230] This was very major progress, but it was still very high by today's standards.

One of the most fundamental changes in Leeds in the period was the process of suburbanisation. In the last three decades of the century central Leeds declined in relative importance as a residential location. While the borough population grew from 259,212 in 1871 to 428,968 in 1901 (an increase of 169,756), under 40,000 of this increase occurred in Leeds township. Virtually all the out-townships at least doubled their populations in these years.[231] As the *Leeds Mercury Jubilee Supplement* remarked:

Of late years great numbers belonging to nearly all classes, have left the more crowded parts of the town, and gone out to the suburbs to live. This is one of the most notable, and, in many respects, beneficial changes which have taken place in the life of the town.[232]

From the 1870s onwards, higher real incomes, shorter working hours, and an expansion of public transport enabled the lower middle classes and the better-off members of the working classes to join the upper middle classes in the northern suburbs. Former villages were engulfed with modern housing occupied by people who had no traditional village ties. Typical was the astonishing growth of Headingley-cum-Burley and Potternewton. The population of Headingley trebled between 1871 and 1901 to over 41,000, while Potternewton grew a remarkable seven-fold to over 26,000. Headingley lost some its select middle-class status as terraces and even a few back-to-backs were built there. The middle classes whom this frightened away, often moved out into Weetwood and Chapel Allerton or beyond the borough boundary into Adel and Roundhay.

Apart from the northern suburbs, a remarkable increase in population also took place in the industrial township of Hunslet, numbers doubling to 69,000 in 1901, while the predominantly working-class township of Armley trebled its population to 27,000 by 1901. D. B. Foster writing in 1897 about housing in Leeds commented on the change in these old industrial villages:

Leeds is made up of many smaller places which have quite a separate life and history. Holbeck, Hunslet, Armley, and several other old villages, while forming part of the larger Leeds, are still on many points as distinct as if they were distant towns, which the rivalry between these places in the world of sport will readily prove. There are people still living who can remember when these places stood altogether apart from Leeds ...Now all this is changed by the intervening spaces being filled up with many thousands of houses; these old villages thus becoming part of the great and crowded City ...The old village property forms some of the worst parts of Slumdom, its lowness and irregularity, coupled with its lack of proper sanitary arrangements, making it very dark and unhealthy. When these houses were surrounded by gardens and fields no doubt they were fairly comfortable homes, but now, hemmed in by higher and more closely-packed buildings, they form a very serious item in the slum problem.[233]

Throughout the discussion of the Victorian period, Leeds has usually been referred to as a town, though, by a host of measures, it manifestly had become a great city. This is because Leeds did not officially become a city until 1893. Civic pride naturally produced civic rivalry. In 1858 Leeds had opened the most magnificent provincial town hall in the country and in 1864 had become an assize town, much to the annoyance of its competitor, Sheffield. In 1888 it had been one of the original ten county boroughs created under the Local Government Act of that year. But, while Birmingham became a city the following year, Leeds had its application in 1890 turned down. Perhaps Leeds councillors were not unduly worried, but in 1892, when they heard that Sheffield was considering applying for a city charter, their claim was rapidly revived. On 5 February 1893 the town clerk was instructed to read a concisely worded memorial to the Queen. The case for Leeds was extemely strong, the petition informed her Majesty that Leeds was the fourth largest municipality in the country and emphasised its antiquity and importance as the capital of the West Riding.

On 6 February 1893 telegrams were sent to both Leeds and Sheffield confirming that they had succeeded in securing city status. Such had been the speed with which the charter had been obtained that there simply had not been time to organise widespread celebrations. The élite could rejoice at the Lord Mayor's Reception and Ball on 10 February, but for the ordinary working man there was nothing. Many expressed complete surprise at the news. On 13 February 1893 Queen Victoria formally sealed the charter and Leeds officially became a city.[234] The *Yorkshire Owl's* weekly diarist voiced a view with which many Leeds loiners no doubt had considerable agreement:

Tuesday. Rummy thing happens. Went to bed last night a mere burgess. Wake up to find am a real citizen. Shouldn't have known this but for the newspaper. See no difference in the town – I mean city. Breakfast as usual – same old bacon and eggs. Same wind on the moor, blowing all the bacca out of your pipe. Meet same girls. Give'em same wink. Get the usual smile back. See the same hollow-eyed crowd hurrying to the same old treadmill, uttering the same old curse against having to get up early. Town – city, should say – just as dirty and dreary and depressing as ever. No difference at all. Yet Leeds is raised to the 'dignity and status' of a city. All the papers careful to explain advantages of the honour. Seem to chiefly consist of sentiment, which warn't butter any parsnips.[235]

The designation of Leeds as a city had one immediate virtue – it solved the problem of finding a name for the new square which the 'City Council', as it was now known, was planning to create at the junction of Park

Colonel T.W.Harding, manufacturer of cards, combs and steel pins at Tower Works, was Lord Mayor of Leeds in 1898-9 and prime mover behind the creation of Leeds Art Gallery and City Square.

Row and Quebec Street. On 14 February 1893 the mayor, Alderman Ward, proposed that it should be known as City Square. The creation of the square made a fitting end to an era in which the rulers of Leeds had found themselves torn between the attractions of wealth, culture and plain utility. From the 1860s many visitors to Leeds, whether in town on business or for leisure, arrived by train. As travellers emerged from Wellington Station they viewed a motley assemblage of buildings of different age, style and quality; a poor first impression of one of the country's most successful towns. Above all, the rapidly deteriorating and largely redundant structure of the Coloured Cloth Hall dominated the south-western corner of the bottom of Park Row, while the Quebec Buildings provided another major eyesore. Acutely aware of the problem, the council wished to create an impressive open space for the town. Negotiations with the owners of Quebec Buildings were long and protracted and this delayed the project. Moreover, the Coloured Cloth Hall needed to be purchased at a cost of £66,000. The finance of the scheme, however, was assisted by the sale of land to the west for a new post office, and to the north for high quality insurance offices.

But what should the square be like? It was the initiative of Colonel T.W.Harding which ensured that from unpromising beginnings the square was to become the city's greatest work of art. He later recalled how the site had been in chaotic unplanned state when he was enjoying spell in Italy:

> I read in a local paper there was a proposal to erect in the middle of it or underneath it a lavatory or tramway waiting room, admirable things of the utilitarian kind which appeal so much to the ratepayer ...I roused myself in my leisure in Italy in making a little plan of what I considered might possibly be done with this site and I sent it to my friend Mr. Bakewell, architect, and asked him to put it into form. Much to my surprise, the Corporation did me the great honour of accepting the plan.[236]

The scheme included a raised circular platform with a balastraded wall and pedestals to two triangular spaces. People were keen that there should be an equestrian statue. Harding, a keen medieval historian, believed that the Black Prince, although he had no connection whatsoever with Leeds, conjured up a vision of chivalry and democracy, a perfect character for such an important position. Better still he generously offered to pay for such a statue on this theme by Thomas Brock, and to provide eight bronze figures based on the models of 'Morn' and 'Even' by Alfred Drury.[237] Subsequently, he offered to complete the scheme by presenting four statues of Leeds Worthies. These he suggested should be Joseph Priestley,

The formal presentation to the City Council of the statues in City Square, 16 September 1903.

The City Square in 1910.

John Harrison, Ralph Thoresby and Dean Hook. Councillor Boston offered to pay for the statue of Harrison, and Richard Wainwright expressed a strong wish to contribute one of the statues, but suggested that James Watt, whose steam engines powered the first mills of Leeds, would be a more appropriate figure than Thoresby. The formal opening ceremony took place on 16 September 1903.[238] Unfortunately, the smoky atmosphere of the town centre soon killed the trees and the statues became covered in soot. For all the wealth and the changes wrought in the Victorian city, one factor remained the same – as a correspondent to the *Yorkshire Evening News* remarked: 'Smoke and Leeds are almost as inseparably connected in the public mind as bacon and eggs'.[239]

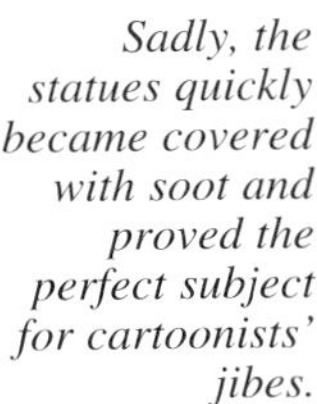

Sadly, the statues quickly became covered with soot and proved the perfect subject for cartoonists' jibes.

References

1. This section on local government is based on the work of Brian Barber which can be found in three principal works: B.J.Barber, 'Leeds Corporation, 1835-1905: a History of its Environmental, Social and Administrative Services' (unpublished Ph.D. thesis, University of Leeds, 1975); 'Aspects of Municipal Government, 1835-1914' in *Modern Leeds*; 'Municipal Government in Leeds, 1835-1914', in D.Fraser, ed., *Municipal Reform and the Industrial City* (Leicester, 1982).
2. 5 & 6 Victoria, cap. 104 (1842).
3. Barber, *op. cit.* (1982), pp. 67-8.
4. *Ibid.*, p. 71.
5. J.Hole, *The Homes of the Working Classes, with Suggestions for their Improvement* (1866), p. 4.
6. R.Baker, *op. cit.* (1842), pp. 21-2; see also, S.M.Barnard, *To Prove I'm Not Forgot: Living and Dying in a Victorian City* (Manchester, 1990) [The story of Beckett Street Cemetery, Leeds], esp. ch. 1.
7. Baker, *op. cit.*(1842), pp. 21-2.
8. *Ibid.*
9. M.W.Beresford, *Walks Round Red Brick* (Leeds, 1980), ch. 8; R.F.Fletcher, 'The History of the Leeds General Cemetery Company, 1833-1965' (Unpublished M.Phil. thesis, University of Leeds, 1975).
10. 5 & 6 Victoria cap. 103 (1842).
11. Barnard, *op. cit.*, pp. 7-8.
12. Barber, *op. cit.* (1982), pp. 68-70.
13. *Ibid.*, p. 65.
14. *Ibid.*, pp. 85-9; R.S.Peppard, 'The Growth and Development of Leeds Waterworks Undertakings, 1694-1852' (Unpublished M.Phil. thesis, University of Leeds, 1973).
15. J.Morgan, 'Demographic Change, 1771-1911' in *Modern Leeds*, pp. 64-8.
16. Barber, *op. cit.* (1980), pp. 303-5.
17. P.P. (1866), XXXIII, J.Hunter, 'Circumstances endangering the Public Health of Leeds'; *Leeds Mercury*, 2 Dec. 1865.
18. Barber, *op. cit.* (1980), p. 302.
19. Leeds Improvement Act, Market Committee Minutes (hereafter, Market Committee Minutes), 3 Aug. 1842.
20. K.Grady, 'Commercial, Marketing and Retailing Amenities' in Fraser, ed., *Modern Leeds*, p. 188.
21. *Ibid.*, p. 190.
22. For a detailed history of the market, see: S.Burt and K.Grady, *Kirkgate Market: An Illustrated History* (Leeds, 1992); G.Rees, *St Michael - A History of Marks and Spencer* (1969), pp. 1-22.
23. *Fenteman's Guide 1858*, p. 43.
24. Grady, *op. cit.*, (1980) p. 192.
25. For a detailed account, see: A.Briggs, *Victorian Cities* (1968), ch. 4 'Leeds, a Study in Civic Pride'.
26. *Ibid.*, p. 177. For a detail contemporary description of the Queen's visit, see: J.Mayhall, ed., *The Annals of Yorkshire, From the Earliest Period to the Present Time* (1878), I, pp. 717-28.
27. D.Fraser, *Power and Authority in the Victorian City* (Oxford, 1979), p. 58.
28. Barber, *op. cit.* (1982), p. 65.
29. E.W.Clay, *The Leeds Police, 1836-1974* (Leeds, 1975), p. 12.
30. *Ibid.*, p. 14.
31. Fraser, *Power and Authority*, p. 59; *Leeds Intelligencer*, 27 Oct. 1838.
32. Clay, *op. cit.*, pp. 16-8; *Leeds Intelligencer*, 1 July 1836.
33. Barber, *op. cit.* (1982), p. 65.
34. *Ibid.*, p. 65: Fraser, *Power and Authority*, p. 59.
35. Mayhall, *op. cit.*, I, pp. 482, 488, 496, 544, 547, 687.
36. *Ibid.*, p. 547, 29 July 1847.
37. Clay, *op. cit.*, pp. 30-1.
38. *Ibid.*, pp. 39-40.
39. *Borough of Leeds Chief Constable's Report*, November 1869.
40. Clay, *op. cit.*, pp. 25-6.
41. *Ibid.*, pp. 30-1.
42. *Ibid.*, pp. 32-4.
43. *Ibid.*, pp. 59-60.
44. *Ibid.*, p. 65.
45. J.H.Pollen, *Narrative of Five Years at St Saviour's, Leeds* (Oxford, 1851), p. 18.
46. *Borough of Leeds Chief Constable's Report*, 1852.
47. P.P. 1843, XIV: *Children's Employment Commission (Trades & Manufacture), Report of J.C.Symons, pp. E 37-9.*
48. *Mayhall*, op. cit., I, pp. 499-500.
49. *Ibid.*, pp. 505-7.
50. *Ibid.*, II, pp. 432-7.
51. *Ibid.*, I, pp. 590-1.
52. *Ibid.*, II, pp. 614-5.
53. *Ibid.*, III, p. 20.
54. *Ibid.*, III, pp. 88-9.
55. *Ibid.*, III, p. 95.
56. *Ibid.*, III, pp. 133.
57. *Ibid.*, III, pp. 155-7, 159.
58. Clay, *op. cit.*, pp. 24, 31-2, 36-7.
59. *Ibid.*, p. 45.
60. *Ibid.*, pp. 53-4.
61. *Ibid.*, pp. 57-8.
62. N.C.Edsall, *The anti-Poor Law Movement, 1834-44* (Manchester, 1971).
63. D.Fraser, 'Poor Law Politics in Leeds, 1833-1855', *Thoresby Soc.*, LIII (1971).
64. *Ibid.*, pp. 27-31. For the Poor Law politics of Leeds in this period set in context, see: D.Fraser, *Urban Politics in Victorian England* (Leicester, 1976), ch. 3.
65. P.Anderson, 'The Leeds Workhouse under the Old Poor Law, 1726-1834', *Thoresby Soc.*, LVI (1980), p. 112.
66. Fraser, 'Poor Law Politics', p. 35.
67. *Ibid.*, pp. 38-49.
68. *Fenteman's Guide 1858*, pp. 99-100.
69. For this quote and the story of the school, see: P.M.Pennock, 'The Evolution of St James's, 1849-94: Leeds Moral and Industrial Training School, Leeds Union Workhouse and Leeds Union Infirmary', *Thoresby Soc.* LIX (1986), pp. 131-48.
70. Fraser, 'Poor Law Politics', p. 38.
71. *Ibid.*, pp. 39-40.
72. *Fenteman's Guide 1858*, p. 116.
73. Mayhall, *op. cit.*, II, p. 25. For a short history of the Union Workhouse, see: Pennock, *op. cit.*, pp. 148-66.
74. *Fenteman's Guide 1858*, p. 78.
75. Mayhall, *op. cit.*, I, pp. 542-3.
76. E.Jackson, *A Pastor's Recollections* (Leeds, 1890), No. 5, pp. 11-12.
77. Mayhall, *op. cit.*, I, pp. 542-4.
78. Jackson, *op. cit.*, p. 15.
79. Mayhall,*op. cit.*, I, pp. 576-7.
80. Pollen, *op. cit.*, pp. 129-30.
81. S.T.Anning, 'Leeds House of Recovery', *Medical History*, Vol. 13, No. 3 (July, 1969), pp. 226-36.
82. Leeds (Group B) Hospital Management Committee, *50th Anniversary of the Opening of Seacroft and Killingbeck Hospitals* (Leeds, 1954).
83. J.Dodgson, *Historical and Descriptive Guide to the Borough of Leeds* (Leeds, 1879), p. 82.
84. *Fenteman's Guide 1858*, p. 116.
85. Pennock, *op. cit.*, pp. 166-76.
86. S.T.Anning, *The General Infirmary at Leeds* (1963), I, esp. ch. 3.
87. *Ibid.*, II, p. 60.
88. For these new institutions, see: Dodgson, *op. cit.*, pp. 82-3.
89. S.T.Anning and W.K.J.Walls, *A History of the Leeds School of Medicine: One and a Half Centuries 1831-1981* (Leeds, 1982), p. 36.
90. *Ibid.*, p. 77.
91. Leeds City Council, *Education in Leeds: A Backward Glance and A Present View: Leeds Education Week Souvenir Handbook* (Leeds, 1926) [hereafter *Education in Leeds*], pp. 10-11; W.B.Stephens, 'Elementary Education and Literacy, 1770-1870' in *Modern Leeds*, pp. 230-2.
92. *Education in Leeds*, p. 26.
93. Stephens, *op. cit.*, p. 243.
94. *Ibid.*, p. 229.
95. *Ibid.*, p. 244.
96. *Education in Leeds*, p. 12.
97. *Ibid.*, p. 11.
98. P.W.Musgrave, *Society and Education in England Since 1800* (1968).
99. *Dodgson's 1879 Guide*, pp. 100-1.
100. *Ibid.*
101. Musgrave, *op. cit.*, pp. 48-9.
102. Leeds School Board, *Central Higher Grade School Prospectus* (Leeds, 1889).
103. *Education in Leeds*, pp. 13-4, 20; A.Elton, 'Sir George Cockburn', 1848-1927', *Thoresby Soc.*, Second Series, 3 (1993).
104. The following details about the Grammar School are found in P.P. 1898, LXVI, *Report on the Endowed Charities of the City of Leeds*, pp. 29-56.
105. *Education in Leeds*, p. 77.
106. For details of the Mechanics' Institute/Modern School, see: E.E.Bullus, ed., *The Modernian: A History of Leeds Modern School, 1845-1931* (Leeds, 1931), pp. 1-14.
107. E.Kilburn Scott, *Leeds Church Middle-Class School: Records from 1870-1907* (Leeds, 1927).
108. *Yorkshire Post*, 24 Jan. 1870.
109. *Education in Leeds*, pp. 90-1.
110. *Ibid.*
111. *Ibid.*, pp. 118-20.
112. *Ibid.*
113. *Ibid.*, p. 93.
114. *Ibid.*, pp. 114-7; A.N.Shimmin, *The University of Leeds: The First Half-Century* (Cambridge, 1954); P.H.J.H.Gosden, 'The Early Years of the Yorkshire College', *Thoresby Soc.*, LIV (1976); P.H.J.H.Gosden and A.J.Taylor, eds., *Studies in the History of A University, 1874-1974: To Commemorate the Centenary of the University of Leeds* (Leeds, 1975).
115. Thoresby Society Annual Reports.
116. LCR: LP710.6 L517, Leeds Horticultural and Floral Society Annual Report, 1837.
117. Leeds Photographic Society, *Centenary Publication* (1952).
118. LCR: LQP 520.6 L517, *Leeds Astronomical Society Journal* (1893).
119. LCR: 590.5 N217, Leeds Naturalists' Club and Scientific Association reports, 1870-1950.
120. T.Steele, *Alfred Orage and the Leeds Arts Club, 1893-1923* (1990).
121. E.A.Elton, 'Leeds Cyclists, 1880-1914', *Thoresby Society Annual Report, 1991.*
122. White, *1837 Directory*, pp. 514-20; Grady, 'Public Buildings', pp. 160-70.
123. W.R.W. Stephens, *Life and Letters of Walter Farquhar Hook* (1878), I, p. 307.
124. A.Elton and E.Foster, *Yorkshire Piety and Persuasion* (Leeds, 1985), p. 7.
125. *Kelly's Directory of Leeds, 1901*, pp. 13-5.
126. W.L.Schroeder, *Mill Hill Chapel* (1924), pp. 60-2.
127. R.Gawler, *History of Blenheim Baptist Church Leeds, 1848-1948* (Leeds, 1948).
128. *Kelly's Leeds Directory 1901*, p. 14.
129. W.Allott, 'Leeds Quaker Meeting', *Thoresby Soc.*, L (1966), pp. 59-70.
130. R.V.Taylor, *Biograhia Leodiensis: Worthies of Leeds* (Leeds, 1865), pp. 368-70.
131. H.W.Dalton, 'Walter Farquhar Hook, Vicar of Leeds: His Work for the Church and the Town, 1837-48, *Thoresby Soc.*, LXIII (1990); W.R.W.Stephens, *op. cit.*, p. 370.
132. W.R.W.Stephens, *op. cit.*, pp. 374-5.
133. Rebuilding of the Parish Church: W.R.W.Stephens, *op. cit.*, p.381; C.Webster, 'R.D.Chantrell, Architects: His Life and Work in Leeds, 1818-1847', *Thoresby Soc.*, 2nd series, II (1992), ch. 5; Dalton, *op. cit.*, p. 43.
134. W.F.Hook, *A Letter to the Parishioners of Leeds* (Leeds, 1844).
135. G.H.Chard, *A History of the Leeds Church Institute* (Leeds, 1907).
136. W.A.Hopwood and F.P.Casperson, *Meanwood* (Leeds, 1986), pp. 30-40.
137. R.V.Taylor, *Ecclesiae Leodiensis* (Leeds, 1875), pp. 63, 500-1.
138. Dalton, *op. cit.*, p. 79.
139. W.R.W.Stephens, *op. cit.*, p. 199.
140. For the story of Hook's problems concerning St Saviour's see: N.Yates, 'Leeds and the Oxford Movement: A Study of "High Church" Activity in the Rural Deaneries of Allerton, Armley, Headingley and Whitkirk in the Diocese of Ripon 1836-1934', *Thoresby Soc.*, LV (1975).
141. R.E.Finnigan, *The Cathedral Church of St Anne, Leeds* (1988), pp. 7, 25.
142. *Ibid.*, p. 17.
143. *Ibid.*, pp. 19-25.
144. *Ibid.*, p. 17.
145. Mount St Mary's Church, *Centenary of the Opening of Mount St Mary's Church, Leeds, 1857-1957* (Leeds, 1957).
146. Finnigan, *op. cit.*, p.27.
147. *Religious Census Returns for 1851.*

148. Yates, *op. cit.*, p. 260.
149. W.Guest, *Rest: or No Rest: A Letter to Working Men on the Sabbath Question, After Ten Months' Sojourn in Continental Cities* (Leeds, 1857), p. 9.
150. *Leeds Mercury*, 29 Dec. 1838.
151. Yates, *op. cit.*, pp. 151-7; Morris, *op. cit.*, pp. 151-7.
152. Jackson, *op. cit.*, p. 51.
153. Quoted in Pollen, *op. cit.*, p. 17.
154. Leeds Parish Church, *Good Shepherd Mission, 1882-1932* (Leeds, 1932), p. 9.
155. Leeds Parish Church, *Railway Arch Mission* (Leeds, n. d.), p. 11.
156. Finnigan, *op. cit.*, pp. 27-39.
157. E.Krausz, *Leeds Jewry: It History and Social Structure* (Cambridge, 1964).
158. Diocese of Ripon, *Report of the Commission Appointed by the Lord Bishop of Ripon* (Leeds, 1900).
159. For an account of the politics of the early Victorian period see: Fraser, *Power and Authority in the Victorian City* (Oxford, 1979), pp.51-8; Fraser, 'Politics and Society in the Nineteenth Century', in Fraser, ed., *Modern Leeds*, pp.279-89.
160. For an account of Chartism in Leeds, see: J.F.C.Harrison, 'Chartism in Leeds', in A. Briggs, *Chartist Studies* (1959); Fraser, in *Modern Leeds*, pp. 285-94.
161. T.Mackay, ed., *The Autobiography of Samuel Smiles* (1905), p. 90.
162. *Ibid.*, pp. 87-96.
163. For these and related disturbances in Leeds, see: Clay, *op. cit.*, pp. 21-3; Mackay, *op. cit.*, pp. 114-23; Harrison, *op. cit.*, pp. 88-90.
164. Mackay, *op. cit.*, p. 123 *et seq.*
165. Fraser in *Modern Leeds*, pp. 289-93.
166. *Ibid.*, pp. 293-8.
167. *Ibid.*, pp. 96-7.
168. Account of the election and Gladstone's subsequent visit to Leeds, see: S.J.Reid, *Memoirs of Sir Wemyss Reid, 1842-1885* (1905), pp. 276-300.
169. G.Ratcliffe, *Sixty Years of It: Being the Story of My Life and Public Career* (1935), p. 22.
170. Fraser in *Modern Leeds*, p. 298.
171. This section on working-class politics is based on T.Woodhouse, 'The Working Class' in *Modern Leeds*.
172. Quoted in E.D.Steele, 'Leeds and Victorian Politics', *University of Leeds Review*, XVII, 2 (1974), pp. 260-1.
173. Mackay, *op. cit.*, p. 104.
174. Woodhouse, *op. cit.*, p. 357.
175. *Ibid.*, p. 356.
176. *Ibid.*, p. 381.
177. *Ibid.*, p.368.
178. *Ibid.*, p. 367.
179. H.Hendrick, 'The Leeds Gas Strike, 1890', *Thoresby Soc.*, LIV (1975).
180. Woodhouse, *op. cit.*, pp. 356-7.
181. S.Burt and K.Grady, *Kirkgate Market: An Illustrated History* (Leeds, 1992), p. 9.
182. Mayhall, *op. cit.*, III, pp 246-50.
183. Barber in *Modern Leeds*, pp. 305-6.
184. M.W.Beresford, 'The Back-to-Back House in Leeds, 1787-1937' in S.D.Chapman, ed., *The History of Working-class Housing: a Symposium* (Newton Abbot, 1971).
185. Barber, *op. cit.*, pp. 309-11.
186. The preceding section on the slums is based on Barber, *op. cit.*, pp. 309-14.
187. *Ibid.*, pp. 302-8.
188. *Dodgson's Guide, 1879*, p. 42.
189. P.P. 1888, LV, *Royal Commission on Market Rights and Tolls*, Vol IV, pp. 433-57, *passim*; Leeds City Council, *City of Leeds Markets and Corn Exchange – the Official Handbook* (1951), p. 41.
190. Leeds City Council, *Opening of the New City Meat Market and Slaughterhouses, 24 July 1899 [brochure]*, pp. 6-8.
191. Leeds City Council, *Opening of the New Market Hall, 1st July 1904 [brochure]*. For the history of the markets in the Victorian period, see: K.Grady, 'Commercial, Marketing and Retailing Amenities' in *Modern Leeds*, esp. pp. 190-4; Burt and Grady, *Kirkgate Market*; Records relating to Leeds markets held at Leeds District Archives.
192. Barber, *op. cit.*, pp. 318-20; S.Bowden, R.Crawford and G.Sykes, 'The Public Supply of Gas in Leeds, 1818-1949', in Chartres and Honeyman, *op. cit.*.
193. *Ibid.*, pp. 320-2 regarding trams.
194. *Ibid.*, pp. 322-4.
195. J.Douglas and K.Powell, 'Boar Lane: Is it Too Late?', *Outlook – Journal of Leeds Civic Trust* (Leeds, 1979); *Yorkshire Weekly Post* Dec. 1899 and 1899 Christmas edition. For Boston's see: *Waddington's Guide to Leeds* (York, 1894), p. 30.
196. Historical Publishing Company, *England's Great Manufacturing Centres: Yorkshire - Leeds and Bradford* (1888), p. 82.
197. Arcades: Documents relating to some of them are on deposit at Leeds District Archives; see also article by J.Hatcher in *Victorian Society West Yorkshire Group Journal* (1981-2), pp. 2-7.
198. *Ibid.*, p. 7; P.Brears, *Images of Leeds* (Derby, 1992), pp. 88-90.
199. Leeds Traders' Special Show Week, *Shopping in Leeds* (1909), p. 27.
200. Clay, *op. cit.*, p. 146.
201. *Ibid.*, pp. 62-4.
202. *Dodgson's Guide 1879*, p. 92.
203. *The Leeds Biographer*, p. 32; *Empire Mail*, July 1926; *Leeds Arts Calendar*, No. 103 (1988).
204. *Illustrated London News*, 27 Oct. 1888.
205. R.Wilkinson, *The Grand Theatre – First Hundred Years* (Leeds, 1978), pp. 9-23.
206. R.Preedy, *Leeds Theatres Remembered* (Leeds, 1981), pp. 27-9.
207. M., J. and B.Marshall, *Recollections: Sixty Years Onwards* (2nd edn., Leeds, 1930), p. 61.
208. *Fenteman's Guide 1858*, p. 9.
209. Leeds City Council Parks Committee, *Woodhouse Moor Centenary Handbook, 1857-1957* (Leeds, 1957).
210. Barber, in *Municipal Reform and the Industrial City*, pp. 78-81.
211. For the early days of football and rugby in Leeds, see: W.G.Rimmer, 'Sport', *Leeds Journal*, Vol. 28 (Leeds, 1957), pp. 77-9, 149-50; A.J.Arnold, 'Shall it be Bradford or Leeds? The Origins of Professional Football in the West Riding Textile District', *Thoresby Soc.*, LXIII (1990).
212. For the origins of the Headingley ground see: J.Marshall, *Headingley* (1970), pp. 1-15.
213. Rimmer, *op. cit.* (Sport).
214. *Guide to Leeds and Its Amusements – Whitsuntide* (Leeds, 1870), pp. 41-2.
215. F.Trowell, 'Speculative Housing Development in the Suburb of Headingley, Leeds, 1838-1914', *Thoresby Soc.*, LIX (1985), pp. 62-72.
216. E.Pitchin, *Leeds Made Uglier* (Leeds, 1882), p. 1.
217. *Ibid.*, title page.
218. See: S.Burt, *An Illustrated History of Roundhay Park* (Leeds, 1983).
219. *Yorkshire Post*, 26 Jan. 1889.
220. Leeds United Working Men's Temperance League, *Seventh Annual Report and Balance Sheet* (Leeds, 1893), p. 10.
221. *Royal Commission on Market Rights and Tolls*, p. 441.
222. S.Wood, *Back-to-Back Memories* (Leeds, 1991); P.Brears, *Yorkshire Food and Tradition*.
223. D.Cole, *Just an Ordinary Life* (Leeds, 1984), p. 21.
224. *The Leeds Mercury Jubilee Supplement*, 20 June 1887, p. 3.
225. Baker, 'Statistical Committee Report' (1839), p. 37; Baker, 'Industrial and Sanitary Economy of the Borough in 1858', pp. 10-6; J.Burnett, *A History of the Cost of Living* (1969), pp. 248-57.
226. Morgan in *Modern Leeds*, pp. 64-68.
227. Baker, *op. cit.* (1858), p. 8.
228. *The Leeds Mercury Jubilee Supplement*, 20 June 1887.
229. Burnett, *op. cit.*, pp. 248-57.
230. Morgan, *op. cit.*, pp. 64-67.
231. Census Returns, 1871-1901.
232. *The Leeds Mercury Jubilee Supplement*, 20 June 1887.
233. D.B.Foster, *Leeds Slumdom* (Leeds, 1897), p. 4.
234. See: A.Elton, 'Becoming a City: Leeds 1893', *Thoresby Soc.*, 2nd ser., 3 (1993).
235. *Yorkshire Owl*, 15 Feb. 1893, p. 285, quoted in Elton, *op. cit.*.
236. G.Black, 'City Square and Colonel Harding', *Thoresby Soc.*, LIV (1975), pp. 106-12.
237. N.G.Morrison, *Edward the Black Prince: A City Square Souvenir* (Leeds, 1903), pp. 9-11.
238. Leeds City Council, *Formal Opening of City Square [brochure]* (Leeds, 1903).
239. *Yorkshire Evening News*, 26 Nov. 1921.

CHAPTER SEVEN

The Twentieth Century

The Expanding City

The process of suburbanisation, which began on a significant scale in the 1870s, has progressed rapidly in twentieth-century Leeds. The increased residential separation of the inhabitants from their places of work and the commercial, administrative and social hub of Leeds, means that for the twentieth century we must look at the city as a whole, rather than focusing primarily on the central built-up area.

When Leeds was given the status of a county borough in 1888 its boundaries remained those of the municipal borough of 1626. During the twentieth century, however, the physical limits of the city were greatly enlarged. The 21,593 acres of 1900 eventually became the 134,916 acres of Leeds Metropolitan District in 1974. The first enlargement of the city was the inclusion in 1912 of the townships of Roundhay, Seacroft, Shadwell, and part of Cross Gates. This was followed by the addition of Middleton in 1919, Adel-cum-Eccup in 1925, and

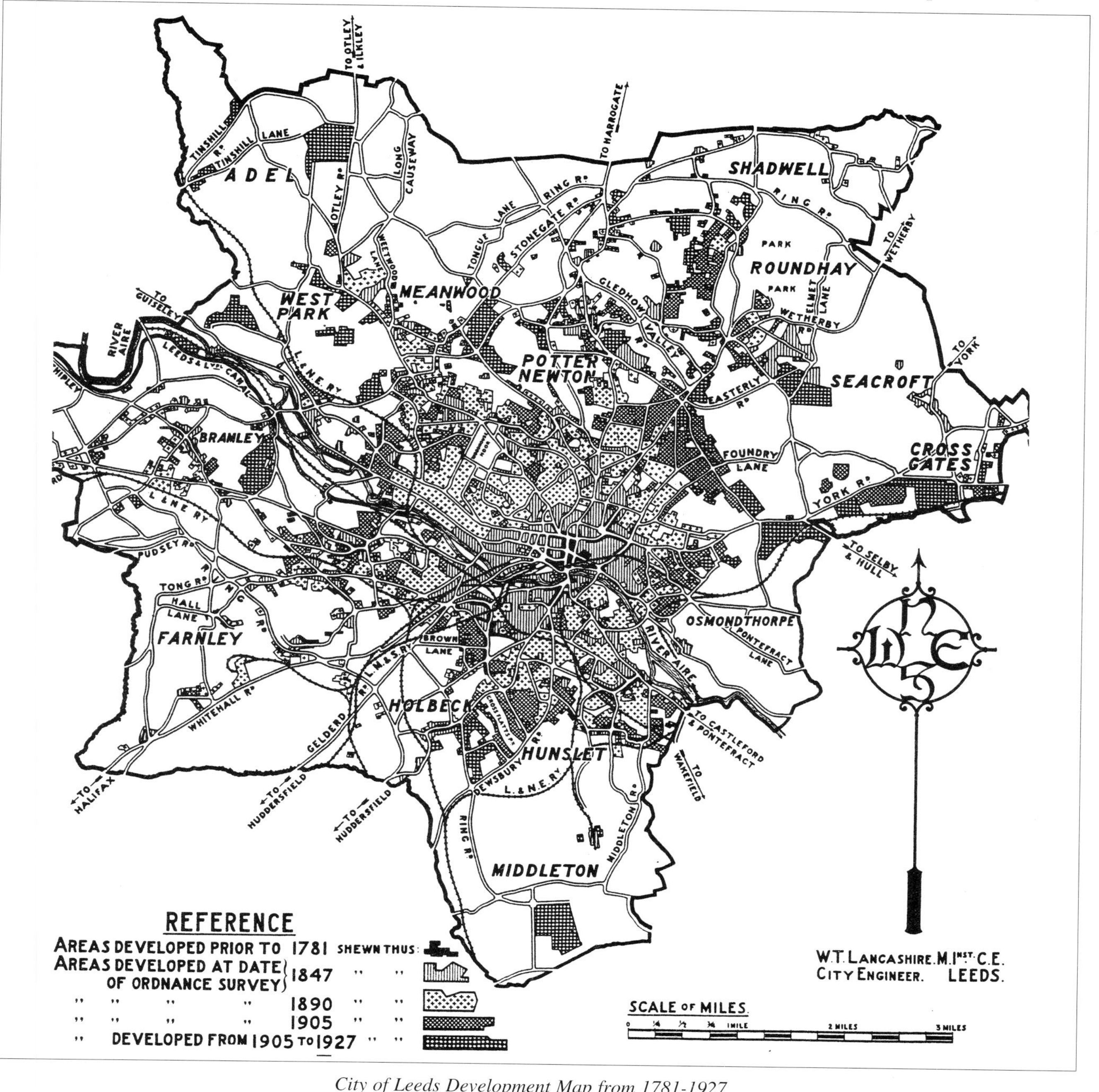

City of Leeds Development Map from 1781-1927

Leeds imperialism defied. Charles Wilson waves goodbye to 'Pudsey' who is jumping over a gravestone to the memory of the Leeds and Bradford Extension Bill which failed to get through Parliament in 1922.

Alwoodley, Temple Newsam, Eccup and part of Austhorpe in 1927. Collectively, these additions enlarged the city to 38,106 acres. In 1937 a further 194 acres comprisingly land in the Borough of Pudsey and the parishes of Austhorpe, Barwick in Elmete, Swillington, Wigton and Arthington were added. The physical area had grown by three-quarters in twenty-five years.[1]

These extensions to the city boundaries occurred for a number of reasons. One was simply political ambition. Charles Wilson, Conservative leader of the council from 1907 to 1928 was an unashamed municipal imperialist. He made it plain that his ambition was for Leeds to control everywhere from the Pennines to the sea. Leeds' neighbours were horrified and spent much of their time between 1919 and 1928 battling against incorporation into the city.[2] The tenor of the opposition was reflected in the controversy over the unsuccessful Leeds and Bradford Extension Bill of 1922, by which Leeds and Bradford between them aimed to gain control of another 17,000 acres and 48,000 people. It was at the local inquiry on this Bill that Alderman Charles Wilson, when asked about the opinion of the people in Leeds, gave the famous reply, 'I am Leeds'. During the parliamentary debate on the Bill, Mr A.R.Barrand, MP for Pudsey and Otley, said he did not know of one individual in Pudsey who wished to be absorbed by Leeds. He asked the House to accede to his constituents' request for protection against this 'unprovoked interference'. 'There was no excuse for annexing what was a self-contained industrial district on the plea that they should be brought into Leeds, and made to contribute to the rates. If Leeds really wanted to get their rich runaway ratepayers, they would have to go to Harrogate and Scarborough. (Hear, hear, and laughter)'. Mr Lane Fox, MP for Barkston Ash, declared the Bill was 'a pure case of the aggrandisement of great boroughs at the expense of their weaker neighbours. The outside areas affected had not been considered or consulted...Bradford had not been a willing accomplice – (hear, hear) – but Bradford knew that if it did not come in, it would have no share at all, and that any area it might wish for would be annexed by its powerful neighbour'.[3]

Despite such strong resistance to the various extensions schemes, there were significant advantages to be gained by both the city and the newly incorporated districts. Much of the area absorbed already depended on Leeds as an economic and social focus, while Leeds depended on it for residential expansion and part of its labour force. Politicians and planners (particularly those concerned with highways) believed it was important to attain administrative control over a wider area. The city's ability to plan and make provision in the spheres of housing, transport infrastructure and industrial expansion was considerably enhanced. Moreover, in the longer term, the economies of scale inherent in the provision of services by the city, enabled a higher standard of public amenities and services, such as gas, electricity, sewerage, and water supply, to be brought more rapidly to these outlying districts than would have been possible had they continued to be run by the smaller units of local government.

One of the most striking features of twentieth-century Leeds has been a dramatic slowing down in the growth of its population. During the nineteenth century the population had grown by over 30 per cent in some decades, and, even though the rate of increase declined after 1870, in each of the last three decades of the century the numbers grew by over 50,000 – a rise of over 16 per cent growth per decade. In the decades from 1901 to 1951, if additions to population due to boundary extensions are excluded, population growth per decade was only in the range of 1 to $4\frac{1}{2}$ per cent. During the 1940s growth almost ground to a halt.The dramatic check to population growth between 1911 and 1921, of course, was partly due to the loss of life and the separation of families during the First World War, but the long-term decline had other explanations. Apart from the nationwide trend towards limitation of family size through birth control, the principal local factor was the shift of population to outlying areas beyond the city boundaries. The 1920s and '30s were the last decades in which the outflow of people beyond the city boundaries, and some migration to other areas in search of work, was sufficiently outweighed by the natural increase of the population, and a net inflow of people from outside the city, to produce significant population growth.

The fall to 1 per cent growth in the 1940s was largely the result of a natural increase in population of around 4 per cent being counteracted by a net outflow of approximately 16,000.[4] Much of the inflow of people in the 1930s came from Scotland and Northern England, whereas the outflow in the 1940s was to the Midlands and the South of England.[5]

Industrial and Business Capital of the North

The most distinctive feature of economic change in Leeds in the twentieth century has been the dramatic decline of manufacturing industry and the rise of a great variety of service industries. The symptoms of such a remarkable change were not readily apparent in the years leading up to the First World War. In 1900, though the textile industry now employed only around a tenth of the borough's workforce and the leather industry was just past its peak as a growth sphere, the other manufacturing sectors were thriving. Engineering, for example, the largest employer with 28,000 workers, employed at least one-fifth of the male workforce, while the factory-made

Blackburn's Olympia Works, Roundhay Road, in 1915, with workers busy on an important order for the Royal Naval Air Service.

clothing industry, with a workforce of over 20,000, was growing at a prodigious rate. Service industries were large employers – transport and traditional domestic service, for example, each employed one in twelve workers. But, even with the growth of commerce and the professions, manufacturing was still clearly dominant. The beginning of the century saw trade at record heights, industry stretched to near capacity, and employment plentiful and remunerative. The Edwardian era was a period of considerable prosperity for Leeds and severe depression was avoided right up to the First World War.[6]

The onset of the Great War emphasised the importance of Leeds as a manufacturing centre. Its factories produced everything from guns, shells, tanks and aircraft to a vast array of clothing. Important new munitions factories were opened at Armley, Newlay, Hunslet and Barnbow, where women and girls formed the majority of the workforce. At its height over 16,000 workers producing shells were employed at Barnbow. Hunslet locomotives supplied the Western Front, while both Kitson's and Fairbairn Lawson adapted or extended their work to meet wartime demand. Greenwood & Batley made rifle cartridges. T.F.Braime & Co of Hunslet made copper shell bands, George Bray's manufactured essential parts for shell fuses, aircraft engines and burners for lamps. Kirkstall Forge manufactured high quality axles. Seventy-five Sopwith Camel biplanes were built in Leeds by March, Jones and Cribb, with further output at Blackburn's Olympia Works. Leeds firms worked round the clock to clothe our soldiers at the front. Not surprisingly, the city became the centre of both the manufacture and distribution of clothing for the troops. Millions of garments passed through the hands of the Northern Area Army Clothing Depot on Swinegate, and in the last year of the war it was handling 750,000 garments a week.[7]

The first significant signs of the long-term decline of the city's manufacturing base came immediately after the short post-war boom — though they were not recognised at the time. In common with the rest of the north of England, Leeds experienced very high levels of unemployment in the period between the First and Second World Wars because of depression in the heavy industries, which suffered severely from foreign competition and the sluggish growth and eventual plummeting of world trade. After hovering around 10 per cent in the 1920s, unemployment shot up to 17 per cent in 1930, following the great stock market crash of 1929, and reached a peak of 21 per cent in 1931. Thereafter it fell back, but was still at 9 per cent in 1937.[8] During these years of acute depression, the engineering industry, the great pride of Leeds, was hardest hit. Its workforce fell from an all time peak of 36,000 in 1921 to only 15,000 in 1926.[9]

It was the hardship experienced by workers in industries such as these which encouraged the participation of many Leeds workers in the General Strike in May 1926 in support of the miners. Around 40,000 Leeds workers were directly involved in the strike, it being the strategy of the strike leaders to call particular industries out stage by stage. The transport workers and most engineering workers came out on strike almost at once, while the clothing and textile workers were not directly affected because they were not in the Trades Union Congress's 'front line'. Despite the efforts of Charles Wilson and the Leeds Volunteer Services Committee, transport in the city almost came to a total standstill. The best that could be managed was to run 150 out of the city's 580 trams, and this only after 60 police were detailed for tram duty. By the time the strike was called off on 12 May some 2,000 of the registered volunteers were in service.[10]

In Leeds the days of the strike possessed little of the light-hearted mood which has been ascribed to it in some other areas of the country. Crowds of workers numbering over 5,000 were involved in riotous scenes in Duncan Street and Vicar Lane in attempts to prevent the movement of transport, and there were serious clashes between volunteers and pickets down at the municipal tram depot in Swinegate. The proprietors of a firm based in Kippax whose 20 buses carried workers at various clothing factories, like Montague Burton's, the Fifty Shilling Tailors and Weaver to Wearer, into Leeds and home again, were warned that they should suspend operations. On an evening shortly after the start of the strike one of the buses got to Leeds, was stopped and stoned by an angry crowd, and the driver and passengers had to be rescued by the mounted police. Shortly after lunch time on that day, the clothing firms closed down and the workers began the eight-mile walk back home. One of the partners in the Kippax garage set out to fetch them, armed with a revolver with which he aimed to threaten the pickets. Fortunately he was stopped by the police four miles from Leeds and sent home for his own safety. In the meantime, the local union leader, also armed, had gone to the Kippax bus depot where he threatened the inspector on duty with his revolver and took charge of the depot. There were no more buses from Kippax until the strike ended.[11]

There was a huge sigh of relief in certain quarters when the strike was called off, for it threatened to ruin the city's Tercentenary Celebrations.[12] But the success of the Tercentenary was small beer when set against the misery of high unemployment in the '20s and '30s. Even in 1936, after the Depression had passed its peak, severe difficulties persisted in engineering. A score of important firms employing 15,000 had been dismantled or left derelict in the previous twenty years, and for almost a decade, locomotive makers, agricultural and general engineers had worked well below capacity.[13]

The economic picture in Leeds in the inter-war period, however, was by no means entirely gloomy, and throughout the period, unemployment in the city remained significantly below that in other major northern towns. Without doubt, the most spectacular success in these years was the clothing industry. From the 1880s several of the city's major mass-production wholesale tailoring firms, such as Blackburn's and Hepworth's, had opened chains of shops. Hepworths, in particular, had 143 shops by 1905.[14] Through these outlets they pioneered wholesale bespoke tailoring, whereby

HRH Princess Royal touring Burton's Hudson Road factory with Sir Montague on 9 October 1934.

Hunslet locomotives could be found all over the world.

customers' measurements were taken in the shops and the suits made back at their factories using mass-production techniques. Despite this innovation, by 1900 these tailoring firms were still primarily manufacturers of ready-made clothes, and wholesale bespoke tailoring still accounted for only around ten per cent of men's factory-made clothing.[15]

The Leeds mass-production bespoke tailoring industry came into its own after the First World War. It experienced prodigious growth under the inspiration of its undoubted king, Montague Burton, 'The Tailor of Taste'.[16] Burton, a Jewish refugee from Lithuania, acquired his first Leeds tailoring factory in 1909, while simultaneously pursuing plans to develop a chain of tailors shops. By 1914 Leeds had become the centre of his activities and he had specialised entirely in the sale and manufacture of bespoke suits. His genius was to organise production so efficiently that, with one-week delivery times, it became only marginally less convenient to buy a made-to-measure suit from one of his shops than to buy a ready-made suit. More importantly perhaps, before the war he was able to produce made-to-measure suits which, at a mere 20-30 shillings, were both within the range of the mass market and could compete in quality with the suits made by traditional bespoke tailors and the stock garments of ready-made producers.

In 1921 he decided to transfer all his production to one new factory at Hudson Road, strategically sited amidst the working-class settlements of Harehills and Burmantofts. By 1925 it was the largest clothing factory in Europe, and became a mecca for the visits of Royalty, entertainers, politicians and sportsmen. The factory was completed in 1934 when the Princess Royal opened what was reputedly the world's largest canteen, which could accommodate 8,000 workers at one sitting, and was said to be able to serve 2,000 cups of tea in five minutes.

Burton's chain of tailors shops, with their stylish fronts and windows, grew rapidly. By 1919 he had 40 shops, rising to 224 in 1926 and no less than 595 by 1939. They spread from the North and Midlands to London and the South-east. Burton was a marketing genius as well as a superb organiser of production, as his detailed advice to his sales assistants indicated:

> Make your customer feel he is welcome and that you are anxious to please him. Avoid the severe style of the income tax collector, and the smooth tongue of the fortune teller. Cultivate the dignified style of the 'Quaker tea blender' which is the happy medium.[17]

Burton was not alone in his activities. Other Leeds firms which became, or already were, household names in this industry, included John Collier, Jackson the Tailor, Price, and Hepworth. In 1927 the industry employed over 30,000 workers, and by the late 1930s it was reckoned that Burton's alone was clothing one-fifth of the male population of Britain.

The importance of the factory-made bespoke tailoring industry to female employment in Leeds was enormous. Such was Burton's demand for female workers that by the late 1930s the firm encountered a saturation of the local supply of labour and was obliged to bus in workers from within a ten mile radius of the city. Its eventual more radical solution was to build factories in Lancashire. In 1939 it employed 10,500 workers at Hudson Road and 6,000 in its three Lancashire factories. The tailoresses became the nationwide stereotype for the female workers of Leeds.

In spite of the poor overall performance of the engineering industry, quite a number of firms prospered by producing new products for wider markets and new patterns of demand. By 1936 Yorkshire Copper Works occupied a 20-acre site at Stourton employing 2,000 people in the largest works in the world devoted solely to the manufacture of drawn copper and brass tubing.[18] Crabtree printing presses were exported to Scandinavia, Singapore and South America. Henry Berry supplied cotton baling machinery to Egypt, Australia, India and Brazil, as well as powerful hydraulic rivetting machines required for the erection of Sydney Harbour Bridge.[19] The Clayton Group made a steel reservoir at the Tallah Waterworks, Calcutta and erected gasholders and oil and water tanks in places as widely separated as Stockholm, the Falkland Islands, Winnipeg and New Zealand.[20] Hathorn Davey's pumps were internationally famous and Kirkstall Forge manufactured axles for the world.[21] Greenwood & Batley's new electric trucks proved popular, while John Fowler switched production from steam ploughs to the manufacture of concrete mixers and equipment for construction work.[22]

The city also had the printing and food processing industries both of which were growth sectors and performed well. Petty's specialised in colour work for advertisers.[23] E.J.Arnold's printed school exercise and text books and supplied all kinds of equipment.[24] Waddington's printed cigarette and playing cards, constantly developing new products including jigsaws (1933), Monopoly (1934) and waxed containers (1936).[25] In the food processing industry firms like William

Moorhouse and Sons, jam producers, moved into larger premises. Their Sunglow Model Factory covered 13 acres and employed over 1000 workers.[26] Lloyd Rakusen and Sons Ltd supplied an increasing proportion of the Jewish market, whilst British Fish Canners on Balm Road produced four-fifths of the canned brisling and sild sardines processed in this country.[27]

In 1938 the Leeds Publicity and Development Department could state with considerable justification that:

> Increasing interest is being given to furniture making (Leeds is fast becoming one of the most important centres in the country in this trade), chemicals, soap manufacture, coach building, ferro-concrete construction, leather, confectionery, medicines, hair-dressing apparatus, cardboard box making, mineral waters, carpets, scientific instruments, cameras, jams and sauces, hats, brush making, watches and clocks, fish canning, button making, electrical appliances and accessories.[28]

The famed diversity of Leeds industries was another factor which helped carry the city through the difficult inter-war period, though it is probable that it was the role of Leeds as a regional centre which sustained these industries rather than their innate vitality. The city continued to offer large numbers of jobs in distribution, building, drink (especially brewing), rail, road and tram transport, entertainment and sport, national and local government administration, banking, insurance and finance. Employment in these sectors flourished in the 1930s and '40s as real incomes rose, business organisation changed, and government functions multiplied. With higher incomes, people in Leeds and the surrounding region were spending more on such items as amusement, travel, and hairdressing.[29]

In the inter-war period the role of Leeds as a regional transport centre was enhanced and its transport facilities both stimulated its economy and generated major employment. The trams remained the most important form of local transport until the early 1950s, but the use of buses increased considerably in the inter-war period. Transport developments came in other spheres too. Improvements to the rail services followed the grouping of the railways into four large companies in 1921. This culminated in the amalgamation of the New Station and Wellington Station to create City Station in 1936, and the rebuilding of the Queen's Hotel, which, with its luxurious accommodation, opened in 1937. Rail links to London were extremely good. In 1937 the fastest train between the two cities was the 'West Riding Limited', which took 2 hours 43 minutes.[30]

The Aire and Calder Navigation also maintained a comfortable profit throughout the inter-war period, and there was considerable bullishness about creating a Leeds Ship Canal to connect Leeds with the sea, on the same lines as the Manchester Ship Canal.[31] After nationalisation in 1947, improvements were made to the navigation in the 1960s and '70s, and it was only with the decline in coal carrying that by the 1990s the future of the navigation was seen in terms of leisure traffic.[32] It was only coal carrying, however, which saved the Leeds and Liverpool Canal from closure in the inter-war period, and it declined rapidly after the Second World War. Though it carried its last commercial traffic in 1973, a brighter future with use by pleasure craft then began to emerge.[33]

In the early 1930s, the creation of the Leeds and Bradford Airport, as a joint enterprise of Leeds and Bradford councils, heralded the dawn of a new age of travel. Two hundred acres of land was purchased at Yeadon, seven miles north-west of Leeds city centre, and in Spring 1931 a licence was obtained to use a portion of the site as a landing ground. A full commercial licence was granted by the Air Ministry in December 1933. By April 1935 there were scheduled flights between Yeadon, Heston, Newcastle and Edinburgh.[34]

The major public utilities, gas, electricity, water and sewage disposal provided increasing levels of employment in these years, both in terms of the construction of the infrastructure and their running.[35] Meanwhile, the role of Leeds as a regional retail centre and entertainment centre continued to grow in importance as a generator of trade and jobs. The slogan 'Leeds Leads' was adopted when the city made renewed efforts to consolidate its position as the chief shopping centre in the West Riding, with its catchment of nearly three and a half million people. Old windows were pulled out, dated buildings demolished and new display techniques instigated.[36]

The *Yorkshire Post's* Guide to the city boasted proudly in 1935 that:

> The centre of Leeds has been transformed since the War. There is still some old property in Briggate, one of the chief shopping streets, but most of the shop fronts have been modernised with the use of striking designs, in which much attention has been paid to the use of metal, glass and concealed lighting ...The same comment can be made of Commercial Street, Bond Street, and, naturally, the big new street, The Headrow, and, to a lesser extent, of some of the adjoining shopping thoroughfare. Electric signs have proved increasingly popular, so that, both by day and night, the city is a great attraction not only to the inhabitants, but to those who live in the densely-populated area outside.[37]

The widening of the Headrow revitalised the entire area, the crowning glory being the construction of the new department store Lewis's, the first building in Leeds to have cost over a million pounds.[38]

The role of Leeds as a newspaper centre was sustained in the inter-war period, despite a long struggle to keep the *Yorkshire Post* viable in the face of competition from national daily papers and local titles based in Manchester. The independence of the *Leeds Mercury* came to an end in 1923 when it was bought up by Yorkshire Conservative Newspapers Ltd, which already published the *Yorkshire Post* and the *Yorkshire Evening Post*. In practice it was difficult for Leeds to support two morning papers, and paper rationing in 1939 provided the opportunity to close down the *Mercury*, though its name lived on for a while as a subtitle of the *Yorkshire Post*.[39] By the mid-1930s, 12 newspapers were printed in Leeds. It had six daily papers – the *Yorkshire Evening News* which had been established as the *Leeds Daily News* in 1873, but changed its name in 1903; the *Yorkshire Post*, and its offshoot the *Yorkshire Evening Post*, which as we have seen was founded in 1890; the *Leeds Mercury*; the *Mid-Day Sporting Special* (Racing); and the *Sporting Pink* (Racing). In addition there were six weekly papers: the *Leeds Catholic Herald*; the *Leeds Guardian*; the *Leeds Weekly Citizen*; the *North Leeds News*; the *Sports Echo*; and the *Sports Post*.[40] The *Yorkshire Evening Post* produced several editions each day, the late, late extra was known as the Buff Final, and eager readers listened out for the paper boy running down the street shouting 'Special!, Special!'. With any luck it would be a murder![41]

The success of newspapers was complemented by the arrival of radio. The BBC had been formed in 1922 and four years later became the first major public broadcasting corporation. The official opening of the Leeds and Bradford Relay Station in July 1924 was a cause of great celebration. From its smart new control centre in Basinghall Street the Lord Mayor, Sir Edwin Airey, was linked to London. He marvelled that only a few years before, wireless telegraphy had been a matter of research in the laboratory but wireless now 'provided amusement and interest for leisure time to thousands of people, and in it were possibilities in the promotion of a wider diffusion of knowledge and culture'.[42] The present generation tends to think of local radio as an innovation of the 1960s, but in fact local broadcasts were not uncommon in the 1920s. The Leeds-Bradford station made a live broadcast of the military tattoo at Roundhay Park during the Tercentenary celebrations in 1926. The local press comment was enthusiastic: 'The orchestra and bands "came over" very well, and one could imagine the wheeling and jumping of the Hussars at the command of the whistle. We could also visualise the entry of the villagers "tripping lightly"; and the roars of laughter from the crowd were unmistakably provoked by the jousting.'[43]

In very broad terms, during the 1920s and '30s the Midlands and the South-east prospered due to innovation and the growth of industries such as electricity supply and electronics, motor vehicles, plastics, and the production of an important range of consumer durable goods. Unfortunately, in many northern towns these industries did not grow. Certainly the manufacture of critically important new products such as motor cars, television sets, vacuum cleaners, etc., did not take firm root in Leeds. This caused problems in the future. Possible explanations for this failure included high property rates, the failure to build the much talked about ship canal, old fashioned ideas, the existence of so much local industry which competed for labour, and particularly the shortage of female workers because so many were already engaged in the clothing industry, shops and offices.[44] But the Second World War arrived in time to postpone concerns about the industrial future of Leeds.

Leeds industry made a vital contribution to the winning of the Second World War. With its commencement in 1939 the city's traditional industries were soon fully at work. John Fowler's worked day and night for nearly six years producing over 1,500 armoured fighting vehicles, including the Matilda, Centaur Crandwell and Comet tanks as well as generating sets, diesel locomotives and petrol engines. Fairbairn Lawson Combe Barbour produced millions of shells and fuses as well as gun and mortar barrels. The Germans identified Kirkstall Forge as a target for their bombers, as well, no doubt, as major firms such as Cohn & Sons, involved in aircraft and engineering works, the Avro works at Yeadon and a number of factories producing components for Blackburn aircraft like the Swordfish, the Stella fighter dive bomber and the Firebrand torpedo aircraft.[45] As a Jew, Montague Burton obviously detested Hitler and Fascism, and enthusiastically supported the war effort. His factories manufactured over 13 million garments of superb quality (a quarter of all uniforms) for the army, navy and airforce. The employees and management purchased a Spitfire known as the 'Montague Bee' which was operational with a Polish Squadron.[46]

The 'Do-it-all' Corporation

The excellent *Tercentenary Handbook* produced by the city council in 1926 to commemorate the 300th anniversary of the creation of the Borough of Leeds, proudly described the council as 'The Do-it-all Corporation'. It waxed lyrical about the development and 'the romance' of the municipal services. Without doubt one of the most striking features of the first eight decades of the twentieth century was the vast expansion of the activities and responsibilities of Leeds City Council. But first let us look at the tussle for political control.

The Reins of Power

The most signal feature of the control of local government in Leeds in the twentieth century has been the way in which the Liberals, the dominant political force for six decades in the nineteenth century, collapsed as a major political force and were effectively replaced by the Labour Party.[47] Only between 1904 and 1907 has the Liberal Party controlled the council. Between 1913 and 1925 it could only muster between 17 and 23 seats of the 68 council seats. In 1926 this representation collapsed to 8 seats, and to 1 to 3 seats between 1933 and 1938. George Ratcliffe was Liberal leader from 1919-33, and, as his autobiography suggests, he was a rather lightweight, complacent leader of the party.[48] During his leadership the Liberal share of the vote in Leeds dropped from 30 to 10 per cent. In truth, the party lacked a recognisable identity and its leaders were incapable of appreciating that need and meeting it. Like the party nationally, the Leeds Liberals were squeezed by the battle between the Conservatives and the burgeoning Labour Party. After the election of 1913, for the first time the Labour Party had more council seats than the Liberals.

For most of the twentieth century, control of the council has see-sawed between the Conservatives and Labour. From 1899 to 1904 the Conservatives only held

Charles Wilson the charismatic Tory leader of Leeds City Council, 1907-28.

Leeds Civic Hall, opened 1933 (architect, Vincent Harris) The council funded this splendid new administrative headquarters through a government grant scheme to create work for the unemployed. It was built by the unemployed building workers of Leeds.

an outright majority on the council by virtue of its monopoly of the aldermanic seats. After the three years of Liberal control, between 1907 and 1928 no party had an overall majority, but in practice the Conservatives held sway under the dynamic and charismatic leadership of Charles (later Sir Charles) Wilson. Gradually the Labour Party gained a firm foothold on the council, winning its first seat in 1903 and increasing the number to 10 in 1908, and 16 in 1913. In 1928 Labour gained control of the council for the first time. The sequence of power then ran: Conservatives 1930-33, Labour 1933-35 and the Conservatives again from 1935-45.

There have been surprisingly few major differences between the policies espoused by the rival political parties in Leeds in the twentieth century. The disagreements have tended to be those of degree rather than general direction. The controlling parties, whether Conservative or Labour, have been primarily concerned with governing and administering the city in a sound and judicious manner. Even when the supposedly radical Labour councillors took control for the first time in 1928, the leader of the Conservatives, Alderman Leslie Owen, was able to comment with some relish, with regard to their budget proposals, that:

> The Socialists have had a majority for twelve months and here we are asked to vote for rates which are certainly not in any sense revolutionary for the simple reason that not one of the things you said you would do have been done. There is nothing in that financial statement which has a vestige of Socialism in it.[49]

But let us return to the start of the century. In the period 1907-28, the council was dominated by the Conservative, Charles Wilson. The *Tercentenary Handbook* produced by the council had a surprisingly frank profile of its leader:

> His critics of the old days, when he first came into the City Council with resonant voice and bellicose attitude, accused him of being 'aspiring and presumptuous'. They recognised presently that he was well-meaning and 'knew his book' ...This sketch aims to show that with all his pushful and vigorous personality, he attained his present position as undisputed governor of the city's affairs without unduly treading on anybody's corns. His opponents are many, but his enemies are few. His political rivals chide him while they secretly and socially admire him. They simulate wrath at his sledge-hammer methods of debate, and, on occasions, they attempt to pull the leg of a gentleman who has the assurance to declare, 'I am Leeds'.
>
> An accountant by profession, he has fallen naturally into the office of local Chancellor of the Exchequer, and, with his famous 'blue pencil' is the terror of every chairman of committee ...If he has a weakness, it is his ambition to see Leeds surpass in size and population any other city in Yorkshire. In seeking to extend the city, no man has ever schemed with such pugnacity.[50]

Charles Wilson presided over many areas of innovation and development in council activities, but it is to the planning for the future growth of the city which we turn first.

The Early Years of Town Planning

Before the twentieth century the council made no attempt to draw up or implement a strategy for the future development of Leeds as a whole. The advent of town planning, in the sense of planning the land-use of the city in a coherent manner, with a view to promoting the economic, social and environmental well-being of the city, was to be a feature of the twentieth century. Municipal town planning began in England in an official sense with the Town Planning Act of 1909. This Act, however, was almost solely concerned with the development of new suburbs. When local authorities obtained specific consent from the Local Government Board, they were permitted to create plans for the layout, amenities, highways, and services of undeveloped land which was deemed to be about to be developed for housing. The 1919 Town Planning Act made the preparation of such plans compulsory, and allowed land already occupied by buildings to be included in the area of a town planning scheme, but the emphasis remained on undeveloped land. There was no question of planning a town as a whole, and the treatment of unhealthy and decrepit districts could still be dealt with only under the Housing Acts.[51]

Leeds enthusiastically made use of the powers under this legislation in guiding the development of the estates of council and private housing in the 1920s and '30s. Indeed, it felt itself to be in the forefront of the new 'science of town planning'. The *Tercentenary Handbook* noted in 1926:

> The science of town planning has indeed arrived, teaching us to look ahead beyond the needs of now and to envisage a future when the Corporation shall be able to say, 'Here shall be the factories, here the workers' homes, here the parks and open spaces, and here the main roads link the town with the suburbs and the outside country' ...Through its new roads and its town-planning scheme generally, the community is now able to guide the growth and control the building development of its own city. In that way, much is now being done to repair the years of uncontrolled development bequeathed by past generations.[52]

It was noted that Leeds had a total area of 30,136 acres, and that the unbuilt-on land amounting to 21,400 acres was to be 'town-planned'. Of this area, 16,447 acres already had town-planning schemes in force and work was proceeding on the other areas. Since this was the era of the expansionist aspirations of Sir Charles Wilson, this emphasis on planning for development at the edge of the city was entirely in keeping with the philosophy of the day.

Of course the efficient operation of the great city and the development of communications with its new territorial conquests depended on improvements to both transport infrastructure and services. These received considerable attention in the 1920s and '30s. Traffic congestion was already a problem at the tail end of the nineteenth century, and was bound to get worse as the number of motor vehicles grew. Nationally, the number of motor vehicles increased from 8,465 in 1903 to 1,195,882 in 1933.[53] Locally, traffic census figures revealed that in 1913 Roundhay Road was carrying 1,703 vehicles a day, but by 1935 the number had leapt to 12,448.[54]

The council turned the high unemployment of the 1920s to a positive benefit by providing jobs for the unemployed on the construction of the city's proposed network of new or improved roads. By 1926 the Ring Road was under construction, though difficulties completing it were anticipated because only half of the 30 mile length was within the city boundaries. The *Tercentenary Handbook* noted that:

> The expenditure has been enormous, but at least one of the beneficial effects is already seen, apart from the facilitation of traffic movement, in the impetus which it has given to house building in areas both rural and suburban ...Cross country traffic will be able to follow it and skirt the City, thus lessening congestion in the centre.[54]

The Ring Road was to be 100 feet wide. Radial roads to it from the city centre were also either being built or widened. By 1926, under the direct labour unemployment relief scheme, £371,000 had been expended on building 10¼ miles of the road. The council was so proud of it that in July 1926 on the rest day of the England-Australia Test Match at Headingley, the Australian cricket team were taken on a motor tour to see it. In addition to work on the Ring Road, by 1926, £940,000 had been spent on 27 miles of arterial roads and road widenings. Gledhow Valley Road, for example was opened in 1926. In many instances only half-widths of the wide roads were being built at that stage so that as great a length as possible could be available at once, but the land had been acquired so that the full width could be built when the necessity arose.[56] A legacy of this decision is that even today some sections of the Ring Road are still only two lanes wide.

For many years Leeds remained primarily dependent on trams to carry people around the city. The trams were cheap, clean and efficient, and, though in 1926 the council's Tramways Committee acknowledged 'the possibilities of the motor omnibus', it argued that tramcars were indispensable in a big city to deal with workers during the 'rush' hours within a radius of from two to three miles from the centre. 'For the gala days at Roundhay Park and the big football and cricket matches in Leeds', it added, 'a system of transport consisting solely of motor omnibuses would lead to hopeless congestion'. The trams, it noted, had performed an inestimable service in bringing such places as Adel, Guiseley, Roundhay Park and Temple Newsam within easy reach of every citizen. Fares were cheap – 'It costs but threepence to make the lovely ten miles tramway trip from Leeds to Guiseley, and thus to reach the delightful scenery of the Wharfe Valley and Otley Chevin. What other city can offer such facilities?'[57]

Several of the new roads planned in the 1920s were to be 125 feet wide to accommodate fenced-off tramways with dual carriageways on either side. The horse trams were taken out of service in 1902, and thereafter the trams were all electric. By 1936 the City Transport Department operated 108 miles of single, electrically equipped track, on which the trams covered over twelve million miles and carried nearly 143 million passengers each year.[58] Despite the council's high opinion of the trams, they did have drawbacks as a means of travel. Keith Waterhouse, the Leeds author and playwright, remembers that the old open-fronted bone rattler trams, some of which were still in service in the 1930s, made passengers sick. Their conductors kept a bag of sawdust under the stairs as a precaution.[59] By 1936 the bus was gaining a firm foothold in the city. In that year there were 107 miles of bus routes within the city, with buses running about 6 million miles a year and carrying over 37 million passengers. By 1936 the Transport Committee was warming to the bus: 'Here, as in many municipalities, there are indications that with the advent of the big capacity bus, the tram, as a much less mobile unit and a prolific source of congestion, will be gradually superseded by the motor unit'.[60] In the event, the trams survived in Leeds until 1959.[61]

In addition to the Ring Road scheme, the problem of traffic congestion in the city centre was tackled in several ways. By far the most spectacular project was the

The Headrow, the grand new avenue of Leeds, designed by Sir Reginald Blomfield in 1925. The major attraction was Lewis's new department store, opened in September 1932 at a cost of £1 million. Its lavish marble floors, bronze decorated staircases, lifts and escalators brought ultra modern style to shopping in Leeds.

monumental venture which created the present-day Headrow. In order to relieve traffic congestion on Bond Street, Commercial Street and Kirkgate, it was decided to build an 80 feet wide street stretching for almost half a mile on the line of Park Lane, Guildford Street, Upperhead Row and Lowerhead Row, between the Town Hall and Mabgate. The property on the north side of these streets, much of it ramshackle, was to be demolished and replaced by a grand unified frontage. The total cost was estimated at half a million pounds. The necessary Act of Parliament was obtained in 1925, but the scheme did not start for a further two years because of the problem of sorting out land ownership. This was a truly grand and ambitious piece of civic design. As the city handbook for 1947-48 commented: 'The project was not without its critics, but now there are few who will say that The Headrow is not one of Leeds's greatest assets, or that it has not been worthwhile.' A large proportion of the cost of the scheme was recovered via rents and sale of land. The northern frontage was designed by Sir Reginald Blomfield and G.W.Atkinson, the only exception being Headrow House, which was not built until 1955.[62]

The flow and regulation of city centre traffic was assisted in additional ways. On 16 March 1928 Leeds became the first town in England to install automatic traffic lights. These were sited at the corner of Park Row and Bond Street. In 1936 a new traffic circulation system was introduced in City Square. This necessitated the removal of the War Memorial, which was tastefully incorporated in a Garden of Rest in front of the Municipal Buildings and Art Gallery.[63]

As well as the provision of good transport and communications, the council continued to see its control and expansion of the major public utilities as vital to the successful development of Leeds. The Corportion Gas Department continued to provide cheap gas for heating, lighting, cooking and for industry. Life was made much easier and cleaner for Leeds people with the gradual replacment of old iron ranges with gas cookers. The area supplied with gas steadily enlarged and by 1939 Scholes, Crossgates, Halton, Seacroft, Alwoodley, Adel, Horsforth, Newlay, Bramley, Stanningley, Pudsey, Rodley and Middleton were all receiving Leeds gas.[64] Electricity, too, was supplied from the Corporation's Whitehall Road works. A huge increase in the number of electrical appliances for the home, and the ease and efficiency of electric lighting led to the number of consumers rising from 14,121 in 1915 to just over 37,000 in 1925. Such was the demand that in 1926 the Redcote Farm Estate, comprising some 104 acres at Kirkstall was purchased by the council, and a splendid new power station was opened there in 1931. By 1937 the department could boast of 148,194 customers.[65]

The council's Water Department continued its sterling work, supplying 18 million gallons of water per day to the city by 1926. The water supply from the reservoirs at Fewston, Swinsty, Lindley Wood and the River Ure in

Wensleydale, passed through Eccup Reservoir on its way to the Weetwood filter beds. In 1926 the department laid new mains to permit the extension of supplies to Moortown Reservoir. The pumping station at Headingley was extremely busy supplying water to the higher districts of Cookridge, Moortown and Bramley, where the demand for water increased as building spread.[66] In 1926, in an article entitled 'The Wonders of Sewage Purification', the council's Sewerage Committee reflected on the other side of the water business. In that year the city's 17¾ million gallons of sewage drained from the city's 534 miles of sewers to the main sewage works at Thorpe Stapleton, Knostrop, which had been extended as a result of the Leeds Corporation Act of 1908. This huge volume was filtered somewhat imperfectly before it was passed into the River Aire.[67] The gross pollution of the River Aire through the inflow of treated sewage effluent is a problem which is still with the city in the 1990s.

But let us return to town planning. The Town and Country Planning Act of 1932 gave local authorities powers to prepare planning schemes for all land within their boundaries, whether undeveloped or not, and required people seeking to build, in an area for which a planning scheme existed or was in preparation, to obtain council permission. Leeds City Council thereby gained enhanced controls over building development. Nevertheless, this was a far cry from empowering the council to coherently plan the future development of the city from an economic, social and environmental point of view. In particular, there was little power to control or direct change in the existing features of the city, whether with regard to buildings or green spaces.

Twentieth-Century Life

The First World War

When war was declared in August 1914 it was greeted with enthusiasm. It was widely felt that war would be over by Christmas and crowds flocked to the recruiting office in Hanover Square to sign up. An illuminated tram car toured the city encouraging all able-bodied men to join up, even theatre performances and football matches were interrupted as appeals were made to young men. Aliens who had failed to take out naturalisation papers were arrested, and over fifty Germans were detained at the Town Hall.

By September 1914, 5,000 Leeds men had enlisted in Lord Kitchener's army and 1,275 had joined the new Leeds City (Pals) Battalion. Leeds, it was observed at the time, wore almost the aspect of a town in military occupation:

> Never before had such sights been seen in Fenton Street, Woodhouse Lane, Claypit Lane and Carlton Hill. Artillery, Engineers, Rifles, Hussars, all were marching hither and thither, undergoing medical examination, receiving instructions, finding billets or being quartered in barracks and schools, in readiness for training, and the central parts of the city were thronged to see and cheer them. Stirring, too, were the scenes on their departure, and inspiring were some of the words spoken by chaplains and commanding officers.[68]

The enthusiasm for the war began to wane as the casualties began to mount. In 1915 the old workhouse in Beckett Street was converted into a 500-bed hospital and in 1916 Chapel Allerton military hospital was opened, but yet more beds were needed. By the end of the war medical facilities for the wounded had been extended to include Temple Newsam House, Gledhow Hall, Roundhay Road School, and Lotherton Hall, plus facilities at Armley, Cookridge, Harrogate, Stokesley, Northallerton and Thirsk. Shortages of many goods also appeared as the months went by. The public houses closed early, beer was in short supply and there were complaints of its low gravity and quality. To supplement food supplies, people began cultivating allotment gardens on land rented from the council, and in the spring of 1917, portions of the parks and golf links were ploughed up and private grounds converted to kitchen gardens.

The people of Leeds of all classes paid a heavy price during the war. Most experienced the tragic loss of a friend or loved one. Of the 82,000 men recruited in Leeds, over 10,000 were killed and many wounded. In particular, the idea of City Battalions had been a bad one, for out of the 1,275 who had joined in 1914, only around

Parade of the West Riding Divisional Service Corps in Park Row, 28 April 1915.

500 survived. When the war officially ended on Armistice Day, 11 November 1918 there was great rejoicing in Leeds. At night there were fireworks and bonfires, shops were illuminated and the hotels, restaurants, theatres and music halls became packed with excited people. But there was no jubilant welcome home for the troops, who returned in dribs and drabs. After months and years in the trenches, they were amazed by the vibrant city which they found:

> They see no sign of the grim spectre of poverty, nor of sadness and melancholy, such as they saw abroad. Thousands of women, presumably out of work, plod daily to the Labour Exchanges, thousands of ex-soldiers (and others) go to and fro on the same errand. In the streets – thronged as perhaps they never were before – predominates the pre-war atmosphere of prosperity, even of luxury. How and why is it? There is no complaint, certainly no wailing on the part of the shopkeepers. Money is about still, and apparently in plenty; if the truth were told, tradesmen were never better off, in spite of four and a half years of war. We do not yet hear of fur coats going to the pawnshop, or of the costly trinkets bought by our prosperous munitioneers finding the same resting-place. Shops, closed 'for the duration', are re-opening. Places of entertainment were never doing better – even in the days when amusement taxes were unknown. And if you gain the confidence of returned soldiers they will tell you quietly of the great change which they feel has come over many of our women and girls; of their over-dress or under-dress, their giddiness and flippancy, the frequent veneer of affected masculinity. Exceptions there are, they admit. But, on the whole, they are not favourably impressed with either the tone or the manners of the majority of girls "they left behind." The development of womanhood, in the hands of those who have professed to be its leaders, does not strike them as being on the right lines. They preferred the pre-war feminine atmosphere.[69]

One of the most striking features of the war was the role of women, who proved themselves capable of doing jobs previously thought of as male occupations. As men joined the forces, women and girls had taken their place. They replaced men as ticket collectors and cleaners on the railways, clerks in the banks and insurance offices, as well as undertaking manual work in warehouses and factories. Many hoped that their vital contribution would be recognised by giving them the vote. Before the war, Leeds suffragettes had campaigned long and hard for enfranchisement. One of their most prominent activists was Leonora Cohen whose memorabilia can be found in the Kirkstall Abbey House Museum. Before the war, she had organised mass meetings on Woodhouse and Hunslet Moors, and achieved international notoriety in 1912 by throwing an iron bar through a jewel case in the Tower of London. The Representation of the People Act of 1918 gave all men the vote at 21, and enfranchised women over the age of 30. While this was an improvement, Cohen felt betrayed because men and women had not been put on an equal footing.[70]

Working-Class Domestic Life Between the Wars

After the celebrations to mark the end of the war, the working classes of Leeds came down to earth with a bang. Despite the distinct improvement in their standard of living in the later years of the nineteenth century, there had probably been little advance in the Edwardian period. Without doubt, they now hoped for a much better life. The paradox of the inter-war years was that for large numbers of people the period brought extreme hardship due to unemployment. At the same time, for those who managed to stay in work, the quality of life improved significantly. Prices nationwide fell sharply – possibly by as much as a quarter on average between 1922 and 1933 – while wages followed them down to a much lesser extent. Between 1918 and 1939 the purchasing power of workers' wages increased between a third and a half.[71] The British Medical Association Committee's Report on Nutrition reckoned that in the mid-'30s a man and wife in Leeds required 19s. a week to meet their household needs (apart from rent), plus 4s. to 5s. 6d. per week for each child according to their age and 8s. for every person of 14 and over.[72] With weekly wages at around £2 10s. 0d. to £2 15s. 0d. for unskilled workers and £3 5s. 0d. to £3 15s. 0d. for skilled workers, a notable though small margin for comfort had appeared in the lives of many working-class people.[73]

The diet of the working classes was much less varied and less nutritious than people are used to today. A survey of Leeds school children between 1902 and 1904 showed that the typical child had white bread and treacle with tap water or weak tea for breakfast, and for the main meal of the day, black pudding, liver and onions, a stew called penny duck consisting of offal meat or fish, or tinned meat with pickles and chips. Recalling the life of his poor but respectable working-class family in the 1920s, Richard Hoggart, a working-class orphan lad from Hunslet who later became an eminent Professor of English Literature, remembered his grandmother's skill at turning even the cheapest food into a nourishing, appetising meal, either a stew, a pie or fried fish. He recalled that only on Sunday would he enjoy cheap streaky bacon for breakfast. Weekday breakfast usually consisted of bread-and-dripping with a cup of tea. Tinned corned beef, cheap blackberry-and-apple jam, sardines and pineapple with condensed milk added variety to the diet. Stews, minces, pies and fried fish were the norm. The only solid meat he recalls eating was the occasional piece of rabbit. Even families with a regular breadwinner would usually only have a joint at Sunday dinnertime.[74]

For many working-class children the acquisition of new clothes was a special event. Indeed, Whitsuntide had special significance as this was the time of year when fortunate working-class children received new clothes. On Whit Sunday visits were made to family and friends to show off the new outfits. For their fathers the inter-war period brought a revolution in clothing. Since the suits made by Burton and, more particularly, his less up-market competitors cost around a week's wages for a working man they were now in the reach of the mass market. In the 1930s and '40s suits became common attire amongst working men at leisure, and it became increasingly difficult to spot the difference between Jack and his master.[75]

For the majority of the working classes their lives were the lives of the back-to-back streets, for even in 1918 over 70 per cent of the city's houses were back-to-backs. The virtue of these homes remained that they were cheap to rent, easy to heat, and provided separate single family dwellings. In these streets close knit communities had developed, providing comfort and support for each other during hard times. Inside, the houses were sparsely furnished with clip-rugs, made of strips of old cloth and clothes pushed through a canvas base, scattered over the floors. Many of these homes had a cellar where food and coal were kept and some had coppers where the water was boiled on wash day. The focus of family life was the fire, often part of a large, black-leaded range, which provided cooking facilities, as well as hot water.

The world of Leeds back-to-backs described by Richard Hoggart was one of gas lamps, rag-and-bone men, horses, and handcarts, and a society in which there was a multiple of fine-gradings of status. People from certain streets, chapels or pubs thought themselves superior to their neighbours. The possession of a side yard, an attic room with bath with tapped water, or the greatest of all distinctions – a through terraced house – were all demonstrations of status. There was a clear hierarchy of working-class occupations – for women, from cleaners, canteen workers and barmaids, to the masses of tailoresses in the middle, and the secretaries, town-centre shop assistants and receptionists at the top. Similar differentiation was to be found in male occupations from the 'pot-bellied' manual worker to the 'five pound-a-week' man.[76]

One of foremost problems for many working-class families remained the poor condition and crampedness of their homes. The Leeds housing reformers of the inter-war period were able to present reports on housing conditions almost as disturbing in their way as those of Baker and Hole in the mid-nineteenth century. Examples were cited in the early '30s of houses where people lay dying in a curtained-off corner of a downstairs room, or where the local doctor had to erect props on each side of a bed with a large dust sheet covering his patient in order to catch the falling bugs. Another unfortunate woman had had to seek the doctor's help when she found rats coming down the chimney and had not dared to leave a night-light (a small candle) on for her baby because its warmth caused the bugs to fall from the ceiling on to the cot.[77]

In 1931 a depressing report was presented to the Housing Committee of the council, which graphically conveyed the impact of housing deficiencies on the lives of many of the working classes:

> The provision of sufficient bedroom accommodation is obviously a primary need for a normal family, and where it is lacking the effects on the younger members of the family are appalling. In many houses of this city the birth of a child must take place in the living room downstairs, for there is no spare bedroom where the mother may lie for her confinement. When death enters the house the body must frequently be laid out in the same living room downstairs, and the clergy who have to visit such houses are accustomed to the sight of the family sitting down to meals, and entertaining the numerous visitors who arrive at such times, in the room where the corpse is laid out. What can the effect be on young children in such a home? Further, it would be easy to gain evidence from school teachers in the city of the terrible effects of lack of sufficient bedroom accommodation at night-time.
>
> Lack of sufficient washing accommodation means that the whole family must wash at the sink in the living room, and the clergy can quote you cases of decent mothers who get up in the morning, prepare the breakfast for the children, and after they have gone off to school lock the door in order that they themselves may partly undress and wash. Of course, there is no supply of hot water in these houses. All must be boiled in the kettle on the fire. Opportunities for taking a bath are difficult to secure. The younger members may be encouraged to go to the public baths; but it is a fact that the parents get very few baths, and as they get older tend to drop the practice altogether. Lavatory accommodation is in many cases woefully inadequate. Families have to share a closet with others usually placed in a passage nearby. They may have to walk down the street past six or eight houses before arriving at the lavatory provided, usually surrounded by the dustbins. Not infrequently they arrive to find the place 'engaged' by one of the neighbours; and children, and not merely the tiny ones, get into the habit of using the street instead. Again, all neighbours are not equally clean, and this tends to make things very unpleasant for the more decent citizens. Such objectionable habits as spitting, not least from those who are suffering from disease of one kind or another, aggravate the situation and do much to increase the work of the Medical Officer of Health. It is sometimes said that slum conditions create revolution; but to many of us the more terrible fact is that the people learn to acquiesce in these sad conditions.[78]

The scale of the problem was massive. In the 1920s the Leeds Medical Officer of Health, Dr Jervis, reckoned that at least 33,000 houses ought to be demolished.

Homes Fit For Heroes

From the city council's view point, up to the end of the First World War the rehousing of the working classes was a large-scale problem with no immediate solution. The private landlords, who owned most of the back-to-backs, had little financial incentive to provide better quality housing, while, for budgetary and philosophical reasons, the council was loth to embark on an extensive house-building programme. Between 1895 and 1914, though the council had cleared 2,300 slum dwellings, it had built only 36 replacement houses. Utopian dreams of a city in which all lived in good quality housing were a long way from being realised.

The entry of the council into the provision of municipal housing and its extensive slum clearance activities were therefore a dramatic feature of the period between the First and Second World Wars.[79] During the last years of the First World War, Lloyd George inaugurated a national campaign to build 'Homes fit for Heroes'. The Addison Act of 1919 required local authorities to survey their inhabitants' housing needs and offered government subsidies towards building costs. Leeds council responded energetically, though the controlling Conservative group had some misgivings,

Three-bedroom, non-parlour council houses built in the late 1920s on the Dewsbury Road Estate.

and under this and subsequent legislation, built almost 4,000 houses to rent and 1,000 for sale by 1926. Council estates with names familiar to us today began to appear – Hawksworth Wood, Wyther House, Meanwood, Cross Gates, Middleton and York Road.[80] By 1930 the council had erected 7,000 houses.

While this sterling effort helped to address the housing shortage, it did nothing for the slum-dwellers. Only the best-off working-class families and the lower middle classes could afford the new accommodation. In 1927 a back-to-back could be rented for under 5s. a week including rates, whereas even the cheapest council property cost over 16s. Dr Jervis complained that 'the class of individual going into the new houses is not the class that stands most in need of improved conditions'.[81]

At the same time, while the Conservative-led council accepted the need for the demolition of the slums, it preferred to concentrate on increasing the housing stock. It believed that it would take at least a generation to remove the slums. A major change in approach came in November 1933 when Labour gained an overall majority on the council. The reason for the change may be summarised in two words – Charles Jenkinson. Jenkinson, a radical Anglican clergyman from the East End of London, became Vicar of Holbeck in 1927, and in 1930 was elected as a Labour member of the council. He was a man with a mission, and had a dynamism and drive not dissimilar to that of Charles Wilson. As a result of his charisma and achievements, he was subsequently to become leader of the Leeds Labour party and a national figure. In the early 1930s he succeeded in making housing policy a priority issue. His day-to-day knowledge of the living conditions of his parishioners in Holbeck gave him an almost unparalleled expertise on the housing problem. He witnessed at first hand the misery and human suffering of those who lived in such appalling conditions.[82]

Jenkinson became chairman of the council's Housing Committee in 1933, and under his impetus the Labour administration proposed its revolutionary intention to demolish more than 30,000 houses within six years. The plan – dubbed the 'Red Ruin' by opponents – proved over-ambitious, but 14,000 houses were cleared away by 1939. The accelerated pace of demolition in the mid-1930s coupled with the build-up of population pressure – numbers had increased by over 20,000 between 1921 and 1931, and rose another 14,000 in the next eight years – necessitated a much more intensive programme of municipal house building. Under Jenkinson's initiative a Housing Department was created in 1934 which pushed ahead rapidly. By 1937 the number of council-built houses, cottages, flats and shops had leapt to over 15,000, and by 1939 there were 24 estates ranging in size from 33 to 3,500 houses.[83]

The key to the successful implementation of the slum clearance programme was to make the replacement houses affordable for the poorer families. In the years 1928-32, the average rent of a house on one of the new estates was 9s. per family per week, whereas the rent of a typical slum house was 4s. 8d.[84] Controversially, Jenkinson introduced a differential rent scheme, whereby every tenant with sufficient income to pay the full economic rent of their council house was required to do so, while those with inadequate incomes were given rent relief – in some cases they paid nothing.[85] For the first time people had the opportunity to transfer directly from the slums to new council housing. The subsidised rents scheme depended on a detailed means test of individual tenants, which, though well-intentioned, caused widespread uproar in the city. The Tories hated the subsidies to the poor, while tenants paying full rents were angered to find some neighbours paying lower rents for identical properties. As a result of the council's slum clearance and house building programmes, over 34,000 people were moved to a new physical and social environment between 1933 and 1940.

In building the new estates, the council was much taken with the contemporary vogue for the creation of airy, spacious, low density 'garden suburbs' on the edge of major towns. The estates were built on high ground, around three or four miles out of the centre – as far as possible out of the blanket of smoke that perpetually smothered the inner city – and had gardens with hedges and one tree. The first estate developed by the Housing Department in 1934 was at Gipton with 3,500 houses, and by 1937 the Seacroft estate, with a target of 11,000 dwellings, was well under way, as were estates each with over 1,000 dwellings at Sandford, Halton Moor and Belle Isle. The density of the houses was approximately 12 per acre, compared to the 70 per acre of the back-to-backs built before 1866, and the 40 to 60 per acre of the later types.[86]

Jenkinson tried to match houses to the individual needs of the tenants. He ensured that on the estates there was a mix of two, three, four and five-bedroomed houses, and special ageing persons' flats. A novel provision were the 'sunshine houses' which were reserved for families containing someone who was medically certified as needing more than the normal amount of sunshine and air. These houses had a bay window in the living room and a large special window in one bedroom, both made with a steel framework which could be folded up completely to let sun and air into the house.[87]

Before moving in, all infested furniture passed through a defestation gas van affectionately called 'Jenkinson's bug van'. The council was so shocked by the poor quality of the furniture possessed by their new tenants that a special scheme was started whereby essential items could be purchased and repayments made by small weekly instalments collected with the rent. A bed with all its furnishings, including a changes of linen, could be bought for £6 17s., around 2½ times the average weekly unskilled wage.[88]

In spite of the vast improvement in the living conditions of the families who were rehoused on these Utopian estates, many had misgivings about the move. In 1914 about 80 per cent of the Leeds population had lived within a two-mile radius of the city centre and its amenities. Close knit communities were broken up and many missed the bustle and convenience of town life. Indeed, in 1938 Labour's newspaper, *The Leeds Weekly Citizen*, noted the discontent of some of the estates' residents:

> Removed from the unhealthy conditions of the congested areas in the central portions of the town, they are at the same time removed from the cinemas, clubs, places of entertainment and the comforting warmth of brightly illuminated shopping centres.[89]

The new estate lacked amenities and the council became concerned about juvenile vandalism. Others complained about the high cost of transport from the suburbs to their place of work.

Keith Waterhouse, who was brought up on the Middleton

Quarry Hill Flats. This massive Utopian council scheme was to house over 3,000 people. The use of the 'Mopin system' of prefabricated blocks of stressed steel and concrete largely removed the need for skilled labour and expensive brickwork. It incorporated lifts and the revolutionary French 'Garchey' automatic waste disposal system which carried domestic refuse and sink waste direct from the flats to central incinerators, and there was a laundry with dryers. The courtyards had playgrounds and lawns, but the proposed tennis courts and bowling greens were never built. The aim of rehousing an entire community here failed as many people decided to stay put in the council houses which had been temporarily allocated to them when their slum homes were demolished. Structural defects and the failure of the 'Garchey' system led to the demolition of the flats only forty years later.

Estate in the 1930s complains that, unlike the streets of Hunslet, the estate streets never felt properly alive. Though the lack of adequate shops encouraged the trade of hawkers and itinerant traders of all sorts ranging from the pea and pieman, and the firewood man to the tea man, the breadman, the pop man and the scissor-grinder, the dreary curves and crescents and the obsession with open space for its own sake, had a deadening effect. The absence of the mixture of housing, retailing, industry and other activities removed the variety and interest of city life.[90]

The pull of city life was a strong one. Even in 1922 some people still lived right in the heart of the city centre, as one *Yorkshire Evening Post* reporter discovered when he visited cottages in North Passage on the north side of the Lowerhead Row in February 1922: 'T would be like uprooting t'owd shire oak to shift me out of here', said an old lady who invited me into a huge living-room where she was busy on her "brasses". 'I've lived all my seventy years within this distance of Kirkgate market, and I don't want to go further afield now. No desire for the country'.[91]

The preference of the working classes to remain within easy reach of the city centre was addressed by the council in one monumental exception to the garden suburb vogue. The building of Quarry Hill flats on the site of the city's most notorious Victorian slums produced perhaps the most revolutionary housing schemes in England. Charles Jenkinson and the Director of Housing, R.A.H.Livett, took as their model Vienna's famous Karl Marx Hof, a new kind of housing estate, consisting of monumental flats and formal courtyards and gardens, communal laundries, kindergartens and playgrounds. When the first stage opened in March 1938 it was the envy of every local authority and became internationally famous.[92]

Mid-1930s low-density council housing on the Gipton Estate.

Dyson's Jewellers. Dyson's clock was one of the best known landmarks in Leeds and a common place to meet.

really "in the country" yet at the same time they have splendid train services (late trains home after the Theatre and the Concerts are special features) that they may almost be regarded as suburbs of the mighty city.'[94]

Some families moved or established their first homes much less far away. While the council was undertaking its impressive programme of municipal house building, an even greater contribution to the growth of the city's housing stock was being made by private enterprise. The low interest rates of the 1930s (a bank/base rate of 2%) produced a great boom in private house-building. Large quantities of the city's present-day private housing stock was built in these years. Almost two-thirds of the 54,000 new dwellings completed in the city between the wars were built by the private sector. In the mid-1920s new semi-detached houses might be bought for in the region of £600-£750, while in the mid-1930s as a result of falling prices the typical range was around £500-£675.[95] Many of the new private sector houses were built in Headingley, Gledhow. Moortown, Alwoodley, Roundhay, Oakwood, Weetwood and Adel, which were thereby confirmed as middle-class areas.

For the working classes the affluence of the city's middle classes was still something to marvel at. The considerable disparity in incomes was most sharply demonstrated by middle-class patronage of city centre shops which were way above the pockets of the working classes. In the 1920s, department stores such as Schofield's, Lillie's and Matthias Robinson catered for 'people with taste', while Marshall's in Bond Street set the seal of distinction on Leeds as a high quality shopping centre. As the *Yorkshire Post* noted

> The afternoon mannequin parades here are an alluring feature. Though generally regarded as an ultra-refinement of luxury shopping, the mannequin parade is essentially a practical institution, appealing to the practical sense which women combine with admiration of dainty finery. Different types of wearers in furs and costumes, evening gowns and cloaks, and French model millinery, show at a glance what is appropriate for individual style, thus guiding selection in an embarrassment of choice and promoting satisfaction in purchase. The attraction of the Fashion House windows is so well known as hardly to need mention; they form a brilliant kaleidoscope of the departmental wealth within.[96]

Ladies who wished to look the part could shop for silks and millinery items at Bridges and Co in Briggate, Lands Lane and Thornton's Arcade, try on evening gowns at Bertie Moor's, purchase 'hats of distinction' from Marian Wilson's or have their hair permed at the Misses Walker on Boar Lane. Other shops became noted for their products – Doyle's china, Denby and Spink's furniture, Peacock's carpets, Longley's beds, Greenwood's jewellery and Saxone shoes.[97] Ladies could

Middle-Class Domestic Life Between the Wars

For the Leeds middle classes, provided they held on to their jobs or their businesses survived, the first half of the twentieth century was a period of increased comfort. Those whose incomes came in the form of salaries, still comfortably out-earned most of the working classes. In the mid-1930s, while male factory workers earned around £130 to £180 per annum, doctors might earn £1,000 a year, administrators and business managers £450, bank clerks £370, clergymen £350, and railway clerks £225.[93]

The trend towards the residential segregation of the working and middle classes increased. Some of the most affluent middle classes took to living even further outside the city. The *Leeds Guide* for 1909 noted: 'There are a score of places within easy reach of the city which are growing in popularity as residential quarters for businessmen.' It proceeded to list the North-Eastern Railway's 'special contract tickets' (season tickets) for one, three, six or twelve months to places such as Cross Gates, Garforth, Scholes, Wetherby, Pool, Thorner, Bardsey, Collingham Bridge, Thorp Arch, Church Fenton, Horsforth, Arthington, Weeton, Pannal, Burley, Ben Rhydding, Harrogate and Ilkley. 'Most of these places', it noted, 'are sufficiently far from Leeds to be

Marshall and Snelgrove, Bond Street and Park Row in 1909. It vied with Schofield's for the title of the city's most prestigious department store.

The Victoria Arcade, on the Headrow, decorated for the Tercentenary Celebrations of 1926.

purchase French perfume, elegant lingerie, hand-made blouses and jumpers.

Tired middle-class shoppers could relax in one of the many fine cocoa houses, coffee shops, cafes and restaurants.[98] One of the finest was Schofield's sumptuous cafe-restaurant where its experienced chef created delicious meals, and in 1926 the diner could relax and listen to the all star Versatiles, a quintet of musicians whose 'renditions are full of variety, and quite removed from the monotony that all too frequently mars the music of similar organisations'.[99] Once refreshed, they could go to Lillies in Albion Street to purchase a new vacuum cleaner, to Jenkins on King Edward Street to buy the latest gramophone, and finish at Eveleigh Bishop's on Briggate where they could inspect:

> an extensive stock of gift goods in the shape of dressing cases (made by the firm) in crocodile leather and beautifully fitted at prices with the astonishing range of from £5 to £500; veritable gems in "period" cabinets of cutlery; tortoiseshell ware; pottery of all the famous makes; cut glass, including one of the fine pieces shown at the Board of Trade Exhibition; hand hammered pewter ware; hand-painted Christmas cards, vanity bags with electric lights, and so on.[100]

Though many men still preferred their shopping done for them, an increasing number of sophisticated retail outlets, with impressive window displays and modern shop fronts attracted the male shopper. Burton's, Hepworth's and Austin Reed's all prospered in the period. Hardy's at 'Number One' Boar Lane provided the sporting gent with golf suits:

> Made from SCOTCH TWEED in the newest Season's Designs. The JACKET is made in the single Breasted Lounge Style, with 2 or 3 button front, Melton under collar, well tailored. All trimmings are made to match. VEST made with 4 pockets and inside note pocket. KNICKERS good smart full cut plus-four style with pleated fronts, Band and Buckle at knee. From 6 guineas to 75/-.[101]

He could stroll over to Albion Street and browse in Rowland Winn's and Francis B.Cox's showrooms where the latest motor cars were on display.[102]

All this was a far cry from the experience of the residents of the back-to-back streets of Hunslet or the new council housing estates. Perhaps the strongest impression conveyed by the autobiographies of working-class lads such as Richard Hoggart and Keith Waterhouse, who grew up in Leeds in the 1920s and '30s, is that, though the city centre was used by all classes of society, it had different associations and different patterns of use for the various social groupings and age groups. All used the same basic grid with its major landmarks, streets and meeting places – Briggate, Boar Lane, City Square, Vicar Lane, the Headrow, the Markets, the major shops, and Dyson's clock – but beyond this, young people headed for the Locarno or the Mecca, the young men-about-town for the bars of Briggate, the middle classes for the 'posh' shops, the cultured for the Grand, concerts at the Town Hall, or a visit to the Art Gallery, and the working classes made for Woolworths, the Market and Lewis's.

Destitution and Ill-health

The high level of unemployment in the inter-war period meant that, however much the standard of living of the working classes had improved since the Victorian period, the possibility of destitution was still not far away. It was not by chance that there were still 77 pawnbrokers shops in Leeds in 1936. Only 6 of them were in the city centre, the rest were conveniently located for their clientele in the working-class areas.[103] The twentieth century has brought radical improvements in the provision for the poor and destitute in Leeds. The foundations of what we know today as the Welfare State were laid in the thirty years before the Second World War. As we have seen, in 1900 the working classes who were destitute or seriously ill had only two lines of recourse: either to the Poor Law Guardians, who would give them out-relief payments or accommodate them in the workhouse or the workhouse hospital, or to local charities which gave financial or medical assistance, the most notable being the General Infirmary. Some workers, of course, were members of benefit societies, but there was a limit to how long assistance from one of these could keep them going.

In 1909, when the Liberal government introduced Old Age Pensions, for the first time many old people were released from the inevitability of destitution. At 5s. per week for individuals over 70 years old and 7s. 6d. for couples, it was clearly not enough to live on without the aid of family and savings, but it was a start. The National Insurance Act of 1911, which for the first time provided ill-health and unemployment benefit payments independent of the Poor Law, however, was a failure. The mass long-term unemployment of the 1920s made it plain to all that many families were reduced to destitution through no fault of their own. In this climate, the Local Government Act of 1929 attempted to end the stigma associated with the Poor Law by abolishing the Boards of Guardians and transferring their powers and duties to the county councils and county boroughs. To mark the change and inculcate a new spirit, the Poor Law service was renamed Public Assistance, and the local authority committees administering it were known as Public Assistance Committees.[104]

On paper at least, the Poor Law and its institutions – the workhouse and the workhouse hospital – ceased to exist. It is rather bemusing to read a town guide or directory for the mid-1930s and find that the buildings which only a few years before were clearly identified as workhouse institutions have discreetly had their names changed. Thus in 1935, homeless men or the infirm aged are accommodated at 'South Lodge' Lane End Place, Holbeck – only recently better known as the Holbeck Union Workhouse and Infirmary. Women are conveyed to the 'North Lodge Institution' – formerly known as Leeds Union Workhouse.[105]

In the effort to remove the stigma from the social support associated with the Poor Law, the government's intention was that the kinds of need which it had addressed in an all-embracing way should eventually be divided into separate services. As part of this strategy, the workhouse hospitals were also transferred to the control of the new Leeds Public Assistance Committee. Henceforth the working classes, whether destitute or not, when they fell seriously ill and could not gain admission to the still charitably funded General Infirmary, were taken to St James's, St Mary's or St George's – none other than the Leeds Union Workhouse Infirmary, the Bramley Union Workhouse Infirmary (in Green Hill Road, Armley), and the Hunslet Union Workhouse Infirmary at Rothwell Haigh.[106] In fact the Leeds Union Workhouse Hospital had changed its name to St James's in 1925, anticipating the coming move to de-stigmatise treatment there. In 1934 all three hospitals were transferred to the council's Health Committee and thereby became municipal hospitals. In 1937 St James' had 1,330 beds, while St Mary's had 206, and St George's 311.[107]

Despite the cosmetics, in the eyes of Leeds people the local authority hospitals still bore the stigma of being former workhouse infirmaries, though Mr (later Sir) George Martin did an enormous amount to alter this situation by arranging for senior staff at the General Infirmary to become approved consultants at St James's. St James's was where many of the poor of Leeds had gone to die for generations and it was perhaps not until the 1960s that the General Infirmary and St James's assumed some sort of parity in the public mind.

By the 1930s the council had built a range of additional medical institutions which complemented the excellent work of the city's voluntary medical institutions. Seacroft Fever Hospital, which dealt with infectious diseases, was created during the years 1893-1904, while Killingbeck Hospital was established in 1900-04 to treat smallpox cases, though from 1913 it specialised in tuberculosis cases. Children with tuberculosis were treated at the Hollies Children's Sanitorium at Weetwood.[108] The Leeds Babies' Welcome Association, founded in 1912, was the first body in the city to interest itself in Motherhood and Child Welfare. In 1916 it amalgamated with the council and by 1926 ran 18 centres for mothers and babies.[109] The Cookridge Hospital, the main wing of which had been built by John Metcalfe in 1869 as ' a Hospital for the Convalescent Poor of Leeds', ran as such until the outbreak of the Second World War, when it became an annexe to the Leeds Maternity Hospital. In 1942 Leeds Corporation took over the lease and it reopened in 1943 with 101 beds for the chronic sick, convalescent and paediatric patients.[110]

For the middle classes, health care continued to be obtained through fee-paying visits to private doctors, or stays in the General Infirmary or in private nursing homes. By the thirties both the Infirmary and St James's took fee-paying middle-class patients, whilst treating the poor for nothing.

At one remove from destitution, there remained the lodging house dwellers. The lodging houses continued to thrive, in practice boosted by the number of men on the move in search of work in the inter-war period. In February 1922 one valiant reporter joined the down-and-outs of Leeds. His report of his night in a lodging house in the Calls has very strong echoes of the Victorian period:

> Our names and our ages were taken, and we were allotted Nos. 37 and 38. Alf was asked where he had dossed the night before, but I was spared the query; so my conscience escaped the burden of another white lie. I paid the tenpences.
>
> 'Time for bed,' says Alf, and we tramp upwards into the darkness. On each landing is a minute glimmer of blue gaslight – just enough to show one or two other shadowy forms in front of us. We enter room after room in search of beds No. 37 and 38. Finally we locate them on the top floor.
>
> Going to bed in a common lodging-house is wonderfully simple. There is no hair-brushing, or teeth-washing, or gargling – symptoms of uncalled-for refinement. Pyjamas are unknown.
>
> Everybody doffs his outer garments and pops into bed in his day-shirt. My room-mates – three including Alf – were asleep in about a minute. The little glimmer of light from the single gas-jet disappeared soon after – turned off at the meter – and I was left to listen to the snoring of my three companions, and others behind partitions, and to count off with rising joy each of the hours struck by the Parish Church clock that bore us towards daylight.
>
> The bed was hard, and the pillow flat as a pancake, but I have slept on many a worse couch in Flanders, so, although my feet protruded at the foot, I endured patiently. After three o'clock I dozed off for a couple of hours ...[111]

Accommodation for those who did not own or rent a house might range from the basic lodging houses to good quality boarding houses where lodgers might have their own room. By 1936 the city directory listed lodging houses under the heading 'Apartments', of which 79 were listed. Under the heading 'Boarding House Keepers', 15 addresses were listed. None of these apartments or boarding houses was situated in the centre. The process of demolition and major demand for central sites for commercial use had greatly reduced the number of common lodging houses – the only ones left in the city centre in the mid-1930s were in Wharf Street and High Court Lane.[112] In 1937 the council embarked on the scheme to build Shaftesbury House in Holbeck, a municipal hostel to meet the needs of people who normally lived in the lodging houses which had been demolished as a result of slum clearance. When opened it had accommodation for 308 men and 196 women.[113]

For the poor who received relief in their own homes, the world of the 1920s and '30s was an era of coupons and visits by officials. Grocery coupons were exchangeable at specified grocers – in Richard Hoggart's case (while his mother was alive and he still lived in Potternewton) the Maypole towards Meanwood – the clothing coupons, usable only at certain shops.[114] It was also a period of charitable handouts in a variety of forms. In the years immediately after the war many parents found it impossible to clothe their children properly, some children even going to school in bare feet. The *Yorkshire Evening Post* and the Education Department worked together to eradicate this problem by starting a 'Boots for the Bairns' charity. Distribution of boots started on 16 November 1921 and in the following six months over 12,000 children received boots and warm socks. Alongside this, approximately 21,000 parcels of nearly new garments were distributed to the needy. One of the difficulties encountered was that the impoverished, heartless parents took these items to the pawnbrokers.[115] By the 1930s the hierarchy of school children's footwear ran from the shoe wearer, to boots for the rougher element, then came clogs, and then plimsolls at the bottom of the social heap.[116]

The raised standard of living of the working classes, better diet, better housing and better health care, was reflected in the greatly improved health statistics in the inter-war period. By 1926 the death rate was down to 15 per thousand each year (compared with 23 per thousand in Leeds township in 1900), and by 1938 it had fallen still further to 13. Infant mortality (the number of children dying under the age of one), which had stood at 200 per thousand in 1900, had declined to 111 per thousand in 1926, 97 in 1929 and 64 by 1938.[117]

Education to 1945

Elementary and Secondary Education

The characteristic which distinctly marked out the working classes from the middle classes of Leeds was their inferior education. In 1900 the working-class children who went on to secondary education were few and far between. As we have seen, in 1902 Leeds School Board had 157 Elementary Schools but only 2 Higher Grade Schools. The Higher Grade Schools and the city's other secondary schools were fee-paying and, with the exception of scholarship children and those given concessionary fees, were essentially schools for the children of the middle classes.

The system of education in Leeds was shaken up as a result of the Education Act of 1902 which was precipitated by a legal ruling that all provision of evening and secondary education by School Boards was illegal. Throughout the country the School Boards were abolished, and county councils and county boroughs such as Leeds became local education authorities.[118] The education of working-class children was improved by the raising of the minimum school leaving age to 11 in 1891, 12 in 1901, and 14 in 1918 when the Education Act of that year completed the emancipation of children by prohibiting their employment below that age in factories, mines and workshops. To cater for the increased numbers of school children, due to both population growth and the broader age range, and to meet the larger geographical spread of the population, the council set about increasing the number of elementary schools, and in the inter-war period began to build them on the new housing estates, notably in the '20s at Cross Gates, Middleton, Hawksworth, Meanwood and Wyther Park.

The major significance of the 1902 Education Act was that it permitted the council's newly established Education Committee to spend money from the rates on secondary schools. It therefore gave the council both the problem and the opportunity of rationalising and increasing the provision of secondary education in the city. The pride of the Leeds School Board, the Central Higher Grade School in Woodhouse Lane and Thoresby High School on Great George Street, remained at the core of secondary provision, while the magnificent Cockburn Higher Grade School in Burton Road, Hunslet/Beeston Hill, which the School Board had opened almost as its final act in 1902, was eventually reorganised purely as a secondary school in 1912. But the council was determined to expand both the scale and the geographical spread of secondary school provision, and to produce a coherent system.[119]

Over the next decade it took over most of the secondary schools controlled by the voluntary sector. Leeds Boys' and Girls' Modern Schools were taken over in 1907, the latter being rehoused in the enlarged premises of Leeds Church Middle Class School in Vernon Road, which was absorbed and ceased as an institution that year. It was clear that secondary schools were needed at Roundhay, Chapeltown and, most urgently, on the west side of the city. West Leeds High School accommodating 600 boys and girls was opened at Armley in 1907. So imposing and well-equipped was the new school that under its photograph in the *Leeds Guide* of 1909 the publishers felt it necessary to place the caption, 'A Council School'![120] In 1914 the council took over Chapel Allerton Girls' High School, and in 1919 it bought up another private school in Roundhay which in 1920 became Roundhay Girls' High School when the council purchased the Ryder estate and used its house as the basis of the enlarged school. In 1926 the Education Committee's initial ambitious plan for the creation of a

West Leeds High School, Armley (architect, F.Broadbent, 1907).

Leeds school children depicting the Romans in Leeds as part of the Tercentenary Pageant at Roundhay Park in July 1926.

network of secondary schools in Leeds was completed when Roundhay School for Boys was opened on the same site. At the same time, £120,000 was being spent on the construction of impressive new buildings for the Boys' Modern School at Lawnswood, in future to be known simply as Leeds Modern School, and the Girls' Modern School, which was renamed Lawnswood High School.[121]

From the point of view of the educational opportunities of the different classes, however, the council's activities largely endorsed the principle that secondary education was essentially for the children of middle-class families and only the brightest of working-class children. The secondary schools – in practice municipal grammar schools – continued to charge fees, and probably less than one-tenth of the city's children were educated in them. The figures for education in Leeds in the mid-1920s are striking. In all there were 121 public elementary schools educating children to the age of 14, of which 70 were council schools, 39 Church of England, and 12 Roman Catholic. Between them they had 67,726 children on the roll. In contrast, there were only 14 secondary schools with 4,579 pupils attending the council schools and 1,701 the non-maintained schools.[122]

Richard Hoggart charts the obstacles which lay between the working-class child and a place in one these schools. When he entered Cockburn High School (on Hunslet Moor) at the age of 11 in the late 1920s, having succeeded in gaining a scholarship place, he was probably one of its thirty-odd scholarship holders a year out of population of 65,000 people who lived in South Leeds. It was the dedication and kindness of some its staff which coaxed him on to higher things. His was one of the rare working-class families (he was brought up by his grandmother and aunts) which resisted the natural inclination and financial pressure to get their children out earning at 14, or to take them out of High School at 16 when they had taken their School Certificate examinations.

The non-maintained, that it is to say independent, secondary schools in Leeds included schools of considerable distinction. Leeds Grammar School, under its reorganised management, began to flourish. A large science wing and new classrooms were added in 1905 and by 1914 the number of boys had increased to 306.[123] Leeds Girls' High School also continued to grow in stature. More extensive provision was also made for the secondary education of Roman Catholic children. Notre Dame Collegiate Secondary School (for girls) on Kingston Terrace, off Woodhouse Lane, had begun life as a pupil teacher school in 1898 and was formally reorganised as a secondary school in 1905. At the same time, St Michael's Roman Catholic College for Boys was founded in 1905 and moved to handsome new buildings on St John's Road, Woodhouse in 1909. Mount St Mary's College at the Richmond Hill also made an important contribution.[124]

The rapidly growing number of pupils and the bid for higher standards meant that there was an urgent need for more teachers. By 1926 the elementary schools alone employed 1,770 teachers. In 1913 the council's magnificent new teacher training college accommodating 480 students opened on the 99 acre site at Beckett Park at a cost of £240,000. Physical training in schools was a rapidly developing feature of children's education and in 1933 teacher training in the city was greatly enhanced by the erection of Carnegie Physical Training College for men in Beckett Park. The capital cost was defrayed by the Carnegie United Kingdom Trust. It provided one-year courses for university graduates and qualified teachers.[125]

Technical, Commercial and Higher Education

As Leeds industry and commerce became increasingly complex and sophisticated, the city required its workforce to be more highly trained in technical and commercial skills. Improved education in these spheres was given a high priority when the council's Education Committee was created in 1903. It soon took over the Technical School of the Leeds Institute, and by 1926 the Central Technical School, as it became known, had departments of chemistry, mechanical and electrical engineering, building, sanitary science, printing crafts, boot and shoe manufacture, and clothing. The evening classes formerly run under the auspices of the School Board had met a real need and were pursued enthusiastically. In 1925 there were around 40 'technical evening schools' providing advanced instruction to some 9,754 students. At the same time the evening teaching in commercial subjects was drawn together to form the Central School of Commerce and Modern Languages, soon to be known as the College of Commerce. By 1925 it had 1,350 evening students and its day department, opened in 1924, had 200 full-time students aged 14 to 18 years by 1926.[126]

The importance of this part-time evening education to the advancement of significant sections of the working classes should not be under-estimated. It gave those with determination the opportunity to fill some of the gaps left by elementary education. By providing minor technical and commercial qualifications, it was enough to raise some of the working classes in self-esteem and earning power above the general mass of unskilled workers or those whose sole qualification was based on manual skill. This process of advancement was also aided by the classes provided by the Workers' Educational Association and the Swarthmore Settlement (founded in Clarendon Road by the Quakers in 1909).[127]

The council also took over the School of Art, and the College of Housecraft, which was transferred from the Yorkshire Ladies' Council of Education. The College of Art, as the School of Art was renamed, had a hand in the training of two of the world's most distinguished sculptors, for Henry Moore was a student there in 1919-21 and Barbara Hepworth a year later – both won scholarships to the Royal College of Art in London.[128]

The quality of these now council run colleges made Leeds a regional centre for higher education – an important contribution to the continuing vitality of the local economy. The handbook prepared for the British Association's conference in Leeds in 1927 noted: 'The Technical College, the College of Commerce, and the College of Art have students in attendance at their courses from places as far distant as fifty miles from the city; while to the City of Leeds Training College and to the College of Housecraft come students from the length and breadth of England.'[129]

With its extensive involvement in primary, secondary and higher education, education became the largest item in the council's budget. In 1936/37 the council's total revenue spending was £4.9 million, out of which education took £1.1 million. The next largest items were: Public Assistance, £600,000; Police and Fire Brigade, £312,000; and Housing, £310,000.[130]

The most prestigious educational institution in Leeds remained the Yorkshire College, the University of Leeds as it became by Royal Charter on 25 April 1904. It went from strength to strength. In 1926 a scheme was prepared to add a magnificent range of buildings in Portland stone with an extensive frontage on Woodhouse Lane. The Mining, Chemistry and Physics Buildings, the University Union, and the splendid circular Brotherton Library, were erected before the war, but work on the Parkinson Building, with its landmark tower, was delayed by the hostilities and not completed until 1951. The Faculty of Medicine remained in the Medical School built in 1894, but the Dental School was added in 1928, and the Algernon Firth Institute of Pathology in 1932. The University was a truly national institution. By 1920-21 it had 2,300 students of whom 1,600 were full-time, 450 part-time and 280 evening students. By 1945-46 the number of full-time students had jumped to just over 2,000, of whom a quarter came from outside Yorkshire.[131]

The possibility of academically talented working-class pupils securing a place at the University was infinitely much more remote than it became after the Second World War, in spite of the availability of council scholarships for the brightest pupils from Leeds secondary schools. Richard Hoggart reckons that when he won his council scholarship to the University in 1936, it was one of only 47 given in that year. The odds against him winning one were further heightened by having to compete against middle-class as well as working-class pupils for the award.[132]

Entertainment for All

In the inter-war period the reduction of working hours and the rise in real incomes had a dramatic effect on the development of leisure pursuits. On average employees worked 46 hours a week in 1934, eight hours less than their parents had done 30 years earlier. While the working classes might not visit the theatre or go to the concerts in the Town Hall due to limited finances or lack of interest, the twentieth century produced one form of entertainment, above all, which brought all social classes together – the cinema.[133] Before the First World War it had been a technical curiosity. In 1905 the film pioneer Sydney Carter started hiring the Coliseum in Cookridge Street for his short season of animated pictures. So successful was the venture, that he went on to buy the freehold and open it as the first full-time cinema in Leeds. In the 1920s cinema attendance figures soared and by 1939 Leeds had 68 picture houses. Cinema changed the pattern of English life, it took people from their homes and eclipsed both church and pub. Women joined their husbands in this pastime, something they had rarely done before, few venturing into a pub or going to watch a match. It was extremely cheap, often only 1d. for two to three hours of entertainment. The seats were usually comfortable, and you did not need to book or dress up. It was a perfect venue for courting couples who purchased the darkness and the privacy and comfort which was not available at home!.

At the start, the black and white films lacked sound, and a pianist played the piano to suit the mood of the scene, though the better class of cinemas like the Lounge, Headingley, had their own orchestra. New purpose-built cinemas like the Majestic, City Square, which opened in 1922, could hold 2,500 people, who not only sat in luxurious surroundings to watch the film, but could enjoy music provided by the Majestic Symphony Orchestra under the direction of Francois Grandpierre, or listen to Harry Davidson on the Grand £5,000 Organ, with all its special effects – all this for between 1s. and 2s. 4d.

The introduction of the talkies in 1928 gradually took their toll on the orchestras: only the famous Wurlitzer organs survived, played by the organist to accompany the selling of chocolates, cigarettes and ice cream. Arguably the most luxurious cinema of its day was the Paramount on the Headrow (now the Odeon). With seating for over 2,500 and its famous Wurlitzer organ, it became a popular venue, and a team of 25 usherettes all wearing blue trousers with red piping, red bows and tam-o'-shanters catered for the needs of the audience.

The arrival of radio created a boon for all classes of Leeds society. Radio gave a new perspective on life to millions of listeners, and in the evening people really did roll up their carpets and dance at home to the finest dance bands in London. Despite the rise of cinema and radio, dance halls, music halls and the theatre remained very popular. In 1926 the Majestic advertised its dinner dances in the Majestic Restaurant. For 3s. you could gain admission to Saturday's 'Dansant'. Powolny's restaurant on Bond Street had music nightly from 7.30 to 11.30. The City Varieties, the Grand, the Empire and the Hippodrome continued to be well patronized, while at the Theatre Royal, King Charles Croft, Francis Laidler's traditional pantomime became a 'must' for the family at Christmas.

With so many new diversions, the number of public

The Scala Cinema, at the junction of Albion Place and Lands Lane, opened in 1922.

Golden Acre Park, near Bramhope, opened 24 March 1932.

houses in the city declined. Moreover, the growth in the number of working men's clubs to 136 by 1926 lured even more men away from their local. People spent less on alcohol and consequently drunkeness was reduced. The Chief Constable of Leeds, in his annual report for 1926, observed: 'There has been a marked decrease in the number of proceedings for drunkeness....I have no reason to vary the opinion expressed in my Report last year that Cinematograph Theatres, Dancing Halls, Wireless entertainments and facilities for outdoor recreation account in large measure for the sobriety of the residents of the City.'[134]

Amateur dramatics were particularly popular in the inter-war period. For the Tercentenary celebrations of 1926 the city's 15 amateur dramatic societies teamed-up to provide a 'spectacle' entitled 'Old Leeds' at the Theatre Royal. Contemporaries were reticent about the merits of the production which combined the diverse talents of societies ranging from the Leeds Art Theatre to the Upper Armley Dramatic Society and no less a body than the Railway Clerks' Operatic Society.[135]

With the advent of the 'Thirties' came fresh attractions. The opening of Golden Acre Amusement Park beside the Otley Road close to the city boundary on 24 March 1932 meant that people no longer had to wait for a trip to the coast or the visit of a fair to enjoy a special day out.[136] Motor launches, rowing boats, canoes, sailing dinghies and a 'drive yourself' motor boat circuit allowed the visitor to enjoy the pleasures of the lake. A miniature railway, nearly 1½ miles long, circled the park with the engines 'Robin Hood' and 'May Thompson' pulling the open carriages and dining car round the circuit. The list of attractions seems endless – tennis, pitch and putt golf, ponies, donkeys, a children's playground, a paddling pool and water chute as well as the exciting aeroflight monorail and mountain glide, and its popular cafe and dance hall, enticed people to visit the park. Unfortunately the park closed after the 1938 season. It lay derelict until 1945 when it was acquired by Leeds City Council.

Cycling continued to be popular, but with the council actively creating playing fields and golf courses the opportunities for other active recreations increased. In 1938 Roundhay Park had facilities for boating, bathing, croquet, cricket, riding, fishing, football, golf, hockey, lacrosse, putting and tennis, and it even had a maze! Its spectacular shows drew thousands, the Military Tattoo of 1926 attracting no fewer than 130,000 people. Leeds became known as 'The City of Public Parks' and by 1937 the council owned 3,175 acres of land, open for public enjoyment.[137] With the expansion of the Scout and Guide movement the delights of hiking and camping were first introduced to an eager audience. Public baths were popular especially with children. By 1937 Leeds had nine public baths and an open air swimming pool at Roundhay Park. Plans were afoot to build swimming baths on the council housing estates at Seacroft, Middleton and Compton Road, and to provide some baths at Beeston Hill, while providing new Central Baths on New York Road and modernising Cookridge Street baths.[138] Leisure facilities were also provided by some of the major employers. Burtons, for example, organised social and sporting activities, a dramatic society, billiard club, tennis club and holiday clubs.[139]

Perhaps the most revolutionary change was the growth in the habit of taking holidays away from home. The middle and upper classes had done this in Victorian times, but after the First World War an increasing number of working-class families went away. Only a small percentage of people had paid holidays, but the 1938 Holidays with Pay Act had a great impact. The usual entitlement was a working week plus public holidays, but many had more than this. Scarborough, Bridlington, Filey, Blackpool and Morecambe were popular destinations though many preferred to go to holiday camps like Butlin's, the first of which opened in Skegness in 1937. For many of the working classes, however, a holiday meant a visit to relatives in another town. Improved transport facilities and lower costs meant that people made an increasing number of trips.[140]

During the Victorian era, religion and activities associated with church and chapel had provided a central focus for the lives of a significant section of the population outside work and home. From what had been a peak of membership in the late Victorian and Edwardian eras, the part played by religion in people's lives began a period of relative decline which became precipitate after 1945. In 1900 perhaps around one-third of the population regularly attended worship, by the mid-1930s this had dropped to about one-sixth, and by 1948 to about one-eighth.[141] Many churches and chapels in the heart of Leeds closed or experienced sharply reduced attendances due to a combination of population movement to the suburbs and declining religious observance. A typical example was Brunswick Chapel which was situated on the northern edge of the city centre shopping area, close to the Leylands. Its centenary brochure observed in 1925:

Right: A special children's charabanc outing, organised by locals at the Lord Raglan, Newlay Street, off Kirkstall Road, c.1930.

Bomb damage to Marsh Lane Station after the air raid on 1 September 1940.

> The problems of today are very great for Brunswick. Through an ever widening zone of Jews, four-fifths of our people come through miles of suburbs to worship in the old place ...One who lives on the outskirts of Leeds in the midst of sylvan quiet told the minister that on a certain Sunday last summer, after a day of brilliant sunshine as he sat in the cool of the early evening in his garden, he remarked to his wife, "This has been a perfect day, I must close it fittingly, I want a service of great quiet, I am going down to Brunswick", and taking a tram he journeyed three or four miles into the stifling heat of the city, through weary streets of brick and ugliness that he might find a retreat for his spirit in the old place.[142]

The fact was that the combination of a less deferential society and increased affluence and mobility, offered the people at large, more inviting prospects on a Sunday than a dull sermon in an uncomfortable church.

Second World War and Overview

Unlike the First World War, there was no euphoria when the start of the Second World War was announced.[143] The people of Leeds had been prepared for the inevitable, and many remembered the miseries of the earlier conflict. This time things were better organised. Though there were queues and shortages throughout the war, the immediate introduction of rationing ensured that the distribution of provisions was better managed. As the troops marched off to war, the Police, Special Constables, Air Raid Wardens and Fire Prevention teams organised the defence of the city. The improvement in aircraft technology meant that the city was in genuine danger of aerial bombardment. Gas masks were issued at once to the population because of fears that the Nazis would use poisonous gas as part of their terror tactics. Meanwhile, over 16,000 air raid shelters were erected giving some measure of protection to more than 300,000 people. Over 1½ million sandbags were filled for the protection of public buildings. Evacuation of vulnerable sections of the population began almost at once. On 1 September 1939, 51 special trains took 18,250 children, 1,450 teachers and 1,350 volunteer helpers to Retford, Lincoln, Doncaster, Worksop, Gainsborough and the Yorkshire Dales. The day after, 45 trains took 8,167 mothers, young children, expectant mothers and blind people to similar locations. Evacuation proved extremely unpopular and within months most of the children

Dancing in the streets near the Town Hall on VJ (Victory over Japan) Day, 15 August 1945.

returned to the city, where the Home Guard had been formed to protect the city in the case of an invasion.

During the war Leeds suffered nine bombing raids. The most violent assault came on the night of 14/15 March 1941. Enemy bombers, flying 10 to 15 miles apart to confuse the defences, crossed the East Coast and made for Leeds. It was a terrifying attack. At 9 o'clock precisely the sirens started to wail, but it was not until 10.45 p.m. that firemen were called to Aire Street to deal with fires started by incendiary bombs. A second bomber showered incendiaries over the city centre causing Schofield's Arcade and premises in the Water Lane district to catch alight. Just before midnight the main thrust of the attack came. Several aircraft dropped more fire bombs, creating havoc as Mill Hill Chapel, the Royal Exchange Building, Denby and Spinks furniture store and the Yorkshire Post's premises were hit. Gipton, Headingley, Woodhouse and Roundhay Road all suffered. Fairbairn Lawson's, Greenwood and Batley's, Wellington Street and Wellington Road railway goods yards and the City and Central stations were all damaged. More enemy bombers soon arrived to drop high explosives bombs. The Infirmary, the Town Hall, the City Museum, Kirkgate Market, St Peter's School, Park Square and Quarry Hill flats were all hit. Fortunately, the damage was comparatively light, only the museum and St Peter's School suffering badly, and few people were killed.[144]

Another particularly notable raid occurred in August 1942 when Kirkstall Forge was bombed. Five workers were killed and the bar drawing shop and rear axle casing shop were badly damaged. Nevertheless relative to other major cities, such as Hull, Sheffield, Liverpool, Coventry, Birmingham and London, Leeds escaped the worst of the wartime air raids. During the course of the war, as a result of the bombing in Leeds, 77 people had been killed, 327 injured, and 197 buildings had been destroyed with a further 7,623 damaged.

On 8 May 1945, VE Day (Victory in Europe Day), the people of Leeds took to the streets, schools closed and workers were given a holiday. Innumerable street parties were held celebrating Peace and Victory. On 13 May 1945 over 2,000 took part in a victory parade, and normality began to return.[145] Once again the people of the city had made an enormous contribution to the war effort. Over £72 million had been raised in National Savings, Leeds industries had performed sterling work, and the Leeds Fire & Rescue services had helped in York, Hull, London, Manchester, Coventry, Liverpool, Sheffield and Birmingham. Many Leeds citizens had sacrificed their lives for the defence of their city and their country.

During the inter-war period the mass of the population of Leeds had experienced improved living conditions. They had better housing, better diet, better health, improved education, more material possessions, better working conditions, and more varied recreation. Nevertheless, life for the poor was still hard and the ladder of opportunity for the social and material advancement of the working classes was still a slender and steep one. In general, life for the working classes was still one full of insecurities, and the memories of mass unemployment and the poverty it brought to many had left an indelible impression on people's thinking. The sacrifices of the war led the people of Leeds to expect a better life when the war was over.

References

1. This account of the boundary alterations is based on: British Association, *General Handbook: Leeds Meeting, 1927* (Leeds, 1927), p. 1; O. Hartley, 'The Second World War and After, 1939-74' in Fraser, ed., *Modern Leeds*, pp.457-9.
2. For the controversy in 1911-12, see: *Yorkshire Evening News*, 10 Oct. 1911, *Yorkshire Post*, 29 Sept. 1911. For the rejection of the Leeds and Bradford Extension Bill in 1922, see: *Yorkshire Post* 12 May 1922. See also: M. Meadowcroft, 'The Years of Political Transition, 1914-39' in Fraser, ed., *Modern Leeds*, pp. 415-6.
3. *Yorkshire Post* 12 May 1922.
4. G.F.Rainnie and R.K.Wilson, 'The Economic Structure' in Beresford and Jones, *Leeds and Its Region* (Leeds, 1967), pp. 215-18.
5. City and County Borough of Leeds, *Development Plan Review: Written Analysis* (1967), [hereafter, *Development Plan Review, 1967*] p. 12.
6. W.G.Rimmer, 'Occupations in Leeds, 1841-1951', *Thoresby Soc.*, L (1967).
7. W.Scott, *Leeds in the Great War* (Leeds, 1923), pp. 172-92; J.Hagerty, *Leeds at War* (Leeds, 1981), pp. 15-17, 29-32.
8. For unemployment in the 1920s and 1930s: Leeds Unemployed Social Work Committee, 'Leeds – Voluntary Work with the Unemployed' (Leeds, 1936); City of Leeds, Report on the Leeds Unemployed 1904-5 (1905); W.G.Rimmer, 'Leeds Between the Wars', *The Leeds Journal* (Oct. 1959).
9. 1926/27 statistics for insured workers, in British Association, *op. cit.*, pp. 272-3 (The figures exclude some specialised forms of engineering.); Leeds Chamber of Commerce, Annual Report, 1928.
10. T.Woodhouse, 'The General Strike in Leeds' *Northern History*, XVIII (1982), pp. 252-62
11. J.Symons, *The General Strike* (1959), pp.89-90.
12. *Yorkshire Weekly Post*, 17 July 1926.
13. Rimmer, 'Leeds Between the Wars', p.352.
14. K.Honeyman, 'Montague Burton Ltd.: The Creators of Well-dressed Men', in J.Chartres and K.Honeyman, *Leeds City Business, 1893-1993* (Leeds, 1993), p.187.
15. E.M.Sigsworth, *Montague Burton: The Tailor of Taste* (1990), pp.28-35.
16. The following account of Burton's development is based on Sigsworth, *op. cit.*, pp. 36, 51, 54-7, 66.
17. *Ibid.*, p.51.
18. *Imperial Review* Oct. 1936, pp.18-19.
19. *Ibid.*, pp.14-15.
20. *Empire Mail*, July 1926, p.439.
21. R.Butler, *The History of Kirkstall Forge* (Leeds, 1945).
22. *Empire Mail*, July 1926, p.442; M.R.Lane, *The Story of the Steam Plough Works: Fowlers of Leeds* (1980).
23. *Yorkshire Post*, November 1983.
24. Anon, '100 Years of School Printing: Arnolds of Leeds', *British Printer*, Vol 76. No.4 (April, 1963), pp.84-8.
25. 'The House of Waddington' in *Leeds Graphic*, I, No.2 (July 1958), pp.36-37; J.Chartres, 'John Waddington PLC, 1890s to 1990s: A Strategy of Quality and Innovation' in Chartres and Honeyman, *op. cit.*.
26. 'William Moorhouse and Son Ltd.', *Leeds Graphic*, I, No.3, (1958), pp.18-19.
27. *Yorkshire Post*, 7 Nov. 1978.
28. Leeds City Council, *Leeds: The Industrial Capital of the North* (Leeds, 1938) [hereafter, *Leeds the Industrial Capital, 1938*, p.13.
29. British Association, *op. cit.*, pp.272-3.
30. *Leeds the Industrial Capital, 1938*, pp.11-12.
31. For ship canal proposals, see Yorkshire Post, *Leeds Tercentenary Supplement* (1926), pp.13, 96.
32. P.L.Smith, *The Aire and Calder Navigation* (Wakefield, 1987), chapter 4.
33. M.Clarke, *The Leeds and Liverpool Canal* (Preston, 1990), chapter 8.
34. *Leeds the Industrial Capital, 1938*, p.33.
35. *Ibid.*, pp.34-8; S.Bowden, R.Crawford and G.Sykes, 'The Public Supply of Gas in Leeds, 1818-1949', in Chartres and Honeyman, *op. cit.*.
36. *Leeds the Industrial Capital, 1938*, p.27.
37. Yorkshire Post, *Guide to the City of Leeds* (Leeds, 1935), p.60.
38. Pyramid Press Ltd., *A Guide to the City of Leeds* (1961), p.339.
39. S.Caunce, 'Yorkshire Post Newspapers Ltd: Perseverance Rewarded', in Chartres and Honeyman, *op.cit.*.
40. *Leeds the Industrial Capital, 1938*, p.62.
41. K.Waterhouse, *City Lights: A Street Life* (1994), p.42.
42. *Yorkshire Post*, 9 July 1924.
43. *Yorkshire Weekly Post*, 17 July 1926.
44. Rimmer, 'Leeds Between the Wars', pp.351-5, 366.
45. Yorkshire Evening News, *Leeds to Victory, 1939-1945* (Leeds, 1946).
46. Honeyman, 'Montague Burton', p.197.
47. For an account of the political scene in Leeds in the twentieth century, see: Meadowcroft, *op. cit.*, esp. pp.424-5; A.J.Taylor, 'Victorian Leeds: an Overview' in Fraser, *Modern Leeds*, pp.402-04; T.Woodhouse, 'The Working Class', in Fraser, *Modern Leeds*, pp.357-64.
48. G.Ratcliffe, *Sixty Years of It* (1935).
49. *Yorkshire Post*, 5 March 1929, quoted in Meadowcroft, *op. cit.*, p.423.
50. Leeds Tercentenary Executive, *The Leeds Tercentenary Official Handbook* (1926) [hereafter, *Tercentenary Handbook*, pp.68-71.
51. For these and subsequent references to town planning legislation, see: G.E.Cherry, Cities and Plans: The Shaping of Urban Britain in the Nineteenth and Twentieth Centuries (1988); G.E.Cherry, *The Evolution of British Town Planning* (1974); W.Ashworth, *The Genesis of Modern British Town Planning* (1968).
52. *Tercentenary Handbook*, pp.123-5.
53. Ashworth, *op. cit.*, pp.215-6.
54. *Leeds the Industrial Capital, 1938*, p.48.
55. *Tercentenary Handbook*, p.125.
56. *Ibid.*, p.125.
57. Yorkshire Post, *Leeds Tercentenary Supplement*, p.33.
58. *Tercentenary Handbook*, p.125; *Imperial Review* (1936), p.7.
59. Waterhouse, *City Lights*, p.5.
60. *Imperial Review* (1936), p.7.
61. N.Proudlock, *Leeds: A History of its Tramways* (Leeds, 1991).
62. *Tercentenary Handbook*, pp.127-9; Yorkshire Post, *Leeds: The Industrial Capital of the North* (1947/48 edition), [hereafter, *Leeds the Industrial Capital 1947/48*], p.46.
63. M.Meadowcroft, 'The Years of Political Transition', in Fraser, *Modern Leeds*, p.429; A Heap, *The Headrow: A Pictorial Record* (Leeds, 1990), p.17.
64. *Leeds the Industrial Capital, 1938*, pp.36-7.
65. *Ibid.*, pp.34-5.
66. *Tercentenary Handbook*, pp.119-22.
67. *Ibid.*, pp.165-7.
68. L.Milner, *Leeds Pals* (1991); W.H.Scott, *op. cit.*; H.and J.and B.Walker, *Recollections: Sixty Years Ago and Onward* (second edition, Leeds, 1930); *Tercentenary Handbook*, pp.49-51.
69. Scott, *op. cit.*, p.16.
70. Manuscript notes of Paul Larkin at Abbey House Museum.
71. J.Burnett, *A History of the Cost of Living* (1969), pp.306-7, 312.
72. H.J.Hammerton, *This Turbulent Priest* (1952), p.115.
73. LCR: Building Centre Committee Report, 'Leeds Housing' (*c.*1936).
74. R.Hoggart, *A Local Habitation: Life and Times, 1918-1940* (Oxford, 1989), p.48.
75. Sigsworth, *op. cit.*, p.71.
76. Hoggart, *op. cit.*, passim.
77. Hammerton, *op. cit.*, p.95.
78. *Ibid.*, pp.73-4.
79. For an excellent account of council house building , see: R.Finnigan, 'Council Housing in Leeds, 1919-39: Social Policy and Urban Change' in M.J.Daunton, ed., *Councillors and Tenants: Local Authority Housing in English Cities, 1919-39* (Leicester, 1984).
80. *Tercentenary Handbook*, pp.130-1; Yorkshire Post, *Leeds the Industrial Capital of the North* (1954 edition), [hereafter, *Leeds the Industrial Capital 1954*], p.76.
81. Finnigan, *op. cit.*, p.114.
82. Hammerton, *op. cit.*, pp.74-5.
83. *Leeds the Industrial Capital, 1938*, p.40.
84. Hammerton, *op. cit.*, p.111.
85. Finnigan, *op. cit.*.
86. *Ibid.*, p.103.
87. *Leeds the Industrial Capital, 1938*, p.42.
88. Hammerton, *op. cit.*, p.103.
89. *The Leeds Weekly Citizen*
90. Waterhouse, *City Lights*, pp.29-31.
91. *Yorkshire Evening Post*, 14 Feb.1922.
92. A.Ravetz, *Model Estate: Planned Housing at Quarry Hill, Leeds* (1974).
93. Burnett, *op. cit.*, pp.298-9.
94. Borough Guides, *City of Leeds Guide, 1909*, pp.58-9.
95. *Yorkshire Evening Post*, 19 March 1926, 23 March 1936.
96. *Yorkshire Post*, 12 Dec.1922.
97. *Tercentenary Handbook*, passim; *Morrison's Leeds Blue Book and City Record to 1929*.
98. D.Tate, *A History of Cafes and Restaurants* (Leeds, 1988).
99. *Tercentenary Handbook*, p.201; R.Schofield, *Schofield's Golden Jubilee, 1901-1951* (Leeds, 1951), pp.5-11.
100. *Yorkshire Post*, 12 Dec. 1922.
101. *Tercentenary Handbook*, p.244.
102. Leeds City Council, *Official Guide to the Leeds Corporation Tramway and Transport System* (Leeds, 1926), p.57.
103. *Kelly's Directory of Leeds, 1936*, p.1280.
104. J.Stevenson, *British Society 1914-45* (1984), chapters 7, 10, 11.
105. *Kelly's Directory of Leeds, 1914*, p.xlviii; *Kelly's Directory of Leeds, 1936*, p.28; *Leeds the Industrial Capital 1947/48*.
106. *Kelly's Directory of Leeds, 1914*, pp.xli, l; *Tercentenary Handbook*, p.157.
107. P.Bedford and D.N.Howard, *St James's University Hospital, Leeds: A Pictorial History* (Leeds, 1985).
108. *Tercentenary Handbook*, p.157.
109. *Ibid.*, pp.157-9; I.Baylis and S.Astbury, *Leed Babies' Welcome Association: A Memoir (Leeds, 1991)*.
110. D.C.Cole, Cookridge: The Story of a Yorkshire Township: Part 2 (Leeds, 1981), p.36.
111. *Yorkshire Evening Post*, 18 Feb.1922.
112. *Kelly's Directory of Leeds, 1936*, pp.1171, 1179.
113. *Leeds the Industrial Capital, 1938*, p.42.
114. Hoggart, *op. cit.*, pp.43-4.
115. *Yorkshire Evening Post*, 28 April 1922.
116. Waterhouse, *City Lights*, p.6.
117. C.J.Morgan, 'Demographic Change, 1771-1911', in Fraser, *Modern Leeds* (Manchester, 1980); City of Leeds, Reports on the Health and Sanitary Administration of the City, 1926 and 1938.
118. Leeds City Council, *Education in Leeds* (Leeds, 1926), [hereafter, *Education in Leeds*], pp.14, 20; British Association, *op.cit.*, p.236.
119. *Education in Leeds*, passim.
120. *Leeds Guide, 1909*, p.69.
121. *Education in Leeds*, passim; British Association, *op. cit.*, pp.236-40; *Kelly's Directory of Leeds, 1936*, pp.1294-5; *Tercentenary Handbook*, pp.147-9.
122. *Tercentenary Handbook*, p.149.
123. *Kelly's Directory of Leeds, 1914*, p.xxxi.
124. *Education in Leeds*, pp.78-9; *Kelly's Directory of Leeds, 1936*, pp.xxvii, 1292-5.
125. *Tercentenary Handbook*, pp.147-9; British Association, *op. cit.*, pp.236-40; *Leeds the Industrial Capital 1947/48*, p.99.
126. *Education in Leeds*.
127. *Ibid.*, p.110; *Kelly's Directory of Leeds, 1936*, p.1292.
128. *Tercentenary Handbook*. p.149; *Education in Leeds*, p.104; R.Lowe, *Past into Present: A Commemorative History of Leeds College of Art and Design* (Leeds, 1993).
129. *British Association*, op.cit., p.239.
130. *Leeds the Industrial Capital, 1938*, pp.28-30.
131. P.H.J.H.Gosden and A.J.Taylor, *Studies in the History of a University* (Leeds, 1975).
132. Hoggart, *op. cit.*, p.181.
133. R.Preedy, *Leeds Cinemas Remembered* (Leeds, 1980).
134. Chief Constable of Leeds, Report of the State of Crime and the Police Establishment for the Year Ending, 31 Dec. 1926, p.27.
135. *Yorkshire Weekly Post*, 17 July 1926.
136. *Yorkshire Evening Post*, 24 March 1932.
137. *Yorkshire Weekly Post*, 17 July 1926; *Leeds the Industrial Capital, 1938*, pp.48-51.
138. *Leeds the Industrial Capital, 1938*, pp.56-7.
139. Sigsworth, *op.cit.*, p.66.
140. J.A.R.Pimlott, *The Englishman's Holiday* (1947).
141. Stevenson, *op. cit.*, pp.361-2.
142. Brunswick Wesleyan Methodist Chapel, Leeds, *Souvenir of the Centenary Celebrations, 1925*, pp.9-10.
143. For Leeds during the Second World War, see: J.Hagerty, *op. cit.*(Leeds, 1981); Yorkshire Evening News, *Leeds to Victory, 1939-1945* (Leeds, 1946).
144. *Yorkshire Evening Post Special: The City Goes to War* (1987).
145. *Yorkshire Evening Post*, 13 May 1945.

CHAPTER EIGHT

Modern Leeds

Leeds Goes Metropolitan

In the years after the Second World War the territorial ambitions of Leeds were curbed for a while at least. A Greater Leeds Plan was devised in 1944-5 which would have doubled the size of the city, but, in the event, there was no expansion in the next thirty years other than the addition in 1956 of 2,321 acres comprising Whinmoor and Austhorpe. The major expansion came in 1974. With local government reorganisation in England, Leeds Metropolitan District was created. This was an amalgamation of Leeds, Morley, Pudsey, Aireborough, Rothwell, Garforth, Horsforth, Otley, and parts of Wetherby, Tadcaster, and Wharfedale. Leeds City Council (in pratice Leeds Metropolitan District Council, but retaining the dignity of the former name) now administered an area containing 748,300 inhabitants. In terms of population it was the second largest Metropolitan District in England, being exceeded only by Birmingham.[1]

The incorporation of Leeds in the new West Yorkshire Metropolitan County recognised the strategic and economic factors which were of mutual concern to Bradford, Calderdale, Kirklees, Wakefield and Leeds. Each was made a Metropolitan District within the new Metropolitan County. In one sense the merchants of seventeenth-century Leeds would have approved. Finally, after three centuries, their ambition to see the areas, once dominated by the Yorkshire woollen and worsted industries, tied together under one authority, had been attained. But Leeds council was not to be the authority controlling West Yorkshire, and the West Yorkshire Metropolitan County's administrative centre was to be Wakefield. Many of the proudly independent inhabitants of the neighbouring small towns such as Morley, Wetherby, and Otley were extremely unhappy about being absorbed by Leeds – and no doubt remain so – but the economic arguments won the day.[2]

Since the Second World War political control of Leeds City Council has changed hands between the Conservatives and Labour on several occasions. From 1945-51 Labour were in control, and thereafter the sequence ran: Conservatives 1951-53, 1967-72, and 1976-80, with the hung council of 1979/80 being Conservative led; and Labour 1953-67, 1972-76 (though the Conservatives were the largest party with the largest number of seats after the elections of 1974 and 1975). In

The smoke-blackened Town Hall and Municipal Buildings and Art Gallery just after the war. The Garden of Rest is dominated by H.C.Fehr's War Memorial which was moved from City Square in 1937.

1980 the Labour Party swept back into power with a large overall majority, a superiority which has held firm to the present and was confirmed at the local elections in May 1994.[3]

Local government reorganisation in 1974 was a disaster as far as many Leeds politicians were concerned. Frank Marshall, the Conservative leader of the council from 1967-72, for example, had wanted Leeds to remain a unitary authority with its control extended to encompass the area from Morley to Pateley Bridge, including the big prize of Harrogate. Instead the more limited extension of its boundaries came at the price of a two-tier system of local government and a 'shotgun marriage' with the other four Metropolitan Districts. The council lost a whole range of powers and responsibilities, such as strategic planning, transport, and the police, to the West Yorkshire Metropolitan County. The council hoped that one of its senior officers might become the chief officer of the Metropolitan County, but this did not come about, possibly because the other Metropolitan Districts feared domination by Leeds. In 1986 the loss of power was reversed when the West Yorkshire Metropolitan County was abolished, but certain major services which benefited from a strategic overview, such as the police and transport, remained within the ambit of county-wide bodies.

The declining rate of population growth in Leeds, which had become established in the inter-war period, became acute in the 1940s and '50s, and was starkly confirmed when the 1971 census showed the first significant drop in the city's population since the plague in 1645. The growth rate of under 2 per cent in the 1950s was largely the result of a natural increase in population of around 4 per cent being counteracted by a net outflow of approximately 11,500.[4] Most of those leaving the city in the 1950s were moving the short distance to privately-built housing just beyond the city boundaries.[5] The population of the borough, which stood at 502,000 in 1951, rose to 511,000 in 1961, but then declined to 496,000 in 1971. This absolute fall in population revealed by the 1971 census was the beginning of a long-term trend. The decline continued over the next two decades, the area now embracing the whole of the Metropolitan District losing over 5 per cent of its inhabitants. By 1991 the enlarged District's population of just over 700,000 had almost fallen back to the level of 30 years earlier.[6]

A particularly notable feature of population change in the city from the late 1950s was the foreign immigration which Leeds experienced in common with many other large English cities. Post-war prosperity led to a shortage of people willing to work in lower-paid jobs such as those in hospitals and on the buses. Active recruiting took place in Britain's former Carribean colonies, encouraging people to come to settle in the city. Further immigrants arrived from India, Pakistan, East Africa, China and eventually even Vietnam. At the 1961 census 2.7 per cent of the population originated from overseas countries, of whom about half were Commonwealth citizens. The passage of the Commonwealth Immigration Act in 1962 greatly reduced this inflow, though the entry of relatives and refugees resulted in a fairly steady increase. Many of the Carribean and Asian immigrants settled in Chapeltown and Harehills, and parts of the Burley and Hyde Park areas. By 1991 the census showed that almost 6 per cent of the Metropolitan District's population belonged to ethnic minority groups. While this represented a sizeable proportion, it was much lower than the 16 per cent for Bradford and 11 per cent for Kirklees.[7]

The Post-War Leeds Economy

When peacetime returned the long-term shift in the structure of the local economy became clear.[8] In 1951 only around half the workforce remained in manufacturing, while well over two-fifths was now in services. The share of the labour force employed by the three largest industries in 1911 – tailoring, engineering and textiles – had fallen from 45 to 30 per cent. This decline in manufacturing continued apace between the late 1940s and the mid-60s. A 15 per cent fall in manufacturing jobs slowed down growth in total employment in the city in these years to only 4 per cent, while employment nationwide grew by 11 per cent (including a growth in jobs in manufacturing). Over the decade up to 1967 the fastest growing industries in Britain were engineering, electrical and metal goods, chemicals, vehicles, food, drink and tobacco. Superficially, Leeds had its share of these, but its specialisms did not tend to be those which were fastest growing and its firms in the growth sectors tended to be small. By 1973 only one-third of the working population of Leeds was employed in manufacturing.

Given this poor performance, Leeds was remarkably prosperous in the 1950s, '60s and early '70s. Unemployment was astonishingly low at less than one per cent in the boom years of 1955, 1961 and 1965 – levels which are almost unimaginable in the 1990s. Job vacancies actually exceeded the numbers unemployed! Indeed, the shortage of labour must have been a deterrent to the expansion of existing firms and the relocation of firms from elsewhere. Such low levels of unemployment were maintained partly because slow growth in employment was matched by slow growth in population, but, above all, because the service industries expanded rapidly. While employment in mainstream engineering remained static, sharp declines in employment in metal and vehicle manufacture, textiles, clothing and footwear were more than counterbalanced by rapid growth in building, gas, electricity and water, the distributive trades, insurance and banking, professional and scientific services, and miscellaneous services. Between 1951 and 1973 while 37,000 jobs were lost in manufacturing, 32,000 were gained in the service industries. In the 1970s this trend persisted. Manufacturing employment declined to 80,000 jobs in 1981, but the strength of the service industries kept employment at high levels by national standards. It was not until the mid-1970s that the impact of a continued decline of manufacturing was reflected in higher levels of unemployment, the rate reaching 5.5 per cent in January 1976.

A small but highly significant feature of the 1960s and '70s was the growth of Leeds as a media centre. In 1968 BBC Television set up its Yorkshire base in Woodhouse Lane, producing programmes such as 'Look North'. In the same year Yorkshire Television began to broadcast from its Kirkstall Road headquarters producing a nightly magazine 'Calendar', an immensely popular soap opera, 'Emmerdale Farm' and successful series such as 'The Darling Buds of May' and 'A Touch of Frost'. Local radio, too, made its mark in the late '60s. BBC Radio Leeds began in 1968 with the aim of providing the city

A production shot of Yorkshire Television's 'Emmerdale Farm', showing 'Alan Turner' in the Woolpack.

with its own personal voice. In 1978 it moved from the Merrion Centre to Broadcasting House, the former Quaker Meeting House in Woodhouse Lane. In 1981 a rival station, Radio Aire, opened in new premises next to Yorkshire Television, nine years later being joined by a pop station, Magic 828.[9]

The change in the composition of employment in Leeds was even more dramatic in the 1980s. Employment in manufacturing declined to 60,000, while employment in the financial sector, for example, grew by two-thirds, reaching 45,000 jobs by 1991. Today, it is the employment in financial and legal services which most catches the eye. As the headquarters of two of the country's leading building societies (the Leeds Permanent and the Leeds and Holbeck) and as home to the Yorkshire Bank and a branch of the Bank of England, the city has a strong institutional base. The recent rapid growth of jobs in accountancy and legal pratices has also been striking. Six of the United Kingdom's top legal firms are based in Leeds and sixteen of the largest accountancy pratices have offices in the city. By 1991 accountancy alone provided almost 4,000 jobs. In 1991, setting aside the numbers employed in energy and water (7,400), distribution, hotels and catering (70,000), transport and communications (18,000) and finance (45,000), there were 95,000 people employed in a whole range of other services – an increase from 80,000 ten years earlier.

Significantly, at the start of the 1990s the largest employers in Leeds were the public sector organisations and the privatised public utilities. Figures produced by Leeds Development Agency showed that the largest employers in Leeds were as follows:

Leeds City Council	35,000
Area Health Authority	14,000
University of Leeds	4.500
Post Office	3,900
Leeds Metropolitan University	2,400
British Gas	2,200
British Telecom	2,000
Central Benefits Agency & Depts of Health and Social Security	2,000
Yorkshire Electricity	1,810
Waddingtons	1,740
Kay and Co Ltd	1,500
Asda	1,500
Yorkshire Rider	1,500
Leeds Permanent	1,500
Yorkshire Post Newspapers	1,100
Yorkshire Bank	1,100
Du Pont Howson	1,100
Joshua Tetley	1,100
Elida Gibbs	1,000

Clearly, the role of Leeds as a regional service centre and a financial and commercial capital has become paramount.

Planning for Utopia

The Second World War brought a great stimulus to British town planning in its modern sense. The extensive damage to cities from bombing was to necessitate the rebuilding of large urban areas. Wartime conditions made rebuilding impossible, but encouraged planning for the future. Invariably the need was stressed to use the opportunity to make improvements comprehensive enough to remedy longstanding defects and weaknesses in the make-up of urban areas. This new approach of comprehensive planning was codified in the Town and Country Planning Act of 1947. Under the Act, Leeds council was required to survey the whole of the city and to prepare, on the basis of the information obtained, a development plan. The first Leeds Development Plan was submitted to the Minister of Housing and Local Government in 1951 and received approval in 1955.[11] It consisted of a report of the survey, a written statement of the proposals for development over the next 20 years, and a large map of the city, indicating on it the land uses proposed. Every acre of the city was allocated to a land use of some sort. The plan showed which settlements were suitable for development and which were best kept at their current size, which areas were to be kept as agricultural land, the areas for housing and industrial

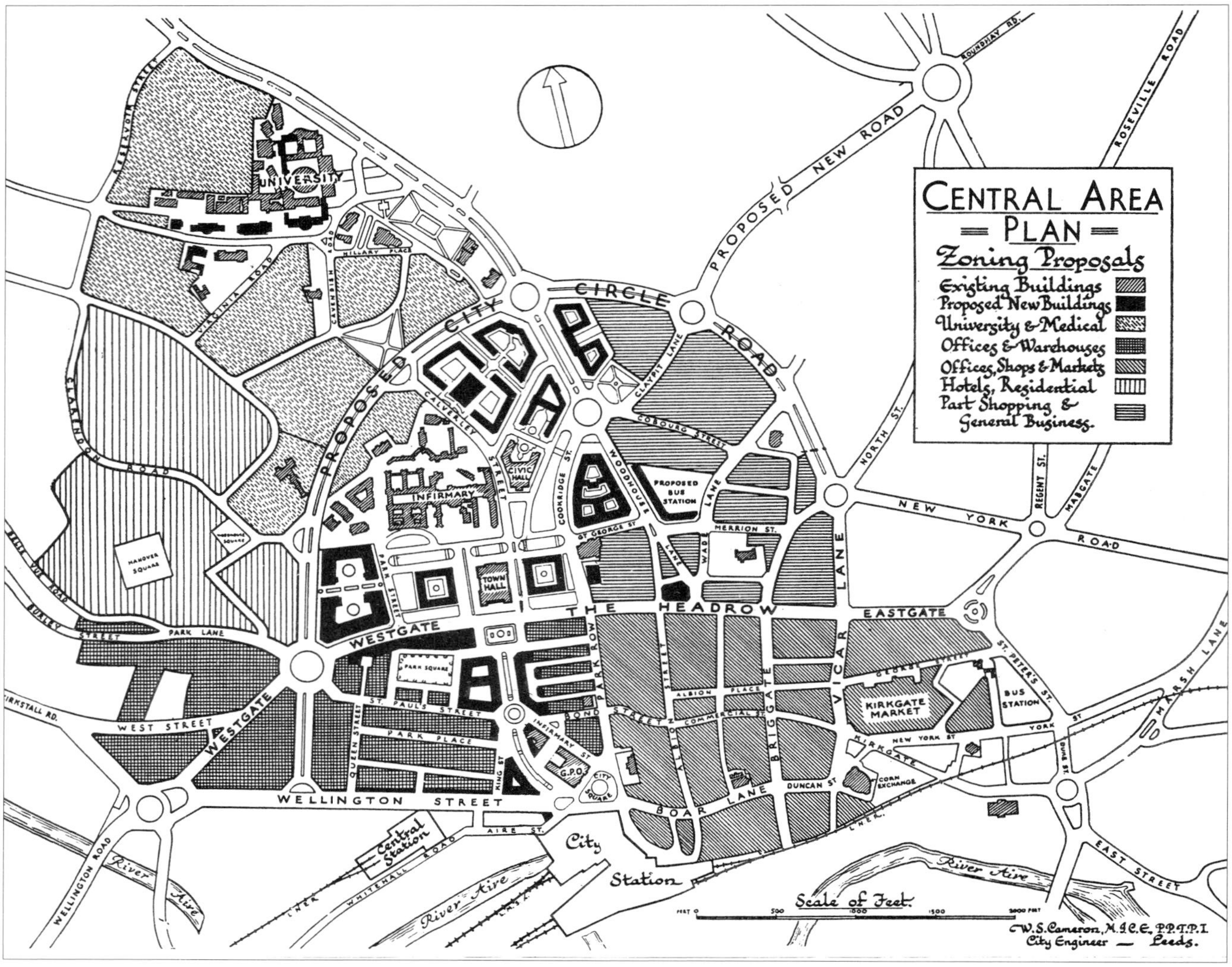

Above: The 1951 Leeds Development Plan proposals for the redevelopment of the city centre.

Right: A contemporary artist's impression of the 1951 Leeds Development Plan's city centre proposals, superimposed on an aerial photograph.

development, the sites of proposed roads, public buildings, airfields, public open spaces, and so on. Particularly notable were the proposals for the zoning of the location of industry with the designation of Light Industrial Estates adjacent to the new housing estates and in close proximity to the Outer Ring Road and other main roads. These confirmed a policy which had begun in Leeds in the mid-1930s. Estates of this sort were designated on Kirkstall Road, Iveson House and at Seacroft.[12] Under the 1947 legislation, private development anywhere in the city was expressly forbidden without the consent of the local authority. Moreover, it gave councils, such as Leeds, the power to place a 'life' on buildings which in the interests of good planning required demolition, and to protect buildings of historic and architectural interest.

The new dimensions which really seemed to embolden the council in its aspirations were the greatly increased local authority powers of compulsory land purchase for comprehensive redevelopment of areas, combined with government assurances to local authorities of large Exchequer grants to assist in such purchases. The most remarkable feature of the Development Plan of 1951 was the grandiose proposals , prepared in 1947, for the redevelopment of the city centre. The whole of the central area was zoned according to land use, and there was to be comprehensive redevelopment of more than a dozen major blocks of property. A grand avenue, 120 feet wide, flanked by imposing new buildings, was to be created from Wellington Street to the Town Hall. Oxford Place Chapel and the Municipal Buildings and Art Gallery on either side of the Town Hall were to be swept away by the building of imposing new civic buildings including a City Museum, Art Gallery and Central Library. On the north and east sides of the Civic Hall large complexes of civic buildings were to be built, free from the noise of through traffic and landscaped with gardens, trees and flower beds. A new bus station and multi-storey car park was to be built on the site which today is occupied by the Merrion Centre. The setting of the University was to be greatly enhanced by the creation of 4½ acres of tastefully laid out public open space between the Parkinson Building and Emmanuel Church, made available by the demolition of the Georgian Blenheim Terrace and other intruding buildings, and the realignment of Woodhouse Lane.[13] In practice most of this extravagant proposal for the redevelopment of the central area was never implemented, though, as we shall see, the proposed inner ring road was built in a modified form some years later.

In keeping with the council's fine record in giving priority to the creation and enhancement of green spaces for public recreation, Leeds was the first local authority outside London to reserve a 'green belt' of land around the developed portion of the city in order to prevent urban sprawl on to agricultural land, and to provide open spaces within easy reach of residents. Its proposals, first put forward in 1944, followed the precedent set by the Green Belt (London and Home Counties) Act of 1938. Under the Leeds Development Plan of 1951, 12¼ square miles of undeveloped land in the suburban areas of the city were reserved as green belt, including 1¼ square miles of land for new public open space. Use was also made of the new powers in the 1947 Act to control ribbon development along major roads.

The new powers in the Act to protect woodlands were also capitalised upon. Provision was made in the Development Plan for driving green wedges from the green belt, alongside streams flowing towards the city centre. The most notable examples being those through Adel and along the Meanwood Valley, and from Roundhay Park along Wyke Beck to Pontefract Lane.[14]

Buchanan and The Leeds Approach

In spite of the council's inter-war road building programme, concern about future traffic congestion in Leeds continued to mount. By the early 1960s, national concern about the long-term problems of traffic in towns led the government to commission Colin Buchanan to report on the issue. Significantly, his report, published in 1963, took Leeds as one of its case studies.[15] Looking at the trend in the growth of traffic to the year 2010, he concluded that only about 40 per cent of the potential demand for car journeys to the central area of Leeds in the long term could be provided for without totally destroying the city's built environment. To avoid the city centre being totally dominated by traffic, three quarters of all workers travelling to the central area would need to travel by public transport.

Buchanan's staggering conclusion, graphically demonstrated in his suggested plan for the city centre, was that even to accommodate his proposed restricted use of cars, almost half the central area would need to be redeveloped and almost a quarter of its land would be taken over by major roads and junctions. Going even further than the council had done in the 1951 Leeds Development Plan, he strongly favoured the comprehensive redevelopment of large sections of the city centre and the inner city, effectively wiping the slate clean in many locations and rebuilding from scratch.[16]

Such extensive redevelopment made it possible for him to enthusiastically advocate the vertical and horizontal separation of vehicles from pedestrians. Under his proposals, City Square, Boar Lane, the Headrow, Briggate, Commercial Street and Kirkgate would have been pedestrianised. At the same time, a road of motorway proportions would have been driven east-west immediately behind the Town Hall along the line of Great George Street and Merrion Street, and a new dual carriage way would have run east-west from the bus station on St Peter's Street and immediately behind the Corn Exchange, running just south of Boar Lane and passing the southern edge of City Square. These would have been linked by two north-south dual carriage ways, one slicing straight through Kirkgate Market, and the other running from Woodhouse Lane down between Park Row and Albion Street. The proposals included the replacement of the city market with an upper level market and shopping area for pedestrians stretching along the east side of Vicar Lane, with a bus station underneath.[17]

While the ideas in the Buchanan Report were being digested by the city council, more immediate steps were taken to deal with traffic problems in the city centre. In the Spring of 1965 the council introduced Leeds' one-way traffic system. The Chamber of Commerce expressed fears about loss of trade in certain streets, and the barrier effect of the one-way streets, but on the whole things seemed to go well without too many traffic problems. On 5 April parking meters made their first appearance in the city centre streets, effectively pushing long-stay parkers out to car parks. The charges were 6d. an hour.[18]

Under the terms of the Town and Country Planning Act of 1962, the council was soon to embark on the first full review of the Leeds Development Plan. A new survey was made of the city and revised proposals were prepared in 1967. As ever the planning process moved slowly and Leeds did not receive government approval for what was known as the Leeds Development Plan Review until 1972. The plan encompassed development proposals up till 1981.[19]

While this work was being undertaken, an extensive appraisal was being made of how to tackle the city's future traffic problems. In 1959 the council had appointed as Deputy City Engineer the man who was to have by far the greatest influence on the planning of Leeds in the second half of the twentieth century – Charles Geoffrey Thirlwall. Thirlwall was a great enthusiast for motorway building and the comprehensive redevelopment of both large areas of the city centre and inner-city housing. It is significant that until the 1970s planning in Leeds was dominated by civil engineers. The City Engineer's Department had responsibility for town planning, road improvements, bridge works, mains drainage and sewage disposal.[20] In 1960 Thirlwall wrote an extremely influential report advocating a system of urban motorways for Leeds, and used his important contacts at national level to promote it. In 1964 he became City Engineer and in 1970, already an immensely powerful figure in city affairs, he became Group Chief Officer, Planning and Technical Services, thereby adding architecture and public transport to his existing portfolio of responsibilities. During these years he enthusiastically promoted co-operation between the council and national government departments in producing a plan to tackle the city's traffic problems. The solution proposed was published in 1968 in a pioneering document entitled 'The Leeds Approach'. The proposals were clearly influenced by the Buchanan Report, but the car restrictions were more severe, the proposed changes to the road system were more modest, and the road alignments had less impact on the city centre. Public transport was to be the salvation of the city. The plan aimed at an 80/20 split between public transport and private cars for journeys to work in the city centre and the central industrial districts.

The 'Leeds Approach' had two main elements.[21] Firstly, the use of cars for getting to work in the centre was to be controlled by restricting the amount of all-day commuter parking. A series of long-stay multi-storey car parks, with a capacity of 11,000 spaces, were to be built around the fringe of the city centre. Short-stay parking for shoppers and business callers was to be provided in multi-storey car parks within the city centre. The second element was to make the bus services more efficient and attractive. In effect, Leeds was to become 'bus city'. 'Fastaway' services (which were introduced in 1968) were to provide fast express services along primary radial roads from the suburbs to the centre. At the same time the buses were to be freed from the general congestion by the introduction of 'bus only' lanes and giving priority to buses at busy road junctions. Meanwhile, the road system was to be improved – where possible placing major new roads in cuttings to avoid disfiguring the appearance of the city.

Accompanying this policy was the central aim of separating traffic and pedestrians. This element, which began its implementation in 1970, aimed at the vertical separation of pedestrian and vehicle circulation at strategic points. Commercial Street at the heart of the shopping area was taken as the natural level at which pedestrians were to circulate. Taking advantage of the gentle slope of the centre down to the river, on the highest ground to the north around the Merrion Centre a mixture of ground level precincts and a subway system which 'dug into' the ground 'to level with the precincts of the Commercial Street area' were to be created. Meanwhile, at the lower southern and eastern parts of the centre, a new level of precincts and arcades raised above the traffic and connected by high level walkways were to be created. Today we know these as the Bond Street Shopping Centre and the Trinity Street Arcade.[22]

In November 1970, 700 yards of public highway (essentially Commercial Street and Lands Lane) were pedestrianised by the introduction of paving across the full width of the street. This it was believed created the largest pedestrianised shopping street in Europe. A second phase was opened in 1972 consisting of the streets between Briggate and Vicar Lane (Queen Victoria Street, Kirkgate, and Central Road). In parts of these areas extensive cleaning of buildings coincided with the paving of the streets to produce a remarkable overall improvement. In both areas, essential service vehicles were allowed access during limited time periods. The Trinity Street Scheme completed in 1974 further extended the shopping precinct to the area between Commercial Street and Boar Lane. In the same year (1974) work started on the Bond Street Centre. Both these schemes used basement servicing to create the opportunity for attractive malls and arcades.[23] While the pedestrianised shopping precincts were to prove immensely successful, the high level walkway was a white elephant. A section was constructed from the Bond Street Centre across Park Row into the pedestrianised Bond Court. Other sections were never completed, and as a result important new buildings such as the Bank of England on York Place have the embarrassment and disfigurement of concrete walkways at first floor level which have never been used.

Motorway City of the Seventies

The Leeds Approach envisaged major road developments and these gradually came on stream. The fact was that, conscious as the city council was of the problem of encouraging traffic, it could not resist the seduction of the trade and business it could bring to the city. Linking Leeds to the motorway network of the country was to become a virtual obsession. In the early 1970s the council depicted Leeds as the 'Motorway City of the Seventies'. By the end of 1972 the extension of the M1 (the South East Urban Motorway) completed the direct motorway link between Leeds and London, and provided motorway access to the heart of the main industrial belt and to within half a mile of the city's shopping centre. The South West Urban Motorway (the M621 programmed to start in 1972) would eventually provide a direct link to the M62 motorway which was soon to run right across the country between Hull and Liverpool. Meanwhile, the £12½ million Inner Ring Road Motorway Distributor, which circled the northern fringe of the city, had been completed.

In the 1980s and '90s it has become commonplace to look back on the 1960s and '70s as an era in which immense damage was done to the built environment of Leeds through insensitive demolition and rebuilding in both the city centre and the inner city. Such changes came about at a time when in certain respects Leeds was looking for a new identity. As we have seen, its manufacturing base was being very seriously eroded and the big hope appeared to be the service industries, especially finance and commerce. It was seen as extremely important that Leeds throw off the cloak of the dirty Victorian city and cultivate the image of a modern city. From the early 1960s onwards, councillors of all political parties combined with council officers to woo developers. Emphasis was placed on the dependability of the council in supporting and facilitating new development. This approach reached a high point in the late '60s. The concentration of administrative and executive power in the hands of a few senior councillors and council officers made for dynamic and purposeful government. The 'big thinking' Frank Marshall, Conservative leader of the council from 1967 to 1972, and Geoffrey Thirlwall promoted an almost romantic vision of Leeds the thriving, thrusting modern city. The publicity brochure for 'Project Leeds', a joint intiative at the beginning of the 1970s, between the city council and the Chamber of Commerce, to promote the development of industry and business in Leeds, reflected the attitude:

> It is a far cry from the grimy old city spawned by the Industrial Revolution to the modern, go-ahead, and continually expanding Leeds of today. Some of the scars left by that ruthless, thrusting age are still in evidence, but the rejuvenation of the city is taking place on a grand and imaginative scale and at a truly staggering pace. New buildings born of new concepts are pushing their white rectangular columns into the sky ...Exciting flyovers and splendid roads twist and spiral their course around

Motorway City of the Seventies. The new road system under construction at Westgate. The view shows the new International Pool (top left) and Park Square (bottom left).

the City Centre and run out to join the great motorways. Everywhere there are signs of improvement and progress. Leeds is surging forward into the 'Seventies.[25]

In this era every letter which left Leeds Post Office was franked with the slogan 'Leeds Motorway City of the Seventies'.

The Price of Utopia

Undoubtedly, the arrival of the motorways and the prolific office building of the 1960s and '70s brought major economic benefits. They bred confidence in the city's future and stimulated investment in it. Likewise the building of the Merrion Centre and the Bond Street Centre, with the pedestrianisation of the city's central streets, maintained the position of Leeds as the premier shopping centre of the north of England. The drawback was the almost unthinking demolition of important features of the city's historic townscape, and the erection of many buildings which less than twenty years later were considered to be blots on the landscape.

With regard to the road schemes, the sinking of the Inner Ring Road into a tunnel as it looped around the northern edge of the city centre was a major success in environmental terms. The bringing of the motorways so close to the southern edge of the city centre shopping area, however, was a mistake. It generated large amounts of traffic wishing to get to the north of the city, which now needlessly clogged the central streets. More permanently damaging, whole swathes of Holbeck and Hunslet were destroyed and dehumanised as the vast road schemes carved through the traditional street patterns and created immense barriers crammed with cars which inhibited pedestrian movement. Thirlwall maintained that he was threading the motorways through areas abandoned by slum clearance and railway line closures, but there was great anger amongst the residents of Holbeck and Hunslet when the motorways sliced chunks off their town moors. The destruction of a sense of place and community, which the slum clearances of the earlier decades had begun, was completed by the tyranny of the motor car.

While the erection of the new shopping centres and offices was probably necessary to sustain the vitality of the city, their scale and location showed an insensitivity to the existing qualities and grain of the city centre. This was reflected in the City Engineer's Department's designation of six Comprehensive Development Areas in the centre between 1962 and 1968 covering 140 acres. The largest of these was the 82 acres along Woodhouse Lane, comprising the land now occupied by the Metropolitan University and the lower part of the Leeds University campus. The two other large ones at 20 and 21 acres respectively were essentially the site of the Merrion Centre, and the Boar Lane/Bond Street site, now partly occupied by the Bond Street Centre.[26] The city council's brochure, *Planning Tomorrow's Leeds,* produced in 1973, suggested that the council recognised the value of the city's historic buildings. Unfortunately, in practice, the perception of the historic core seemed to be largely restricted to the area bounded by Albion Street, the Headrow, Vicar Lane and the south side of Commercial Street and Kirkgate, and the buildings recognised to be of historic importance tended to be flamboyant Victorian

City of tower blocks. This view shows City Square and Boar Lane in 1975 and the cleared comprehensive redevelopment site which was to house the Bond Street Shopping Centre.

and Edwardian building rather the plainer but extremely important Georgian buildings.[27]

Large numbers of buildings were demolished, which without doubt by the 1980s would have been given listed building protection by the Department of the Environment.[28] Though it has to be said that in the 1960s and '70s the council showed little compunction in approving the demolition of buildings which it had itself identified as being of architectural and historic importance in its lists prepared in 1960, 1962 and 1963. Almost a third of the buildings on Park Row, described in the 1880s as the 'Pall Mall' of Leeds, were replaced by modern office blocks – one of the most notable losses being the fine Gothic Beckett's Bank in 1965. The integrity of City Square was destroyed as first the Royal Exchange at the junction of Park Row and Boar Lane, and Standard House were demolished to be replaced by two towering office blocks, Royal Exchange House and Norwich Union House. The former was then the tallest building in Leeds, and the latter, by the 1990s, was regarded as the ugliest building in the city centre. In truth, neither was unusual or particularly ugly by the standards of the 1960s and '70s. Their crime was to be built in such insensitive locations and to be poor replacements for buildings of significant architectural interest. Throughout this period planners and designers seemed to have lost their appreciation of the importance of the scale and massing of buildings in producing a harmonious townscape. The huge tower blocks which shot up, today stick out like sore thumbs against the roofscape of the historic heart of Leeds.

The Battle to Protect Historic Leeds

The loss of important historic buildings in Leeds in the early 1960s, most notably Beckett's Bank, prompted the founding of Leeds Civic Trust in 1965.[29] The trust's object was to stem the tide of the destruction of the city's historic buildings, and to promote high quality architectural design and town planning in the city, and the improvement of public amenities. At the beginning of the 1970s it had notable successes in defeating plans to demolish Barran's Moorish warehouse in Park Square, the Bank of England in South Parade, and the circular Midland Bank building in City Square, but glaring losses continued including the centre of the facade of the Empire Theatre which was quite barbarously chopped out of its Briggate frontage and replaced with a modern shop front.

The Merrion Centre, the first of the city's modern shopping centres, opened in 1963. A product of another of the post-war comprehensive redevelopment schemes.

A row of early eighteenth-century merchant houses on the west side of Lower Briggate. The nine-bayed house in the centre with the 'Sold' sign is Thomas Lee's house, which was shown on Cossins' Plan of 1726. All were demolished in the late 1970s.

In the early 1970s developers brought forward a scheme to demolish all the buildings between Boar Lane and the railway viaduct to clear the way for a new shopping centre on the site. Battle was waged at a public inquiry in 1974 by Leeds Civic Trust and the Victorian Society in a joint effort to save the fine buildings on Boar Lane. But the battle was lost. Due to the economic uncertainties of the late 1970s and the early 1980s, and fortuitous bankruptcies amongst the site owners, the shopping centre was not built and the Boar Lane buildings survived. Nevertheless, the buildings behind were demolished to make way – almost inevitably in the climate of the day – for surface car parking on the cleared site. At a stroke, one of the last surviving merchant houses which had graced the borders of John Cossins' Plan of Leeds of 1726, Thomas Lee's house, and two houses of a similar age, were flattened with their accompanying historic yards. More of the Briggate yards were soon to follow with the comprehensive redevelopment of the area for the Trinity Street Arcade. Such buildings had survived for two and a half centuries, and were demolished perhaps less than 20 years before a change in attitudes to building conservation at both national and local level would have made their demolition unthinkable.

Under the Civic Amenities Act of 1967 local authorities were empowered to designate 'Conservation Areas' – areas containing buildings many of which might not be of sufficient architectural merit or historic importance to be 'listed' individually, but which as a group had considerable historic character. In future buildings in such designated areas could not be demolished or substantially altered without planning permission from the local authority. The city council adopted these powers and by mid-1973 it had created 14 Conservation Areas and was considering designating another 29. By 1993 Leeds had 63 Conservation Areas.[30] The vitally important enhancement studies for each area, which were intended to promote their sensitive conservation and improvement, however, have never been produced. This has weakened the protection of historic buildings especially in the suburban Conservation Areas. Important buildings had continued to disappear in the meantime, but at a gradually diminishing rate. The greatest battle of the late 1980s was that successfully waged principally by the market traders and Leeds Civic Trust, though with immense support from the general public, against the incorporation of Leeds Market in a huge shopping centre. Following the rejection of the scheme by a public inquiry, the city council and the Norwich Union implemented a high quality scheme to renovate and refurbish the markets.

Running in parallel to the battle to protect historic buildings and areas were efforts by members of the public to combat the dire environmental consequences of proposed road widening schemes. Perhaps the most celebrated campaign of all was that to prevent the A660 (the road from the city centre through Headingley to Otley) being converted to an expressway. This would have involved the creation of a Headingley By-pass. The scheme which featured in the council's proposals in the late 1940s, was the subject of furious public debate in the early 1970s and early 1980s. On each occasion the proposals were shelved. The phase 'the A660 Joint Council exists to co-ordinate informed opposition to such plans' must over the years have given many a transport planner a heavy heart! Unlike Holbeck and Hunslet, the A660 corridor had the advantage of one of the most articulate middle-class populations in Britain.[31]

Another change which has had a dramatic impact on both the appearance and the health of the city has been the virtual abolition of smoke pollution. From the passing of the Clean Air Act in 1956, smoke control measures compelling the use of only smokeless fuel were introduced into the city. The first smoke control area was introduced in 1959 and by 1973 there were 109 control areas.[32] The cleaner environment encouraged property owners to clean their buildings, and from the mid-1970s the architectural glory of many of the city's buildings has emerged from the grime. The most striking of all was the cleaning of the Town Hall. Remarkable though it may seem, there was a heated debate about the cleaning of Leeds Town Hall. Indeed, the Civic Trust strongly opposed it preferring that its blackness should 'stand as a symbol of the city's industrial past and as a reminder to future generations of the air pollution which the city is so successfully combatting'.

Planning for the Future

With the creation of the West Yorkshire Metropolitan County in 1974, responsibility for planning became shared between the West Yorkshire County Council and Leeds City Council. The county council provided the broad framework for land use and transport policy within Leeds and West Yorkshire by means of the West Yorkshire Structure Plan. The city council worked out the detailed policies within the Structure Plan framework and set these out in 'Local Plans' which it sought to implement by controls on development.[33] Though the loss of some planning powers was regretted by some, a major advance was made in 1974 when for the first time the city council established a Department of Planning entirely separate from the City Engineer's Department. At last, consideration of good town planning, architecture and design was established as a counterweight to civil engineering considerations. As we have seen, when the metropolitan county was abolished in 1986, full planning powers reverted to Leeds. In 1989 the city planners were required to prepare a Unitary Development Plan for the future development of the city to the year 2001 and beyond. The draft document was placed on deposit in the summer of 1993 ready to be considered at a public inquiry.

Housing, Health and Education

There can be no doubt that since the Second World War the people of Leeds as a whole have gained in prosperity at a greater rate than at any comparable period in the past. The improvement has been most marked in the well-being of the working-classes. Indeed, the levels of income, dress, and styles of life of significant sections of the working and middle classes have become so similar, at least superficially, that even the Prime Minister talks with enthusiasm about creating a classless society. Despite the genuine blurring of the distinctions, and the attempts by the 'political correct' to obscure them, both the working classes and the middle classes alike have little doubt into which class they might be grouped. Quite properly many of the citizens are unashamedly proud of their working-class stock and their important contribution to the well-being and life of the city. It is perhaps the middle classes who view the distinction with a degree of embarrassment in what is supposed to be an age of equality.

The working classes benefited greatly from the practically full employment of the 1950s and '60s, a well developed social security system, and wages which moved ahead of the relatively low rates of inflation. There was a distinct levelling-up of incomes as the earnings of clerical occupations, semi-skilled and

families owned a washing machine, 80 per cent a deep freeze, 98 per cent a television, and 75 per cent central heating.[34]

Post-War Housing

The Second World War aggravated the housing problem in Leeds, as ambitious schemes like one for multi-storey flats in Marsh Lane had to be abandoned. After the war, however, council house building gathered momentum at a prodigious rate, once building materials greatly increased in supply in 1953. The council built well over two-thirds of the dwellings erected in the city between 1949 and 1972, some 45,000 houses. Large estates like Armley Heights, Spen Hill, Moor Grange and Tinshill were created around the Outer Ring Road, while further extensions were made to the council estates at Belle Isle and Seacroft. By 1961 Seacroft alone had a population of around 40,000.[35]

Inevitably, the war delayed the council's programme of slum clearance. After hostilities ceased, the Marsh Lane site was cleared to make way for Saxton Gardens, a complex of seven parallel slab blocks of flats, five to ten storeys in height. In 1954 there was the large-scale redevelopment of the York Road district and the adjacent area of old Burmantofts which was renamed Lincoln Green. Major slum clearance, however, did not get fully under way until the 1957 Housing Act obliged the council to advance slum clearance with vigour. As a result 9,000 were cleared between 1955 and 1961, and a further 10,000 between 1961 and 1966.

Awaiting the bulldozer. Residents struggle on amidst the boarded-up back-to-backs of Servia Mount, Woodhouse, c.1970. The view looks across to Buslingthorpe.

Unfortunately for many working-class families, the council, irrespective of which party was in control, became almost irrationally obsessed with demolishing back-to-back houses and older terraces, regardless of their location or condition. Of course the demolition of such properties and their replacement with modern, roomier council houses was a good thing in principle, but much less commendable was the sweeping away of large areas of houses in one go, thereby destroying whole communities and major components of the urban face of Leeds. Admittedly, Leeds was a pioneer of housing renovation on a large scale by using Housing Act grants and declaring General Improvement Areas – between 1958 and 1973 over 13,000 dwellings were improved with grant aid – but the principal object was to extend the useful life of what was regarded as slum property for around 15 years pending its demolition.[36] The council was convinced that large-scale housing renewal could only be successfully achieved by starting with cleared sites.[37] A further 17,500 houses were demolished between 1967 and 1972, clearance rates hitting the high point of 3,000 a year in 1970-72.

Finally, in 1972 the people's backlash came when the Conservative-led council prepared, without any public consultation, the Provisional Housing Renewal Programme for 1971-75. This threatened over 30,000 houses, mainly back-to-backs, – over one-sixth of the city's entire housing stock. The proposals, which were meant only for the eyes of councillors, were leaked to the press. David Austick, Liberal councillor for Hunslet, sounded the alarm bells: 'The community of West Hunslet is going to be abolished and there are no plans for rebuilding. People who have lived there for years and

unskilled workers increased by more than the average and by considerably more than those of professional and other middle-class groups. Between 1951 and 1975 the purchasing power of a manual worker's wage increased by three-quarters, while many of the white collar jobs that before the war might have commanded salaries around double those of manual workers, now provided incomes often significantly less than 50 per cent higher (see appendices).

As we will see, during the 1950s and '60s and the decades thereafter, the majority of the people of Leeds have become better housed, better educated, and significantly healthier. Their material possessions have increased greatly. In 1991, approximately 90 per cent of have spent money on improving their homes face the destruction of their surroundings without anything positive in the way of the redevelopment of the area.' Alderman Sir Frank Marshall, in the controlling Conservative group's defence, replied that: 'All we are doing is designating areas of clearance in a rolling programme for several years ahead. We have plans for the city over the next 20 years. It is not only Hunslet but many other areas of the city that are affected. All that the Liberals are trying to do is to inflame the minds of people by what they are pleased to call community politics.'[38]

Community politics or not, the working-class rebellion was on. Literally thousands of residents packed meetings all over the city – they had had enough! Burley, Armley, Stanningley, Bramley, Burmantofts were all areas where over the next two years residents campaigned for the improvement of their homes rather than their demolition. There were more residents' associations and societies formed in 1972 than in the previous quarter of a century. The residents of Woodhouse were perhaps the most resolute campaigners of them all. In February 1972, Robert Simpson, the Vicar of Woodhouse, warned:

> There seems to be a plan to knock down Woodhouse almost completely in two stages from 1972-76 and from 1977-81. It appears that after knocking down houses and redistributing the community, the land cleared would lie fallow for ages. Then more houses would be built and people brought back. The new residents will not form a community. They will just be a large number of people living in the same place. We don't grumble at redevelopment. It's just that we think the council should phase out small areas gradually, building up and re-accommodating people as they go.[39]

When Labour gained control of the council in 1972, it was almost split down the middle by the slum clearance issue, and the policy of wholesale slum clearance was moderated. The result was that more than half of the 30,000 houses scheduled for demolition were removed entirely from the proposals and others phased in later quinquennial periods. Nevertheless, house clearance continued at a rate of around 2,000 a year until the late 1970s, despite the fact that the council had thousands of people on the waiting list for council houses. From the mid-1970s onwards the council's policy started to shift towards the gradual renewal of housing areas and emphasised the refurbishment and improvement of older property. The council's Urban Programme, begun in 1978, specifically aimed at regenerating the inner city areas and promoting community involvement rather than tearing communities apart. The programme of grant assisted projects focussed on the older industrial areas around the core of the city centre: Hunslet, Holbeck, Beeston Hill, Armley, Burley, Woodhouse, Chapeltown, Burmantofts, Harehills and Osmonthorpe, and some of the inter-war council estates, Middleton, Belle Isle, Halton, Cross Gates, Gipton and Seacroft. By 1983 the *Leeds Planning Handbook* could say with confidence that the era of large-scale housing redevelopment was over.[40]

For many people in the 1950s and '60s, the move from a back-to-back to a new council dwelling meant a vast improvement in the quality of their accommodation, but not for all. The drawback for some was the vogue for erecting multi-storey blocks of council flats in this period. Between 1958 and 1964, for example, of 11,427 dwellings erected by the council, 4,543 were multi-storey flats. For many families, life in the more modern and spacious back-to-backs, in communities in which they felt at home, seemed infinitely preferable to being stuck ten or more floors in the air in soulless blocks of flats. Moreover, in some cases the high rise flats were so badly built that council tenants demanded to be rehoused. The most notorious instance was the Hunslet Grange flats in Leek Street, which suffered such great problems of damp, structural defects and vandalism that, though built only in 1965, by the early '70s the council was obliged to try to persuade students to occupy them, and in 1985 finally demolished them. In the mid-'60s the council began to recognise the absurdity of placing families with young children in high rise flats, and the opening of Cottingley Towers in 1968 brought the high rise flat era to an end.

By 1970 virtually all the pre-1870 back-to-backs had been demolished, and many of the houses which were cleared in the 1970s were perfectly capable of being up-

Hunslet Grange Council Flats, Leek Street, built in 1965. Within 20 years, structural defects, vandalism and the refusal of tenants to occupy them, led to their demolition.

graded to provide desperately needed low-cost housing. Today there are still some 23,000 back-to-backs in Leeds, which in a modernised state provide perfectly adequate and pleasant low-cost homes. Ironically, the inter-war housing estates, built to solve the problem of the back-to-backs, are in a state of physical and social decay.[41]

The post-war period saw a major increase in the building of private houses, particularly in the northern suburbs, where Alwoodley, Cookridge, Shadwell, Oakwood and Roundhay proved especially popular locations.[42] Around 20,000 were built between 1953 and 1972 at a rate of about 1,000 a year. For those who could afford to buy, Leeds houses were excellent value for money. In 1976 a 3-bedroom terrace could be bought for just over £6,000, while a 3-bedroom semi-detached house would cost around £9,500.[43] Between 1949 and 1972 the council and the private sector together erected 65,000 houses, while 34,000 were demolished.

The net effect of all these activities was a major change in the geographical distribution of the city's inhabitants. The inner city experienced heavy population losses as a result of slum clearance and the reduction of overcrowding. Between 1949 and 1961, for example, Woodhouse lost 9,000 inhabitants, while Armley lost 7,200. Correspondingly, there were marked increases in the populations of the outer suburbs. Municipal development accounted for large increases at Seacroft and Beckett Park, for example, while private house building produced major growth at Cookridge and Lawnswood. Alwoodley and Moortown gained some 7,000 due to both public and private sector building. This trend in the redistribution of the population has continued to the present day.

The financial security given by the low levels of unemployment in the 1950s and '60s, and the considerable rise in the spending power of the population as a whole, has contributed to a major rise in home ownership. Probably only 10 per cent of the city's houses were owner-occupied in 1914. As a result of the major building for owner occupation, particularly in the 1930s, this proportion rose to about 30 per cent by 1950. Since then the figure has risen sharply, reaching 40 per cent in 1961, 53 per cent by 1981 and just over 61 per cent by 1991.[44]

Post-War Welfare

The lives of all the citizens of Leeds were very significantly improved after the war by the establishment of the Welfare State. The steps which had already been taken before the war to destigmatise the relief of poverty, and to extend the safety net to a greater range of services, were greatly developed under the inspiration of the Beveridge Report of 1942. The major legislation between 1944 and 1948 created a comprehensive and universal system of National Insurance, Family Allowances, National Assistance and the National Health Service, and these were backed by the housing, education, health and other welfare services provided by local authorities at the behest of the government. The emphasis shifted greatly to national provision administered at a local level, with the local authorities being the junior partner.

With the creation of the National Health Service in 1948 all the Leeds hospitals, both voluntary and municipal, passed into State ownership and were merged under the Regional Hospital Board. Under the new system, teaching hospitals, like the Infirmary, were given special autonomy in that their boards of govenors were appointed directly by the Minister of Health. The General Infirmary came under control of the Board of Governors of the United Leeds Hospitals with Sir George Martin as its first chairman. This group also included the Women's Hospital, the Leeds Maternity Hospital, the Dental Hospital and the Ida and Robert Arthington Hospital. There can be no doubt that these hospitals and their patients benefited from the change, for the tremendous expense of future developments in diagnosis and treatment could not have been borne by institutions dependent on voluntary contributions. At the same time St James' came under the management of the Leeds (A Group) Hospital Management Committee which had responsibility for five hospitals with a total bed complement of 2,073 of which 1,679 were at St James' North and South. In the late 1960s, moves to expand the Leeds University Medical School set in train the development of St James' as a teaching hospital. Accordingly, in 1970, Britain's largest general hospital, became St James' University Hospital.[45] There can be no doubt that the reorganisation of health care in Leeds as a result of the creation of the National Health Service greatly improved the lot of the masses. At long last, the family doctor, previously too expensive for many poor people, had become available free and integrated into a more comprehensive system. Treatment by dentists and opticians also became readily available to the whole of the population.

Post-War Education

There was also a radical shake up in the system of education in Leeds immediately after the Second World War as a result of the 1944 Education Act. This provided for the reclassification of the city's schools: primary schools for children up to the age of 11 years, and secondary schools for children over that age. The secondary schools were to be of three types: grammar schools providing an academic type of education; technical schools providing an education of a similar standard, but designed to prepare pupils for commercial or technical careers; and secondary modern schools giving an education euphemistically described as 'for those who are unlikely to seek a professional career'. The system which, from the viewpoint of a later generation, harshly branded some children failures at the age of eleven was born.

The total reclassification of the city's schools was held back by the dislocation and shortage of resources following the Second World War, but the city produced a £21 million development plan which was gradually implemented. By 1947 the city had 120 primary schools, 8 secondary grammar schools, 2 secondary technical schools and 5 secondary modern schools. In addition there were two independent and three direct grant secondary schools.

In the sphere of primary and secondary education the main pressure post-war was from the increase in pupil numbers. In 1939-40 there were 53,188 children between the ages of five and fourteen. In 1971-72, before the second raising of the leaving age, there were 79,397 children aged five to fifteen. In order to find sufficient resources, the city's excellent nursery education system disappeared shortly after the war.

The reputation of the city's colleges continued to grow after the war. In 1946 the College of Art celebrated its centenary. It had a fine reputation and by then included a School of Architecture. The College of Commerce was one of the few colleges in the country whose examinations were recognised by professional bodies for exemption purposes. The College of Technology, with 4,000 students, not only prepared students for City and Guild qualifications and for professional courses, but was recognised by the University of London for external degree purposes in engineering and scientific subjects.[47] These institutions continued to grow strongly in the next two decades. By 1969 the recently amalgamated City of Leeds and Carnegie Colleges had 1,300 full-time students, while the College of Technology had 718 full-time and 4,984 part-time. The College of Art had 598 full-time and 976 part-time students, while the College of Commerce had 831 full-time and 5,000 part-time. The Yorkshire College of Education and Home Economics (affectionately known to successive generations of students as 'the Pud School') was also flourishing.[48] On 1 January 1970 the council's long-term ambition of creating one central college for higher education embracing all subjects was realised when the Colleges of Technology, Commerce, Art, and Education and Home Economics were amalgamated to become Leeds Polytechnic.[49]

In common with other civic universities, Leeds University experienced a dramatic growth in its numbers in the 1950s and '60s. With its strong science base, it in particular benefited from the government's enthusiasm for the development of science and technology. Between 1952 and 1972 the number of students rose from 3,000 to over 9,000. By the 1970s it had emerged as the largest university in England.[50]

This remarkable array of institutions of higher education were well complemented in 1970 by the council's Colleges of Further Education. These had been established in the late 1950s and the 1960s as branches of the established colleges to teach their subjects at a lower level. The College of Building; Jacob Kramer College (renamed Leeds College of Art and Design in 1993); Kitson College of Engineering and Science; and Park Lane College, specialising in commercial and secretarial courses, offered excellent teaching, as did Thomas Danby College, providing courses for nurses and nursery nurses, housekeepers, catering and food technology, and hairdressing; and the Music Centre in Cookridge Street (which subsequently became Leeds City College of Music).[51] By the 1970s, Leeds had a formidable mass of students in higher and further education, and its provision in this sphere was probably unrivalled in outside London.

In 1972 Leeds' primary and secondary education system was reorganised yet again. A three-tier comprehensive system of schooling was introduced. Children were to transfer from Primary School to Middle School at the age of 9 and from Middle to High School at 13. Many were sad to see the maintained grammar schools disappear in this reorganisation, but, in spite of the national political debate about education in the 1960s, this change does not appear to have been a particularly contentious issue at local level. The Conservative reorganisation scheme was implemented by Labour after 1972 with only small differences of emphasis.

Education in Leeds since the 1960s seems to have been in a perpetual state of flux. Recent years have brought two further major changes. The first has affected schools. The piecemeal expansion of the Leeds Education Department meant that by 1990 it had a bewildering array of Nursery, Infant, Junior, First, Middle and Secondary Schools under its control. Already under pressure from central government to reduce the number of vacant places in the schools as a result of the decline in the birth rate, the time seemed right for a restructuring of the city's schools into uniform age bands. In this reorganisation, which took place during the academic year 1991/92, middle schools were abolished and the city reverted to the former two-tier system of primary and secondary schools, with children changing schools at age eleven. The second major change came in 1989 when Leeds Polytechnic was freed from Leeds City Council control. In 1992 Leeds was raised to the dignity of a two-university city when the Polytechnic became Leeds Metropolitan University.

Post-War Leisure

The greater affluence of Leeds people since the war, shorter working hours, labour-saving devices in the home, and paid holidays for almost all full-time workers, have greatly increased the opportunities for leisure. The greater comforts of home and widespread ownership of radios, record players and televisions, accentuated the trend begun in the inter-war period for leisure to become much more home-centred. Until after the war, television remained a pleasure only for the affluent, but thereafter ownership grew rapidly. By 1961 three-quarters of all households in Leeds had sets.[53]

Television had a devastating impact on cinema and theatre attendances, as well as reducing numbers at sporting events. It could be blamed for the closure of the Theatre Royal in 1957 and the Empire in 1961. In the 1960s, cinema after cinema closed, quite a number being converted to Bingo Halls. The decline was rapid: from a high point of 68 cinemas in 1939, the number fell to 20 by 1967. Though the decline slowed, by 1980 there were only were 15 cinemas left in Leeds, and today there are only five.[54] Against the odds, the almost terminal fall in attendances has been reversed in recent years and the surviving long-established cinemas – the Odeon and the MGM in the city centre (both now multi-screen cinemas) and the Cottage Road, the Lounge and the Hyde Park Cinema in Headingley – are well patronised. Even the opening in 1990 of the modern multi-screen Showcase Cinema on the southern fringe of the city has done little to dent their popularity.

Greater affluence has brought an increase in the habit of eating out. For even the working classes, by the 1960s eating out had begun to mean something more exotic than eating at a fish and chip parlour, or 'meat and two veg.' in a cafe. In 1961 a Leeds guide, after noting that the best cuisine in Leeds was to be found in the Queen's Hotel, the Hotel Metropole and the Parkway, commented that the city had a 'cosmopolitan range of eating places, many of them open until 11 p.m., to cater for the after-theatre crowds ...Currently popular are Chinese dishes ...whilst Cypriot and other specialists help to cater for the gourmet eating on a tighter pocket.'[55] Today there is even more diversity. Italian, French, Greek, Vietnamese, Caribbean, Polish, Indian and Thai cooking compete against excellent traditional fish and chip restaurants like Nash's Tudor Restaurant in town and Bryan's in Headingley. The 1990s has seen the development of high quality riverside bars and restaurants catering for the more affluent diners.

For sports enthusiasts the city's amenities improved steadily. The jewel in the crown was the Leeds International Pool opened in 1967; the city boasted that it had the only pool of exact international length in the country. By this date the city possessed 174 soccer, 40 rugby and 74 cricket pitches, 159 tennis courts, 50 bowling greens and 6 putting greens. Long-established golf clubs like Headingley, Sandmoor, Moor Allerton and Cobble Hall, supplemented by municipal courses at Gott's Park and Middleton, proved incapable of coping with the demand.[56] These facilities have been very successfully enhanced by the provision of a dozen excellent municipal sports centres in the suburbs, with squash and badminton courts, gym facilities, swimming pools, sauna suites and solariums.

For those interested in spectactor sports, the phenomenal success of Leeds United, in the 1960s and '70s during the Revie era, and the great popularity of Test and County Cricket at Headingley, made Leeds a nationally renowned centre for sport. The city's rugby teams, especially, Leeds Rugby League Football Club and Headingley Rugby Union Club, also set high standards and drew considerable followings.

For the teenagers and younger adults the 1960s brought some major new attractions. The Top Rank Bowling Alley and Silver Blades Ice Rink on Kirkstall

The Glory Years. Don Revie's famous Leeds United team, which won the Football League Championship in 1968-69 and 1973-74, the FA Cup (1972), the League Cup (1967-68), and the European Fairs Cup in 1967-68 and 1970-71. The glory has returned under Howard Wilkinson. In 1991-92 Leeds became League Champions once again.

Hero of Yorkshire and England! Geoffrey Boycott reaches his hundredth hundred in the England-Australia Test Match at Headingley in August 1977.

Road, opened in 1962, were extremely popular; though in 1967 the ice rink was converted to the Olympic Roller Skating Rink. Ten pin bowling alleys were also opened in the Merrion Centre, the Arndale Shopping Centre in Headingley, and at Seacroft. Though ten pin bowling faded as a pastime in the 1970s, it is currently undergoing a revival in the city with alleys at AMF Bowling in the Merrion Centre and L.A. Bowl on Sweet Street.

Then, of course, there were the dance halls and, the new craze, the discotheques and night clubs, where the younger parts of the population danced the nights away. Jimmy Savile, one of the great Leeds personalities, made his name as one of the country's first disc jockeys at the Mecca Ballroom in the County Arcade in the late '50s and early 1960s. Discipline there was such that on Saturdays, the Teddy Boys used to pay 6d. a time at the nearest barber's to have their sideboards trimmed to regulation length, lest they failed to pass the scrutiny of the Mecca's bouncers. Those that failed used to gather in the rougher pubs nearby, where the the Saturday night 'punch-up' was not an infrequent occurrence.[57] In this era the Manchester night clubs were regarded as superior to the nightlife offered by Leeds, but towards the end of the '60s the city's night club scene was boosted by the opening of the purpose-built 'Cinderella/Rockerfella' complex behind the Merrion Centre. 'Nightbird' James Towler noted the difference in atmosphere between its two halves: 'In Cinderella's the volume is loud, the pace is fast and the atmosphere spells action with a capital 'A'. But move through the door into the adjoining Rockerfella's and you are in another softer and more sophisticated world'.[58] Today, Leeds is one of the top night spots in the country. Most clubs are situated in the city centre. The Warehouse, The Gallery, Mister Craig's, Digby's, Ritzy's and 'Back to Basics' nights in the Music Factory have an outstanding reputation. The council is actively promoting Leeds as a 24 hour city, extending licensing hours to encourage people of all ages to come back into the city at night. Because of the night life, the police reckon that there are more people in New Briggate at 3.00 a.m. in the morning than there are at lunchtime.

The city has in late years lost much of its reputation as a night time haunt of disorderly youths, tramps and alcoholics. Traditional pubs in the city centre, such as Whitelock's, the Adelphi and Duck and Drake continue to prosper. The city centre pubs' singing rooms of former years have been replaced by new feature evenings with jazz, folk and rock bands. Compact disc jukeboxes, live football on large televisions, and karaoke talent competitions and quiz nights are increasingly used to lure the drinkers through the door.

For those interested in cultural activities, the city's facilities and institutions progressed to new heights in the 1960s and '70s, and today are almost unrivalled outside London. The Leeds Playhouse, established in the shell of a new sports hall at Leeds University in 1970, proved such a great success that it was replaced in 1990 by the splendid £13½ million West Yorkshire Playhouse at Quarry Hill with its 2 theatres and excellent ancillary facilities.[59] The triennial Leeds International Piano Competition, established in 1963, has become an immense international success, receiving live coverage on national television. In 1978 the city's music enthusiasts were delighted by the establishment of English National Opera North at the Grand Theatre. Its marvellous nine productions each year have continued to thrill packed houses of opera goers. The city's

Victorian music hall tradition continues at the City Varieties, England's oldest music theatre. TV's longest running music show, The Good Old Days, was filmed there from 1953-1983.

A scene from Opera North's 1992 production of Benjamin Britten's 'Billy Budd'. One of many outstanding performances.

Genesis performing at Roundhay Park in 1992.

international concert season at the Town Hall brings the world's best orchestras to Leeds. In 1985 Leeds Leisure Services Department could proudly boast that there would be a musical event in Leeds every forty hours. Meanwhile, the city has not neglected pop music. In 1982 the arena at Roundhay Park became one of the country's biggest outdoor rock venues when the Rolling Stones played to a 90,000 sell out audience. Since then it has been host to concerts by international stars, including Michael Jackson, Genesis and Madonna. The city's lack of a major permanent pop venue was at last overcome in 1993 when the Coliseum in Cookridge Street became the Town and Country Club.

Since the war, car ownership has grown dramatically. In 1938 there were 18,000 private cars licensed in Leeds. By 1966 there were 68,000. Today almost 60 per cent of Leeds households have one or more cars.[60] The positive side of the traffic predicament that these vehicles created was the greater mobility given by mass car ownership. More people began to visit stately homes, and take trips into the countryside, and the seaside. People travelled further afield for their holidays too and caravaning became popular. Wallace Arnold Tours Ltd has gone from strength to strength as national and international tour operators. Founded in the charabanc days, its first continental holiday ran to Germany in 1935. By 1963, with over 200 coaches, it had developed continental 'Teens and Thirties Holidays' and 'Dream Holidays for

The Chapeltown Caribbean Carnival on August Bank Holiday Monday each year is one of the great events of the Leeds calendar.

the Elderly'.[61] The arrival of cheap charter flights and low-cost package holidays have brought foreign holidays within the reach of the masses. Today people who might once have gone to Blackpool or Scarborough for a week's holiday, now fly off to Spain or Greece or even more exotic places.

Perhaps not surprisingly, with all these counter attractions, the decline in the place of religion in the lives of Leeds people has continued. The extent of this decline was highlighted most clearly by the change in national legislation in 1993 which made it legal for all shops to open on Sundays. The people of Leeds may now do their supermarket food shopping on a Sunday if they wish. At the beginning of the 1950s probably about 11 per cent of women and 7 per cent of men were regular church goers.[62] By the mid-1980s there were reckoned to be about 40,000 – 45,000 regular church attenders in the city out of a total population of just over 700,000. This further fall in attendance has been exacerbated by the ageing of the church congregations. The city still has over 200 churches, and these are complemented by the places of worship of other world religions, many of which have sprung up as a result of immigration in the last few decades. The Jewish community in the city numbers some 16,000 (the third largest in Britain), while there are some 10,000 Muslims, 6,000 Sikhs, 4,000 Hindus, and smaller groups of Buddhists, Bahais and other faiths.[63]

Disparities in wealth and income

The graffiti on a railway bridge spanning Burley Road in the early 1990s used to read 'Neither Work Nor Leisure'. The point was well made – however splendid the entertainments offered by Leeds, if you did not have a job, you could not afford to fill your spare time by making the most of them! Despite the material gains of the inhabitants of Leeds since the war, the increased affluence has not been evenly distributed. In terms of quality of life, the gap has widened between the affluent suburbs and the increasingly deprived inner-city districts and ageing council estates. Today residents in the old industrial areas of Hunslet, Holbeck, Burmantofts, Burley, Armley, the outer council estates of Belle Isle, Middleton, Gipton and Seacroft, and the multi-racial, multi-cultural areas of Harehills and Chapeltown – collectively known as the Urban Priority Areas – lead markedly different lifestyles from those in other parts of the city.

The downturn in the economy in the late 1970s meant that unemployment increased most significantly in areas such as Chapeltown. On certain streets there, not one adult male had a job.[64] Poverty, racism, Thatcherism and the lack of a local organisation which could express the grievances of the people led to frustration and bitterness. This found expression in the Chapeltown Riots on the nights of 11/12 and 13/14 July 1981. Huge crowds of black youths, supported by white teenagers from nearby estates, attacked the police and fought pitched battles with stones and petrol bombs. Three hundred police officers with riots shields were deployed in an attempt to quell the riots. Several shops and businesses were burned and looted, and damage estimated at £2 million was inflicted on a stunned community.[65] George Mudie, the Labour council leader, called together the ethnic community leaders in the hope of solving some of Chapeltown's problems. Progress was certainly made in improving conditions in the area, but today prostitution, drugs and street crime are a major problem, though a new police task force has recently been formed to try to tackle the problem more intensively.[66]

In such inner-city Urban Priority Areas, problems of poor housing persist.[67] According to the 1986 Housing Investment Programme there were still over 27,000 unfit houses in the city of which 2,600 households lacked either a bath, inside toilet, sink or hot and cold water, most of them in these areas. In 1986 in the Leeds Urban Priority Areas, with a population of around 200,000, there were to be found 40 per cent of the city's elderly, 50 per cent of the city's single parents, 60 per cent of the unemployed, and 75 per cent of the city's houses in need of major repair. Fifty-five per cent of the city's reported crime occurred in these districts. In the city as a whole in December 1988, 1,109 people in the city were categorised as homeless, in addition to which the accommodation of some left much to be desired. In February 1986 the *Leeds Weekly News* highlighted the plight of a 93-year-old widow, who was so infirm she could not move from her ninth-floor flat, was too poor to afford a telephone, and had to contact friends by hanging a cloth from a balcony!

While the creation of the Welfare State did a great deal to alleviate poverty and its associated problems, some of the advances it made have been eroded in recent years as a result of government policy. The disparities in income across the city, notably between those in employment and those unemployed, are still very substantial. Attempts to make statistical comparisons are fraught with difficulties but perhaps the following give some sort of useful impression. In April 1992 the average household disposable income in Yorkshire and Humberside was around £15,500 per annum. On Income Support plus Housing Benefit (the social security payments made to those not eligible for unemployment benefit) a husband and wife with two children would at that date have received the equivalent of approximately £6,500 a year. Put in another way, at that date the average gross annual full-time earnings of an adult male were approximately £16,000 (around £12,000 after deduction of tax and national insurance). In contrast an adult male on Income Support would receive £2,184 a year, plus housing benefit equivalent to rent payments of around £1,500 per annum. The stark fact is that in very broad terms, those on living on social security in Leeds in the early 1990s receive at best between one-third and one-half of the income of a those families with a least one member in work. With an unemployment rate of over 10 per cent in the city as a whole, and around 25 per cent in the Urban Priority Areas, and more than one-third of the city's unemployed having been out of work for more than a year, it is not surprising if life is miserable and difficult for a significant section of the population. Leeds is still a city of 'haves' and 'have nots'.

Though the problems of poverty and deprivation are not comparable with those of the Victorian era, the relative deprivation in Leeds of a significant proportion of the population is sufficient to give rise to a sense of hopelessness. Whilst experts and politicians argue about causal links between deprivation and crime, the city like the rest of the country has seen an enormous increase in crime in the last decade. Perhaps the price the more affluent citizens of Leeds pay for the unequal distribution of the city's income and wealth is the perpetual and regularly justified fear that their houses will be burgled and their cars stolen. In the final annual report of the Chief Constable for the City of Leeds in 1973 the total recorded number of indictable offence was 29,293. This figure is likely to be exceeded in just the Killingbeck and Millgarth divisions of the city alone in 1994.

Leeds Past, Present and Future

Viewed from a historical perspective, perhaps one of the most striking features of Leeds today is the greatly diminished role and influence of the city council compared with the first half of the twentieth century. We have seen how over the centuries the principal inhabitants strove to gain control of the town affairs and to reduce the influence of outsiders. In the ninteenth century the reformed corporation, partly through necessity and partly through enthusiasm, not only extended its powers of regulation, but began to provide a host of municipal services. By the 1920s and '30s the council referred to itself with pride as 'the Do-it-all Corporation'. The story of the last fifty years, and particularly the last two decades, has been the steady erosion of this power and influence. Perhaps least debilitating has been the loss of control of the public utilities. The council's gas and electricity undertakings were nationalised in the 1940s, and in 1974 its water and sewage undertakings were transferred to the Yorkshire Water Authority. These changes made sound economic and technical sense, and even when these public utilities were privatised in the 1980s the impact on the city was minimal. Much more serious has been the council's loss of control of public transport in the city. The city's transport services were first transferred to the West Yorkshire Metropolitan County in 1974 and then privatised and deregulated in 1986. At a time when the council is anxious to limit the damaging expansion of motor vehicle traffic in the city, it is unable to provide a coherent integrated public transport system, and its valiant efforts to implement a comprehensive transport strategy, including supertrams and guided buses, is very much at the mercy of the whims of central government.

In recent years central government has also limited the council's powers to act in many other ways. In the Victorian period the council had the discretion to spend lavishly on major projects which it felt were important for the prestige and well-being of the city. These might be anything from building the Town Hall to the improvement of the city waterworks or the building of an art gallery. Today the national system of rate-capping (or 'Council Tax capping') ensures that councils, whose spending is deemed by central government to be excessive, have their government grants reduced. Though Leeds has never been rate-capped, the threat of it is sufficient to prevent the council financing through local taxation or borrowing, prestigious civic projects such as the building of a new concert hall or exhibition centre, or a new city museum. In this situation, council-owned buildings which were once the pride of Leeds are left to go to rack and ruin, or sold off for private uses, for want of adequate finance to maintain and adapt them for new public purposes. Large council-owned sites in the city centre, which offer the opportunities for much needed open spaces or sites for public amenities, end up being disposed of to raise much needed cash. The 'family silver' is being sold off to meet the short-term rather than long-term needs of the city.

The ability of the council to provide housing has also become severely limited. Earlier in the twentieth century, the provision of municipal housing was absolutely critical to providing large numbers of working-class people with decent homes. In recent years, the Conservative Government's bid to create a 'property owning democracy' has forced councils throughout the country to sell off large quantities of council housing to their tenants under the 'right to buy scheme'. In a city desperately short of cheap rented accommodation, these sales have exacerbated the shortage. Most galling of all, the council has not been permitted to use the proceeds of council house sales to build new housing. Thus in a period when private housebuilding has been depressed, the council has been unable to meet the shortfall of accommodation. The increased activity of housing associations in Leeds has been important, but, at a time when the city needs around 1,900 new houses every year, the council and housing associations between them build less than 500 houses a year.[69]

In education too the council's role has been diminished. The government's granting of independent status to Leeds Polytechnic in 1989 has taken higher education out of the council's hands, probably for the better. But fortunately, from the point of view of maintaining a coherent system of primary and secondary education in the city, the government's attempts to encourage primary and secondary schools to opt-out of local authority control have failed so far. On the other hand, in health matters the council's already diminished influence has been dented by the conversion of the two major hospital groupings, based on the General Infirmary and St James' Hospital, to self-governing hospital trusts.

Perhaps the greatest indignity which the council has suffered in recent years occurred in 1988, when its planning powers over a large area of south and central Leeds (south of Boar Lane) and the Kirkstall Valley were transferred to an unelected government appointed quango – the Leeds Development Corporation. The creation of the corporation was bitterly opposed both by the council and the Leeds Chamber of Commerce. For many months the *Yorkshire Evening Post* ran a vitriolic 'Behind Closed Doors' campaign which finally forced the corporation's board to open its meetings to public scrutiny. Public disapproval of what was judged to be the board's high handed attitude was manifested in particular by the establishment of the Kirkstall Valley Campaign, through which the residents of Kirkstall attracted national attention in their battle to prevent the valley, which the council had envisaged as a green park, being turned into a development site.

The creation of the corporation could not make for good coherent planning, especially in the city centre, but eventually the council and the Development Corporation have reached a fairly amicable accommodation with each other. Despite the problems, the results the corporation has achieved in south Leeds and the city centre have mainly been beneficial. Large sums of central government money have been ploughed into these areas, and particularly around the waterfront the regeneration, which the city council had begun, has progressed well. The Conservative government is unlikely to have made such large sums available to the city's Labour council, and the investment must be regarded as a bonus. Moreover, even if the money had been made available to the council, as a body answerable to the electorate, it is unlikely to have had the political will to focus the spending on such a tightly defined area, given the many other demands on the public purse.

Turning to local party politics, as we have seen, Leeds is a city in which there has been a strong political concensus throughout most of the twentieth century. Generally, political argument has been over the method and speed with which policies should be implemented rather than about their general direction. Even in the 1980s, when a city such as Liverpool was brought to chaos by an extreme left-wing Labour council, the Leeds Labour councillors placed sound administration and the promotion of the well-being of citizens and industry and commerce above doctrinaire political attitudes. Perhaps it is this political concensus which in part explains why the city's prominent businessmen or women now take little part in local government. Today, it would be hard to find a councillor with major business interests. On the other hand, possibly it is the greatly diminished influence of the council, which discourages many people from making the virtually full-time commitment that is, for example, involved in being the chairman of a major council committee.

The influence of local businessmen on the future of the Leeds economy has also been greatly reduced since the Second World War. Many of the strong personal ties which formerly gave the city's business and professional leaders a stake in the future of the city have disappeared. With a few notable exceptions, most of the city's major firms are no longer in family ownership and very often are controlled by national or multi-national companies. The investment decisions affecting these firms are most likely to be made outside the city. This combined with the council's loss of control over some major aspects of city affairs, has produced the problem of how Leeds people can protect the future economic well-being of the

Leeds Waterfront from Crown Point Bridge in the late 1960s – a derelict backwater.

Leeds Waterfront from Crown Point Bridge today. The riverside has undergone a remarkable transformation in the late 1980s and the 1990s.

city and how key decision takers can be induced to develop a sense of commitment to Leeds.

The city council has worked hard in association with the Leeds Chamber of Commerce to launch the concept of the corporate city – the idea of a partnership between the city council, the business sector, national government departments, and the city's major institutions to present and market Leeds to the rest of the country and the world, and to work together in promoting the mutually beneficial improvement of the city as a whole. The vehicle for this, established in 1990, is known as the Leeds Initiative. It is interesting to reflect that the select membership of this body, which meets at breakfast time each month to nibble croissants and bacon sandwiches while hearing progress reports on an array of initiatives to improve the city and discussing topics of mutual concern, must constitute, in the city council's view, the most influential players in the city's future prospects. In addition to the city council itself, the bodies represented are: Leeds Chamber of Commerce and Industry, Leeds Development Corporation, Leeds Chamber of Trade, the Department of the Environment, the Department of Trade and Industry, the Department of Employment, the Leeds/Bradford City Action Team, Leeds University, Leeds Metropolitan University, Yorkshire Television, Yorkshire Post Newspapers, the Regional Trade Union Congress, and Leeds Training and Enterprise Council, with occasional representation from Leeds Civic Trust, the West Yorkshire Police, British Rail, and the West Yorkshire Passenger Transport Executive.

Against this background, the recent performance of the local economy, measured by national standards, has been remarkably good. Throughout its history, the secret of Leeds' success has been its outstanding ability to introduce new industry and adapt older ones when patterns of demand have changed and new opportunites have arisen. Its regional role and the much famed diversity of the economy have been extremely important factors in its ability to buck recessions and the possibility of long-term decline. Like many towns and cities around the country, since the 1970s the performance of the Leeds economy has been a source of unease as its manufacturing base has continued to be eroded. In the 1980s and early 1990s, Britain has experienced severe economic problems with sustained high levels of unemployment at 10 per cent or more. The remarkable resilience of Leeds in changing economic circumstances is underlined by its levels of unemployment compared to those in some of the country's other major cities. In April 1991, while unemployment in Leeds was 10.3%, unemployment in Bradford was 12.3%, in Greater London 12.5%, Sheffield 14.3%, Birmingham 16%, Newcastle 17.2%, Manchester 20.2% and Liverpool 24%.[70]

Anyone visiting Leeds city centre in the last five or six years would have been surprised to hear that these were hard times. The rapid expansion of Leeds as a regional centre for commercial and financial services, higher education, national and local government administration, medical services, retailing, and leisure has encouraged large amounts of investment in the city centre. At a time, when many towns and cities have experienced decline, the cranes have kept working in what is a veritable renaissance of the city centre. The regeneration of the city centre waterfront has been quite amazing, with a combination of the adaptation and renovation of old warehouse and dock buildings for flats, offices, hotels and restaurants, and the erection of new buildings to serve similar functions. The waterfront, a semi-derelict backwater less than ten years ago, is rapidly becoming a major tourist attraction. The opening of Granary Wharf, a craft market in the Dark Arches, has been followed by the opening of Joshua Tetley's Brewery Wharf visitor centre on the south side of the river opposite the Calls. Work is already under way on building the £40 million Royal Armouries Museum which is due to open in 1996. Quite remarkably, the Calls, so many times referred to in this book as a centre of low life in the city, has become one of the fashionable eating areas in the city centre.

The combination of the efforts of conservation groups and a more sensitive approach by city planners has in good measure stemmed the tide of the destruction of the historic fabric of the city centre. The most emphatic demonstration of the new found sensitivity in the 1980's was the arrival of the 'Leeds Look', villified by some and warmly welcomed by others. In an attempt to soften the impact of new office and retail developments and to make them blend more happily into the fabric of the city centre, the city council adopted an informal policy that, in considering planning application within the city centre, preference would be given to buildings built in traditional materials. This changed emphasis effectively brought an end to erection of re-inforced concrete buildings in the centre. The building boom of the mid- to late 1980s has brought a plethora of buildings clad in red brick, with stone dressings and grey slate hipped roofs, and by the end of the decade Leeds stood in serious danger of becoming an incredibly bland city because of the excess of this architectural style. Fortunately, a more receptive attitude to innovative design combined with many splendid refurbishment and conservation schemes, finding new uses for important Georgian and Victorian buildings, is now bringing much new interest, vitality and style to the city centre.

In the central shopping streets, the main pedestrianised area of Lands Lane and Commercial Street has recently been expensively refurbished in a controversial manner, while the Corn Exchange, the County Arcade, the Queen's Arcade, Thornton's Arcade, and the City Markets have all undergone major high quality refurbishments. The most remarkable project has been the roofing over of Queen Victoria Street with a stunning stained glass canopy, effectively making it a cathedral-like arcade linked to the County Arcade and the Cross Arcade. All these shopping and market facilities were looking extremely shabby and neglected just a few years ago, and their rejuvenation has been part of deliberate effort by both the city council and commercial interests to stem the decline of the city centre's shopping area, which has resulted from the creation of out-of-town shopping centres locally, and mega shopping centres in or near other towns, most notably the Meadowhall Centre on the edge of Sheffield.

The south side of Boar Lane too has just undergone a major renovation. The character of the street has been preserved by the retention of the facades of the Victorian buildings, and new life has been found in the form of a hotel, offices and shops. Meanwhile, purposeful attempts are being made to arrest the serious decline of Briggate as the city's principal shopping street, resulting from the counter-attractions of the pedestrianisation of other streets, the decline in popularity of its major department stores, and the movement of major shops into shopping malls such as the Bond Street Centre, and latterly the

The 'Leeds Look', the city's predominant building style from the late 1980s. To the left is Westgate Point, one of the more elegant buildings in the style, and, to the right, the most eccentric – the Magistrates' Court (opened in 1993).

Regional capital and city of culture, Quarry Hill viewed from York Street in 1994. The cleared site of Quarry Hill flats is now occupied by the West Yorkshire Playhouse (opened in 1990) and Quarry House, the massive national headquarters of the Departments of Health and Social Security, completed in 1993.

Schofields Centre and the St John's Centre. In 1993 significant improvements were made in the street furniture and paving of both Briggate and Vicar Lane to give them a more cared-for and stylish air, and the pavements of Briggate were widened and vehicle access to the street between Boar Lane and the Headrow was restricted to buses and taxis.

For those who have money in their pockets, Leeds is a splendid city to live in. Its excellent shops, schools and colleges, hospitals, leisure facilities, and its parks and easily accessible countryside, all make it an extremely convenient, attractive and interesting city. A common enjoyment and appreciation of these attributes appears to give people of all classes a shared pride in the city. In looking to the future, the anxiety which exists concerns the deprivation in the inner city areas, where high levels of unemployment, lack of financial security and almost perpetual dependence on social security payments, must surely breed amongst many of their residents, resentment against society at large. The city appears to be developing an 'under-class' which has little stake in Leeds, and which in its way is surely as spiritually deprived and detached from the main stream of local society in relative terms as the Victorian under-class was from the middle classes over a century ago. As in other British cities, this is reflected in escalating levels of

A triumph for conservation. The Corn Exchange superbly converted to a shopping centre in 1990.

crime and high levels of vandalism, drug addiction, and lawlessness in what are virtually police 'no-go areas' in certain inner-city districts. Unless this problem is solved, there is a timebomb ticking away. At present the situation seems to be deteriorating year by year. As well as being an intolerable situation for this unfortunate minority of Leeds, its social consequences are a growing and tangible threat to the more fortunate majority's enjoyment of life in the city.

Looking positively towards the future, the city council has produced a series of strategies – for transport, the economy, environmental matters, the countryside, nature conservation, and tourism – all of which form part of the largest strategy of them all, the Leeds Unitary Development Plan. The leader of the city council, Jon Trickett, aspires to make Leeds a European city of note, and to develop the continental style and economic links befitting a major European regional centre of the future.

Queen's Court, a Briggate merchant's yard, saved for posterity in the late 1980s.

The term 'Leeds loiner' is said to derive from the fact that Leeds had many principal streets called lanes (pronounced 'loins') – Boar Lane, Vicar Lane, Call Lane, and so on – and that the townspeople used to gather at the junctions, the lane ends, to gossip – hence 'Leeds lane-enders'.[70] We must await the twenty-first century to see whether the bid to return the people to the lane ends to relax and eat and drink away the evenings and weekends in continental style will be a success. What is more certain, however, is that just as the Leeds merchant community created the Aire and Calder Navigation in 1699 to improve the town's commercial links with the Continent, Leeds once again sees its future as one inextricably linked with Europe.

Leeds Goes Continental. Albion Place refurbished as part of the controversial 'Landmark Leeds' project, implemented in 1991/92 to revitalise the pedestrianised shopping streets. West Riding House, the biggest planning blunder of the mid-1970s, towers above the fine Victorian and Edwardian city centre streets.

References

1. Leeds City Council, *Leeds: The Capital of the Centre of Britain* (1976), [hereafter, *Leeds: Capital of the Centre*], p.11.
2. West Yorkshire Metropolitan Council, *West Yorkshire: Official County Guide* (1977) [hereafter, *West Yorkshire Guide*].
3 O.Hartley, 'The Second World War and After', in Fraser, *Modern Leeds*; *Yorkshire Evening Post*, Council election reports.
4. G.F.Rainnie and R.K.Wilson, 'The Economic Structure' in Beresford and Jones, *Leeds and Its Region* (Leeds, 1967), pp.215-18.
5. City of Leeds, *Development Plan Review: Draft Written Analysis* (1967) [hereafter, *Development Plan Review, 1967*], p. 12.
6. See appendix for sources of population figures.
7. *Development Plan Review, 1967*, p.15; E.Butterworth, 'Area Reports on Cities and Boroughs with Substantial Immigrant Settlements: No.2, Leeds', Supplement to the Institute of Race Relations Newsletter, March 1964; Central Statistical Office, *Regional Trends 28* (1993 edition), p.161.
8. This account of the development of Leeds industry since 1945 is based on : W.G.Rimmer, 'Occupations in Leeds', *Thoresby Soc.*, L (1967), pp.171-5; Rainnie and Wilson, *op. cit.*, p.221; R.Wiener, 'The Industrial Base of Leeds', (WEA Leeds, 1980); *Development Plan Review, 1967*; M.Sawyer, 'The Economy of Leeds in the 1990s', in J.Chartres and K.Honeyman, *Leeds City Business, 1893-1993* (Leeds, 1993).
9. *Yorkshire Life* (August, 1968), p.15; *Yorkshire Evening Post*, 7 Dec. 1978; *Leeds and Yorkshire Topic* (Sept., 1981), p.74.
10. Statistics provided by Leeds Development Agency.
11. Leeds City Engineer's Department, *Development Plan for Leeds: Town and Country Planning Act, 1947* (1951), [hereafter, *Leeds Development Plan, 1951*], approved 1955.
12. *Leeds the Industrial Capital, 1938*, pp.34-40.
13. *Leeds the Industrial Capital 1947/48*], pp.25-31, and 1954 edition, pp.22-30.
14. *Leeds the Industrial Capital 1947/48*], pp.33-8; City of Leeds, Planning and Property Department, Town Planning Division, *Planning Tomorrow's Leeds* (Oct. 1973) [hereafter, *Planning Tomorrow's Leeds*], p.45.
15. Ministry of Transport, *Traffic in Towns: A Study of the long term problems of traffic in Urban Areas* (HMSO, 1963) [hereafter, *Traffic in Towns*], pp.80-111.
16. *Ibid.*, p.198.
17. *Ibid.*. pp.100-05.
18. Leeds Chamber of Commerce, *The Leeds Journal*, Feb.- April 1965.
19. *Development Plan Review, 1967*; *Leeds Development Plan Review, Written Statement, 1972 [hereafter,* Development Plan Review, 1972].
20 .Pyramid Press Ltd., *Leeds: A Guide to the City* (1963) [hereafter, *Leeds Guide, 1963*].
21. *Planning Tomorrow's Leeds*, pp.21-3.
22. *Ibid.*
23. *Leeds: Capital of the Centre*, p.51; Leeds City Council, *Planning Handbook, 1984*, p.62.
24. *Planning Tomorrow's Leeds.*
25. Leeds City Council, *Project Leeds: Leeds Motorway City of the Seventies* (Leeds, 1971), pp.3-5.
26. *Development Plan Review, 1972.*
27. *Planning Tomorrow's Leeds*, p. 41.
28. The following details of buildings demolished and the battle to save others are drawn from Leeds Civic Trust Annual Reports, 1966-1993.
29. This section is largely based on Leeds Civic Trust Annual Reports.
30. *Planning Tomorrow's Leeds*; Leeds City Council, Department of Planning, *Moving Ahead: Leeds Planning Handbook, 1993.*
31. Leeds Civic Trust Annual Reports.
32. Leeds City Council, *Planning Statistics* (1975), p.22.
33. *West Yorkshire Guide*, pp.34-6.
34. *Regional Trends 28* (1993 edition), p.108.
35 .Paragraph based on: *Development Plan Review, 1967*, ch. 3; *Planning Tomorrow's Leeds*, p.53.
36. *Planning Tomorrow's Leeds*. p.25; *Development Plan Review, 1967.*
37. *Development Plan Review, 1967*, p.39.
38. *Yorkshire Post*, 7 Feb. 1972.
39. *Ibid.*
40. Community Housing Working Party Report, 'Gradual Renewal in Leeds' (March, 1976) and 'The Better Way: An Approach to Gradual Renewal in Leeds' (1978); Leeds City Council, Report of Housing Working Party on Gradual Renewal (June 1976); Leeds City Council, Report on Gradual Renewal and its Application to Woodhouse (June 1978).
41. Leeds City Council, Department of Planning, *Leeds Unitary Development Plan: Issue 1: Housing* (1990).
42. For post-war housing statistics, see: *Planning Tomorrow's Leeds*, pp.53-4; *Development Plan Review, 1967 and 1972.*
43. *Leeds: Capital of the Centre*, p.55.
44. M.Boleat, *The Building Society Movement* (1986), p.33; *Regional Trends 28* (1993 edition), p.172; *Moving Ahead: Leeds Planning Handbook, 1993*, p.116.
45. P.Bedford and D.N.Howard, *St James' University Hospital* (Leeds, 1985), p.23; S.T.Anning, *The History of Medicine in Leeds* (Leeds, 1980), pp.6-16.
46. *Leeds the Industrial Capital 1947/48*], p.98.
47. *Ibid.*
48. E.J.Burrow, publishers, *Guide to the City of Leeds* (1970), [hereafter, *Leeds Guide, 1970*], pp.28-33.
49. *Leeds: Capital of the Centre*, pp.59-60.
50. *Leeds the Industrial Capital 1954*, p.98; Gosden and Taylor, *Studie in the History of a University*, pp.28-9, 34-41.
51. *Leeds Guide, 1970*, p.5.
52. Hartley, *op. cit.*, pp. 450-3; *Leeds: Capital of the Centre*, p. 57.
53. *Yorkshire Evening Post*, 26 Sept. 1979.
54. *Development Plan Review, 1967*, p.155; R.Preedy, *Leeds Theatres Remembered* (Leeds, 1981), pp.11, 29.
55. Pyramid Press Ltd, *Guide to Leeds* (1961) [hereafter, *Leeds Guide, 1961*], p.347.
56. E.J.Burrow, *Guide to the City of Leeds* (*c.*1968), [hereafter, *Leeds Guide, 1968*], pp.44-5.
57. We are indebted to Colin Stewart for this reminiscence.
58. *Yorkshire Evening Post*, 6 Oct. 1979.
59. *Ibid.*, 8 March 1990.
60. *Development Plan Review, 1967*, pp.34, 98; *Regional Trends 28* (1993 edition), p.183.
61. *Leeds Guide, 1963*, p.91.
62. A.Marwick, *British Society Since 1945* (1990), p.106; *Development Plan Review, 1967*, pp.154-5.
63. Leeds Churches Community Involvement Project, *Faith in Leeds: Searching for God in Our City* (1986), pp.10-11, 24-6.
64. P.G.Bell, 'Leeds the Evolution of a Multi-cultural Society' (1982).
65. M.Farrer, 'Towards a History of Harehills and Chapeltown Riot and Revolution – the Politics of an Inner City', *Revolutionary Socialist* (Winter, 1981/82).
66. *Yorkshire Evening Post*, 10 March 1994.
67. For an excellent survey of inner-city deprivation in Leeds in the 1980s, see: *Faith in Leeds* (1986) already cited and its 1989 supplement.
68. The following figures were calculated by the authors from a range of official statistics.
69. *Moving Ahead: Leeds Planning Handbook* (1993), p.116.
70. J.H.Wilkinson, *Leeds Dialect Glossary and Lore* (Leeds, 1924), p.140.

Appendices

Appendix 1

Glossary of Textile Terms (not explained in the text)

Bearskin A shaggy form of woollen cloth, used for overcoats.

Barragan A waterproof cloth of coarse wool.

Bay (Baize) Originally a fabric of a finer lighter, texture than that common today.

Camblet A light stuff (i.e. worsted), formerly much used for women's clothes, made of long wool, hard spun, sometimes mixed in the loom with cotton or linen yarn.

Coatings Woollen material for coats.

Everlastings A hard wearing, strong, twilled stuff, also called lasting.

Flannel An open woollen stuff, of various degrees of fineness, usually without a nap.

Gill A flax comb. The machine commonly called the gill was employed for preparing, drawing and roving flax and hemp.

Hackling The action of combing flax.

Kersey Very like, but inferior in quality to, the broad cloth, but was longer and narrower.

Northern Whole Broadcloths Contained 23-25yds x 1¾yds 'and being well scowered, thicked, milled, and fully dried, shall weigh 66lb at the least'. Northern Dozens: Length 12-13yds breadth 1¾yds; weight 33lb. In the seventeenth century, broadcloths were the highest grade of Northern fabrics, made of the best wool, chiefly drawn from Lincolnshire or the other southern counties. In the early part of the century they sold for 4s to 5s per yard.

Puke The very best sort of woollen cloth, of which gowns were made.

Raven duck A kind of canvas.

Serge French for twill, also a term applied to fabrics of a twill nature and of rough make as distinct from the finer make of material.

Shalloon A light woollen cloth used as linings for coats, liveries, etc., usually 30-40 inches wide and 36 yards long. Dyed in browns and blacks principally.

Slay To set a warp.

Tammy A fine worsted cloth of good quality, often with a glazed finish.

Tawny Dyed cloth of a browny-yellow colour.

Appendix 2
The Vicars Of Leeds

c. 1110 Thomas
c. 1145 Ailsi
c. 1167 Paulinus, ('Priest of Ledes')
1215-16 Henry de Cerne
c. 1239 Hugo de Ebor, ('Vicarius de Ledes')
1242 Alanus de Schireburn.
1250 Johannes de Faversham.
1281 Galfrides de Sponden.
1316 Gilbertus de Gaudibus.
1320 Alanus de Berewick.
c. 1342 Ralph Poteman.
1372 Thomas Daynyll.
1392-93 William Minfield.
1393 William Brunby.
1394 John Snyfall.
1408 Robert Passelew.
Robert Newton.
1418 William Saxton, S.T.B.
1424 John Herberd.
James Baguley.
John Thomson
1430 Thomas Clarell.
1470 William Eyre.
1482 John (Frazer), Bishop of Ross.
1499 Martyn Collyns, Dec, Doc.
1500 Robert Wrangwash, B.A.
1508 William Eyre.
1535 John Thomson.
John Thornton.
1556 Christopher Bradley.
1559 Alexander Fascet.
1590 Robert Cooke, S.T.B.
1614-15 Alexander Cooke, S.T.B.
1632 Henry Robinson, S.T.B.
1646 Peter Saxton, M.A.
1652 William Styles, M.A.
1661 John Lake, D.D.,
Bishop of Sodor and Man, 1682;
Bristol 1684; Chichester 1685.
1663 Marmaduke Cooke, D.D.
1667 John Milner, S.T.B.
1690 John Killingbeck, S.T.B.
1716 Joseph Cookson, M.A.
1751 Samuel Kirshaw, D.D.
1786 Peter Haddon, M.A.
1815 Richard Fawcett, M.A.
1837 Walter Farquhar Hook, D.D.
Dean of Chichester, 1859.
c. 1859 James Atlay, D.D.
Bishop of Hereford, 1868.
1868 James Russell Woodford, D.D.
Bishop of Ely, 1873
1873 John Gott, D.D.
Dean of Worcester, 1886.
Bishop of Truro 1891.
1886 Francis John Jayne, D.D.
Bishop of Chester, 1889.
1889 Edward Stuart Talbot, D.D.
Bishop of Rochester, 1895.
Southwark, 1905, Winchester 1911.
1895 Edgar C. Sumner Gibson, D.D.
Bishop of Gloucester, 1905.
1905 Sasmuel Bickersteth, D.D.
Canon of Canterbury.
1917 Bernard O.F.Heywood, M.A.
Bishop of Southwell, 1926, Hull, 1931, Ely, 1934.
1926 William Thompson Elliott, M.A.
Canon of Westminster, 1938.
1939 Wilfred Marcus Askwith, M.A.
Bishop of Blackburn, 1942.
Gloucester, 1954.
1943 Arthur Stretton Reeve, M.A.
Bishop of Lichfield, 1953.
1954 Christopher Bolckow Sampson, M.A.
1961 William Fenton Morley M.A.
1971 Ronald Graham Gregory Foley B.A.
1982 James John Richardson, B.A.
1991 Stephen Oliver
(first 'Rector of Leeds')
1992 Christopher Cornwell
(first 'Vicar of St Peter's, Leeds')

Appendix 3
Aldermen, Mayors and Lord Mayors of Leeds

Aldermen: First Charter, 2 Charles I, 1626

July
1626 Sir John Savile, *Knight.*
1627 Samuel Casson
1628 Robert Benson
1629 Richard Sykes
1630 Thomas Metcalf
1631 Joseph Hilary
1632 Benjamin Wade
1633 Francis Jackson
1634 John Harrison
1635 Samuel Casson
1636 Richard Sykes
1637 Thomas Metcalf
1638 John Hodgshon
1639 Joseph Hillary
1640 Francis Jackson
1641 John Hodgshon
1642 Ralph Croft
1643 John Dawson
1644 Francis Allanson
1645 John Thoresby
1646 John Thoresby
1647 John Thoresby
1648 John Thoresby
1649 Robert Brooke
1650 James Moxon
1651 William Marshall
1652 Richard Milner
1653 John Thwaits
1654 Martin Iles
1655 Henry Roundhil
1656 Marmaduke Hicke
1657 Francis Allanson
1658 William Fenton
1659 William Fenton
1660 Paul Thoresby

Mayors: Second Charter, 13, Charles II, 1661

November
1661 Thomas Danby

September
1662 John Dawson
1663 Benjamin Wade
1664 Henry Skelton
1665 Daniel Foxcroft
1666 Marmaduke Hicke
1667 Edward Atkinson
1668 Christopher Watkinson
1669 Godfrey Lawson
1670 Richard Armitage
1671 Thomas Dixon
1672 William Hutchinson
1673 William Busfield
1674 Samuel Sykes
1675 Martin Headley
1676 Anthony Wade
1677 John Killinbeck
1678 William Pickering
1679 Joseph Bawner
1680 Henry Skelton

October
1681 Marmaduke Hick

September
1682 Thomas Potter
1683 William Rooke
1684 Joshua Ibbetson

Third Charter, 36, Charles II, 1684

December
1684 Gervase Nevill

September
1685 Joshua Ibbetson
1686 William Sawer
1687 Henry Stanhope
1688 Thomas Kitchingman

Second Charter Restored, I, William and Mary, 1689

September
1689 William Massie
1690 Michael Idle
1691 John Preston
1692 William Calverley
1693 Thomas Dixon
1694 Marmaduke Hick
1695 Henry Iveson
1696 John Dodgson
1697 William Milner
1698 Caleb Askwith
1699 John Rontree
1700 Thomas Lazenby

1701 John Gibson
1702 James Kitchingman
1703 Samuel Hey
1704 Edmund Barker

October
1705 Thomas Kitchingham

September
1706 Jeremiah Barstow
1707 Rowland Mitchell
1708 Rowland Mitchell
1709 Henry Iveson
1710 John Dodgson
1711 John Atkinson
1712 William Cookson
1713 William Rooke
1714 Solomon Pollard
1715 Croft Preston
1716 Edward Iveson
1717 Thomas Peas
1718 Benjamin Wade
1719 Scudamore Lazenby
1720 Thomas Brearey
1721 Robert Denison

October
1722 James Kitchingman

September
1723 Edmund Barker
1724 Jeremiah Barstow
1725 William Cookson
1726 Thomas Sawer
1727 Soloman Pollard
1728 Edward Iveson
1729 John Blayds
1730 George Dover
1731 Edward Kenion
1732 John Douglas
1733 William Fenton
1734 Henry Scott
1735 Thomas Micklethwaite
1736 John Brooke
1737 Robert Denison
1738 William Cookson
1739 Henry Atkinson
1740 Thomas Sawer
1741 John Snowden
1742 John Watts
1743 Robert Smithson
1744 Richard Horncastle
1745 Timothy Smith
1746 Edward Kenion
1747 William Fenton
1748 Henry Scott
1749 Edward Gray
1750 John Firth
1751 Henry Hall
1752 Thomas Micklethwaite
1753 Sir Henry Ibbetson, *Baronet*

October
1754 John Brooke
1755 Robert Denison

September
1756 Thomas Denison

October
1757 Walter Wade

September
1758 William Denison
1759 Edmund Lodge
1760 Thomas Medhurst
1761 John Blayds
1762 William Wilson
1763 Samuel Harper
1764 Samuel Davenport
1765 Joshua Dixon
1766 James Kenion
1767 Luke Setchwell
1768 Edward Gray
1769 William Hutchinson
1770 William Dawson
1771 Edmund Lodge
1772 John Calverley
1773 Thomas Medhurst
1774 John Blayds
1775 John Beckett
1776 John Wormald
1777 Joseph Fountaine
1778 Gamaliel Lloyd
1779 John Micklethwaite
1780 Thomas Rea Cole
1781 William Smithson
1782 Arthur Ikin
1783 William Cookson
1784 Jeremiah Dixon
1785 John Calverley
1786 John Markland, *afterwards,* Entwistle
1787 William Hey
1788 Edward Sanderson
1789 Edward Markland
1790 John Plowes
1791 Wade Browne
1792 Richard Ramsden Bramley
1793 Alexander Turner
1794 John Blayds
1795 Whittell Sheepshanks, *afterwards,* York
1796 Henry Hall
1797 John Beckett
1798 John Calverley
1799 Benjamin Gott
1800 John Brooke
1801 William Cookson
1802 William Hey, F.R.S.
1803 Thomas Ikin
1804 Wade Browne
1805 John Wilson
1806 Richard Ramsden Bramley
1807 Edward Markland
1808 Thomas Tennant
1809 Richard Pullen
1810 Alexander Turner
1811 Charles Brown
1812 Henry Hall
1813 William Greenwood
1814 John Brooke
1815 Whittell York
1816 William Prest
1817 John Hill
1818 George Banks
1819 Christopher Beckett
1820 William Hey, F.R.S.
1821 Lepton Dobson
1822 Benjamin Sadler
1823 Thomas Tennant
1824 Charles Brown
1825 Henry Hall
1826 Thomas Beckett
1827 Thomas Blayds
1828 Ralph Markland
1829 Christopher Beckett
1830 Robert William Disney Thorp
1831 William Hey
1832 Thomas Tennant
1833 Benjamin Sadler
1834 Griffith Wright

Municipal Corporation Act, 5 and 6 William IV, Cap. 76. 1835.

January
1836 George Goodman

November
1836 James Williamson, MD
1837 Thomas William Tottie
1838 James Holdforth
1839 William Smith
1840 William Smith
1841 William Pawson
1842 Henry Cowper Marshall
1843 Hamer Stansfield
1844 Darnton Lupton
1845 John Darnton Luccock
1846 Charles Gascoigne Maclea
(Resigned January 1847, and term completed by George Goodman.)
1847 Francis Carbutt
1848 John Hope Shaw
1849 Joseph Bateson
1850 George Goodman
1851 George Goodman
(Resigned March 1852, and term completed by J.H.Shaw.)
1852 John Hope Shaw
1853 John Wilson
1854 Joseph Richardson
1855 Thomas Willington George
1856 John Botterill
1857 Peter Fairbairn
1858 Peter Fairbairn
1859 William Kelsall
1860 James Kitson
1861 James Kitson
1862 Joseph Ogden March
1863 Obadiah Nussey
1864 John Darnton Luccock
1865 Henry Oxley
1866 Andrew Fairbairn
1867 Andrew Fairbairn
(Resigned September 1868, and term completed by T.W.George.)
1868 Thomas W.George
1869 William Glover Joy
1870 John Barran
1871 John Barran
1872 Henry Oxley
1873 Henry Rowland Marsden
1874 Henry Rowland Marsden
1875 Samuel Croft
1876 Richard Gallsworthy
1877 Edward Hamer Carbutt
1878 Robert Addyman
1879 George Tatham
1880 George Tatham
1881 George Tatham
1882 Edwin Woodhouse
1883 Edwin Woodhouse
1884 John Richard Bower
1885 Edwin Gaunt
1886 Edwin Gaunt
1887 Archibald Witham Scarr
1888 John Ward
1889 William Emsley
1890 Alf Cooke
1891 William Boothroyd
1892 John Ward
1893 Thomas Richmond Leuty
1894 Peter Gilston
1895 The Rt. Hon. Wm.Lawies Jackson, MP
1896 Sir J.Kitson, Bart, MP

Lord Mayors
In June 1897, the name, style, and title of 'Lord Mayor' was conferred upon the Chief Magistrate.

June
1897 Sir James Kitson, Bart., MP
1898 Thomas Walter Harding
1899 John Gordon
1900 Frederick William Lawson
1901 Ambrose Edmund Butler
1902 John Ward
1903 Arthur Currer Briggs
1904 Robert Armitage
1905 Edwin Woodhouse, D.L.
1906 Joseph Hepworth
1907 Wilfred Lawrence Hepton
1908 Frederick James Kitson
1909 William Penrose-Green
1910 William Middlebrook, MP
(Resigned 21 November, Frederick J.Kitson elected 25 Nov. resigned 12 Dec, and William Middlebrook re-elected 19 Dec.)
1911 William Nicholson
1912 Albert Wellesley Bain
1913 Edward Allen Brotherton
1914 James Edward Bedford
1915 Charles Lupton
1916 Edmund George Arnold
1917 Frank Gott
1918 Joseph Henry
1919 Thomas Beveridge Duncan
1920 Albert Braithwaite

1921 Willie Hodgson
1922 Frank Fountain
1923 Sir Edwin Airey
1924 Charles Granville Gibson
1925 John Arnott
1926 Hugh Lupton
1927 George Ratcliffe
1928 David Blythe Foster
1929 Nathaniel George Morrison
1930 Arthur Hawkyard
1931 Fred Brown Simpson
1932 Robert Holliday Blackburn
1933 Albert Edward Wilkinson
1934 William Hemingway
1935 Percival Tookey Leigh
1936 Tom Coombs
1937 John Badlay
1938 Rowland Winn
1939 Charles Humphrey Boyle
1940 Willie Withey
1941 Hyman Morris
1942 Arthur Clark (Died 9 Nov.)
Jessie Beatrice Kitson (Elected 18 Nov.)
1943 Albert Hayes
1944 Charles Vivian Walker
1945 David Beevers
1946 Sir George William Martin, KBE
1947 George Brett
(Term of office extended pursuant to provision of the Representation of the People Act, 1948.)

May
1949 Norman Douglas Vine
1950 Francis Hugh O'Donnell
1951 Francis Eric Tetley, DSO
1952 Frank Barlow Burnley
1953 Donald George Cowling, MBE
1954 Henry Sidman Vick
1955 Sir James Croysdale
1956 Thomas Austin Jessop
1957 Joseph Hiley
1958 Mary Pearce
1959 Gertrude Annie Stevenson
1960 Lillian Hammond
1961 Percival Arthur Woorward
1962 Harold Watson
1963 Edwin John Loy Wooler, MBE
1964 Lizzie Naylor
1965 William Richard Hargreave
1966 Joshua Samuel Walsh
1967 Lawrence Turnbull
1968 John Rafferty
1969 Allan Roberts Bretherick
1970 Arthur Brown
1971 John Trevor Verity Watson
1972 Albert Smith
1973 Kenneth Travis Davison
1974 Jean de Carteret
1975 Alan Pedley
1976 Ernest Howard Morris
1977 William Hudson
1978 Harry Booth
1979 Christine Mary Thomas
1980 Eric Atkinson
1981 Patrick Crotty
1982 Doreen Jenner
1983 Martin Dogson
1984 Douglas Ernest Gabb
1985 Sydney Symmonds
1986 Rose Lund
1987 Doreen Wood
1988 Arthur Vollans
1989 Les Carter
1990 Bill Kilgallon
1991 Ronnie Feldman
1992 Denise Atkinson
1993 Keith Loudon
1994 Christiana Myers

Appendix 4
Members of Parliament

L = Liberal C = Conservative Lab = Labour

Parliaments summoned by Oliver Cromwell

Date	
1654	A.Baynes
1656	A.Baynes

Reform Act of 1832

Leeds appointed two Members of Parliament

Date		
1832	J.Marshall Jnr. (L)	T.B.Macaulay (L)
1834	E.Baines (L)	Sir J.Beckett (C)
1835	"	"
1837	"	Sir W.Molesworth (L)
1841	W.Aldam Jnr (L)	W.Beckett (C)
1847	J.G.Marshall (L)	"
1852	M.T.Baines (L)	Sir G.Goodman (L)
1857	"	R.Hall*
1859	E.Baines (L)	G.S.Beecroft (C)
1865	"	"
1868	"	R.M.Carter (L)
1874	W.St.James Wheelhouse (L)	"
1876	J.Barron (L)	W.L.Jackson (C)
1880	"	W.E.Gladstone (L)**

* died - replaced by G.S.Beecroft
** Appointed First Lord of the Treasury and Chancellor of the Exchequer. Replaced by H.J.Gladstone (L)

Redistribution Act of 1885 divided the borough into five divisions, each returning a single member.

Date	Central	North	East	West	South
1885	G.W.Balfour (C)	W.L.Jackson (C)	R.Dawson (C)	H.J.Gladstone (L)	Sir L.Playfair (L)
1886	"	"	J.L.Gane (L)	"	..
1892	"	"	"	"	"
1895	"	"	T.R.Leauty (L)	"	J.L.Walton (L)*
1900	"	"	H.S.Cautley (C)	"	"
1906	R.Armitage (L)	R.Barran (L)**	J.O'Grady (Lab)	"	"
Jan 1910	"	"	"	T.E.Harvey (L)	W.Middlebrook 1910(L)
Dec 1910	"	"	"	"	"

* replaced Sir L.Playfair in the 1892 by-election.
** first elected in the by-election of 1902.

Wards reorganised into six divisions

Date	Central	North	South East	West	South	North East
1918	R.Armitage (L)	A.C.Farquharson (L)	J.O'Grady (Lab)	J.Murray (L)	W.Middlebrook (L)	J.D.Birchall (C)
1922	A.Willey (C)	H.M.Butler (C)	"	"	H.C.Charlton (Lab)	"
1923	C.Wilson (C)	G.Beckett (C)	"	T.W.Stamford (Lab)	"	"
1924	"	"	H.Slesser (Lab)	"	"	"
1929	R.D.Denman (Lab)	O.Peake (C)	J.Milner (Lab)	"	"	"
1931	"	"	"	S.Adams (Nat.Un.)	B.Whiteside (C)	"
1935	"	"	"	"	H.C.Charlton (Lab)	"
WAR	-	-	-	-	-	-
1945	G.Porter (Lab)	"	"	T.Stamford (Lab)	H.Gaitskell (Lab)	A.Bacon (Lab)

Wards reorganised into seven divisions

Date	Central	North	South East	West	South	North East	North West
1950	G.Porter (Lab)	O.Peake (C)	J.Milner (Lab)	T.Pannell (Lab)	H.G.Gaitskell (Lab)	A.Bacon (Lab)	D.Kaberry (C)
1951	"	"	"	"	"	"	"

Reverts to six divisions

Date	North East	East	West	South	South East	North West
1955	O.Peake (C)	D.Healey (Lab)	T.Pannell (Lab)	H.Gaitskell (Lab)	A.Bacon (Lab)	D.Kaberry (C)
1959	K.Joseph (C)	"	"	"	"	"
1964	"	"	"	M.Rees (Lab)	"	"
1966	"	"	"	"	"	"
1970	"	"	"	"	S.Cohen (Lab)	"
Feb 1974	"	"	J.Dean (Lab)	"	"	"
Oct 1974	"	"	"	"	"	"
1979	"	"	"	"	"	"

Reorganisation

Date	Central	North East	East	West	Morley + Leeds	Pudsey	North West	Elmet
1983	D.Fatchett (Lab)	Sir K.Joseph (C)	D.Healey (Lab)	M.Meadowcroft (L)	M.Rees (Lab)	G.Shaw (C)	K.Hampson (C)	S.Batiste
1987	"	T.Kirkhope (C)	"	J.Battle (Lab)	"	"	"	"
1992	"	"	G.Mudie (Lab)	"	J.Gunnell (Lab)	"	"	"

Appendix 5

The Population of Leeds in the Twentieth Century

	Borough	Metropolitan District
1901	428,968	–
1911	445,550	–
1921	458,320	–
1931	482,900	–
1939	497,000	–
1951	502,700	–
1961	511,600	–
1971	496,009	738,931
1981	–	697,000
1991	–	706,000

Sources: British Association, *General Handbook: Leeds Meeting, 1927* (Leeds, 1927); Leeds City Council, *Planning Statistics* (1975); Central Statistical Office, *Regional Trends 28* (1993 edition); Beresford and Jones, *Leeds and its Region* (Leeds, 1967).

Appendix 6

Some Twentieth-Century Wage Rates

1926

	Weekly Wages Men	Weekly Wages Women
Ready-made tailoring	59s.6d.	28s.5d.
Engineering	49s.3d.	28s.5d.
Woollen Industry	47s.6d.	27s.10d.
Railway Porter	40s.	–
Railway Linesman	64s.	–

Source: *Ministry of Labour Gazette*, Vol.XXXIV (1926).

Mid-1930s

Unskilled male workers	£2 10s. – £2 15s. (weekly)
Skilled male workers	£3 5s. – £3 15s.

Source: Building Centre Committee, 'Leeds Housing' (*c.*1936).

1975

Average male manual worker	£54 per week (*c.*£2,800pa)
Shorthand typists and clerks	*c.*£2,000pa
Auditors, Accountants, Welfare Officers	£3,000 – £3,500

Source: *Yorkshire Post* and *Yorkshire Evening Post.*

Appendix 7

Leeds House Prices in the Twentieth Century (£)

	Back-to-back	Terrace 3 bedrooms	Semi-detached 3 bedrooms	Detached 4 bedrooms
1925/26	–	–	600-750	–
1935/36	300-350*	–	500-675	–
1976	–	6,000	9,500	–
1994	20,000-35,000	35,000-60,000	45,000-80,000	130,0
150,000**				

Sources: *Yorkshire Evening Post* 19 April 1926, 18 March 1935, 23 March 1936, May 1994.; Leeds City Council, *Leeds: The Capital of the Centre of Britain* (1976).

Appendix 9

Some Notable People Associated With Leeds

(not referred to in the text)

Joseph Aspdin (1779-1858)
Leeds stone mason famous for inventing 'Portland' cement.

Sir Nathan Bodington (1848-1911)
First Vice-chancellor of the University of Leeds.

Atkinson Grimshaw (1836-93)
Landscape painter who painted many views of Leeds. Lived near Woodhouse Ridge and then at Knostrop Old Hall.

Jacob Kramer (1892-1962)
The influential artist, who trained at Leed School of Art, and founded the Yorkshire Luncheon Club. He painted portraits of Delius, J.B.Priestley, Sybil Thorndike, Gracie Fields and Mahatma Gandhi.

Thomas Osborne, Duke of Leeds (d1712)
Created Duke of Leeds in 1694 for services to the State. Though he owned ground rents in Leeds, he had little involvement with the town.

Louis Aime Augustus Le Prince (1842-90)
The pioneer of cinematography. In 1888 he made the world's first moving pictures when he filmed traffic coming over Leeds Bridge.

Phil May (1864-1903)
A skilled artist who became famous in the 1890s for his cartoons. In 1895 he joined the staff of *Punch* and became a weekly contributor.

John Smeaton (1724-94)
Mechanical and civil engineer. Most famous for building the Eddystone Lighthouse, but involved in many projects including major improvements to the Aire and Calder Navigation. Lived at Austhorpe Hall.

Appendix 8

Medieval Leeds Map Reconstructions

The map reconstructions of 1086, 1350 and 1650 are based on the OS 6" to the mile map of 1851, surveyed in 1847. The Leeds Tithe Award of 1847 at Leeds District Office of the West Yorkshire Archive Service (RD/RT 142/1) proved particularly helpful. The 1560 Plan of Leeds is far more accurate than at first imagined and helped establish the general shape of the open fields in the Woodhouse area. Cossins' Plan of 1726, the Giles' Plan of Leeds in 1815, Fowler's Plan of 1831, and the Baines and Newsome, Map of the Borough in 1834, were also consulted. Innumerable maps at Leeds District Archives added fine detail, the majority being found in the DB/Maps Calendar.

The map of the town of Leeds in the late medieval period is based on the Giles Plan of 1815. The OS five foot to the mile plan of Leeds in 1850, shows the location of the medieval chantry chapels and town bars. Further information was gleaned from a range of sources including Thoresby's *Ducatus* (1715), J.Wardell, *The Antiquities of the Borough of Leeds* (Leeds, 1853) and J.Le Patourel, 'Documents Relating to the Manor and Borough of Leeds'.

The first clue to the existence and location of the manor house of Kirkgate-cum-Holbeck was found in York Minster Library (Hailstone Mss. Add. 205). Maurice Beresford assisted the authors in establishing the exact site of the building, which was confirmed by Deed Parcel 3946 at Leeds District Archives.

Appendix 10

Population of Leeds Townships, 1775-1901

	1775	1801	1811	1821	1831	1841	1851	1861	1871	1881	1891	1901
Leeds	17,121	30,669	35,951	48,603	71,602	88,741	101,343	117,566	139,362	160,109	177,523	177,920
Armley	1,715	2,695	2,941	4,273	5,159	5,676	6,190	6,734	9,224	12,737	18,992	27,521
Beeston	862	1,427	1,538	1,670	2,128	2,175	1,973	2,547	2,762	2,928	2,962	3,323
Bramley	1,378	2,562	3,484	4,921	7,039	8,875	8,949	8,690	9,882	11,055	14,787	17,299
Chapel Allerton	833	1,054	1,362	1,678	1,934	2,580	2,842	3,083	3,847	4,324	4,377	5,841
Farnley	540	943	1,164	1,332	1,591	1,530	1,722	3,064	2,964	3,608	3,590	4,351
Headingley-cum-Burley	667	1,313	1,670	2,154	3,849	4,768	6,105	9,674	13,942	19,138	29,911	41,561
Holbeck	2,055	4,196	5,124	7,151	11,210	13,346	14,152	15,824	17,165	19,150	20,630	28,249
Hunslet	3,825	5,799	6,393	8,171	12,074	15,852	19,466	25,763	37,289	46,942	58,164	69,064
Potternewton	419	509	571	664	863	1,241	1,385	1,878	3,457	5,107	9,269	26,004
Wortley	894	1,995	2,336	3,179	5,944	7,090	7,896	12,058	18,923	23,530	26,854	27,456
Coldcotes and Osmondthorpe		114	131	147	155	180	247	284	395	491	446	379
Totals	30,309	53,276	62,665	53,943	123,548	152,054	172,270	207,165	259,212	309,119	367,505	428,968

Source: C.J.Morgan, 'Demographic change' in D.Fraser, ed., *A History of Modern Leeds* (Manchester, 1980)

Bibliography

1. **Manuscript Sources**

Borthwick Institute, York.
Inventory of Croft Preston's estate, 1726

Brotherton Library, University of Leeds
Leeds White Cloth Hall Papers
MS. No. 18: W.Linley, 'Number of Steam Engines ...in Leeds and its Immediate Vicinity ...March 1824'.

Hertfordshire County Record Office
T4951: Report of surveyors to Earl Cowper on his Leeds estates, 1819.

Leeds Central Reference Library
Diary of John Lucas, 1712-50 – Master of Leeds Charity School.
A sketch of the late Samuel Kirshaw (1788).
J.Wray, 'A Compilation of facts illustrative of Methodism in Leeds, 1735-1833'.
'Leeds: a Poem by Mr. McGeorge' *c.*1760.
William Boyne's *History of Leeds* (grangerized edition of works by Thoresby, Whitaker and other Leeds historians).
Newspaper cuttings about the Leeds Jewish tailors' strike, 7-23 May 1888.

Leeds District Archives:
DB 213/47: Littlewood petition regarding moot hall, 1598.
TN: EA/12, 14; F/8 Temple Newsam papers.
TN/LA/6: Papers relating to the Kirshaw-Scott dispute.
LDA, TN/PO/3C/5: Lord Lieutenant's correspondence.
LDA, TN/PO/3C/7.
FW/211, Leeds White Cloth Hall.
LC/M1-3: Leeds Corporation Court Books, 1662-1835.
LC/QS: Leeds Borough Quarter Sessions Order and Indictment Books, 1662-1835.
Leeds Parish Church Vestry Minute Books, 1716-1844.
LO/M1-6: The Minutes and Order Books of the Workhouse Committee for Leeds, 1726-1826.
Diary of the Revd Henry Crooke.
Acc. 2720: Diaries of law clerk articled with Bloome and Gatcliff of 15 Commercial Street, 1834-9.

The Leeds Library
Lists of Persons entitled to Vote in the election of Members for the Borough of Leeds (Leeds, 1832).
Poll Book of the Leeds Borough Election, July 1837 (Leeds,1837).

Thoresby Society Library
Mss. Box IV, 29: Papers relating to the Mixed or Coloured Cloth Hall.
22B6: Pitt Club Dinner 1825: Printed programme.
W.F.Hook, *A Letter to the Parishioners of Leeds* (Leeds, 1844).

Yorkshire Archaeological Society Archives
Mss. 723: Ensign Storr's Orderly Book.

2. **Printed Transcriptions of Manuscript Records**
'The Court Books of the Leeds Corporation', *Thoresby Soc.*, XXXIV (1933)
First and Second Decrees for a Committee of Pious Uses in Leeds, 1620 and 1661: transcribed in J.A.Symington, *Old Leeds Charities* (Leeds, 1926).
'West Riding Poll Tax Returns, 1379', *Yorkshire Archaeological Journal*, VII (1882).
'The Manor and Borough of Leeds, 1425-1662: An Edition of Documents', J.W.Kirby, ed.,*Thoresby Soc.*, LVII (1983).
'Documents Relating to the Manor and Borough of Leeds, 1066-1400', J.Le Patourel, ed., *Thoresby Soc.*, XLV (1956).
'St John's Church, Leeds: The Trustees' (Feofees') Account Book, 1660-1766', *Thoresby Soc.*, XXIV (1919).
'Leeds Friends Minute Book, 1692-1712', J.E. and R.Mortimer, eds., *Yorkshire Archaeological Society Record Series*, CXXXIX (1980).
T.Fairfax, 'Short Memorials of the Civil War', *Yorkshire Archaeological Journal*, VIII (1884).
Sir Thomas Fairfax, *The Memoirs of General Fairfax* (1776).
Underhill, T.(printer), *A True Relation of the Passages at Leeds on Munday the 23 of January* (1643).
Clay, J.W., 'The Royalist Composition Papers', *Yorkshire Archaeological Society Record Series*, XV (1893), XVIII (1895), XX (1896).
Lumb, G.D., ed., 'The Registers of the Parish Church of Leeds from 1639-67', *Thoresby Soc.*, VII (1897).
W.T.Lancaster, ed., 'Letters to Ralph Thoresby', *Thoresby Soc.*, XXI, (1912).

3. **Parliamentary Papers**
P.P. 1806, III, *Reports from the Select Committee ...(on) the State of the Woollen Manufacture in England.*
P.P. 1833, XX, *Queries Addressed by the Factory Commissioners for the Northern Districts to Mill Owners.*
P.P. 1834, XIX, *Royal Commission on Employment of Children in Factories.*
P.P. 1835, XXIII, *Reports from Commissioners on Municipal Corporations in England and Wales.*
P.P. 1842, XXIX, *Sanitary Enquiry, R.Baker, 'Report on the State and Condition of the Town of Leeds'.*
P.P. 1843, XIV, *Children's Employment Commission (Trades and Manufacture).*
P.P. 1845, XIII, *Select Committee on Smoke Prevention.*
P.P. 1866, XXXIII, *J.Hunter, 'Circumstances endangering the Public Health of Leeds'.*
P.P. 1867, XXXIII, *Third Report of the Commissioners appointed to Inquire into the Best Means of Preventing the Pollution of Rivers (River Aire and Calder).*
P.P. 1888, LV, *Royal Commission on Market Rights and Tolls,* Vol. IV.
P.P. 1898, LXVI, *Report on the Endowed Charities of the City of Leeds.*

4. **Newspapers and Magazines**
Empire Mail.
Imperial Review.
Leeds Biographer.
Leeds Graphic.
Leeds Intelligencer
Leeds Mercury.
Leeds Weekly News.
Morning Chronicle.
Yorkshire Evening News
Yorkshire Evening Post
Yorkshire Post
Yorkshire Weekly Post

5. **Trade Directories and Town Guides**
1781 W.Bailey, *Bailey's Northern Directory* (Leeds Section, pp.221-25).
1784 W.Bailey, *Bailey's British Directory* (Leeds Section, pp.560-4).
1793 P.Barfoot and J.Wilkes, *The Universal British Directory* (Leeds section pp.532-41) (London).
1797 G.Wright, *A Leeds Directory.*
1800 Binns and Brown, *A Directory of Leeds.*
1806 J.H.Leach, *A Walk Through Leeds or Stranger's Guide.*
1806 J.Ryley, *Leeds Guide.*
1807 G.Wilson, *A New and Complete Directory for Leeds.*
1809 Edward Baines, *The Leeds Directory for 1809.*
1817 Edward Baines, *Directory, General and Commercial of the Town and Borough of Leeds.*
1822 Edward Baines, *History, Directory and Gazetteer of the County of York.*
1826 *W.Parsons,* General and Commercial Directory of Leeds.
1830 Parsons and White, *Directory of the Borough of Leeds.*
1834 Baines and Newsome, *General and Commercial Directory of Leeds.*
1835 J.Heaton, *Walks Through Leeds.*
1837 W.White, *History, Gazetteer, and Directory of the West Riding of Yorkshire*
1842 W.White, *Directory and Topography of the Borough of Leeds.*
1842 *The Parliamentary Gazetteer*
1849 Charlton and Archdeacon's, *Directory of the Borough and Neighbourhood of Leeds.*
1853 W.White, *Directory and Gazetteer of Leeds, Bradford ...*
1858 T.Fenteman, *An Historical Guide to Leeds and its Environs.*
1870 *Guide to Leeds and Its Amusements – Whitsuntide.*
1879 J.Dodgson, *Historical and Descriptive Guide to the Borough of Leeds.*
1889 R.Jackson, *Guide to Leeds.*
1892 Robinson, Son & Pike, publishers, *Leeds – Illustrated* (Brighton).
1894 *Waddington's Guide to Leeds.*
1901 *Kelly's Directory of Leeds* (and for many subsequent years).
1909 Borough Guides, *City of Leeds Guide.*
1926 Leeds Tercentenary Executive, *Leeds Tercentenary Official Handbook.*
1935 Yorkshire Post, *Guide to the City of Leeds*
1938 Leeds City Council, *Leeds: The Industrial Capital of the North*
1947/8 Yorkshire Post, *Leeds: The Industrial Capital of the North.*
1954 Yorkshire Post, *Leeds: The Industrial Capital of the North.*
1961 Pyramid Press Ltd., *Guide to the City of Leeds*
1963 Pyramid Press Ltd., *Leeds: A Guide to the City.*
1968 E.J.Burrow Ltd, *Guide to the City of Leeds.*
1970 E.J.Burrow Ltd, *Guide to the City of Leeds.*
1971 Leeds City Council, *Project Leeds: Leeds Motorway City of the Seventies*
1976 Leeds City Council, *Leeds: The Capital of the Centre of Britain*
1977 West Yorkshire Metropolitan Council, *West Yorkshire: Official County Guide.*
1992 R.Ratcliffe, ed., *Leeds Fax: The Complete Handbook to Life in Leeds.*
Note: From the 1840s there are Leeds directories for most years. The above list is complete up to 1842 and thereafter refers to those used as sources for this book.

6. **Acts of Parliament to 1842**
Acts Local and Personal relating to Leeds
1755 28 Geo. II, cap. 41: *For Enlightening the Streets and Lanes, and Regulating the Pavements.*
1790 30 Geo. III, cap. 68: *For Better Supplying the Town with Water and for More Effectually Lighting and Cleansing the Streets.*
1809 49 Geo. III, cap. 122: *For better supplying of the Town with Water, and for the more effectually lighting and cleansing the Streets and*

for erecting a Court House and Prison..
1815 55 Geo. III, cap. 42: *For erecting a Court House and Prison, to provide for the Expence of the Prosecution of Felons in certain Cases; and to establish a Police and Nightly Watch.*
1824 5 Geo. IV, cap. 124: *For Lighting, Cleansing and Improving the Town.*
1842 5 & 6 Victoria, cap. 103: For Improving the Town.
1865 28 & 29 Victoria, cap. 251: North- eastern Railway (Leeds Extension).

7. **Books, Pamphlets and Articles Published Before 1900**

Atkinson, D. H., *Old Leeds: Its Bygones and Celebrities by an Old Leeds Cropper* (Leeds, 1868).
Atkinson, D.H., *Ralph Thoresby the Topographer: His Town and Times* (Leeds, 1887).
Baines, E., *The Extraordinary Life and Character of Mary Bateman, the Yorkshire Witch* (Leeds, 1820).
Baines, E., *The Social, Educational and Religious State of the Manufacturing Districts* (1843).
Baines, Edward, jnr., *The Life of Edward Baines* (1851).
Baines, E. jnr., *The Woollen Manufacture of England: With Special Reference to the Leeds Clothing District* (Leeds 1858).
Baker, R., *Report to Leeds Board of Health* (Leeds, 1833).
Baker, R., 'The Industrial and Sanitary Economy of the Borough of Leeds in 1858', *Journal of the Statistical Society of London* (1858).
Bede, *Historia Ecclesiastica*, ed. Plummer (1896).
Bell, R., ed., *Memorials of the Civil War* (1849).
Bradley, T., *Old Coaching Days in Yorkshire* (1889).
Cartwright, J.J., ed., *The Diary of John Reresby* (1875).
Defoe, Daniel, *A Tour Through the Whole Island of Great Britain (1724-6)* (Penguin edition, ed. P.Rogers, 1971).
Foster, D.B., *Leeds Slumdom* (Leeds, 1897).
Green, M.A.E., *Letters of Queen Henrietta Maria* (1857).
Guest, W., *Rest: or No Rest: A Letter to Working Men on the Sabbath Question, After Ten Months' Sojourn in Continental Cities* (Leeds,1857).
Historical Publishing Company, *England's Great Manufacturing Centres: Yorkshire – Leeds and Bradford* (1888).
Hole, J., *The Working Classes of Leeds: An Essay on the Present State of Education in Leeds, and the Best Means of Improving It* (1863).
Hole, J., *The Homes of the Working Classes, with Suggestions for their Improvement* (1866).
Jackson, E., *A Pastor's Recollections* (Leeds, 1890).
Leeds Band of Hope League, *Annual Report* (Leeds, 1870).
Leeds City Council, *Opening of the New City Meat Market and Slaughterhouses, 24 July 1899 [brochure].*
Leeds Corporation Statistical Committee, 'Report upon the Condition of the Town of Leeds, 1839', *Journal of the Royal Statistical Society*, II (1840).
Leeds Horticultural and Floral Society Annual Report, 1837.
Leeds Naturalists' Club and Scientific Association Reports, 1870-1950.
Leeds School Board, *Central Higher Grade School Prospectus* (Leeds, 1889).
Leeds United Working Men's Temperance League, *Seventh Annual Report and Balance Sheet* (Leeds, 1893).
Leland, J., *Leland's Itinerary* (1710).
London Printing & Engraving Company, *The Century's Progress: Yorkshire Industry and Commerce* (1893).
Marshall, T., 'Leeds Chantries of the Blessed Virgin Mary', *Thoresby Soc.*, IV (1895).
Mayhall, J. ed., *The Annals of Yorkshire, From the Earliest Period to the Present Time* (1878).
Miall, J.G., *Congregationalism in Yorkshire* (1868).
Myers Gardiner, J., *History of the Leeds Benevolent or Strangers' Friend Society, 1789-1889* (Leeds, 1890)
Oastler, R., *A Well-seasoned Christmas Pie for 'the Great Liar of the North'* (Bradford, 1834).
Orage, A.R., 'A Study in Mud' in A.T.Marks, ed., *Hypnotic Leeds* (Leeds, 1894).
Osburn, W., *An Account of the Egyptian Mummy preserved in the Museum of the Leeds Philosophical and Literary Society* (Leeds, 1828).
Parsons, E., *The Civil, Ecclesiastical, Literary, Commercial and Miscellaneous History of Leeds*, 2 vols, (Leeds, 1834).
Pitchin, E., *Leeds Made Uglier* (Leeds,1882).
Priestley, J., *Historical Account of the Navigable Rivers, Canals, and Railways of Great Britain* (1831).
Pollen, J.M., *Narrative of Five Years at St Saviour's, Leeds* (Oxford, 1851).
Puckler, H., *Muskau Prince, Tour in Germany, Holland and England, 1826, 1827, 1828* (1832).
Rusby, J., *St Peter's at Leeds* (Leeds, 1896).
Sadler, M.T., *Memoirs of the Life and Writings of M.T.Sadler* (1848).
Sales, H.H., *A Description of the Royal Exchange in Leeds* (Leeds, *c*.1872).
Sheracy, R., 'The White Slaves of England: The Slipper Markets and Tailors of Leeds', *Pearson's Magazine*, II (1896).
Skene, W.F., *Chronicles of the Picts: Chronicles of the Scots* (1867).
Stephens, W.R.W., *Life and Letters of Walter Farquar Hook* (1878).
Taylor, R.V., *Biographia Leodiensis: Worthies of Leeds* (Leeds, 1865).
Taylor, R.V., *Ecclesiae Leodiensis* (Leeds, 1875).
Thackrah, C T., *The Effects of the Principal Arts, Trades and Professions and of Civic States and Habits of Living on Health and Longevity: with particular reference to the Trades and Manufacturers of Leeds* (Leeds, 1831; enlarged edition 1832).
Thoresby, R., *Ducatus Leodiensis* (1715); second edition, ed. Rev. T.D.Whitaker (Leeds, 1816).
Thoresby, R., *Vicaria Leodiensis or the History of the Church of Leedes in Yorkshire* (1720).
Thoresby, R., *Diaries* (J.Hunter, ed., 1830).
Tomlinson, J., *Some Interesting Yorkshire Scenes* (1865)
Wardell, J., *The Municipal History of the Borough of Leeds in the County of York* (Leeds, 1846).
Wemyss Reid, T., *Memoir of John Deakin Heaton, M.D.* (1885).
Wesley, John, *The Journals of the Revd John Wesley*, (ed. N.Curnock, 1938).
Whitaker, T.D., *Loidis and Elmete* (Leeds, 1816).
Wilkinson, Tate, *The Wandering Patentee: or A History of the Yorkshire Theatres from 1770 to the present time* (1795).
Wilson, E., 'A Leeds Law Suit in the Sixteenth Century', *Thoresby Soc.*, IX (1899).
Wright, T., *The Autobiography of Joseph Lister* (Leeds, 1842).

8. **Twentieth Century Books, Pamphlets and Articles**

Allott, W., 'Leeds Quaker Meeting', *Thoresby Soc.*, L (1965).
Anderson, P., 'The Leeds Workhouse under the Old Poor Law, 1726-1834', *Thoresby Soc.*, LVI (1980).
Anning S.T., *The General Infirmary at Leeds* (1963).
Anning, S.T., 'Leeds House of Recovery', *Medical History*, Vol.13, No.3 (July, 1969).
Anning, S.T., 'The Leeds Public Dispensary', *Thoresby Soc.*, LIV (1975).
Anning, S.T., *The History of Medicine in Leeds* (Leeds, 1980).
Anning, S.T., and Walls, W.K.J., *A History of the Leeds School of Medicine: One and a Half Centuries 1831-1981* (Leeds, 1982).
Arnold, A.J., 'Shall it be Bradford or Leeds? The Origins of Professional Football in the West Riding Textile District', *Thoresby Soc.*, LXIII (1990).
Ashworth, J.W., *The Jubilee of South Parade Baptist Chapel* (1877).
Ashworth, W., *The Genesis of Modern British Town Planning* (1954).
Barber, B.J., 'Municipal Government in Leeds, 1835-1914', in D.Fraser, ed., *Municipal Reform and the Industrial City* (Leicester, 1982).
Barnard, S.M., *To Prove I'm Not Forgot: Living and Dying in a Victorian City: The story of Beckett Street Cemetery, Leeds* (Manchester, 1990)
Barnes, G.D., 'Kirkstall Abbey, 1147-1539: An Historical Study', *Thoresby Soc.*, LVIII (1984).
Baylis, I.and Astbury, S., *Leeds Babies' Welcome Association: A Memoir* (Leeds, 1991).
Baynes, J., *The Jacobite Rising of 1715* (1970).
Bedford, P. and D.N.Howard, *St James's University Hospital, Leeds: A Pictorial History* (Leeds, 1985).
Beckwith, F., 'A Forgotten Eighteenth Century Baptist Chapel in Leeds', *Baptist Quarterly*, IX (1939).
Beckwith, F., The Beginnings of the Leeds Library', *Thoresby Soc.*, XXXVII (1941).
Beckwith, F., 'The Population of Leeds during the Industrial Revolution', *Thoresby Soc.*, XLI (1945).
Beckwith, F., 'Thomas Taylor: Regency Architect', *Thoresby Soc.*, Monograph I (1949).
Beckwith, F., 'An Account of the Leeds Intelligencer, 1754-1866', *Thoresby Soc.*, XL (1953).
Bell, P.G., 'Leeds the Evolution of a Multi-cultural Society' (1980).
Bennett, H.S., *Life on the English Manor* (Cambridge, 1937).
Beresford, M.W., *The Leeds Chambers of Commerce* (1951).
Beresford, M.W., 'Prosperity Street and Other Streets', in M.W.Beresford and G.R.J.Jones, eds., *Leeds and its Region* (Leeds, 1967)
Beresford, M.W., 'The Back-to-Back House in Leeds, 1787-1937' in S.D.Chapman, ed., *The History of Working-Class Housing: a Symposium* (Newton Abbot, 1971).
Beresford, M.W., 'The Making of a Townscape: Richard Paley in the East End of Leeds, 1771-1914', in C.W.Chalklin and M.A.Havinden, eds., *Rural Change and Urban Growth, 1500-1800* (1974).
Beresford, M.W., 'Leeds in 1628: A "Ridinge Observation" from the City of London', *Northern History*, X (1975).
Beresford, M.W., *Walks Round Red Brick* (Leeds, 1980).
Beresford, M.W., 'The Face of Leeds, 1780-1914' in D.Fraser, ed., *History of Modern Leeds* (Manchester, 1980).
Beresford, M.W., 'Prometheus Insured: the Sun fire Insurance Agency in Leeds during Urbanization, 1726-1826', *Economic History Review*, 2nd ser., XXXV (1983).
Beresford, M.W., 'East End, West End: The Face of Leeds During Urbanisation, 1684-1842', *Thoresby Soc. Monograph*, LX an LXI (1988).
Beresford, M.W., 'The Urban Garden in Leeds', in P.Swan and D.Foster, *Essays in Regional and Local History*.
Beresford, M.W., 'A Tale of Two Centenaries: Leeds City Charter and City Square, 1893', *University of Leeds Review*, Vol.36 (1993/94).
Beresford, M.W., and Jones, G.R., eds., *Leeds and Its Region*, (Leeds, 1967).
Black, G., 'The Leeds Eye Dispensary', *Thoresby Soc.*, LIV (1975).
Black, G., 'City Square and Colonel Harding', *Thoresby Soc.*, LIV (1975).
Boleat, M., *The Building Society Movement* (1986).
Bolton, J.L., *The Medieval Economy, 1150-1500*, (1980).
Bonser, K.J., *The Leeds Permanent Building Society: A Centenary Booklet* (Leeds, 1948).
Bonser, K.J., 'Spas, Wells and Springs of Leeds', *Thoresby Soc.*, LIV (1974).
Bowden, S, Crawford, R, and Sykes, G., 'The Public Supply of Gas in Leeds, 1818-1949', in Chartres and Honeyman, *Leeds City Business, 1893-1993*.
Brears, P.C.D., *The Gentlewoman's Kitchen: Great Food in Yorkshire, 1650-1750* (Wakefield, 1984).
Brears, P.C.D., *Yorkshire Food and Tradition* (Edinburgh, 1987).
Brears, P.C.D., *Of Curiosities and Rare Things: The Story of the Leeds City Museums* (Leeds, 1989).
Brears, P.C.D., 'Ralph Thoresby: A Museum Visitor in Stuart England', *Journal of the History of Collections*, I, No.2 (1989).

Brears, P.C.D., *Images of Leeds* (Derby, 1992).
Briggs, A., *Victorian Cities* (1968).
Briggs, A., 'Local and Regional in Northern Sound Broadcasting', *Northern History*, X (1975).
British Association, *General Handbook: Leeds Meeting, 1927* (Leeds, 1927).
Brunswick Wesleyan Methodist Chapel, Leeds, *Souvenir of the Centenary Celebrations, 1925*.
Buckman, J., *Immigrants and the Class Struggle: The Jewish Immigrant in Leeds, 1880-1914* (Manchester,1983).
Bullus, E.E., ed., *The Modernian: A History of Leeds Modern School, 1845-1931* (Leeds, 1931).
Burnett, J., *A History of the Cost of Living* (1969).
Burnett, J., *A Social History of Housing, 1815-1970* (1978).
Burt, S., *An Illustrated History of Roundhay Park* (Leeds, 1984).
Burt, S., *Criminal Leeds: From Earliest Records to 1879* (Leeds, 1985).
Burt, S., and Grady, K., *War, Plague and Trade — Leeds in the Seventeenth Century* (Leeds, 1985).
Burt, S., and Grady, K., *The Merchants' Golden Age: Leeds 1700-1790* (Leeds, 1987).
Burt, S., and Grady, K., *Kirkgate Market: An Illustrated History* (Leeds,1992).
Butler, R., *The History of Kirkstall Forge*, (Leeds, 1945).
Butler, T., *The Diary of Thomas Butler of Kirkstall Forge, Yorkshire, 1796-99* (1906).
Butterworth, E., 'Area Reports on Cities and Boroughs with Substantial Immigrant Settlements: No.2, Leeds', Supplement to the Institute of Race Relations Newsletter (March, 1964).
Cambridge Group for the History of Population, *The Plague Reconsidered* (1977).
Carus-Wilson, E.M., 'An Industrial Revolution of the Thirteenth Century', *Economic History Review*, XI (1941).
Caunce, S., 'Yorkshire Post Newspapers Ltd.: Perseverance Rewarded' in Chartres and Honeyman, *Leeds City Business, 1893-1993*
Central Statistical Office, *Regional Trends 28* (HMSO, 1993 edition).
Chadwick, S.J., 'Some Papers Relating to the Plague in Yorkshire', *Yorkshire Archaeological Journal*, XV (1900).
Chalklin, W., *The Provincial Towns of Georgian England, 1740-1820* (1974).
Chard, G.H., *A History of the Leeds Church Institute* (Leeds, 1907).
Chartres, J., 'Joshua Tetley and Son, 1890s to 1990s: a Century in the Tied Trade', in Chartres and Honeyman, *Leeds City Business, 1893-1993*.
Chartres, J., 'John Waddington PLC, 1890s to 1990s: a Strategy of Quality and Innovation', in Chartres and Honeyman, *Leeds City Business, 1893-1993*.
Chartres, J., and Honeyman, K., eds., *Leeds City Business, 1893-1993* (Leeds, 1993).
Cherry, G.E., *The Evolution of British Town Planning* (1974).
Cherry, G.E., *Cities and Plans: The Shaping of Urban Britain in the Nineteenth and Twentieth Centuries* (1988).
Clark, E.K., 'A Brawl in Kirkgate', *Thoresby Soc.*, IV (1895).
Clarke, M., *The Leeds and Liverpool Canal: A History and Guide* (1990).
Clay, C.T., 'The Early Abbots of Yorkshire Cistercian Houses', *Yorkshire Archaeological Journal*, XXXVIII (1952).
Clay, E.W., *The Leeds Police, 1836-1974*, (Leeds, 1975).
Clay, J.W. 'The Gentry of Yorkshire at the Time of the Civil War', *Yorkshire Archaeological Journal*, XXIII (1914-15).
Clay, J.W., 'Events in Yorkshire during the Civil War', *Yorkshire Archaeological Journal*, XXIII (1914-5).
Cliffe, J.T., *The Yorkshire Gentry from the Reformation to the Civil War* (1969).
Cole, D., *Cookridge: The Story of a Yorkshire Township* (Leeds, 1981).
Cole, D., *Just an Ordinary Life* (leeds, 1984).
Collins, M., 'The History of the Leeds Permanent Building Society, 1893-1993', in Chartres and Honeyman, *Leeds City Business, 1893-1993*.
Collinson, J.M., 'Weetwood and the Foxcroft Family', *University of Leeds Review*, Vol 30 (Leeds, 1987/88).
Collyer, C., 'The Leeds District and the Rebellion of 1745', *University of Leeds Review*, III, No.2 (1952).
Collyer, C., 'Yorkshire and the '45', *Yorkshire Archaeological Journal*, XXXVIII (1952).
Community Housing Working Party, 'Gradual Renewal in Leeds' (March, 1976).
Community Housing Working Party, 'The Better Way: An Approach to Gradual Renewal in Leeds' (1978).
Connor, W.J., 'The Architect of Holy Trinity Church, Leeds', *Thoresby Soc.*, LIV (1979).
Corfield, P.J., *The Impact of English Towns, 1700-1800* (1982).
Copley, J., 'The Theatre in Hunslet Lane', *Thoresby Soc.*, LIV (1974).
Copley, J. 'The Theatre in Hunslet Lane II', *Thoresby Soc.*, LIV (1976).
Cross, C., 'The Development of Protestantism in Leeds and Hull, 1520-1640: the Evidence of Wills', *Northern History*, XVIII (Leeds, 1982).
Cross, C., 'Urban Magistrates and Ministers: Religion in Hull and Leeds from the Reformation to the Civil War', *Borthwick Papers*, No.67 (York, 1985).
Crump, W.B., ed., *The Leeds Woollen Industry, 1780-1820* (Thoresby Society Monograph, 1931).
Curtis, S.J., *History of Education in Great Britain* (1967).
Dalton, H.W., 'Walter Farquhar Hook, Vicar of Leeds: His Work for the Church and the Town, 1837-48', *Thoresby Soc.*, LXIII (1990).
Dawson, F., 'Paganini in Leeds, January 1832', *Thoresby Soc.*, XXXIII (1935).
Dews, D.C., 'Two Eighteenth Century Baptist Chapels', in *Lantern Slide Leeds* (Thoresby Society Occasional Publication, 1984).
Dews, D.C., *Oxford Place Methodist Centre, Leeds, 1835-1985* (Leeds, 1985).
Dillon, T., 'The Irish in Leeds, 1851-1861'. *Thoresby Soc.*, LIV (1973).
Diocese of Ripon, *Report of the Commission Appointed by the Lord Bishop of Ripon* (Leeds, 1900).
Dobson, R.B., 'Yorkshire Towns in the Late Fourteenth Century', *Thoresby Soc.*, LIX (1985).
Douglas, J., 'Catholic Churches in Leeds, 1783-1900', *Victorian Society: West Yorkshire Journal* (1983-4).
Douglas, J., and Powell, K., 'Boar Lane: Is it Too Late?, *Outlook – Journal of Leeds Civic Trust* (Leeds, 1979).
Driver, C., *Tory Radical: The Life of Richard Oastler* (Oxford, 1946).
Duckham, B.F., *The Yorkshire Ouse* (1967).
Edsall, N.C., *The Anti-Poor Law Movement, 1834-44* (Manchester, 1971).
Elton, A., and Foster, E., *Yorkshire Piety and Persuasion* (Leeds, 1985).
Elton, A., 'Leeds Cyclists, 1880-1914', *Thoresby Society Annual Report*, 1991.
Elton, A., 'Sir George Cockburn, 1848-1927', *Thoresby Soc.* 2nd ser., Vol.3 (1993).
Elton, A., 'Becoming a City: Leeds 1893', *Thoresby Soc.*, 2nd ser., 3 (1993).
Farrer, M., 'Towards a History of Harehills and Chapeltown: Riot and Revolution: The Politics of an Inner City', *Revolutionary Socialism* (Winter, 1981-82).
Finnigan, R.E., 'Council Housing in Leeds, 1919-39: Social Policy and Urban Change', in M.Daunton, ed., *Councillors and Tenants* (Leicester, 1984).
Finnigan, R.E., *The Cathedral Church of St Anne, Leeds* (1988).
Forster, G.C.F., 'Parson and People: Trouble at Leeds Parish Church', *University of Leeds Review*, VII (1961).
Forster, G.C.F., 'The Early Years of Leeds Corporation', *Thoresby Soc.*, LIV (1979).
Forster, G.C.F., 'Holy Trinity Church in the History of Leeds, 1727-1977', *Thoresby Soc.*, LIV (1979).
Forster, G.C.F., 'The Foundations: From the Earliest Times to c.1700' in D.Fraser, *A History of Modern Leeds* (Manchester, 1980).
Fraser, D., 'Poor Law Politics in Leeds, 1833-1855', *Thoresby Soc.*, LIII (1971).
Fraser, D., 'The Leeds Churchwardens, 1828-50, *Thoresby Soc., LIII (1971).*
Fraser, D., 'Improvement in Early Victorian Leeds', Thoresby Soc., LIII (1971).
Fraser, D., 'Fruits of Reform: Leeds Politics in the 1830's', *Northern History*, VII (1972).
Fraser, D., *Urban Politics in Victorian England* (Leicester, 1976).
Fraser, D., *Power and Authority in the Victorian City* (Oxford, 1979).
Fraser, D., ed., *A History of Modern Leeds* (Manchester, 1980).
Freeman, M., *Leeds Jews: The First Hundred Years* (Leeds, 1992).
Friedman, T.F., 'A Noble and Magnificent Statue, *Leeds Arts Calendar*, No.72 (1973).
Friedman, T.F., 'The Ingenious Mr Lodge's View of Leeds', *Leeds Arts Calendar*, No.79 (1976).
Friedman, T.F., 'Jacques Parmentier in Leeds: A Newly Discovered Drawing', *Leeds Arts Calendar*, No.94 (1984).
Gawler, R., *History of Blenheim Baptist Church Leeds, 1848-1948* (Leeds,1948).
Gibb, M.A., and Beckwith, F., *The Yorkshire Post: Two Centuries* (1954).
Gosden, P.H.J.H., and Taylor, A.J., eds., *Studies in the History of a University, 1874-1974: To Commemorate the centenary of the University of Leeds* (Leeds, 1975).
Gosden, P.H, J.H., 'The Early Years of the Yorkshire College', *Thoresby Soc.*, LIV (1976).
Grady, K., 'Profit, Property Interests and Public Spirit: The Provision of Markets and Commercial Amenities in Leeds, 1822-9', *Thoresby Soc.*, LIV (1976).
Grady, K., 'Commercial, Marketing and Retailing Amenities, 1700-1914', in D.Fraser, ed. *History of Modern Leeds* (Manchester, 1980).
Grady, K., 'The Georgian Public Buildings of Leeds and the West Riding', *Thoresby Soc. Monograph*, LXII (1989).
Hadfield, C., *The Canals of Yorkshire and North East England* (1972).
Hadfield, C., and Biddle, G., *The Canals of North West England* (2 vols., 1970).
Hagerty, J., *Leeds at War* (Leeds, 1981).
Hammerton, H.J., *This Turbulent Priest: Charles Jenkinson* (1952).
Hargrave, E., 'The Early Leeds Volunteers', *Thoresby Soc.*, XXVIII (1928).
Hargrave, E., 'The Gentlemen Volunteer Cavalry, 1797', *Thoresby Soc.*, XXVIII (1928).
Hargrave, E., 'Leeds Volunteers, 1803-1808', *Thoresby Soc.*,XXVIII (1928).
Hargrave, E., 'Leeds Local Militia, 1808-1814', *Thoresby Soc.*, XXVIII (1928).
Hargrove, C., *The Unitarian Chapels of Yorkshire*.
Harrison, J.F.C., 'Chartism in Leeds', in A.Briggs, *Chartist Studies* (1959).
Harrison, J.F.C., *Early Victorian Britain, 1832-51* (1979).
Hartley, O., 'The Second World War and After, 1939-74', in Fraser, *Modern Leeds* (Manchester, 1980).
Hartley, W.C.E., *Banking in Yorkshire* (1975).
Hatcher, J., *Victorian Society West Yorkshire group Journal* (1981-2).
Heap, A., *Briggate: A History in Pictures* (Leeds, 1988).
Heap, A., *The Headrow: A Pictorial Record* (Leeds, 1990).
Heaton, H., 'The Leeds White Cloth Hall', *Thoresby Soc.*, XXII (1931).
Heaton, H., *The Yorkshire Woollen and Worsted Industries* (2nd edn, Oxford, 1965).
Hendrick, H., 'The Leeds Gas Strike, 1890'.*Thoresby Soc.*, LIV (1975).
Hennock, E.P., *Fit and Proper Persons* (1973).
Hoggart, R., *The Uses of Literacy* (1957).
Hoggart, R., *A Local Habitation: Life and Times, 1918-1940* (Oxford, 1989).
Hopwood, W.A., and Casperson, F.P., *Meanwood* (Leeds, 1986).
Honeyman, K., 'Montague Burton Ltd: The Creators of Well-dressed Men', in Chartres and Honeyman, *Leeds City Business, 1893-1993* (Leeds, 1993).
Honeyman, K., 'Soapy Joes': the History of Joseph Watson and Sons Ltd., 1893-1993', in Chartres and Honeyman, *Leeds City Business, 1893-1993* (Leeds, 1993).
Hornsey, M.A., 'John Harrison, The Leeds Benefactor and his Times', *Thoresby Soc.*, XXXIII (1935).
Jenkins, D.T., *The West Riding Wool Textile Industry, 1770-1835: A Study in*

Fixed capital formation (Pasold Research Fund Ltd., 1975).

Jenkins, E.W., 'David Forsyth and the City of Leeds School', *Thoresby Soc.* 2nd series, Vol.1 (1991).

Johnston, C.P., 'The Charity School, the Church and the Corporation: Aspects of Educational Provision for the Poor in Eighteenth Century Leeds', *Thoresby Soc.* 2nd series, Vol.3 (1993).

Jones, G.R., 'To the Building of Kirkstall Abbey', in M.W.Beresford and G.R.Jones, eds., *Leeds and its Region* (1967).

Keen, M., *English Society in the Later Middle Ages, 1348-1500* (1990).

Kilburn Scott, E., *Leeds Church Middle-Class School: Records from 1870-1907* (Leeds, 1927).

Kilburn Scott, E., *Matthew Murray, Pioneer Engineer: Records from 1765-1826* (Leeds, 1928).

Killick, J.R., and Thomas, W.A., 'The Provincial Stock Exchanges, 1830-70'.*Economic History Review,* XXIII (1970).

Kirby, J.W., 'The Manor and Borough of Leeds, 1425-1662: An Edition of Documents', *Thoresby Soc.*, LVII (1983).

Kirby, J.W., 'The Rulers of Leeds: Gentry, Clothiers and Merchants, c.1425-1626', *Thoresby Soc.*, LIX (1985).

Kirby, J.W., 'A Leeds Élite: The Principal Burgesses of the First Leeds Corporation', *Northern History*, XX (1984).

Kirk, G.E., *History of the Parish Church of St Mary, Whitkirk, Leeds* (Leeds, 1935).

Kitson Clark, E., *The History of 100 Years of Life of the Leeds Philosophical and Literary Society* (Leeds, 1924).

Kitson Clark, E., *Kitsons of Leeds, 1837-1937* (1938).

Krausz, E., *Leeds Jewry: Its History and Social Structure* (Cambridge, 1964).

Lackey, C., *Quality Pays: The Story of Joshua Tetley & Son* (1985).

Lane, M.R., *The Story of the Steam Plough Works: Fowlers of Leeds* (1980).

Le Patourel, J., ed., 'Documents Relating to the Manor and Borough of Leeds, 1066-1400', Thoresby
Soc., XLV (1956).

Le Patourel, J., 'The Norman Conquest of Yorkshire', *Northern History*, VI (1971).

Leeds Building Centre Committe Report, 'Leeds Housing' (*c.*1936).

Leeds Chamber of Commerce, Annual Reports.

Leeds Chief Constable, Report on the State of Crime and the Police Establishment for the Year Ending, 31 Dec. 1926.

Leeds Churches Community Involvement Project, *Faith in Leeds: Searching for God in Our City* (1986 and 1989).

Leeds City Council, *Formal Opening of City Square [brochure]* (Leeds, 1903).

Leeds City Council, *Opening of the New Market Hall, 1st July 1904 [brochure].*

Leeds City Council, Report on the Leeds Unemployed 1904-5 (1905).

Leeds City Council, *Official Guide to the Leeds Corporation Tramway and Transport System* (Leeds, 1926).

Leeds City Council, *Education in Leeds: A Backward Glance and a Present View: Leeds Education Week Souvenir Handbook* (Leeds, 1926) [hereafter *Education in Leeds].*

Leeds City Council, Reports on the Health and Sanitary Administration of the City, 1926 and 1938.

Leeds City Council, *City of Leeds Markets and Corn Exchange – the Official Handbook* (1951).

Leeds City Council Parks Committee, *Woodhouse Moor Centenary Handbook, 1857-1957* (Leeds, 1957).

Leeds City and County Borough, Development Plan Review: Draft Report of Survey, Written Analysis (1967).

Leeds City and County Borough, Development Plan Review, Written Statement, 1972.

Leeds City Council, Planning and Property Department, Town Planning Division, *Planning Tomorrow's Leeds* (Oct. 1973).

Leeds City Council, *Planning Statistics* (1975).

Leeds City Council, Report of Housing Working Party on Gradual Renewal (June 1976).

Leeds City Council, Report on Gradual Renewal and its Application to Woodhouse (June 1978).

Leeds City Council, Department of Planning, *Leeds Unitary Development Plan: Issue 1: Housing* (1990).

Leeds City Council, Department of Planning, *Moving Ahead: Leeds Planning Handbook* (1993).

Leeds City Engineer's Department, Development Plan for Leeds: Town and Country Planning Act, 1947 (1951), approved 1955.

Leeds Civic Trust Annual Reports, 1966-1993.

Leeds (Group B) Hospital Management Committee, *50th Anniversary of the Opening of Seacroft and Killingbeck Hospitals* (Leeds, 1954).

Leeds Parish Church, *Railway Arch Mission* (Leeds, n.d.).

Leeds Parish Church, *Good Shepherd Mission 1882-1932* (Leeds, 1932).

Leeds Photographic Society, *Centenary Publication* (1952).

Leeds Sketches and Reviews (Leeds, 1902).

Leeds Traders' Special Show Week, *Shopping in Leeds* (1909).

Leeds Unemployed Social Work Committee, Leeds – Voluntary Work with the Unemployed (1936).

Lenman, B., *The Jacobite Risings in Britain, 1689-1746* (1980).

Linstrum, D., *West Yorkshire, Architects and Architecture* (1978).

Lockwood, A., 'The Origins of Gas in Leeds: the Leeds Gas Light Company, 1817-35', *Thoresby Soc.*,LVI (1980).

Lonsdale, A., 'The Last Monks of Kirkstall Abbey', *Thoresby Soc.*, LIII (1973).

Lovell, V. M. E., 'Benjamin Gott of Armley House, Leeds, 1762-1840: Patron of the Arts', *Thoresby Soc.*, LIX (1986).

Lowe, R., *Past into Present: A Commemorative History of Leeds College of Art and Design* (Leeds, 1993).

Lumb, G.D., 'The Family of Harrison the Leeds Benefactor', *Thoresby Soc.*, (1909).

Lumb, G.D. 'Leeds Manor House and Park', *Thoresby Soc.*, XXIV (1917).

Lumb, G.D., 'The Old Hall, Wade Lane: Leeds and the Jackson Family', *Thoresby Soc.*, XXVI (1924).

Lumb, G.D., 'York or East Bar Leeds', *Thoresby Soc.*, XXVI (1924).

McGuire, A., and Clark, A., *The Leeds Crosses* (Leeds City Museums, 1987).

McLynn, F.J., *The Jacobite Army in England: The Final Campaign, 1745* (Edinburgh, 1983).

Mackay, T., ed., *The Autobiography of Samuel Smiles* (1905).

Manning, B., *The English People and the English Revolution* (1978).

Marshall, J., *Headingley* (1970).

Marshall, M.J., and B., *Recollections: Sixty Years Onwards* (2nd edn., Leeds, 1930).

Marwick, A., *British Society Since 1945* (1990).

May, B.C., 'Waggonways and Staiths: The Impact of the Middleton Colliery on the Township of Hunslet, *c.*1750-1800', *Thoresby Soc.* 2nd series, Vol.3 (1993).

Meadowcroft, M., 'The Years of Political Transition, 1914-39', in D.Fraser, *History of Modern Leeds* (Manchester, 1980).

Meiklejohn, A., *The Life, Work and Times of Charles Turner Thackrah: Surgeon and Apothecary of Leeds, 1795-1833* (1957).

Middleton Railway Trust, *A History of Middleton Colliery Railway, Leeds* (5th edn, 1973).

Mitchell, B.R., and Deane, P., *Abstract of Historical Statistics* (Cambridge, 1962).

Milner, L., *Leeds Pals* (1991).

Mount St Mary's Church, *Centenary of the Opening of Mount St Mary's Church, Leeds, 1857-1957* (Leeds, 1957).

Moir, E., *The Justice of the Peace* (1969).

Morgan, C.J., 'Demographic Change, 1771-1911' in D.Fraser, ed., *History of Modern Leeds* (Manchester, 1980).

Morris, C., ed., *The Journeys of Celia Fiennes* (1949).

Morris, R.J., Leeds and the Crystal Palace', *Victorian Studies,* 13 (1970).

Morris, R.J., 'Middle-class Culture, 1700-1914' in Fraser, *Modern Leeds* (Manchester, 1980).

Morris, R.J., *Class, Sect and Party:* The Making of the British Middle Class, Leeds 1820-1850 (Manchester, 1990).

Morrison, N.G., *Edward and the Black Prince: A City Square Souvenir* (Leeds, 1903).

Mortimer, J.E., 'Thoresby's "poor deluded Quakers": the Sufferings of Leeds Friends in the Seventeenth Century', *Thoresby Soc.* 2nd series, I (1991).

Mortimer, J.E., 'Joseph Tatham's School, Leeds', *Thoresby Soc.*, 2nd ser., I (1991).

Musgrave, P.W., *Society and Education in England Since 1800* (1968)

Newman, P.R., 'The Royalist Army in Northern England, 1642-5' (Unpublished Ph.D. thesis)

Newman, P.R., 'The Defeat of John Belasye', *Yorkshire Archaeological Journal*, 52 (1980).

Norcliffe, C.B., 'Inventory of the Goods of John Pawson', *Thoresby Soc.*, IV (1895).

Oliver, R., *Leeds-Holbeck: The First Wisp of Steam* (Leeds, 1980).

Outhwaite, R.B., *Inflation in Tudor and Early Stuart England* (1969).

Parris, H., 'Leeds and its Industrial Growth, No.11. Leeds and its Railways', *The Leeds Journal,* Vol.26 (1955).

Patterson, M., *The Ham Shank [Life at the Bank in the early twentieth century]* (Bradford, 1993).

Pearson, R., 'Knowing One's Place: Perceptions of Community in the Industrial Suburbs of Leeds, 1790-1890', *Journal of Social History*, Vol.27 (1993).

Pelling, H., *A History of Trade Unionism* (1963).

Pemberton, H., 'Two Hundred Years of Banking in Leeds', *Thoresby Soc.*, XLVI (1963).

Pennock, P.M., 'The Evolution of St James's, 1849-94: Leeds Moral and Industrial Training School, Leeds Union Workhouse and Leeds Union Infirmary', *Thoresby Soc.*, LIX (1986).

Perrie, C., *The Jacobite Movement* (2nd edn, 1948).

Phelps Brown, E.H. and Hopkins, S.V., 'Seven Centuries of Building Wages', *Economica*, (1955).

Pimlott, J.A.R., *The Englishman's Holiday* (1947).

Place, J.B., 'Woodhouse in the Manor of Leeds', *Thoresby Soc.*, XXXVII (1945).

Ponting, K.G., ed., Edward Baines, *The Woollen Manufacture of England with special reference to the Leeds Clothing District, 1848* (Newton Abbot,1970).

Port, M.H., *Six Hundred New Churches: a Study of the Church Building Commission, 1818-1856* (1961).

Postan, M.M., *The Medieval Economy* (1975)

Preedy, R., *Leeds Cinemas Remembered* (Leeds, 1980).

Preedy, R., *Leeds Theatres Remembered* (Leeds, 1981).

Price, A.C., *A History of Leeds Grammar School from its Foundation to the end of 1918* (Leeds, 1919).

Proudlock, N., *Leeds: A History of its Tramways* (Leeds, 1991).

Rainnie, G.F., and Wilson, R.K., 'The Economic Structure' in Beresford and Jones, *Leeds and its Region* (Leeds, 1967).

Ramsden, G., 'Two Notes on the History of the Aire and Calder Navigation', *Thoresby Soc.*, XLI (1953).

Ratcliffe, G., *Sixty Years of It: Being the Story of My Life and Public Career* (1935).

Ravetz, A., *Model Estate: Planned Housing at Quarry Hill, Leeds* (1974).

Rees, G., *St Michael – A History of Marks and Spencer* (1969).

Reid, S.J., *Memoirs of Sir Wemyss Reid, 1842-1885* (1905).

Rimmer, W.G., 'Middleton Colliery, near Leeds, 1770-1830', *Yorkshire Bulletin of Economic and Social Research*, VII, No.1 (1955).

Rimmer, W.G., 'Sport', *Leeds Journal,* Vol.28 (Leeds, 1957).

Rimmer, W.G., 'The Woollen Industry in the Nineteenth Century', *Leeds Journal*, 30 (Leeds, 1959).
Rimmer, W.G., 'Leeds Between the Wars', *The Leeds Journal* (Oct. 1959).
Rimmer, W.G., 'Workingmen's Cottages in Leeds, 1770-1840', *Thoresby Soc.*, XLVI (1960).
Rimmer, W.G., *Marshall's of Leeds: Flax-spinners, 1788-1886* (Cambridge, 1960).
Rimmer, W.G., 'Leeds Leather Industry in the Nineteenth Century', *Thoresby Soc.*,XLVI (1961).
Rimmer, W.G., 'Alfred Place Terminating Building Society, 1825-43', *Thoresby Soc.*, XLVI (1963)
Rimmer, W.G., 'Occupations in Leeds, 1841-1951', *Thoresby Soc.*, L (1967).
Rimmer, W.G., 'The Industrial Profile of Leeds 1740-1840', *Thoresby Soc.*, L (1967).
Rimmer, W.G., 'The Evolution of Leeds to 1700', *Thoresby Soc.*, L (1967).
Roberts, A.W., 'Leeds Liberalism and Late Victorian Politics', *Northern History*, V (1970).
Russell, D., 'The Leeds Rational Recreation Society, 1852-9: "Music for the People" in a mid-Victorian City', *Thoresby Soc.*, LVI (1981).
Savage, S., and Tyne, C., *The Labour of Years: The Story of St Saviour's and St Hilda's, Leeds* (Oxford, 1976).
Sawyer, M., 'The Economy of Leeds in the 1990s', in Chartres and Honeyman, *Leeds City Business, 1893-1993.*
Schroeder, W.L., *Mill Hill Chapel, 1674-1924* (Leeds, 1925).
Schofield, R., *Schofield's Golden Jubilee, 1901-1951* (Leeds, 1951).
Scott, W., *Leeds in the Great War* (Leeds, 1923).
Scottorn, J.J., *A Short History of South Parade Baptist Chapel, 1779-1979* (Leeds, 1979).
Shimmin, A.N., *The University of Leeds: The First Half-Century* (Cambridge, 1954)
Shrewsbury, J.F.D., *A History of the Bubonic Plague in the British Isles* (1970).
Sigsworth, E.M., 'The Brewery Trade During the Industrial Revolution: The Case of Yorkshire', *Borthwick Papers*, No.31 (York, 1967).
Sigsworth, E.M., *Montague Burton: The Tailor of Taste* (1990).
Smiles, S., *The Autobiography of Samuel Smiles* (ed. T.Mackay, 1905).
Smith, P.L., *The Aire and Calder Navigation* (Wakefield, 1987).
Sprittles, J., 'Leeds Music Festivals', *Thoresby Soc.*, XLVI (1961).
Sprittles, J., 'Links with Bygone Leeds', *Thoresby Soc.*, LII (1969).
Steele, E.D., 'Leeds and Victorian Politics', *University of Leeds Review*, XVII, 2 (1974).
Steele, E.D., 'The Irish Presence in the North of England, 1850-1914', *Northern History*, XII (1976).
Steele, E.D., 'Imperialism and Leeds Politics, *c*.1850-1914', in D.Fraser, *History of Modern Leeds* (Manchester, 1980).
Steele, E.D., 'E.S.Talbot and the Silver Age of Anglicanism in Leeds', *Northern History*, XXV (1989).
Steele, T., *Alfred Orage and the Leeds Arts Club, 1893-1923* (1990).
Stephens, W.B., 'Elementary Education and Literacy', in D.Fraser, ed., *History of Modern Leeds*, (Manchester, 1980).
Sterne, E., *Leeds Jewry, 1919-29* (Leeds, 1989).
Stevenson, J., *British Society 1914-45* (1984).
Symons, J., *The General Strike* (1959).
Tate, D., *A History of Cafes and Restaurants* (Leeds, 1988).
Tate, W.E., *The Parish Chest* (third edition, 1969).
Thomas, J., 'The Leeds Clothing Industry', *Yorkshire Bulletin of Economic and Social Research*, Occasional Paper No.I (1955).
Thomas, W.A., *The Provincial Stock Exchanges* (1973).
Thompson, E.P., *The Making of the English Working CLass* (1968).
Thompson, F.M.L., *The Rise of Respectable Society: A Social History of Victorian Britain, 1830-1900* (1988).
Tomlinson, W.W., *The North Eastern Railway* (1914).
Transport, Ministry of, *Traffic in Town: A Study of the long term problems of traffic in urban areas* (HMSO, 1963).
Trease, G. *Portrait of a Cavalier: William Cavendish, First Duke of Newcastle* (1979).
Treen, C., 'The Process of Suburban Development in North Leeds, 1870-1914', in F.M.L.Thompson, ed., *The Rise of Suburbia* (Leicester, 1982).
Trowell, F., 'Speculative Housing Development in the Suburb of Headingley, Leeds, 1838-1914', *Thoresby Soc.*, LIX (1985).
Turnbull, G.L., 'Provincial Road Carrying in England in the Eighteenth Century', *Journal of Transport History*, IV (1977-8).
Unwin, R.W., 'The Aire and Calder Navigation, Part I: The Beginnings of the Navigation', *Bradford Antiquary*, XLII (1964).
Unwin, R.W., 'The Navigation in the Pre-canal Age' *Bradford Antiquary*, XLIII (1967).
Unwin, R.W., 'Leeds Becomes a Transport Centre' in D.Fraser, ed., *History of Modern Leeds*, (Manchester, 1980).
Upton, A.F., *Sir Arthur Ingram, 1565-1642: a Study of the Origins of an English Landed Family* (1961).
Versey, H.C., 'The Postal History of Leeds', *Thoresby Soc.*, L (1968).
Wainwright, P., 'Chas. F.Thackray Ltd.: Suppliers to the Surgeons' in Chartres and Honeyman, *Leeds City Business, 1883-1993.*
Walton, J.K., *The English Seaside Resort: A Social History, 1750-1914* (Leicester, 1983).
Ward, D., 'Environs and neighbours in the "Two Nations": Residential Differentiation in Mid-Nineteenth Century Leeds', *Journal of Historical Geography, 6 (1980).*
Ward, J.T., 'Richard Oastler on Politics and Factory Reform, 1832-1833', *Northern History*, XXIV (1988).
Waterhouse, K., *City Lights: A Street Life* (1994).
Webster, C., 'R.D.Chantrell, Architects: His Life and Work in Leeds, 1818-1847', *Thoresby Soc.*, 2nd series, II (1992).
Wenham, P., *The Great and Close Siege of York, 1644*,
West, E.G., *Education in the Industrial Revolution* (1975).
West Yorkshire Metropolitan County Council, *West Yorkshire: an Archaeological Survey to A.D.1500*, 2 Vols, (Wakefield, 1981).
Wiener, R., 'The Industrial Base of Leeds' (W.E.A., Leeds, 1980)
Wilkinson, J.H., *Leeds Dialect Glossary and Lore* (Leeds, 1924).
Wilkinson, R., *The Grand Theatre – First Hundred Years* (Leeds,1978).
Wilson, R.G., 'Transport Dues as Indices of Economic Growth, 1775-1820', *Economic History Review*, XIX (1966).
Wilson, R.G., 'Records for a Study of the Leeds Woollen Merchants, 1700-1830', *Archives*, VIII, No.37 (1967).
Wilson, R.G., 'Merchants and Land: The Ibbetsons of Leeds and Denton, 1650-1850', *Northern History*.
Wilson, R.G. *Gentlemen Merchants: The Merchant Community in Leeds, 1700-1830* (Manchester, 1971).
Wilson, R.G., 'The Denisons and the Milneses: Eighteenth-Century Merchant Landowners', in J.T.Ward and R.G.Wilson, *Land and Industry* (Newton Abbot, 1971).
Wilson, R.G., 'The Supremacy of the Yorkshire Cloth Industry in the Eighteenth Century' in N.B.Harte and K.G.Pontings, eds., *Textile History and Economic History* (Manchester, 1973).
Wilson, R.G. 'The Corporation of Leeds in the Eighteenth Century', *Thoresby Soc.*, LIV (1979).
Woledge, G., 'The Medieval Borough of Leeds', *Thoresby Soc.*, XXXVII (1945), pp.288-309.
Wood, R.G., 'Leeds Church Patronage in the Eighteenth Century', *Thoresby Soc.*, XLI (1954).
Wood, R.G., 'Leeds Church Patronage in the Eighteenth Century: A Further Note', *Thoresby Soc.*, L (1968).
Wood, S., *Back-to-Back Memories* (Leeds, 1991).
Woodhouse, T., 'The General Strike in Leeds', *Northern History*, XVIII (1982).
Woodhouse, T., 'The Working Class', in D.Fraser, *History of Modern Leeds* (Manchester, 1990).
Wright, D.G., 'Leeds Politics and the American Civil War', *Northern History*, IX (1974).
Yarwood, R., 'The Historical Landscape of Colton and Newsam', *Leeds Arts Calendar*, No.92 (1983).
Yasumoto, M., 'Urbanisation and Population in an English Town', *Keio Economic Studies*, X (1973).
Yates, N., 'Leeds and the Oxford Movement: A Study of "High Church" Activity in the Rural Deaneries of Allerton, Armley, Headingley and Whitkirk in the Diocese of Ripon 1836-1934', *Thoresby Soc.*, LV (1975).
Yates, N., 'The Religious Life of Victorian Leeds', in Fraser, *Modern Leeds*.
Yorke, H., *A Mayor of the Masses: History and Anecdotes of Archibald Witham Scarr* (Leeds, 1904).

9. **Unpublished Works**

Barber, B.J., 'Leeds Corporation, 1835-1905: A History of its Enviromental, Social and Administrative Services' (unpublished Ph.D. thesis, University of Leeds, 1975).
Connell, E.J., 'Industrial Development in South Leeds, 1790-1914' (unpublished Ph.D. thesis, University of Leeds, 1975).
Dews, D.C., 'Methodism in Leeds, 1791-1861', (unpublished M.Phil. thesis, University of Bradford, 1984).
Fletcher, R.F., 'The History of the Leeds General Cemetery Company, 1833-1965' (unpublished M.Phil. thesis University of Leeds, 1975).
Greaves, B., 'Methodism 1740-1851' (unpublished Ph.D. thesis, University of Liverpool, 1968).
Meadowcroft, M., 'Transition in Leeds City Government, 1903-1926' (Unpublished M.Phil thesis, University of Bradford, 1978).
Peppard, R.S., 'The Growth aand Development of Leeds Waterworks Undertakings, 1694-1852' (unpublished M.Phil. thesis, University of Leeds, 1973).
Pearson, R., 'The Industrial Suburbs of Leeds in the Nineteenth Century: Community Consciousness among the Social Classes' (unpublished Ph.D thesis, University of Leeds, 1986).
Treen, C., 'Building and Estate Development in the Northern Out-townships of Leeds, 1781-1914' (unpublished Ph.D. thesis, University of Leeds, 1977).
Ward, M.F., 'Industrial Development and Location in Leeds North of the River Aire, 1775-1914' (unpublished Ph.D. thesis, University of Leeds, 1972).

Index

Numbers in **bold** type indicate illustrations